SEARCH FOR SANITY

SEARCH FOR SANITY
The Politics of Nuclear Weapons and Disarmament

edited by Paul Joseph and Simon Rosenblum

SOUTH END PRESS   BOSTON

Grateful acknowledgement is made for permission to reprint the following material:

"Reagatomics or How to 'Prevail'" by Christopher Paine. *The Nation*, April 9, 1983. Copyright 1983, *The Nation* magazine, The Nation Associates, Inc.

"First Strike: An Interview with Daniel Ellsberg" Reprinted from *Inquiry*, April 13, 1981. Copyright 1981, *Inquiry* magazine.

"Strategic Thinkers" by Fred Kaplan. *The Bulletin of the Atomic Scientists*, December, 1982. Copyright 1982 by the Educational Foundation for Nuclear Science, Chicago Ill., 60637.

"The Baroque Arsenal" by Mary Kaldor. Reprinted by permission of Hill and Wang.

"First Strike: Myth or Reality" by Edward Anderson. *The Bulletin of the Atomic Scientists,* November 1981. Copyright 1981 by the Educational Foundation for Nuclear Science, Chicago, Ill., 60637.

"Nuclear Errors and Accidents" by Louis Rene Beres. Reprinted from *Apocalypse* by permission of the University of Chicago Press.

"Wasting Space: Countdown to a First Strike," by Michio Kaku. Copyright, 1983. Reprinted by permission from *The Progressive*, Madison, WI, 53703.

"The Terrifying Prospect: Atomic Bombs Everywhere" by Daniel Yergin, *The Atlantic*, April, 1977. Copyright 1977. Reprinted by permission of the Helen Brann Agency, Inc.

"Nuclear Decapitation," by John Steinbruner, *Foreign Policy*, 45 (Winter 1981-82) Copyright 1981 by the Carnegie Endowment for International Peace.

"Can Nuclear War Be Controlled?" by Desmond Ball. Abridged version of *Adelphi Papers*, No. 169, The International Institute for Strategic Studies, London, 1981.

"The Illusion of Survival" reprinted by permission of Jack Geiger and the Physicians for Social Responsibility.

"War, Militarism and the Soviet State" by David Holloway. World Policy Institute 1980.

"From the Other Shore" reprinted by permission of Suzanne Gordon and *Working Papers*.

"East, West—Is There A Third Way" by E.P. Thompson. Reprinted by permission of Pantheon Books.

"A False Start" by Christopher Paine. *The Bulletin of the Atomic Scientists*, August-September 1982. Copyright 1982 by the Educational Foundation for Nuclear Science, Chicago, Ill., 60637.

"Call To Halt The Nuclear Arms Race" reprinted by permission of Randall Forsberg and the Institute for Defense and Disarmament Studies.

"A Nuclear Freeze Isn't Enough" by Michael Klare. *The Nation*, September 25, 1982. Copyright 1982, *The Nation* magazine, The Nation Associates, Inc.

TABLE OF CONTENTS

PART I: DYNAMICS OF THE ARMS RACE

PART II: SPECIFIC ISSUES OF THE ARMS RACE

PART V: OPPOSING THE ARMS RACE

LIST OF TABLES

Introduction

Adm. Gene LaRocque (ret.)

I have been concerned for many years that Americans do not appreciate the danger of nuclear war. For decades governments have cloaked the dreadful reality of nuclear war and nuclear weapons in reassuring and soothing language. Many Americans, including political and military leaders, have failed to understand the tremendously destructive nature of nuclear weapons. Americans have come to believe that a war with nuclear weapons could be controlled, won, and survived.

The traditional role of the military in all countries, in case of war, is to win. The military professional has always sought superiority. They tend to be uncomfortable with notions of military balance or equilibrium. They constantly seek to strengthen the defense of their countries and to maintain advantages. But my experience in the United States military has convinced me that nuclear weapons have changed the traditional rules of warfare. Despite this, the United States and the Soviet Union continue to approach the accumulation of military power in the nuclear age very much as they have in the past. Both countries constantly seek to improve their nuclear and conventional forces.

Many of us are shocked and sobered by the mad nuclear

scramble of the superpowers. It seems so obvious that they have diminished their own security in the nuclear competition. We all know that a balance of terror provides a precarious peace.

The Soviet Union and the United States are, in part, victims of modern military technology. Advances in weaponry, particularly better delivery systems, have dramatically compressed time and space. Thus, military leaders believe they must maintain large forces on a close-to-war status. In a nuclear war, each nation could destroy the other in 30 minutes. Nuclear missiles launched from submarines could land within 15 minutes. There is no defense, regardless of who strikes first. The latest generation of first strike weapons such as the MX, the Trident II, and the Pershing II is accelerating the hair trigger quality of preparedness for instant nuclear war. The prospect of immediate mass destruction seems to compel high states of military readiness and this situation inspires mutual suspicion and rhetorical harshness.

Continuation of the nuclear arms race is also made possible by widespread apathy about the danger of nuclear war. Many people believe that nuclear weapons will never be used. But the fact of the matter is that the military in both the U.S. and the Soviet Union sees nuclear weapons as a central instrument of military policy. Troops in both countries constantly train and practice for nuclear war.

Failure to appreciate the revolution in warfare and international affairs brought about by nuclear weapons has been and still is a fundamental problem, although in recent years there has been a salutary increase in public education about the nature of nuclear weapons and the consequences of nuclear war. More people are aware that a nuclear war would be unlike any other war in American history. Many are beginning to realize that we will not go to war next time—it will come to us. While most know that a nuclear war would be a war without winners, the majority of Americans apparently support the construction of thousands of new weapons each year. Paradoxically, there is a growing demand among informed people to slow, stop, and reverse the arms race.

But I fear that the shift in public attitudes has yet to make any substantial impact on the thinking of those who are currently in charge of the U.S. military establishment. Official policy remains enamored of nuclear weapons and continues to be based on attempts to pursue military advantage in the nuclear age. The fuzzy ideology of deterrence is proclaimed in public while strenuous efforts are made to prepare to try to fight and win a nuclear war.

This is not new with the Reagan Administration. The dominant thrust of U.S. military policy for decades, whether Republican or Democratic, liberal or conservative, has been to tie the U.S. ever more closely to preparation for nuclear war.

Opposition to the Vietnam war in the early 1970s helped to bring about a climate of public opinion for a time which sought to de-emphasize a militarist foreign policy. Americans learned some "lessons" from Vietnam, but it is noteworthy that none of these lessons had much impact on the generally very negative view that most Americans held of the Soviet Union. We rejected the Vietnam war but we also continue to reject the Soviet Union as a true collaborator in building international peace. The perceived need to contain the Soviet Union and fear of Soviet military power remained. We were only to be somewhat more cautious and restrained in our involvement in the Third World.

The Vietnam war ended in 1975. Already at that time there was far from unanimity about the direction U.S. foreign and military policy should take after Vietnam. Henry Kissinger had not given up seeking "strategic" confrontation with the Soviet Union and its client states in all parts of the globe. Former Defense Secretary James Schlesinger was actively pursuing plans for fighting a so-called limited nuclear war and developing new weapons for such purposes. Schlesinger, among others, was quick to reassert the necessity of America's global mission: "Without the constable there can only be anarchy." Nuclear weapons, both strategic and tactical, were to play a central role in the post-Vietnam U.S. policy.

The loss in Vietnam was a traumatic experience for the American people. While Americans finally came to reject the war and devoutly wish its termination, many Americans came to support increased U.S. military spending to compensate for the failure in Vietnam. A measure of paranoia over Soviet successes in a few small countries loomed large in the American mind because while we did not want to get involved in another war in a far away place again neither did we want the Soviets to extend their hegemony while we were still recovering from Vietnam.

U.S. relations with the Soviet Union were lukewarm in the early 1970s, a period when massive Soviet military aid to our opponent in Vietnam continued and when Allende was overthrown in Chile. It is only in retrospect that one can, with exaggeration characterize this period as one of detente. Senate ratification of the SALT I treaty in 1972 was accompanied by a stepping up of the U.S. nuclear weapons program, as the late Senator Henry Jackson, Defense Secretary Melvin Laird, and others continually warned of the danger of Soviet military power and the vulnerability of U.S. nuclear forces. The Joint Chiefs of Staff extracted funding from the U.S. Congress for an expanded nuclear buildup as the price for their support of SALT I. The important economic ties that the Soviets sought never materialized.

Missed opportunities have typified U.S.-Soviet relations since World War II. Opportunities to limit the nuclear weapons competition have frequently been lost since the days of Krushchev and Eisenhower. We could have had a comprehensive nuclear test ban in the early 1960s. We could have had a ban on MIRV in the early 1970s. The underlying fear and suspicion between the peoples of the two countries—fanned to emotional peaks on occasion by the leaders—have continually limited or destroyed possibilities for sustained improvement in relations. Seemingly accidental events such as the U-2 affair in 1960 or the Korean plane incident in 1983 have played a major role.

The loss in Vietnam coupled with the visible emergence of the Soviet Union as more or less a military equal of the U.S. was a most unsettling experience for the U.S. Beginning in 1969 President Nixon and other U.S. leaders spoke of the existence, and American acceptance, of strategic nuclear parity between the U.S. and the Soviet Union. Despite this rhetoric, many Americans were uncomfortable that the U.S. should settle for military equality with a country whose domestic practices and frequent international acts were so repugnant to our own values. Such a compromise or accommodation with "evil" was not to be easily accepted.

U.S. military leaders were also far from comfortable with the reality of U.S.-Soviet military equality. A dominant view was that because of the alleged inferiority of the U.S. and its allies in non-nuclear military forces, it was necessary for the U.S. to retain some exploitable nuclear edge over the Soviet Union. It was also believed that the U.S. world role required nuclear superiority. The U.S., with some fifty or so military allies around the world, many to whom the U.S. has committed a "nuclear umbrella," allegedly could not maintain this alliance system on a basis of nuclear stalemate with the Soviet enemy. The U.S. could not afford to be complacent about pushing the pace of nuclear weapons development or about accepting coercive Soviet nuclear capabilities.

Thus, despite the sweet words of nuclear parity and arms control treaties, the reality of U.S.-Soviet nuclear competition over the past 15 years is one of constant momentum and constant innovation. It is very far from the presumed ideal of nuclear balance. Ceaseless pursuit of advantage is the reality, not restrained compliance with stalemate.

The Reagan Administration has differed from its predecessors more in the frankness (or carelessness) of its rhetoric than in its actual nuclear weapons policies. Caspar Weinberger was probably representative when he said, "You show me a Secretary of Defense who's planning not to prevail and I'll show you a Secretary of Defense who ought to be impeached." Richard Wagner, Assistant to the Secretary of Defense for Atomic Energy, was even blunter in testimony before the House Armed Services Committee in March 1983:

> What it comes down to in the end is to keep their (Soviet) image of themselves inferior to their image of us, so that if a crisis comes they will have the gut feeling that they won't measure up to us. It is often said that the Soviet leaders are conservative. They are when they feel inferior.

In this view, any sort of Soviet self-confidence is viewed as dangerous for the U.S. and we should continually strive to keep the Soviets on edge and worried.

General John W. Vessey, Chairman of the Joint Chiefs of Staff, has also explicitly gone on the record on the need for a U.S. nuclear edge: "We don't want to be paralyzed by the fear of war...In the event deterrence fails, adequacy will be measured by its ability to win." General Vessey quotes an American basketball coach for guidance: "Everyone has the will to win, but few have the will to prepare to win."

However, the idea of seriously pursuing arms control, which acquired respectability in the U.S. for the first time in the last half of the 1960s, did constitute a major step forward. For the first time even some military leaders entertained the idea that certain steps of nuclear arms control could serve U.S. interests. It became plausible that there were some areas of common U.S.-Soviet interest in limiting the nuclear arms race.

But psychologically, most Americans, including political and military leaders, could not help but view any U.S. steps toward cooperation with the Soviets as a favor granted by the U.S. toward the morally inferior and backward Russians. If the Russians behaved better we would continue to dispense the favor of arms control agreements and limited cooperation. If they misbehaved and did not reform their evil ways we would withdraw our favors. This has been the basic American attitude from the beginning.

So it is no surprise that as international events unfolded during the 1970s and 1980s innumerable instances of Soviet

misbehavior occurred, from Angola to Afghanistan to Poland
to the Korean plane incident. There has hardly been a period of
more than a few months over the past dozen years when the
Soviets have not done something, or been accused of doing
something, that outrages millions of Americans.

Accusations large and small have filled the newspapers.
The Soviets have been accused of bombarding our embassy in
Moscow with harmful radiation, of sneaking combat troops
into Cuba, of cheating on all their arms control agreements
with the U.S., of incarcerating sane dissidents in insane
asylums, of using poison gases against civilians in Asia, of
using slave labor to build the gas pipeline, of attempting to kill
the Pope, of plotting a nuclear first strike, of habitually lying to
foreign leaders, etc. The list could be extended indefinitely.
Although many people would reject one or more accusation, the
cumulative impact of the nearly constant barrage of revelations
about Soviet misconduct cannot but affect nearly everyone.
Emotional American reactions in recent years have been exacerbated by the idea that somehow the Russians deceived us, that
they had promised to be good guys and then were found to have
lied about it.

All of this reflects the American tendency to look for
symbolism in foreign policy, our history of crusading fervor, our
ideals of eternal peace, denials of basic realities, and exaggerated fears in response to events abroad. Americans have
often used foreign policy as a vehicle for expressing unresolved
internal tenions.

But the problem of the Soviet Union is also real. There is
probably no more complex decision facing both individuals and
nations than how to assess and relate to the Soviet Union. From
the Bolshevik revolution led by Lenin in 1917 through the
Stalin era of extraordinary oppression and World War II to the
time of peaceful coexistence under Krushchev and since, the
Soviets have presented the most contradictory and disturbing
face to the world. Acceptance of the Soviets as a legitimate
power has only come grudgingly and painfully slowly. It was
not until 1933 that the U.S. took the elementary step of
establishing diplomatic relations with the Soviet Union.

Even today, with Ronald Reagan as President, the idea
that the communist regime in the Soviet Union can and should
be a transitory phenomenon is far from dead. The view that the
Soviet troublemakers are ultimately responsible for conflict
and discord in the world is also still widespread. These are not
simply the eccentric views of Mr. Reagan. At an emotional level
they reflect the deep repugnance that most people in the West

feel about what they know of Soviet society and the oppression of the individual in the Soviet system. We just cannot bring ourselves to place the Soviets on the same moral plane as ourselves. We are suspicious of nearly everything the Soviets do.

Actually, we have little competence to measure Soviet attitudes and little interest in doing so. The sad state of Soviet studies in the United States reflects our basic indifference to learning what the Soviets are really thinking. Dr. Robert Legvold of the Council on Foreign Relations summed up the situation:

> The gaps in our knowledge are enormous and they are growing...In the absense of serious, carefully research-ed studies, our view of the Soviet Union is shaped increasingly by popular impressions, *a priori* analyses, built from superficial reflections on the Soviet actions that most catch the eye, and traditional habits of thought.

Even Senator Dan Quayle, a conservative Republican from Indiana, says he is struck by "the incredible lack of knowledge about the Soviet people and Soviet history" that pervades the Congress.

We must make up our minds once and for all that the Soviet Union is here to stay and somehow we and the Russians must learn to live together. We are deluding ourselves to think as Hitler did, in talking to his generals, that "We have only to kick in the front door and the whole rotten edifice will come tumbling down!" This does not mean that we cannot hope for positive internal evolution in the Soviet Union.

As a result of the Korean plane incident in September 1983 we have learned again how deep and tenacious are the anti-Soviet feelings that Americans have. Fear and mistrust of the Russians is the dominant American foreign policy attitude. Sometimes these feelings are below the surface and latent and at other times they boil to the top and exercise a decisive influence. There is a long and complex history to anti-com-munist and anti-Russian sentiments in the U.S. It is paradox-ical that so many Americans would be willing to go to war with the hated Russians in light of the heightened awareness of the dangers of nuclear war that has come about recently. Some Americans apparently still think of war in World War II terms and do not fully appreciate the suicidal nature of nuclear war.

Emotions play a major role in foreign policy, although they are frequently ignored in academic analyses. Military studies in particular neglect the unpredictable or unquantifiable dimensions. Rationality and reasoned self-interest are usually thought to determine—even when we know better—the policies of modern states. But a major lesson of the Korean plane incident is the volatility of public opinion, notably in the United States. Americans seem to be spoiling for a fight, for an opportunity to strike down the "villain." If the Korean airplane had been a U.S. plane, then bellicose attitude in the U.S. could have elicited some form of military response which could have triggered a series of escalating steps which might have been difficult to stop.

More than anything else the Korean plane incident demonstrates the danger of letting U.S.-Soviet relations deteriorate to the point that in a crisis one side or the other is tempted to shoot first and ask questions later. We are all at risk in a climate of such intense tension. This is true regardless of the allocation of ultimate blame for the shooting down of a civilian airliner by the Soviet military. We should learn from history how often the onset of war is linked with misperception and misinformation.

Complacency about the stability of peace has been widespread. Most people, including leaders, have shared a certain confidence that East and West can continue to co-exist and that there will be no nuclear conflagration. Even in the face of the widespread anti-nuclear movements, the prevalence of confidence in peace has been the dominant mood of public opinion in the West. We have no scientific measure of public attitudes in the Soviet bloc but we may suspect that the vast majority of people in the Soviet Union and elsewhere also fundamentally do not believe in a high probability of nuclear conflict between East and West. Perhaps to preserve our sanity, most people seem to think that no matter what happens it will all come out all right in the end.

American military policy in the years since World War II has been articulated chiefly in the concept of deterrence. Defense Secretary Caspar Weinberger stated, in March 1983, "We are simply maintaining the calculus of deterrence." Deterrence has a reassuring sound to it. It is evoked on any and all occasions.

The most striking aspect about deterrence is that even though everyone talks about it, nobody can say what it consists of. Who knows what is necessary to deter? Who knows how much is enough? No one knows, and in part for this reason, we (and the Soviets) have accumulated essentially unlimited nuclear arsenals and work constantly in a very determined way to acquire still more weapons, new means of delivery, and new stratagems to use these weapons.

Deterrence is such a vague term that it can be used, and has been used, to justify everything we do. It is now purely a slogan. It has no real value as a guide to what we should do or what we actually do in our policy toward the Soviet Union. Actions we have taken in the name of deterrence have almost invariably been perceived by the Soviets as threatening and provocative and have resulted in stepped-up military responses by them. One person's deterrent is another person's threat.

In the current conditions of public and official ferment over nuclear issues, openings have been created for major departures from traditional approaches. The new opportunities have arisen unexpectedly, but there are real possibilities to mobilize broad political support for containing, limiting and nearly eliminating the nuclear arms race. The Reagan Administration, with its nuclear excesses, has ironically played the major role in making possible these changes.

But at the same time we move forward with arms negotiations we need to start dealing with the basic issue of how to facilitate peaceful coexistence between the United States and the Soviet Union. Fear and mistrust are at the heart of the nuclear arms race. They are at the heart of our deterrence policy theories which assume an aggressive intent on the part of the Soviet Union. We cannot go far toward slowing the nuclear arms race if the current level of fear and tension continues. Even at greatly reduced numbers of nuclear weapons, the world will not really be much better off if we and the Soviets continue to engage in hostile confrontation.

We are torn in contradictory directions by our anti-Soviet impulses and our desire for self-preservation. We have often let our revulsion against Soviet practices cloud our recognition of the mutual interests we share with the Soviets in opposing the enemy of nuclear war. Our feelings of moral superiority have frequently led us to act as if rejection of the Soviet way of life offers practical guidance as to how best to control nuclear weapons.

We need to be looking toward and actively planning for a future where East-West cooperation and understanding are strengthened as the fundamental basis for peace. We should be starting to move from a policy of deterrence based on fear and threat to a policy of mutual deterrence built through interdependence, mutuality of interest, trade, and cooperation in dealing with shared problems.

Editors' Introduction

Our planet is increasingly filled with tension. Presently, some forty local wars are being fought around the world. To greater and lesser degrees each one contains the ominous possibility of engaging superpower involvement and triggering a nuclear holocaust. The international economy is unstable with more and more nations unable to pay their debts. Recession may leapfrog into a world economic crisis. The dynamics are different but both superpowers are losing control over their "spheres of influence"—whether it be in Eastern Europe or Latin America. This is a positive development, but one that contributes to world tension. Many experts predict that at least one nuclear bomb will be detonated before the end of the century. The typical American isn't optimistic either. Approximately half of the adult population feels that the U.S. and the Soviet Union will go to war and that nuclear weapons will be used. Eugene Rostow, a former official in the Reagan administration believes that we are living in a "pre-war and not a post-war world." Clearly these are dangerous times. Without considerable progress in establishing a more stable and humane world, it is probably only a matter of decades before this heightened conflict concludes in a decisive shattering of world peace as we presently "enjoy" it.

The most immediate and pressing world issue at this moment in history is the global danger posed by the current escalation of the nuclear arms race. The danger of nuclear war in the 1980s is awesome. Not only are inherently more dangerous nuclear weapons being built—"first strike" weapons with built-in pressure to "use them or lose them"—but nuclear strategies are being developed and refined which make it increasingly likely that these weapons will be drawn into superpower conflicts throughout the world. The list of flash-points for nuclear war is a long one. We must join in condemning what Randall Forsberg, founder of the nuclear freeze movement, has characterized as "the hubris, the arrogance, the almost criminal carelessness of the men who pursue this policy in the confidence that they can play 'nuclear chicken' forever without losing control of the situation once." If we are to survive this century, the policies of the Pentagon must be decisively reversed.

This book is a very modest contribution to the task before us all. We have organized the book into five sections. The *first* presents different explanations for the arms race. The range of opinion reflects our feeling that the development of a critical perspective capable of illuminating the dynamics of the arms race is of critical importance, but also that an adequate theory does not yet exist. The *second* part examines some of the specific problems associated with nuclear weapons. They are offered in the spirit that many "technical" issues, such as missile accuracy and verification procedures, are in fact issues of substance and should be understood by the peace movement. The *third* section examines the impact of the arms race on American society and some of its institutions. The *fourth* discusses international issues and includes a short symposium on the nature of the Soviet threat, discussions of the Euromissile debate, and analyses of the movements, in both Western and Eastern Europe, attempting to resist the deployment of those missiles. The *last* section of the book focuses on issues of vital concern to the peace movement here in the United States.

As with most books there are many people who have been important to the project. First and foremost we thank all our contributors who have been without exception a pleasure to work with. Special thanks go to Carl Conetta of South End Press for his valuable editorial assistance, and to Hayes Gladstone who helped with much of the proof-reading. Without the efforts of Carmen Sirianni this book would still be a tree. He has been our "shadchan" (Yiddish for matchmaker) who suggested to each editor individually that such a book would be valuable and then brought us together to jointly undertake the project. Equally valuable has been Carmen's mediator role in points of disagreement between us. Needless to say, all errors of omission and judgement are his alone.

This book invites response from you the reader. The nuclear arms race is at a fundamental crossroads. We are about to enter a whole new era of nuclear weaponry which will dramatically lower the nuclear threshold and may make nuclear war only a matter of time. Or we can join the tens of millions who have demonstrated on behalf of halting and then reversing the arms race through a nuclear freeze and major—but balanced—reductions. The future of this planet hangs in the balance. We all have an obligation to ourselves and future generations to reduce significantly the risk of nuclear war. As Dr. Helen Caldicott of the Physicians for Social Responsibility has advised: "If you love this planet, you must change the priorities of your life."

PART I

DYNAMICS OF THE ARMS RACE

Introduction

The U.S. now possesses approximately 10,000 strategic warheads (and another 20,000 tactical bombs). Together they have an explosive power of more than half-a-million bombs of the type detonated over Hiroshima at the end of World War II. How many of these bombs are needed to deter, or prevent, a Soviet attack on the United States? Most experts, and even the Defense Department, agree that the number is comparatively small. The prospect of having some four hundred warheads exploded over and on one's territory is sufficient to deter an attack. No one seriously questions the capacity of the U.S. to destroy the Soviet Union should that country ever attack us. As Paul Joseph and Hayes Gladstone reveal in their analysis of the nuclear balance, there are no serious vulnerabilities jeopardizing America's nuclear deterrent. In fact, the United States is ahead of the Soviet Union in most areas that measure strategic superiority.

So why do we have so many atomic bombs? Why do we accumulate so much overkill? Why do we modernize our weapons? Why do we develop different types of bombs, different systems for delivering those bombs, and improve the accuracy of those bombs so they can land more exactly where they are aimed? Have confidence. We already know we can create Armageddon. Why then does the arms race move inexorably forward? This section tries to provide some answers.

One important fact is that American nuclear strategy was never, as Allan Krass and Dan Smith explain, based on a doctrine of pure deterrence. The U.S. was never satisfied only with making sure that it could respond to a Soviet attack. In fact, the possible first use of nuclear weapons has been an underlying premise of U.S. foreign policy ever since 1950, when Paul Nitze (now a leading arms negotiator for President Reagan) wrote a top-secret, presidentially approved National Security memorandum (NSC-68): "Our overall policy (on nuclear weapons) at the present time may be described as one designed to foster a world environment in which the American system can survive and flourish." Although he disagrees with the wisdom of the choice, Daniel Ellsberg argues much the same thing: the explicit threat of using nuclear weapons to give the U.S. the upper hand in political conflicts has been an underlying premise of American foreign policy. This doctrine of *extended deterrence*, or what arms race historian Michael Mandelbaum calls "strategic mercantilism," has involved the potential first use of nuclear weapons in an effort to protect American strategic interests in Europe and the Third World. The credibility of U.S. extended deterrence depended upon American nuclear superiority "at all points along the spectrum of violence." It was considerably less successful in counselling Soviet caution in local conflicts after the American loss of overwhelming nuclear superiority in the late 1960s. Nuclear threats were a less effective trump card when the Soviets possessed the ability to retaliate to an American first strike.

Christopher Paine examines the current desire for a nuclear war-fighting capability ("Reagatomics") and finds it a quest to recreate the old nuclear superiority that the U.S. enjoyed over the Soviet Union until the late 1960s. American plans for the more selective use of strategic weapons—as envisaged, for example, by the Schlesinger doctrine of 1974 and Carter's Presidential Directive 59 of 1980—show that the U.S. is trying to escape from the restrictions of a near parity. Washington is trying to restore political utility to its strategic forces.

Such a strategy depends upon counterforce, or the ability to destroy Soviet military forces and command centers. Counterforce itself is not new. Krass and Smith indicate that it has been a major part of American nuclear targeting for a long time. But a viable counterforce threat depends on the "house address" accuracy necessary to destroy hardened silos. Only now is nuclear weapons technology advanced enough to at least potentially possess such a capability. It is extreme accuracy that permits the U.S. to credibly threaten nuclear attacks at various levels of conflict and the ability to dominate at each level if the nuclear exchange is escalated.

This theory of escalation dominance suggests a tidiness of categories of nuclear weapons and escalation processes that belongs more to the theoretical scenarios of strategic analysts than to the realities of a world in the midst of nuclear war. Krass and Smith correctly point out the danger of a strategy based upon being able to "dismount at will". The existence of counter-force weapons systems on both sides not only greatly increases the likelihood of new U.S.—U.S.S.R. nuclear confrontations, but as Chris Paine notes, the Soviets are now much less likely to back down in a clash of "vital interests". "The impending new stage of the military confrontation," according to American foreign policy critic Richard Barnet, "is likely to make the world of the 1970s look in retrospect like a Quaker village." The current American drive for nuclear superiority will be increasingly destabilizing and is quickly putting the arms race on a hair trigger. This greater readiness to rely on nuclear weapons to achieve foreign policy ends has caused Paul Warnke, chief arms control negotiator during the first two years of Carter's presidency, to ask, "Do we want to reenact *High Noon* with nuclear weapons?"

The drive for U.S. nuclear superiority is a major but by no means complete answer to the question of what fuels the arms race. Many now talk of the inner and independent momentum of the arms race. Indeed the competition between the superpowers is based upon the worst possible scenario of what weapons the other side has or is developing. The result obviously is a race to keep ahead or not to fall too far behind. The technological escalation in nuclear weapons is also thought to have an independent existence. As Robert Oppenheimer once said, when scientists spot something "technologically sweet," they tend to go ahead and develop it and think about the consequences afterward. It is necessary to caution against a rigid technological determinism—technology has no mind of its own. The decision to pursue first-strike weaponry, for example, was widely discussed and decided upon by military and political officials. Yet it is also true that new weaponry may open up a range of possibilities unperceived by those who originally sought their acquisition.

The existence of inter-service rivalries, and the pressures from the so-called "military-industrial-complex," have also served to create far more nuclear weapons than are needed for simple deterrence. Fred Kaplan discusses the ongoing conflict between the Air Force and Navy over which nuclear strategies should be adopted and ultimately which service will have what weapons. Quite often, "peace" between them is achieved by giving both most of what they request. Now that Trident II will allow the Navy to get in on counterforce planning, we may see less doctrinal rivalry between the services. Both services will get practically everything they want!

When Eisenhower left office he sounded the major alarm about the military-industrial-complex—the Iron Triangle composed of big defense contractors (General Dynamics, Lockheed, McDonnell-Douglas, etc.), procurement officers in the Pentagon, and the politicians whose communities have become more dependent on defense spending. The revolving door between the Pentagon and the defense corporations has bred what James Fallows calls a "culture of procurement." Mary Kaldor discusses the increasing dependency of government on these corporations "to tell them what they need." And the competition between these large corporations has intensified technical "improvements" in weapons capability. But as Kaldor argues, many of these complex "improvements" have resulted in weapons that are more expensive and less reliable.

Our list of factors supporting the arms race should not be seen as all encompassing. The realm of state politics has not yet been adequately studied. For example, Carter gave the green light to the MX at least partly to win Senate approval of SALT II. Earlier the decision to build 1200 Minuteman missiles (twice the number that McNamara and his "whiz kids" thought necessary) was made so that the Kennedy administration could maintain a "credible" relationship with Congress and the Joint Chiefs of Staff. And we must not ignore the influence of the strategists from brain trusts like Rand. The "nuclear war priesthood" has concocted varied and elaborate plans for nuclear war-fighting, all of which demanded an increased number of nuclear weapons—in the name of "deterrence," of course!

Chapter 1

Reagatomics, or How To "Prevail"

Christopher Paine

Over the last two years, the Reagan Administration has made clear its unequivocal intention to equip U.S. nuclear forces with the kinds of weapons and control systems that will enable them not only to survive an initial thermonuclear exchange—this criterion having long been satisfied—but also to "endure" in a "protracted" nuclear war, enabling America to "prevail" over the Soviet Union in post-holocaust ruins.

While this strategy is not quite the radical departure from SALT-era doctrines that some exiled Democratic Party defense officials would have us believe, it does represent a mindless intensification of established trends toward nuclear warfighting—trends which were moderated in the past by the competing notion of "stable" deterrence achieved through a negotiated balance of mutually invulnerable retaliatory forces.

The Reagan Administration's belief that one side or the other might actually prevail in some meaningful sense in a nuclear war is not a novel idea for either American or Soviet strategists. What is new is that this ghoulish delusion is being pursued in a time of overall nuclear parity between the superpowers—and of growing Soviet-American capabilities for conventional as well as tactical nuclear intervention overseas.

Unlike the outcome of the Cuban missile crisis, in 1962, it is far from clear today that the Soviet Union would be willing to back down when its "vital" foreign interests clash with those of the United States. And both sides are becoming increasingly equipped for combat at every level of violence—conventional, chemical and nuclear—on the ladder of escalation leading to all-out nuclear war.

American Postwar Nuclear Policy

"Winning" a nuclear war was certainly American defense policy during the period from 1945 until the late 1960s, when the United States had first a nuclear monopoly and then massive but gradually waning superiority. Throughout most of this period, it possessed enough warheads and delivery vehicles to pre-emptively and severely damage both the conventional and nuclear war-making potential—military forces and war-supporting industry—of the Soviet Union.

Regardless of the possible consequences of such an American attack for Europe, and for the few American urban targets that might have been struck even then by Soviet nuclear weapons, U.S. leaders used their nuclear superiority as the basis for a policy promising massive retaliation against the Soviet Union in the event that its conventional forces threatened American interests abroad.

The Reagan Administration's belief that from the nettle of nuclear holocaust it can pluck the flower of victory, regardless of the millions of dead on both sides, is an idea as old as the atomic age itself. Indeed, much of what the Reagan Administration is saying and doing about nuclear weapons is alarmingly consistent with the views of those who were beguiled by the coercive possibility of nuclear superiority in the mid-1950s. Thus Paul Nitze, Reagan's chief negotiator at the intermediate nuclear forces talks in Geneva, argued in a 1956 issue of *Foreign Affairs* that despite the Soviet ability to deploy thermonuclear weapons a thousand times more powerful than the bomb that destroyed Hiroshima, it would still be possible to "win decisively" when "the word 'win' is used to suggest a comparison of the postwar position of one of the adversaries with the postwar position of the other adversary." Nitze added, "The victor will be in a position to issue orders to the loser and the loser will have to obey them or face complete chaos or extinction."

Throughout the 1960s, even as Defense Secretary Robert McNamara was publicly enunciating that deterrence of nuclear attack through the threat of "mutual assured destruction" was all that could be reliably achieved by either side, the Pentagon continued to emphasize strikes against Soviet nuclear and conventional military installations. "Most of our planned targets were military forces," recalled Henry Rowen, former Deputy Assistant Secretary of Defense and former president of the Rand Corporation, in a mid-1970s government study.

The Kennedy Administration did make an effort to move away from the massive retaliation doctrine of the Eisenhower years, chiefly by increasing reliance on conventional forces, but also by trying to introduce a measure of flexibility into the Pentagon's Single Integrated Operational Plan (SIOP), the U.S. master blueprint for all-out nuclear war. Nevertheless, the small number of nuclear "options" that were devised, including a distinct "counter-military" option, "involved thousands of weapons," Rowen admitted. Given the relative inaccuracy of the then-new intercontinental and submarine launched ballistic missiles, the megaton-range yields of most warheads in the strategic arsenal and the location of important military targets in and around cities, McNamara's Rand-inspired vision of a counterforce "no cities" option made little headway. The Air Force's traditional doctrine of an "optimum mix" of weapons delivered more or less simultaneously against "nuclear threat," "other military forces" and "urban-industrial" targets remained dominant.

But by the end of the 1960s, Rowen wrote, "increases in the number, hardness, and mobility of Soviet long-range nuclear forces...resulted in a decline in damage expectancy for this class of (military) targets." In other words, American nuclear superiority was ebbing. The Soviet Union was acquiring an increasing capacity to mount a devastating retaliation even after absorbing an American pre-emptive attack. Thus the United States was no longer able to threaten nuclear attacks on Moscow's military forces without worrying about the so-called "bonus" effects on Soviet civilians and industry. If the threats to use nuclear weapons in response to Soviet conventional attacks on overseas U.S. interests were to be preserved, some plausible way of managing and controlling nuclear escalation had to be found.

In 1974, Secretary of Defense James Schlesinger announced that U.S. nuclear war plans had been revised to take account of these new realities. Since the United States could no longer count on disarming the Soviet Union in a pre-emptive strike, and since antimissile weapons and civil defense schemes were technological and fiscal pipe dreams, some other means had to be developed for maintaining the credibility of U.S. nuclear threats.

It would be secured, Schlesinger announced, by instituting an array of preplanned "limited nuclear options," "tailored"to the scale of various Soviet provocations. In other words, the threat of Soviet nuclear retaliation or escalation might be "controlled" through the use of limited nuclear attacks that would redress the particular military situation at issue while providing the Soviet Union with an "incentive"—or at least an opportunity—to back down before destruction became widespread.

During the Carter Administration, this tit-for-tat strategy— which Schlesinger indicated could be "enhanced" by improved "hard-target kill capability"—took on an increasingly counter-military cast. Described by Secretary of Defense Harold Brown as the "countervailing strategy," it was formally endorsed as government policy in Presidential Directive 59, signed by Carter in July 1980. According to a *New York Times* account by Richard Burt, who at the time was the paper's national security correspondent and now is Assistant Secretary of State for European Affairs, PD-59 "requires American forces to be able to undertake precise limited nuclear strikes against military facilities in the Soviet Union, including missile bases and troop concentrations...(and) to develop the capacity to threaten Soviet political leaders in their underground shelters in time of war."

The Reagan Administration's Modernization Programs

Thus the trend toward a nuclear war-fighting posture was already well entrenched in the national security establishment by the time the wild-eyed practitioners of Reagatomics descended on Washington from their outposts at TRW, Boeing, Bechtel and the Committee on the Present Danger.

Nevertheless, a fair number within this "neo-hawk" fraternity believe that countervailing nuclear threats—the Nixon/ Ford/Carter strategy—are not enough. They argue that to be fully credible, the U.S. nuclear deterrent must have the capability of limiting damage to the United States in a protracted nuclear war. Ideally, they say, this capability would be composed of an imposing pre-emptive threat against Soviet missile silos, submarines, bombers, warning systems, command and control systems and air defenses; an "active" antiballistic missile (ABM) defense against any "residual" Soviet re-entry vehicles that escaped destruction in a pre-emptive U.S. attack; and "passive" civil defense measures such as evacuation from "high risk" areas and "expedient shelters" against fallout from any nuclear warheads that penetrate the ABM system and explode on American territory. Looking toward the future, they advocate yet another layer of defense be deployed in space—the zone thay call the "high frontier"—to further reduce the size of any residual Soviet retaliatory attack. With such an imposing array of offensive and defensive military capabilities behind them in a crisis, we are told, U.S. leaders would appear less afraid of war—and therefore more willing to pursue vital national interests eyeball-to-eyeball and fireball-to-fireball with the Russians.

As described in Congressional testimony by Richard De-Lauer, Undersecretary of Defense for Research and Engineering and a former TRW vice president, a strategy of fully credible nuclear deterrence means that "we must improve the capability to control U.S. forces throughout crisis situations *up to and including protracted nuclear war*, improve the survivability and endurance of strategic offensive forces and intelligence resources, protect the U.S. population in order to reduce the risks of coercion and blackmail, and counter Soviet capabilities and initiatives by exploiting their weaknesses." (emphasis added.)

The President's strategic program, DeLauer testified, "is designed to take control of the U.S./Soviet strategic balance and shape it to our benefit." To implement this program, Reagan would like the nation to buy 100 B-1B strategic bombers at an estimated total program cost of $40 billion; more than 100 radar-evading, hi-tech "stealth" bombers ($56 billion); 100 MX missiles ($20 billion); 20 Trident submarines ($30 billion); 480 Trident-2 submarine-launched missiles ($30 billion-plus); 3,400 air-launched cruise missiles (ALCMs) and advanced stealth ALCMs ($8 billion); 3,000 sea-launched cruise missiles ($7 billion); bomber, missile and civil defense systems ($29 billion); and "enduring" nuclear command, control and communications and intelligence (C^3) systems ($22 billion)—for a grand total of at least $242 billion. And that is just the beginning: recently the Administration has been toying with plans for the deployment of possibly thousands of lightweight and potentially mobile single-warhead intercontinental missiles that would cost another $30 billion to $40 billion. Then there is Reagan's provocative and risky proposal to deploy an ABM system in space—a project that could cost hundreds of billions of dollars for research alone.

In defense of this extremely expensive and unabashedly aggressive program, Gen. John W. Vessey, Chairman of the Joint Chiefs of Staff, testified before Congress in 1982 that the crux of America's security problem is that Soviet acquisition of a massive and survivable nuclear retaliatory force allows Moscow "to build an atmosphere in which they can pursue their own political objectives in the world without the United States threatening to interfere with their pursuit of those objectives." In a classical explication of the object of U.S. strategy, Vessey added: "We don't want a war and we certainly don't want a nuclear war. But at the same time we don't want to be paralyzed by the fear of war as we pursue our economic, political, social and cultural objectives."

Eliminating constraints on U.S. freedom of action in the global arena while imposing such constraints on the Soviet Union is what most American policy makers mean when they speak of "maintaining deterrence." For Eugene Rostow, recently fired as chief of the Arms Control and Disarmament Agency, this means "confronting Soviet expansion...with the prospect of unacceptable risk, to which they have always responded with prudence." In effect, maintaining deterrence has become a quest for nuclear weapons and doctrines that will somehow convince Moscow that in moments of extreme crisis U.S. leaders might not be daunted by the prospect of unacceptable risk. Maintaining an ability to sow such doubts in the minds of Soviet leaders, we are told, is the essence of deterrence. When U.S. "vital interests" are at stake, these must somehow be made to appear more vital than even the immunity of American and allied citizens to nuclear attack; that is, the unacceptable risk of nuclear war must be manipulated in such a way to make it appear less unacceptable to us than it is to the Russians.

Given the existence of massive conventional forces and tactical nuclear munitions on the Soviet side, and given the steady growth of an invulnerable long-range Soviet second-strike capability, the Pentagon's strategic logic now dictates that threats to begin the process of nuclear escalation—ostensibly to defend American interests in specific overseas threats—can only be rendered credible by continuous modernization of U.S. nuclear and conventional warfighting capabilities "across the full spectrum of conflict," from brush-fire engagements to major regional conflicts and then to protracted intercontinental nuclear wars.

In order to convince the Russians that the United States is prepared to use its nuclear deterrent, America's vital interests must be shown to be at stake. This is the mission of U.S. "power projection" forces—the Rapid Deployment Forces and other units formed for military intervention overseas. Once deployed, these forces must appear to be such a firm expression of Washington's commitment to protect its interests that the

Russians could reasonably expect nuclear retaliation should they succeed in over-running them.

To heighten such Soviet fears, the Reagan Administration is modernizing the tactical nuclear weapons stockpile and accelerating the production of "dual-capable" delivery systems, which could deliver nuclear or conventional munitions. Old F-4 Phantom attack planes in the Marine Air-Ground Task Force that were not certified for delivering nuclear weapons are being replaced by F-18 Hornets that are certified. Non-nuclear AV-8A Harrier jump-jets are being replaced by nuclear-capable AV-8Bs. Non-nuclear 105-millimeter howitzers are being replaced by the dual-capable 155 millimeter gun, almost doubling the Marines' nuclear artillery arsenal. Army and Marine 8-inch howitzers will also be equipped to fire the W-79 "neutron" warhead, about 800 of which are now being stockpiled in the United States for potential deployment overseas.

Pentagon planners fear, however, that the threat to use these and other tactical nuclear systems may not appear particularly convincing in view of the matching capabilities of the Soviet Union. Indeed, the Reagan Administration believes that the credibility of this nuclear "first-use" threat needs to be reinforced by regional and intercontinental nuclear forces designed to destroy Soviet nuclear forces or, failing that, at least to deprive the Soviet Union of limited nuclear options of the sort envisioned by former Defense Secretary Schlesinger.

Developing Regional Forces

Prime candidates for the regional warfare role in the Reagan Administration's nuclear master plan include the B-52H bomber and, beginning in 1986, the B-1B "long-range combat aircraft"; precision-guided Pershing-2 intermediate-range ballistic missiles; and ground- and sea-launched cruise missiles (GLCMs and SLCMs). These weapons provide the intermediate links in what Pentagon strategists like to think of as the "seamless web" of deterrence, falling between "conventional warfare options" and "execution of the Single Integrated Operational Plan."

Some Pentagon officials are evidently worried that Reagan's offer to forgo deployment of land-based intermediate-range missiles in Europe as part of a zero-option agreement with the Soviet Union could undermine the credibility of the "seamless web." According to Richard Perle, Assistant Secretary of Defense for International Security Policy, the President's proposal "will leave a gap. There is no question about that. We will not be able in the aftermath of the zero option, should that be approved in treaty form, to attack missiles from Western European territory and strike targets in the Soviet homeland, and I know there is a concern about that." Perle hastened to reassure the Senate Armed Services Committee, however, that "the benefits (of this option) are significant benefits. They would leave our theater nuclear forces far more survivable than they are under circumstances of the SS-20 threat and we will retain other means of attacking targets in the Soviet homeland."

One of the other means Perle is counting on is the nuclear version of the Tomahawk cruise missile, a sea-launched variant of the missile Reagan is ostensibly offering not to deploy in Europe. Quite apart from the debate over comparative U.S.-Soviet nuclear warfighting capabilities in Europe, the mere existence of the program places the President's vaunted zero option in a rather different light. Incredibly, the only reference to the nuclear SLCM program in Defense Secretary Caspar Weinberger's fiscal 1984 "Annual Report to Congress" is this brief comment: "For the near term, we plan to deploy sea-launched cruise missiles with nuclear warheads on attack submarines and surface ships. These missiles will strengthen our nuclear capabilities by providing survivable forces that can strike the full range of enemy targets." Discussion of the nuclear Tomahawks in Weinberger's 1983 report was equally brief and unenlightening, making no reference to their deployment on surface ships, but suggesting that "these weapons will provide some near-term hard-target kill capability" while contributing to a "strategic reserve." (A "strategic reserve" is the force the Pentagon plans to withhold from the SIOP in order to maintain a nuclear force for "large protection and coercion" in the "post-attack environment.")

According to Adm. Frank B. Kelso, director of the Navy's Strategic Submarine Division, "We plan to deploy a small number of nuclear-armed cruise missiles on SSNs (nuclear attack submarines) starting in 1984...None of these cruise missiles will be dedicated to SIOP. Nuclear SLCMs will be part of the strategic reserve force and will be available for reconstitution and retargeting, if necessary, during the post-SIOP periods." Admiral Kelso testified that these weapons would help the United States "retain a measure of coercive power in the post-exchange environment." Kelso did not indicate what would be left to shoot at after the United States had blanketed the Soviet Union with thousands of nuclear warheads.

A less bizarre but more provocative role for the nuclear Tomahawk was also described by Admiral Kelso. This role, no doubt, is the real one. Since this missile is "not planned for commitment to the SIOP or the NATO general strike plan, it will be available for selective release in non-SIOP options...to provide extremely accurate strikes against theater targets." In other words, the nuclear SLCM could be used as at least a partial substitute for the land-based cruise missiles that would be prohibited by the President's zero-option proposal.

According to recent newspaper accounts, the Pentagon's long-range plans call for deployment of some 3,000 to 4,000 sea-based cruise missiles of all types by the early 1990s. The Administration suggested in 1982 that perhaps 400 of these might be nuclear armed; more recently it announced that the number has been raised to 1,000. How many ultimately will be produced and armed with nuclear warheads is anybody's guess, including the Russians. The flagrant irresponsibility of this program can scarcely be exaggerated: several thousand cruise-missiles deployed on more than 200 Navy vessels, all capable of delivering nuclear warheads to Soviet territory. How will the Russians be able to tell which Tomahawks are conventional and which are not? The nuclear SLCM represents a monstrous and wholly gratuitous complication for arms control—which is perhaps why the Reagan Administration is so enthusiastic about it.

And these are merely the current plans. Given the enormous nuclear potential of the SLCM force, one may take it for granted that—short of a nuclear freeze, which would prevent production of cruise missile warheads—the Soviet Union will probably feel compelled to plan for the worst case and place additional missiles on its ships. As a result, U.S. forces will be more vulnerable and the surest American response will be a further, more dangerous expansion of its cruise missile arsenal. In the end it means running formidable risks to obtain what retired Admiral Elmo Zumwalt and Worth Bagley call "a long-range strike weapon for deterring regional aggression."

Zumwalt and Bagley suggest that the purpose of the nuclear SLCM is to create greater freedom of action for U.S. sea-based power to projection forces. To rid themselves of the SLCM threat, the admirals argue, "the Soviets would have to launch simultaneous attacks against the (nuclear) strike-capable ships dispersed widely over regional waters. It is an impossible task." Not being able to prevent nuclear retaliation from the sea, they say, "Moscow cannot be expected to risk the use of nuclear weapons against our naval forces defending regional interests." In effect, the SLCM is being sold as the ticket to regional nuclear superiority.

War Escalation Capability

Because the Soviet Union also possesses intermediate-range weapons for fighting regional wars—such as SS-20 missiles and Backfire bombers—the outcome of regional conflict would by no means automatically favor the United States and its allies. This being the case, Pentagon planners reason that accurate U.S. intercontinental strategic nuclear weapons could pre-emptively destroy the Russian's ability to wage conventional and tactical nuclear war in specific theaters, while holding "collateral damage" in the rest of the Soviet Union to levels low enough to provide Moscow with an incentive for not escalating the conflict even further. Pentagon planners now appear to believe that as long as both sides are able to maintain control over a significant portion of their nuclear forces, they would stop short of launching an all-out nuclear attack on cities. These strategists believe, moreover, that a nuclear war confined largely to military targets could become quite protracted—lasting for days, weeks or even months.

If they are right, then the United States must have the ability to deter Moscow from launching limited strategic nuclear attacks by threatening the prompt destruction of Soviet counterforce weapons, particularly the more accurate ICBMs deployed in hardened silos. From a nuclear war-fighting perspective, if these missiles and their command and control systems are perceived as being vulnerable, an American president or a Soviet premier might be less inclined to threaten their deliberate limited use in a crisis, out of fear that such threats might spark a pre-emptive attack. It follows from such reasoning that the side with the most accurate and survivable weapons will be able to "dominate" the process of nuclear escalation and achieve its national objectives, before the conflict becomes an all-out nuclear war.

As interpreted by Gen. Bennie L. Davis, commander of the Strategic Air Command, this outlook means that "for combatant commanders to meet today's defense policy requirements, they must possess...strategic forces which are capable of destroying, neutralizing or disrupting the enemy in a measured and selective manner across the conflict spectrum, whether nuclear or conventional, spasmodic or protracted." In contrast with the strategy of the 1960s and early 1970s, Davis noted, "today we must provide flexible targeting options which destroy hard and soft targets, yet keep civilian fatalities at the lowest possible level."

This is the principal reason, Davis explained to the Senate Armed Services Committee, that the Pentagon seeks deployment of the highly accurate MX missile. "As we go from a strategy of assured destruction to one which stresses war-fighting capability, that is, the priority targeting of military and leadership targets, you need weapons that are more accurate—that give you a capability against Soviet military and leadership elements."

It is essential, Davis argued, that we have ICBMs "with the accuracy, yield and range to place Soviet silos and launch control facilities at risk. We must insure our systems are so structured that the Soviets cannot perceive their nuclear threat to the U.S. is afforded sanctuary status, either by time or by distance." Because the newest generation of Soviet land-based missiles—SS-17s, SS-18s and SS-19s—are deployed in hardened protected silos, "we need MX as a prompt hard-target killer." Some aircraft weapons are also hard-target killers, he noted, but they are too slow. Only the MX "puts those fourth-generation (Soviet) missiles at risk."

Davis's sentiments were echoed by Deputy Under Secretary of Defense James P. Wade, who testified that the United States needs the MX because older missiles "do not have the accuracy to significantly help influence Soviet behavior in a crisis."

Like other military leaders, Davis invoked the "window of vulnerability"—the theoretical vulnerability of U.S. land-based ICBMs to a pre-emptive Soviet strike—as the driving force behind the Administration's big nuclear buildup. In reality, the Pentagon's imposing charts, with the ominous trend lines documenting the existence of the "window," are a setup. If we look at the counterforce capabilities of both superpowers, the "window of vulnerability" is actually wider on the Soviet side: the United States poses a greater pre-emptive threat to the *total* Soviet nuclear deterrent than the Soviet Union poses to the *total* U.S. deterrent. This is because two thirds of the 7,500 Soviet strategic warheads are concentrated on 668 land-based SS-18 and SS-19 missiles. By contrast, only about one fourth of the 9,200-odd U.S. strategic warheads are concentrated in 1,054 silos, making the U.S. deterrent considerably less vulnerable to destruction by surprise attack.

Once the MX and other counterforce weapons are in production, the next step on the Reagan agenda is acquiring a defensive, warfighting capability, combining an anti-ballistic missile system and civil defense. Although always described as defensive weapons, ABMs could play an *offensive* role in a U.S. first strike, reducing the efforts of the Soviet retaliation by intercepting enemy missiles that survive an initial U.S. assault.

In such a scenario, civil defense measures would provide shelter for the population from any Soviet weapons that do penetrate the ABM system.

In line with this long-term perspective, top military and civilian officials in the Reagan Administration have become openly hostile to the exisiting ABM treaty. Secretary of Defense Weinberger, for example, incorrectly informed the Senate Armed Services Committee last December that "there is no change in the treaty needed" if the Administration opts for an ABM system to defend the proposed "dense pack" MX deployment. Displaying (or feigning) ignorance of the fact that the 1972 ABM treaty and its 1974 protocol permit the U.S. to move its ABM system from Grand Forks, North Dakota, *only* to Washington, D.C., he testified, "Instead of Grand Forks, we could put an ABM system on Fort Warren, in Wyoming." Weinberger further declared, "I am fully prepared to make that notification any time it is determined that an ABM system be constructed...The sooner we get to it, the better I like it."

According to Maj. Gen. Grayson Tate, the Army's Ballistic Missile Defense (BMD) Program manager, "this Administration has made it very plain that they intend to restore some sort of balance between offense and defense." For fiscal 1984, the Administration is requesting $709.3 million for BMD development, and the proposed funding for 1985 more than doubles that amount to nearly $1.6 billion. The only explanation Weinberger's fiscal 1984 annual report offers for this large expenditure in a field supposedly foreclosed by treaty is that the "program is structured...so that we could field an advanced and highly effective BMD system quickly should the need arise."

Indeed, this "need" could arise much sooner than most supporters of the ABM treaty would like. Having already discarded some thirty-five previous options in its search for a survivable MX basing mode, the Reagan Administration could well decide to forge ahead with a plan to deploy a low-altitude BMD system for the controversial missile.

And that is only one BMD option being studied. In his television address on March 23, President Reagan proposed an open-ended program to develop a whole array of anti-missile systems. The efforts, which according to Reagan "may not be accomplished before the end of this century," would make use of lasers, particle beam weapons and other spacewars technology.

If President Reagan or his successors manage to abrogate the ABM treaty and deploy a ballistic missile defense system, then the only stone missing from the Administration's nuclear warfighting arch would be a serious civil defense program.

Predictably, the purveyors of Reagatomics have not neglected this area either. The Administration regards civil defense as a kind of psychic swagger stick for American leaders in a crisis, to convince Soviet leaders that we are quite as capable of self-delusion as they are, and therefore equally immune to nuclear coercion.

What is most disturbing, however, is the evidence that the President and his civil defense director, Louis Giuffrida, actually believe that civil defense would be effective. According to Giuffrida, the President had directed that the U.S. civil defense program be strengthened so as to "reduce the possibility that the United States could be coerced in time of crisis," and to "provide for survival of a substantial portion of the U.S. population in the event of a nuclear war...and for the continuity of government."

Also critical to the attainment of the Administration's nuclear warfighting agenda is a major step-up in the testing and production of new nuclear warheads and bombs. According to Maj. Gen. William W. Hoover, director of the Office of Military Application in the Department of Energy, the nuclear weapons production complex is a "corporation" that would rank "in the top quarter of the Fortune 500," with sales of a "product line" that currently includes nine warheads. Strategic munitions now in production include the W-76 warhead for the Trident 1 missile, the W-78 warhead for the improved Minuteman 3 and the W-80 warhead for the air-launched cruise missile. Several other warheads are in the final stages of development, including the W-87 for the MX missile's advanced ballistic reentry vehicle (ABRV) and the B-83, a "modern strategic bomb that will be capable of high-speed, low-altitude delivery."

The Energy's Department's theater nuclear product line currently includes a new lower-yield warhead for the ground-launched cruise missile and an "air burst-surface burst" warhead for the Pershing 2. Also in production are enhanced radiation warhead for the Lance battlefield missile (W-70) and the 8-inch nuclear artillery projectile (W-79). The W-82 warhead for the widely deployed 155-millimeter howitizer is in the developmental stage, as is the W-81 warhead for the Navy's Standard 2 air defense missile.

All told, the Reagan Administration is planning the production of an estimated 17,000 new nuclear warheads over the next decade and the retirement of about 11,000 older warheads—a net increase of some 6,000, expanding the total arsenal from 26,000 to 32,000 warheads and bombs. Commenting on the huge increase in workload imposed by the Administration's "strategic modernization" program, General Hoover testified that the response of his organization, "like the rest of American industry, is to improve productivity." He added, "We feel strongly that we must have more new automation and computer-aided design and manufacturing techniques and robotics."

Conclusion

The Reagan Administration seems bent on resurrecting what Herman Kahn once called a "not-incredible first-strike" capability—an ability to counter the threat of Soviet conventional or limited nuclear attacks with a range of pre-emptive nuclear strikes that could "disarm" or at least severely damage Soviet nuclear forces in all theaters of operation. The Reagan Administration and its allies in the Pentagon and the weapons complex apparently believe they can approach this goal by judiciously manipulating the strategic balance through carefully circumscribed arms "reductions" while modernizing the American nuclear arsenal across the board.

The nuclear orthodoxy now propping up the newest round of the arms race is open to challenge on many fronts, not the least of which is that the composite sketched here lends Reagatomics a degree of intellectual coherence it rarely achieves in practice. Reagatomics is actually a highly improvised intellectual pastiche whose chief function is to rationalize long-standing technocratic, industrial and anti-Soviet political interests.

Nuclear warfighting doctrine can be opposed on many grounds. First, placing the burden on Moscow of making a rational moral choice about whether to escalate in a dire crisis may not be the way to insure U.S. security; second, none of the nuclear warfighting weapons are likely to perform with the degrees of accuracy and reliability that the scenarios require; third, limiting a nuclear conflict requires assured communication with the enemy as well as one's own forces, something that is likely to be impossible in the radioactive frenzy of the nuclear battlefield; and fourth, efforts to negotiate meaningful arms control agreements will surely be overtaken by the rush to deploy new warfighting systems on both sides.

It may be safely predicted that this Administration will not attain a reliable and useable nuclear warfighting capability. But the Soviet-American enmity and the potential for miscalulation engendered by the quest for it contain the seeds of an unprecedented genocidal castastrophe.

Chapter 2

Fallacies in Deterrence and Warfighting Strategies

Allan Krass and Dan Smith

In the attempt to understand nuclear strategy and new developments in the field of nuclear weapons, the term 'deterrence' now serves as much to cause confusion as to enlighten. In Western countries, the popular conception of deterrence is that it is fundamentally defensive and reactive: nuclear weapons would be used by the West only in retaliation, and are possessed only so that the threat of overwhelming retaliation will deter agression.

However, there are several different doctrines for nuclear weapons which can all be referred to under the label of deterrence. The concept has undergone continual and profound changes over the past three decades. The doctrines which have now emerged are barely distinguishable from the coercive strategies of threat and counter-threat which have characterized the politics of the industrialized world for over a century—with the crucial exception, of course, that the armed forces to which they relate now possess vastly more destructive power.

Through the tangled web of different doctrines all calling themselves "deterrence" it is possible to distinguish two basic models. One is the reactive and defensive strategy popularly understood to be the intrinsic nature of nuclear deterrence -- we shall refer to this as "pure" deterrence. The other is a more complex and flexible approach to the question of the use of nuclear weapons and can be referred to as a "war-fighting" doctrine or "counterforce" strategy (so-called because of the importance it gives to destroying the other side's *forces*). Like pure deterrence, war-fighting or counterforce strategies mount a threat to a potential aggressor which is intended to deter that aggressor, but the nature of the threat is different. At its most direct, we can say that the threat entailed in pure deterrence is a threat of *punishment*, while the threat entailed in counter-force strategy is a threat of *defeat*. Defeat for one side implies victory for the other: thus it is necessary to prepare to fight and win a nuclear war. Pure deterrence is not interested in victory, only in inflicting upon the aggressor whatever annihilation the deterring state itself has suffered.

The basic difference between punishment and defeat is reflected in different doctrines about the employment of and the requirements for nuclear weapons. Pure deterrence supposes that nuclear weapons would only be used in retaliation for a nuclear attack, and, seeking to inflict enormous damage in return, requires powerful "city-killing" weapons with no very stringent demands in terms of accuracy. By contrast, a counterforce or war-fighting strategy is more flexible: nuclear weapons might be used in retaliation, but they might be used before the other side has launched a nuclear strike; they might be used in overwhelming force, or in relatively limited ways; it is therefore necessary to have a wide range of types of weapons, and to have the greatest accuracy possible.

In this context, it should be noted that for as long as NATO has had nuclear weapons in Europe (since the early 1950s) it has reserved the option of using them whether or not the Warsaw Pact has already launched nuclear strikes. NATO's doctrine of deterrence, that is, includes the willingness to retaliate with nuclear means against non-nuclear aggression, and thus to start a nuclear war. Similarly, in the 1950s and again in the 1970s and today, U.S. doctrine for strategic nuclear forces has included the possible "first use" of nuclear weapons. In this essay we shall first look at the problems of pure deterrence. These problems are partly due to flaws and contradictions within the theory of nuclear deterrence itself, partly the result of pressures on deterrence in practice. One of the major pressures comes from the seemingly irresistible onward march of technology, constantly creating problems for deterrence, constantly making available strategic options which seem to make counterforce more attractive. We shall then consider the flaws in counterforce strategy, the immense risks that are taken on the basis of elaborate theories which seem simply to ignore the problems and dangers they are generating. And then we shall turn to a summary of the technological developments of the 1970s which have all moved nuclear doctrine towards counterforce.

In fact, we must begin by realizing that pure nuclear deterrence has never really been practiced, although the doctrine of "mutual assured destruction" in the USA in the 1960s came close to it. But the popular conception of deterrence as essentially defensive and reactive has been reinforced by numerous statements and writings, of which one stands out as having particular historical significance, made by U.S. Secretary of State, John Foster Dulles, in 1954:

> The way to deter aggression is for the free community to be willing and able to respond vigorously at places and with means of its own choosing...to depend primarily on a great capacity to retaliate instantly, by means and at places of our choosing.[1]

Similarly, on the Soviet side, also in 1954:

> If, however, the aggressive circles, relying on atomic weapons, should decide on madness and seek to test the strength and might of the Soviet Union, then it cannot be doubted that the aggressor would be crushed by that very weapon...[2]

These statements leave no doubt that deterrence is a system based on threat. But to understand how deterrence has shifted since 1954, it is essential to understand the dual nature of threats: they can be defensive or offensive, deterrent or coercive.

It would be impossible to explain the development of modern nuclear weapons if one insisted on defining deterrence as purely defensive and reactive. We must now learn to think of deterrence as "flexible" and "extended," containing capabilities for "second-strike counterforce" and "sub-holocaust engagements." It has come to be accepted in the USA that nuclear deterrence must be addressed to threats far below the level of destructiveness of strategic nuclear warfare, and some writers close to the Reagan administration have been willing to go further:

> (T)he West needs to devise ways in which it can employ strategic nuclear forces coercively, while minimizing the potentially paralyzing impact of self-deterrence. U.S. strategic planning should exploit Soviet fears insofar as is feasible from the Soviet perspective...[3]

Soviet views are more difficult to ascertain; but they seem to have been more consistent and less ambiguous (at least on the surface) than American views. Most interpreters of Soviet nuclear doctrine agree that the USSR has never made much of an intellectual effort to distinguish between concepts of deterrence and war-fighting. The Soviet Union has certainly recognized the deterrent value of its military power, but appears to have assumed that this arises ultimately from its power to fight and win wars. Whether a Western interpreter chooses to focus on the deterrent or the war-fighting aspect seems to depend more on the political preferences of the observer than on any inherent doctrinal distinction or preference in Soviet thinking itself.

The Problems of Pure Deterrence

On the face of it, "pure" deterrence seems to hold out a relatively benevolent prospect, in which the states of both NATO and the Warsaw Pact would be deterred from nuclear aggression. If this could be extended to cover non-nuclear aggression (although it would be preferable to deter non-nuclear aggression through non-nuclear means), it would seem that a stable situation of mutual deterrence and mutual non-aggression would result. This would not be the best of all possible worlds—the system might break down and lead to war through technical accident, miscalculation or sheer mischance, but it might be argued that technological safe-guards together with political dialogue and the 'hot-line' system of crisis-communications could sharply reduce those risks. It would seem to provide a way of living with nuclear weapons in a divided world, and it might provide the basis for steadily reducing nuclear weapons by mutual agreement.

Many advocates of nuclear arms control and most of those who believe the West's nuclear strategies are strategies of pure deterrence seem to believe that this is an accurate picture of the present. To understand why it is not accurate one needs to understand the problems of pure deterrence, problems which have been exposed by critics on two sides—by those who have gone on to argue for nuclear disarmament, and by those who have gone on to argue for different doctrines for the deployment of nuclear weapons.

The first problem is the essentially defensive and reactive nature of a pure deterrent posture. Looked at one way, this seems like its basic attraction, the foundation on which the stability of mutual deterrence could be built. But looked at differently, it results in a strategy which leaves all the initiative to the adversary and deprives the possession of nuclear weapons of any real political value: in a purely deterrent posture, nuclear weapons become useless as coercive implements. In the USA, this criticism had been thoroughly aired even before the first public enunciation of the doctrine of massive retaliation in 1954. Indeed, in the same speech, from which we have already quoted, Dulles took pains to reassure his audience that the new doctrine did not abandon the initiative to the other side:

> Now the Department of Defense and the Joint Chiefs of Staff can shape our military establishment to fit...*our* policy, instead of having to try to be ready to meet the enemy's many choices. That permits...a selection of military means instead of a multiplication of means...

But these reassurances were not convincing then, and they are not convincing today.

The second problem is suggested by the requirement that, to be deterred, the enemy "must understand what behavior of his will cause the violence to be inflicted and what will cause it to be withheld."[4] In other words, the deterrent threat must be both unambiguous and credible. But by being unambiguous, by being explicit about just what is being deterred, and by making an irrevocable commitment to carrying out the threat, a national leader totally loses flexibility; this is a position in which no political leader will ever willingly be placed, and which again risks ceding the initiative to the adversary. The criterion of credibility proved too full of logical flaws to survive analysis. Simply stated, the problem is how a nation credibly commits itself to retaliation by suicide, to saying, in effect, "One step further and I'll shoot (myself)." Attempts to solve this problem led to some of the more bizarre proposals of the 1950s in the form of 'doomsday machines' which would automatically unleash nuclear retaliation against the appropriate form of aggression. Early on, it was recognized that assigning the task of retaliation to computers could eliminate the unpredictable factors of human fear, remorse or compassion.

The third problem is revealed exactly by such proposals, which carry pure deterrence to its full technological and logical conclusions: its utter moral repugnance. Naturally, this was initially exposed more by advocates of disarmament than by advocates of war-fighting concepts, but the latter have also often relied on moral objections to mass murder to sustain their arguments. It is a measure of the way in which the debate has shifted that, especially in the USA, advocates of arms control and disarmament now find themselves often forced to defend, on practical political grounds, a strategy based on threats to destroy civilian populations which fundamentally conflicts with their own moral convictions.

The fourth problem follows from these three—the effect of deterrence on the morale of the political leadership, military establishment and civilian population. The morale of political leaders cannot help but be reduced by a strategy which effectively puts the most vital issues of security beyond their control and commits them to mass murder, while civilian morale must certainly be undermined by a strategy which leaves civilians as helpless victims of a constantly threatening destruction against which defense is both impossible and (if the doctrine is taken seriously) undesirable. But equally important would be the effect on military morale. A pure deterrent posture would put the military into an impossible position: it recognizes the possibility of war and, indeed, postulates the adversary's aggressive predilictions, but then leaves all the initiative to that adversary to decide when, where and how the war will be fought. The doctrine would deny the possibility or desirability of pre-empting, weakening or resisting the attack and, in effect, say to military officers: You must sit and wait for the enemy to attack; then you must sit and watch the enemy's missiles destroy your planes, ships, missiles, communications facilities and so on; then your job is to gather together everything you have left and send it off to kill defenseless civilians in the enemy's country; the more defenseless civilians you kill, the better you will have done your job; if the enemy kills defenseless civilians in your country, that is not your concern and is irrelevant to the completion of your task.

These four problems in pure deterrence constitute strong arguments against it. But a fifth problem, concerning technological advance, makes it extremely difficult to sustain a stable basis for deterrence. Pure deterrence might be expected to create stability between two adversaries, and to some extent this stability is necessary for the continuation of mutual deterrence. But the world does not actually stand still. Developments in technology make new capabilities available to the military on each side, and thus also provide new problems for the other. Thus, improved missile accuracy has fueled the debate in the USA about the vulnerability to a Soviet strike of American inter-continental ballistic missiles, providing the justification for the concept of mobile basing for the new MX missile. The invulnerability of submarine-launched missiles may be open to question as the counter-measures and counter-counter-measures of anti-submarine warfare develop apace. Anti-satellite technologies raise doubts about the survivability of satellite-based communications and therefore about the ability even to order, let alone plan and coordinate a retaliatory strike. Each new development demands a response (and then a counter-response), so that there can never be a fixed answer to the famous question which poses the central issue of planning for nuclear deterrence—how much is enough?[5]

At one level, pure deterrence demands continual techno-logical innovation, to provide ever re-strengthened deterrence against the adversary's developing capabilities. Yet this con-tinual process of innovation consistently undermines pure deterrence, as the adversary responds in turn. At the same time, of course, technology is also driven forward, not by rational strategic calculation (or any kind of strategic calculation), but by the institutional interests around the technologies. These, the corporations in the USA and design bureaus in the USSR, in alliance with groups within the military, bureaucratic and political leadership can only justify their continued existence by continued innovation. And this process of innovation, whether it is marginal or providing technological breakthroughs, pro-vides new possibilities in nuclear planning. Critically, in the 1970s, technological developments have offered the possibility of thinking about nuclear weapons in a different light, the temptation to move away from pure deterrence and the con-straints of passivity and inflexibility into more flexible fields.

If these arguments are correct, and pure deterrence is unsatifactory over the long term, what are the alternatives? Clearly, they are either nuclear disarmament or the adoption of a more 'flexible' approach to nuclear deterrence, leading into strategies which prepare for nuclear warfare, for fighting and winning it. There can be little doubt which course the super-powers have taken.

The Lure of Counterforce

As the term implies, counterforce targeting is a policy of targeting nuclear forces against the armed forces (especially nuclear) of the other side. The opposite form of targeting would be counter-city. American doctrine also refers to counter-value or countervailing targeting, which embraces both counterforce and counter-city.

It is essential to understand at the outset that American nuclear strategy has always included counterforce targeting, under the doctrines of massive retaliation and mutual assured destruction in the 1950s and 1960s no less than under the doctrines of the 1970s and now. A counterforce *strategy*, however, is one which emphasizes the element of counterforce targeting and links it to the concepts of limited nuclear war-fighting which now abound in western strategic circles. It is distinct from the notion of pure deterrence we have just been discussing, but it does not exclude deterrence. It is both easy and intellectually respectable to argue that the deterrent function is a product of the ability to fight a nuclear war and win it. But, as we noted at the outset, the basic deterrent threat is different: it is the threat of defeat, not of simple punishment. And the deterrent function as such becomes conceptually less distinctive and effectively more incidental to the primary war-fighting function.

The pursuit of a nuclear counterforce strategy derives from a continuing desire to make nuclear weapons useful as instruments of war, coupled with an understanding, either explicit or implicit, of the inadequacies of pure deterrence. So the attractions of counterforce are to some extent the mirror images of the deficiencies of deterrence, but there is a significant additional set of motivations which have to do with an undiminished belief in the utility of military force in international affairs and an unquestioned faith that the most powerful weapon ever invented must be capable of making a major contribution to this utility.

The desire to make nuclear weapons militarily useful is as old as the weapon itself. The first major doctrinal battles within the U.S. government were being fought even as the public was adjusting to the new idea that nuclear weapons had made the future wars "unthinkable." In fact they were as thinkable as ever, and the discussion of how nuclear weapons were to be employed quickly accommodated itself to the political environment of the U.S. military. The battle lines were drawn between air power enthusiasts in the Air Force and the traditional Army-Navy hierarchy.

The argument was not about counterforce versus deterrence, but about different conceptions of the best counterforce applications of the new weapons. The U.S. Air Force attempted to gain a monopoly control over nuclear weapons by stressing their usefulness in strategic attacks on the enemy heartland, while the Army emphasized their potential for battlefield use.

However ardently the U.S. Air Force may have wished for a counterforce mission in the 1940s and 1950s, technological, economic and political constraints produced a strategic posture which looked much more like deterrence. But the deterrence doctrine was then, as it has been ever since, a doctrine of necessity, enforced more by technological constraints than by any desire to renounce counterforce as a viable military posture. The persistence of the search for a counterforce capability can be traced through all U.S. administrations. In the Kennedy administration, Robert McNamara, Secretary of Defense, promoted the concept of 'damage limitation' or 'no-cities' warfare. This proposed that, after nuclear deterrence had failed and nuclear war begun, it would be possible to limit damage to the USA by refraining from attacking Soviet cities and thus holding them 'hostage,' continuing the war meanwhile by counterforce attacks.[6] When McNamara came to understand the technological limitations which made 'damage limitation' unworkable, he set in motion a determined effort to overcome them, opting in the interim for the doctrine of "mutual assured destruction"—the embodiment of the balance of terror in U.S. nuclear strategy.

Richard Nixon came to Washington as President, advocating 'superiority' over the USSR; the subsequent softening of this word to 'sufficiency' had more of a cosmetic than an operational significance. The leadership of Melvin Laird and James Schlesinger in the Pentagon carried on the development of counterforce capabilities, leading to the declaration of a strategy of limited options—that is, options for the limited use of nuclear weapons—by Schlesinger in January 1974. Under the Presidency of James Carter, Harold Brown at the Pentagon continued this basic thrust, formally codified by the release of Presidential Directive 59 in the summer of 1980.[7] Counterforce thinking, planning and weapons procurement were modified only in detail during the Carter-Brown years.

Thus, over the years, it is only the technical means of achieving the mission which have from time to time been reevaluated: the mission itself has not been questioned. There seems very little likelihood that it will be questioned under Reagan.

The USSR has moved along a similar course. It would appear that in the battle for the post-Stalin leadership in the 1950s, arguments about nuclear deterrence were instrumental in Nikita Khrushchev's successful efforts to oust Premier Malenkov. With support of the Soviet Army, Khrushchev argued that pure or 'minimal' deterrence would lead to 'complacency' and 'defeatism' and that it was essential for Soviet foreign policy to maintain the belief that defense was possible and nuclear war was winnable. But this was followed by Khrushchev's own adoption of 'minimal' deterrence, which may have been a genuine doctrinal preference on his part, or merely a concession to the USSR's technological limitations.[8] In any case, the counterforce course has certainly been followed by the USSR, and with considerable vigor, in the years since the fall of Khrushchev.

However, it is still possible to identify important differences between U.S. and Soviet doctrines. The growing American emphasis on limited nuclear wars involving counterforce targeting was clearly stated by James Schlesinger in 1975:

> In answering the question, 'Do you think it is possible to have a limited nuclear war, just to exchange a couple of weapons?' the Secretary said, 'I believe so.' He added, it is easier to think of the circumstances in which limited use might occur than it would be to think of a massive all-out strike against the urban industrial base of another nation, which has the capability of striking back.[9]

And although, as Defense Secretary, Harold Brown made it clear that he thought there could be no guarantee that a limited nuclear war would remain limited, he continued to assert the need for the USA to have options for the limited use of nuclear weapons—that is, for limited nuclear war.[10] It is clear that a preponderance of U.S. military and civilian strategists favor this approach, but no similar tendency can be identified in Soviet strategic declarations, and this is naturally a matter of some concern to U.S. strategists. The Soviet reaction to the enunciation of the strategy of limited options in 1974 was uniformly hostile, and included the criticism that the strategy was insensitive to the realities of nuclear warfare. This reaction, moreover, was well in keeping with the main lines of long-standing Soviet doctrine on nuclear war which is, as one writer has noted, "a highly institutionalized body of official precepts":

> Soviet military writings countinue to assert that in any nuclear engagement, theater or global, Soviet nuclear forces will strike simultaneously at the strategic capabilities, political-military command infrastructure, and economic-administrative centers of the adversary. Moreover, they reveal no trace of interest in the notions of intra-war bargaining, graduated escalation, and crisis management which play a heavy role in current U.S. strategic theorizing.[11]

In the face of this unfortunately intransigent refusal to play the counterforce game, the American hope seems to be that improvements in Soviet technology will tempt the USSR into playing this game according to American rules. As two influential American analysts have put it:

> Russian commentators once scoffed at the idea that there could be a substantial conflict in the NATO area

that would not immediately become nuclear. After much invective on the subject, they eventually admitted the need to plan for nonnuclear engagements. For good reason, we might witness the same phenomenon with respect to other forms of limitation, for example, within nuclear conflict. Now a great deal of Soviet rhetoric flows about the absurdity of the notion of limiting the use of nuclear weapons; on the other hand there is no real evidence that the Soviets would abandon all caution in a nuclear or any other conflict.[12]

On the other hand again, there is 'no real evidence' to support any of this theorizing, posturing, procuring and deploying. We do not refer to the 'the American *hope*' facetiously: counterforce strategies and options for limited nuclear war are built entirely on hope—that the weapons will work as they are supposed to, that control will be maintained and both sides will keep to the game-plan, that once war starts both sides will somehow recognize a common point where the calculations of cost and benefit balance out so they can both stop the game, but above all else that when it comes to it, when it's 'eyeball to eyeball', 'they' will 'blink' first, and 'we' will win without a shot being fired.

The Problems of Counterforce

A counterforce strategy may include (as it does now in the West) the option of launching the first nuclear strike, but it is by no means a strategy necessarily based on the launching of an all-out first strike aimed at the total incapacitation of the enemy's own nuclear forces -- a 'disarming first strike', as it is charmingly called in the trade.

Even so, the first defect of counterforce lies precisely here, in the high premium it places, even unintentionally, on a first strike. The weapons and support systems required for a flexible counterforce strategy are indistinguishable from those required for a 'disarming first strike'. Thus, if one side does not trust the other's declared strategy, and looks beneath it to assess the hardware, there will be a great deal of justification in concluding that, if the political situation deteriorates to the point where war seems imminent, it will face an attempt at a 'disarming first strike' against it.

The problem is compounded by the increasingly accurate multiple independently-targeted re-entry vehicles or warheads (MIRVs) which both sides now deploy. MIRVing provides large numbers of warheads on relatively few systems—for example, 160 warheads on each U.S. Poseidon submarine, and as many as 250 or more on each of the planned Trident submarines. Yet it only takes one shot (and not necessarily a nuclear one) to destroy a single submarine. In principle, one could calculate that the USA's 9,000 strategic warheads could be destroyed by about 1,200 well-aimed Soviet warheads, while the USSR's 6,000 strategic warheads might be destroyed by approximately 1,500 successful U.S. shots.[13] Thus the USA has about six times as many warheads as it needs to destroy the Sovet strategic force, and the USSR has about five times as many warheads as it needs to do the same to the USA. The significance of these ratios should not be overstressed, because the success of such an enormously risky and complex enterprise would depend on far more than the simple ratio of warheads to targets.

However, if one assumes high reliability and accuracy for the weapons used in the first strike, the ratios do reveal a growing disparity between the losses which will be suffered by the side which strikes first and the losses whcih will be suffered by the side which strikes second. Accordingly, if each side has forces which, whatever the declaratory doctrine, reveal a potential for a disarming first strike, and if war seems imminent, either side may conclude that the other is indeed about to launch a first strike, and therefore conclude it can only cut its losses by launching its own first strike. Either side may conclude that its own only rational option is to "get its retaliation in first." As a result, we can only conclude that counterforce strategies weaken deterrence and make war more likely in times of crisis—which are exactly the times when deterrence should be strongest.

The second major problem of a counterforce strategy is its dependence on theories of intra-war bargaining, intra-war deterrence and controlled escalation, theories which have fundamental logical flaws. As it has been put:

> It is the nature of escalation that each move passes the option to the other side, while at the same time the party which seems to be losing will be tempted to keep raising the ante...Once on the tiger's back we cannot be sure of picking the place to dismount.[14]

Yet it is integral to the idea of limited nuclear warfare, and to the currently fashionable concept of 'escalation dominance', that we can mount and dismount the tiger at will. There is a surface plausibility in the idea that since each side will be concerned to limit the damage to itself, both sides will be interested in fighting a limited nuclear war rather than a total war. But this plausibility vanishes once one tries to identify the moment at which one side would decide to leave the other with the final say, the final shot. And if it therefore seems likely that neither side will wish to pull out leaving the other with the 'advantage', then why should either side bother with limited war at all? It is surely more likely that both sides would conclude that, since the most likely outcome is a non-limited war, the best option is to make an all-out strike immediately. Despite the pseudo-scientific appearance of theories of intra-war bargaining, they lack all rational foundation. And their irrationality is merely emphasized by the lack of interest in such theories displayed by the USSR.

A third flaw in the logic of counterforce lies in the require-ment for efficient, reliable and speedy performance of assigned missions involving high accuracy. Despite remarkable prog-ress in counterforce capabilities, doubts must remain about this requirement. Reminders of military and technological fallibil-ity recur with alarming regularity: the failure of the U.S. rescue mission in Iran, the false alerts generated by the U.S. warning system, and the recent revelation that for 18 months in the 1960s most of the warheads on U.S. Polaris submarines were inoperative.[15]

An article in 1980, based on interviews with knowledgeable ex-officials in the U.S. military establishment, argued that the accuracies claimed for inter-continental nuclear missiles are exaggerated.[16] The argument may be somewhat overstated (too easily dismissing counterforce capabilities and potential vul-nerability of submarines) but it provides a firm basis for skepticism about the public claims of accuracy and reliability made by the military. Most tellingly, inter-continental missiles have never been tested over their expected wartime flight courses. U.S. missiles are tested on an east-west track from California to the Marshall Islands in the Pacific, while Soviet missiles are tested west-east, from west of the Urals to the Kamchatka Peninsula or beyond. Thus, guidance systems have been checked and calibrated over regions of the Earth with different gravitational anomalies from the regions over which they would fly in war. And while U.S. and Soviet geodetic and other satellites have been mapping the gravitational field for many years, it requires a substantial leap of faith to believe that a missile can be given pinpoint accuracy over a range of 10,000 kilometers on the very first shot simply by programming this information into its guidance computer.

It may be argued that these problems are purely technical, and therefore amenable to ultimate, if not imminent, technical solution. Reliability is another matter. The history of military technology is a history of poorly designed equipment, slovenly maintenance and regular breakdowns. Moreover, however limited the planned nuclear strike, the stakes in ordering it would be so great that it is hard to imagine a national leader doing so unless the situation were desperate. But in a desperate situation, thoughts will turn to massive strikes rather than limited ones: saturation is the traditional military remedy for doubts about accuracy and reliability.

The logic of counterforce is therefore undermined by a series of other inter-locking logics of far greater plausibility. Counterforce strategies require the precise, surgical use of nuclear weapons, but for several reasons, some of them technical, nuclear weapons cannot be scalpels -- they are sledge-hammers, and the danger is that far too many strategists and political leaders appear to be dreaming these massive, blunt instruments could actually be used with surgical delicacy. It can be added, however, that the entire counterforce posture is based on weapons and theories which have never been tested under the conditions in which they will have to be used. While generals have often been accused of preparing to fight the last war, preparations are now being made to fight a war in which the old process of learning by trial and error is impracticable. This is certainly one major reason why nuclear weapons have not been used since Nagasaki over 35 years ago. The non-use precedent grow stronger with the passing of time, and presents even greater obstacles to plans for the controlled use of nuclear weapons. It is an essential part of the 'self-deterrence' which most of us find comforting, but which many analysts find increasingly inconvenient.

Deterrence, Counterforce and Disarmament

It is, of course, possible that the 1980s will not show the same course of technolgical development as the 1970s did. It is possible that different choices will be made, and a different path will be followed. If the possibility of choice is to exist, it will be because the politics and institutions of the armament process are subjected to a sharp, massive and sustained challenge. Essentially, the choice is between three different positions about nuclear weapons—one arguing for pure deterrence, one arguing for counterforce, and one arguing for disarmament.

It is clear from our arguments above that a strategy of pure nuclear deterrence is desperately flawed. It has too many unattractive aspects for political leaders, the military and civilians alike. It is effectively dysfunctional for the pursuit of the political interests it is established to protect. The flaws in pure deterrence suggest that to the extent that it is necessary it is inherently unstable and, conversely, to the extent that it is stable it is probably unnecessary. It suffers from the paradox of declaring nuclear weapons to be unuseable while demanding massive resources for their development and sophistication. It is constantly weakened by the very process of technological development it sets in motion, and this process weakens it further by tempting decision-makers into counterforce strategies which reassert the utility of nuclear weapons.

Yet the flaws of counterforce strategy are even greater than the flaws of pure deterrence. Even if the claim is made that counterforce strengthens deterrence, and even if this is genuinely believed by the military and political decision-makers, the effect of counterforce is to weaken deterrence at exactly the times when it should be strongest, at times of crisis. All the intricate theorizing about the possiblity of rational use of nuclear weapons cannot remove the dangers and flaws of counterforce. Even if the declared strategy does not actively contemplate a disarming first strike, the deterioration of a political crisis to the point where war is looming could make it seem that the only 'rational' action is to strike first, throwing all theories of limited nuclear war out the window in the process. It is not the logical rigor of theories of limited nuclear war and the utility of nuclear weapons which is the problem: what is worrying is the apparent absorption and even obsession with such theories, despite their evident illogicality.

At one level it can be argued that this is the result of technological momentum which is essentially non-rational, which derives not from any strategic logic but from the technical possibilities available at any given time, from the power of institutions promoting and profiting from the technology, and from the dazzling effect of shiny new gadgetry on political decision-makers. Yet it is also true that the quest for doctrines asserting the utility of nuclear weapons is linked to the political and strategic assumption that military power is essential to the pursuit of the interests of the nation-state. Nuclear weapons are seen as indispensable and central components of military power—one could say, they have to be seen that way by the states which deploy them—and it is therefore axiomatic that they be useable components. Technological developments can seem to have such a powerful influence on strategy because they appear to provide solutions to problems which deeply concern decision-makers.

What is particularly worrying at the present time is the connection between these assumptions and the re-emerged assertion that the confrontation between the USA and the USSR is fundamental and essentially irreducible for the foreseeable future. Increasing multipolarity in world affairs has consistently eroded the credibility of this view. Yet it is precisely this view that lies at the heart of the Reagan administration's international perspectives. There is every sign of that administration wanting to cut through the tangled undergrowth of world politics as if everything could be reduced to the U.S.-Soviet dimension. In so doing, it will cause a great deal of damage and, because it is not attacking the objective it thinks it is, it will not improve what it appears to see as a weak American position. Along that path lie continuing frustrations in world affairs and ever-renewed bouts of hysteria. With the administration also wanting to make nuclear weapons into useable instruments of a misguided policy, the result could be tilting at windmills in an increasingly dangerous fashion.

Thus consideration of the immediate situation and of the fundamental flaws of counterforce make it essential that a decisive turn away from counterforce is made. Yet the instabilities of pure deterrence cannot be just wished away. A "return" to pure deterrence cannot be contemplated: to attempt it would be, if our arguments are correct, merely to establish the process which would lead strategy back into counterforce within a relatively short period.

Two things follow. Firstly, it is clear that genuine reductions of nuclear forces require not only turning aside from counterforce but also rejecting the concept of stable nuclear deterrence. The alternative is to establish the pragmatic as well as the moral basis for nuclear disarmament. Secondly, it is also clear that it is possible to do just that—to advance pragmatic as well as moral arguments for nuclear disarmament and, indeed, to tie the two strands inextricably together. The dangers of counterforce bring home the impossibility of relying on nuclear deterrence, and therefore emphasize the need for nuclear disarmament. The increasing political breadth of concern about nuclear weapons in western Europe, focusing in the first place on the decision to deploy Pershing II and cruise missiles, is evidence for that assertion.

This provides us with a rather optimistic conclusion to an essay which has otherwise been necessarily grim. It may be that our optimism will be criticized on the grounds that our argument in this concluding section has relied heavily on rationality, a reliance which can be irrelevant in a world where irrational fears, distrusts and fantasies of power are easily exploited by massively powerful institutions whose own rationality relates only to short- and medium-term goals, not to long-term outcomes. This is not an easy criticism to answer. But it cannot be allowed to discourage those who wish to prevent nuclear war.

While it is a truism that nobody wants a nuclear war, this has not prevented the military, political and technological establishments of the great powers (and some lesser ones) from preparing for it. If the truism is true, it seems the main tasks of those who wish to prevent nuclear war are to understand what forces are operating to make such a war more likely and to show that rational and logical alternatives exist. In the last analysis, we can only rely on human rationality to draw the correct conclusions.

Footnotes

1.) J.F. Dulles, speaking before the Council on Foreign Relations, 12 January 1954, reprinted in R.G. Head and E.J. Rokke, eds,. *American Defense Policy*, John Hopkins University Press, 1973.

2.) G.M. Malenkov, Chairman of the Council of Ministers of the USSR, speaking on 27 April 1954, quoted in H. Dinnerstein, *War and the Soviet Union*, Praeger, 1962, p. 74.

3.) K.S. Gray and K. Paine, 'Victory is Possible,' *Foreign Policy*, no. 39, summer 1980.

4.) T. Schelling, *Arms and Influence*, Yale University Press, 1966, p. 10.

5.) See A.C. Enthoven and K.W. Smith, *How Much is Enough? Shaping the Defense Program 1961-1969*, Harper & Row, 1971.

6.) See *U.S. Department of State Bulletin*, 9 July 1962; also W.W. Kaufmann, *The McNamara Strategy*, Harper & Row, 1964, p. 26.

7.) See H. Brown, *Department of Defense Annual Report Fiscal Year 1982*, pp.38-43.

8.) See H. Dinnerstein, *War and the Soviet Union*, ch. 3; also *World Armaments & Disarmament: SIPRI Yearbook 1974*, MIT Press, 1974, ch. 5.

9.) *World Armaments & Disarmament: SIPRI Yearbook 1975*, Almquist & Wiksell, 1975, p.44.

10.) See Harold Brown's posture statement for FY 1982 (cited above, no. 7) and also for FY 1981; for a discussion of the tension within Brown's views, see E. Rothschild, 'The American Boom', in E.P. Thompson and D. Smith, eds., *Protest and Survive*, Penguin, 1980.

11.) B.S. Lambeth, 'Selective nuclear operations and Soviet strategy,' in J.H. Holst and U. Nerlich, eds., *Beyond Nuclear Deterrence: New Aims, New Arms*, Macdonald & Jane's, 1977, pp. 80 & 87.

12.) H.S. Rowen and A. Wohlstetter, 'Varying response with circumstances,' in Holst & Nerlich, eds., *Beyond Nuclear Deterrence,* pp. 226-7.

13.) Figures are taken from *World Armaments & Disarmament: SIPRI Yearbook 1981*, Taylor & Francis, 1981; the difference between the number of warheads required by each side in a theoretical first strike results from the different make-up of the two forces, with the USA having a much larger number of warheads based in missile-firing submarines; calculations based on the figures are further complicated by the presence of U.S. nuclear warheads in Europe which are not included here.

14.) L.H. Gelb and R.K. Betts, *The Irony of Vietnam: The System Worked*, Brookings Institute, 1979, p.111.

15.) W. Pincus in *International Herald Tribune*, 4 December 1978.

16.) A. Cockburn and A. Cockburn, 'The myth of missile accuracy,' *New York Review of Books*, 20 November, 1980.

Chapter 3

Nuclear Weapons and Global Intervention

Daniel Ellsberg

Daniel Ellsberg began his career as specialist for the Pentagon on nuclear command and control systems. He drafted the policy guidance memorandum for the 1961 operational plan for strategic warfare. His public release of the "Pentagon Papers" in 1971 marked his break with a career that spanned the administration of four presidents. Now he devotes himself to speeches and direct action for nuclear arms limitation.

Q: *America now controls more than 30,000 nuclear warheads: about 22,000 tactical (short-range) weapons with the same average yield as the Hiroshima/Nagasaki bombs, and more than 10,000 strategic (intercontinental) weapons with yields of up to 500 times that size. Do we need all those to deter a Soviet attack on the United States?*

Ellsberg: No. That's not what most of our weapons are for, and—contrary to what most Americans suppose—it never has been. Consider these facts: A single Poseidon submarine at sea, with 224 warheads, could destroy every Soviet city with population of 100,000 or over. We have about 30 Poseidon and Polaris submarines at sea on alert at all times, and the Russians don't have the antisubmarine warfare capability to track and destroy a single one of them.

Four or five of these submarines, enough to keep two at sea at all times, carry just 10 percent of our actual inventory of strategic warheads. The other 90 percent, including all our land-based missiles and our bombers—and the thousands of strategic warheads that Carter and now Reagan propose to add on: MX, Trident, and cruise missiles—probably don't add anything at all to the deterrence of a nuclear attack on this country. But, I repeat, in the eyes of war planners and the proponents of these weapons, that's not what there for.

Q: *What are most of these weapons for, then?*

Ellsberg: To threaten or carry out counterforce attacks, that is, attacks on Soviet military capabilities—air bases, missile launching sites, sub pens, command posts, air defenses, and so forth—primarily in the context of a U.S. first strike. By that I don't mean U.S. "preventative war," an aggressive attack out of the blue, but a U.S. initiated attack on the Soviet homeland, either escalating an ongoing conflict or in anticipation of a possible escalation by the Soviets. In either case, the major object would be to destroy Soviet nuclear missiles and planes before they had been launched.

Q: *Haven't various presidents committed us to not carrying out a first strike?*

Ellsberg: No. Never. Our military strategy has been based, ever since the debut of atomic weapons in 1945, on our possible first use of nuclear weapons to back up and complement any nonnuclear defense or intervention that we might make. Our planners have never allowed for an extreme firebreak between nuclear and conventional weapons. As our adversaries and allies know well, but our own public much less so, every President has refused to pledge "no first use" of nuclear weapons—though the Soviets have repeatedly proposed this as a bilateral commitment—and indeed, each has explicitly reaffirmed our commitment to first use in at least some circumstances, such as an attack on our NATO allies.

Our NATO plans have always been explicitly premised on a U.S. first strike in response to a Soviet nonnuclear attack that NATO couldn't contain with conventional or tactical nuclear warfare (the latter we might refer to as NATO "first use," to distinguish it from a strategic "first strike" against a superpower's retaliatory forces). For most of the era since 1949, when NATO was formed, the United States promised a first strike to come within hours or days of the onset of any sizable Soviet attack. Remember that our Strategic Air Command (SAC) was set up immediately after World War II to drop atomic bombs, if need be, on Russia at a time when the Soviets were not expected by our military or President Truman to deploy any nuclear weapons for a decade or more. SAC's *only* mission in that initial period was to threaten or carry out a U.S. first strike; *not at all* to deter or retaliate for a nuclear attack on the United States or anywhere else.

Even after the Russians' first test in 1949 and their H-bomb tests in the mid-fifties, the U.S. ability to threaten or carry out a first strike amounted to a monopoly until as late as the mid-sixties, because our superiority in delivery capability was so overwhelming. In 1961, the year of the predicted "missile gap," the U.S. had within range of Russia about 3,000 bombers, over 40 ICBMs, 48 Polaris missiles, and another 100 long-range missiles in Europe. The Soviets had about 190 intercontinental bombers (the same ones they're flying today) and exactly *4* ICBMs—four soft, nonalert, liquid-fueled ICBMs, at one site at Plesetsk that was vulnerable to a small slow U.S. attack with conventional weapons. When Kennedy urged the American people to prepare fallout shelters during the Berlin crisis that year, it was not for a nuclear war that would be started by the Soviets.

Q: *Were these "gap" alarms—which we've heard again in the last few years—simply manipulated, then? What was their object?*

Ellsberg: Warnings of the imminent Russian "superiority" were conscious exaggerations amounting to hoaxes, and this is just as true of the warnings we hear today (from some of the same people, such as Paul Nitze), though the reality now is parity, or "rough equivalence," rather than the past overwhelming U.S. superiority. It was not only the desire for profits, jobs, and votes associated with war production that led to these alarms, though of course these motives did figure as well. Planners, presidents, and "statesmen" in the corporate world saw an ominous possibility as the Soviets tested new weapons and vehicles—usually, then as now, four to five years behind our development and deployment. Their fear was that the Soviets might some day achieve a retaliatory capability roughly *equivalent* to ours, eliminating our decisive first-strike superiority. To head off that possibility, these planners had to reject arms control proposals that would have constrained our own advances—like a comprehensive test ban agreement of a "freeze" on all new missile testing and deployment. They also had to whip up public fears of imminent U.S. "inferiority," to mobilize support for vastly expensive arms spending that would assure us, in fact, of a continued U.S. superiority.

Q: *You're saying that our planners have always been seeking U.S. superiority?*

Ellsberg: Yes. Superiority at every level of nuclear confrontation, including theater nuclear warfare—that's what the proposed, highly precise Pershing intermediate range missiles and the ground launched cruise missiles for Europe are all about; that and strategic counterforce, first strike capability. In other words, a superior ability to destroy the opponent's retaliatory forces. As Henry Kissinger put it in late 1979 in a revealing speech before the International Institute of Strategic Studies: "Our strategic doctrine has relied extraordinarily, perhaps exclusively, on our superior strategic power. The Soviet Union has never relied on its superior strategic power...Therefore, even an equivalence in destructive power, even assured destruction for both sides, is a revolution in NATO doctrine as we have known it." He goes on to endorse the development of weapons like the MX missile that promise, with their highly accurate, high-yield warheads, to help America regain its lost superiority in first strike capability.

Q: *When did we lose that superiority?*

Ellsberg: Starting in 1967, when the Russians finally began protecting their retaliatory force by installing missiles in hardened, concrete silos. This Soviet buildup, from close to nothing sixteen years ago into the nuclear era to 1400 hardened land-based ICBMs today, could probably have been prevented at various times along the way if we had accepted Soviet proposals for a comprehensive ban on warhead testing or missile testing or both, adequately monitored by U.S. national means of detection. Brezhnev, displacing Khrushchev in 1964, seems to have promised the Soviet military to spend whatever it would take to avoid inferiority, in the absence of arms limitation agreements that put a ceiling on U.S. forces. The Soviets proceeded to outspend us in the seventies, when they finally duplicated the huge investments in strategic capabilities that we had made in the fifties and the sixties. At great sacrifice, they have at last bought "equivalence" and removed the American first strike threat. Now we're being mobilized for the big effort to buy that threat back unilaterally by adding MX and Trident to our anti-submarine capability.

Q: *Might we achieve that?*

Ellsberg: We can't buy back our monopoly of the fifties, or even our overwhelming superiority of the mid-sixties, but for a couple of hundred billion dollars we might get back a first-strike capability something like that of 1967-1969, if the Russians stood still for this, which they probably won't.

Q: *Why would anyone think that was worth the money?*

Ellsberg: To back up the credibility of our first-use threat; to initiate local, tactical nuclear war where that is needed to keep our conventional forces from being overwhelmed either by the Soviets or local non-Soviet forces.

Q: *But how could we make first-use threats credible against Soviet troops, or elsewhere in the world where our adversaries are likely to be allies of the Soviet Union? In other words, how can we keep from being deterred ourselves by the prospect of Soviet retaliation?*

Ellsberg: That really comes down to the question of how we can ensure that our use of tactical nuclear weapons, or our threatened use, would remain one-sided, rather than leading to a two-way exchange, the prospect of which would deter us in the first place. Or if some retaliation does occur, how can we keep it very limited, to a level acceptable to ourselves? The Pentagon's answer is that we must have a threat of escalating the conflict that is more credible than the Soviets can make, should they choose to match us in the local area with nuclear retaliation. This means being able not only to escalate, say, to a theater-wide level, but to escalate again and again, if necessary, to a level where the Soviets will be afraid to match us. That calls for forces that are superior to those of the Soviets at virtually every level of nuclear conflict, up to a fully disarming first strike or a campaign of annihilation.

Q: *Are you saying, in other words, that nuclear weapons are seen as viable and realistic weapons for actual war fighting?*

Ellsberg: Well, yes and no. One doesn't actually have to be optimistic about how the conflict would come out. I don't think that the people who back these weapons are awfully optimistic about that, but they don't think that's necessary. The key thing, as they see it, is to confront the Soviets with at least a significant uncertainty as to whether we might escalate the conflict in the face of their obvious capability to reply. These people want the Soviets to think that U.S. planners and decision makers *might* escalate, given our advantage in weapons.

Q: *So they hope to have the Soviets back down before we would ever get to the point of actually having to use the weapons?*

Ellsberg: That's right, precisely. Again, this attitude doesn't depend on a certainty that in an actual two-sided exchange we would really come out well. But just by trying hard enough, we might get back what Herman Kahn once called "A not-incredible first-strike capability." The theory is that after seeing us work so hard to sell the feasibility of a "war-winning" capability to various skeptical constituencies, and after we've spent so much money to achieve it, the Soviets would have to tread cautiously lest we be foolish enough to believe our own calculations. Sounds complicated, but I would have to admit it might work. Then again it might not.

Q: *Is this all just a bluff, then?*

Ellsberg: Unfortunately not. Our efforts to increase the credibility and effectiveness of these threats commit us to a whole range of actions that—unless our threats always work perfectly, which they won't—make it likely that sooner or later we ourselves will turn a nonnuclear conflict into a nuclear one, or a local nuclear exchange into a global one. With the Soviets having bought parity, it's much harder and more expensive than before to make our threats look credible, and no matter how much we commit ourselves, the threats are more likely to fail at some point, and then have to be carried out. When that happens, the consequences will be far more dangerous for us and for the whole world than when we first adopted this strategy twenty to thirty years ago.

Q: *What makes these risks look worthwhile to anyone? Why are we continuing with this approach, in the face of the Soviet determination to match us?*

Ellsberg: For the same reasons that led us to adopt it in the first place, and a few new ones. The oldest reason, which still applies, is the desire to defend Western Europe without investing the additional money needed to provide an adequate nonnuclear defense against a Soviet nonnuclear attack. Given the military and economic resources of the NATO alliance, much larger than those of the Warsaw Pact, the conventional alternative is certainly feasible, but also very expensive. The newest reason is the collapse of our strategy for assuring our control of the distribution of Middle East oil by supporting the shah's dictatorship in Iran. By ourselves we are unable to protect with non-nuclear forces our "vital interests" in northern Iran and neighboring regions since they border on Russia, and are very far from our own supply lines.

Our current dilemma merely exposes the fact that our previous strategic nuclear monopoly, definitely a thing of the past, permitted and encouraged us to claim what amounted to a global "sphere of predominant influence" that ran right up to the borders of Soviet occupation everywhere in the world, including northern Iran. There is no adequate military alternative if we are going to continue to assert a right and intention to intervene militarily in a corner of Russia's borders where we lack the allies and bases of Western Europe. Thus Harold Brown, in the last administration, assured us that the Carter Doctrine was no bluff by asserting our readiness to use nuclear weapons if necessary, and accompanying those words with deployments of nuclear-equipped carriers and bombers to the Indian Ocean. Defense Department officials candidly describe the proposed Rapid Deployment Force as a "tripwire" to what would be a regionally "limited" Doomsday Machine. And already President Reagan has pointed to the extension of that wire to SAC headquarters in Omaha by warning that a Russian challenge to the U.S. forces he proposes to base in the Middle East would inescapably incur a "risk of World War III."

Q: *You say that you don't have a military alternative to propose?*

Ellsberg: No adequate, unilateral U.S. military proposal. But making commitments and taking actions that measurably increase the likelihood of blowing the lid off the Northern Hemisphere doesn't strike me as an acceptable approach to any objective whatever—even to detérring outright Soviet aggression against "our" oilfields in the Middle East. Instead we must rely on diplomatic, economic, and multilateral sanctions, along with reducing Western dependence on oil. If that doesn't sound adequate, all I can say is that this is not the only problem in the world for which there is *no* adequate U.S. military solution. Possible Soviet aggression against Poland is another, much more immediate example, one that is extremely anguishing to me.

Q: *Are there other reasons for our build-up that apply outside Europe and the perimeter of Russia?*

Ellsberg: The broadest reason of all: the prospect of wars in the future like those we have actually fought since World War II, wars against non-Soviet and nonnuclear adversaries. I think that the Reagan administration—like the Carter administration, really—recognizes a future need for "more Vietnams." Not that they hope for this—although, accepting the inevitable, some, may see early "demonstrations" of efficient brutality as desirable: El Salvador may suffer the burden of this.

This administration sees it as inescapable that the United States will have to pursue its "interests" abroad by sending expeditionary forces when other means of influence such as trade and finance and CIA intervention fail. But these future Vietnams must be planned with an eye to the lessons of Vietnam, which include the political lesson that for reasons of economics and domestic public opinion we can't count on sending 500,000 or more U.S. troops abroad. Which means that there must be a much more effective and brutal and early use of American firepower backed up—in places, *unlike* El Salvador, that are far from our logistical base—by the clear threat and the willingness to employ tactical nuclear weapons to support these troops.

Q: *Would a President seriously consider using nuclear weapons against a country that didn't possess them?*

Ellsberg: First, that's how Harry Truman used them, in August 1945. Second, it safer than using them against the Soviets. Third, every President from Truman on (with the exception of Ford) has had occasion in an ongoing, urgent crisis to direct serious preparations for possible imminent U.S. initiation of tactical nuclear warfare, preparations in every case "leaked" to the enemy, and in several cases accompanied by secret, explicit, official threats.

In the cases involving the Russians directly, the warnings and preparations were public: the Berlin crisis of 1961, the Cuban missile crisis of 1962, the Carter doctrine last year, and now, Reagan's comments on strategy for defending the Middle East. But a larger number of cases involved threats or preparations against non-nuclear adversaries who were, however, supported by the Soviets, so that our tactical threats needed backing by our strategic near-monopoly. A public instance was Truman's warning in December, 1950, that we were considering using nuclear weapons, the day after the Chinese surrounded marine units at the Chosin Reservoir in Korea.

The other cases were highly secret at the time, but are documented now in memoirs or declassified papers. They include Eisenhower's secret threat to the Chinese that he would drop nuclear bombs on their homeland if they did not meet his terms in negotiations at Panmunjom, Korea, in the spring of 1953. In 1954 Dulles offered Premier Georges Bidault of France three U.S. tactical nuclear weapons for the defense of Dienbienphu in Indochina. In 1958, Eisenhower directed the Joint Chiefs of Staff to plan on the use of tactical nuclear weapons against Chinese shore batteries blockading the offshore islands of Quemoy if the Chinese attempted to invade Quemoy or if they continued an effective blockade. In 1968, the Joint Chiefs advised Johnson that nuclear weapons would have to be considered if a final assault were made on the marines surrounded at Khe Sanh, in South Vietnam, when the weather was unsuitable for close air support.

In 1968 and later, as H.R. Halderman has revealed in his

memoirs and other officials have confirmed, Richard Nixon was determined to win the Vietnam War the same way his former boss, Eisenhower, had ended the Korean War. Starting in 1969, Nixon made direct, secret threats to the Hanoi regime that as of November 1969, he would escalate the war massively, including the possible use of nuclear weapons, if it did not accept the terms Nixon describes in his own memoirs as his "November ultimatum." Roger Morris, who worked on these escalation plans under Henry Kissinger, reports seeing the actual mission folders, including photographs, for nuclear targets recommended to the President—one of them a railhead in North Vietnam a mile and a half from the Chinese border.

Q: *How is it then, that no nuclear weapons have actually been used since Nagasaki?*

Ellsberg: The meaning of the historical record I've just described is that nuclear weapons, both tactical and strategic, *have* been used, again and again—in the way a gun is "used" when you point it at someone's head in a direct confrontation, whether or not the trigger is pulled. Reagan is using our weapons now—and not for deterring an attack on the United States—when he tells inteviewers that the Russians are risking World War III if they move further in the Middle East. Presidents buy these weapons because they expect to use them, based on their knowledge of a largely secret history—which both they and their adversaries know better than the American public does—cf how past presidents threatened their use, and often with some significant success.

As for why the threats weren't actually carried out: in most cases they didn't have to be, perhaps because they were effective. The marines fought their way out at Chosin Reservoir and they weren't assaulted at Khe Sanh; the Chinese accepted our armistice terms in Korea and later ended their daily shelling of Quemoy.

Q: *So such threats can work?*

Ellsberg: Sure. My objection to this whole approach is not that it can't possibly work. In fact, for most of that period our strategic superiority was so overwhelming that such a threat, from the country that had attacked Hiroshima, was far more likely to work than a lot of critics of Dulles' "massive retaliation" strategy and brinksmanship could possibly imagine. Their false belief, fostered by hawks in both parties, was that the Russians were already equal to us and about to move decisively ahead.

By the same token, we should note that the 1969 threat in Vietnam—which like the Carter Doctrine, demonstrated that

U.S. presidents continued to rely on nuclear threats after our loss of superiority—did *not* succeed. Hanoi never did accept the terms of Nixon's November ultimatum; yet Nixon's own discussion, and his actions later, indicate strongly that it was not a bluff.

Why was that escalation not carried out? Nixon himself gives the reason: there were too many Americans on the streets, peacefully protesting the war. On October 15, and again on November 15, 1969 in the moratorium and the Washington March Against Death, the protests happened to straddle his secret November 1 deadline. As he saw it, they kept him from ending the war, his way, his first year in office. From another point of view, the protests—whose power Nixon kept as secret frrm the public as his ultimatum—may have prolonged the moratorium on the combat use of nuclear weapons by more than a decade.

Q: *Why didn't Truman and Eisenhower make their threats public at the time—they were no secret to the enemy!—and take credit for success, revealing our actual superiority and the need to maintain it?*

Ellsberg: Because they knew that too many citizens would have reacted against what seems all the more true now: the fact that the threats were not ever *certain* to work; that cumulatively, each one raised the likelihood of our own eventual initiation of nuclear war; that the credibility and effectiveness of this strategy would drop sharply and its risks rise sharply when the Russians acquired a strong retaliatory force, as has finally happened; and that to pursue superiority was to ensure an indefinitely prolonged arms race, increasing the chances of proliferation, nuclear weapons accidents, false alarms, and small wars triggering big ones.

Meanwhile the chances for success are going down—which is still not to say that our first-use and first-strike threats cannot succeed in a given case—temporarily saving "our" oil in the Middle East in some future years of crisis, for example at the risk of World War III. At the same time, the costs are going up. The hundreds of billions of dollars to be spent pursuing superiority are hardly even worth counting next to the truly relevant long-run price: the continued postponement of a global effort *led* by the United States to stop and then reverse the arms race and proliferation, and to delegitimize and eliminate preparations to initiate nuclear war under any circumstances, by anyone.

Thirty years ago, our national leaders pioneered a strategy based on threats of regional genocide: the indiscriminate, massive slaughter of innocents forseeable even in the most "limited" of nuclear wars. The pursuit of superiority in the face of current Soviet forces is meant to prolong that reliance on nuclear threats into an era when such threats will be vastly more dangerous than before; likely now to be suicidal as well as genocidal, yet more likely to be challenged and then carried out.

Faced with this shocking awareness, we may cling all the harder to the leadership, the values, and the strategy that have worked so well up till now. Or we can awaken at last to the reality of what we are doing and where we are heading, and discover, in a different direction, a way for us all to survive together on this earth.

Examples of Presidential Threats to Employ Nuclear Weapons

Korea

On November 30, 1950, Truman told a press conference that the United States would use every weapon in the arsenal to counter "Chinese aggression" in Korea. Later, during the Korean war, the U.S. government worked out specific plans to use nuclear weapons against Korea, the People's Republic of China, and the Soviet Union. General Omar Bradley, then Chairman of the Joint Chiefs of Staff, confirmed in secret testimony to the Senate Foreign Relations Committee on Febuary 10, 1953, that "we have discussed many times the use of the atomic bomb, tactically," in the Korean war. As soon as a "suitable target" in Korea was found, he added, the U.S. "would have to consider very seriously the use of the A-bomb." President Dwight Eisenhower apparently agreed with Bradley's assessment. Eisenhower told Bradley and Secretary of State John Foster Dulles that "we should consider the use of tactical atomic weapons in the Kaesong area," as area that had been designated through armistice negotiations as a "sanctuary."

Berlin

During the first crisis over Berlin in 1948, the U.S. government raised the issue of the possible use of nuclear weapons by deploying six B-29s to Britain. Press reports described these bombers as "atomic capable." In 1959, and again in 1961, in response to Soviet threats to Berlin, the U.S. government threatened to use nuclear weapons. In March 1959, U.S. Defense Secretary McElroy stated that "it would be impossible to limit war over Berlin, and raised the specter of a preventive war by the West if the U.S.S.R. was perceived as preparing an attack."

Taiwan

The Eisenhower administration risked global war over Taiwan and other offshore Chinese islands twice, in 1954 and in 1958. Both times, Eisenhower deployed strategic bombers in the Western Pacific to "reassure" the Taiwanese government in a conflict with the Chinese government. The 1954-1955 conflict escalated, and Eisenhower sent the Seventh Fleet into the area. *U.S. News and World Report* wrote at the time: "If fighting starts in the waters around this island (Taiwan), the first atom-armed fleet in world history will bear the brunt of it. That is the role assigned to the U.S Seventh Fleet." The article warned that "the entire China coast would be open to...attack by the Seventh Fleet's planes," and there would be no "privileged sanctuaries." In conclusion, *U.S. News and World Report* told its readers that "the Communist leaders are aware of the fleet's power," and are unlikely to fight against "an antagonist that so far overshadows any force they can throw against it."

In the 1958 Taiwan crisis, in addition to deploying SAC planes in the Western Pacific, Eisenhower stationed nuclear-capable howitzers on Quemoy Island in order to protect counter-revolutionaries in Taiwan...The howitzers were a clear message that Taiwan "could not be taken by amphibious assault, if the United States should decide to defend it by the use of tactical nuclear weapons." China eventually backed down, but only after several months of heightened danger of nuclear war.

The Suez Crisis and Lebanon and Jordan

In October 1956, the Eisenhower administration directed an "overt and explicit threat" against the Soviet Union to prevent it from becoming involved in the Suez crisis. Two years later, the simultaneous political crisis in Lebanon, Jordan, and Iraq prompted Eisenhower to threaten again the use of atomic weapons.

Cuban Missile Crisis

In 1961, after the U.S. government-sponsored invasion, Cuba turned to the Soviet Union for military help. The next year, the Soviet government decided to place nuclear weapons in Cuba. The Kennedy administration threatened an all-out war if the Soviet ships bearing the missiles continued to move towards Cuba. The Soviet government gave in, and the U.S., in return, undertook not to invade Cuba.

Vietnam

Less than a year after the Korean war ended, Eisenhower prepared for the use of nuclear weapons again. He offered Mark 21 tactical nuclear weapons to the French for use against the Vietnamese forces which had surrounded French colonial troops at Dien Bien Phu.

In 1968, President Johnson was advised by the Joint Chiefs of Staff that he might have to order the use of nuclear weapons to free U.S. troops who were surrounded at Khe Sanh, about 25 miles from Quang Tri, and only a few miles south of the 1954 cease fire line. General William Westmoreland, then commander of U.S. forces in South Vietnam thought the use of nuclear weapons might help end the war quickly. He stated in his memoirs that Khe Sanh would indeed have been an almost ideal occassion to use tactical nuclear weapons. "If Washington officials," Westmoreland wrote, "were so intent on 'sending a message' to Hanoi, surely small tactical nuclear weapons would be a way to tell Hanoi something, just as two atomic bombs had spoken convincingly to Japanese officials during the World War II and the threat of atomic bombs induced the North Koreans to accept meaningful negotiations during the Korean war."

In public, President Nixon maintained that it was "ridiculous" to suggest that he was considering the use of nuclear weapons. But on July 15, 1969, he sent a message to Ho Chi Minh: "Unless some serious breakthrough had been achieved by the November 1 deadline," Nixon would regretfully find himself "obliged" to have recourse "to measures of great consequence and force," i.e. the use of the atomic bomb. A few weeks later, Secretary of State Henry Kissinger repeated that message to Vietnamese negotiators in Paris.

The Yom Kippur War

The Nixon administration brought the world close to the brink again in 1973 during the October Israeli-Arab war. According to Kissinger's memoirs, a nuclear alert was issued to all U.S. forces under the direction of Kissinger himself along with White House Chief of Staff Alexander Haig.

Examples adapted from *CounterSpy*, July-August 1982 by Hayes Gladstone. Also see, *Force Without War* by Barry Blechman and Stephen Kaplan (Brookings, 1978)

Chapter 4

Interservice Rivalry and the Arms Race

Fred Kaplan

Among those who ponder the size of nuclear arsenals and the wisdom of nuclear arms control, the question most commonly debated is "How much is enough?" Yet too often neglected is the more pertinent question: "Enough for what?"

Those who point only to the superpowers' nuclear "overkill" believe that one side has "enough" nuclear weapons when it can demolish the other side's major cities in a retaliatory second strike—a prospect so horrifying that it will deter an enemy from launching a nuclear first strike even under desperate circumstances. Yet American strategic thought—and strategic policy—has long been governed by the premise that these weapons might one day be used and, if they are, that the United States should somehow emerge victorious, or at least alive and breathing. Thus, how to *fight*—and, some would add, win—a nuclear war has always been the first question for many officials. And that approach presents an entirely different formula for calculating how much is enough.

The Birth of Deterrence

Those who believe that deterrence should be the sole policy and that this requires only a small nuclear arsenal generally take their cues from the earliest writing of Bernard Brodie, the father of nuclear strategy, who in 1946, just months after Hiroshima, wrote:

> The first and most vital step in any American security program for the age of atomic bombs is to take measures to guarantee to ourselves in case of attack the possibility of retaliation in kind. The writer...is not for the moment concerned about who will *win* the next war in which atomic bombs are used. Thus far the chief purpose of our military establishment has been to win wars. From now on its chief purpose must be to avert them. It can have almost no other useful purpose.[1]

Brodie also said:

> The number of critical targets is quite limited...that does not mean that additional hits would be useless but simply that diminishing returns would set in early; and after the cities of, say, 100,000 population were eliminated, the returns from additional bombs would decline drastically...If 2000 bombs in the hands of either party is enough to destroy entirely the economy of the other, the fact that one side has 6000 and the other 2000 will be of relatively small significance.[2]

Yet only a few years later, Brodie himself, in a development not widely acknowledged or known by many of his celebrators, started to adopt a different standard for assessing atomic adequacy.

As the 1950s began, the Soviets had virtually no atomic bombs and the United States had a few hundred. The fear among the American military was not that the Soviets would attack the United States but that they would invade Western Europe, economically prostrate after World War II, physically unable to defend itself. Since the United States had no conventional forces to speak of, and certainly none that could quickly be mobilized to Western Europe, the only hope for defense and deterrence was the atomic bomb.

Brodie was briefly a consultant to Air Force Chief of Staff General Hoyt Vandenberg at the beginning of the decade, and was assigned the task of examining the atomic war plan.[3] Brodie discovered that virtually no one had figured out precisely how the bomb was to push back or wipe out the Soviet military. The U.S. Strategic Air Command (SAC), according to the war plan, was simply to drop all of its bombs as quickly as possible on targets inside the Soviet Union, destroying as many key factories and—as long as they were close to other targets

—military facilities as it could in a single volley. The Air Force called the strategy "the Sunday Punch," and saw it as the optimal way of "killing a nation."[4]

Brodie had doubts. For one thing, the Soviets were in the process of acquiring their own atomic arsenal. If the United States responded to Soviet conventional aggression by "killing" the Soviet Union, the Kremlin would almost certainly retaliate in kind. Thus to execute SAC's war plan would be tantamount to committing suicide. The nineteenth-century warrior-philospher, Karl von Clausewitz, had said that "war is the continuation of politics by other means." Brodie, an admirer of Clausewitz, interpreted that to mean that wars must be fought to accomplish rational objectives and that the degree of destruction should be proportional to the value of the objective. National suicide, of course, was hardly a rational objective, whatever the value of the stakes. The SAC plan, therefore, was not only a fatuous war strategy; it might not even serve well as a deterrent, since the Soviets might suspect that no sane U.S. President would carry out such a self-defeating threat.[5]

Brodie conceived an alternative plan: If the Soviets, say, invaded Western Europe, the United States should fire only a few of its nuclear weapons—perhaps against Soviet troops on the battlefield, certainly *not* against Soviet cities. The United States should also have deployed a highly secure, essentially invulnerable reserve force of nuclear weapons. After this limited strike, the United States should insist that the Soviets stop their aggression at once, and threaten to use the reserve force against Soviet cities, if they did not stop. The hope was that this carrot-and-stick combination would effect a Soviet surrender or, short of that, keep the battle limited to the battlefield.[6]

In the early 1950s, neither the Air Force nor the rest of government paid much attention to Brodie's idea. Indeed, a few years later, President Eisenhower and Secretary of State John Foster Dulles proclaimed a policy of "massive retaliation" very similar to the SAC war plan.[7]

But Brodie did influence others. In 1951 he joined the Rand Corporation, an Air Force-sponsored "think tank" specializing in military research. There several other budding strategists were attracted by his ideas. One was Herman Kahn, who later explored nuclear warfighting scenarios in three influential books: *On Thermonuclear War, On Escalation* and *Thinking about the Unthinkable.*[8] Another was Andrew Marshall, since 1974 director of the Pentagon's net assessment office. Marshall later had a major role in drafting the controversial "Defense

Guidance" by Secretary of Defense Caspar Weinberger, which calls for the ability to fight a "protracted" nuclear war.[9]

Brodie had dealt more with what targets should *not* be hit with nuclear weapons than with those that should. An answer to the latter question presented itself—not so much to Brodie as to his colleagues—in 1953, when the Soviet Union detonated its first hydrogen bomb. The United States had exploded one a year earlier, with several times the power of the first Soviet effort. But the Soviet test indicated that they were much farther along than the United States in developing a hydrogen bomb that could be attached to an intercontinental ballistic missile (ICBM).[10] Suddenly, America was entering a new state of vulnerability. And to some of the Rand strategists the appropriate target for Brodie's limited-strike strategy was clear: the Soviet strategic nuclear arsenal. Sparing Soviet cities in a nuclear attack might induce the Soviets to avoid American cities; knocking out their long-range weapons would *prevent* them from doing so.

Thus, the tentative beginnings of what would later be known as a "counterforce/no-cities strategy" began to penetrate the strategic community at RAND. More systematic thinking about the issue was inhibited, however, by the concern that the United States would never be able to find all the Soviet military targets, making such a strategy unworkable.

By the end of the 1950s this obstacle collapsed. The U-2 spy plane and the impending development of the Discoverer reconnaissance satellite—which a few at Rand, including Marshall, knew about—made counterforce seem feasible. The theory was taken up again, most actively by a Rand historian and political scientist named William W. Kaufmann. Like his former teacher Bernard Brodie, Kaufmann had done a great deal of writing on limited (conventional) warfare in the mid-1950s.[11]

For a few bright, ambitious officers in the Air Force staff, Kaufmann and counterforce came along at just the right time. The Air Force was facing, from the U.S. Navy, a fearsome threat, far more severe than any the Soviets had ever posed. This was the Navy's new Polaris submarine. Unlike SAC's bombers, which sat on airfields that were increasingly seen as vulnerable to attack, Polaris moved underwater, undetected. Its submarine-launched missiles (SLBMs) travelled at hypersonic speeds in a ballistic trajectory and were therefore invulnerable to Soviet air defenses as well. And Polaris could destroy Soviet cities and many other targets just as easily as the bombers could. Since SAC's war plan called for hitting urban and

military targets simultaneously—with an emphasis on destroying industrial plants in enemy cities—SAC seemed dangerously on the edge of obsolescence.

A new strategy was needed at once, and Rand counter-
force/no cities idea seemed just the thing.[12] By late 1960,
counterforce/no cities became the official Air Force policy.[13]
The Air Force liked counterforce because one weakness of
Polaris was that its missles were dreadfully inaccurate; they
could not be relied upon to strike military targets without
hitting nearby cities as well. It was questionable whether SAC's
bombers would be perfect at the task, either, but they would
have a much better chance.

The Navy had its own "new strategy," designed to rationalize Polaris and further discredit SAC. Called "finite deterrence," its tenets were explained in a widely circulated but
classified document called Naval Warfare Analysis Group
(NAVWAG) Study No. 5, "National Policy Implications of
Atomic Parity."

The idea was in essence a refinement of the strategy that
Brodie had outlined 15 years earlier in *The Absolute Weapon:*
deterring an enemy nuclear attack required having enough
nuclear weapons so that in the event of an enemy first strike the
United States could obliterate the urban-industrial society of
the aggressor with the weapons that survived. The most
efficient way to accomplish this, according to the NAVWAG,
was to have a relatively small number of nuclear-armed
submarines stationed at sea at all times.

That was all we needed; no matter how many weapons the
Soviets built, the United States would be in fine shape as long as
the submarines were there. Building more bombers or land-
based missiles would only guarantee an unending arms race![14]

Against this last point the Air Force had no argument. An
arms race was exactly what they wanted—as long as they were
given the money and weapons to win it. For them, the beauty of
counterforce was that—unlike finite deterrence—it prescribed
no logical limit to the number of weapons that were "needed."
As long as both sides kept building weapons—as they almost
certainly would—there would be more and more targets, requiring more and more weapons with which to destroy them.

McNamara and Interservice Rivalry

By the time John F. Kennedy took office in January 1961,
the issues of nuclear strategy had become thoroughly intertwined with a major interservice rivalry over which branch of
the military would receive the bigger budget. This Air Force-

Navy competition would dominate the U.S. side of the nuclear arms race and the strategic debate through the 1960s.

When Robert McNamara became Kennedy's Secretary of Defense, he initially liked the idea of "finite deterrence": It provided a clear measure of how much was enough, and systematic guidance on how tightly he could rein in the military, over which he wanted to establish complete control.[15] But McNamara had also hired some Rand strategists as his top assistants—most notably Charles Hitch as comptroller and Alain Enthoven as Hitch's deputy of systems analysis. Advocates of the counterforce philosophy, these two were distressed by McNamara's penchant for finite deterrence. They persuaded their boss to give William Kaufmann's views a hearing and set up an appointment for February 10, 1961.

A week earlier, McNamara had visitied SAC headquarters in Omaha for a briefing on the Single Integrated Operational Plan (SIOP), the military's nuclear war plan. Basically it was only a slight variation on the old SAC plan—kill and destroy as much as possible in the Soviet Union, Red China and Eastern Europe, as quickly as possible; there were virtually no provisions for more limited options. McNamara was appalled by the massive devastation called for, by the straitjacket in which it would strap a President in a crisis. He was looking for some way to give the President more options—and Kaufmann's briefing showed him how.

McNamara adopted the counterforce/no-cities strategy in his first few years as Defense Secretary, espousing its philosophy at Athens in a top secret speech to the NATO Defense Ministers in May 1962 and in a public commencement address at the University of Michigan the following June.[16]

At the same time, however, McNamara was cutting Air Force programs by the handful—the B-70 bomber, various primitive cruise missiles, the Skybolt air-launched ballistic missile—and limiting the number of B-52 bombers and Minuteman ICBMs to be deployed.[17] The Air Force had its counterforce strategy, but not the budget or the weapons for which it had adopted counterforce as a rationale. Top officers started to apply ferocious pressure on McNamara, all the while using his own endorsement of counterforce to support their demands for more money.

The Secretary fought back by dispensing with counterforce rhetoric. He and his systems analysts defined a new measure of nuclear adequacy called "assured destruction" which, over the years became known as "mutually assured destruction" or MAD. It stated that the United States had enough nuclear weapons when, following a Soviet first strike, it could still kill one fourth of the Soviet population and half its industry. This task required—so went their calculations—the equivalent of 400 one-megaton bombs. McNamara extended this to note that there should be 400 "equivalent megatons" on each leg of the strategic Triad—the intercontinental ballistic missiles (ICBMs), submarine-launched ballistic missiles (SLBMs) and bombers —so that if two legs failed or were destroyed, there would still be one that could wreak the required devastation. Assured destruction thus would be met by 1,200 equivalent megatons surviving a Soviet attack.[18]

McNamara's aides worked out this calculation most formally in 1964. As it happened, his five-year defense plan for that year—which recommended several hundred fewer nuclear warheads than the military wanted—provided enough weapons so that by 1969, after a fairly successful Soviet first strike, the United States could respond with exactly 1,200 equivalent megatons.[19] The assured-destruction philosophy was, in essence, a political technique that appeared to give scientific justification to McNamara's own weapons plan in the face of Air Force opposition.

At the same time, McNamara was having genuine doubts about counterforce. A top secret study (since declassified), titled "Damage Limiting," was produced in 1964 by General Glenn Kent, under the auspices of Harold Brown's Directorate of Defense Research and Engineering. It suggested that even with a very good U.S. counterforce strike—supplemented by air, anti-ballistic-missile (ABM) and civil defense—the Soviets, in a retaliatory strike, could still inflict tremendous damage. Moreover, if the United States spent a great deal more on these defensive efforts, the Soviets could nullify the additional expenditure much more cheaply by adding only slightly to their strategic offensive forces.[20] Counterforce, in short, appeared to be a loser's game.

In addition, it appeared from their own writings that the Soviets did not believe in using nuclear weapons as tit-for-tat instruments, or in carefully differentiating urban from military targets. It took two to play the counterforce game, and if the Soviets refused to go along, it made no sense at all.

Nevertheless, even as McNamara's disenchantment grew and as assured destruction became the *declaratory* strategy, the *actual* strategy—as reflected in the targeting plan at SAC — remained predominantly counterforce. And new weapons were built to accommodate it. As the Soviets built more and more ICBMs in the 1960s, the United States responded by building

MIRVs (multiple independently targetable reentry vehicles) that allowed a single missile to strike several different targets hundreds of miles from one another.[21] As the Soviets began to follow America's prudent example of encasing their ICBMs in hardened silos, the United States built new inertial guidance systems that made its missiles—theoretically, anyway—more accurate.

MIRVs and improved guidance systems were approved by McNamara, mainly as part of a political trade-off in which the Air Force agreed to hold the line at 1,000 Minuteman missiles. It was, in retrospect, a shortsighted deal, for the two programs kept the flame of counterforce burning.

A Consensus on Counterforce

By the 1970s, a mismatch cropped up in U.S. strategic forces. The Soviets had built still more ICBMs and hardened their silos even further. The United States had continued to MIRV hundreds of Minutemen missiles and to improve the guidance systems. But it still wasn't enough: 1,650 warheads on 550 Minuteman III missiles could not destroy all 1,400 Soviet ICBM silos. (It is generally estimated that at least two warheads are needed to destroy a single hardened missile silo, since some will fall outside the "lethal radius" and some others will not work at all.)

So the Air Force, in 1973, asked for a new ICBM—the MX —which would have ten warheads and still better accuracy. With 200 MX missiles—or even 100 combined with the Minuteman IIIs—counterforce could be feasible once more.

Meanwhile, in the 1970s, the Navy had also equipped its submarine-launched ballistic missile force with MIRVs: Poseidon and Trident I. As a result, the Navy had more warheads than were required for assured destruction or for the NAVWAG-5's strategy. Yet not even in theory were these missiles accurate enough to destroy hardened silos. In the mid-1970s as the second Poseidon submarine went to sea—each with 16 missiles carrying up to ten warheads per missile—Admiral Gerald Miller, then deputy director of SAC's Joint Strategic Target Planning Staff, complained to an aide: "Hell, what are we going to do with all of those?" New targets had to be created for new weapons—not the other way around.

So the Navy had no objection when, in the late 1970s, Andrew Marshall, the Rand veteran who had become director of Pentagon net assessment, started lobbying for a program to improve SLBM accuracy to give it "hard-target-kill capability." The result was the Trident II missile, now in research and development, scheduled for operations in the late 1980s.

The Navy could now afford to get into the counterforce business, since the strategy was no longer a source of interservice rivalry. Even the Army grew cooperative when all agreed that the anti-ballistic missile, the Army's only piece of the strategic-nuclear pie, might play a part in helping to protect the MX from nuclear attack. The entire military establishment could comfortably close ranks around a common stake in counterforce. The link between strategy, force levels and higher budgets suited all.

Modifying Counterforce Strategy

However, several theorists—and a small number of military officers—were beginning to detect further problems with counterforce. The Soviet Union had built so many ICBMs (1,000 by 1967) that a full-scale U.S. counterforce strike would require firing at least 2,000 nuclear warheads. The problem was that the Soviets would probably be unable to distinguish such a massive strike from an all-out attack against their cities and would probably order full-scale retaliation. Thus, by the late 1960s, the requirements of a successful counterforce mission had become inconsistent with the philosophy underlying that strategy.

Thomas Schelling, a strategic theorist from Rand and Harvard, recognized this potential contradiction as early as 1960. His solution: if nuclear weapons are to be used, fire small-scale, shot-across-the-bow strikes.[22] The idea was the same as that outlined by Brodie in 1951: Inflict pain, threaten more pain as a way of coercing the Soviets to stop their aggression, but do so in a way that avoids striking Soviet cities and thus compels the Soviets to keep the conflict limited.

The idea appealed to another Rand theorist, James Schlesinger, who elaborated on it in a series of Rand studies, done in association with the Air Force in the late 1960s, known as NUOPTS, or Nuclear Operations. By the time Schlesinger became Secretary of Defense in 1973, several officials in the national security-bureaucracy had become interested, and Schlesinger was determined to make it policy.

The result was a series of National Security Decision Memoranda, beginning with NSDM-242 in January 1974 and climaxing in 1980 with President Carter's controversial Presidential Directive 59.[23] The 1982 "Defense Guidance" signed by Weinberger is only a slight elaboration of the strategy of counterforce and small-scale strikes first articulated in the 1950s.

Force requirements for this sort of nuclear strategy are less elaborate than for the full-scale counterforce plan, in that a military adopting such a strategy would not need so many weapons since it would not have to hit all of the adversary's counterforce targets. But they are more elaborate in that the weapons would have to be even more precise, and because the command-control-communications network would have to be almost unimaginably extensive and durable.

Both sides would need intelligence facilities—satellites and sensors—that could immediately inform their top officials of what targets were hit and what weapons remained. The links connecting the officials and the weapons would have to remain under firm centralized control for days, weeks or longer. This is practically impossible, given the inevitable confusion of large-scale organizations, the inherent unreliability of much military electronic gear and the vulnerability of this equipment to a wide array of nuclear effects, including blast, radiation and electromagnetic pulse. Indeed, these systems are so *inherently* vulnerable that after one or two nuclear "exchanges," chances are very high that escalation will slip completely out of anyone's control.[24]

The strategy also shares certain problems with those of the counterforce philosophy: How do you get the Soviets to play according to the same rules? Does this combination of strikes and threats really coerce the other side? Couldn't the other side fire back equally small-scale strikes—or simply pretend to ignore our "signals"—and try to coerce us instead? Finally, how do you end such a war, on what terms, on what basis of shared trust? After the initial volley, strategy vanishes; only luck and prayer remain.

Some theorists have argued that Soviet surrender would be facilitated if the U.S. targeting plan were geared to destroy the political infrastructure of the Soviet Union; that we should "take out" command posts and other key facilities of the party and military apparatus; that then the Soviet Union would collapse.[25] The real-life technicians of nuclear targeting—the Joint Strategic Planning Staff in Omaha—have considered these suggestions but have discovered no way to make them work. Furthermore by destroying the enemy's command-control network, we might be eliminating the only means by which the Kremlin could communicate with us and signal a desire to end the fighting. We would also be destroying the means by which the top Soviet political leaders could keep their own military officers under control. Authority to use nuclear weapons might automatically fall to some "mad marshal" or "crazy colonel," making further escalation and mutual destruction more likely.

Nuclear Weapons on the Battlefield

Finally, there are those, mainly in Army circles, who talk of fighting a nuclear war on the battlefield. The idea goes back to the early 1950s, when a number of scientists and theorists— Bernard Brodie among them but more notably J. Robert Oppenheimer and later Henry Kissinger—wanted to avoid the holocaust of the hydrogen bomb and city-bombing by "bringing the battle back to the battlefield."[26]

But after 30 years of thinking, nobody has devised a way of doing this. Towns in West Germany, where a theater nuclear war would probably be fought, are only two kilotons apart, so to speak. If tactical nuclear weapons were used on a militarily meaningful scale, millions of West Europeans would die—and that assumes no Soviet retaliation.[27] Moreover, pressure would logically build to "take out" Soviet SS-4, SS-5 and SS-20 missiles, the weapons that most lethally threaten Western Europe. Those missiles lie inside the Soviet Union; once Soviet territory is hit, American territory would almost certainly be next. Then the problems of the counterforce and small-strike strategies start all over again.[28]

In one sense, it is understandable that some analysts have sought in earnest for the rational war-fighting option. No one, after all, really knows what deters war, not even nuclear war; and if nuclear war does come, surely a president should have —and, in fact, does have—choices beyond "suicide or surrender." The problem, however, is that there simply does not appear to be any way that one can fight, much less win, a nuclear war. For an arms controller, that conclusion has inspiring potential. The vast bulk of both sides' nuclear arsenals—practically the entire land-based ICBM force, for example—need not exist except for the pupose of war-fighting. Therefore, if both sides ever begin to comprehend the futility of the war-fighting mission, the prospects for serious mutual arms reductions should shine with hope.

However, the bright lights dim once again with a quick look at the political realities that underlie the arms race. The military and its allies—not only in the United States, but doubtless in the Soviet Union as well—have an immense stake in the war-fighting mission and the weapons that become "requirements" as a result. Since these interests play a powerful role in both sides' politics, especially their arms control politics, the vision of massive reductions will—short of a drastic change in these politics—certainly not be realized for a very long time.

Footnotes

1.) B. Brodie, *The Absolute Weapon*, (Harcourt Brace, 1946) p. 76.

2.) B. Brodie, p. 48.

3.) For Brodie's Air Force experiences, communication to David A. Rosenberg, August 22, 1977 in *Bernard Brodie Papers*, Box 9, Pending folder, UCLA. Brodie's switch to thinking about fighting, not just deterring, war actually occurred a few years earlier. See also Brodie, "The Atom Bomb As Policy Maker," *Foreign Affairs* (Oct. 1948); "New Techniques of War and National Policies," in W.F. Ogburn, ed., *Technology and International Relations* (University of Chicago Press, 1949). Later in life he reverted to an anti-warfighting position; see Brodie, "The Development of Nuclear Strategy," *International Security* (Spring 1978).

4.) Robert F. Futrell, *Ideas, Concepts, Doctrine: A History of Basic Thinking in the United States Air Force, 1907-64*, (Air University, 1971) p. 122.

5.) *Brodie Papers*, "Characteristics of a Sound Strategy," March 17, 1952; "Changing Capabilities and War Objectives," Box 12; Brodie. Also communication to Rosenberg.

6.) *Brodie Papers*, Box 12.

7.) John Foster Dulles, "The Evolution of Foreign Policy," *Department of State Bulletin*, Jan. 25, 1954.

8.) Herman Kahn, *On Thermonuclear War*, (Princeton University Press, 1960); *Thinking About the Unthinkable*, (Horizon Press, 1962); *On Escalation*, (Praeger, 1968).

9.) Richard Halloran, "First Strategy for Fighting a Long Nuclear War," *New York Times*, May 30, 1982. That Marshall was involved comes from my own interviews.

10.) The evidence was that traces of lithium were found amid the radioactive fallout from the test, indicating that the Soviet H-bomb, unlike our own, did not require a massive refrigeration unit, suggesting that it was farther along the way toward becoming a usable weapon. Roy Neal, *Ace in the Hole: The Story of the Minuteman Missile*, (Doubleday, 1962), with interviews.

11.) W.W. Kaufmann, *Military Policy and National Security*, Princeton University Press, 1956; B. Brodie, "Unlimited Weapons and Limited War," *The Reporter*, Nov. 18, 1954.

12.) *Thomas White Papers*, Library of Congress communications: General Thomas Power to General White, May 9, 1959, and General Hewitt to General Charles Westover, May 12, 1959, both in Box 27, SAC folder; White to Power, May 11, 1959, Box 29, 1959 Top Secret File Folder (recently declassified).

13.) *Thomas White Papers*, communication, White to Frank Collbohm, Aug. 12, 1960, Box 37, Rand folder; "Air Force Information Policy Letter" Oct. 1, 1960, Box 37 Commanders' Conference folder; "Subjects of Major Importance for Discussion at the Commanders' Conference,

17-18 November 1960," Tab A, Nov. 1, 1960, Box 41, 1960 Top Secret File Folder (recently declassified).

14. "Unclassified Summary of NAVWAG Study No. 5," Jan. 22, 1958, White House Office files, Office of Staff Secretary, Subject Series, Alpha Subseries, Box 21, Nuclear Exchange (1) folder, Dwight Eisenhower Library.

15.) McNamara got a briefing endorsing finite-deterrence position, Jan. 26, 1961, from the Weapons Systems Evaluation Group, which had just completed a major strategic study called WSEG-50.

16.) The Athens speech is now declassified; for Ann Arbor speech see William W. Kaufmann, *The McNamara Strategy*, (Harper & Row, 1964).

17.) Alain C. Enthoven and K. Wayne Smith, *How Much is Enough*, (Harper and Row, 1971).

18.) Enthoven and Smith.

19.) Robert McNamara, communication to Lyndon Johnson, "Recommended FY 1965-69 Strategic Retaliatory Forces," Dec. 6, 1963; "Recommended FY 1966-1970 Program for Strategic Offensive Forces, Continental Air and Missile Defense Forces, and Civil Defense," Dec. 3, 1964 (recently declassified).

20.) Director of Defense Research and Engineering, *Damage Limiting: A Rationale for the Allocation of Resources by the U.S. and the USSR*, Jan. 21, 1964 (recently declassified); interviews.

21.) MIRVS were justified publicly as ABM penetrators, but they were always intended as weapons that could cover an expanding Soviet strategic force without having to build more missiles. See John S. Foster, quoted in Ralph Lapp, *Arms Without Doubt*, (Cowles Book Co., 1970) p. 21.

22.) Thomas Schelling, *The Strategy of Conflict*, (Oxford University Press, 1960) pp.252-53; interviews.

23.) Desmond Ball, "Counterforce Targeting: How New? How Viable?" *Arms Control Today*, Feb. 1981; Fred Kaplan, "Going Native Without a Field Map," *Columbia Journalism Review*, Jan./Feb. 1981.

24.) Desmond Ball, "Can Nuclear War Be Controlled?" *Adelphi Paper*, 169, International Institute for Strategic Studies, Fall, 1980; William J. Broad, "Nuclear Pulse -- Parts I, II, III," *Science*, May 29, June 5, June 12, 1981; John Steinbruner, "National Security and the Concept of Strategic Stability," *Journal of Conflict Resolution*, Sept. 1978; Fred Kaplan, "Nuclear War Strategy Not New -- or Practical," *Boston Globe*, June 13, 1982.

25.) Colin Gray and Keith Payne, "Victory Is Possible," *Foreign Policy*, Summer 1980.

26.) The slogan of Project Vista, a 1951 report from the California Institute of Technology in which Robert Oppenheimer played a major role. See Philip M. Stern, *The Oppenheimer Case*, (Harper & Row, 1969). Also, Henry Kissinger, *Nuclear Weapons and Foreign Policy*, (Harper Bros., 1957).

27.) This has been the result of virtually every war game involving tactical nuclear weapons in Europe; see Edouard Le Ghait, *No Carte Blanche to Capricorn*, (Brookfield House, 1960).

Chapter 5

The Military-Industrial Complex and the Baroque Arsenal

Mary Kaldor

The Relationship Between Free Enterprise and the Military

"Baroque" armaments[1] are the offspring of a marriage between private enterprise and the state, between the capitalist dynamic of the arms manufacturers and the conservatism that tends to characterize armed forces and defense departments in peacetime. On the one hand, soldiers and weapons designers have clung to particular notions about how wars should be fought and the kinds of weapons with which they should be fought. These notions are largely drawn from the experience of World War II; they justify certain military roles, the existence of military units to carry them out, and the maintenance of certain types of industrial capacity. On the other hand, competition to win contracts and stay in business together with rivalry between the armed services and the various branches of government, has led to an ever-increasing technological effort. The consequence is what is sometimes called "trend innovation"—perpetual improvements to weapons that fall within the established traditions of the armed services and the armorers.

As it becomes more and more difficult to achieve "improvements," the hardware becomes more complex and sophisti-

67

cated. This results in dramatic increases in the cost of individual weapons. But it does not increase military effectiveness. On the contrary, "improvements" become less and less relevant to modern warfare, while cost and complexity become military handicaps: sophisticated weapons are difficult to handle; they go wrong; they need thousands of spare parts; they absorb funds that could otherwise be used for training, practice, pay, ammunition, etc.; and they are prime targets.

The industrial base of the modern armament sector was created in World War II. It consisted of the dominant companies of the period, mainly the manufacturers of automobiles and aircraft. By maintaining and even expanding this base, military spending has helped to preserve the industrial structure of the 1940s. In the first two postwar decades, this may have helped to mobilize resources for investment and innovation and to avoid the crises to which rapidly changing capitalist economies are prone. But this is no longer true. Baroque military technology artificially expands industries that would otherwise have contracted. It absorbs resources that might otherwise have been used for investment and innovation in newer, more dynamic industries. And it distorts concepts of what constitutes technical advance, emphasizing elaborate, custom-built product improvements that are typical of industries on the decline instead of the simpler mass-market process improvements which tend to characterize industries in their prime. It has thus contributed to the slowdown of capital investment and productivity growth and to the gradual degeneration of the American economy.

The Anatomy of the Defense Contract System

The design, development, and production of weapons systems is, by and large, undertaken by a handful of companies known as prime contractors. With a few significant exceptions the prime contractors are generally the manufacturers of weapons platforms—aircraft, shipbuilding, automobile, or engineering companies. They assemble the complete weapons system, subcontracting subsystems, like the gun or missile, the engine and the electronics and components, and so create an interdependent network of big and small companies. The prime contractors are generally among the largest industrial companies. Since World War II, between forty and fifty companies have regularly appeared both on *Fortune's* list of the top one hundred United States companies and on the Pentagon's list of the one hundred companies receiving the highest prime contract awards. The stability of the primes has been widely noted. Since the war, firms have disappeared through merger or, in Europe, through nationalization, but there have been vitually no closures and virtually no new entrants.

Very often, prime contractors and their families of sub-contractors dominate a region, so that the economic impact of producing a weapons system may be very great. Boeing is the biggest company in the state of Washington. Several aircraft companies—Lockheed, Rockwell, Douglas, for example—are located in Southern California. McDonnell dominates manu-facturing in St. Louis, while Bath Ironworks, which makes destroyers, is the most important employer in Maine. Hundreds and thousands of people may work on a single contract. At Electric Boat in Groton, Connecticut, 31,000 people are esti-mated to work on the Trident submarine. And this does not include the people employed by subcontractors or the ripple effect on the producers of consumer goods purchased by the people employed or the capital goods acquired by the contract-ors. In the 1960s, it was estimated that, although military contracts accounted directly for only 8 percent of California's employment, the total impact including indirect employment by subcontractors and indirect employment among producers of consumer and capital goods was 40 percent.[2] And if we also take into account the fact that many small firms which produce both military and civil goods are dependent on the military market to insure their survival, then it is evident that the defense industry is deeply embedded in the economy as a whole.

The weapons system is subject to a technological dynamic characteristic of its industrial environment. As the social structure of industry and the armed forces converge, the competition which epitomizes private industrial enterprise per-vades the various institutions which make up the organization of defense. The National Security Industrial Association, an organization of American defense contractors, reports:

> Within DoD (the U.S. Department of Defense) itself, competition is a very active force. This is reflected in DoD's drive to stay ahead of our potential enemies by fielding weapons which incorporate the latest possible technology; in DoD's relationships with other govern-mental departments; in the efforts of the military services to protect and expand their respective roles and missions and to obtain a larger share of the defense budget; in the relationship between the military ser-vices and the Office of the Secretary of Defense; and in the competition among the branches, commands, ar-senals, yards, centers, and laboratories of the military services.

For industry, competition is keen because the overall total of defense business is seldom adequate to
support the available capacity of even the hard-core
defense contractors, thus forcing the companies into a
continuous life-and-death struggle to obtain defense
contracts. Defense programs often are of gigantic magnitude, which results in competition more intensely
concentrated than is typically encountered in the commercial marketplace.[3]

The consequence of this competition is rapid technical
change, in which every component part of successive weapons
systems is pushed up to and beyond the "state of the art." It is
the fantastic space-age dimensions of much modern weaponry
which so awes the soldier and the civilian observer. And yet the
direction of technical change, it can be argued, is confined
within limits that are defined by the persistence of military and
industrial institutions. The stability of prime contractors and
their customers has helped to preserve traditions about the kind
of military equipment that is considered appropriate. Indeed,
the very sophistication and complexity of hardware may be a
sign of conservatism and narrow perspective. In peacetime, in
the absence of external necessity imposed by war, decisions
about what constitutes technical advance are necessarily subjective. They tend to be taken by people who make and use the
weapons systems, whose ideas are necessarily shaped by
institutional experience and interest in survival. "We have,"
writes John Downey, an eminent British soldier,

a situation in which the nature of present strategy
(deterrence) precludes the acid test of war, while complexity invalidates the rough and ready evaluations of
public opinion.[4]

The consequence is that,

the system is almost completely introverted, concentrating on the perpetual perfection of itself against
some future day of judgment. The dynamic tensions,
commonly regarded as necessary in all systems, must
also be generated internally and can only come from
debate between vigorous minds. But although the
system strives hard to recruit able people, it chooses
and trains them in its own image.[5]

This is what we mean by baroque technology. "Baroque"
technical change consists largely of improvements to a given
set of "performance characteristics." Submarines are faster,
quieter, bigger, and have longer ranges. Aircraft have greater

speed, more powerful thrust, and bigger payloads. All weapons systems have more destructive weapons, particularly missiles, and greatly improved capabilities for communication, navigation, detection, identification, and weapon guidance. Even the development of nuclear weapons can be regarded as an extension of strategic bombing. While the basic technology of the delivery system has not changed much, such marginal improvements have often entailed the use of very advanced technology, e.g., radical electronics innovations such as microprocessors or nuclear power for submarines, and this has greatly increased the complexity of the weapons system as a whole.

The Cost of Military Technology

The outcome of this contradictory process, in which technology is simultaneously promoted and restrained, is gross, elaborate, and very expensive hardware. The Trident program will cost the American taxpayer over $30 billion (in 1980 prices). The latest nuclear-powered aircraft carrier, the subject of controversy, will cost, together with its associated ships and aircraft, more than $60 billion. An Air Force F-15 fighter costs $19 million; the Navy F-14 costs $22 million. The Air Force F-16 and Navy F-18, which were originally designed as cheap, lightweight fighters, are currently estimated to cost $11 million and $18 million, respectively. These costs are several times greater than the cost of World War II predecessors, even when inflation is taken into account. One well-known estimate suggests that if current trends continue, the U.S. Air Force will be able to afford only one plane in 2020.[6] Bombers cost two hundred times as much as they did in World War II. Fighters cost one hundred times or more than they did in World War II. Aircraft carriers are twenty times as expensive and battle tanks are fifteen times as expensive as in World War II. A Gato class submarine cost $5,500 per ton in World War II, compared with $1.6 million per ton for the Trident submarine.[7]

These costs primarily reflect amazing sophistication and technical complexity. And the complexity means thousands and thousands of parts, each part a servicing and logistical problem. The F-4, for example, the predecessor to F-14 and F-15, required 70,000 spare parts. In Vietnam, despite the most extensive logistical operation ever mounted, there were always shortages. All military aircraft are much less reliable than commercial aircraft. They break down more often; they require more maintenance, more repairs, more spares, and more fuel. Tanks are much less reliable than tractors, and warships are much less reliable than merchant ships. As weapons systems become complex, particularly as they incorporate more electronic equipment, reliability declines and operational costs increase at an exponential rate (despite the increased reliability of solid-state devices and improved automated maintenance).

Complex weapons systems are also complex to operate. And yet training hours, combat exercises, and firing practice are reduced because of high operating costs as well as the risk of an expensive accident. And families of weapons systems are increasingly dependent on complex systems of communication which are also costly to operate and maintain.

The Trident, perhaps, is the best example, because most people would think that nuclear-firing missile submarines represent just about the best that modern military technology has to offer. The Trident submarine is huge. It is 560 feet long, longer than the Washington Monument, and six inches too deep to get out of the Thames Channel in Connecticut from its building site to the sea. It is faster than its predecessors, the Polaris/Poseidon submarines. It carries more missiles with a longer range. It has a natural circulation nuclear reactor which is significantly quieter at normal patrol speeds. Its size and its large complement of missiles, however, may actually increase its vulnerability, since it will be easier to detect than its predecessors. Its top underwater speed (25 knots) is still significantly slower than that of attack submarines (30 knots), and in any case, it is so noisy at top speed that it would have to go slow to avoid detection. The increased missile range is of dubious advantage since, for the foreseeable future, Soviet anti-submarine warfare forces cannot detect submarines within the operating area of the current Poseidon.

The weapon system, in perfecting itself along the lines projected by user and producers seems to have overreached itself. It has become big, costly, elaborate, and less and less functional. It serves a certain social purpose, in creating an ever more complicated set of connections between soldiers, sailors, officers, managers, designers, workers, and bureaucrats. And it retains a certain grandeur, a certain ability to instill social awe, that is often to be found in the baroque, whether art, architecture, or technology—a grandeur that may portend degeneration.

In the United States, the tendency towards baroque weaponry is futhered by a number of important institutional arrangements. Foremost among these is the follow-on system.

The Follow-On System

The argument that procurement was necessary to maintain

a capacity to design, develop, and produce weapons became institutionalized in the follow-on.[8] Essentially, this means that as soon as work is completed on one weapons system, work begins on its successor. Hence, Boeing produced the B-47, followed by the B-52, followed by the Minuteman ICBM. Lockheed produced the F-80 and the F-104 fighters, and a famous series of heavy transports. North American produced the P-51 Mustang, followed by the F-86, followed by the F-100. As one Air Force colonel said, "there is always someone working on the follow-on at the Pentagon, it's an article of faith."

The follow-on system is often explained in bureaucratic terms. The mission of each military unit and the organization of its officers and men is built around a particular weapons system. When the weapons system comes to the end of its useful life, the military unit needs a successor to justify the unit's continued existence. While this explains the attachment to particular types of weapons systems and particular performance characteristics, it does not explain the pace of technical advance, the length of the useful, the emphasis on "quality" rather than quantity, the "cost and complexity" syndrome. There are, after all, many military men who favor numbers and simplicity and a slower rate of replacement. For the corporations, however, it is continuous development of weapons systems, rather than continuous use, on which their existence depends. Hence, there are reasons for supposing that it is the corporations that have had a decisive influence on the pace of the follow-on system.

To ensure continuous work, all defense companies have planning groups, whose sole function it is to choose suitable successors for the weapons that are currently being produced and who work closely with similar groups in the services. The planning group is supposed to predict what a particular branch of the armed services might require when current projects come to an end, and the various ways the corporation might meet that requirement. Because of the relationship with the armed forces, particularly during the so-called concept-definition phase, the prediction tends to become a self-fulfilling prophecy. As one corporate vice president said, the government "depends on companies like ours to tell them what they need."

Despite these efforts, the follow-on system does not function smoothly. If it did, the efforts would be unnecessary. Indeed, interruptions are a paradoxical consequence of the workings of the system. The struggle for continuous employment of industrial capacity also entails the tendency for continuous expansion. As competition spurs further "improvements" in design, so the weapons system become bigger and heavier, more expensive and more elaborate. Teams of engineers expand and additional layers of management are inserted. Each engineer pushes his own idea, each manager competes to attract more funds for his own section, and so more improvements, in a self-perpetuating manner. In war, the acid test of battle proves which improvements are useful and which are not. In peace time, the only limits to the improvements that can be offered are the available technology and the size of the military budget. In fact, those limits are consistently overreached as the advocates of particular programs—the defense contractors and their military allies—underestimate the cost of their program and overestimate the technological possibilities. This is why cost overruns which, during the 1970s *averaged* 100 percent, are a permanent feature in defense contracting.[9]

Military Spending and Economic Decline

Planned obsolescence could be said to be a sign of technological stagnation, a sign that the technologies of car making, aircraft manufacture, and shipbuilding, at least in the United States, have reached a point, which all technologies reach sooner or later, of diminishing returns, where new investments yield ever smaller improvements in productivity and hence competitiveness, where quality becomes more important than quantity, because new markets cannot be captured and old markets can only be preserved through apparent qualitative improvements. This is a characteristic of industries during the declining phase of a long wave. Baroque military technology could be seen as an extreme form of planned obsolescence. Because the consumer is the government, tastes can be more easily imposed, and there is almost no external discipline, as there is in a commercial market, on the so-called improvements which can be offered.

Since the automobile and aircraft industries dominate the U.S. economy, the consequences of baroque technology, this manifestation of technological stagnation, are pervasive. After World War II, the dynamism of the early twentieth century was never regained. To be sure, the 1950s and 1960s were a boom period. Military spending may have contributed to the boom, stimulating demand and providing technological spin-off, especially in the electronics industry. But the signs of economic decline could already be detected. From 1950, productivity growth lagged well behind Europe and Japan, and investment as a share of GNP was lower than in any other advanced industrial country. (Japan had the fastest productivity growth and the lowest rate of military spending as a share of GNP.) America continued to be the highest spender on research and development (R&D), but a large share of this spending was devoted to military purposes. In the late 1960s, Germany and Japan overtook the United States in the share of the GNP devoted to civilian research and development. Furthermore, most of the German and Japanese R&D went to the fast-growing sectors of chemicals and electronics and was undertaken by private corporations, whereas in the United States the bulk of civilian R&D went to aerospace and was financed by the government.[10]

Military spending, as we have seen, was partly a response to the problems of the defense-related sectors. And these, in turn, were the dominant industries. High military spending could thus be viewed as a consequence of economic decline. But the causal connection need not be only one-way. If military spending played a role akin to overseas investment in the cumulative process of Britain's decline, might the same be true for the United States? It has been widely argued that the U.S. overseas investment is both a cause and a consequence of the slowdown in the American rate of growth. The same might also be true of military spending. For example, American preeminence in aircraft and electronics is due, in part, to the sheer volume of military resources. And yet the military orientation of these industries—and indeed the military market as a whole—impedes current and future commercial developments which provide the economic basis for military spending.

The result can be generalized. American military power has been based on the strength and dynamism of American industry. It is probably true that, in the postwar world, American military power was needed to underwrite the Western economic system and the spectacular long boom. But the form and cost of American military power cannot be so directly related to the international economy and geopolitics. The ritualistic replay of World War II in the acquisition of ever more sophisticated aircraft and tanks and in the imaginary extension of strategic air missions as the nuclear armory grew more grotesque was peculiarly an outcome of the American industrial structure. It has served to preserve this structure, and to extend it, ironically, in ways that were probably quite alien to its original creators. World War II marked the beginning of a kind of self-consciousness about American achievements that prevented their ever being repeated. After World War II, technological stagnation and hence periodic recession led to increased military spending—a reassertion of American predominance with the symbols of military power which were also the products of the depressed sectors. And increased military spending further channelled technical change in what might be called decadent directions, reinforcing stagnation and establishing the conditions for worse recessions in the future.

Footnotes

1.) The term "baroque" in relation to armament was first used by Herbert York, one of the nuclear physicists who developed the atom bomb, former Director of the Livermore Radiation Laboratory and top United States government official, when he wrote of "baroque, even rococo varieties of A-bombs and H-bombs." (*Race to Oblivion*, New York, Simon and Schuster, 1970) p. 44.

2.) Charles M. Tiebout, "The Regional Impact of Defense Expenditure: Its Measurement and Problems of Adjustment," in Roger E. Bolton, *Defense and Disarmament: The Economics of Transition* (Englewood Cliffs, Prentice-Hall, 1966.)

3.) Quoted in J.R. Fox, *Arming America: How the U.S. Buys Weapons* (Cambridge, Harvard University, 1974) pp. 100-101.

4.) *Management in the Armed Forces: An Anatomy of the Military Profession* (London, McGraw-Hill, 1977) p. 195.

5.) *Ibid.*, p. 198.

6.) Norman R. Augustine, "One Plane, One Tank, One Ship: The Trend for the Future," *Defense Management Journal,* April 1975.

7.) Aerospace Systems Analysis, McDonnell Douglas **Astronautics** Corp., *Cost of War Index*, (Santa Monica, 1968.)

8.) The idea of the follow-on imperative as an intellectual concept was originated by James Kurth. See his "Why We Buy the Weapons We Do," *Foreign Policy,* No. 11, 1973.

9.) U.S. Congress, House of Representatives, Committee on Government Operations, "Inaccuracy of Department of Defense Acquisition Cost Estimates," 9th Report, 96th Congress, first session, No. 96-656, (Washington D.C., 1979).

10.) OECD, *Patterns of Resources Devoted to Research and Development in the OECD Area,* 1963-71, (Paris, 1973).

Chapter 6

The Strategic and Theater Nuclear Balance

Paul Joseph and Hayes Gladstone

Forming the basis of any discussion of the nuclear arms race between the United States and the Soviet Union is the concept of the "military balance." Defining this apparently straightforward term has proved elusive because of the number and types of factors involved. For instance, does the accuracy of an American Minuteman III compensate for the megatonnage of a Soviet SS-18? Do the greater number of American warheads on submarines counter the greater number of Soviet warheads on land-based missiles? What about geography? Allies? What is the impact of leads in technology or conventional military strength on the nuclear balance?

The mass media often present a bewildering array of statistics which claim to make a definitive statement on the superpower military balance. However the numbers are frequently manipulated to suit a particular stance. Depending on the expert, the U.S. may be found to be dangerously behind the U.S.S.R.; there may be rough military parity, with each side holding distinct advantages and disadvantages; or the U.S. may hold a decided edge. More importantly, does any calculation of the military balance become obsolete when considered in the light of the gross overkill capabilities of each side?

Our position has two fundamental premises. Each is based on a distinct concept of what "being ahead" in the arms race actually means. The first sense of being ahead is that one or the other country would be in a position to actually win a nuclear war. The victorious country could then issue orders to the defeated country. On this point, the evidence accumulated by the Physicians for Social Responsibility, Congress, and the U.S. Arms Control and Disarmament Agency indicates that the enormous casualities and destruction of nuclear war, while impossible to detail in advance, would nonetheless be so overwhelming as to dictate the conclusion that there can be no winner in this classic military sense.[1] Each side would face terrifying destruction. Each side would lose. Thus our first premise is that the *reality* of the arms race is one of rough parity, a parity based on the fact that being "ahead" or "behind" has little if any meaning should a nuclear war ever start.

A second sense of being ahead concerns the possibility of threatening to use nuclear weapons to gain political influence. One side is ahead when it can use its perceived advantage in the nuclear arena to good advantage on other military or foreign policy issues. For example, it might be easier to use conventional military force without fear of a response from the other superpower. Or it might threaten to use its nuclear force so that its political and economic ends are achieved. Paul Nitze, a member of the Reagan administration, has argued that this translation of presumed military advantage to political influence is comparable to "a game of chess. The atomic queens may never be brought into play; they may never actually take one of the opponent's pieces. But the position of the atomic queens may still have a decisive bearing on which side can safely advance a limited-war bishop or even a cold-war pawn"[2] In this sense, the U.S. is ahead if it can create, in the deliberations of the Soviet leaders, a credible threat that it will use nuclear weapons first. Frightened by such a possibility, Moscow will lower its determination to counter an American effort to exert its influence and the U.S. will have gained an advantage in global politics.

This game of nuclear maneuver is being played by both sides, although in different ways. Only one side, the United States, is trying to gain an advantage that is usable politically. The Soviet Union is trying to stay even in order to deny the U.S. political leverage. The game is played by attempting to gain leads on the different measures used to judge the military balance. Examples of such measures include throw-weight,

FIGURE 6-1
THE NUCLEAR BALANCE SHEET:
U.S. and Soviet Strategic Nuclear Forces

— United States —

	Delivery Vehicles	Warheads	Approximate Explosive Power in Hiroshima-Bomb Equivalents
Intercontinental ballistic missiles	1,052	2,152	123,000
Submarine-launched ballistic missiles	520	4,800	23,000
Bombers	350	2,600	130,000
TOTAL	1,922	9,552	276,000

— Soviet Union —

	Delivery Vehicles	Warheads	Approximate Explosive Power in Hiroshima-Bomb Equivalents
Intercontinental ballistic missiles	1,400	5,500	270,000
Submarine-launched ballistic missiles	950	1,900	59,000
Bombers	150	400	33,000
TOTAL	2,500	7,800	362,000

Source: Stockholm International Peace Research Institute. *The Arms Race and Arms Control,* *1982;* Center for Defense Information. *U.S. — USSR Strategic Nuclear Forces,* 1982: *The New York Times,* April 2. 1982.

total megatonnage, number of missile launchers, number of warheads, accuracy of those warheads, and the like.

Our second premise is that these measures used to judge the military balance are both misleading and real. They are misleading because quantitative leads on one or another measure are rarely related to specific military missions, that is, to what the U.S. or the U.S.S.R. can or cannot do with this lead in the actual conditions of nuclear war. There is no advantage on any measure of military superiority that alters the fact that either side can destroy the other. If intended to convey a decided advantage, then a lead in throw-weight, or number of warheads, is misleading.

These measures are also real in the sense that they can help form the *perceptions* of whom is ahead or behind. These perceptions are important. American military propagandists claim that the U.S. is behind on some of the measures so that political support can be mobilized to support the ambitious weapons program that is needed in the (futile, but very dangerous) attempt to establish a policy of using nuclear weapons as political instruments. The various measures are thus part of the reality of politics. The point is illustrated by looking at Figure 1.

Leading Measures of the Arms Race

The size and composition of the strategic forces of the Soviet Union and the United States are different. One area where the U.S.S.R. is "ahead" of the U.S. is in the total explosive power of its nuclear bombs (362,000 to 276,000 Hiroshima equivalents). But what does this lead signify? On August 6, 1945, the first atomic bomb was detonated over Hiroshima. Over 80,000 people perished from that single bomb and thousands more died from radiation-related causes. In addition, the city was structurally decimated. Presently, the two superpowers possess 638,000 times the explosive power of the first Hiroshima bomb. This enormous destructive capacity boggles the imagination. Given the carnage at Hiroshima, it is impossible to grasp what two or three hundred thousand times that damage actually means. It is even more difficult to grasp the significance of a "lead" of some 75,000 Hiroshima bomb equivalents. Therefore, the differential between the U.S. and U.S.S.R. in terms of total megatonnage is of negligible significance. Each side possesses more than enough to destroy the other.

The Soviet Union is also ahead of the U.S. in the total launchers or delivery vehicles (2,500 to 1,922), in the subcategory of number of land-based ICBMs (1,400 to 1,052), in the subcategory of number of sea-based ballistic missiles (950 to 520), and, in a category not shown in the table, that of total throw-weight (throw-weight is the total payload that sits on top of the last stage of the missile).

The United States is ahead in total number of warheads or actual bombs (9,552 to 7,800), in intercontinental bombers, in warheads that these bombers carry, and in the number of warheads based at sea (4,800 to 1,900). The U.S. has more warheads, even though the Soviet Union has more missiles, because the American systems are more fully MIRVed. More of the U.S. missiles are capable of carrying multiple warheads (MIRV stands for Multiple Independently Targeted Reentry Vehicles).

When presented in isolation, numbers such as these can be drawn upon selectively to support different political perspectives. Those supporting an arms buildup can point towards Soviet "advantages". Liberals can argue that the two force structures are in rough parity with each side trading off strengths and weaknesses. Our own position is that these numbers cannot be considered apart from specific historical and political context. On close examination it is the U.S. that is ahead of the Soviet Union, not in the sense of being able to win a nuclear war, but in blustering the first use of nuclear weapons in order to gain political influence.

Let us examine the perceived Soviet advantages. Its lead in throw-weight, for example, is in compensation for the lack of miniaturization of guidance systems and less efficient rocket engines. In the past, American military planners considered and explicitly rejected building a new "heavy" missile, largely because the technological lead of the U.S. permitted development of smaller but more accurate weapons.

What about the Soviet "lead" in land-based missiles? Moscow has more but this situation is more the product of political decisions made within each country's military establishments than U.S. acquiescence to the Soviet Union. In part to placate inter-service rivalry *within* the Pentagon, in part because it is more flexible, the U.S. has remained committed to preserving a strategic "triad" in which each leg—land-based missiles, sea-based missiles, and bombers—can deliver extensive damage to the Soviet Union. Due to geographic constraints (lack of warm-water ports) and a history of invasions, Moscow has been more committed to ICBMs stationed away from its borders. A full 75 percent of its warheads are on land-based missiles. Twenty percent are at sea, and only five percent can be found on long-range bombers. (Washington's warheads are more evenly distributed among sea-based missiles, 50 percent; land-based missiles, 25 percent; and bombers, 25 percent.)

Moscow has let its intercontinental bomber fleet atrophy. Its long-range bombers are 1950s vintage and propeller driven. The main U.S. bomber, the B-52, was also produced in the 50s but is powered by jet engines and has been modernized in many ways. Besides being able to fly longer distances than its Soviet counterpart, the B-52 can refuel in the air since the U.S. has over 600 KC135 tankers.[3] In contrast the Soviet Union has only 30 long-range tankers. In addition, Washington is producing an entirely new bomber, the B-1, and still another, the so-called Stealth or Advanced Technology Bomber, is being developed.

Another disparity is the Soviet lead in the number of missile launchers. It is a result of complex arms control negotiations conducted during the Nixon administration. Moscow was (and still is) concerned about U.S. nuclear forces in Europe which American negotiators showed little interest in including in arms limitation talks. From the standpoint of the Soviet Union, an imbalance existed because the U.S. systems stationed in Europe could hit their territory, yet there was no equivalent weapon that threatened the U.S. The U.S. claimed a distinction between strategic systems, based in the U.S. or the oceans, and tactical, or forward-based systems such as those stationed in Europe. Moscow did not admit to such a distinction because each category could hit their territory. Eventually a deal was worked out. In exchange for Soviet agreement to exclude the U.S. forward-based or tactical systems from U.S./ Soviet strategic talks, Moscow was permitted several hundred additional launchers to offset Europe.[4] Among themselves, U.S. strategists felt that their lead in exploiting MIRV technology would permit them, by loading each missile with multiple warheads, to more than compensate for the Soviet advantage in number of missile launchers. At that time the U.S. enjoyed a lead in number of warheads by better than three to one (see Figure 6). Furthermore, to secure military support for an arms control agreement that conferred even a superficial advantage to Moscow, President Nixon agreed that the Navy could proceed with the production of the new Trident submarine.

The U.S. enjoys important advantages in the quality of its weapon systems. Warhead accuracy is one example. Accuracy is measured in terms of circular error probability (CEP) or the radius of the circle within which 50 percent of the warheads aimed at a given target will fall. (Note that there is no assumption that the center of that circle will sit exactly upon the target itself. A missile may be accurate in the sense of

FIGURE 6-2
PRINCIPAL STRATEGIC AND EUROSTRATEGIC MISSILES

Type	Name	Year	Number of Warheads	Power of Each Warhead (Kilotons)	Range (km)	CEP (m)
Strategic:						
U.S.						
ICBM	Titan II	1963	1	9,000	11,500	1,300
	Minuteman II	1966	1	2,000	13,000	400
	Minuteman III	1970	3	170	13,000	300
	Minuteman III with Mk 12A	1976	3	350	13,000	200
	MX	proj - 1986	10	350	13,000	*100
SLBM	Polaris-A3	1964	1	600	4,500	900
	Poseidon-C3	1970	10	50	7,500	500
	Trident I	1980	8	100	7,500	500
	Trident II	proj - 1989	14	150	11,000	*500
ALCM	—	1983	1	200	**1,800	30-90
USSR						
ICBM	SS-9	1966	1	18,000	12,000	1,000
	SS-11	1966	1	1,000	10,500	1,500
	SS-13	1969	1	1,000	8,000	1,300
	SS-17	1977	4	900	9,000	300-600
	SS-18	1976	8	2,000	10,000	300-600
	SS-19	1976	6	500	9,000	300-450
SLBM	SS-N-6	1968	1	1,000	3,000	2,000
	SS-N-8	1973	1	1,000	8,000	1,000
	SS-N-18	—	3	1,000	7,500	600

FIGURE 6-2
PRINCIPAL STRATEGIC AND EUROSTRATEGIC MISSILES CONTINUED

	Type	Name	Year	Number of Warheads	Power of Each Warhead (Kilotons)	Range (km)	CEP (m)
Eurostrategic::							
U.S.	BM	Pershing 1A	1962	1	60-400	750	450
		Pershing II	1983	1	10-20	1,600	45
	GLCM	Tomahawk	1983	1	200	2,500	30-90
USSR	BM	SS-4	1959	1	1,000	3,000	2,400
		SS-5	1959	1	1,000	3,700	1,250
		SS-12	1969	1	1,000	800	—
		SS-20	1977	3	150	4,000	400
	SLBM	SS-N-5	1964	1	1,000	1,200	—
U.K.	SLBM	Polaris-A3	1967	1	600	4,500	900
France	SLBM	S-3	1971	1	150	3,000	—
	BM	M-20	1977	1	1,000	5,000	—

* Terminal Guidance Systems are known to be being developed for these missiles. If these are deployed, the CEP will reduce to a few tens of meters.

** In the case of ALCMs, the range of the carrying aircraft should be added to this figure.

Source: IISS— The Military Balance. 1980-1981. SIPRI... Yearbook. 1980

producing a "tight" patterning of shots, but inaccurate in the sense that wind, gravitation, magnetic fields, and other factors combine to produce a bias pushing the distribution of that pattern away from the intended target.) Accuracy is much more important than megatonnage as a measure of destroying a given target. Increasing the yield of a bomb will increase the probability of destroying a hardened target only slightly; doubling the accuracy will increase the probability of destroying that target by a factor of eight. The 1980 Report on Nuclear Weapons of the Secretary General of the United Nations noted that the "megatonnage alone is a very misleading measure of one side's capability. Of equal or more importance is missile accuracy."

Figure 2 gives some of the accuracies achieved by different missile systems of each side. It is important to note that accuracy is not important for retaliating at cities or industrial targets; accuracy is of paramount importance when establishing the ability to hit military targets that are hardened to withstand the shock of a near miss. Note that the CEPs of the most modern U.S. systems—Minuteman III, the MX, Trident II, the Pershing II, and the Tomahawk cruise missile—are a quarter a mile or less. Of the Soviet systems, only the SS-20 and the most modern version of the SS-18 have a theoretical capacity to destroy hardened targets.

Another example of an important but unrecognized U.S. edge is in anti-submarine warfare, an area where the Soviet Union makes little serious effort. Elsewhere in this volume, Robert Aldridge makes the argument that the Soviet submarines are becoming vulnerable. If this would ever happen, the U.S. would be much closer to achieving a genuine first-strike capability.

Geography also favors the U.S. since its submarines can quickly reach deep water from either coast while the Soviet subs must travel through narrow chokepoints where they can be much more easily monitored. Sea-launched ballistic missiles represent 50 percent of America's nuclear force. In the case of a preemptive attack by the Soviet Union, the submarines would be almost impossible to destroy because of their mobility and poor Soviet anti-submarine technology. As President Carter said in 1979: "Just one of our relatively invulnerable Poseidon submarines—less than two percent of our total nuclear force of submarines, aircraft, and land-based missiles—carries enough warheads to destroy every large and medium-sized city in the Soviet Union."[5] The American submarine advantage is compounded since the Soviet Union only maintains nine to ten submarines at sea. These hold less than 300 nuclear weapons. This tactic is opposed to the U.S. practice of keeping close to three thousand sea-based nuclear weapons in position to attack the Soviet Union.[6]

Selective Use of Data

The disparities between the U.S. and U.S.S.R. on measures outlined above permit the possibility of manipulating data to support the adoption of particular weapon-systems. Nowhere has this sleight-of-hand been more evident than in reporting of the "need" to fund the MX in order to close a missile gap that

FIGURE 6-3
THE NUCLEAR BALANCE WITHOUT MX:
Existing Strategic Forces, U.S. Government Estimates

	United States	Soviet Union
Land-based intercontinental ballistic missiles (ICBM) launchers	1,053	1,398
ICBM warheads	2,100	6,000
Submarine-launched ballistic missiles (SLBM)	544	950
SLBM warheads	5,000	1,500
Bombers	410	345
Total missiles	**1,597**	**2,348**
Total missiles and bombers	**2,007**	**2,693**
Total missile warheads	**7,100**	**7,500**

Source: *New York Times*, 1982

allegedly exists between the two superpowers. President Reagan has claimed that "...unless we demonstrate the will to rebuild our strength and restore the military balance, the Soviets, since they are so far ahead, have little incentive to negotiate with us..."[7] Shortly afterwards, *The New York Times* printed a table (see Figure 3) in its "Week In Review" section which purported to reveal the present Soviet strategic advantage. Notice in particular the Soviet lead in ICBM launchers and warheads. (The figures differ from those given in Figure 1 because *The New York Times* chart includes the Backfire bomber as a strategic system.) The reader is certainly left with the impression that a "window of vulnerability" exists and that the MX may be the best solution for it.

But *The New York Times* chart excludes various factors which distort its accuracy. Despite listing ICBM and SLBM warheads, it neglects to account for nuclear weapons attached to American strategic bombers. Yet, the U.S. bomber force contains six and one-half times more warheads than their Soviet counterpart. Moreover, unlike the Soviet bombers, a third of the Strategic Air Command planes are on continuous alert. A calculation of the strategic balance that allows for U.S. advantages—the fact that Soviet submarines are in port more often than American nuclear submarines, and that American forward-based (tactical) bombers are capable of striking the Soviet Union—indicates that the U.S. maintains an advantage in deliverable nuclear weapons of 10,350 to 6,340 (see Figure 4).

Despite this U.S. lead, the brutal fact is that neither side can escape overwhelming destruction if the other side chooses to launch its nuclear forces. This point is conveyed in clear fashion in Figure 5. The first column of the table depicts the numbers of strategic warheads available to the U.S. and U.S.S.R. and their distribution on each of the three legs of the strategic triad. The second column indicates the number of warheads remaining after a U.S. first strike; the third, the number after a first strike by the Soviets. After a U.S. first strike, the U.S.S.R. would still have more than 1000 warheads, enough to cause enormous damage. After a U.S.S.R. first strike, the U.S. would have more than 3000 warheads. While the U.S. is "ahead" by these calculations, the most important factor is that both sides would retain, even after the worst possible case of receiving a first strike from its enemy, the capacity to respond at a level the attacker would find unacceptable.* Most defini-

---

*The argument advanced by Robert Aldridge elsewhere in this volume is that U.S. offensive and defensive capabilities are advancing so rapidly that it will be possible, in the near future, for the U.S. to initiate

FIGURE 6-4
DELIVERABLE NUCLEAR WARHEADS*

— United States on the Soviet Union —

ICBMs	2,150
SLBMs	3,000
Strategic bombers	2,600
Tactical bombers	2,600
Total	**10,350**

— Soviet Union on the United States —

ICBMs	5,600
SLBMs	300
Strategic bombers	290
Backfire bombers	150
Total	**6,340**

* Excluding submarines in port; including U.S. forward-based bombers.

Source: *Defense Monitor*, Volume XI, 6, 1982.

tions of unacceptable damage are set at 25 percent of the civilian population and between 50 and 75 percent of the industrial capacity—a level of destruction that can be achieved by as few as 400 bombs. Imagine a line drawn across figures at 400 warheads. Note in this regard that *each leg* of the U.S. arsenal can deliver unacceptable damage, even *after* a Soviet first strike. The main point of the table, and indeed of the arms race generally, is that neither side is vulnerable to a disarming first strike.

a first strike without receiving unacceptable damage in return. Of course, the definition of what is "unacceptable" is crucial here.

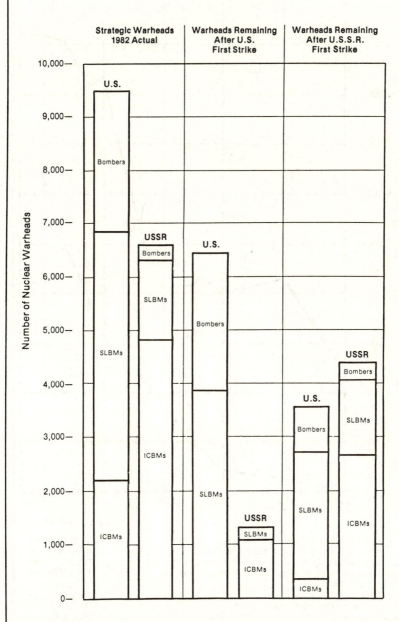

Source: *Scientific American*, November 1982

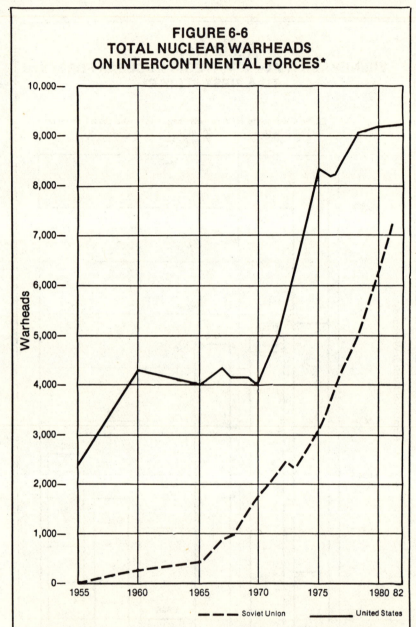

**FIGURE 6-6
TOTAL NUCLEAR WARHEADS
ON INTERCONTINENTAL FORCES***

– – – Soviet Union   **United States**

* Warhead estimates are unavoidably uncertain because (1) the number of bombers
in service and the number of bombs loaded on each bomber vary considerably and
(2) some warheads are stockpiled, but not deployed on delivery vehicles. Some
studies have estimated that U.S. warheads exceeded 7,000 in the early 1960s and
11,000 by the mid-1970s.

Source: International Institute for Strategic Studies, *Military Balance 1982-1983;* Stockholm International Peace Research Institute, SIPRI *Yearbooks 1976-1980;* and Robert P. Berman and John C. Baker, *Soviet Strategic Forces,* Washington: Brookings Institution, 1982), pp. 42-43.
Adapted from *Living with Nuclear Weapons* (New York: Bantam, 1983), p. 74.

History

The capacity of each side to destroy the other, independent of the circumstances, is called mutually assured destruction, or MAD. MAD has not always been an accurate description of the strategic balance between Moscow and Washington. Despite protests from scientists who contributed to the bomb such as Leo Szilard and Niels Bohr for an international arms control body, the U.S. government steadfastly refused to yield control. Rather than limit the number of bombs and delivery vehicles, the American military developed the medium-range bomber in 1948 and the hydrogen bomb in 1952. Since the first atomic explosion in Los Alamos, a pattern has evolved: the Americans have been far ahead of the Soviets in the research and development of nuclear weapons. After the unveiling of an American weapons system, the Soviet Union would accelerate the development of parallel projects in order to "catch up" with the U.S. Nonetheless, until the mid fifties, the U.S. possessed a monopoly on the delivery of nuclear weapons. Through the mid sixties, the U.S. enjoyed overwhelming superiority.

Figures 6, 7, and 8 depict some features of the arms race over the postwar period. Of the three measures, the most important is the number of warheads (Figure 6). Note the huge lead the U.S. enjoyed over the Soviet Union, especially before the late-sixties. Indeed, it is the achievement, not of strict parity, but of the ability to absorb a first blow from the United States and still be assured of inflicting unacceptable damage in return, that has sharply reduced the ability of Washington decision-makers to threaten the first use of nuclear weapons during the crisis situations. During the 1962 Cuban Missile Crisis, for example, the U.S. had approximately 4,500 warheads while the Soviet Union had only 300. It has been estimated that the Soviet Union had less than 10 missiles during the crisis. No wonder that President Kennedy was able to force Krushchev to order the withdrawal of Soviet missiles from Cuba.

Figure 7 shows that the Soviet Union has caught up to and finally surpassed the United States in the number of strategic launchers (remember in this regard that the U.S. has forward-based systems in Europe that are not counted in the strategic total, while the Soviet Union has nothing comparable to threaten the U.S.). Since the mid seventies, confined by arms control agreements, neither side has increased its number of launchers. (These agreements have not constrained warheads as effectively and both sides have continued to add to their arsenals.)

Figure 8 shows the total megatonnage of both sides and

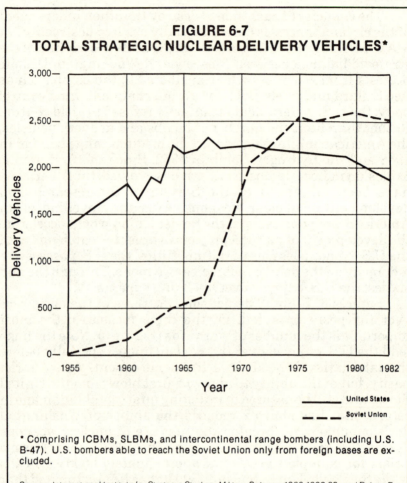

FIGURE 6-7
TOTAL STRATEGIC NUCLEAR DELIVERY VEHICLES*

United States
Soviet Union

* Comprising ICBMs, SLBMs, and intercontinental range bombers (including U.S. B-47). U.S. bombers able to reach the Soviet Union only from foreign bases are excluded.

Source: International Institute for Strategic Studies. *Military Balance 1960-1982-83*, and Robert P. Berman and John C. Baker. *Soviet Strategic Forces* (Washington: Brookings Institution, 1982), pp. 42-43. Adapted from *Living with Nuclear Weapons* (New York: Bantam, 1983), p. 75.

clearly indicates a Soviet advantage, although there is little significance to this lead. Since the early 1960s, the U.S. has *reduced* its total megatonnage. This is more a sign of technical prowess than it is one of unilateral disarmament. The largest land-based warhead in U.S. possession sits on our oldest missile, the Titan II (see Figure 1). Warheads sitting on the newer missiles are smaller in explosive yield, but more accurate and form part of a MIRV package. As pointed out above, it is far more destabilizing to have several smaller and more accurate warheads than it is to have a single large warhead. In the late seventies, American megatonnage began to increase again.

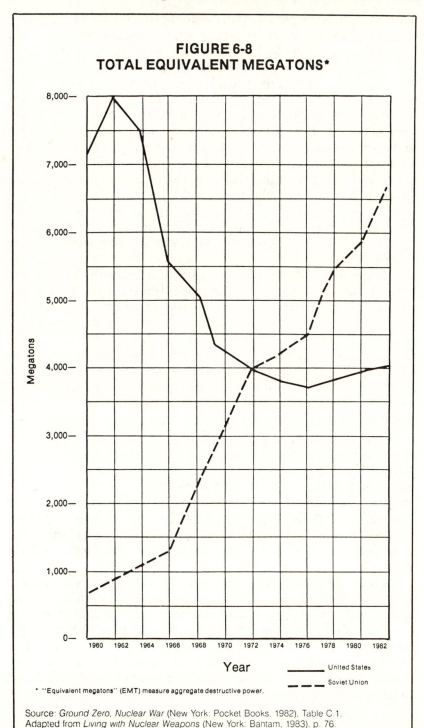

FIGURE 6-8
TOTAL EQUIVALENT MEGATONS*

* "Equivalent megatons" (EMT) measure aggregate destructive power.

Source: *Ground Zero, Nuclear War* (New York: Pocket Books. 1982), Table C.1.
Adapted from *Living with Nuclear Weapons* (New York: Bantam, 1983). p. 76.

This change is the result of introducing the Mark 12A warhead, which combines both accuracy and a larger yield, on the Minuteman III missile. The Soviet Union relies more heavily on huge blockbuster weapons and larger total megatonnage, although there are some indications that as the Soviet Union modernizes its forces and introduces MIRVs on its missiles, its megatonnage is beginning to drop as well.[8] The two points to keep in mind concerning megatonnage are that both sides have more than enough and that it is not the best indicator of superiority—indeed, in some respects it is a counter-indicator. It is useful to keep in mind the response of Secretary of Defense Caspar Weinberger, who when asked by the Senate Foreign Relations Committee if he would trade the U.S. nuclear arsenal for the Soviet arsenal, responded: "I would not for a moment exchange anything because we have an immense edge in technology."

A summary of the strategic situation between the U.S. and U.S.S.R. would be as follows: the most fundamental fact is that each side can destroy the other, no matter the circumstances; of the various measures used to show strategic superiority the U.S. is ahead in most of those that capture technical superiority; the U.S. also holds certain geographic and alliance advantages; as a consequence the U.S. is closer to creating a situation that its leaders believe will translate into greater political influence.

Europe

The European military balance is the source of much controversy. It is focused particularly on the December 1979 NATO "double-track decision" to deploy Pershing II and cruise missiles and pursue arms control negotiations with the Soviet Union. The political and military considerations surrounding the NATO decision are detailed elsewhere in the volume by Dan Smith. The goal of this brief section is to illustrate some of the considerations involved in defining the Eurostrategic or theater military balance.

There are more than 10,000 nuclear weapons in Europe and over 70 different types of delivery systems. The U.S. has about 6,000 warheads deployed on submarines and aircraft carriers in the Atlantic Ocean, the Mediterranean, and in Europe itself. Government officials estimate that the Soviet Union has between 3 and 6 thousand weapons for use in Europe. Great Britain and France also have nuclear weapons but with much smaller arsenals, probably on the order of 500 weapons each.[9]

FIGURE 6-9
U.S. CALCULATION
OF NATO AND WARSAW CAPABILITIES

U.S. Calculation of NATO Capabilities	U.S. Calculation of Soviet Capabilities
— Aircraft in Europe —	— Aircraft in Europe —
F-111 164	Nuclear-Capable Fighter planes (Fender, Flogger, Fitter) 2,700
F-4 265	
A-6/A-7 68	Backfire Bomber 45
	Badger/Blinder Bombers 350
— Aircraft in U.S. —	
F-111 63	
— Intermediate Missiles —	— Intermediate Missiles —
none	SS-20 250
	SS-4/5 350
	SS-12/22 100
	SS-N-5 30
Total 560	Total 3,825

Source: *Atlantic News.* November 25. 1981

In the fall of 1981, President Reagan claimed that the Warsaw Pact enjoyed a six-to-one advantage over NATO in medium-range nuclear capable systems (medium-range is between 1,000 and 5,000 kilometers). In November of that year, Richard Burt, director of the U.S. State Department Bureau of Political/Military Affairs, detailed Reagan's claim (see Figure 9). The U.S. focused in particular on the newest Soviet intermediate range missile, the SS-20, which, it was claimed, was powerful and accurate enough to intimidate Western Europe. NATO had nothing to counter the threat posed by the SS-20 and, as a result, those countries were subject to political blackmail from the East. In response, the U.S. insisted on deploying 108 Pershing II and 464 cruise missiles against the SS-20s. In Washington's view, these intermediate range missiles were necessary to restore the European balance.

Some participants in the European peace movement have countered with arguments that the new missiles free the U.S. to conduct nuclear war against the Soviet Union with Europe as the battleground. The Pershing II and cruise enable the U.S. to devise scenarios for limited nuclear war that do not involve the continental United States, and even, particularly in the case of the Pershing II, for a disarming first strike.

The Soviet Union has not been forthcoming in its explanation of why it has deployed so many SS-20s. Some analysts have argued that the new missile, which carries three warheads and is mobile, in fact contributes to European crisis stability because it is less vulnerable and hence is less provocative a target to NATO missiles than the obsolete, liquid-fueled SS-4s and 5s. In addition, some of the SS-20s are deployed against China and should not be included in calculations of the European balance. Finally, since there is no new mission that the SS-20 can perform that the older missiles cannot, deployment of the new system does not change the theater balance.[10]

If a Soviet first strike should occur in Europe, the existing NATO forces would be capable, without the Pershing II and cruise missiles, of inflicting unacceptable damage on the Soviet Union.[11] In fact, Dieter Lutz of the Institute for Peace Research and Security Policy argues that it would take even fewer bombs than normally supposed to cause unacceptable damage to the U.S.S.R. This situation is due to the density and distribution of the population, industrial structure, production of raw materials and energy, transport, communications systems, and agriculture. Lutz argues that all of these sectors of Soviet life are

FIGURE 6-10
SOVIET CALCULATION
OF NATO AND WARSAW CAPABILITIES

Soviet Calculation of NATO Capabilities	Soviet Calculation of Warsaw Capabilities
— Aircraft in Europe —	**— Aircraft in Europe —**
F-111............... 172	(Backfires, Blinders, Badgers)............. 461
F-4.................. 246	
A-6/A-7............. 240	
French Mirage......... 46	
British Vulcans......... 55	
— Aircraft in U.S. —	
F-111................ 65	
— Intermediate Missiles —	**— Intermediate Missiles —**
British................ 64	SS-20................ 243
French................ 98	SS-4/5............... 253
	S-N-5................. 18
Total.................. 986	**Total................. 975**

Source: *Die Zeit, New York Times, Bulletin of Atomic Scientists*

located in the European part of Russia which is within striking distance of NATO's existing nuclear force. Lutz concludes that even after a Soviet first strike, NATO (excluding the American strategic arsenal) would still have 259 MIRV warheads of 50 kilotons, 62 MIRV warheads of 200 kilotons, and 26 warheads of one megaton, or more than enough to destroy the 30 largest cities in the U.S.S.R. and about 40 percent of its industry.[12] NATO's deterrence, in other words, is already adequate.

In early 1982, the Soviet Union published its calculation of the European balance which it finds to be in rough parity (see Figure 10). The differences between the U.S. and Soviet versions are less over numbers of each weapon system—in fact there is little disagreement at this level—but over which systems should be included in the calculations of the theater balance and which should be excluded. Of particular significance is the Soviet's desire to include French and British nuclear weapons systems in the European balance. The U.S. wants to negotiate an *American-Soviet* balance in Europe. Moscow points out that even an agreement restricted to intermediate-range European missiles must include the 162 missiles (64 British and 98 French) in the West that are not American.

Inextricably linked to the nuclear arms balance in Europe are conventional forces. Those who advocate an increased deployment of nuclear arms in Europe believe that NATO nuclear superiority is obligatory in the face of a powerful Warsaw Pact army. They claim that despite a NATO conventional force located in the Federal Republic of Germany, the Warsaw Pact nations can effect a *blitzkrieg* as efficiently as the Germans over 40 years ago. Therefore, an advantage in tactical nuclear weapons is necessary to deter the Russians. This logic is skewed on several accounts.

Why would the Warsaw Pact nations invade Western Europe and risk almost certain nuclear war? The U.S. government has failed to provide an adequate answer. Even if the Soviet Union decided to invade Central and Western Europe through a *blitzkrieg* maneuver, their efforts would be thwarted by NATO forces. The Warsaw Pact has more divisions than NATO (57 to 28) on the central front but, due to the fact that there are far fewer men in each Warsaw Pact division, the Pact only has a 1.2:1 manpower advantage over NATO. Most Western military analysts argue that to execute a successful *blitzkrieg*, it is necessary to maintain at least a 3:1 manpower ratio.[13] The Soviet's own army manuals indicate that an 8:1 ratio of force superiority is necessary.

Another popular notion is that due to the enormous Soviet

FIGURE 6-11
MILITARY RESOURCES
OF NATO AND THE WARSAW PACT*

	NATO	Warsaw Pact
Population	626 million	380 million
GNP	$5,975 billion	$2,020 billion
Military spending	$256 billion	$202 billion
Military manpower	5.8 million	4.8 million**
Strategic nuclear weapons	10,000	7,800
Total nuclear weapons	31,000	20,000
All tanks	29,000	63,000
Anti-tank weapons	400,000+	data not available
Other armored vehicles	54,000	83,000
Heavy artillery	17,000	24,000
Combat aircraft	12,000	12,000
Helicopters	12,400	4,500
Major surface warships	428	281
Attack submarines	232	298

* NATO totals include France and Spain.
** Excludes some 560,000 Soviet border guard, internal security, railroad, and construction troops.

Source: NATO, IISS, DOD, CIA, CDI, Chart by Center for Defense Information.

advantage in tanks, they will be able to roll quickly over Europe. But NATO possesses over 400,000 anti-tank weapons.[14] And NATO possesses other advantages: the combined population of the allies is almost twice that of the Warsaw Pact; the combined GNP of NATO countries is double that of the Eastern bloc; and presently NATO has a 1 million man advantage in total military manpower (see Figure 11). Thus there is little reason to believe that the Soviet Union or the Warsaw Pact will think that they can successfully invade the West.

Conclusion

In brief, there is overall military parity between the United States and the Soviet Union. This parity is based on the fact that either side can destroy the other. Neither country can win a nuclear war. But most American policy-makers refuse to accept this nuclear fact of life. They persist in the attempt to build an arsenal that carries the credibility of first use. They believe that this capability will increase U.S. political influence. In mobilizing political support in Congress, in the press, and among the American people for new weapon systems, these policy-makers claim that the Soviet Union is ahead. On close examination, the measures used to support that claim are bogus. If anything, it is the U.S. that is "ahead." The effort to gain a significant lead to increase political influence, to play nuclear chess, is futile. The Soviet Union learned its lesson in Cuba in 1962. Humiliated by Kennedy, the Soviet Union became determined to catch the United States. Referring to the successful U.S. effort to force the withdrawal of Soviet missiles from Cuba, a Soviet negotiator told his American counterpart, "You will never be able to do this to us again." The Soviet Union will match every American buildup. Every new ICBM deployed will become a new target and therefore only reduce the security of American citizens and those of other countries. Balancing numbers is not the answer. Security can be achieved only by creating the political will to reduce those numbers.

Footnotes

1.) A literate summary of these findings can be found in Jonathan Schell, *The Fate of the Earth* (New York: Knopf, 1982).

2.) Paul Nitze, "Atoms, Strategy, and Policy," *Foreign Affairs*, January 1956.

3.) See "U.S.-Soviet Military Facts," *Defense Monitor*, vol. XI, no. 6, 1982; p. 3.

4.) See John Newhouse, *Cold Dawn: The Story of SALT* (New York: Holt, Rinehart and Winston, 1973).

5.) *Defense Monitor*, p.3.

6.) Randall Forsberg, "A Bilateral Nuclear-weapons Freeze," *Scientific American*, November 1982, p. 54.

7.) Transcript of President's Address on Nuclear Strategy Toward Soviet Union, *The New York Times*, November 23, 1982.

8.) *Defense Monitor*, p. 1.

9.) Estimates drawn from David Holloway, "Nuclear Weapons in Europe," *Bulletin of the Atomic Scientists*, April 1983.

10.) Forsberg, *op. cit.*

11.) Dieter Lutz, "A Counterforce/Countervalue Scenario—Or How Much Destructive Capability is Enough?," *Journal of Peace Research*, Vol. 20, No. 1, 1983, p. 23.

12.) *Ibid*; p. 25

13.) John Meansheimer, "Why the Soviets Can't Win Quickly in Central Europe," *International Security*, Summer, 1982, pp.7-10. There are other aspects of Meansheimer's argument that are worth summarizing. The NATO forces are deployed along the East German and Czech borders. They are divided into the Northern Army Group (NORTHAG) and the Central Army Group (CENTAG). These groups are divided into eight corps sectors with approximately four divisions in each sector. It is doubtful that the Soviet army would attempt to drive through CENTAG since this area contains German and American troops who are the best trained of all NATO forces. Furthermore, this area is mountainous and contains canals which would make an armored attack nearly impossible.

    Alternatively, if the Soviet army should attempt a multipronged attack on NORTHAG, their success would be limited because of the Harz Mountains, the Luneberger Heath, and the city of Hanover which would necessitate urban warfare which is advantageous to NATO forces. The "force-space" ratio is also advantageous to NATO in this area. A brigade can hold an area from 7 to 15 kilometers long. The length of the NORTHAG front is 225 km and there are 30 brigades. This translates into one brigade every 7.5 km—an almost optimum force-to-space ratio.

14.) *Defense Monitor*, p. 1.

PART II

SPECIFIC ISSUES OF THE ARMS RACE

Introduction

Exactly how accurate are land-based missiles? What is the significance, and how effective is U.S. anti-submarine warfare? Is it possible to build an effective defense, especially one based in space, against incoming missiles? Is it possible to mesh those offensive and defensive capabilities into an effective first strike? How prone to significant errors and accidents is the U.S. nuclear arsenal? Is it possible to carry out a "decapitation strike," that is, to knock off the enemy's commanding head and thus paralyze the retaliatory arms and legs? Can nuclear war be controlled once it starts? What are the dangers of proliferation? And finally, given the complexities of modern nuclear weapons, is it possible to verify arms control agreements?

These are important questions. Yet to many they seem technical, perhaps even overly technical, in nature. The essays in this section attempt to answer the questions listed above. We believe that they do so in a manner that remains accessible to the typical reader of this book.

Robert Aldridge addresses the issue of whether the U.S. can achieve a first strike. A first strike can be defined as an offensive capability sufficiently overwhelming that the Soviet Union cannot retaliate, or can retaliate only at a level that is considered "acceptable." Improved defensive measures are also part of a first strike for they keep the level of retaliation damage low. While no serious analyst, Aldridge included, argues that the U.S. currently possesses a first-strike capability (the reality is mutually assured destruction), there are alarming trends that indicate that the U.S. is moving in that direction. Aldridge documents some of the necessary components in such a capability. Foremost among these is the development of missiles accurate enough to hit hardened silos and military command posts. Aldridge points out that improvements to the guidance system of the existing Minuteman III missiles, the production of the new MX, and the planned Trident II missile are part of the development of the necessary offensive. He also argues that the U.S. is developing defensive capabilities, such as anti-submarine warfare, that will place the Soviet retaliatory force in jeopardy, and that quantum leaps are being made in the sophistication of the satellites and computers necessary to coordinate the complexities involved in a first strike.

It is precisely the difficulties associated with coordination and questions concerning the reliability of complex systems that lead Edward Anderson to conclude that a first strike is impossible to achieve. The consequences of missing just one percent of the other side's warheads (now numbering close to ten thousand on each side) would be disastrous. Anderson develops persuasive arguments that lead us to be skeptical of the chances that hundreds of offensive missiles could all hit their chosen targets. The limitations include irregularities in the earth's magnetic and gravitational fields, fratricide (the destruction of incoming warheads by others exploding nearby), geographic terrain, inability to test over the actual North-South missile path, and human error. In addition, new research conducted independently by teams of Soviet and American scientists indicates that the consequences of exploding some one thousand megatons (necessary in any full-scale first strike) would create dust, smoke and fire, and produce as a result a phenomenon known as a "nuclear winter." Thus, a first strike, even if "successful" in the sense of destroying the other side's retaliatory forces, would eventually doom the attacking as well as the defeated power. The danger, as *both* Anderson and Aldridge point out, is that a country's leadership can come to believe that the theoretical level of performance can be achieved in reality, ignore the scientific evidence concerning the impact of such an attack on the earth's climate, and mistakenly conclude that a first strike is possible.

In the meantime, the development of accurate offensive

systems that threaten missiles and military command posts encourages the adoption of a launch-on-warning policy. Such a policy would change the current reliance on human decision to launch a missile and replace it by computers that would both assess information to decide if an attack had been launched and order a response. This policy is motivated by the fear that an incoming offensive would destroy all or most of the existing land-based forces before they could get out of their silos. A launch-on-warning policy is also very dangerous, as Louis Rene Beres points out in his essay, in part because of the extraordinary number of errors and accidents regarding nuclear weapons that have occurred within the U.S. military establishment. These accidents include the mishandling of nuclear weapons and a number of full-scale alerts produced by false readings of impending attacks. Beres's contribution is to situate these accidents, not in the fallacy of some autonomous machine, but in the context of U.S. nuclear policy.

In no other area are the fallacies of the technological fix as readily apparent as in the plans of the Reagan administration to militarize space. Michio Kaku's article documents both the importance of space-based weapons to the Reagan administration's efforts to achieve superiority over the Soviet Union, and the ease with which these efforts can be overcome. Kaku demonstrates how space-based systems are extremely vulnerable to the various effects of nuclear weapons. In addition, plans to use lasers or particle beam weapons against Soviet missiles, even assuming that the enormous logistical problems associated with their actual deployment are overcome, can be frustrated by comparatively simple devices such as placing reflectors or parasols on the missiles. Nonetheless, the effort to develop space-based capabilities provides an important clue to the plans and intentions of the Reagan administration.

The technical and logistical difficulties associated with the development of space-based weapons also help explain exactly why it is impossible to keep nuclear war carefully controlled. Desmond Ball's somber assessment of the varied effects that accompany the detonation of a nuclear warhead, taken in combination with the vulnerabilities of modern electronics to the effects, dictate pessimistic conclusions concerning the survivability of satellites, the complex communications systems between national and local leaders and the computers that are necessary to assess the extent of damage and carry out the orders to respond. Even the hotline between Washington and Moscow that would be used to negotiate an end to hostilities is vulnerable. Yet these components are the basis for the Reagan administration's plans for developing the capacity for waging a protracted and/or limited nuclear war. Ball's conclusion that as few as thirty nuclear warheads will lead to spasmodic, uncontrolled responses on both sides is terrifying indeed.

The enormous chaos and uncertainty associated with nuclear war raises another danger: the possibility that one side might launch comparatively few, but extremely accurate, warheads at the other side's military and political leadership, and set off nuclear explosions high over the country so that it would be bathed with a short but intense electromagnetic pulse. The object of such a "decapitation strike" would not be a full first strike capable of taking out all of the other side's retaliatory forces, but an attempt to prevent the order to retaliate from passing between the leadership and local military command. The possibilities of such a strategy actually working have not received much public discussion. Yet it is a strong fear in both capitals. The procedures by which authorization to fire nuclear weapons can be delegated to subordinates are among the most closely held secrets in both the U.S. and the Soviet Union. Much of President Kennedy's concern during the Cuban missile crisis was to prevent the Soviet Union from establishing a base that would put Washington on short-term risk. Moscow's fears regarding the Pershing II missile now being deployed in Germany are precisely the same. Once again the real danger is not that a decapitation strike can be successfully carried out, but that in some future international crisis the political leaders are briefed or believe that such a strategy is a viable option. We endorse John Steinbruner's conclusion that as long as both sides have nuclear weapons, stability is best preserved by taking steps that will reduce the vulnerability of the command system.

At the moment, the nuclear club includes both the United States and the Soviet Union, as well as Britain, France, China and India. Israel is suspected widely of having a bomb and South Africa may have that capacity as well. In addition, some ten to fifteen other countries are considered as capable of manufacturing and delivering a bomb by the end of the century. Some of the nuclear weapons held by the U.S. overseas are open to possible theft and misuse, thus increasing the chances that groups not formally under the control of a nation-state may acquire a bomb, or manufacture a crude one, and threaten to use it. Daniel Yergin's essay on proliferation points out these and other dangers associated with the spread of nuclear weapons. Yergin also establishes the links between the nuclear reactors and nuclear weapons, arguing convincingly that there are not two different atoms, one peaceful, the other for war, but only one atom and a dangerous one at that. We cannot expect to control proliferation until the U.S. and U.S.S.R. agree to alter the arms race itself.

One of the greatest sticking points in the development of arms control treaties between the U.S. and U.S.S.R. is the issue of verification. The opponents of SALT II successfully raised the spectre of verification difficulties in helping to scuttle the treaty. Karl Pieragostini's essay on verification makes three important points: first, it is neither realistic nor necessary to establish "iron clad" verification, that is, agree only to those clauses where there is one hundred percent chance of catching a prospective cheater. Cheaters can be deterred even where the chances for being caught are lower. Second, the more comprehensive the treaty the easier the task of verification. A comprehensive freeze that establishes well-defined limits to testing, development and deployment multiplies the chances of catching a cheater. A freeze would be probably easier to verify than SALT II. Third, treaties establishing specific verification procedures also create a pattern of cooperation between the parties and, as a consequence, make future verification issues easier to handle. These points, together with Pieragostini's review of the impressive technical facilities available to the U.S., should allow us to approach verification with greater confidence.

Chapter 7

First Strike: The Pentagon's Strategy for Nuclear War

Robert Aldridge

Let us start with two important defintions—that of "counterforce" and that of "first strike." As a nuclear strategy, counterforce means aiming attack missiles at military targets. The word means to *counter* the enemy's military *forces* which include missile silos, command posts, nuclear storage depots, strategic air bases, communications centers, and submarine pens. Many of these targets are called "hard" because they are buried deep in bunkers and silos and are reinforced with steel and concrete. Weapons used to destroy hard targets would have to be extremely precise. Although counterforce weapons are not necessarily first strike weapons, counterforce does have offensive connotations because many counterforce targets would have to be destroyed *before* they are used or their destruction would be of no significance. Furthermore, these are the installations which would be targeted if either the U.S. or the U.S.S.R. were contemplating an unanswerable nuclear first strike.

First strike is an ambiguous term which has been assigned several meanings. In one sense it is used to describe whatever country initiates nuclear war. It is also associated with a (hoped for) limited use of nuclear weapons to stop a massive attack with conventional armament. This is most often called "first-use."

Use of the term "first strike" in this article will be in the more technical military sense of a strategic first strike: a capability to inflict a *disarming* or *unanswerable* first strike against a rival nation.

Counterforce is not necessarily equated with first strike because there are degrees of counterforce. The ability to destroy bomber bases, for instance, would require counterforce weapons or counterforce targeting. But destroying a bomber base does not constitute a disarming first strike because silo-based and submarine-based missiles would be certain to retaliate.

A disarming first strike capability would require an arsenal of counterforce weapons capable of destroying the entire strategic force of the other superpower. Although counterforce does not necessarily mean first strike, first strike is counterforce in its maximum sense.

The scenario for a disabling first strike is as follows: very precise strategic weapons to destroy Soviet land-based missiles in silos and other critical targets, anti-submarine warfare (ASW) to sink Russia's missile-launching submarines before they can fire their weapons, and anti-ballistic missile (ABM) and bomber defenses to stop any weapons that survived the first assault and were launched in retaliation. Let us examine these in turn.

The land leg of the U.S. strategic triad is currently made-up of 1,054 intercontinental ballistic missiles (ICBMs). They are stationed in concrete and steel silos which are buried deep underground. The latest version Minuteman ICBMs—the Minuteman-3s—occupy 550 of these silos; each missile holding three warheads which can be sent to different targets. The accuracies achieved by the Minuteman-3 are sufficient for counterforce targeting. The remaining silos contain 450 Minuteman-2 missiles equipped with a single one-megaton bomb each, and 54 Titan-2s which are each loaded with a gigantic nine-megaton device. But it is the planned MX missile that stands out among land-based missiles as the most suitable for a first-strike role.

Pentagon spokesmen describe the MX as an advanced, large throw-weight, MIRVed ICBM which would be capable of fulfilling U.S. military requirements into the 21st century. It was originally proposed as a three stage, solid propellant missile but the Air Force has added a fourth liquid-fueled stage. MX will be 92 inches in diameter, 72 feet long and will weigh 95 tons (195,000 pounds)—over twice the weight of Minuteman-3. It will deliver a payload in excess of four-and-one-half tons over a range of at least 7,000 nautical miles. Although the weapon

has been promoted and justified because of its survivability—
its capacity to ride-out a Soviet-first strike—it will be capable of
a degree of accuracy that will place it in the vanguard of a U.S.
first-strike. Survivability could be achieved without increasing
accuracy—presuming that the true rationale for this weapon is
purely defensive.

To help obtain the accuracy needed for a first-strike capability, MX will have a new guidance package called the
Advanced Inertial Reference Sphere. Weighing only 115 pounds
this package will be physically smaller than the Minuteman-3
guidance system and provide a midcourse positioning within
100 feet for dropping off MIRVs. That will give a target Circular
Error Probability (CEP) no greater than 600 feet—some experts
say as small as 400 feet. Pentagon officials have also testified
that MX will be designed to use Navstar navigational satellite
fixes to insure high accuracy. That will bring the CEP down to
300 feet.

The fact that the MX could threaten Soviet silo-based
ICBMs has frightening implications. A Congressional Budget
Office paper elaborated on MX's prompt counterforce capability:

> The MX ICBM and the Trident-2 submarine-launch-
> ed missile, both highly accurate ballistic missiles plan-
> ned for future deployment in survivable basing sys-
> tems, would provide a "prompt" counterforce capa-
> bility, one that would provide the means to retaliate
> against reserve Soviet ICBMs within minutes of a
> Soviet first strike. Such prompt counterforce capability
> *would give the Soviets little time to launch a second-
> round attack* before the arrival of counterattacking
> U.S. missiles.[3] (Emphasis added)

Another CBO paper noted how such a second strike counterforce capability would also have the potential for a disarming
first strike against Soviet land targets:

> ...It would be virtually impossible to deploy a force of
> MX ICBMs large enough to provide a significant
> second-strike retaliatory capability yet small enough to
> avoid posing a counterforce threat to the Soviet silo-
> based ICBM force.[4]

Some military planners and government official: recognize
the destabilizing aspect of MX with its first strike co interforce
potential. In 1977, then Defense Secretary Brown highlighted
the risk of having such a weapon:

> Before I leave the subject of land-based ballistic mis-
> siles, I would like to turn to another matter of percep-

tions—how the Soviets might perceive the threat to them of a U.S. preemptive strike. They may calculate that a first strike would result in a (missile) ratio adverse to them, just as we calculate that a Soviet first strike would result in a ratio adverse to us. To the extent that this is so, either side will, during the next decade, have a so-called "advantage" in firing first...[5]

What Secretary Brown is saying in his roundabout way is that (1) the U.S. would have a military advantage in being able to shoot first but (2) in developing that capability we risk the chance that the Soviets might fire first in desperation before they lose all their missiles. MX is a very visible program and there is no doubt that the Soviets recognize its first-strike potential. That "perception," as Secretary Brown called it, might prompt the Soviets to embark on a course of action more drastic than they would otherwise consider.

When he was Research and Development Chairman of the Senate Armed Services Committee, former Senator Thomas J. McIntyre sounded the warning in more forthright language. He noted that because the MX could destroy the Soviet ICBM force—which contains three-quarters of all Soviet strategic warheads—in thirty minutes, the Soviets might feel a military need to strike first. "In a period of crisis," he explained, "the Soviets would be faced with the choice of either using their missiles or losing them." That "would put a hair trigger on nuclear war."[6]

In addition to the MX, the United States is developing counterforce capabilities on its newest submarine—the Trident. Submarine-launched ballistic missiles would be among the first, if not the very first, weapons used in a limited nuclear exchange during some future crisis. The characteristics that make SLBMs likely to be the first weapons used are the same that make them the most probable choice to initiate a strategic first strike. First, the location of the submarine which launches them is much less certain to the Soviets than the U.S. silo-based missiles. Soviet radar would have to provide surveillance in all directions from which a SLBM might possibly come. It is possible that they would not even detect a SLBM until it was too late. That would mean that Soviet land-based missiles would be destroyed before they could be launched. Likewise, communications centers could be annihilated before they could send the launch command to Soviet missile-carrying submarines.

The second very important advantage of SLBMs over land-based ICBMs in destroying land targets is their shorter flight time. That is made possible by the shorter range from which they can be fired. Whereas ICBMs take about thirty minutes to get from one continent to another, SLBMs travel from submarine to their target in as little as ten to fifteen minutes. This pares down warning time from 25 minutes for an incoming attack by land-based ICBMs to as little as five minutes for a SLBM attack. Because it takes some time to launch a missile after receiving a warning of attack, the offensive use of SLBMs could reduce the margin for reaction to zero.

Because of the decided advantage of SLBMs in a first strike it is important that they be very accurate and that the submarines remain undetected. Trident is the U.S. Navy's newest attempt to bring greater accuracy and elusiveness to the sea-based leg of the strategic triad.

There are many facets to the Trident Weapons system. The most visible programs are a new fleet of some undetermined number of submarines and two generations of submarine-launched ballistic missiles. In addition, the Navy has plans for such exotic technology as maneuvering warheads and a new type of communication system which will penetrate the ocean to depths of several hundred feet.

Currently, the Navy is deploying the Trident-1 missile. The Reagan Administration's guidance document for fighting a protracted nuclear war, drafted by Defense Secretary Caspar Weinberger, also directs the deployment of a newer Trident-2 missile, in 1988.[7]

Trident-2's range goal is 4,230 nautical miles with a full load of bombs. Its size will stretch to a 42-foot length and swell to 82 inches diameter. It will weigh 126,000 pounds and only fit into the new submarines.

To highlight the destructive potential of Trident-2 let us look at its prospective payload. One of the warhead "mixes" being considered is fourteen hydrogen bombs of 150 kilotons each.[8] Another is eight 300-kiloton bombs.[9] Each can be sent to a different target. Trident-2's 1988 operational date will allow it to use the Navstar global positioning system to deliver those warheads within 300 feet of their targets. But exploding the equivalent of fifteen Hiroshima bombs within rock-throwing distance of missile silos is not the end of Pentagon ambitions. It is also developing manuevering reentry vehicles (MARVs) which will whittle that miss distance to just a few feet. That means the warheads can be smaller and more of them can be put on each missile. My best estimate is that Trident-2 will be able to carry seventeen MARVs with an explosive force between 75 and 100 kilotons. Any of these mixes add up to tremendous kill power.

The destabilizing effect of developing such precise warheads was pointed up in the President's *Fiscal Year 1979 Arms Control Impact Statements*:

...If deployed in sufficient numbers (they) would threaten a large share of the Soviet retaliatory forces, and could be perceived by the Soviets as indicating a U.S. intention to develop a total first strike capability against their ICBM force.[10]

As if this situation were not destabilizing enough, there are indications that MARVs themselves may be equipped to receive fixes from the Navstar satellite navigation constellation. That being true, the warhead accuracy would then be within 30 feet of the target. The President's report reads:

If difficult technical problems were solved, Navstar GPS might make a significant contribution to the Navy's SLBM capabilities. This technology could then be applied to the Trident-1 and Trident-2 missiles currently in development and possibly incorporated into the design of a new maneuvering reentry vehicle (MARV).[11]

and,

...(Navstar) improvements could be applied to ballistic missiles and possibly incorporated into the design of maneuvering reentry vehicles (MARVs)...[12]

Clearly, MARVs, especially with the help of Navstar, will be a strong stride towards a destabilizing first strike counterforce capability.

The relative power of the U.S. SLBM systems, both existing and projected, can best be appreciated by comparing them to Soviet systems. The Delta submarine with its SS-N-8/18 missiles has been proffered as the counterpart of Trident. The only aspect of the Soviet system which is in any way comparable, however, is the 4,000-plus nautical mile range of the missiles. This range is a few hundred nautical miles greater than Trident-1's full-load range. But it is less than Trident-1's reduced-payload range. There is no point, however, of flying a missile that far to destroy a counterforce target if it can't hit close enough to accomplish that feat. And it is the Trident-2, now in development, that will achieve counterforce capabilities.

The MX and the Trident are two systems that serve as the cornerstones of the offensive in a first-strike scenario. What about defense capabilities?

Anti-Submarine Warfare

The role of anti-submarine warfare (ASW) in a first strike strategy is to destroy all hostile missile-launching submarines at sea—those in port could be annihilated with strategic missiles. Most people believe that submarines are invulnerable. That is still true for U.S. subs but not those of the Soviet Union. I started investigating ASW in 1976—searching out the sensors, weapons and carriers that the U.S. Navy has or soon will have. The outcome of that first study unnerved me. It indicated that, if all the programs in progress came to a successful conclusion, the United States, by the early 1980s, would be able to locate and track every Soviet missile-launching submarine in the ocean. From there it would not be difficult to destroy those vessels on command. Developments in the meantime tend to substantiate that prediction.

Navy expenditures for ASW development jumped from $3 billion a year during the early part of the 1970s to somewhere between $4- and $7-billion by 1978.[13] The Navy's fiscal 1979 budget contained approximately $7.4-billion for ASW.[14] Frost & Sullivan, a market research firm in New York, has forecast that U.S. spending for ASW will total $46.2-billion during the six-year period ending with fiscal 1983. All of this does not include unknown amounts buried in the budgets of such agencies as the Department of Energy, the National Aeronautics and Space Administration, the National Oceanic and Atmospheric Administration, and the National Science Foundation.

Our discussion of the place of U.S. anti-submarine warfare activities in a first strike strategy must begin with an assessment of how many Soviet submarines would have to be instantaneously destroyed to sap the Soviet Union's SLBM capability. In his fiscal year 1983 posture statement, General David C. Jones, then Chairman of the Joint Chiefs of Staff, said the Soviet Union has 70 modern nuclear-powered ballistic missile-launching submarines of which 62 would be accountable under SALT-2. There are another 15 diesel-powered submarines which carry ballistic submarines. These latter poke along at ten miles per hour submerged and have to surface every night to recharge their batteries, and are so easy to track that they are not counted in SALT quotas. Even if the total Soviet missile launching force becomes significantly larger by the latter 1980s, it will pose no real challenge to the U.S. anti-sub capability currently under development.

The anti-submarine warfare system can be divided into three basic groups: sensors, weapons, and carriers. *Sensors* will be described first. Just as the name implies, sensors are the devices by which anti-submarine forces "see" and "hear" what is happening beneath the waves. They not only detect submarines but pinpoint their location and determine if they are friend or foe. The sensing function (or surveillance) is divided into two regimes: escort and open-ocean.

Escort surveillance is supposed to be a defensive activity to protect ships, convoys and task-forces from hostile submarines. It is ostensibly confined to a limited ocean area of about sixty miles radius around the ships. The sensors are specifically designed for short-range detection so that a hostile sub in the area can be pinpointed and destroyed. Sensors are now so precise that they can determine the class of submarine.

Open-ocean surveillance uses different types of sensors to determine, with a sixty-mile radius of error, the position of all submarines in the ocean. These two types of sensing systems would work hand-in-glove during a preemptive first strike. Open ocean surveillance would detect all the Soviet submarines and put escort surveillance forces on their tail which, in turn, would set them up for the kill.

The mainstay of the Navy's open-ocean sensing system is SOSUS (SOund SUrveillance System)—a system of passive underwater listening devices which are permantly fixed on the continental shelf of the United States and friendly countries. The information picked up by SOSUS listening devices—called hydrophones—travels through underwater cables to shore stations. SOSUS dates back to the 1960s but it has undergone continuous improvements. The Navy has invested well over a billion dollars in SOSUS and, although its original mission has changed, it still remains an effective and important system.

SOSUS can spot a sub anywhere in the ocean when conditions are favorable and pinpoint it within a sixty-mile radius. It can also interact with ASW aircraft and escort surveillance ships. But conditions are frequently not favorable and there are limits to the sensitivity of SOSUS. For that reason the Navy has two additional systems to enhance open-ocean ASW—the *SURveillance Towed Array Sensor System* (SUR-TASS) and, currently under development, the *Rapidly Deployable Sensor System* (RDSS). It is my impression that they will use a new sonar which will focus on the cavitation noises generated by the turbulent flow of water around large and fast submarines, as opposed to detecting engine noises and other sounds that originate from within the vessels.

SURTASS went into service in 1980. These arrays are pulled around the ocean by slow tuna-clipper-type boats and have sensors tuned for long distance sound detection. Data is relayed from the towing ship though a communications satellite to the shore station where it is processed and analyzed. SURTASS provides a geographic mobility which SOSUS does not have. There will eventually be 18 of these arrays complete with their towing ships (designated T-AGOS and AGOS).

RDSS arrays are buoys with passive sensors that can be readily deployed by aircraft, surface ships, or submarines in selected areas during times of crisis. This system, originally called moored arrays, is scheduled for deployment in the late 1980s. Assistant Navy Secretary Gerald A. Cann recently called RDSS a system "flexible to the needs of the operational users so that surveillance can be provided where and when needed. (Deleted) RDSS will provide a long life, moored capablity with excellent detection capabilities (deleted)."[15] I believe this system will have particular application in the Barents Sea where the Soviet Delta submarines tend to patrol. That is the location of greatest challenge to U.S. ASW efforts.

New advances in laser optics are also being applied to ASW. ORICS (Optical Ranging, Identification and Communications System) is a laser system used not only to find hostile subs but to communicate with friendly ones. It operates in the blue-green wavelength of the visible light spectrum. That seems to be the tuning that allows maximum penetration of seawater. An ASW helicopter tested ORICS off the Florida keys in late 1976 and was reportedly successful in locating a submarine.

The development of ORICS has sparked speculation on the use of lasers for open-ocean surveillance. In the mid-1960s, the Defense Advanced Research Projects Agency (DARPA) conducted a study called *Deep Look* to address some basic obstacles to light travel through the ocean. Its goal was to define the practical limits to underwater imaging and then demonstrate a rudimentary system that would perform near those limits. DARPA discovered that the depth of ocean penetrated by the laser it developed was limited mainly by the power of the beam.

On July 23, 1972 the first *Landsat* earth resources satellite was put in orbit. Ostensibly a tool to help solve the world's food and energy problems, Landsat also photographed scenes of military interest such as the Chinese missile launch complex at Shuang-Cheng-Tzu and the Soviet bases at Kapustin Yar and Pletsetsk.

Skylab was launched the following year and was subsequently occupied by three different space crews. Both Landsat and Skylab viewed the earth's surface with a variety of color frequencies and some of their photographs show the ocean bottom in shallow water near the coast. These pictures were made using a laser scanner operating close to the blue-green wavelength that gives maximum seawater penetration.

In 1976, I received a letter from a colleague working in the satellite communications field that noted the new advances in laser photography of the ocean floor. I will quote several passages: "...refinement of tracking has given the Navy another fine tune focusing capability for precision control of short duration (2 weeks) laser camera orbital satellites. Camera angle (side looking)...was the breakthrough that scored success in the Navy mission to photograph the ocean floor. It's real. It exists. I have seen the photographs...The laser photo that I saw was tuned to the frequency spectrum of seawater. As such it simply nulled out seawater, leaving exposed the ocean floor..." The letter went on to explain that given the ability to photograph the ocean bottom it would also be possible to detect a submarine.

That letter ties in with a statement made by the former Under Secretary of Defense William Perry in early 1980. He said that research into nonacoustic means of detecting submarines included methods of remotely measuring ocean depths and determining the presence of objects under the surface. [16]

The placement of infrared sensors on spacecraft or high-flying aircraft capable of spotting the thermal wake of submarines may provide another means of tracking submarines. According to *Air Force Magazine*, space-borne infrared sensors can tell the difference between submarines in port that have their reactors in a standby mode and those that are running up their reactors to get under way.[17] Defense analyst Norman Freedman of the Hudson Institute predicts: "Probably the ultimate in remote ASW surveillance systems will, in time, be satellite-based and employ some type of nonacoustic sensor. Nonacoustic sensors, such as those which home in on the thermal wake of a submarine, have been on the drawing board for a long time."[18] DARPA's Fiscal Year 1983 report said that it had an intensive effort aimed at "submarine detection based on observable changes in the ocean environment caused by recent passage of a target."[19]

As can be seen, sensor development has taken sinister leaps since its proof test on the automated battlefields of Southeast Asia. They have now been refined for use in homing maneuvering warheads, as the eyes for navigating and targeting various weapons, and many other applications to be discussed in later chapters. Anti-submarine warfare has reaped its share of this technology. The main obstacle to simultaneously sinking all Soviet missile-carrying submarines is the ability to find them, identify them, and shadow them. Sensors in development will soon make this possible. Let's take a look at a likely scenario for such a search and destroy mission.

After a Soviet submarine has been detected and identified by open-ocean surveillance, a patrol aircraft, ship or attack sub is sent to pinpoint it and stay on its tail. Should hostilities erupt between the two superpowers, U.S. anti-submarine warfare forces would then be set up for the kill. Weapons for that purpose include both nuclear and conventional torpedoes (launched from submarines, surface ships, or aircraft), mines, depth bombs, and anti-submarine missiles. Current development efforts include torpedoes that integrate computers and advanced acoustic sensing arrays, maneuverable torpedoes, and torpedoes that can be placed in a casing on the ocean floor to lie in wait for "hostile" craft.

In comparing U.S. and Soviet anti-submarine activity, what is immediately apparent is that the Soviets tend to concentrate their efforts closer to their own territory and shipping lanes. They apparently have no open-ocean ASW forces.[20] Meanwhile, the U.S. has a commanding lead in ASW capabilities because it possesses a significant technological advantage in ASW sensors, ASW weapons, and submarine quieting.[21] Former Defense Secretary Brown noted that although Russian subs are becoming quieter and harder to detect, "our Navy has maintained and, in some cases, even widened our technological lead."[22] The Soviets even lag the U.S. in the more traditional acoustic sensing technology.[23] Finally, because of its two-ocean coastline which provides easy access to sea lanes, and its large network of overseas bases and allies, the U.S. enjoys a decided geographical advantage.[24] The open-ocean ability to locate and track subsurface craft has aggressive connotations because if that can be accomplished those submarines could be summarily destroyed at the appropriate signal. The implication of such a U.S. capability was raised by a U.S. Library of Congress report:

> ...If the United States achieves a disarming first strike capability against Soviet ICBMs, and also develops an ASW capability that together with attacks on Naval facilities could practically negate the Soviet SSBN force, then the strategic balance as it has come to be broadly defined and accepted would no longer be stable.[25]

The final leg of the emerging U.S. first-strike posture is the ability to detect, track, and destroy those Soviet missiles and bombers that may escape a counterforce strike. Programs aimed to provide precise land-, sea-, and space-based detection and interception capabilities are currently underway. As the U.S. approaches a first-strike posture we can be certain that the U.S.S.R. will strive for the same objective. Once the two superpowers face each other in a first-strike stand-off, with weapons systems and decision making highly automated, an international crisis, such as we have every few years, may provide the impetus for a "preemptive" leap into nuclear war.

Footnotes

1.) *Hearings on Military Posture and HR 11500, Fiscal Year 1977*, before the House Armed Services Committee, February 10, 1976, Part 1, p. 1334.

2.) *Ibid*, p. 1333.

3.) *Counterforce Issues for the U.S. Strategic Nuclear Forces*, Congressional Budget Office background paper, January 1978, p. 50.

4.) *Planning U.S. Strategic Nuclear Forces for the 1980s*, Congressional Budget Office budget issue paper, June 1978, p. xv.

5.) *Department of Defense Appropriations for 1978*, hearings before the Defense Subcommittee of the House Appropriations Committee, Sept. 15, 1977, Part 7, p. 146.

6.) "MX Development Termed 'Disastrous Mistake'," *Aviation Week & Space Technology*, October 17, 1977, p. 16.

7.) See Richard Halloran, "Pentagon Draws Up First Strategy for Fighting a Long Nuclear War," *New York Times*, May 30, 1982, p.1.

8.) *The Military Balance 1979/80*, published by the International Institute for Strategic Studies, London England.

9.) Speech by Deputy Assistant Secretary for Defense Dr. Thomas A. Brown at the "Defense Issues Forum" convened in Santa Cruz, CA by Congressman Leon Panetta.

10.) *Fiscal Year 1979 Arms Control Impact Statements*, June 1978, pp. 56 & 58.

11.) *Ibid*, p. 110.

12.) *Fiscal Year 1980 Arms Control Impact Statements*, March 1979, p. 125.

13.) James Coates, "Oceans Bristling With Deadly Weapons," *Chicago Tribune*, December 4, 1977, p. 21. Also see "The High Stakes Business of Antisub Warfare," *Business Week*, May 8, 1978, p. 50B.

14.) *Department of Defense Appropriations for 1979*, hearings before the House Appropriations Committee, March 15, 1978, Part 6, p. 97.

15.) *Department of Defense Appropriations, Fiscal Year 1982*, hearings before the Senate Appropriations Committee, April 30, 1981, Part 4, p. 589.

16.) *The Fiscal Year 1981 Department of Defense Program for Research Development and Acquisition*, a statement by William J. Perry, Under Secretary of Defense for Research and Engineering, February 1, 1980, p. V-9.

17.) *Air Force Magazine*, August 1979, p. 20.

18.) Norman Freedman, "The Navy's RDT&E Program," *Sea Power*, April 1980, p. 52.

19.) *Fiscal Year 1983, Research and Development Program*, op. cit., p. III-29.

20.) *Evaluation of Fiscal Year 1979 Arms Control Impact Statements*, p. 115.

21.) *Ibid*, p. 104.

22.) Cited by Joel S. Wit, "Advances in Anti-submarine Warfare," *Scientific American*, February 1981, p. 35.

23.) *Fiscal Year 1981 Arms Control Impact Statements*, May 1980, p. 359.

24.) *Evaluation of Fiscal Year 1979 Arms Control Impact Statments*, op. cit., p. 107.

25.) *Evaluation of Fiscal Year 1979 Arms Control Impact Statements*, op. cit., p. 119.

Chapter 8

First Strike: Myth or Reality

Edward Anderson

A U.S. Air Force colonel recently asked me the rhetorical question: "Wouldn't we be safer with first-strike capability because the Soviets would fear loss of their equipment?" Even though I had strongly suspected that some officials in the U.S. Department of Defense wanted to achieve first-strike capability, I was in disbelief.

From a two-hour radio debate with a representative of the Air Force MX office and from *Aviation Week,*[1] I know that the Air Force is telling the public that it believes the MX missile will be accurate enough and reliable enough to give the United States first-strike capability. They conclude that the Soviet Union has achieved first-strike capability and consequently that the Minuteman missiles in the western United States are vulnerable. The solution therefore is to deploy the MX.

In a speech on March 22, 1976, then Secretary of State Henry Kissinger said:

> Indeed neither side has even tested the launching of more than a few missiles at a time; neither side has ever fired in a North-South direction as they would have to do during wartime. Yet initiation of an all-out surprise attack would depend on substantial confidence that

thousands of re-entry vehicles launched in carefully coordinated attacks—from land, sea and air—would knock out all their targets thousands of miles away, with a timing and reliability exactly as predicted, before the other side launches any forces to preempt or retaliate and with such effectiveness that retaliation would not produce unacceptable damage. Any miscalculation or technical failure would mean national catastrophe. Assertions that one side is "ahead" by the margins now under discussion pale in significance when an attack would depend on decisions based on such massive uncertainties and risks.[2]

Nevertheless, the Air Force insists that technology has advanced so rapidly in only a few years that it has become imperative that the MX system be deployed.

If one really believes, as Secretary Weinberger apparently does, that the Soviet Union can—and may be motivated to—destroy a very high percentage of the Minuteman and Titan missiles in one blow, there is reason for the utmost urgency in getting the MX program underway. But before we emulate Chicken Little and run to tell the king that the sky is falling, we need to study the possible success—and the consequences—of a first-strike attack as it must be viewed from the vantage point of the Soviet high command.

The Air Force position is that basic information, enough to convince them that the Soviets have achieved first-strike capability, is classified. We, the general public, who have "no need to know," are asked to take their word for the "need" and for the expenditure of tens of billions of dollars.

Among strategic systems, this one stands alone in the complexity of its justification. But I believe that unclassified information can be used to show that the problem of a Soviet first-strike is greatly exaggerated.

What kind of attack?

Logically, if the Soviet leadership were to contemplate a first-strike attack on the United States, they would need to attempt the destruction, in one blow, of all U.S. strategic systems capable of reaching their territory, before the U.S. could launch a counter-attack. The well-documented consequences of such an attack would be enormous.[3] Even the Air Force official to whom I spoke acknowledged that it would cause the deaths of over half the population of the United States.

As Henry Kissienger has said, with the "massive uncertainties" involved in such an attack the Soviet leadership would recognize that in retaliation an unknowable number of American nuclear bombs would probably explode on their territory. And even a few would produce devastating effects. An all-out first strike would mean nuclear war on a massive scale. It could be provoked only in a desperate situation in which the Soviet leaders thought they were about to become victims of an American first strike, and were persuaded that a preemptive attack would be necessary to limit damage to their own territory. The Air Force representative acknowledged that such an all-out attack would be irrational and that the MX is not designed to counter such an attack but only lesser attacks.

The often-discussed lesser attack is one targeted only at the 1,052 land-based ICBM silos. The theory is that the Soviets could destroy these silos and the missiles in them in one "surgical" strike and then demand from the President certain concessions. Knowing that the Soviets still had enough ICBMs to destroy the major American cities, the President would then presumably stay his hand, since not to do so would mean assured destruction.

If this theory is plausible, it can be carried one step further: the Soviet leader could simply call the American President one day and tell him to get U.S. forces out of Europe or face certain destruction of, say, our major electrical power plants (easier targets than missile silos), and should any U.S. missiles be detected heading for the Soviet Union, their rocketry would be immediately unleashed to destroy all major U.S. cities. If the President would surrender in the first situation would he also not surrender in the second? Could our entire triad of strategic forces be so easily checkmated?

The effects of the attack on the attacker

While motivation for a selective attack on only the land-based ICBMs appears thin, such an attack is theoretically possible. Its consequences and probability must be pursued further. The largest ICBM warheads the Soviet Union has in quantity are reported to yield in the range of 1.5 megatons and are mounted on MIRVed SS-18 missiles. If one of these warheads were exploded by impact fusing (assuming that it can be done reliably) at each of 1,052 ICBM silos, I estimate that up to one-quarter of a cubic mile of radioactive dust would enter the atmosphere. The Office of Technology Assessment estimated that, depending on the direction and magnitude of the wind and other uncertainties, such an attack would kill within a month between two and 20 million Americans. In no way could such an attack be viewed as "surgical," destroying only missiles. The Soviet high command would have to believe that the President, even though confronted with a calamity of this magnitude, would be intimidated into surrender. If they misjudge, and the United States retaliates, the results are suicidal.

There would be other direct consequences of the attack. The Soviet Union could no longer buy grain from North America. Radioactive dust would circle the earth, cooling the atmosphere and decreasing their own crop production by an indeterminate amount. The ozone layer would be depleted. The attack would throw the world's population into a state of panic. All remaining military forces would be placed at maximum readiness. The Soviets would be accused of responsibility for the most awesome crime ever committed against humanity. Even if the Soviets were to take over other lands, they would experience difficulties that would make their problems in Afghanistan pale by comparison. If, as recently reported, the Soviets anticipate a labor shortage in the mid-1980s, where could they recruit troops for occupation duty?[4] Would these possibilities add to the credibility of deterrence?

Testing

Confidence in military hardware and operations can be obtained only through adequate, realistic testing. While Soviet ICBMs are tested from operational silos, it is common knowledge that U.S. ICBMs are not. Minuteman tests from operational silos were attempted on four occasions years ago, and they failed each time.[5] These missiles are now shipped to Vandenburg Air Force Base for testing where, the Air Force insists, operational conditions are so well simulated that tests from operational silos are not necessary.

But are the tests enough? Had a production line been maintained to produce one Minuteman per week after the first 1,000 were deployed, and the results of the testing were then used to make engineering changes on a regular basis, there would be no discussion of an aging Minuteman system. Complete Minuteman missiles have not been fired often enough to obtain high confidence in their reliability, and the Titan missiles haven't been fired at all. Statistical theory relates the range of uncertainty in the reliability of a large number of missiles to the reliability measured by testing a smaller number, if test conditions duplicated operational conditions. But when one compares the operational conditions of missile crews in hundreds of missile silos—crews that have to be in constant readiness over a period of years—with occasional testing of missiles, it becomes clear that the statistical formulae are not valid. Mathematics is not magic; it cannot predict the results in a simultaneous firing of enough missiles to constitute a first strike on 1,000 missile silos on any basis other than a series of such firings.

Greater confidence would be obtained if the advice of statisticians were followed on the required number and conditions of the tests. But Congress has been unwilling to appropriate the necessary funds for such activities. Even if more testing were done, it would still not be possible to have the test missiles carry real nuclear warheads, so the fusing systems cannot be tested under operational conditions. Yet the Air Force argues flatly that their testing is adequate, even though it is clear that it must be subsystem, never full system, testing.

The irony of the MX missile is that a larger, more expensive missile, because of budget limitations, will be tested even less often, so that genuine confidence in its performance will be even less. The desire of certain Senators for "heavy" missiles makes no sense from the viewpoints of vulnerability and confidence. Other military equipment can be tested frequently. The ICBM can be tested the least, but the consequences of an error on estimated performance are the greatest.

The probability of success of a first strike is the probability of success if all of the missiles function as expected (dependent upon accuracy) multiplied by the probability that all of them do perform as expected. The first of these is the kill probability with 100 percent reliability; the second is commonly called the reliability. Suppose the former is 0.95 or 95 percent. As will be shown, this is very optimistic. If the reliability is 90 percent, the real kill probability is 0.95 x 0.90 or 0.855. This means that 855 of 1,000 Minutemen will be destroyed, and 145 Minutemen will survive—enough to devastate the Soviet Union. But assuming that only, say, 50 Minutemen would survive—that the real kill probability were 0.95—the reliability would have to be higher than 95 percent. If, by multiple targeting, it were increased, to say, 98 percent, the kill probability with 100 percent reliability would have to be 97 percent. We see that the number of surviving missiles almost triples—from 50 to 145—as the reliability decreases from 98 to 90 percent. Yet an enormous amount of realistic testing would be needed to keep the uncertainty and knowledge within such a range. This is one basis for Kissinger's phrase, "massive uncertainty." Thus simple mathematics illustrates why a first strike attacker must expect a devastating response—unless the attacker believes with very high confidence that the attacked country will not respond at all.

Fratricide

To increase the real kill probability, it is obviously desirable to fire more than one warhead at each silo. But as is often discussed in the literature, it is highly likely that the first of a series of warheads to explode will destroy other warheads in the vicinity before they can explode.[6] Between the time that the shock wave from the first explosion has run its course and its mushroom cloud develops there is apparently a "window" where a second warhead may get through, and it is possible to estimate the duration of that window. But remarkable coordination would be needed to hit such windows 1,000 times, and the proof of performance would require atmospheric testing in a manner not attempted before: firing a number of ICBMs with live warheads at intercontinental range in sequence and detonating them at ground level.

The consequence is that confidence can be placed only in the first warhead to explode. If more than one is fired—which of course is necessary—the reason can only be to increase reliability. If single-shot reliability is, say, 0.7, the double-shot reliability increases to 0.91.

The Miss Probability

I define miss probability as one minus the kill probability with 100 percent reliability. The miss probability depends on the destruct radius of the bomb; the random error, usually referred to as the "circle of equal probability"; and the systematic, or bias error. The circle of equal probability, the radius of which is called the CEP, is a circle centered on a large number of missile impact points that contain half the impact points. Thus it is equally probable for a missile to impact inside or outside this circle. The CEP is a measure of precision; the bias error is a measure of accuracy.

The destruct radius of the bomb varies as the cube root of its yield and the height of the burst. The figure is drawn under the assumption of 100 percent reliable impact fusing. Since the TNT explosion occurs over a period of about 100 microseconds (the nuclear explosion is much faster), an ICBM warhead hitting the ground typically at 10,000 feet per second will travel about one foot during the explosion process. This appears to indicate that impact fusing is possible, but it is complicated by the fact that an ICBM on a minimum-energy trajectory enters the atmosphere at an angle of about 22 to 23 degrees. Thus, there is a chance that the warhead could hit the downslope side of a hill and be destroyed before detonating.

Moreover, since the radioactive fallout from 1,000 one-megaton ground bursts may kill up to 20,000,000 Americans, it would be very difficult for the Soviet leadership to follow the "surgical-strike" concept. Thus, the idea has been brought forward that, to reduce fatalities in a limited first strike, air bursts would be used. But the destruct radius of bombs in the one-megaton range varies little for bursts from ground to about 1,000 feet, above which it falls off very rapidly. Because of the very high re-entry speed, pressure operated fuses are not practical and radar altimeters could be jammed.[7] Therefore, the use would probably be activated by a timer. Fusing then would depend on timing the 1,800-second flight to an accuracy of 10 to 20 milliseconds. (A 10 millisecond change in the flight time is produced by a launch flight-path-angle change of about three seconds of an arc.)

For these reasons, the destruct radius of the bomb cannot be accurately known. The Test-Ban Treaty makes it impossible to test explosions of thermonuclear bombs at various heights and distances from ICBM silos of varying degrees of hardness and shockmounting. Thus, the attacker must make a very conservative estimate of the destruct radius based on theoretical calculations of a very complex phenomenon.

The Air Force has frequently reported the MX missile CEP as 300 feet. Study of miss probability curves (see Figure) leads to the conclusion that the CEP must be as low as 300 feet to obtain low miss probability. The CEP is a result of many possibilities for error: in the initial angular alignment; in instrumentation; in the calculated flight time; in the magnitude and direction of the burn-out velocity; and in knowledge of the terminal atmosphere.

As one example, for a purely inertially guided missile (the guidance system now used), the initial angular-alignment error that produces a 100-foot error (all errors must add to less than 300 feet) in a 6,000-nautical-mile flight is about three microradians. To visualize this, consider shining a searchlight on a building one mile away. If the searchlight beam is rotated through an angle of three microradians, the spot on the building moves two-tenths of an inch. The angular orientation of the inertial guidance system must be determined to this accuracy with respect to the local vertical and the earth's spin axis, and held in part by star sighting and optical transference of angular data. Changes in temperature, humidity, vibrations or earth shocks and human events are some of the ways the alignment can be thrown off. To achieve and maintain such alignment would be remarkable indeed.

We know, however, that the United States plans to bypass this extreme alignment problem, in part, through midcourse corrections made possible by forthcoming navigation satellites

(NAVSTAR). There has been no public information indicating that the Soviet Union is planning such an error-correcting system.

The bias, or systematic error, is the distance from the center of the circle of equal probability to the target. It is due to uncorrected gravitational field anomalies, errors in the model of the terminal atmosphere, magnetic drift due to unknown electronic charge on the re-entry vehicle—and anything else that has not been thought about. It can be corrected by flying the polar trajectories planned for the first strike, but short of that impossible test procedure, bias can be estimated only by unverifiable theoretical calculation. Thus, the Soviet high command, in planning a first strike, must take on faith the opinions of many layers of bureaucracy. With such grave consequences in view, this is a risky prospect indeed.

With these definitions of the three factors that determine the miss probability, again consider the figure, drawn under the assumption that the re-entry vehicle descends vertically onto the target. In reality, the vehicle approaches the target at an angle of around 22.5 degrees to the ground, making the destruct area not a circle but an ellipse of about 38 percent of the area it would have if the missile came in vertically. For this reason, and because the calculation assumes 100-percent reliable impact fusing, the miss probability taken from the chart will be too small. The miss probability is plotted against the ratio of destruct radius to the CEP for various values of the ratio of bias to CEP. The destruct radius of a ground-exploded 750-kiloton bomb is about 550 feet. [8] Using the cube-root law, knowledge of this value permitted a scale of bomb size for 300-foot CEP to be drawn parallel to the horizontal scale.

If an attack by Soviet 1.5 megaton bombs (presumably SS-18 rockets), with a hypothetical 300-foot CEP (reportedly 600 to 1,000 feet) is considered, the destruct radius is about 700 feet, and the corresponding ratio of destruct radius to CEP is 2.3. If the bias were estimated to be an optimistic 300 feet, the ratio of bias to CEP is one, and we are at point A on the figure corresponding to a miss probability of about 0.1. Suppose, however, that the actual CEP and bias are both twice these very small values. Then we move to point B, for which the miss probability is 0.6; doubling the errors has increased the miss probability by a factor of six! Aiming at a fleet of 1,000 Minutemen, the Soviet high command would realize that if the errors were actually the more conservative second set instead of the first, the first strike would leave 600 Minutemen unharmed, not 100. Conservatism is necessary, but it produces the result

FIGURE 8-1
MISS PROBABILITY

The miss probability — plotted on the vertical axis of the figure — is the fraction of a large number of missile shots that will miss their targets. It depends on two quantities: the ratio of the destruct radius of the bomb to the CEP, and the ratio of the bias error to the CEP. It is plotted above against the first of these ratios for values of the second ratio ranging from 0 to 6. For a given CEP, the ratio on the horizontal axis increases as the cube of the yield of the bomb. The bomb yield is therefore plotted for CEP = 300 feet.

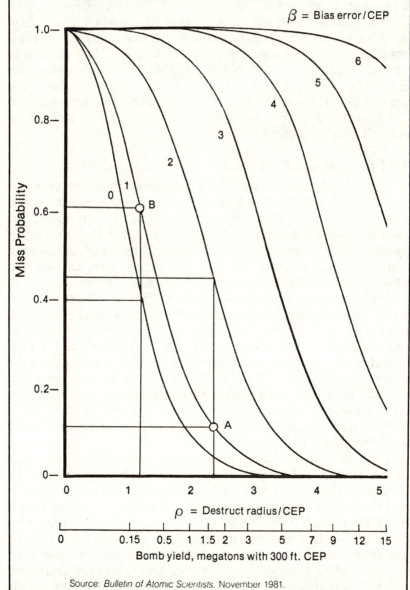

β = Bias error / CEP

Miss Probability

ρ = Destruct radius / CEP

Bomb yield, megatons with 300 ft. CEP

Source: *Bulletin of Atomic Scientists*, November 1981.

that the attack would fail. Here again we see the massive uncertainty referred to by Kissinger.

Since the MX warheads are reported to yield 350 kilotons, it is worthwhile to estimate their corresponding miss probability by the same method, if their circle of equal probability is about 0.43. If, despite the problems of fratricide, it were assumed with perfect certainty that the "window" could be hit, the miss probability for two shots at each target is 0.43 squared or 0.18; 18 percent or more than 250 of the 1,398 Soviet land-based ICBMs would be left standing (assuming perfect reliability) following an American first strike.[9] This is enough to permit a counterstrike of enormous damage. NAVSTAR is expected to provide a midcourse correction for ICBMs that would reduce the CEP to 90 feet, presumably with a bias error of the same magnitude.[10] If that were true, the ratio of the destruct radius to CEP for the MX is increased to 4.7, a value for which the miss probability is negligible.

The Perception of a Threat

When backed into a corner with these arguments, even the most hawkish of the intelligentsia admit that they do not "even pretend to believe" that a Soviet first strike would occur, but insist that there is a perception of a threat.[11] If Minuteman appears vulnerable to world leaders, they may perceive a weakness in American determination and may, in negotiations, lean, if only subtly, toward the Soviet Union.

Based on published information on Soviet CEPs, on their lack of a comprehensive navigation-satellite system, and on the many other factors presented, a Soviet first-strike capability is not close at hand and may never be. On the other hand, based on confident U.S. Air Force assurances of their accuracies with the forthcoming NAVSTAR system and the Navy's extensive and growing deep-water anti-submarine-warfare capability, it has become increasingly clear that the Department of Defense has been working toward first-strike capability, now confirmed by the Secretary of Defense.

I do not believe that an honest assessment of the probability of success of a first strike can produce high confidence in the results. But what I believe does not matter. What matters is what the Secretary of Defense and the President believe, based on information handed to them. Since they have neither the time nor the training to understand all the factors involved, their decision will be intuitive and ideological. The moment they are led to believe that the collateral damage from the Soviet Union to the United States resulting from an American first strike is "acceptable"—and assuming they really believe, as they publicly say, that the Soviets are close to first-strike capability—in a future tense international situation the finger on the button will itch. Moreover, much of the decision process, because of the short time involved, will be computerized. The world indeed races dangerously closer to the ultimate holocaust.

Footnotes

1.) Paul Mann, "Panel Reexamines ICBM Vulnerability," *Aviation Week and Space Technology*, July 13, 1981, pp.141-148.

2.) Reprinted in *International Security*, Vol. 1: 1, Summer, 1976, p. 187.

3.) "The Effects of Nuclear War," Office of Technological Assessment, May, 1979.

4.) Seweryn Bialer, "The Politics of Stringency in the USSR," *Problems of Communism*, May-June, 1980.

5.) James Fallows, *National Defense,* (New York: Random House, 1981) p. 149.

6.) John D. Steinbruner and Thomas M. Garwin, "Strategic Vulnerability: The Balance Between Prudence and Paranoia," *International Security,* op.cit.,178-181.

7.) "Strategic Vulnerability," p. 160.

8.) Bernard T. Field and Kosta Tsipis, "Land Based Intercontinental Missiles," *Scientific American*, Vol. 241:5, Nov. 1979.

9.) Such an attack would require 2,800 warheads more than the United States now has but fewer than would be available following deployment of the MX.

10.) Robert C. Aldridge, *The Counterforce Syndrome*, 2nd ed., Institute for Policy Studies (Washington, D.C., 1978).

11.) *National Defense*, p. 162.

Chapter 9

Nuclear Errors and Accidents

Louis Rene Beres

Nuclear war might begin by accident. No matter how well the United States and the Soviet Union satisfy the requirements of a credible nuclear deterrence posture, their "success" will not reduce the likelihood of accidental nuclear war. Indeed, it may actually *increase* its likelihood.

Also the availability of nuclear weapons allows for the possibility of accidents which, while they may not lead to nuclear war between the superpowers, could still produce a calamitous nuclear explosion. Accidents of this type could be triggered by mechanical and/or human malfunction in the operation of nuclear weapon systems.

As the nuclear arms race continues, the chances of nuclear accidents grow. The number of nuclear weapons in the world, and their accompanying command/control systems become more and more complex. At the same time to maintain a credible deterrence posture strains the safeguards which are designed to prevent accidental nuclear weapons detonations. Yet, our very survival depends upon the presumption that nuclear weapons systems (i.e., the weapons themselves and the personnel who are charged with responsibility over these weapons) can *never* fail since even a single accident involving nuclear weapons could be overwhelmingly catastrophic.

No mechanical system, however carefully constructed and monitored, can be presumed to be infallible. As a recent publication of the U.S. Arms Control and Disarmament Agency puts it: "We all know that no matter how much we spend in care and resources, mechanical things, from simple tools to sophisticated systems, can malfunction."[1] The same point, of course, can be made about the individual human beings who exercise custody and control over nuclear weapons. They, too, are fallible. What we have, then, is a system of nuclear deterrence in which certain sorts of mechanical, electrical, or human malfunction cannot be tolerated, but where malfunction is distinctly possible, even probable.

Any nuclear weapon accident may have catastrophic effects. So far, we have been lucky. Consider the American record of accidents involving nuclear weapons, at least as far as the record is known. According to the Department of Defense:

> There has been a total of 33 accidents involving U.S. nuclear weapons throughout the period that the U.S. has had these weapons. Because of the inherent safety features, the control features, the administrative procedures designed into U.S. nuclear weapons systems and the precautions taken during operations with these weapons, there has never been a case where a nuclear detonation has occurred in a nuclear weapon accident. During the last ten years, due in part to the Department of Defense's comprehensive program to improve nuclear weapon safety, only six accidents have occurred...
>
> Of the six accidents occurring in the last ten years, two accidents, involving B-25 aircraft, resulted in the dispersal of fissile material. These accidents were at Palomares, Spain in 1966 and in Thule, Greenland, in January 1968. Cleanup operations were undertaken at both locations and the areas were completely decontaminated.[2]

According to the Center for Defense Information, however, there is evidence of many other nuclear weapon accidents that have gone unreported or unconfirmed. In the words of *The Defense Monitor:* "Serious students of the problem estimate that an average of one U.S. nuclear accident has occurred every year since 1945, with some estimating as many as thirty major nuclear accidents and 250 minor nuclear accidents during that time."[3] Some of the specific incidents follow.

"Broken Arrows": Nuclear Accidents Admitted By The Pentagon

1.) *Aircrash over Palomares, Spain.* On January 17, 1966, an American B-52 bomber collided with a KC-135 refueling tanker causing the deaths of five crewmen and the dropping of four hydrogen bombs which were recovered after an intensive ground and sea search. Radioactive leakage and conventional explosions occurred in the area.

2.) *Bomb accidentally dropped over South Carolina.* On March 11, 1958, a B-47 bomber accidentally dropped a nuclear weapon in the megaton range over Mars Bluff, South Carolina. The conventional explosive "trigger" of the nuclear bomb detonated leaving a crater 75 feet wide and 35 feet deep. One farmhouse was obliterated. Luckily no nuclear radiation leakage was detected, no nuclear explosion occurred, and no one was killed.

3.) *Bomarc missile burned in fire.* On June 7, 1960, a fire at the McGuire Air Force Base led to a series of shattering explosions and the destruction of one of 56 nuclear armed Bomarc missiles. Although no nuclear explosion occurred, there was a small amount of radioactive leakage creating a temporary health hazard.

4.) *Twenty-four-megaton bomb safety devices sprung.* In 1961 a near catastrophe occurred at Goldsboro, North Carolina when a B-52 bomber had to jettison a 24-megaton bomb. Five of the six interlocking safety devices were set off by the fall. A single switch prevented the bomb from exploding, an explosion which would have been over 1,800 times more powerful than the Hiroshima bomb.

5.) *Greenland aircrash scatters plutonium.* On January 21, 1968, a B-52 attempting an emergency landing at Thule Air Force Base, Greenland, crashed and burned on the ice of North Star Bay. The high explosive components of all four nuclear weapons aboard detonated producing a plutonium-contaminated area of at least 300-400 feet wide and 2,200 feet long.

6.) *The Damascus, Arkansas incident.* In September 1980, a technician accidentally dropped a wrench, puncturing a Titan II missile, causing it to ignite and explode. The blast blew a 740-ton cover off the silo and created a non-nuclear fireball that was visible for thirty miles. Two men were killed and the missile's 9-megaton warhead was hurled 200 yards away.[4]

With this record of "broken arrows" (major nuclear weapons accidents) as a background, consider the number and complexity of nuclear weapons held by the superpowers. The United States alone has approximately 30,000 nuclear weapons dispersed across the oceans, in Europe and Asia, and within its own borders. What are the odds that none of these weapons (or those in the huge Soviet arsenal) will ever be accidently fired? While such odds can, of course, never be calculated with certitude or precision, we surely know enough to realize that they are not so favorable as to warrant the ultimate gamble.

Safeguards Against Accidental Detonation

The principal steps taken to avert accidental use of nuclear weapons by American forces include maintaining strict custodial control of these weapons and implementing a considerable array of redundant safety features.[5] These features are incorporated into the chain of command and into the weapons themselves. Precautions in regard to the chain of command include: a so-called two-man concept whereby no single individual has the ability to fire weapons, a control system whereby each individual with nuclear weapon responsibility must be formally certified under the Human Reliability Program,[6] and the use of "secure codes." Precautions pertaining to the weapons themselves emphasize "highly secure coded locking devices."[7] Moreover, although the exact release procedure for nuclear weapons are highly classified, it is known that safeguards against accidental nuclear firings do vary somewhat from one weapon system to another.

For example, all tactical nuclear weapons that are deployed overseas include mechanical or electrical devices which prevent their firing in the absence of a specially coded signal issued by higher command. Absence of the coded signal physically precludes firing the weapon. Strategic nuclear weapons under Air Force jurisdiction incorporate somewhat different sorts of command/control devices that nonetheless serve the same purpose as those associated with theater-nuclear forces. Additionally, all nuclear weapons—tactical and strategic—incorporate some sort of "environmental sensing device" that is designed to prevent unwanted detonations. These include switches that respond to acceleration, deceleration, altitude, spin, gravity, and thermal forces.[8]

The submarine-based nuclear weapons, however, are unique in one very important sense: these missiles can presumably be fired without receiving a coded signal from the continental United States.[9] Hence, nuclear missile submarines apparently comprise the only component of the strategic nuclear triad in which firing can be accomplished without activation by remote electronic switch turned on by higher command.[10] The reason for this is simply the problem associated with transmitting electronic signals to submerged submarines. Safeguards against accidental firings on American nuclear missile submarines are thus essentially limited to the use of an electrical firing circuit which requires collaborative action within close time tolerances on the part of several men on board who are certifiably "reliable."

But aren't these sufficient safeguards? After all, the captain cannot fire the missiles by himself. His key closes just one of several switches on the firing circuit. Before the missiles can be launched, several other officers on board must "vote" by turning their respective keys, and the weapons officer must pull the trigger.

Before answering, consider the following story of a former Polaris captain: Back at the time of the Gulf of Tonkin incident, in August of 1964, an American nuclear missile submarine cruising somewhere in the Pacific received the order to hold a missile drill. The officer on duty, however, misread the message and announced to aboard that this was the real thing. The captain quickly checked the message himself, discovered the error, but decided to preserve the impression of the "real thing" in order to "see how the crew does." The weapons officer and the officer in launch control were told of the deception so that "nothing could happen," and "the whole thing went off perfectly." According to the former captain, the practice of failing to identify a missile drill as a drill is not uncommon.[11]

The outcome would surely have been different if the captain had repeated the mistake of the officer on duty; if the captain detected the mistake but generalized the subsequent deception to include the weapons officer and the officer in launch control; or, if a genuine Emergency Action Message had been mistakenly sent to the submarine in the first place.

On a mechanical level, there is always the possibility that there could be a malfunction in the firing circuit.

Another hazard to be considered concerns collisions involving nuclear submarines. Such collisions are already a matter of record. The House Intelligence Committee's suppressed final report states that United States nuclear submarines have collided with nine "hostile vessels" in Soviet waters during the last ten years. Of these, five collisions are known to have involved Soviet nuclear submarines bearing either nuclear missiles or nuclear torpedoes.[12] According to reports, in one of these incidents, the U.S. nuclear submarine *Gato* collided with the Soviet nuclear submarine at the entrance to the White Sea in November 1969. The "*Gato* prepared for action with nuclear torpedoes but the Soviet crew was so confused about what had been encountered that the Americans were able to steal away."[13]

Even the most carefully monitored written procedures during missile drills cannot guard against errors completely. Nothing can insure against an Emergency Action Message being transmitted by mistake, or a malfunction occurring in the firing circuit of a nuclear weapons submarines that might lead to the firing of missiles.

In addition, how can we know for certain that no predelegation of authority to use nuclear weapons has been given to submarine commanders in situations of extreme duress? How can we ever be sure that our own system of safeguards is matched by that of the Soviet Union? And how much faith can we place in the continuous running of test procedures and checks? In the absence of "the real thing," such procedures and checks can never be regarded as proof positive of reliability. The entire system of safeguards is built upon procedures and equipment that can never be tested completely until the time comes when they are called into action.[14]

There is still another reason to fear nuclear missile submarines from the standpoint of accidental nuclear war between the superpowers. Because in the years ahead, an increasing number of nuclear weapon countries will turn to sea basing of their strategic forces, it will be exceedingly difficult to identify the country-source of a submarine launched ballistic missile attack. Thus, it would be fairly easy for a "small" nuclear power to provoke nuclear war between the superpowers, creating what is customarily referred to as "catalytic" war.

Members of the "nuclear club" could also inadvertently catalyze war between the superpowers. Such countries, confronted by the prospect of a disarming first strike by other members of the club might seek security through the deployment of "hair trigger" launch mechanisms (automatic systems of nuclear retaliation based upon the processing of electronic warnings by computers) and through the adoption of "launch on warning" strategies with launch authority delegated to field commanders. With such measures the probability of an unintended nuclear attack on one of the superpowers by a third-party state would increase substantially.[15]

What all of this suggests is that we do indeed have a

problem. While the weapons engineers and the military authorities must be commended for the fact that none of these
accidents resulted in a nuclear explosion, there is no reason to
expect such good fortune to persist indefinitely.

Furthermore, there is the Soviet Union to consider. What
about their system standards? For example, how strict and how
reliable is their system of codes and communications? What
sorts of safety devices are built into the Soviet weapons
themselves? What kind of "human reliability program" is
operative among Soviet personnel who deal with nuclear
weapons? What sort of redundancies are built into Soviet
command/control procedures for nuclear weapons expenditure? And what is the Soviet safety record to date?

ICBM Fallibility

The land-based missile component of the strategic triad
must also be considered from the standpoint of accidental
nuclear war between the superpowers. Unlike the manned
bomber, these missiles cannot be recalled once launched.[16] This
suggests, of course, that every conceivable measure must be
taken to prevent inadvertent launches in the first place. Presently, before a Minuteman missile can be launched, "at least
two missile combat crew commanders must authenticate launch
orders and activate necessary controls." Moreover, "all launch
crew personnel must work separately and individually, but
within very close time tolerances to carry out their tasks."[17]

What can go wrong?[18] There is always the possibility that
the missiles will be launched because of the mistaken belief that
a disabling first-strike attack is on the way. In the United
States, there have already been at least five major incidents
involving false warnings that have been publicly reported:

BMEWS. On October 5, 1960, the central defense room
of the North American Air Defense Command (NO-
RAD) received a top priority warning from the Thule,
Greenland, Ballistic Missile Early Warning System
station indicating that a missile attack had been
launched against the United States. The Canadian Air
Marshall in command undertook verification, which
after some 15 to 20 minutes showed the warning to be
false. The radars, apparently, had echoed off the moon.

NEWC. On February 20, 1971, the National Emergency
Warning Center at NORAD headquarters transmitted
an emergency message, authorized by the proper code
for that date, directing all U.S. radio and TV stations to

cease normal broadcasting immediately by order of the President. The message, designed for use only in grave national emergencies such as enemy attack, was not cancelled until 40 minutes after its nationwide transmission. The same NORAD headquarters complex is the point of transmission for messages to trigger nuclear retaliation in the event of enemy attack.

SECT.   On at least two occasions during 1971, Submarine Emergency Communications Buoys, accidently released from U.S. Polaris nuclear missile submarines, signalled that the submarines involved had been sunk by enemy action.[19]

On November, 9, 1970, mechanical error sent "war game" information into the sensing system that provides early warning of nuclear attack. The "war game" tape, which was loaded into the North American Air Defense Command (NORAD) computer in Colorado Springs, Colorado, simulated a missile attack on North America. Read as a "live launch," the error initiated a sequence of events to determine whether the United States was actually under attack. It took six minutes, during which the country was in a low-level state of "nuclear war alert," to discover the error. A spokesman for NORAD stated that he could not recall another incident in which an alert had actually gone out from the NORAD complex to the command centers of the vast American defense chain. On the day following the incident, Tass, the official Soviet press agency, criticized the error and warned that another error "could have irreparable consequences for the whole world."

In view of (1) the steadily increasing accuracy and power of ICBMs, and (2) the fact missiles cannot be launched on warning to insure their survival, the amount of time available to decision-makers who must decide whether or not to retaliate is extremely limited. Coupled with the understanding that the missiles cannot be recalled, these developments point to a very serious hazard in the area of accidental nuclear attack. This hazard is aggravated during periods of peak tension and alert, when the need for quick reaction is most apt to impair the safeguards of redundant verifications and authorizations.

As a potentially vulnerable component of the strategic triad, land-based missiles leave decision makers with the least amount of time to decide what to do. Hence, the relative vulnerability of these missiles heightens the probability of their accidental use, either by American or Soviet forces. Faced with the understanding that a first-strike attack might succeed in obliterating its land-based nuclear missiles, each superpower is placed under intense pressure to launch these missiles when an attack is threatened or believed to be impending. The more survivable triad systems, therefore, are substantially less subject to the harmful effects of reduced decision time than are the land-based ICBMs.

The pressure of false alarms can bring about accidental nuclear war between the superpowers even where it does not lead to an immediate launch of vulnerable missiles. Consider the following scenario:

> American radar warning systems mistakenly sound an alarm (the problem might be something as ridiculous as the rising of the moon, the fall of meteors, a flock of geese or a mechanical error). In response, all triad forces are placed on alert. The Soviets, of course, witness these preparations and respond in kind. A chain reaction of preparations and counterpreparations ensues that ultimately fulfills the original mistaken "prophecy"—nuclear war between the superpowers.

The false alarm scenario could take a different, more bizarre, form. Consider the following:

> In response to false warnings, the United States begins to launch its nuclear missiles against Soviet targets. Almost immediately after the launching process begins, Amerian officials confront the terrible truth that a grievous mistake has been made. Aware, however, that a Soviet retaliation is certain, the American National Command Authority decides that the only "sane" course is to press forward with a full-scale, no-holds-barred, nuclear assault. To do otherwise, i.e., to immediately announce the error to the Soviets while ceasing all further hostilities would simply be too risky. The logic of "damage minimization" compels the initiation of unrestrained nuclear attack. An irreversible nuclear holocaust begins.

This scenario, of course need not be limited to situations involving false warnings. It could be played out wherever nuclear missiles—whether land-based or sea-based—are launched by accident.

Land-based nuclear missiles are also subject to the same hazards of proliferation as sea-based missiles. With the anticipated increase in nuclear weapons countries in the years ahead, it would be extremely difficult to identify positively the country source of an ICBM attack. Under these conditions, a secondary nuclear power could actually "catalyze" a nuclear war between the superpowers, whether by deliberate choice, by unauthorized use of weaponry, or by inadvertent action occasioned by the deployment of "hairtrigger" launch systems and the adoption of risky "launch-on-warning" strategies.

Finally, there is the risk of accidents involving tactical nuclear weapons. The United States has maintained an arsenal of approximately 7,000 tactical nuclear weapons in western Europe since the 1950s. Most of these, about 5,000, are in West Germany while the rest are in all NATO European countries with the exception of Norway, Denmark, Luxembourg, and France. The United States also has tactical nuclear weapons in Asia (approximately 1,700 in South Korea, the Philippines, Guam, and Midway), on board U.S. Navy combat ships (approximately 2,500), and in the custody of selected Army, Navy, and Air Force units in this country (approximately 10,800).

Despite the seemingly innocuous sound of the word "tactical," these weapons range from "small" systems with blast effects that are equivalent to only 100 tons of TNT to one megaton systems that are 80 times as powerful as the Hiroshima bomb. Indeed, the principal difference between tactical and strategic weapons concerns range rather than yield. In certain instances, tactical weapons are actually more powerful than strategic ones.

The wide dispersion of this type of weapon (not to mention the coming deployment of 572 Pershing II and ground-launched cruise missiles) suggests a substantial risk of catastrophic accidents. Tactical nuclear weapons could be involved in air crashes; they could accidently be dropped from aircraft or jettisoned; they could be burned in fires at weapons storage sites; or they could be damaged in explosions on board carrier ships or at artillery, surface-to-surface, or surface-to-air installations.

In view of the continuing American policy of "first use" (as distinguished from "first strike"), tactical nuclear weapons also heighten the prospects of escalation to strategic nuclear war and greatly increase the incentive of Soviet-Warsaw Pact forces to strike first.

In the event of false warnings, the presence of tactical nuclear weapons might make the consequences of "retaliation" extremely costly. This problem (which is already exacerbated by the use of Quick Action Alert Aircraft, QRA) would be especially great during times of crisis.

And the hazards inherent in the proliferation of tactical nuclear weapons are the same as those for land-based and sea-based strategic missiles. The greater proliferation, the more difficult it becomes to identify an attacking country. Hence, another tactical nuclear power could "catalyze" a nuclear exchange between the superpowers, again, by design, by inadvertant action, or by unauthorized use of weapons.[20]

What more can be done about the problem of the accidental use of nuclear weapons by the United States? The answer is as simple as it is disappointing: little, if anything, beyond what is already being done. The "fault" lies neither with the existing system of American safeguards (they are surely as sound and well maintained as is humanly possible) nor with the military people who oversee these safeguards (they are certainly dedicated and capable), but rather with the underlying strategy of peace through nuclear deterrence. The implementation of even more stringent measures to prevent the accidental use of nuclear weapons would in most cases certainly impair the credibility of this country's nuclear deterrence posture. As long as we continue to base our hopes for peace and security on the ability to deliver overwhelming nuclear destruction to a Soviet aggressor, the risk of accidental nuclear war and of other nuclear weapon accidents will simply have to be endured.

Footnotes

1.) See U.S. Arms Control and Disarmament Agency, *Arms Control: Moving Toward World Security* (Washington, D.C.: Government Printing Office, 1975), p.10

2.) From U.S. Department of Defense undated press release sent to the author by W.Y. Smith (Lieutenant General, USAF, and assistant to the chairman of the JCS), on June 16, 1976.

3.) See *The Defense Monitor* 4, no. 2, (February 1975), p. 9

4.) Ibid.

5.) However, no matter how reliable American safety systems are presumed to be, security from accidental nuclear war is still contingent upon the reliability of Soviet safety systems. Since we know very little about the character of Soviet safety systems, considerable uncertainty necessarily surrounds the issue of security from accidental nuclear war between the superpowers.

6.) I received special briefings on this program from the USAF Directorate of Nuclear Surety at Kirkland AFB, New Mexico, on May 11, 1976, and from the SAC office at Headquarters, Offut AFB, on May 13, 1976. They revealed that each armed service is charged with enforcing such a program pursuant to DOD directives 5210-41 and 5210-42. The Air Force's Human Reliability Program stipulates a scrupulous and continuing review of every pertinent individual's medical and personnel records, although it is not necessary that each individual under review be examined by a psychological professional. The basic judgement of reliability rests with the commanding officer. At SAC, a total of approximately 1,500—2,000 individuals screened under its Human Reliability Program are disqualified annually for nuclear weapon assignments. Of these, about one-third are disqualified at the initial screening and two-thirds during the first two years of service. There is very little disqualification after two years of service have been completed.

7.) See U.S. Department of Defense, *Nuclear Weapons Safeguards*, a publication issued by the Deputy Assistant to the Secretary of Defense, (Washington, D.C.: Government Printing Office, n.d.).

8.) This information is based on the author's May 11, 1976 briefings by the USAF Directorate of Nuclear Surety.

9.) Although this point is generally accepted in the declassified literature on the subject (see especially Phil Stanford, "The Deadly 'Move to Sea,'" *The New York Times Magazine,* September 21, 1975, pp.16-17, 44-69; and "The Talk of the Town," *The New Yorker*, May 3, 1976, p.29), the Department of Defense has refused to corroborate it for me. It is a highly classified piece of information.

10.) With respect to the ICBM force, however, there once did appear to be some difference between the Minuteman and Titan forces. At the special Command Control Briefing conducted for me at SAC's Underground Command Post on May 3, 1976, I was told that while coded switches were already operative in the Titan forces, their installation in Minuteman forces would not take place until 1977. Both elements of the strategic bomber force—B-52s and FB-111s—are allegedly governed by coded switch systems that transmit firing capability as well as firing authority. Of course, all elements of triad are safeguarded by the requirement that at least two (and usually more than two) individuals who are certifiably "reliable" must act in concert within very close time tolerances.

11.) Stanford, "The Deadly 'Move to Sea,' " pp.16-17

12.) See the unofficial publication of the House Select Committee on Intelligence Report (the Pike Papers after Committee Chairman Otis Pike) presented in a 24-page supplement of *The Village Voice*, 21, no. 7 (February 16, 1976): 88. In reply (March 12, 1976) to my inquiry to the Department of Defense about the accuracy of the House Intelligence Committee's final report, Brig. Gen. William B. Maxson states: "We do not possess any information on collisions involving U.S. nuclear submarines."

13.) See *The Indianapolis Star,* February 16, 1976.

14.) See Lloyd J. Dumas, "National Insecurity in the Nuclear Age," *Bulletin of the Atomic Scientists,* 32, no. 5 (May 1976): 28.

15.) For an interesting discussion of some of these problems see the statement by Herbert F. York prepared for the Committee on International Relations, House of Representatives, 94th Cong., 2d sess., March 18, 1976.

16.) Nor are these missiles equipped with in-flight destruction mechanisms, since an adversary might learn the secret signal and render the attacking missiles impotent.

17.) *SAC Information*, July 1, 1975, p. 16.

18.) Based on my briefings by USAF Directorate of Nuclear Surety and SAC officers, the prospects of an accidental launch by launch crew members would be minimal for a number of reasons: ICBMs cannot be launched out of a single silo; several launch crew members must "vote" within very close time tolerances (in the case of Minuteman missiles, at least four individuals operating out of two launch control centers must be involved); launch crew members are under continual screening by the Air Force's Human Reliability Program; each launch crew member has an "inhibit capability" whereby an improper launch vote by any other crew member can be nullified; and since 1977, no ICBM has been capable of firing without a coded release by authorities outside the launch control facility itself.

19.) See Dumas, "National Insecurity in the Nuclear Age," pp. 28-29.

20.) It should be noted that this discussion of tactical nuclear accidents has been conservative, since it has assumed the reliability of permissive action links, environmental sensing devices, human reliability programs, and the two-man concept. Moreover, there is also considerable danger from the possibility of accidents involving Soviet tactical nuclear weapons (although Soviet deployment is almost certainly less extensive.) Presently, we know very little about Soviet safety measures in this area.

Chapter 10

Wasting Space: Countdown to a First Strike

Michio Kaku

The "space wars" speech delivered by Ronald Reagan on March 23 may represent the most enormous gamble of his Administration—and our lives. In committing the United States to the development of massive space-based antiballistic defense systems, Reagan raises the stakes of the contest between American and Soviet weaponry to a level all but unimaginable.

One possible outcome offered by Reagan is attractive: this country will be perpetually protected from nuclear devastation by Soviet missiles. Another possible outcome, feared by many scientists and strategic thinkers, is disastrous: the arms equilibrium between the two superpowers will be disturbed to the point where a nuclear first strike becomes inevitable.

In either event, Reagan's laser-beam proposal, which the Soviet Union immediately denounced as a violation of the 1972 Antiballistic Missile Treaty, must be understood as a profound departure from the balance-of-terror doctrine that has prevailed for the past three decades. Reagan's speech set the arms race on a wholly uncharted course.

The strategic rationale underlying the space wars proposal can be found in a glossy, 175-page document called *The High*

Frontier (published last year by the right-wing Heritage Foundation). Here, retired Lieutenant General Daniel O. Graham, former director of the Defense Intelligence Agency, advocates a policy of "ensured survival" to replace the current doctrine of "assured destruction," which leaves the United States vulnerable to wholesale destruction by Soviet nuclear warheads.

To ensure survival, Graham recommends a system of 400 satellites that would constantly circle the globe, armed with a lethal array of energy beams capable of shooting down Soviet missiles within five minutes of their launching. The energy beams would consist of light (driven by hydrogen flouride lasers), particle beams (of charged or neutral subatomic particles), X-rays (driven by an atomic explosion and focused by lasers), microwaves, and EMP (electromagnetic pulse generated by a nuclear detonation).

In addition, Graham would have the Pentagon deploy killer satellites capable of blinding or destroying Soviet satellites in outer space, as well as ground-based "energy cannons" capable of knocking down enemy missiles before they reach their targets in the United States. A massive civil defense program would also be developed, just in case any Soviet missiles managed to penetrate the antimissile arsenal.

The U.S. military point with pride at the advances in laser technology that have supposedly placed satellite antiballistic missile systems within reach—at a research cost of about half a billion dollars. They cite a test conducted five years ago in San Juan Capistrano, California where a hydrogen flouride laser was used to blast three anti-tank missiles traveling through the air at 450 miles per hour.

However, the military efficacy of space weapons, let alone their advisability as a new stage in the arms race, is a matter of much dispute. It is no great feat, critics note, for ground-based lasers to shoot down airborne antitank missiles. It is much easier to destroy a slow-moving, preprogrammed missile that is easily tracked by radar than to intercept from outer space thousands of Soviet missiles launched simultaneously and speeding at thousands of miles per hour over a vast area. The feasibility of space wars weapons against targets of this sort has never been demonstrated.

It took an entire building to house the 300-watt power supply for the San Juan Capistrano tests. A genuine laser cannon could require from 100 billion to one trillion watts, and might entail placing several nuclear power plants in orbit—an impractical assignment at best.

Furthermore, the space-based beams can easily be neutralized by inexpensive countermeasures. Warheads coated with highly reflective paint can diminish the usefulness of laser beams. Decoys and chaff can confuse radar. For every ruble the Soviets might spend on such cheap diversions, the United States would have to spend millions of dollars on devices that can differentiate between real warheads and duds. And there is always the possibility—some would say the likelihood or even the certainty—that the Soviets would destroy U.S. satellites with killer satellites or space mines of their own.

Finally, it may be that the laws of physics simply rule out the successful development of space weaponry. Because a satellite takes ninety minutes to complete an orbit around Earth, only a fraction of the laser fleet would be in position to act in case of an enemy attack. Within a few minutes, the small number of satellites must locate enemy missiles with pinpoint accuracy, separate out the decoys and dummies, focus the destructive beam long enough to destroy a warhead, confirm the kill, and repeat the process hundreds or thousands of times. It may be impossible to do all that.

What makes the new space war strategy such an ominous development, though, is not the high cost, dubious effectiveness, or great vulnerability of the weaponry, but the potential escalation of the arms race to a new, destabilizing level.

The mere *perception* by one side that the other has achieved a first-strike capability or a foolproof ABM system may suffice to provoke nuclear war. The Soviet Union, understandably fearful that the United States is preparing a knock-out first strike, could decide to jump the gun and fire first. Former U.S. strategic arms negotiator Paul Warnke has said, "There is no question in my mind that we could have a war in space within a decade unless we devise a treaty that will stop it." And a war in space would inevitably become a war that devastates the Earth.

Satellite Warfare

Neither the skepticism of most scientists nor the profound misgivings felt by many strategic analysts seem to have had any impact on President Reagan. His preoccupation is with the Soviet Union and the possibility that it may forge ahead in the arms race. For him, the space wars scenario seems to hold out the hope of perpetual, foolproof protection for the United States.

The Soviet military might entertain similar visions. For decades, both superpowers have secretly studied the black arts of antisatellite (ASAT) and ABM warfare, hoping to find security on the ground by placing the proper weaponry in space.

When the Soviets launched their first Sputnik in October

1957, the United States immediately embarked on a crash program called SAINT (for satellite interceptor). SAINT was abandoned in 1962 only because nuclear-tipped ASAT missiles based on Kwajalein Atoll and Johnston Island in the Pacific seemed to offer a more promising way of attacking Soviet space satellites. Though the use of such missiles was explicitly banned by the Outer Space Treaty of 1967, they were kept in place until 1975, when the Pentagon came to the embarrassing realization that the electromagnetic pulse generated by nuclear detonations would wreak indiscriminate havoc among American as well as Soviet satellites.

Today, the U.S. ASAT program calls for use of an F-15 fighter jet equipped with a miniature rocket that is capable of soaring 200 miles into outer space and homing in on Soviet satellites. The rocket, called the MHV (miniature homing vehicle), is now undergoing final flight tests.

In addition, the Space Shuttle has increasingly taken on a role as a space wars weapon. Its heavy involvement in military applications dates back to May 13, 1978, when President Carter signed Presidential Decision Memorandum 37, calling for "activities in space in support of [the U.S.] right of self-defense, thereby strengthening national security, the deterrence of attack, and arms control agreements." With substantial funding from the military budget, the Space Shuttle now serves as a vehicle to beam-weapon experimentation. The Soviets have protested, to no avail, that this violates existing treaties.

ASAT systems will be ready for deployment in the 1990s, but beam weapons are at a less advanced stage and their current status is shrouded in secrecy. We do know that the Defense Advanced Research Projects Agency (DARPA) set up Project See Saw as long ago as 1958 to investigate particle beam ABM systems. After more than a dozen years of exploratory work, See Saw was abandoned in 1972 when researchers concluded that the costs of such weaponry would be prohibitive.

In the 1970s, the Army started its own program, first called Sipapu (a Native American word for "sacred fire") and later renamed White Horse. The Navy set up the mysterious Chair Heritage Project, which runs a test series called Dauphin at the Lawrence Livermore weapons laboratory in California.

Three years ago, Dauphin dispelled the long-held assumption that it was impossible to generate X-ray lasers. In the first successful test of its kind, Dauphin demonstrated that a small underground nuclear charge could be used to pump an X-ray laser at a wavelength of .0014 microns. This breakthrough helped persuade the Pentagon and the Reagan Administration that an elaborate space wars program might be feasible. In an X-ray laser, a nuclear detonation creates huge numbers of soft X-rays that can be channeled through hundreds of laser tubes into directed X-ray beams. When used in space, however, the nuclear explosion kills the satellite itself, so a laser cannon of this sort can be used only once.

Predictably, we know even less about the Soviet Union's space war efforts than about our own government's, but there is no doubt that the Russians, too, have explored techniques of destroying enemy satellites. Instead of using conventional jet fighters to launch ASAT weapons, the Soviets have been experimenting since 1968 with maneuverable satellites capable of firing conventional charges to destroy enemy vehicles in space.

On April 13, 1976, Cosmos 814 was borne aloft on an F-1M missile launched from the sprawling Tyuratam space port. After only one orbit, Cosmos 814 maneuvered within striking distance—one kilometer—of the previously launched Cosmos 803. It was a stunning display of satellite virtuosity, and it prompted President Ford to approve funding for the Pentagon's MHV program.

Still, Soviet ASAT efforts cannot be construed as a serious threat to the security of the United States. The Soviet weapons can effectively be directed only against low-altitude satellites in orbit at 200 miles or less, while most important U.S. communications satellites are in synchronous orbits at 20,000 miles— beyond the reach of either Cosmos or MHV. What's more, Soviet killer satellites are unsophisticated machines, able to home in only on carefully preprogrammed dummy satellites locked into special orbits.

Soviet efforts to manipulate satellites in outer space can easily be tracked on radar, but the progress of space beam research on the ground is a matter of speculation and interpretation of aerial reconnaissance.

The Reagan Administration's claims that the Russians are "ahead" in laser ABM technology rests almost exclusively on a single scrap of disputed evidence. In 1972, Major General George Keegan, then in charge of the $3 billion-a-year U.S. Air Force intelligence apparatus, alleged that satellite photos of a Soviet base sixty kilometers south of Semipalatinsk proved beyond doubt that the Russians were out in front in development of particle beam weaponry. Keegan cited four large holes in the ground and two spherical structures that he described as energy storage tanks for particle beams.

Keegan's assertions were investigated by the Central Intelligence Agency, which decided his evidence was marginal and inconclusive. The CIA skeptics designated the Soviet facility as URDF-3, for "unidentified research and development center number three," leaving Keegan virtually alone in insisting that the Soviets had a twenty-year jump on the United States. It was only with the advent of the Reagan Administration that Keegan's charges started receiving a respectful hearing, and the retired general recently put in a return appearance on the CBS television program, *Sixty Minutes*.

The Laser ABM and First Strike Strategy

The hard-line scientists who have played a role in persuading the Reagan Administration to commit itself to space wars are not fools. They are aware of the doubts voiced by their colleagues and they understand the formidable obstacles that stand in the way of effective satellite weapons. They surely realize that no laser ABM systems will ever be able to destroy all Soviet missiles immediately after launch, and that a failure rate of even 1 per cent would inflict catastrophic damage on targets in the United States.

Why, then, are they pushing the ABM system, and why is the Administration heeding their advice? The answers are to be found in the arcane theories and peculiar ratiocinations of the Nuclear Warfighting strategists.

The laser ABM, with all its limitations, may have effective applications in conjunction with the launching of a preemptive first strike.

The Nuclear Warfighters' reason that an American first strike, no matter how successful, could never destroy all of the Soviet retaliatory force. That's where the space weapons would come into play: the 10 to 20 per cent of Soviet missiles that might manage to escape a U.S. first strike could be shot down by laser ABM systems. In Nuclear Warfighting jargon, this is called Strategic Defense.

The arithmetic is simple: the Soviet Union has about 8,000 strategic warheads aimed at targets in the United States. In the near future, the land-based MX missile and the submarine-launched Trident II will be accurate enough to drop two hydrogen bombs in each of the Soviet SS-18 and SS-19 missile silos.

Still, there are some uncertainties: to what extent will magnetic and gravitational anomalies over the North Pole divert the attacking U.S. missiles from their flight paths? Until the missiles actually are sent on their course, no one will know. It must also be assumed that at least 10 per cent of the Soviet nuclear submarine fleet will survive a first strike. In sum, there is a likelihood that about 1,000 of the 8,000 Russian warheads would still be available to retaliate against the United States.

With all its faults, the laser ABM system can reasonably be expected to handle most of those remaining 1,000 Soviet warheads. The few missiles that might elude both the first strike and the laser ABM provide the rationale for the Administration's new emphasis on civil defense and relocation plans; the purpose of such programs is to preserve U.S. industrial capacity for the "post-attack era."

State Department consultant Colin S. Gray, one of the Nuclear Warfighters, has neatly summed up the doctrine:

> The United States should plan to defeat the Soviet Union and to do so at a cost that would not prohibit U.S. recovery. Washington should identify war aims that in the last resort would contemplate the destruction of Soviet political authority and the emergence of a post-war world order compatible with Western values...A combination of counterforce offensive targeting, civil defense, and ballistic missile and air defense should hold U.S. casualties to approximately 20 million, which would render U.S. strategic threats more credible.

The objective, in other words, is not merely a first strike —though that is an essential component—but a comprehensive mix of first-strike targeting, antimissile weaponry, and civil defense measures that will guarantee, in the Administration's view, that the United States will "prevail" in a nuclear exchange.

That is the "security" promised by Reagan's space wars program—not the security of peace, but the security of American victory in a nuclear war rendered all but inevitable.

Chapter 11

Can Nuclear War Be Controlled?

Desmond Ball

For the greater part of the nuclear age, Western strategic thought focused on deterrence and other means of avoiding strategic nuclear war. The principal concerns of the strategic studies community were the conditions of viable mutual deterrence and crisis stability, the prevention of accidental nuclear war, and the promotion of nuclear non-proliferation to limit the danger of catalytic war. Virtually no consideration was given to the conduct of nuclear war in the event that deterrence failed or that for whatever the reason, nuclear strikes were initiated. It was assumed, at least implicitly, that any significant use of nuclear weapons by either the United States or the Soviet Union against the territory or military forces of the other would inevitably develop into an all-out nuclear exchange limited only by the size of their respective nuclear arsenals.

During the last decade, however, there has been a radical shift in this thinking. Today, the principal concerns of the strategic studies community relate to the period *following* the initiation of a strategic nuclear exchange—i.e. to questions of nuclear warfighting, such as targeting plans and policies, the dynamics of escalation during a strategic nuclear exchange, and the termination of any such exchange.

Controlled escalation has become the central operational concept in current U.S. strategic doctrine. This concept requires the U.S. to be able to conduct very selective military operations, initially focusing on the protection of vital American interests immediately threatened, but also aimed at foreclosing opportunities for further enemy aggression. The intention is to "deter escalation and coerce the enemy into negotiating a war termination acceptable to the United States by maintaining our capability to effectively withhold attacks from additional hostage targets highly valued (or) vital to enemy leaders, thus limiting the level and scope of violence by threatening subsequent destruction."[1] Controlling escalation requires *both* adversaries to exercise restraint, and current U.S. policy is to offer a combination of measures involving a mixture of self-interest and coercion.

The capabilites for command-and-control, and the conditions which enable control to be exercised throughout a strategic nuclear exchange are critical to the viability of the current U.S. strategic doctrine. Without survivable command, control and communication (C^3) systems, for example, any limited nuclear operations involving control, selectivity, discrimination and precision would rapidly become infeasible.

Concern with the command-and-control of the U.S. strategic nuclear forces is of course not entirely novel. In 1961-1962, for example, much official attention was devoted specifically to this issue. In April 1961, a task force was established within the Pentagon to study the whole field of command-and-control and in November 1961 a major report was completed which contained plans for a national command-and-control system designed to survive nuclear attack and provide the President of the U.S. with instantaneous command over vital American military forces.[2] Implementation of these plans over the following years produced the underground SAC and NORAD headquarters at Omaha, Nebraska and Cheyenne Mountain, Colorado; alternative command posts at sea and in the air; and redundant communications links to all elements of the U.S. strategic forces. In fact, over the past two decades some $40 billion has been spent on C^3 systems for the U.S. strategic nuclear forces.[3] However, this expenditure was directed towards a variety of ends, such as improving the safety of strategic weapons or simply taking advantage of new technological developments, not all of which served to enhance the prospects for controlling nuclear escalation.

Three particular (though closely related) aspects of the current interest in strategic command-and-control are especially noteworthy. First, the concern with command-and-control is now at the center of U.S. strategic planning. Previous considera-tion of nuclear warfighting focused essentially on two vari-ables: the targets to be attacked in any nuclear exchange (counterforce or countervalue), and the rate at which the attack was to proceed (massively or slowly and selectively.)[4] Of course, various aspects of control were important to both these vari-ables. At least in some formulations, counterforce strategies were closely associated with damage limitation and "city avoidance," and required the exercise of discrimination and restraint for successful implementation. And demands on capabilities to control rates of fire would be particularly great if the decision was to conduct the exchange slowly and selec-tively, holding forces in reserve rather than launching the entire nuclear stockpile simultaneously. Both variables—tar-gets and rates of fire—were to be essentially determined before the outbreak of war, and little change would have been possible during the actual exchange. Now, however, the concern is much more with the dynamics of escalation and the capabilities and conditions for managing the exchange as it progresses. Com-mand and control are obviously central to this.

Second, the concern with command-and-control now has a new dimension—that of endurance. As the Nuclear Targeting Policy Review (NTPR) concluded in 1978, the U.S. command, control, communication and intelligence (C³I) system "should have much greater endurance than the present system."[5] At least since 1961-1962, substantial resources have been devoted to improving the survivability of U.S. command and control systems. Most particularly, command centers were hardened and alternative systems deployed to ensure that command capabilities would survive a Soviet nuclear attack and that the order for a retaliatory strike could be given and executed. But endurance was not required of command and control systems beyond perhaps a few days or a week, whereas the current requirement is measured in terms of weeks and even months.

Third, there has been a significant shift in the prevailing rationale for the continued (and increasing) allocation of resources to command-and-control systems. The rationales that dominated command-and-control programs in the 1950s and 1960s were to prevent accidental or unauthorized nuclear war and to enhance deterrence by maintaining a survivable cap-ability for ensuring retaliation; only infrequently did concern emerge for a serious ability to conduct nuclear strikes other than massive and indiscriminate ones. The notion of deterrence is still invoked, but it is now seen as involving much more than simply maintaining an unambiguous second strike assured destruction capability. Greater attention is now given to the requirements for deterring both quite limited attacks (such as a strike against some ICBM silos), against which the threat of massive destructive responses might be incredible, and also theater nuclear conflict, particularly on the NATO/ Warsaw Pact front. More fundamentally, however, as the spectrum of contingencies to be deterred has widened, so has the nature of the concept itself. Whereas in the 1960s, for example, the concept of deterrence was starkly contrasted with that of defense, both are now seen as integral parts of a continuum. The capacity for nuclear warfighting is now regarded as an essential ingredient of successful deterrence. Insofar as this reformulation depends on maintaining survivable and endurable C^3, the new rationales are extremely sensitive to the vulnerabilities of strategic command-and-control.

The recognition that the command-and-control network is the most vulnerable component of the U.S. strategic forces has generated an extensive effort to correct some particular deficiencies. However, many C^3 systems are inherently susceptible to a wide range of physical and electronic threats. These vulnerabilities impose very severe physical limits on the extent to which a nuclear war could be controlled.

Various operational strategic, military and political considerations also work against the possibility of controlling a nuclear war. The collateral damage involved in even quite controlled, precise and discriminating nuclear strikes is likely to be both substantial and somewhat unpredictable; there must be great doubt as to whether nuclear weapons can be designed and employed in ways that constitute an unambiguous and fully coherent signalling mechanism—at least when more than a handful are involved. In any case, the control of escalation requires that all participants in the conflict have both the capabilities and the willingness to exercise restraint. Although the Soviet capabilities for control improved markedly during the 1970s, there is still a very real question mark over whether Soviet strategic doctrine can accommodate the requisite restraint.

Moreover, the dynamics of a nuclear exchange are likely to generate military and political pressures for the relaxation of restraints, even where both adversaries agreed at the outset that it was in their mutual interest to avoid unwanted escalation. There are compelling military arguments both against the highly graduated application of force and for attacking the command-and-control infrastructure of the adversary's strategic nuclear forces. Differences in interests and perspectives among the various groups and individuals that comprise the respective national leaderships (as well as between those leaderships) would make intra-war bargaining and conciliation an extremely difficult exercise.

It does not follow that all limited or selective nuclear operations would necessarily lead to an all-out nuclear exchange. Small, carefully conducted attacks designed to demonstrate political resolve could well have a salutary effect. However, it is difficult to envisage the maintenance of control in situations beyond the detonation of several tons of nuclear weapons.

C³ and Strategic Doctrine

The principal official rationalization of U.S. strategic command-and-control programs is the support of the declared national strategic doctrine. It is very difficult, however, to delineate any single or consistent relationship between the U.S. strategic command-and-control architecture and that doctrine. For one thing, strategic doctrine has itself rarely offered clear and coherent guidance for the design and development of command-and-control systems and procedures. For another, U.S. strategic doctrine has been extremely transitory, periodicly oscillating between relatively simple notions of countervalue deterrence (such as Massive Retaliation or Assured Destruction) and more complex and more demanding notions of flexible response, nuclear warfighting and escalation control. The lead times for the design, development and deployment of modern sophisticated command-and-control systems are such that the rare periods when the guidance has been clear enough have generally been too brief for any systematic overall relationship to be effected.

It is less difficult, however, to describe the general command-and-control requirements of particular types of strategic policies; and it is possible to provide at least some specific examples of command-and-control systems that have been directly generated by the demands of strategic doctrine.

At one extreme, a simple first-strike plan based on a policy of massive pre-emption would require a minimal command-and-control system; indeed, a simple capability to communicate the launch order to the strategic forces would be virtually sufficient. The command-and-control requirements of Massive Retaliation or Assured Destruction differ from this in only one critical respect: since these notions are based on the ability of the strategic forces to *respond* to a nuclear attack, they require command-and-control systems with sufficient survivability to guarantee the communication and implementation of the response order in a second strike. Because the target structure can be pre-determined, however, and is essentially insensitive to any technical or political undulations in the course of the exchange, the provision of anything beyond this is quite unnecessary. Most especially, there is no need for the command-and-control system to have any endurance beyond the retaliatory strike; there is no need for two-way communciations between the strategic forces and the national command authorities; and there are no immediate demands on the system, since no battle management is involved.

The command-and-control requirements of concepts such as flexible response, damage limitation, nuclear warfighting, and controlled escalation are obviously much more complex and elaborate. The ability to respond to a nuclear strike in such a way as to blunt any subsequent strikes or to inflict some proportionate level of punishment imposes a number of requirements: reliable tactical warning, post-strike reconnaissance, attack- and damage-assessment systems; the means to rapidly retarget one's own strategic forces without wasting firepower on damaged or empty missile silos and airfields, or to strike targets of equivalent value to those damaged or destroyed by the adversary; and two-way communications between the National Command Authorities and the strategic forces, so that at any time the NCA can know the latter's status for both damage assessment and force employment purposes. Communications with the adversary are also desirable, so as to clarify confusing events and provide a channel for negotiations and the control of escalation, and the command-and-control system needs sufficient endurance to co-ordinate and control the successive strikes, which could proceed over weeks or even months. These strategic notions also require the continuous and immediate injection of political considerations into the selection of targets, the determination of firing rates, and decisions on the operational configuration of one's own forces so as not to produce misapprehension in the mind of the adversary.

War Termination

In so far as command-and-control systems have been generated and shaped by the demands of strategic doctrine, the effort has been rather unbalanced. The great bulk of the developments have been concerned with the beginning and the early phases of a nuclear exchange and have been designed to enable the U.S. NCA to take the initiative during that period in the sense of determining the parameters of the escalatory process. The Secretary of Defense declared in his FY 1981 report to Congress that "strategic C^3 must also facilitate termination of nuclear strikes," but the impact of this admonition has evidently been relatively slight.[6]

The principal capacity which has officially been identified with facilitating war termination is a direct communications link between the respective U.S. and Soviet national command authorities—the so-called "hot line" between Moscow and Washington.[7] However, despite this system's critical importance to war termination, no special measures have been taken to protect it from the collateral effects of a nuclear exchange.

The termination of a nuclear exchange also requires the strictest NCA control over the strategic forces themselves. Communications with FBM submarines attempting to launch their missiles in the face of enemy anti-submarine warfare (ASW) activity, or with SAC bombers flying at low altitudes within Soviet airspace, could be very difficult, and, at least in these situations, the ability to countermand orders or to disengage forces could be very tenuous. The deployment of UHF AFSATCOM terminals on SAC B-52s and FB-111s will considerably improve this situation with respect to the bombers, but ICBMs and SLBMs, once launched, obviously cannot be recalled and lack any mechanism for destruction in flight.[8] It is possible to imagine an intra-war pause or armistice being nullified by such deficiencies.

The Vulnerabilities of C^3 Systems

The viability of any strategic policy of controlled nuclear warfighting depends, *inter alia*, upon the ability of C^3 systems to survive throughout the nuclear exchange. The survivability need not be absolute. Some elements of the U.S. and Soviet command-and-control networks are of only marginal strategic value, while others are so redundant that the loss of any particular one would not degrade the system's overall operational effectiveness. On the other hand, it is obviously desirable that the potential capabilties of the residual strategic forces should not, at any given point in the nuclear exchange, be constrained by deficiencies in the C^3 systems.

Current U.S. strategic policy requires that the strategic command-and-control systems have sufficient survivability and endurance to operate for several months from the start of a strategic nuclear exchange—the 90 days which is the nominal endurance imputed for planning purposes to the strategic forces themselves, plus an additional period when the command-and-control system is intended to support the reconstitution of the residual strategic forces. This requirement might, in fact, be impossible to realize. The strategic forces themselves are, in comparison, rather easy to protect; they can be dispersed, buried underground in hardened silos, or deployed in some mobile mode, either on the ground, under the water in submarines, or on board aircraft. But these systems are generally not applicable to C^3 systems. Many of them (such as early-warning radars, the VLF communication system for the FBM submarines, and satellite ground control facilities) are inherently large, fixed and soft. Some elements (such as underground command posts) can be hardened, sometimes to withstand a blast overpressure (pressure over and above normal atmospheric pressure) of as much as 3,000-5,000 pounds per square inch (psi) but, as ballistic missile accuracies fall below about one-tenth of a nautical mile, the survivability of even these becomes problematical; and the cables and antennae with which they communicate can never be hardened to anywhere near the same extent as the underground facilities themselves. Some elements can be dispersed and others can be made mobile, but this invariably makes the commUnciation links between them more difficult to engineer, and in any case these links are themselves vulnerable to various forms of interruption and interference. Finally, there will always be some critical nodal points—e.g. where commUnciation links connect to the command posts and, most especially, where the chain of command-and-control originates at the national command level—which can neither be hardened nor duplicated. It is axiomatic that the chain of command is only as strong as its weakest link.

Command-and-control systems are in fact vulnerable to all the threats to which the strategic forces are subject as well as others more peculiar to command structures and telecommunications systems. (Indeed, some of the elements will succumb to effects which are quite unpredictable and unintentional.) Essentially, they are vulnerable to direct physical attack (and to the collateral effects of attack upon the strategic forces) and to operational failures that must be expected to occur. Physically, they are open to nuclear effects (blast and radiation), attack with conventional weapons and sabotage. Operationally, they are vulnerable both to unintended effects—human error, natural phenomomena and equipment failure—and to intentional jamming or exploitation of failures in security.[9]

MOLINK: The Moscow-Washington Hot Line

Control of a strategic nuclear exchange between the Soviet Union and the United States would be rather easier if a continuous communications link could be maintained between the respective NCAs. As Secretary Schlesinger testified in March 1974 in support of the doctrine of limited nuclear warfighting: "If we were to maintain continued communications with the Soviet leaders during the war, and if we were to describe precisely and meticulously the limited nature of our actions, including the desire to avoid attacking their urban-industrial base...political leaders on both sides will be under powerful pressure to continue to be sensible."[10] Continued communications would enable the clarification of confusing events, and provide a channel for negotiations and the control of escalation, including the negotiations of war termination.

The possible consequences of the lack of a direct communications link (DCL) between Moscow and Washington became apparent during the Cuban missile crisis of October 1962, when President Kennedy and Chairman Krushchev were forced to communicate with each other through clumsy diplomatic channels, with messages sometimes being delayed many hours and often being overtaken by the rapid movement of events. As a result, agreement was reached to establish a so-called "hot line," which went into service on August 30, 1963.

The Washington terminal of the hot line (designated MOLINK, a contraction of "Moscow link") is in the National Military Command Center (NMCC) in the Pentagon, from which there is also now a connection to the White House; the Moscow terminal is evidently in the Chairman's Office in the Communist Party headquarters building.[11] The hot line originally had two main routings: the primary one—based on underwater and terrestrial cables running through London, Copenhagen, Stockholm and Helsinki—and a radio back-up circuit via Tangier, Morocco. Both were duplex teletype circuits.[12]

The value of the DCL was first demonstrated during the June 1967 war in the Middle East. On the morning of June 5, at the very outset of the war, Premier Kosygin contacted President Johnson and expressed his strong interest in both the Soviet Union and the United States using their influence "to bring hostilities to an end." On June 8, when Israel attacked the USS Liberty, President Johnson used the hot line to inform Mr. Kosygin that the U.S. was aware that Israel was responsible and that American aircraft were scrambling from carriers in the area only to aid the stricken ship. And on June 10, President

Johnson used the link to tell Mr. Kosygin that the U.S. had received assurances that the Israeli counterattack against Syria would stop short of Damascus—and hence that any Soviet intervention would be unwarranted. Without a hot line, a direct U.S.-Soviet confrontation would clearly have been a possibility.[13] The line was next used on December 12, 1971, during the Indo-Pakistani War. The U.S. informed Moscow that unless pressure was put on India to accept a standstill cease-fire and immediate negotiations, the U.S. would proceed unilaterally, which might produce "consequences neither of us want."[14] It was also used by President Brezhnev in response to the U.S. nuclear alert of October 24-26, 1973, during the Yom Kippur War, which President Nixon has described as "perhaps the most serious threat to U.S.-Soviet relations since the Cuban missile crisis eleven years before."[15]

The cable and radio links that constituted the hot line from 1963 to 1978 were quite vulnerable to accidental interruption as well as to possible sabotage or direct attack. Six separate accidental interruptions have been publicly reported for the period 1964-1966 alone. In 1964, a thief snipped out a 20-foot section of the cable near Helsinki; later the same year a thunder storm reportedly put the line out of commission by damaging a power station in southern Finland; in 1965 a fire in a manhole at Rosedale, Maryland cut the circuit; also in 1965, a farmer in Finland ploughed through the cable; in 1966 a Finnish postal workers' strike reportedly interrupted the circuit for several hours; a few months later a Soviet freighter severed the cable when it ran aground in Denmark.[16] Although in none of these cases was the hot line actually out of operation for more than a few seconds (since the radio back-up was always available) they did prompt efforts to establish a more secure and reliable system.

On September 30, 1971, the U.S. and the U.S.S.R. agreed to improve the hot line by replacing the cable and radio teleprinter links with a satellite communications system comprising two independent and parallel circuits and four ground stations. This system became operational in January 1978. The United States provides one circuit via an *Intelsat* IV satellite, with ground stations at Etam, West Virginia, and Moscow; the Soviet Union provides the other circuit through a *Molniya* II satellite, with ground stations at Vladimir and Fort Detrick, Maryland. Telephone cables from the ground stations complete the Washington-Moscow connection.[17]

The satellite link is probably more secure and reliable than cable from the point of view of accidental interruption, but it is probably also more vulnerable to disruption in the event of any nuclear exchange—the very situation in which it would be desperately needed. As Secretary Rumsfield testified in January 1977, "the system is not designed to survive a direct attack."[18] The ground stations and the *Molniya* II satellite are particularly vulnerable. Both the satellites operate at a somewhat higher frequencies than the UHF band, so that the communication links between them and the ground stations would be relatively unaffected by any black-out induced by nuclear detonations, hence, as Dr. Dinneen testified, "We may still have a propagation path after a massive attack."[19] However, the *Molniya* II satellite has a perigree of only 300 miles and would be very vulnerable to any exo-atmospheric nuclear detonations at the outset of a nuclear exchange.

There would be little strategic rationale for any direct attack against the four ground stations. However, these stations and the associated ground links and terminals are naturally quite soft (less than 5 psi) and could well be incidental casualties of strikes against nearby targets. As Dr. Dinneen said: "The ground terminals, of course, are here in Washington, so most likely they are not going to be there. Unless we have some way of getting into that hotline from the Airborne Command Post, then you would have to assume that after the first impact on Washington the hotline is available.[20]

The irony is that the DCL is only likely to remain operational during the period in a nuclear exchange when restraint is already being exercised for other reasons; once restraint is abandoned, and an exchange progresses to any large-scale level, the availability of the hot line could not be relied upon. Yet it is from this point on that casualties are likely to be several times greater than for the phase when the DCL was available.

Conclusions

A strategic nuclear war between the United States and the Soviet Union would involve so many novel technical and emotional variables that predictions about its course—and especially about whether or not it could be controlled—must remain highly speculative.

To the extent that there is a typical lay image of a nuclear war, it is that any substantial use of nuclear weapons by either the United States or the Soviet Union against the other's forces or territory would inevitably and rapidly lead to all-out urban-industrial attacks and consequent mutual destruction. As Carl-Friedrich von Weiszacker recently wrote, "as soon as we use nuclear weapons, there are no limits."[21]

Among strategic analysts on the other hand, the ascendant view is that it is possible to conduct limited and quite protracted nuclear exchanges in such a way that escalation can be controlled and the war terminated at some less than all-out level. Some strategists actually visualize an escalation ladder, with a series of discrete and clearly identifiable steps of increasing levels of intensity of nuclear conflict, which the respective adversaries move up—and down—at will. Current U.S. strategic policy, although extensively and carefully qualified, is closer to this second position: it is hoped that escalation could be controlled and that more survivable command-and-control capabilities should ensure dominance in the escalation process. Indeed, reliance on the ability to control escalation is an essential element of U.S. efforts with respect to extended deterrence.

Escalation is neither autonomous and inevitable nor subject completely to the decisions of any one national command authority. Whether or not it can be controlled will depend very much on the circumstances at the time. The use of a few nuclear weapons for some clear demonstrative purposes, for example, could well not lead to further escalation. However, it is most unrealistic to expect that there would be a relatively smooth and controlled progression from limited and selective strikes, through major counterforce exchanges, to termination of the conflict at some level short of urban-industrial attacks. It is likely that beyond some relatively early stage in the conflict the strategic communications systems would suffer interference and disruption, the strikes would become ragged, uncoordinated, less precise and less discriminating, and the ability to reach an agreed settlement between the adversaries would soon become extremely problematical.

There is of course no immutable point beyond which control is necessarily and irretrievably lost but clearly the prospects of maintaining control depend to a very great extent on whether or not a decision is taken deliberately to attack strategic command-and-control capabilities.

Command-and-control systems are inherently relatively vulnerable, and concerted attacks on them would very rapidly destroy them, or at least render them inoperable. Despite the increased resources that the U.S. is currently devoting to improving the survivability and endurance of command-and-control systems, the extent of their relative vulnerability remains enormous. The Soviet Union would need to expend thousands of warheads in any comprehensive counterforce attacks against U.S. ICBM silos, bomber bases and FBM submarine facilities, and even then hundreds if not thousands of U.S. warheads would survive. On the other hand, it would require only about 50-100 warheads to destroy the fixed facilities of the national command system or to effectively impair the communication links between the National Command Authorities and the strategic forces.

This figure would permit attacks on the National Military Command Center, the major underground command posts (including the Alternative National Military Command Center and the NORAD and SAC Command Posts), the critical satellite ground terminals and early warning radar facilities, the VLF communication stations, etc. as well as 10 or 20 high altitude detonations designed to disrupt HF communications and generate EMP over millions of square miles. Any airborne command posts and communication links that survived the initial attack could probably not endure for more than a few days. Soviet military doctrine suggests that any comprehensive counterforce attack *would* include strikes of this sort. U.S. strategic targeting plans involve a wide range of Soviet command-and-control facilities, and, while attacks on Soviet national leadership would probably only be undertaken as part of an all-out exchange, it is likely that attempts would be made to destroy the command posts that control the strategic forces, or at least to sever the communication links between the Soviet NCA and those forces at a much earlier stage in the conflict.

In fact, control of a nuclear exchange would become very difficult to maintain after several tens of strategic nuclear weapons had been used, even where deliberate attacks on command-and-control capabilities were avoided. Many command and control facilities, such as early warning radar, radio antennae and satellite ground terminals would be destroyed, or at least rendered inoperable, by nuclear detonations designed to destroy nearby military forces and installations, while the widespread disturbance of the ionosphere and equally widespread generation of EMP would disrupt HF communications and impair electronic and electrical systems at great distances from the actual explosions. Hence, as John Steinbruner has argued, "regardless of the flexibility embodied in individual force components, the precariousness of command channels probably means that nuclear war would be uncontrollable, as a practical matter, shortly after the first tens of weapons were launched."[22] Moreover, any attack involving 100 nuclear weapons that was of any military or strategic significance (as opposed to demonstration strikes at isolated sites in northern Siberia) would produce substantial civilian casualties. Even if cities were avoided, 100 nuclear detonations on key military or war supporting facilities (such as oil refineries) would probably cause prompt fatalities in excess of a million people.

The notion of controlled nuclear warfighting is essentially astrategic in that it tends to ignore a number of realities that would necessarily attend any nuclear exchange. The more significant of these include the particular origins of the given conflict and the nature of its progress to the point where the strategic nuclear exchange is initiated; the disparate objectives for which a limited nuclear exchange would be fought; the nature of the decision-making processes within the adversary governments; the political pressures that would be generated by a nuclear exchange; and the problems of terminating the exchange at some less than all-out level. Some of these considerations are so fundamental and so intemperate in their implications to suggest that there can be no possibility of controlling a nuclear war.

The origins of a nuclear exchange are relevant because, for example, a strategic nuclear strike by the United States or the Soviet Union against targets in the other's heartland—no matter how limited, precise, or controlled it might be—is most unlikely to be the first move in any conflict between them. Rather, it is likely to follow a period of large-scale military action, probably involving substantial use of tactical nuclear weapons, in an area of vital interest to both adversaries, and during which the dynamics of the escalation process have already been set in motion. Some command-and-control facilities, communications systems and intelligence posts that would be required to control a strategic nuclear exchange would almost certainly be destroyed or damaged in the conventional or tactical nuclear phases of a conflict. And casualties on both sides are already likely to be very high before any strategic nuclear exchange. In the case of a tactical nuclear war in Europe, possible fatalities range from 2 to 20 million, assuming extensive use of nuclear weapons with some restraints and up to 100 million if there are no restraints at all.[23] The capabilities of the Warsaw Pact forces (using large and relatively "dirty" warheads) and the Warsaw Pact targeting doctrine make it likely that the actual figure would lie at the higher end of this range.

A war involving such extensive use of nuclear weapons in Europe would almost inevitably involve attacks on targets within the Soviet Union. Indeed, it has long been U.S. policy to use nuclear weapons against the Soviet Union even if the Soviet Union has attacked neither U.S. forces nor U.S. territory. As

Secretary Brown expressed it in January 1980, "We would not want the Soviets to make the mistaken judgment, based on their understanding of our targeting practices, that they would be spared retaliatory attacks on their territory as long as they did not employ strategic nuclear weapons or attack U.S. territory.[24] The U.S. would attempt to destroy the Soviet theater nuclear forces, including the MRBMs, IRBMs and bombers based in the western USSR, the reserve forces, and POL and logistic support facilities. Soviet casualties from these attacks could amount to several tens of millions. The prospects for controlling any subsequent strategic exchange would not be auspicious.

In addition to these technical and strategic considerations, the decision-making structures and processes of large national security establishments are quite unsuited to the control of escalatory military operations. The control of escalation requires extreme decisional flexibility: decision-makers must be able to adapt rapidly to changing situations and assessments, and must have the freedom to reverse direction as the unfolding of events dictates. Their decisions must be presented clearly and coherently, leaving no room for misinterpretation either by subordinates charged with implementation or by the adversary leadership.

These are not attitudes that are generally found in large national security establishments. In neither the United States nor the Soviet Union are these establishments unitary organizations in which decisions are made and executive commands given on the basis of some rational calculation of the national interest. They are made up of a wide range of civilian and military individuals and groups, each with their own interests, preferences, views and perspectives, and each with their own quasi-autonomous political power bases. The decisions which emerge are a product of bargaining, negotiation and compromise between these groups and individuals, rather than of any more rational process. The heterogeneous nature of the decision-making process leads, in the first instance, to a multiplicity of motives and objectives, not all of which are entirely compatible; and resolving them generally involves the acceptance of compromise language acceptable to each of the contending participants. The clarity of reception among the adversary leadership is consequently generally poor, and the reactions invariably different from the responses initially sought. The "fog of war" makes it extremely unlikely that the situation to which NCA believe themselves to be reacting will in fact correspond very closely to the true situation, or that there will be a high degree of shared perception between the respective adversary leaderships. In these circumstances it would be most difficult to terminate a nuclear exchange through mutual agreement between the adversaries at some point short of all-out urban-industrial attacks.

Of course, the pressures to which decision-makers are subject do not come only from within the national security establishment. In the event of a nuclear exchange, the national leadership would also be subject to the pressures of popular feelings and demands. The mood of horror, confusion and hatred that would develop among the population as bombs began falling on the Soviet Union and the United States and casualties rose through the millions would inevitably limit the national leaderships' freedom of maneuver. Whether the horror would force them to recoil from large-scale attacks on urban-industrial areas or the hatred would engender rapid escalation must remain an open question—but neither mood would be conducive to measured and considered actions.

The likelihood that effective control of a nuclear exchange would be lost at some relatively early point in a conflict calls into question the strategic utility of any preceding efforts to control the exchange. As Colin Grey has argued, it could be extremely dangerous for the United States "to plan a set of very selective targeting building blocks for prospective rounds one, two, and three of strategic force application" while rounds four and five entail massive urban-based strikes.[25] Implementation of such a plan, no matter how controlled the initial rounds, would amount "in practice, to suicide on the installment plan."[26]

The allocation of further resources to improving the survivability and endurance of the strategic command-and-control capabilities cannot substantially alter this situation. Command-and-control systems are inherently more vulnerable than the strategic forces themselves, and, while basic retaliatory commands would always get to the forces eventually, the capability to exercise strict control and coordination would inevitably be lost relatively early in a nuclear exchange.

Furthermore, the technical and strategic uncertainties are such that, regardless of the care and tight control which they attempt to exercise, decision-makers could never be confident that escalation could be controlled. Uncertainties in weapons effects and the accuracy with which weapons can be delivered mean that collateral casualties can never be calculated precisely and that particular strikes could look much less discriminating to the recipient than to the attack planner. The uncertainties are especially great with respect to the operation of particular C³ systems in a nuclear environment. The effects of EMP and transient radiation on electrical and electronic equipment have been simulated on many components but rarely on large systems (such as airborne command posts). Moreover much of the simulation of nuclear effects derives from extrapolation of data generated in the period before atmospheric nuclear tests were banned in 1963.

Given the impossibility of developing capabilities for controlling a nuclear exchange through to favorable termination, or of removing the residual uncertainties relating to controlling the large-scale use of nuclear weapons, *it is likely that decision-makers would be deterred from initiating nuclear strikes no matter how limited or selective the options available to them.* The use of nuclear weapons for controlled escalation is therefore no less difficult to envisage than the use of nuclear weapons for massive retaliation.

Of course, national security policies and postures are not designed solely for the prosecution of war. In both the United States and the Soviet Union, deterring war remains a primary national objective. It is an axiom in the strategic literature that the criteria for deterrence are different from those for warfighting and capabilties which would be deficient for one purpose could well be satisfactory for the other.[27] The large-scale investment of resources in command-and-control capabilities, together with high-level official declarations that the United States would be prepared to conduct limited, selective and tightly controlled strategic nuclear strikes (perhaps in support of extended deterrence), could therefore be valuable because they suggest U.S. determination to act in limited ways—the demonstrable problems of control notwithstanding. However, viable deterrent postures require both capabilities and credibility, and it would seem that neither can be assumed to the extent that would be necessary for the concept of controlled nuclear warfighting to act as a deterrent. Rather than devoting further resources to pursuing the chimera of controlled nuclear war, relatively more attention might be accorded to another means of satisfying the objectives that limited nuclear options are intended to meet. This is likely, in practice, to mean greater attention to the conditions of conventional deterrence.

Footnotes

1.) Testimony of Dr. William Perry, Under Secretary of Defense for Research and Engineering, in Hearings before the Senate Armed Services Committee, *Department of Defense Authorization for Appropriations for Fiscal Year 1980,* Part 3, March-May 1979, p. 1437.

2.) See Desmond Ball, *Politics and Force Levels: The Strategic Missile Programme of the Kennedy Administration* (Berkeley: University of California Press, 1980), chapter 9.

3.) Harold Brown, *Department of Defense Annual Report Fiscal Year 1981,* (USGPO, Washington D.C., 1980), p.71.

4.) See Michael D. Intriligator, "The Debate Over Missile Strategy," *Orbis,* (vol. XI, no.4), Winter 1968, pp. 1138-1159.

5.) Senate Armed Services Committee, *Department of Defense Authorization for Appropriations for Fiscal Year 1980* (January-February 1979), p. 298.

6.) Harold Brown, *Department of Defense Annual Report Fiscal year 1981,* January 29, 1980, p. 140.

7.) *Ibid.*

8.) Testimony of General Jones, House Appropriations Committee, *Department of Defense Appropriations for 1977,* Part 1, p. 152.

9.) Nicholas T. Lampos, "Telecommunication Systems Surviability," *Electronic Warfare/Defense Electronics,* January 1978, p. 98.

10.) Senate Foreign Relations Committee, *US-USSR Strategic Policies,* March 4, 1974, p. 13.

11.) Richard Hudson, "MOLINK is Always Ready," *New York Times Magazine,* August 26, 1973, pp. 14, 18, 20, 24, 26, 29.

12.) John G. Whitman and William W. Davison, "The New Hotline-via Satellite Direct Communications Link," *Signal* March 1974, p.52

13.) Lyndon Baines Johnson, *The Vantage Point: Perspectives on the Presidency 1963-1969* (London: Weidenfeld & Nicolson, 1971), pp. 287-303.

14.) Henry Kissinger, *The White House Years* (London: Weidenfeld & Nicolson, 1979), p. 910.

15.) Richard Nixon, *The Memoirs of Richard Nixon* (New York: Grosset & Dunlap, 1978), p.938.

16.) *Op. Cit.* in n. 11, p. 20.

17.) *Op. Cit.* in n. 12, pp. 52-53.

18.) Donald H. Rumsfeld, *Annual Defense Department Report FY 1978,* January 17, 1977, p. 146.

19.) House Appropriations Committe, *Department of Defense Appropriations for 1980,* Part 3, March 1979, p.105.

20). *Ibid.*

21). Carl-Friedrich von Weiszacker, "Can a Third World War be Prevented?", *International Security* (vol. 5, no. 1), Summer 1980, p.205.

22.) John Steinbruner, "National Security and the Concept of Strategic Stability," *Journal of Conflict Resolution* (vol. 22, no. 1), September 1978, p. 421.

23.) Alain C. Enthoven, "U.S. Forces in Europe: How Many? Doing What?", *Foreign Affairs* (vol. 53, no. 3), April 1975, p. 514; Alain C. Enthoven and K. Wayne Smith, *How Much is Enough?: Shaping the Defense Program, 1961-1969*, (New York: Harper and Row, 1971), p. 128.

24.) Harold Brown, *Department of Defense Annual Report Fiscal Year 1981* (January 29, 1980), p. 92.

25.) Colin S. Gray, "Targeting Problems for Central War," *Naval War College Review)* (vol. 33, no. 1), January-February 1980, p. 9.

26.) *Ibid.*, p. 7.

27.) See Andre Beaufire, *Deterrence & Strategy,* (London: Faber & Faber, 1965), p. 24; and Glenn H. Snyder, *Deterrence & Defense: Toward a Theory of National Security,* (Princeton, New Jersey: Princeton University Press, 1961), pp. 3-6.

Chapter 12

Nuclear Decapitation

John Steinbruner

U.S. strategic policy has arrived at an unusual and consequential moment of political drama. A new president strongly committed to increasing U.S. strategic strength is facing the hard realities of financial constraint and entrenched military programs. Although this clash of fresh impulse and established position is routine for any new administration, the circumstances this time are not. The president is encountering submerged security problems that if fully grasped and consistently pursued will likely alter profoundly his own judgements and the ultimate course of U.S. policy.

A similar situation has arisen at least once before in recent memory. In 1961 John F. Kennedy encountered in his first budget cycle an unexpected clash among his established commitments, the political mood of the moment, and the deeper security interests of the country. He had gained office promising new vigor in national security policy. Amidst fears that the Soviet Union was on the verge of gaining a dangerous military advantage, he had made the state of U.S. strategic missile forces a primary symbol. He inherited an extensive strategic missile procurement program from the Eisenhower administration, but he increased it through supplemental budget requests during his first six months in office.

By September, America was in confrontation with the USSR. The Bay of Pigs affair and the unfortunate Vienna summit meeting had set a tone of conflict that was ripening into a crisis over Berlin; the Soviets had just begun a series of nuclear weapons tests in the atmosphere, thereby providing a provocative strategic context for the crisis. This situation seemingly impelled Kennedy even more powerfully into expanding U.S. forces.

There was, however, a new underlying fact. The intelligence agencies had established that U.S. intercontinental ballistic missile (ICBM) deployments were substantially ahead of Soviet ones and would be so for the foreseeable future. As a result, the central problem became not the procurement of more strategic forces, but rather the imposition of some sensible limit on U.S. deployments. Very little internal analysis or public discussion had prepared the complex machinery of the U.S. government to deal with that problem.

Ronald Reagan is in an analogous situation, despite differences in partisan roots and historical context. Reagan finds a lingering public mood that encourages his political commitment to expand U.S. forces. Nonetheless, he too will have to ponder deeper national security problems where policy requirements contradict his political impulses and lead in directions for which the U.S. political system is poorly prepared. Moreover, there is an important additional burden: the consequences of Kennedy's solution are now part of Reagan's problem.

Between 1961 and 1965, the Kennedy administration and its immediate successor did impose a limit on U.S. strategic force deployments and in the process worked out a justifying logic. U.S. strategic forces, it was asserted, must be maintained at a level sufficient to deter war by threatening appropriate retaliation to an attack of any size even after absorbing the damage that attack would entail. The mix of forces provided—ICBMs, ballistic missile submarines, and bombers—were judged adequate to meet that standard.

The Reagan administration has assumed the same standard, now elaborated and deeply entrenched. But the administration has also accepted a prevailing judgement that the United States must undertake a major reconstruction of its ICBM force and a substantial modernization of the other strategic force elements. This commitment is now necessary to meet the Kennedy standard, administration officials assert, because of recent increases in the level of the Soviet threat. The administration is now attempting to translate this general commitment into specific military programs.

In so doing, Reagan must also face some pertinent facts that substantially change the character of the problem. These have to do with the vulnerability of the U.S. command structure—the organizational and technical network that provides coherent direction for U.S. strategic forces. These facts will not again be presented in the sudden, decisive fashion of the 1961 intelligence breakthrough. But if fully appreciated, they are more dramatic in their implications, more corrosive of prevailing conceptions, and more demanding of new dimensions in national security policy.

This situation presents a severe test of the Reagan administration and of the U.S. political system as a whole. If the analogy to the Kennedy administration is a reasonable guide, the consequences for national security policy will emerge over the course of a decade or more, and many specific decisions and associated policy discussions must ensue before clarity and national consensus can appear.

The Most Vulnerable and Valuable Targets

The basic elements of the command structure problem are easily stated. The United States does not have a strategic command system that could survive deliberate attack of a sort that the Soviet Union could readily undertake. Fewer than 100 judiciously targeted nuclear weapons could so severely damage U.S. communications facilities and command centers that form the military chain of command that the actions of the individual weapons commanders could no longer be controlled or coordinated. Some bomber crews, submarine officers, and ICBM silo launch officers could undertake very damaging retaliation and hence continue to pose a deterrent threat. Nonetheless, even 50 nuclear weapons are probably sufficient to eliminate the ability to direct U.S. strategic forces to coherent purposes.

The Soviet Union has had the offensive capability to undertake an attack against U.S. command structure since the mid-1960s. With the improvements of the 1970s, neither the scale of the attack nor the technical weapons requirements would be particularly demanding for the deployed Soviet forces. Moreover, the Soviets have also signaled an appreciation of command vulnerability and its importance both in their writings on military strategy and in extensive investments to protect their own command facilties.

Unfortunately, a pre-emptive attack on the U.S. command

structure is a rational defensive act for the Soviets once they have judged that nuclear war can no longer be avoided. Although it would preclude a bargained end of war, it offers two important advantages: First, by eliminating central coordination it sharply reduces the military effectiveness of opposing strategic forces; second, it offers some small chance that complete decapitation will occur and no retaliation will follow. The later possibility, however slight, is probably the only imaginable route to decisive victory in nuclear war. U.S. policy makers must assume that the Soviets have long realized that the U.S. command structure is the most vulnerable and valuable target and that they have planned strategic attacks to take advantage of the fact.

While developing attack strategies focused on the U.S. command system, the Soviets have also displayed great sensitivity to the vulnerability of their own command structure, and for understandable reasons. In addition to physical facts that render major command center and communications assests inherently vulnerable to nuclear weapons, a number of circumstances make the Soviet forces particularly susceptible to disruption. As a result of long tradition and deeply ingrained policies, for example, the management of Soviet military forces is highly centralized. The loss of central coordination would therefore probably have even greater consequences for the operation of Soviet forces than it would for those of the United States. Moreover, under most circumstances, including the crises experienced since World War II, Soviet strategic forces appear to be kept under unusually tight operational restrictions well short of the final preparations necessary for full-scale combat. Significant numbers of bombers and submarines are held in base areas, exposed to the possibility of surprise attack. As a result, these force components depend on the command system to initiate a timely protective dispersal. This observable pattern for the bombers and submarines may have more subtle analogues for the ICBM force.

Furthermore, the United States has base areas in Western Europe from which it might launch a carefully coordinated attack with very little tactical warning. Although the Soviets have made extensive investments in measures to protect their command systems and, whether by intention or necessity, have utilized relatively primitive communications equipment significantly less sensitive to nuclear weapons effects, the consequence of their systematic attention to the subject appears to be awareness of exposure rather than confidence in secure protection.

U.S. military planners have long understood the vulnerability of the U.S. command structure, the existence of an organized Soviet threat to it, and to a lesser extent the vulnerability of Soviet commanders. For technical, economic, and political reasons, however, U.S. strategic weapons deployment policies have not given this problem the central prominence it would seem to demand. First, the importance of command coordination for overall strategic capabilities is not easily calculated and cannot be included in standard measures of the strategic balance. This situation has retarded the development of any consensus on its significance.

Second, the protection of a command network against the effects of nuclear weapons is very difficult and expensive. Some dimensions of the problem were discovered relatively late in the process of strategic force development. If taken seriously, the problem might require re-investments large enough to threaten funding for powerfully supported weapons programs. Third, the centralization inherent in strategic command structure development runs counter to strong U.S. military traditions. U.S. military communications are not centrally managed, and political advocacy for investment in the area is correspondingly weak. All these reasons have left the topic dramatically underdeveloped U.S. strategic policy.

The resulting imbalance in policy is placing increasing strains on the logic and pattern of investment that underlie the U.S. strategic posture. It does not make sense to undertake a $30-50 billion program to reduce the apparent vulnerability of ICBM launchers while making only marginal improvements in protecting command structures on which the utility of the surviving ICBMs necessarily depends. Similarly, it does not appear militarily wise to undertake a provocative deployment of strategic missiles in Western Europe, where the U.S. command system is particularly exposed and vulnerable. Defense planners have nonetheless proposed this dubious allocation of effort in projecting the development of U.S. strategic forces—with considerable encouragement from then-candidate Reagan.

In announcing his own strategic weapons program on October 2, 1981, Reagan indirectly signaled that his judgements were beginning to alter. He postponed an attempt to solve the problem of ICBM vulnerability, and he upgraded investment in command structure assets, defining that investment as top strategic priority. He also proposed cruise missile deployments on submarines and thereby undermined the North Atlantic Treaty Organization commitment to a land-based deployment of these systems. These decisions are not sharp changes, but they suggest that the problems of command vulnerability are emerging into prominence as a new administration faces a new decade of U.S. strategic force deployment.

Potential Strains

Assuming that command vulnerability is the most significant problem of modern strategic forces, a number of important implications emerge. First, the conceptions of the strategic balance that have prevailed over the past 20 years are seriously misleading, and the U.S. reading of the history of these two decades must be revised accordingly. None of the popular measures of relative U.S. and Soviet strategic capability—delivery vehicles, warheads, equivalent megatonnage, lethal area coverage, hard target potential, or postattack force balances—takes command performance into account, even though it is undeniably a critical element of actual capability. No one at the moment can know with much precision how the balance would appear if an accurate quantitative assessment of command performance were made. Some general judgements, however, emerge.

The substantial superiority, for example, that the United States believed it possessed in the 1960s was sharply mitigated in reality by command vulnerability, which was particularly acute at the time. The then numerically and technically inferior Soviet forces could have done far more damage with judicious targeting than was ever acknowledged in the official U.S. public reviews of the strategic situation. Moreover, the sharp increase in Soviet offensive power that has occurred since the mid-1960s has not proportionately increased this vulnerability. Since only modest numbers of weapons are required to threaten the U.S. command system, increases beyond that level have little effect. U.S. strategic forces have always been seriously vulnerable to an initial attack, and the 1980s will not produce unusual dangers in this regard, as is often alleged.

Second, residual strategic forces—those surviving an initial attack and not used in immediate retaliation—have very limited military value because they cannot be coherently directed. U.S. investments designed to guarantee large residual forces are misguided, and crisis decisions to hold strategic forces in reserve are unrealistic unless the U.S. command structure can survive an attack or be rapidly reconstituted. Although Reagan has announced his intention to create such a command structure, an actual program to do so has not yet been technically defined or financially authorized.

Third, command vulnerability has produced powerful incentives within the U.S. military planning system to conduct full-scale strategic operations at the outset of any serious nuclear engagement. This bias is very likely strong enough and deeply enough entrenched to defeat any attempt to utilize strategic forces in limited engagements of significant size. Hence, once the use of as many as 10 or more nuclear weapons directly against the USSR is seriously contemplated, U.S. strategic commanders will likely insist on attacking the full array of Soviet military targets. Political motives for engaging in limited strategic attacks will not likely prevail against the risks of leaving a vulnerable command system exposed to counter-attack from a severely provoked enemy.

In effect, this situation means that the aspirations for survivable, highly flexible strategic capability, articulated in recent years as a requirement of deterrence under a counter-vailing strategy and officially mandated in 1980 by Presidential Directive (PD) 59, are so far from realization that they do not provide a realistic standard for managing current forces. If national commanders seriously attempted to implement this strategy in a war with existing and currently projected U.S forces, the result would not be a finely controlled strategic campaign. The more likely result would be the collapse of U.S. forces into isolated units undertaking retaliation on their own initiative against a wide variety of targets at unpredictable moments over a period of time that might last from several days to several weeks.

Soviet strategic forces are subject to the same pressures for pre-emption and immediate, full scale commitment in the event of war. But these pressures are acknowledged in a Soviet doctrine. As best can be judged from a distance, the Soviet Union has not attempted to resist these inherent pressures with commitments to nuclear operations that are sharply limited in scale. Thus, although the Soviet Union faces a similar strategic problem, it does not appear to be subject to the same doctrinal tensions that occur in the United States.

Fourth, under conditions of intense crisis, the existing U.S. command system is subject to strains powerful enough to trigger an unintended war. The command system is designed technically and organizationally to achieve two purposes. In peacetime, the objective is to establish negative control—to prevent unauthorized use of nuclear weapons while allowing for constant operational exercises. The system allows bombers to fly, submarines to cruise, and ICBM launch silos to be continuously manned with tolerably low risk that an accident or mutiny will occur.

Under imminent threat of war, the prevailing command system objective would necessarily shift to that of guaranteeing positive control—that is, the transmission of deliberate and effective instructions to undertake strategic attacks. Current capabilities can guarantee only the most rudimentary form of positive control: the initial communication of presidential authority to weapons commanders. In fact, even that capability could be rendered uncertain if a presidential decision is delayed or genuine tactical surprise is achieved.

These two objectives are thrust into conflict under crisis circumstances. If the elaborate procedures designed to guarantee negative control in peacetime are preserved right to the brink of actual war, the risk would be significantly increased that a pre-emptive Soviet attack might severely degrade, even possibily prevent, coherent retaliation. If these negative control procedures are effectively relaxed in the process of bringing weapons to a high state of readiness—a powerful institutionalized instinct in response to a crisis—then the possibility that war would be triggered unintentionally is increased. Military officers responsible for the execution of strategic missions want to secure positive control. Political officials powerfully motivated to avoid war want to maintain negative control.

As yet there is no experience adequate to gauge the power of these potential strains and no theory of behavior robust enough to yield a confident prediction. However, there are reasons for serious concern. For all the wonders of modern technology central leaders cannot direct the elaborate operations of the opposing U.S. and Soviet strategic organizations in exhaustive detail and cannot entirely subordinate those operations to strategic logic. The forces are operated by the decentralized actions of many different individuals and organizational units. They are not immune to the confusion, miscalculation, failure of coordination, and unintended consequences historically associated with military forces in crisis and war. Given their inherent vulnerability, they may be far more prone to such occurences.

These four implications of the command vulnerability problem all bode significant grief for current strategic policies. If elaborated and taken seriously, they would inevitably motivate striking changes in conceptions of the strategic balance, in the pattern of investment in nuclear forces, in principles of crisis management, in declaratory doctrine, and in the fundamental assumptions on which national security ultimately rests. At the very least, these implications set an agenda for serious reflection and public discussion.

A Priority Objective—Stabilization

In the strategic program Reagan announced on October 2, 1981, $18 billion was to be committed to maintaining and developing the strategic command structure over the course of the five year defense plan. At least $15 billion for additional command structure development has been proposed in connection with PD 59, but has not yet been incorporated into the defense budget. Complete implementation of all these programs optimistically might allow the command system to survive moderate levels of attack (50-150 weapons) and to exercise coordinating functions for a few hours to a few weeks. Even if achieved, that improvement would not eliminate the fundamental problem, but would alleviate the pressures of an intense crisis.

The ultimate effect of command system improvements depends on the context of security policy in which they are undertaken. Apparently desirable improvements could actually worsen the situation if the broader security implications are ignored or mismanaged.

This dependence on broader policy results from the lack of a purely tecchnical solution. Currently, a degree of protection consistent with the prevailing standard for strategic weapons themselves is not in prospect for the entire command system. First, it is much more difficult to preserve an operating national network than individual isolated units. If critical elements are lost, the network disintegrates even if significant portions should remain intact.

Second, some critical elements of the existing network are inherently vulnerable. Normal operations of the U.S. government require that its constitutional leadership be exposed most of the time. Immediate military commanders are less exposed, but it is in the nature of organizational hierarchy that they be fewer in number than the weapons commanders they direct. Communications equipment is necessarily exposed, not only to the standard weapons effects, but also to a variety of electromagnetic effects. In particular, a very small number of high altitude explosions (one to five) could subject the entire United States to short but intense electromagnetic pulses in the range of 25,000-50,000 volts per meter. Solid state circuitry of contemporary design heavily utilized in U.S. military technology and in critical civilian technology is particularly vulnerable to damage from these pulses.

Third, it is extremely difficult to protect space satellites against dedicated efforts to destroy them. Severe tradeoffs in peacetime performance are necessary to achieve high confidence protection of these systems, and none of the existing programs is designed for this purpose. As a result, the United States will remain vulnerable as long as current space programs are implemented and relied upon. In all, a high confidence technical solution to command system vulnerability cannot be achieved at feasible cost.

Given this circumstance an effective program for marginal improvements to the U.S. command structure must include a diplomatic dimension. The Soviet Union could probably offset the effects of a modest unilateral program to increase protection of the American command structure simply by adjusting Soviet operational plans and increasing the allocation of weapons from existing inventories to command and control targets. Should the Soviets choose to add weapons to their existing forces to negate the U.S. effort, neither existing arms control arrangements nor internal budget would impose effective constraint. An adequate American policy therefore requires careful consideration of the Soviet response and probably means influencing it.

The relative ease with which the Soviet Union could negate improvements in protection of the U.S. command structure is not in itself a decisive objection to pursuing those improvements. Raising the threshold of Soviet requirements for command structure attacks and reducing the confidence Soviet planners could reasonably have in the ultimate effectiveness of such an attack would benefit deterrence marginally. Deterrence and the prevention of war, however, are not the same thing. Soviet leaders could be powerfully deterred from war, and yet still conclude in the midst of a crisis that war will inevitably occur against their will. In that case, they would be strongly motivated to initiate a command structure attack to reduce the damage they would ultimately suffer. Thus, significant tradeoffs exist between the requirements of deterrence and of stablizing a crisis. The former requires manipulation of threat, the latter manipulation of reassurance.

As seen from current Soviet perspective, an extensive U.S. program to prepare the command structure to support a nuclear campaign will be understood as a sign of increased willingness to initiate war. That impression would intensify crisis pressures on the Soviets and might convince them of the inevitability of nuclear war at an earlier point in a serious crisis and on the basis of less compelling information. If that situation occurs, it can outweigh the marginal benefit to deterrence of less vulnerable command and control systems and can severely damage overall U.S. security.

These tradeoffs between deterrence and crisis management make the overall context of policy measures designed to address the command structure vulnerability problem extremely significant. If stark confrontation becomes the dominant theme of U.S.-Soviet relations and if political commitments are so defined that conflicts beyond the established lines of engagement in Europe and Asia become a potential occasion for using strategic nuclear forces, then there is strong reason to fear the ultimate effects of a major program to improve command structure protection. The degree of protection actually provided would inevitably be quite modest; the provocation to the Soviet Union potentially quite severe. Under those circumstances, the Soviets must be expected to match any improvements on the U.S. side with offensive force increases.

If, however, constructive stabilization of the U.S.-Soviet political relationship can be achieved, then increased command structure protection undertaken on the basis of an explicit bilateral understanding would markedly improve overall security. Stabilization of the U.S.-Soviet relationship is thus a necessary condition for an effective program of command structure protection and a priority objective of U.S. security policy.

Even if such stabilization should elude the most serious sustained professional efforts to achieve it, a minimum diplomatic requirement must be preserved as an imperative of security. Namely, a complete, simultaneous alert of U.S. and Soviet strategic forces under circumstances of political crisis must be prevented. Given the vulnerabilities of current forces and the strains to which they are subject, a full two-sided alert in crisis must prudently be considered tantamount to war and should not be undertaken for reasons less powerful than those required to justify war itself. This principle requires strict discipline over impulses to use strategic forces to send signals of resolve. It also mandates diplomatic efforts to keep strategic forces disengaged from secondary issues where the interests at stake are not sufficient to justify their actual use. Linkage of strategic forces to political conflicts in the Third World is not desirable policy and should not be considered a political inevitability; rather, it is a threat to be resisted.

The United States can ill afford emotions or illusions of any sort in dealing with the problems of command vulnerability. Purging security policy of such influences and establishing a realistic grasp of the circumstances in which the United States finds itself should be the overriding commitment of the coming decade.

Chapter 13

The Terrifying Prospect: Atomic Bombs Everywhere

Daniel Yergin

In an automobile accident there is the long moment before impact, when you see the other vehicle coming toward you, and you realize that a collison is imminent, and you cannot believe what is going to happen. At last, you hear the sound of colliding metal, and you know that it is too late.

The people of the world are at such a moment, on course for a nuclear collison. The question is whether it is already too late to change direction. Nuclear warfare has been a possibility for more than three decades. But suddenly the threat has intensified—not because of political instability, but simply because of the prospect of widespread proliferation of nuclear armaments. It is not too much to say that we are entering the Second Nuclear Age—the age of proliferation.

While many countries use nuclear energy as a source of power, there are only six "nuclear weapon states" today—the United States, the Soviet Union, Britain, China, France, and India. But recent technical, economic and political changes have brought nuclear weapons within easy reach of many others. Israel seems very close to a nuclear weapons capability though it feels safer being secretive on the subject. A host of other countries could soon qualify for admission to what newspapers call "the nuclear club"—countries such as South Korea, Iran, Pakistan, South Africa, Brazil, Argentina, Taiwan, and Spain. Turkey's defense minister has publicly discussed his country's developing nuclear weapons and the Yugoslav Communist Party newspaper not long ago suggested that some atomic bombs would contribute to the nation's security. A number of Arab countries are exploring ways to obtain nuclear weapons. Libya's president has said that in the future "atomic weapons will be like traditional ones, possessed by every state according to its potential. We will have our share of this new weapon." So eager is Libya that a few years ago it actually went shopping for a bomb. Both France and China are reported to have refused to sell.

In the First Nuclear Age, a country that wanted a bomb had to mount an expensive, complex program. In the Second Nuclear Age, a country acquires the capability to produce a nuclear weapon with relative ease as a by-product of developing nuclear power. According to present plans, some forty countries will have nuclear energy programs by 1985. Each program would produce enough nuclear material for three or more bombs. Most of them would have enough material for thirty or more bombs.

Looking to 1990, projections indicate that reactors in the Third World alone would be producing enough nuclear material for 3,000 Hiroshima-type bombs a year. In such circumstances, so-called "sub-national" groups—terrorists—could take as hostages not planes but a reactor, or even an atomic bomb, or nuclear waste products, and then their terror would reach to an entire city or even a nation. The problem gets worse year by year. In 1995, up to a hundred nations could have the knowledge, facilities, and raw material that, with little extra effort, would enable them to manufacture a bomb.

David Lilienthal is now seventy-seven years old. His experience with nuclear energy goes back almost to its beginnings. In 1946, he helped to draft America's first plan to control nuclear weapons and became the first chairman of the Atomic Energy Commission. He once shared the dream that the atom could bring good as well as bad into the world. But he now looks with something akin to horror at what is happening. He recently described the proliferated world as "the terrifying prospect for the young men and women who are looking to a future."

"I am glad," he added, "I am not a young man, and I am sorry for my children."

The Second Nuclear Age

On that day, shortly after nine in the morning, the Indian

foreign minister received a phone message: "The Buddha is smiling." An hour or so earlier, in an underground site in the Rajasthan desert, a hundred miles from the Pakistan border, the Indian Atomic Energy Commission had set off a nuclear device. It was officially announced to the world as a "peaceful nuclear explosive experiment." But there is no discernible difference between a "peaceful nuclear explosion" and the detonation of a prototype for an atomic bomb. Indeed, no satisfactory peaceful use has yet been found for nuclear explosions. India had become, in the words of an official in the U.S. Arms Control and Disarmament, "a fourth-rate nuclear power." The Indian device was similar in design and power to the Nagasaki bomb, and, while lacking a large arsenal or sophisticated delivery systems, India is certainly more advanced than the United States was after Hiroshima and Nagasaki.

Mrs. Gandhi congratulated her scientists: "They worked hard and have done a good, clean job." The Indian newspapers headlined, "Nation is Thrilled" and "Indian Genius Triumphs." Canada, which had shared its technology with India, expressed shock that a country with so many economic problems, and in the face of assurances it had given Canada, would divert precious resources in order to develop nuclear weapons. The Indians said they had not violated any assurances because they had used uranium mined in India to make the explosive. Canada suspended and then cancelled its $100 million a year assistance program with India.

The Indian test in the Rajasthan desert ushered in the Second Nuclear Age. It dramatized the fact that we could soon be living in the midst of what has been called "a nuclear weapons crowd." As the director of the Indian Institute for Defense Studies reminded the rest of the world, "The nuclear powers thought they could simply lock up technology. It was absurd."

Powerful forces have promoted the spread of nuclear technology. To make sense of them, we need first to back up several months from the Indian explosion to the "October Revolution" effected by the OPEC oil cartel in the autumn of 1973. The October revolution revealed several dangers to most industrial and developing countries. These countries were highly vulnerable for they were dependent primarily on a small number of Middle Eastern producers for their supplies. The price hikes delivered a stunning blow to their economies, and many people became convinced that the world would run out of oil within a few decades.

Fortunately, or so it seemed at the time, a "deus ex

technologica" was standing in the wings to rescue the world from dependence on OPEC oil—nuclear power. "With the increase in the world of both population and industrialization, we will have no choice for the years after 2000 but to accept nuclear energy," observed a senior official concerned with energy for the European Community in the autumn of 1975. "Everybody is convinced that nuclear energy will develop very quickly."

But as the renewed drive for nuclear power took shape, relatively few people were willing to face up to a most alarming fact—that when a country develops a nuclear capability, it is much of the way toward developing a nuclear device. "A great many countries," the strategist Albert Wohlstetter of the University of Chicago has pointed out, "as a result of their civilian nuclear energy programs and the policies of nuclear exporters, can come within days or hours of assembling nuclear explosives without breaking any of their promises to abstain from making or receiving them."

"There are not two atoms, one peaceful and one military," he said. "They are the same atom."

The Plutonium Economy

The central problem is the "nuclear fuel cycle." This term suggests something pleasing, fulfilling, natural. It is not natural, for it involves tampering with natural uranium to create a new form of uranium as well as a number of elements that do not exist in nature and are very dangerous.

The cycle has, depending on how detailed one gets, between seven and eleven steps. The first several involve the mining of uranium and its preparation for the reactor. Then comes its actual use as fuel. The last step involves the storage and disposition of the nuclear waste—that is, the leftovers after the uranium has done its job.

Two points in this fuel cycle intersect with the manufacture of an atomic bomb. Both stages produce what is variously known as fissionable or "fissile" material, which could be used as an explosive rather than a source of nuclear power.

As it is mined, uranium is not quite suited for nuclear reactors. It consists mostly of the stable U-238, with typically a .7 percent concentration of the isotope U-235. It needs to be "enriched" to about 3 percent U-235 in order to sustain a controlled chain reaction in the type of reactor developed in the United States. A nation that has enrichment facilities can go ahead and enrich uranium to a concentration of U-235 much higher than 3 percent. Then it is in a state suitable for use as the explosive core of an atomic bomb. Highly enriched uranium was the material used in the Hiroshima bomb.

Further along in the fuel cycle, at what is called "the back end," after the enriched uranium has been consumed, there is the nuclear waste or ash, containing many different radioactive and toxic materials. Some of these wastes can be chemically separated and used again as fuel in the reactor. The two principal materials so recoverable are uranium and plutonium, a man-made element. Plutonium was the substance of the Trinity and Nagasaki bombs.

The most intense concern focuses on the plutonium at the back end. Uranium enrichment is a costly, complex process. While it is not easy to extract plutonium from other wastes, it can be done through what is now the rather standard and less costly process of chemical separation. So even nations dependent on outside sources of enriched uranium can use it to produce their own plutonium.

Plutonium is the nub of the proliferation problem today. It has two uses. It can be separated for use as a fuel in a reactor, and there are those who think such plutonium will become a major nuclear fuel in the future. (Currently, reprocessing for this purpose is being carried out only on a small-scale developmental basis in Europe and the United States. No one has yet found the procedure economical.) But plutonium can also be used as one of the two basic materials for an atomic bomb.

The important point is that no country need decide that it specifically *wants* to accumulate stocks of plutonium. In buying a reactor from country Y, country X does not have to make a conscious decision to acquire nuclear weapons. The thought can be a mere haze, neither analyzed by planners in the foreign ministry nor costed by the economists in the budget office. The opportunity is simply handed over with the keys to the reactor. All that needs to be done is to start up the reactor, and plutonium becomes one of the country's resources. The plutonium used in the core of the Indian bomb was chemically separated from the radioactive exhaust materials produced in reactors outside Bombay.

A good-sized but still standard reactor could produce 200 kilograms of plutonium a year, while a crude implosion bomb requires a mere ten kilograms of plutonium. It is the contrast between these two numbers that causes so much alarm. For they indicate that a satisfactory operating atomic reactor would produce enough material for the explosive core of a bomb every two or three weeks. And in *The Last Chance*, William Epstein suggests that a plant for separating plutonium for the purpose of making a bomb could be constructed for as little as $3 million. If current plans and developments for nuclear power go ahead, there will be such a plutonium glut—as a source of fuel, in international trade, and in waste products—that people have begun to speak of the dangers of a widespread "plutonium economy." Plutonium will become extravagantly widespread if the breeder reactor comes into use.

"The real problem of proliferation today is not that there are numerous countries 'chomping at the bit' to get nuclear weapons," Albert Wohlstetter noted. "But rather that all the non-nuclear nations, without making any conscious decision to build nuclear weapons, are drifting upwards toward higher levels of competence."

Incentives

The October Revolution gave another kind of boost to atomic energy. The East-West split has been the historic impetus for the nuclear arms race of the last three decades. The United States, Britain, and France on one side, and the Soviet Union and China on the other, built up their stockpiles primarily to deter the other side. (Although, in the last several years, China and Russia of course have also been deterring each other.) But the October Revolution dramatized a different division—between North and South—pitting the Northern Hemisphere against the Third World "developing nations" in the Southern Hemisphere. In the United Nations and many other councils, the Third World countries have been asserting their independence, proclaiming on the subject of their equality, and, in general, blaming the First World for all their problems. Some of them believe that the acquisition of nuclear weapons is one of the most visible ways to assert their power and influence. It does no good for Westerners to express worry about the dangers for everybody in the spread of nuclear weapons, for the Third World responds (in the words of a leading Indian spokesman) that such concerns are "modern versions of the doctrine of the white man's burden." Nuclear weapons are taken as a sign of prestige and influence. After all, it was not Mrs. Gandhi but Charles de Gaulle who announced, on the day of its first nuclear explosion, that France was "stronger and prouder since this morning." But it is not only countries such as India that want to augment their prestige and influence with nuclear weapons. Now, as a result of the drastic increase in oil prices, a country such as Libya has not only the desire but also the wherewithall in cash to buy nuclear technology.

There are more specific incentives at work as well. Such

countries as India, Brazil, and Iran are striving for what is now known as "regional hegemony." Nuclear weapons are one way to assert their seigniorial rights. But such steps of course only encourage further proliferation. Just as China's nuclear test in 1964 helped induce India's effort to make the bomb, so India's test a decade later had much the same effect on Pakistan, whose prime minister warned that if India took any more steps in the direction of building an atomic arsenal, "We will eat leaves and grass, even go hungry, but we will have to get one of our own." Pakistan is now strenuously seeking to assure itself that it too has the weapons option.

There is a final incentive. For decades a number of nations have lived and prospered under America's "nuclear umbrella." It has been understood, or implicitly guaranteed by treaty, that if their security is at stake, the U.S. nuclear arsenal stands behind them. But the umbrella has lost some of its covering in recent years. South Korea is not sure that it is protected anymore. Taiwan worries that it will soon be excluded. Therefore, as nations fear that they will be standing in an exposed place, they are sorely tempted to raise their own umbrellas, to develop an independent deterrent.

Living in a Nuclear Crowd: Bad Dreams

Even if we cannot predict how a conflict might occur, we can develop likely possibilities.

1.) *Undermining the balance of terror.* So long as there was a sharp distinction between the nuclear weapons states and all the rest, a kind of stability—absurd but real—prevailed. The superpowers have, at least to date, been in agreement on an implicit rule to contain crises. The closest they ever came to breaking that rule was over Cuba in 1962. But as more and more states acquire nuclear capability, more and more nations (including our own) will feel a heightened sense of insecurity. Nuclear proliferation raises havoc with all the calculations about the nuclear relationship between the United States and the Soviet Union. Current defense thinking is based on the notion that in order to have nuclear stability, there must be parity and balance between the two superpowers, so that no intelligent person will make a mistake.

"There cannot be a balance where there are many different parties with many different objectives and with entirely different levels of technology," says scientist Herbert York, who has been involved in the American atomic weapons program since World War II. "So if there is—and there does seem to have been—a stability in the nuclear relationship between the

United States and the Soviet Union, the stability will be wiped out by proliferation. Even its theoretical underpinnings will be wiped out."

On a visit to China before he became secretary of state Cyrus Vance pointed to one form of the danger when, in a discussion with Teng Hsiao-p'ing, he said, "The hazards of accidental launch are real and could have devastating effects if one didn't know where the weapon was launched from. Accidental launching will become more likely with the indiscriminate spread of nuclear weapons."

2.) *The chain reaction.* One can easily imagine Israel being pushed to the wall. Arab forces are advancing on Tel Aviv. The Israelis begin assembling nuclear weapons. The Russians learn of this and dispatch warheads. The United States in turn detects the Soviet warheads in transit. And the world is on the edge of destruction. But the chain can start with any client states. Both Iran and Iraq could become nuclear weapons states. In a nuclear clash between these two states, how long could the superpowers stay out? Where would it all end?

3.) *The easing of the taboo.* The world slowly becomes accustomed to the idea that nuclear weapons are not merely for deterrence, but actually of considerable value in war. Perhaps India and Pakistan go to war, or Brazil and Argentina. Each side uses nuclear weapons, millions are killed, but one side emerges a decisive winner. While the superpowers are not drawn in, this spectacle reduces the taboo and makes it easier for other ambitious leaders to contemplate the use of nuclear weapons.

4.) *Microproliferation.* A terrorist group or even the Mafia attempts to steal plutonium—despite toxic risks—from either a power station or a reprocessing plant, or while it is in transit. This they use to blackmail one or more governments, either for money or for some political aim. Physical security is never perfect. Not long ago, a lunatic walked unnoticed into the control room of a French nuclear plant and randomly threw several switches before being detected. Such a danger is so real that in the United States guards now have shoot-to-kill orders at fourteen federal nuclear installations. As the number of power stations increases, as the trade in nuclear material and the plutonium economy expand, and as a covert, semilegal "grey market" in sensitive items grows, the threats become so serious that they result in security measures that have a corrosive effect on democratic institutions, for people come to fear that the dangers could not be met without a more authoritarian political system.

The microproliferation threats, however, are more likely to occur in the unstable political systems of the Third World. Thomas Schelling of Harvard University engaged in some chilling speculations in the journal *International Security*. How different might the course of events have been in Lebanon in late 1975 and early 1976, he asked, had the country had even a small pilot plant for extracting plutonium from spent fuel? "Who would have guarded the facilities? Who would have destroyed them, from nearby or from afar, at the risk of spreading deadly plutonium locally to keep bomb material from falling into mischievous hands? What outside country might have invaded if the spoils of war would have included a nuclear-weapon capability, even only to deny that capability to some other greedy neighbor?

"One thing is certain: in years to come there will be military violence in countries with sizable nuclear power industries."

America's Two Atoms Policy

From 1949, when the Americans realized that the Russians had the bomb, until 1974, when the Indians exploded their device and the Buddha smiled, proliferation was not of much concern in Washington. This omission seems very odd. After all, one would think that the United States, as progenitor of nuclear weapons and nuclear power, would have had some proprietary interest in the subsequent spawning and that special attention would be given to the relationship between atomic power and the atomic bomb. Such was indeed the case in the years immediately after World War II. In 1946, Robert Oppenheimer pointed out that the "heart of the problem" of international control was "the close technical parallelism and interrelation of the peaceful and the military applications of atomic energy."

But this connection was quickly forgotten. After Hiroshima and Nagasaki, there was a powerful emotional drive to find peaceful uses, something good to do with the atom, in order, somehow, to compensate for its horrors. Furthermore, once the Russians had the bomb, the worst seemed to have happened, and fears about the spread were forgotten. There were also strong economic incentives. And so, in 1953, President Eisenhower proposed Project Plowshare and Atoms-for-Peace. The next year, the United States approved the export of nuclear power technology to other countries.

Thereafter, American interests in this realm were defined by a nuclear energy Establishment: government agencies such as the Atomic Energy Commission and the Defense Department; the congressional Joint Atomic Energy Committee; and such industrial allies as Westinghouse and General Electric. Both the AEC and the Joint Committee were committed to the "maximum" utilization of atomic energy. The Joint Committee may well have been the most powerful congressional committee in history. It certainly did a masterful job of pushing a disproportionate share of government research funds into nuclear energy, to the detriment (as we know today) of other forms of energy research. Since the Establishment wanted to promote nuclear power on a worldwide basis, little thought was given to proliferation or to nuclear waste disposal. It has only recently been discovered that the Atomic Energy Commission lost track of sizable quantities of weapons-grade material leased to a score of foreign countries in the 1950s and 1960s. "For twenty years," said Victor Gilinsky, a member of the Nuclear Regulatory Commission, "(the nuclear export bureaucracy) had been freewheeling through the domains of diplomacy and international commerce—out of public view, and under the protection of a myopic Atomic Energy Commission and its own congressional committee."

When an organization or a group of organizations wants to "sell" something badly enough, whether it be nuclear power or a new drug, eyes tend to be shut to possible side effects, especially if they seem far off. Such is what happened with the Atoms-for-Peace program. "Many mistakes were made in the way we executed the idea," observed Fred Ikle, former director of the Arms Control and Disarmament Agency. "We now can see many forks in the road, many points where we could have taken a different technological direction. We could have chosen a course that might have greatly reduced the risks of nuclear proliferation without any loss in terms of economical operation of power reactors."

But we did not. The conventional American reactor, the so-called light-water reactor, is, after all, a spin-off from the World War II atom project, for which plutonium was a highly desired end product and, more directly, from the subsequent development of the Navy's nuclear-powered submarines. Habit was strong, and little thought was given to designing reactors that would not involve the dangerous steps in the fuel cycle.

"What is used for reactor design in the United States today is not the same design as for making plutonium for military purposes," said the late George Kistiakowsky, one of the most prominent scientists in the Manhattan Project and subsequently science adviser to President Eisenhower, and professor emeritus of chemistry at Harvard. "But our commercial light-water reactors are derivative copies of the submarine reactor.

This is the result of the AEC's having been staffed with people who had worked on Admiral Rickover's nuclear submarine program. There could have been other pathways. The Canadian design is in some ways less risky, because its spent fuel is not very desirable for plutonium extraction. The British design is different again. But there was a determined drive by the AEC to adopt the light-water reactor because people in the AEC were to a large degree Rickover's people." In addition, General Electric and Westinghouse were eager to capitalize commercially on their experience in the Navy's reactor program.

Those in the nuclear Establishment held to an underlying faith that the appropriate technological "fixes" would be found for all problems—at the appropriate time. Furthermore, proliferation dangers seemed pretty far away. By the 1960s, the United States was not much worried that it allies in the First World, beyond the French and the British, would seek their own nuclear arsenals. Certainly there was no need to worry that the Russians would be so reckless as to trust *their* potentially unreliable allies in Eastern Europe with nuclear weapons. And it is difficult to imagine in the 1950s and the 1960s that Third World nations would organize themselves sufficiently and acquire the wherewithal and skills to move on to a nuclear weapons capability. That was a severe miscalculation.

After the first Chinese test in 1964, President Johnson, at the instigation of Defense Secretary Robert McNamara, appointed a high-level committee under Roswell Gilpatric to assess the dangers of proliferation and recommend whether or not non-proliferation should be made a top priority of U.S. foreign policy. The preliminary international negotiations for a nuclear non-proliferation treaty (the NPT) had already begun. Johnson was also looking for gestures before the November presidential election that would show that he was "doing good."

How Safe are Safeguards?

Finally, in 1968, the United States did reach agreement with the Soviet Union and other states on a non-proliferation treaty. It went into force in 1970. The International Atomic Energy Agency became the "executive" for the NPT. Headquartered in Vienna, the IAEA was founded in 1957 as a result of the drive to find a peaceful atom that would do good around the world. The agency was supposed to promote peaceful uses of atomic energy, but at the same time to apply "safeguards" to prevent the diversion of peaceful developments to military purposes.

Since the technological and economic barriers to proliferation are coming down, the effective potential barriers are political, and the most important is certainly the non-proliferation treaty. Unhappily, it is a product of the First Nuclear Age, and is not very effective in the Second.

The NPT system has a number of notable problems. While the IAEA has been getting stronger all the time, it is still not up to the new pressures thrust upon it. It was fine in a world of relatively few nuclear states, but it will need many more trained people to carry out safeguards in a world with hundreds of reactors, and it is not at all obvious where such people will come from.

One can also read too much into safeguards. The IAEA can evaluate plans for atomic facilities, review records of the movement and use of nuclear material, and carry out inspection and surveillance of plants—where and when allowed by the host country. It is an accounting system. What this comes down to is a threat, "the deterrence of nuclear materials diversion by detection." But detection can be evaded, and agreements canceled. What would happen if cheating were discovered? IAEA officials have no definite channels for making their findings public. To whom would the information be conveyed? Who would be the policeman? That mysterious and often sluggish creature "world public opinion"? What would be the punishment? Even if the United States and the USSR got together to apply heavy pressure on the violator, would not many nations see this as rather hypocritical—as two nations with tens of thousands of nuclear weapons getting mad at some developing country that only wants two or three little ones?

There is another problem with safeguards: reprocessing large quantities of plutonium for commercial use in a reactor is still a relatively complicated and demanding undertaking. But to reprocess for just a few bombs is a much easier task. The quantities needed are so much smaller. The requisite facility might require only a dozen people to operate it.

The rationale of safeguards—and here is the critical point—is that the diversion from peaceful use will be discovered well before the violator reaches a nuclear weapons capability, thus exposing him to the risks of international reaction. And yet when a nation has not only reactors and low-enriched uranium but also a stockpile of separated plutonium or facilities for separation, then the value of safeguards—accounting and inspection procedures—is greatly diminished. Even though safeguarded and stockpiled for peaceful future uses, this plutonium is only a short step away from use as an explosive.

"Should the owner decide, for whatever reason, on a sudden

move to appropriate the material for illicit purposes," Victor Gilinsky has said, "the time between diversion of plutonium and complete weapons can be sharply reduced to what might be a matter of weeks, or conceivably days. Under thse circumstances, even if it were assumed that IAEA inspection and monitoring systems were improved, it is hard to imagine that an international reaction could be mustered before the assembly of nuclear weapons was completed."

The second problem with the NPT is that although over a hundred countries have ratified the treaty, China, France, India, Argentina, Brazil, Pakistan, Saudi Arabia, Israel, and Spain have given no indication of signing.

The NYT and the IAEA are caught in a contradiction. On the one hand, they aim to prevent the proliferation of nuclear weapons. On the other hand, they are charged with encouraging peaceful uses. But to repeat, there is only one atom. So the NPT system encourages the diffusion of the *capability* to become a nuclear weapon state swiftly, even while trying to prevent it. Also, a nation can opt out after having benefited from sharing the technology of other members. "I don't think withdrawal would be lightly treated," said one U.S. official much involved with the NPT. But after all, a country need give only ninety days' notice, and then it can legally quit the NPT.

What Is To Be Done

"As forces for proliferation are rising, our historical leverage to impose restraints is eroding," warned the secret memorandum that was the basis for the turn-around of the Ford administration. Such sentiments were faced by the Carter administration: How much power over proliferation does the United States have in the Second Nuclear Age. The Reagan administration has done little about the problem.

Many argue that it is already too late. "The technology is not all that magical, and we're not a monopoly," William Anders, a former chairman of the Nuclear Regulatory Commission has said. "The only way to have our way is to be involved, to not opt out, to set the pace, to set the moral tone, if you will." Those who stand to make money from nuclear technology— industry—agree, and are even more outspoken. They argue that the best way we can continue to influence events is by competing aggressively in the marketplace.

This is a distortion. The United States continues to hold dominant power. "We are still *numero uno*," said NRC Commissioner Gilinsky. The United States holds about 70 percent of the nuclear business worldwide. The reactor industries of the other

major exporters—France, West Germany, Canada—are all
deeply involved with the U.S. industry and technology, and of
course these nations are our partners in the Western security
system. A United States that put "anti-proliferationism" at the
top of its agenda would have a profound effect.

There is no single solution of course, but a great number of
initiatives can be taken to induce dramatic change and help
reduce dangers. (Deftness is also required, especially as the
United States does not come to the subject with an unblemished
record. "We have to work out a political approach that doesn't
set us up as morally superior," says a State Department official.
"The sledgehammer approach is not the best way of getting
others to see the problem the way we do. In fact, it will have
exactly the opposite effect of what we want.")

There are a number of other political options.

1.)*The demonstration effect.* By one estimate, the United
States has some 30,000 nuclear weapons. In current lingo, the
accumulation of nuclear weapons is known as "vertical proliferation." Some of those most worried about "horizontal
proliferation" scoff at the notion that vertical proliferation has
any relevance to the problem. But, in the minds of Third World
citizens, the connection is real. Why should they be denied
nuclear weapons, Third World leaders ask themselves, when
the superpowers go along building up their arsenals? Under the
NPT, the superpowers are obliged to reduce their own arsenals,
but this obligation has not exactly been observed. When James
Schlesinger was Secretary of Defense, he talked about creating
a "credible response"—that is, suggesting that nuclear weapons are not merely weapons of last resort but also have a
rather precise role to play in limited battlefield conditions. This
sounded as if the United States was saying that nuclear
weapons are after all quite useful tools. If it is true for the United
States, the Third World countries say, it is also true for them. A
serious effort to control the nuclear arms race between the
superpowers would have major meaning for the proliferation
problem. As Michael Nacht of Harvard's Program in Science
and International Affairs has said, "Progress in SALT will
positively affect the perception of some "have-nots" toward the
'haves' and should influence the domestic debate in threshold
countries in favor of restraint."

2.)*The prohibition effect.* Prohibit all nuclear explosions,
even the "peaceful" underground variety. The United States
and the Soviet Union signed a treaty banning tests above a
threshold of 150 kilotons in 1974. But this "threshold" is more
than *ten times higher* than the strength of the Hiroshima bomb.

Unfortunately, the Russians continue to hold to the mistaken belief that "peaceful nuclear explosions" can work wonders, like changing the direction of Siberian rivers, although, increasingly, it seems that such explosions are uneconomic, unbelievably crude for the task at hand, and dangerous. If the United States and the U.S.S.R. agreed to do away with all peaceful nuclear explosions, it would help to remove the cloak behind which India can disguise its weapons tests.

The Decisive Step?

Yet all these proposals could well prove inadequate. Even if they are all acted upon, we might nevertheless in the 1980s be living in a world glutted with plutonium. "At last we've reached the point where the people making decisions recognize the problem," observed Professor Irwin Bupp of the Harvard Business School's Energy Research Project, a leading analyst of the nuclear industry. "But they are putting more faith in institutional solutions than is justified. It's unlikely that you're going to be able to prevent further proliferation through international organizations and controls. The inevitable result of spreading nuclear power is a world of abundant plutonium, and that means a very high risk of malevolent use."

There is a final bold step that the United States could take: a retreat from nuclear power itself. A number of responsible observers have already called for such action. "We must hold back on a great expansion of nuclear power until the world gets better," said George Kistiakowsky. "It's just too damn risky right now."

When one looks at the decline in orders for new reactors in the United States one could conclude that such a retreat is already on. But the United States could go further and announce a moratorium on the new development of conventional fission nuclear power. (This would not preclude continuing research.) When all the doubts—about economics, safety, nuclear waste disposal, and proliferation—are added up, it becomes reasonable to ask whether fission power, at a billion dollars or so per reactor, is the wisest way to allocate resources for future needs.

An American moratorium could have a powerful demonstration effect, significantly slowing the spread of nuclear weapons competence. A moratorium would announce that the world's technological leader, the progenitor of atomic power, had examined it and found it wanting. Then many other countries would surely recalculate their own programs and look in other directions. It is already clear that nuclear energy makes little sense for the Third World. (Several studies now suggest that it is nothing short of ludicrous for a developing country to make the huge capital investment required for nuclear power.) In Western Europe and Japan, as in the United States, nuclear development lags far behind the expectations of only three or four years ago. As in the United States, the delays result from concern about cost, safety, and proliferation.

It is a commonplace conclusion that nuclear warfare could extinguish civilized life. Yet the fact today is imbued with new urgency. While there is no way to stop proliferation, there are many things to be done that could help to manage the Second Nuclear Age. Even in sum, they may not be enough. Yet there is no choice but to try, and swiftly, when the alternative is the terrifying prospect of atomic bombs almost everywhere.

Chapter 14

Treaty Verification: Why? How? And How Much Is Enough?

Karl Pieragostini

Much recent debate in the US on arms control has centered on verification as a litmus test for proposed and existing arms control agreements. But there is obvious disagreement over the nature of the test. President Reagan tells the public that a comprehensive freeze is dangerous because it is unverifiable. Former senior intelligence officials William Colby and Herbert Scoville, Jr., however, say a freeze is good arms control and can be verified. This disagreement stems from profoundly different views of what verification can and should do.

Verification is the means by which the US, or any other state, determines whether its security interests are better served within an arms control treaty relationship with others, or outside it. Those who actually oppose arms control, however, often use verification as a weapon in their fight against agreements. They do so in two ways: by inflating the degree of verification needed; and implying that verification is dependent upon "trusting the Russians." They mislead the public on both counts.

In entering into an arms control agreement with the Soviet Union, the US agrees to restrict current or future actions in return for reciprocal, self-imposed restraint by the Soviets. It is

209

a bargain based on mutual self-interest, and verification protects those interests. No state can be expected to remain party to a treaty which has come to threaten, rather than protect its security.

"Adequate" Verification is Better Than "Iron Clad"

No treaty, however, can be "absolutely" verifiable. The United States cannot be certain at all times that all aspects of every treaty provision are being honored to the letter by the Soviets. No state operates in an environment of complete information. The "iron clad" verification President Reagan called for in his November 1982 address to the nation is an unattainable goal which if actually pursued will prevent any meaningful negotiated arms control or disarmament. During the debate over ratification of SALT II, opponents of the treaty attempted to redefine the criteria for verification by arguing that the US had to have the capability of detecting virtually any Soviet breach of the treaty, no matter how small. They were largely successful. If this revisionist view is allowed to stand, meaningful arms control will remain out of reach. "Adequate" verification is more realistic than "iron clad" verification. It is also a standard that will better promote our national security. Let us see why.

Richard Nixon, not a person often accused of being soft on the Soviets, sent his negotiators to the first SALT session in 1969 with instructions that "any agreed measures must be subject to *adequate* verification."[1] This was defined as the ability to determine Soviet compliance with treaty provisions "to the extent necessary to safeguard our security." George Seignious, as Director of the Arms Control and Disarmament Agency (ACDA) re-emphasized this before the Senate Foreign Relations Committee a decade later, arguing that the US required a capability "to ensure that any Soviet non-compliance will be detected before it can pose a significant military risk or adversely affect the strategic balance." [2]

Deciding if a certain activity by the Soviets is militarily significant for the US is a matter of determining the effect of that activity on US capabilities. Here it becomes important to determine if US nuclear policy is one of deterring a Soviet attack or creating a war-fighting capability. A treaty which controls nuclear weapons meant for deterrence is easier to verify. One ironic advantage of the enormous size of the nuclear arsenals amassed by the two super-powers is that small changes to the force structures of either side will have no effect on deterrence. The nuclear balance is insensitive to such tinkering. If, on the other hand, one wanted to preserve the war-fighting capabilities of nuclear weapons, more stringent verification would be required. It would be necessary to ensure that a war-fighting edge were preserved, and any cheating which gave the Soviets a marginal advantage would be important. US nuclear weapons policy, either deterrence or war-fighting, will provide the yardstick for "significant" cheating, and the more significant the possible cheating, the more stringent the verification requirements will have to be.

Verification As a Process

Verification's most familiar aspect is the sophisticated monitoring technologies used. But there is more to verification than a technologically derived answer to a technical question. Verification is actually a larger process which involves political judgments and, hopefully, the cultivation of goodwill.

The process has reasonably discreet steps. During treaty negotiation, agreement is reached on the restrictions to be imposed and cooperative measures which can assist in their verification.[3] Once the treaty is in force, monitoring of the agreed restrictions is undertaken to collect data on possible breaches of the treaty. This collected data is then analyzed to determine what is disclosed about the activities of the parties. A further, broader judgment is then made of what this means in terms of the treaty's effectiveness. Finally, a suitable response is decided upon and implemented.

Most of the steps in the process would be accomplished even if there were no need for verification.[4] The US intelligence community would still gather and analyze the data, and government officials would make judgments about its meaning and the need for a response. Verification places few new burdens on the intelligence and surveillance capabilities of the US.

Cheating

Verification plays two complementary roles. It provides the capability for timely detection of violations and, because of this, also deters cheating through the threat of discovery and unwelcomed military or diplomatic reactions by the other side. A prospective cheater approaching the problem in a very deliberate way would carefully weigh the likely costs and benefits of cheating.

Any concerted effort to cheat on a treaty would incur costs—even if the cheater were not caught. For example, a clandestine effort would require money, materials and workers, probably more of each than would be the case if the effort were open. Additionally, certain testing procedures would have to be changed or even foregone, adversely affecting the performance of the clandestinely produced weapon. A program to produce secretly a new missile and warhead, for example, could not include the normal quota of warhead explosive tests and missile flight tests without drastically increasing the likelihood of detection. Without full testing, the cheater could not have high confidence the weapon would perform as designed. A cost would be less confidence in the system's reliability than would normally be accepted.

If caught, the cheater faces markedly greater costs. What would the other side do in response? What would happen to the cheater's standing in the international community?

Generally speaking, the more to be gained through cheating, the larger the effort needed. The result is a greater probability of being caught prematurely and having to pay the price. Harold Brown described this as the "double bind" of cheating: the less likely it is that cheating will be detected, the more likely it is that the result of this cheating will be insignificant; and, conversely, the more significant the effort, the more likely it will be detected.[5]

The alternative of not cheating has attractions which must be weighed. Money will probably be saved because of reduced arms expenditure, and one's security will probably be enhanced because of constraints placed on the other side. There could also be a reduction in tensions which is generally welcomed.

Few individuals, let alone governments, make decisions in such a rational way. There is never enough time or information to consider all the possible consequences of certain actions. We usually do what seems to suffice at the time. Additionally, government decisions are often compromises made among individuals and departments, none of whom would have made that particular decision if allowed to act alone. Furthermore, actions which may appear from the outside to be the result of high level decisions, may in fact be due to autonomous decisions made at a much lower level in the hierarchy. Such "irrational" decision-making could result in cheating by one side despite a high likelihood both of being caught and of sufffering the consequences of the other side's response. It would benefit everyone, therefore, if a treaty promoted as rational a process of decision-making, at as high a level, as possible. This can be done in several ways.

An agreement could provide for an initial exchange of data

on weapons covered and require that this information be updated periodically. SALT II, for example, requires that data in ten areas be updated every six months. In this way, a prospective cheater is required every six months to reconfirm the decision to cheat. Knowing that cheating would not be a single act, but would require a semi-annual lie, would help promote more careful consideration of the original decision to cheat.

The more comprehensive an agreement, the more likely the decision to cheat would have to be made deliberately. A freeze on the testing, production and deployment of new systems, for example, would provide numerous hurdles where positive decisions to cheat would have to be made. For a completely new missile system, six separate decisions could be required: (1) to produce the required fissile material, (2) to test the necessary warheads, (3) to produce them in sufficient quantity, (4) to test a delivery system, (5) to produce it in quantity, and (6) to build silos for deploying them. If an agreement permitted all these activities to continue unrestrained except for the actual building of silos, cheating would be based on a lone decision, not a series of them. The more conscious decisions required, the more likely the result will be reasonably rational.

The demonstrated vigilance of one side will also encourage more rational and carefully considered decisions by the other. If the US routinely brings up for discussion every ambiguous activity it detects, the Soviets will come to appreciate the importance the US attaches to compliance with the strict letter of the treaty. This will encourage the higher echelons in the Kremlin to exercise strict control over activities that could be perceived as cheating. It would be useful to establish that evidence suggesting even insignificant and unintended cheating will require explanation.[6]

Breakout

The specter of "breakout" is often raised in connection with cheating. Breakout is the hypothetical case in which the Soviet Union secretly amasses a militarily significant nuclear force while the US faithfully adheres to treaty provisions. Once amassed, this force is suddenly unveiled by the Soviets, who make demands backed up by their clandestinely acquired nuclear advantage. With the state of the current arsenals, however, effective breakout would require a clandestine effort of enormous size. A few additional missiles will not, by themselves, prove significant. And the larger the effort, the more likely it will be detected before fruition.

Comprehensiveness helps here, too. The more comprehensive a treaty, the less likely breakout could occur. Treaties limited in scope allow the continuation of many activities associated with increasing a nuclear weapons inventory. In President Reagan's START proposal, for instance, no restrictions are placed on the production of fissile material, the testing and production of warheads, or the production of additional missiles. It appears to concentrate on deployed systems alone. It is conceivable, therefore, that the Soviets could, while remaining within the letter of START, develop, test and produce a new ICBM warhead, and a new missile on which to mount these warheads, limited only by storage availability. They could conceivably even develop, test and produce a new mobile launcher. This could result in a large number of mobile ICBMs and launchers *produced for storage* either as a hedge against future collapse of the agreement, or in preparation for breakout, and yet START would not have been infringed. A comprehensive freeze, however, would explicitly prohibit this sort of production for storage thereby making breakout much more difficult.

Responses

Responding to suspected cheating is part of the verification process. The object is to halt current cheating and deter future cheating by demonstrating that it is not in the best interests of the other side.

There are a range of possible responses. Most important for the long-term future of a treaty is, as has already been mentioned, the need to bring up all cases of suspected cheating or ambiguous data. In this way, concern for strict adherence to the treaty can be established. But if discussion brings neither a halt to the worrisome activity nor provides an acceptable explanation, other measures would be required.

The ultimate sanction is abrogation of the entire treaty. The threat to abrogate a treaty in response to any form or level of cheating, like the threat of a massive counter-city nuclear attack, is not always credible. This does not mean that abrogation is out of the question. If it were decided that compliance with treaty provisions had collapsed and the treaty as a whole was no longer in the interests of the US, then abrogation would be the logical decision. But such a decision need not be a blunt, irreversible, "bolt from the blue." SALT II, for example, includes a requirement that six months notification be given of intent to leave the treaty. This allows one side to demonstrate how seriously it views the other's actions, while leaving open the option of rescinding its notification if developments in the ensuing six months allow.

Other responses to cheating do not involve discarding the entire treaty. They involve more flexibility, allowing one to tailor the response to fit the violation. The object would be to prompt a reappraisal by the other side of what is, and is not, in its own best interests to do.

If the Soviets cause concern by breaking a provision of the treaty which is of sufficient importance to the US, Washington could respond with actions calculated to cause the USSR a similar amount of concern. The US could, for example, decline to provide information required by the treaty, or refuse to allow on-site inspections called for by the treaty. Alternatively, the selective infringement could be of the same type as Soviet cheating. For example, if the Soviets were to conduct an underground nuclear explosive test, the US could do the same. In either case the US would be responding in kind and/or degree. In most circumstances this would be a more credible alternative than total abrogation. It would be important, however, to ensure that a response did not appear as escalation.

Actions outside the realm of a treaty could include, for example, placing second strike strategic forces in a higher alert status. More submarines could be put to sea and a certain number of bombers could be kept in the air at all times. Other actions might involve conspicuous acceleration of certain research and development programs not covered by the treaty. Additionally, the testing, production and deployment of select-ed conventional weapon systems could be accelerated. Finally, putting one's case before the United Nations in an attempt to bring world opinion to bear should not be discounted, although experience shows that this alone will not suffice.

Other suggested responses stray from the subject of arms control, and are less likely to be effective: closing Soviet consulates; reinstating full travel restrictions on Soviets in the US; halting agricultural shipments; cancelling contracts or withholding shipments of manufactured goods; concluding agreements with foes of the Soviet Union, such as the Chinese; or re-establishing restrictions on Soviet bloc shipping.[7] The US experience in halting grain shipments, embargoing US gas pipe-line technology, and boycotting the Moscow Olympics in response to Soviet "misdeeds" indicates that linking diverse subjects is unlikely to prove successful.

To oversee the process of determining suitable responses, an independent, expert group might prove useful. Much critic-ism of SALT I focused on compliance issues. This criticism did not allege that US monitoring capabilities were not up to the job, but that there was a lack of will on the part of US officials to do anything about evidence which indicated possible cheating. Any arms control agreement will be subjected to such attacks, although genuine concern can be allayed if the public has confidence in the process through which compliance issues are handled. An "advisory commission on compliance" composed of members of the Cabinet, Congress, and the public has been suggested.[8] It could review cases of suspected cheating, judge whether cheating was taking place, and recommend appropriate action. It would be important for the commission to retain the confidence of the public, but it would also be helpful if it could deliberate in secret in order to encourage the Soviets to continue a frank discussion of compliance issues. The tension between these two requirements might be partially eased if the commission were composed of people of recognized integrity, independence and diversity.

Verification Capabilities

What assets would such a commission have at its disposal for the monitoring of a treaty? A treaty is monitored mainly through the use of sophisticated sensing technologies and special agreed procedures, although espionage and other activities also play a role. Anyone looking seriously at verification should have a general understanding of these assets, if only to avoid being intimidated by "expert" opinion.

Remote Sensors

The US employs a variety of imaging and non-imaging sensing techniques from four types of platforms: satellites, ground stations, ships, and aircraft. These represent the "national technical means" (NTM) often referred to in relation to verification.

Perhaps the most familiar of the imaging techniques is visible light photography. Cameras onboard at least three different types of US satellites can take high resolution photographs of objects on the ground.[9] The most sensitive can take pictures from an altitude of about 100 miles with a ground resolution of between four and six *inches.*

Not all satellite photography, however, uses such high resolution. As with other imaging sensors, cameras perform two monitoring tasks: "search-and-find", and "close-look". In the first, a wide area is covered in an attempt to discover indications of interesting activity. This requires a large field of view and usually means only moderately good resolution. Once something interesting is detected by a search camera, a high resolution, close-look camera can be called on to provide a more detailed picture. A low resolution search camera, for example, might take pictures which indicate construction activity of some sort near a Soviet ICBM field. A close-look camera could subsequently be used to take more detailed pictures of the area. Until the 1970s, the US used separate satellites to perform these two tasks. Now, however, a single satellite, "Big Bird", has the capability for both "search-and-find" and "close-look" photography.

Such cameras, however, detect only reflected light. They are useless at night, cloud cover can drastically reduce their effectiveness, and they can be fooled by camouflage. The use of systems sensitive to infra-red (IR) radiation helps fill part of this gap.

Thermal and photographic IR are exploited in verification. Thermal IR is radiated by anything emitting heat, such as an aircraft engine. It allows detection of heat emitting objects which are in the dark, under roofs, and beneath the earth's surface. Photographic IR is, like light, radiation from the sun reflected by an object. Special cameras use infra-red photography in conjunction with visible light to beat camouflage, although the resolutions attainable using IR are not as good as those using visible light alone. Several US satellites use IR sensors for "search-and-find" purposes. Additionally, US early warning satellites depend on IR sensing of missile plumes to warn of a Soviet attack.

The potential for exploiting IR emission in monitoring has been markedly increased through the use of devices called "mosaic infrared detectors". These detectors consist of millions of tiny cells which are extraordinarily sensitive. They are connected to integrated microelectronics which process the collected information. By recording what each element "saw", an image of the whole picture can be created in a fashion similar to the way newspaper pictures are made up of many black and white dots. These detectors will greatly increase satellite detection "telemetry".

Communications intelligence (COMINT) involves listening capabilities.

The KH-11 satellite carries a "multispectral scanner" that combines infra-red and visible light photography using mosaic detectors. The scanner is sensitive to a spectrum of radiation. During daylight hours, several pictures are taken simultaneously at a variety of wavelengths. These images are converted into digital form and transmitted to earth for further analysis. A different color is assigned to each image. The different images are superimposed to create a highly detailed "false-color" photograph which can reveal camouflage. For example, a mobile missile site might be hidden by a cover painted green to resemble the surrounding foliage. Neither the human eye nor conventional photography is likely to detect a difference between the cover and surrounding leaves. False-color photography, however, causes the paint to appear blue and the foliage bright red. The multispectral scanner on the KH-11 satellite probably attains a ground resolution of between five and ten feet.[10]

Radar is also important for verification because it can "see" at night and through clouds. Its major drawback is resolution. Because it uses microwaves, which have a relatively long wavelength, its resolution is much poorer than that attainable by a camera with a similar size aperture.[11] The aperture of a radar is controlled by the size of the antenna. The bigger the antenna, the bigger the aperture, and the better the resolution. But enormously large, movable antennas are not practical. Instead, large new static radar antennas use many small transmitting and receiving elements in an array linked to a powerful computer. The computer phases the transmissions and receptions to produce artificially the effect of a moving antenna. These "phased array" radars also provide a *continuous* picture of the target area, rather than the observable "sweep" seen on conventional radar scopes.

Ground and ship-based phased array radars are crucial in US monitoring of Soviet missile test flights. The "Cobra Dane" phased array radar on Shemya Island in the Aleutians can detect a basketball sized object at 2000 miles. Together with a ship-based phased array radar, "Cobra Judy" on board the USNS *Observation Island*, "Cobra Dane" can determine the missile's trajectory, velocity, acceleration, and number of warheads. The radars can even determine characteristics of the fuel by monitoring the effects the missile's exhaust flames and combustion have on the ionosphere.[12]

All of the "imaging sensors" outlined above can provide initial indications of interesting activity. Such tip-offs, however, also come from other, non-imaging means, such as "signals intelligence" (SIGINT).

SIGINT is information gleaned from the analysis of intercepted signals, including radio communications and radar emissions. These signals are collected by very sensitive receivers found in US satellites, onboard aircraft, and at ground stations around the world. There are different types of SIGINT, grouped by the source emitting the signal; the most important being COMINT, ELINT, and listening in on peoples' radio conversations. The conversations may be in code, and if the code is broken, important information may be revealed. Even if the code is not broken, the mere fact that certain facilities have begun communicating with others may indicate activity of interest. For example, an increase in communications between a Soviet missile test launch site and a down range impact site probably means that a missile test is in preparation. This could be deduced even though the exact information contained in the messages was encoded and therefore inaccessible.

Electronic intelligence (ELINT), on the other hand, involves listening to the transmissions of other people's electronic equipment not associated with communications, such as radars. An ELINT receiver in a US satellite, for example, might detect transmissions normally associated with a Soviet radar used at surface-to-air missile (SAM) sites. If the transmissions come from a location not before identified as a SAM site, a satellite-borne camera could shoot detailed pictures to determine if a new SAM site has been built. Naval ships are often tipped-off about the presence of other ships by the interception of their radar transmissions.

Another type of electronic transmission, telemetry, has been of direct use in monitoring the SALT treaties. Telemetry is information sent by radio signal from a test missile in flight, giving details of the missile's performance. In Soviet tests the information is transmitted in more than fifty separate streams, each containing a particular type of data to be analyzed by Soviet missile engineers. This telemetry, however, is also heard by US analysts, who can estimate the missile's launch-weight, throw-weight, range, type of fuel, and number of warheads, among other things.[13]

This is assuming the telemetry is sent "in the clear". The Soviets, however, have "encrypted" (coded) some telemetry from some missile tests. This began in the mid-1970s, and was of concern to US SALT II negotiators. Without access to unencrypted telemetry, US analysts would have had more difficulty in gauging the throw-weight of a missile, or the number of warheads it was capable of dispensing, both of which were to be limited by the SALT treaty. The Soviets, for their part, did not want the US to have access to information concerning capabilities not limited by SALT, such as missile accuracy. After much sensitive negotiation it was agreed that either side could encrypt only that telemetry which was not needed by the other to verify compliance with the treaty. For instance, the Soviets could encrypt information regarding accuracy, but not that regarding throw-weight or warhead numbers.

Two final types of remote, non-imaging sensors should be mentioned, as they are used to monitor nuclear explosions, an important subject for arms control. Such explosions can be detected from afar in essentially two ways: by detecting the emissions from the explosion itself, or by detecting and measuring the shock waves transmitted through the earth.

A nuclear explosion gives off neutrons, gamma rays and x-rays. It also causes an enormous flash of light due to the fireball, as well as a burst of electromagnetic energy called an electromagnetic pulse (EMP). Sensors mounted in US satellites can detect all of these emissions.

Nuclear explosions underground can be detected by seismometers located a considerable distance away. Seismometers also detect earthquakes, however, and the monitoring problem becomes one of distinguishing one type of seismic event from the other. Nuclear explosions differ from earthquakes in the type and relative strengths of the several waves generated, and these differences can be seen on seismometers.[14] Additionally, in many cases the geographic location and/or depth of an event distinguish it clearly as an earthquake. A recent study suggests that the current US world-wide seismic network can detect and identify underground explosions down to a yield of about one kiloton in hard rock.[15]

While this is an impressive array of capabilities, the US does not rely on NTM alone.

Cooperative Measures

US experience in negotiating with the Soviet Union shows that very important cooperative measures are available to augment "national technical means". Precedents have been established for measures to foster resolution of treaty related problems, to increase the effectiveness of NTM, to provide for some forms of on-site inspection, and to allow the emplacement of so-called "black box" sensors.[16]

Perhaps the most important result of US and Soviet cooperation has been the precedent of a treaty discussion forum, the Standing Consultative Commission (SCC), initially created by the ABM Treaty. Such a forum provides a means to establish the procedures needed to implement treaty provisions, and to discuss in detail possible helpful changes in these procedures or in the treaty itself. Additionally, prescribed treaty review can be accomplished, and an SCC-type forum is also a useful place in which to discuss new circumstances, the details of which could not be foreseen.[17] Most importantly, such a forum provides the opportunity to discuss questions of compliance with treaty provisions. It is not a court or third party for making judgements on compliance issues, but rather a mechanism for discussing, clarifying and resolving matters of concern, including ambiguous situations. These matters can be raised and discussed in a full and frank manner, and a consensus arrived at before irreparable damage is done to the confidence either side has in the operation of the treaty. To facilitate discussion and encourage consensus, it is helpful if compliance related matters are dealt with in private, which is the practice of the SCC. In this way, a discussion forum may act to promote consensus prior to either side taking its case before the public.

The SCC has dealt with questions and complaints concerning compliance. Regarding SALT I, every complaint brought to the SCC by either side in the 1970s was resolved by either a halt in the questionable activity or a satisfactory explanation of it. The Reagan Administration initially refused to bring SALT II related matters to the SCC for fear that doing so would legitimize a treaty the President had said was "fatally flawed." Once the efficacy of this forum became apparent to the new Administration, however, questions of compliance were placed before the SCC. The SCC has been one of the few unqualified successes of recent arms control efforts.

In SALT II negotiations, agreement was reached on important measures to aid NTM. These included pledges to refrain from hindering the collection of treaty related information by either interfering directly with NTM sensors or using deception to conceal relevant information from these sensors. Additionally, the two sides worked out definitions, "worst-case" counting rules, and special earmarking design features to assist the counting and evaluating of weapons by NTM.[18]

As noted earlier, US and Soviet negotiators have also established the precedent of a periodic exchange of information related to a treaty. Such an exchange of data, and its regular up-dating, can help by both enhancing the technical capabilities of NTM, and by providing a given base-line from which analysis can begin. For example, the Threshold Test Ban Treaty includes agreement to exchange data on geographic boundaries and geological characteristics of designated test sites. It also calls on the parties to share data from a certain number of tests to allow the calibration of seismic equipment. This information would undoubtedly improve the capabilities of seismic monitoring, but because the US has not ratified the Treaty the exchange has not occurred. Also, SALT II requires each side to provide and periodically update data information in ten areas which would help eliminate future disagreements.

Former high officials in the CIA point to another important type of information exchange. It involves the notification and confirmation of events. For example, SALT II required that prompt notification be given of the first and last (or twenty-fifth) test launches of the one new ICBM allowed. The Peaceful Nuclear Explosions Treaty requires *post*-event confirmation of the actual time of the explosion and the data derived from it. Advanced notification allows the monitoring side to ready its sensors to monitor certain activities. It could also be used by one side to advise the other of impending activities it does not want misconstrued. The more advanced information one side gets of the other's actions, the less likely it is that intentions will be misread. Post-event confirmation provides a useful check on the data collected by NTM. This would assist the monitoring of allowed missile test flights, and if agreement could be reached on the closure of certain military facilities, formal confirmation of closures would be helpful. For these reasons, former intelligence officials strongly argue that the US should try to get as many notification and confirmation provisions in a treaty as possible.

Much recent discussion on arms control has centered on the use of on-site inspection (OSI). OSI is a much more intrusive form of monitoring than is NTM, or even NTM aided by the cooperative measures outlined above. It involves the actual presence of foreign nationals in or near sensitive military related facilities, and is most useful in well-defined, restricted applications. It is neither a panacea nor a hobgoblin for arms control efforts.[19] "General OSI" is the most sweeping, and the least likely to be negotiated initially. It allows unrestricted access at any time by one side to the other's facilities and weapons systems constrained by the treaty. The very intrusive and wide-ranging nature of such inspection arrangements makes them unlikely candidates for adoption at the outset of an agreement. For this reason, opponents of arms control often call for general OSI, hoping it will scuttle the effort.

That is not to say that it is impossible to negotiate. The Antarctic Treaty bans any military activity on that continent. To ensure compliance, inspectors from each signatory are allowed access at any time to any and all areas of Antarctica including all stations, installations, equipment, ships and aircraft. It was possible to agree on such intrusive OSI partly because the agreement is a preclusive one, in that it prohibits potential activity rather than putting constraints on current practices. In this context general OSI is more acceptable, as it does not involve the presence of foreign nationals in or near permitted, but sensitive existing facilitites. "Selective OSI" places greater restrictions on the activities of inspectors. It is used to monitor specific constraints on specific weapons or facilities. The Peaceful Nuclear Explosions Treaty (PNE) and the Non-Proliferation Treaty (NPT) provide examples. The PNE has detailed provisions for selective on-site inspection. For certain explosions, inspectors from the monitoring side are allowed prior access to the site to inspect and to install monitoring equipment.[20] The treaty, however, has not been ratified by the US and is not, therefore, formally in effect. Central to the NPT's safeguards program are selective on-site inspections by personnel of the International Atomic Energy Agency. The program is designed to deter the diversion of nuclear material from peaceful to weapons purposes, and is based on a comparison of information provided by the inspected country and that gained through independent inspections by these IAEA personnel. In a decision of potentially great importance for future verification, the Soviets recently agreed to IAEA safeguards on some of their civilian nuclear power facilities. The IAEA already has safeguards on some US facilities.

Based on past experience, even selective OSI would present problems in US/USSR negotiations. The US would seek numerous, highly intrusive inspections, arguing that a few regularly scheduled inspections would be ineffective against determined cheating. The Soviets, on the other hand, would see in such an argument the desire to cloak espionage in the more respectable attire of arms control. The use of "control posts" also faces this difficulty.[21] Inspection "by challenge" has been suggested as a way out of this problem. It is based on the notion that it is easier to prove your own innocence than somebody else's guilt. When one party suspects another of infringing a treaty provision this suspicion is made known and the accused party is expected to provide sufficient information to allay the other's fears, including, if needed, an invitation to on-site inspection. During the negotiations on a comprehensive test ban, the US and Soviet Union agreed to the use of OSI by challenge.

It is sometimes mistakenly assumed that there are only two forms of monitoring: non-intrusive remote sensing from satellites and other such platforms, or intrusive on-site inspections by foreign nationals. There is, however, a third way which has the accuracy of on-site inspection without the same degree of intrusiveness. That is, the use of on-site, tamper-proof remotely monitorable devices which has already been agreed upon in principle by the US and Soviet Union. In 1978 at the tri-lateral Comprehensive Test Ban (CTB) negotiations, after much internal discussion, the Soviets agreed to a US proposal that each party accept ten seismic stations on its territory for the duration of the treaty. Seismic data would be transferred to the monitoring nation by satellite relay.[22] These negotiations, however, were subsequently suspended by the US.

In addition, the US Arms Control and Disarmament Agency (ACDA) and the IAEA have been testing a new monitoring system called "REmote COntinuous VERification", or RECOVER for short.[23] It uses remotely monitored, tamper-proof cameras and locks to assist the IAEA's surveillance and containment measures. In 1981, as director of ACDA, Eugene Rostow noted that continuous television monitoring could be used for on-site verification of future strategic weapons treaties between the US and USSR. The concept certainly provides the basis for a future system of remotely monitored, precise, on-site verification that could be both credible to the United States and acceptable to the Soviet Union, but the US government has shown little interest since Rostow's initial remark.

Other Means

National technical means and cooperative measures are not the sole means by which evidence of possible treaty violations can come to light.

Both the US and Soviet Union maintain large intelligence gathering agencies which use covert methods. Additionally, citizens of one side occasionally defect to the other, bringing with them classified information which could have a bearing on treaty compliance. Or a disgruntled citizen with access to evidence of cheating might simply make this available to the other side. Furthermore, an accident could unintentionally reveal to one side suspicious activity by the other. These agents, "whistle blowers", and blunderers, therefore, also have a role to play.

Former senior US intelligence officials say there is evidence the Soviets are very concerned about agent penetration of their highest policy levels. Much of this concern stems from the operations of Oleg Penkovsky, a Soviet official who acted as a U.S. agent. Penkovsky is credited with supplying information which helped in reassessing downwards the Soviet missile threat during the early 1960s, and he provided further information which helped lead to the discovery of Soviet missiles in

Cuba.[24] In contemplating their chances of successfully cheating, the Soviets would be at least partially deterred by memories of Mr. Penkovsky. "Whistle blowers" and blunderers are also a worry to the prospective cheater. If either side engages in activity that is contrary to the treaty, there is always a chance that someone connected with the activity will either defect or simply pass damaging evidence to the other side. A simple mistake or accident could also reveal cheating without the need for agents or informers. The more people involved in the activity, the greater the risk such revelations will occur.

As Secretary of Defense, Harold Brown summarized these verification "assets" in 1979 Congressional hearings: "The Soviets would also have to face the possibility that a clandestine effort could be compromised by a defector, an intelligence source, or an accident which revealed the nature of the activity. The larger the scale of the effort and the longer it went on, the more people would be involved and the greater the possibility of compromise would become. This serves as a further disincentive to cheat." [25]

Cruise Missiles

Cruise missiles present important problems for verification. Some would even say they herald the beginning of the end for verifiable arms control. Certainly, their small size, portability, and dual-capable nature make adequate verification much more difficult, but the problem is not necessarily an insuperable one. We cannot simply throw up our hands in despair. A combination of constraints should be sought which make cheating complicated and risky enough that it is not worth the effort. Closely monitoring cruise missile production or testing would be very difficult, and it would be better, therefore, to concentrate on deployment limitations. Nevertheless, the inclusion of bans or restrictions on production and testing would increase the problems faced by the prospective cheater, and should be viewed as useful supplements to deployment bans.

The SALT II process established the precedent of "worst case" counting rules for air-launched cruise missiles (ALCMs) on bombers, although the scheme could be used for missiles on any type aircraft. Using the SALT rules, a maximum allowed missile load for each type of aircraft of this type would be considered to have this missile load, regardless of what it actually carried, thereby eliminating the need to count individual missiles. Any aircraft detected with a configuration suggesting it could accommodate more than the maximum allowed number would be grounds for suspicion that cheating was being attempted. All Soviet ALCMs are currently externally mounted, making the detection of altered missile loads relatively easy to detect. The task would become more difficult were the Soviets to develop internal mountings, although a development of this sort would probably be detected when the aircraft were being modified. Again, any such alteration would be grounds for suspicion and demands for an explanation.

A ban on further deployment of sea-launched cruise missiles (SLCMs) would be monitored in a similar way. Like an ALCM, a SLCM is tied, so to speak, to an easily identifiable launch platform. As with aircraft and ALCMs, a maximum allowable loading could be established for ships and their SLCMs. Unlike aircraft, however, ships store all their cruise missiles internally, not externally where they can be counted. It w)uld be difficult to determine, therefore, if any individual ship was breaching the load limit. This uncertainty could be lessened through restrictions on SLCM launchers, which would be much easier to count than the missiles themselves. The launcher is an integral part of the ship, where it is, for the most part, distinguishable from afar. The US and Soviet Union could agree on which type launchers were used for nuclear capable missiles, and set a limit on the number of such launchers that could be deployed on any single ship of a certain class.

Submarine-launched SLCMs are not as amenable to such launcher counting, as the newer type of cruise missile is launched from the submarine's torpedo tubes. Nevertheless, a maximum allowable loading could be established. The prospective cheater would have a higher probability of success in beating this limit, but a submarine is not the roomiest of vessels, and any attempt to increase the missile loading significantly would probably cause a severe degradation of the submarine's operational capabilities, representing an unacceptable cost.

Monitoring a ban on further deployment of ground-launched cruise missiles (GLCMs) presents different monitoring problems. Once in the field, these missiles are not embedded in any large, identifiable launch platform such as an aircraft or ship, and the same type of counting rules could not apply. That is not to say that their size is insignificant. While each Tomahawk GLCM, for example, is less than twenty feet long, the TEL vehicle (its "transporter/erector/launcher") which carries four missiles is itself about 50 feet in length. Furthermore, each Tomahawk GLCM combat unit consists of sixteen missiles loaded on four TELs, accompanied by two fifty-foot mobile launch control center vans (LCCs) which provide communications and computer support. Such a group of vehicles would be considerably easier to detect than a single missile. A ban on further deployment should, therefore, concentrate on the launch vehicles for verification.

GLCMs are not, of course, always trundling about the countryside. In non-crisis periods they will be grouped at their secure main bases. The Tomahawk, for instance, will be stored in hardened concrete shelters housing four TELs and two LCCs each. To restrict the possibility of illicit deployment further, it would be useful to place a ban on the construction of additional storage sites. It would also be useful for verification purposes to restrict the deployment and exercising of GLCMs to specific agreed geographic areas.

When viewed in isolation, the deployment of cruise missiles poses significant monitoring difficulties, but these problems would be eased by a comprehensive agreement such as the freeze. A comprehensive freeze would place a series of hurdles in the way of a prospective cheater, not just one. To be successful, the cheater would have to produce the plutonium or uranium secretly, and clandestinely fashion it into a warhead. Any warhead testing would also have to be illicit. Furthermore, there is inherent in a comprehensive freeze an "intra-agreement" deterrent to cheating on the less easily monitorable elements. The prospective cheater must consider that to be caught violating, or even suspected of violating, one element of an agreement could jeopardize other elements. For example, the Soviet Union could be deterred from cheating on cruise missile deployment because of a fear that it might result in the US unilaterally renouncing parts of the treaty the Soviets greatly value. It is also in the interest of the US to conclude an agreement on cruise missiles sooner rather than later. The verification problems are greater, at the moment, for the Soviets than for the US, as the US is years, perhaps as many as 10-15, ahead of the Soviets in exploiting the potential of this technology.

Conclusions

In monitoring an arms control agreement, the only realistic goal is adequate verification. "Iron-clad" verification is an enemy of arms control. Those who advocate it, or anything approaching it, are making meaningful agreement less likely. The United States, like any other state, will remain within the bounds of a treaty only as long as its security is better protected inside than outside. Verification's role is to provide enough information to ensure that this judgement can be safely made.

An arms control treaty, especially one between the superpowers, is a consensual arrangement, with each side giving something for something in return. There is no third party or set of laws which governs the nature of the treaty, or rules on subsequent compliance. It is important, therefore, that the parties to a treaty regularly confer on its operation, exchanging information and sharing concerns, to ensure that each side retains confidence in it as a positive contribution to their security.

The means to provide adequate verification are available. The remote sensors, or "national technical means", of the US are impressive and improving. Of equal importance are the numerous cooperative measures available. Perhaps the most important of these is a discussion forum in which complaints may be discussed in private.

Adequate verification is also assisted by the comprehensive nature of a treaty, and in this regard Colby and Scoville are right and President Reagan is wrong. Comprehensiveness is a two-sided coin. Critics of the freeze argue that its coverage of so many weapons is a weakness of the proposal. They maintain that the more weapons covered, the more extensive the verification needed. In fact, the US intelligence community would endeavor to keep track of all Soviet weapons systems whether or not a freeze were in place. The additional burden on US monitoring resources created by a comprehensive agreement is less than it may initially seem. In fact, the coverage of numerous *aspects* of a single system allows the cumulative nature of probabilities to work against the prospective cheater, and thereby help verification. This other side of the coin would be a powerful disincentive to cheat.

A country contemplating cheating on a comprehensive agreement faces a series of hurdles: for example, production of the fissile material, testing and production of the warhead, testing and production of the delivery system, and deployment of the whole system. The probability of getting caught at one activity may be greater than at another. The US is better, for example, at monitoring the testing of delivery systems than it is at monitoring their production. Nevertheless, all these probabilities accumulate to present the prospective cheater with a gloomy picture. The cheater's task is analogous to the flipping of a coin. The odds that "heads" will be flipped are one in two for each throw. The odds that "heads" will be flipped six times *in a row*, however, are one in sixty-four. Figuratively speaking, the cheater has to flip "heads" six times straight, as the monitoring side need catch the cheater at only one point.

Finally, verification has nothing to do with "trusting the

Russians". The successful operation of a treaty as revealed by adequate verification, however, should build trust in the process of arms control and disarmament.

FOOTNOTES

1. "Verification of SALT II Agreement," *Special Report no. 56*, August 1979, Bureau of Public Affairs, Department of State, p.1, emphasis added.

2. "The SALT II Treaty," *Report of the Committee on Foreign Relations, United States Senate*, 96th Congress, 19 November, 1979, Exec. Report no. 96-14, henceforth SFRC, p.189.

3. For example, a treaty could prohibit all nuclear explosive testing, and provide for the installation of seismic devices on the territory of the parties to the treaty to assist verification.

4. This is contrary to the contention of some. For example, see Richard N. Perle, "What is Adequate Verification?", in *SALT II and American Security*, Institute for Foreign Policy Analysis, Inc., Special Report, October 1980, Cambridge, p.61.

5. SFRC, p. 221.

6. A balance would have to be made between questioning all ambiguous events and protecting intelligence sources. It would seem, however, that for verification purposes the more extensive the questioning the better compliance is likely to be.

7. William H. Kincade, "Verification and SALT II," in Institute for Foreign Policy Analysis Inc., op. cit., p. 34.

8. Kincade, op. cit., p. 51.

9. Resolution refers to the sensitivity of the camera system; the "higher" the resolution the smaller an object which can be detected. Resolution is usually expressed as the width of the finest line which can be detected.

10. "Verifying SALT Agreements," Bruce G. Blair and Garry D. Brewer, in William C. Potter, ed., *Verification and SALT*, Boulder Colorado, Westview Press, 1980, pp. 25-26.

11. The angular resolution of any transmitting or receiving system is limited by the size of its aperture. The greater the aperture, the better the resolution at a given distance.

12. Blair & Brewer, op. cit., pp. 31-32.

13. Les Aspin and Fred Kaplan, "Verification in Perspective", in Potter op. cit., pp. 181-183.

14. Two wave types, P and S, move through the solid body of the earth. Two other types, Rayleigh and Love, move over the surface. An earthquake causes predominantly S waves, while an underground explosion is a source of nearly pure P waves. An earthquake generates both Rayleigh and Love waves, while a simple explosion causes only the former.

15. Lynn R. Sykes, in testimony at the Federation of American Scientists Hearings, 7 March 1983; see also Lynn R. Sykes and Jack F. Evernden, "The Verification of a Comprehensive Nuclear Test Ban," *Scientific American*, October 1982, vol. 247, no. 4.

16. This discussion of cooperative measures is taken from the author's "Cooperative Verification," *Arms Control Today*, vol. 13, no. 5, June 1983.

17. This is particularly important now that new space-based laser ABM systems are being touted by the US President. One of the Agreed Statements appended to the ABM Treaty provides for SCC discussion of any future ABM systems based on physical principles other than those in use at the time of signing. The ABM Treaty also requires that it be reviewed at five-year intervals, and the first two such reviews were conducted by the SCC, in 1977 and 1982.

18. The design features are of two types: "functionally related observable differences" (FRODs) which physically limit the capabilities of a weapon system so it cannot be confused with another; and "externally observable design features" (EODFs) which signal to the other side one's intentions but do not actually limit a weapon's capabilities.

19. A. Crawford, F.R. Cleminson, D.A. Grant, E. Gilman, "Compendium of Arms Control Verification Proposals," Second Edition, *ORAE Report No. R81*, March 1982, Department of National Defence, Canada.

20. Inspectors are permitted for group explosions with a planned aggregate yield over 150 kt, and any explosion with a planned yield of more than 100 kt but less than 150 kt that the two parties deem appropriate for on-site inspection. These inspectors would be present to confirm that the explosion is in fact for peaceful purposes, and to verify that no single explosion exceeds 150 kt in yield.

21. The use of "control posts" is similar to selective OSI in that the freedom available to inspectors is limited, but different from it in that the inspectors from one country are actually stationed on the soil of another. Inspectors or teams of inspectors could continually monitor crucial junctures in the transportation network, or important weapons facilities where they would be given enough access to ensure that prohibited activity was not underway, but not so much that military secrets were put in jeopardy. Both the US and USSR have proposed the use of control posts to monitor mutual force reductions in Europe, but disagreements have arisen over how long the posts would remain in operation.

22. Unfortunately, the agreement subsequently ran into problems over the number and location of stations on British territory, although participants believe these could have been overcome.

23. See the author's "RECOVERing Verification," *Arms Control Today*, vol. 12, no. 11, December 1982.

24. Blair and Brewer, op. cit., p. 37.

25. SFRC, op. cit., p. 191.

PART III

IMPACT OF THE ARMS RACE

Introduction

The Physicians for Social Responsibility (PSR) have become well known for their challenge to the illusion that it is
possible for our society to survive and—yes—perhaps even
"prevail" in a nuclear war. According to a recent report from the
World Health Organization more than a billion people would
die and another billion would be mutilated in an all-out nuclear
war using at least half of the present weapons stockpiles. A
recent study published in *Science* is even more pessimistic.
According to Carl Sagan and the other authors, the detonation
of one thousand megatons will lead to devastating climatic
effects known collectively as "nuclear winter." (One thousand
weapons is only a small fraction of the global nuclear arsenal.)
The implication is that there can be no rational military
strategy that relies on nuclear weapons. Jack Geiger's article
indicates the medical implications of nuclear war in the context
of one major U.S. city and argues that preventive medicine (i.e.
disarmament) is the only prescription that a reasonable doctor
can offer. After a nuclear holocaust the survivors will envy the
dead.

Although increasingly challenged, economics is in no
danger of losing its place as the "dismal science." To many

235

people, military expenditures are seen as giving a boost to the economy, but as Joe Joseph argues, military spending saps America's economic strength. Not only does investment in nuclear weapons produce far less jobs than alternative investment opportunities—costing the U.S. 270,000 jobs according to one study—but military outlays starve the rest of the economy of desperately needed investment dollars. Additionally, the social costs are enormous. We now know that throughout the world—whether it be in the slums and tenements of the great industrial cities of the Northern hemisphere or among the impoverished people of the Southern hemisphere—the consequences of the arms race are not potential eventualities but must be acknowledged as present and real. Malnutrition, disease, illiteracy, indeed the whole range of conditions that we describe as underdevelopment, are the legacy of an arms race that serves not only to divert scarce resources but also to sustain and entrench an unjust economic order.

Less widely discussed are what Morris Schwartz refers to as the social-psychological effects of the arms race. His discussion of the sanitization of military strategy language in the nuclear age ("damage limitation," and the MX as "Peacekeeper," etc.) is part of what Robert Jay Lifton and Richard Falk have labelled "nuclearism"—the "psychological, political and military dependence on nuclear weapons, the embrace of the weapons as solution to a wide variety of human dilemmas, most ironically that of 'security.' " Nuclearism, as Schwartz explains, depends upon delusions and deceptions—the polarization of the enemy as "evil incarnate" and a kind of collective numbing of the public psyche. No place is the impact greater than on youth, who increasingly believe that their natural lives will be interrupted by nuclear war. The "fallout" resulting from this belief will have a significant, but not yet really understood impact on their transition into adulthood.

Chapter 15

The Illusion of Survival

Jack Geiger

To attempt to measure and describe the consequences of a thermonuclear attack on a major American city is to confront a paradox.

On the one hand, the nature and magnitude of the effects of hypothetical—but eminently possible—nuclear attacks are entirely specifiable. The calculations are straightforward and only moderately complex. Indeed, over the past two decades, these consequences have been described in exquisite detail in hundreds of scientific journals (including *The Bulletin of the Atomic Scientists*), books and government publications.[1]

On the other hand, despite the specificity, these effects—the numbers of killed and injured, the destruction of the physical environment, the damage to the ecosphere—are unfathomable. In short, it is almost impossible fully to grasp the reality they represent, the implications they carry.

This is not merely because the numbers are so large as to be incomprehensible: close to 10 *million* people killed or seriously injured, for example, in consequence of a single 20-megaton explosion and the resulting firestorm on the New York metropolitan area. The difficulty occurs primarily because we are attempting to describe and understand an event that is without human precedent.

No "Outside" to Rely Upon

Hiroshima and Nagasaki do not serve as precedents for any probable nuclear war scenario. The weapons used on those cities approximated 13 kilotons of explosive force each. At one megaton—a small weapon by contemporary standards—we are trying to imagine 70 simultaneous Hiroshima explosions. At 20 megatons we are trying to imagine 1,400 Hiroshima bombs detonated at the same moment in the same place.

Hiroshima and Nagasaki were single events, with effects decaying over time; today we are faced with the possibility of multiple events—a thermonuclear explosion at 10 a.m. and another at 4 p.m. At the time Hiroshima, there was one nuclear power and the world's total arsenal comprised two or three weapons; today there are at least six nuclear powers and the total arsenal is—conservatively—in excess of 50,000 warheads.

But most important, Hiroshima and Nagasaki were isolated, limited disasters. They could, in time, be saved and reconstructed with help from outside. Always, we think of an "outside" this is our intuitive model of disasters, for our historical experience is confined to single-event phenomena of limited range, duration and effect—hurricanes, earthquakes, World War II bombings, even Hiroshima and Nagasaki—in which both short-term and longer-term relief efforts could be mounted.

In any full-scale contemporary nuclear exchange, however, *there will be no "outside" that we can rely upon.* We cannot safely assume that there will be unaffected major areas within reach of targeted cities that will have resources that can be mobilized effectively to help the stricken targets, or that are likely to regard even making the effort as a rational enterprise. In a population-targeted attack, every major population center may be effectively destroyed.

A Case Study: San Francisco After a Nuclear Attack

In attempting to comprehend the consequences, it is useful to consider the case of a single weapon and a single city. One specifies the megatonnage, the nature of the attack (air burst or ground burst, single or multiple strike), the time of year, the day of the week (workday or weekend), the time of day, the atmospheric conditions (clear or cloudy, raining or dry), and the wind patterns. The magnitudes of blast (in pounds per square inch above atmospheric pressure), heat (in calories per square centimeter) and radiation are determined at various distances from ground zero. These distances are the radii of a series of concentric circles extending outward from the point of explosion. Within each circle, given the physical forces, the nature of the buildings and terrain, and the population concentration, it is possible to calculate the numbers killed and seriously injured.

The U.S. Arms Control and Disarmament Agency has made such calculations for every city in the United States with a population of 25,000 or more, at weapon sizes varying from 50 kilotons to 20 megatons.[2] In San Francisco, for example, the Agency calculates that a single one-megaton air burst would kill 624,000 persons and seriously injure and incapacitate 306,000. A single 20-megaton air burst would kill 1,538,000 and seriously injure 738,000.

However, these figures are serious understatements. They are based on a census population distribution, that is, they make the implicit assumption that everyone is at home, when in fact a population-targeted attack is much likelier to occur on a weekday during working hours, when the population is concentrated in central-city areas closest to ground zero. And they do not allow for the probability of a firestorm or mass conflagration as the secondary consequence of a nuclear attack. A firestorm—like those at Hiroshima, and at Dresden and Hamburg after conventional bombings during World War II —may burn for days, with ambient temperatures exceeding 800 degrees centigrade. It increases the lethal area *five-fold*.[3] It also makes all conventional sheltering attempts worse than useless. At these temperatures, and with the exhaustion of oxygen supplies and the accumulation of toxic gases, shelters become crematoria. In Dresden and Hamburg, the only survivors were those who fled their shelters.

A 25 percent increase in the numbers of killed and seriously injured would be a conservative adjustment for these two factors. Thus corrected the figures for San Francisco would be that:

□ A one-megaton air burst would kill 780,000 persons (22 percent of the total Bay Area population) and seriously injure 382,000 (10.5 percent), for total casualties of 1,162,500, or 33 percent of the population.

□ A 20-megaton air burst would kill 1,923,000 persons (53 percent of all the people in the Bay Area) and seriously injure 874,000 (24 percent) for total casualties of 2,797,000, or 77.4 percent of the population.

The figures illustrate the lack of precedent. There is no identifiable event in human history when a million people have been killed in one place at one moment. There is no previous situation in which there were 400,000 seriously injured human beings in one place.

The nature of these injuries further illustrates the magnitude of the problem. Among the "survivors" there will probably be tens of thousands of cases of extensive third-degree burns. And in this kind of injury, survival and recovery depend almost entirely on the availability of specialized burn-care facilities, highly and specially trained medical and allied personnel, complex laboratory equipment, almost unlimited supplies of blood and plasma, and the availability of a wide range of drugs. No such facilities would remain intact in San Francisco; the number of Bay Area burn casualties would exceed by a factor of 10 or 20 the capacity of all the burn-care centers in the United States.

In addition to third-degree burns, hundreds of thousands of "survivors" would suffer crushing injuries, simple and compound fractures, penetrating wounds of the skull, thorax and abdomen, and multiple lacerations with extensive hemorrhage, primarily in consequence of blast pressures and the collapse of buildings. (Many of these victims, of course, would also have serious burns.) A moderate number would have ruptured internal organs, particularly the lungs, from blast pressures. Significant numbers would be deaf in consequence of ruptured eardrums, in addition to their other injuries, and many would be blind, since—as far as 35 miles from ground zero—reflex glance at the fireball would produce serious retinal burns.

Superimposed on these problems would be tens of thousands of cases of acute radiation injury, superficial burns produced by beta and low-energy gamma rays, and damage due to radionuclides in specific organs. Many would die even if the most sophisticated and heroic therapy were available; others, with similar symptoms but less actual exposure, could be saved by skilled and complex treatment. In practical terms, however, there will be no way to distinguish the lethally-radiated from the non-lethally-irradiated.

Finally, this burden of trauma will occur in addition to all pre-existing disease among "survivors," and this list of problems is not based on consideration of the special problems of high-risk populations—the very young and the very old, for example—which are particularly vulnerable.

These are the short-range problems to which a medical response must be addressed. But who will be left to respond?

Physicians' offices and hospitals tend to be concentrated in central-city areas closest to ground zero. If anything, physicians will be killed and seriously injured at rates greater than those of the general population, and hospitals similarly have greater probabilities of destruction or severe damage. Of the approximately 4,000 physicians in San Francisco County, perhaps half would survive a one-megaton air-burst; of the 4,647 hospital beds in the county, only a handful would remain. At 20 megatons, there would be only a few thousand physicians left in all of San Francisco, Alameda, Marin, San Mateo and Contra Costa Counties to try to care for 874,000 seriously wounded.

One carefully detailed study of an American city suggests that there would be 1,700 seriously injured "survivors" for every physician—and that includes physicians of all ages, types of training, states of health and location at the time of the attack.[4] If, conservatively, we estimate only 1,000 seriously wounded patients per surviving physician, if we further assume that every physician sees each patient for only 10 minutes for diagnosis and treatment, and if each such physician worked 20 hours a day, it would be eight days before all the wounded were seen—once—by a doctor. Most of the wounded will die without medical care of any sort. Most will die without even the simple administration of drugs for the relief of pain.

A closer look at these calculations reveals that they are absurd—and the absurdities have implications that extend far beyond issues of medical care.

Thus, the calculations assume that every surviving, uninjured physician would be willing to expose himself or herself to high levels of radiation. They assume that every physician will be able to identify the areas in which medical help is needed, get there with no expenditure of time, and find every one of the 1,000 patients. It is further assumed that physicians will spend no time on uninjured or mildly injured patients, on those with pre-existing illness requiring care, on those with acute illness unrelated to the bombing, or on those who merely believe they are injured, all of whom will demand his time and attention.

And all of this is happening in an area where there is no electricity, no surviving transportation system. What is left of the buildings is lying in what is left of the streets; the bridges are down; subways and tunnels are crushed; there is no effective communication system; there are no ambulances and no hospitals.

Finally, in each ten-minute patient visit, the "medical care" will be dispensed without x-rays, laboratory equipment, other diagnostic aids, supplies, drugs, blood, plasma, beds and the like. There will be no help from "outside." There will be no rational organization even of this primitive level of care. In short, this is not medical care at all, as we commonly understand it.

Secondary Effects of a Nuclear Attack

It is important to examine medical care scenarios not merely as an element in the essentially hopeless task of response to a nuclear attack, but as a metaphor for *all* complex human—that is to say, social—activities in the post-attack period. *What becomes clear is that all such activities require an intact social fabric*—not merely the infrastructure of electric power, transportation, communications, shelter, water or food but the social enterprises, the complex human interactions and organizations supported by that infrastructure. That social fabric is ruptured, probably irreparably, by even a single nuclear weapon. Medical care is impossible in any real sense, not only because of the damage to the physical and biological environments, but most of all because it is a complex activity that requires a high degree of social organization.

The same is true of most other important human activities in complex urban societies. It follows that the only true meaning of "survival" is social, not biological. Simply to tally those who are still alive, or alive and uninjured, is to make a biological body-count that has little social meaning. The biological "survivors" in all probability have merely postponed their deaths—by days, weeks, months, or at most a few years—from secondary attack-related causes. Life in the interim will bear no resemblance to life before a nuclear attack.

In the period of days to months after an attack, other problems of both social and medical significance will rapidly emerge. Without functioning transportation, even assuming that effective social organization continues on the "outside," no food will come into the stricken area; remaining undestroyed stocks will be depleted rapidly. Extreme water shortages will occur almost at once. The average citizen of a modern American city uses between 50 to 150 gallons of water a day; in the post-attack period, a quart a day per survivor would be generous, and there will be no easy way to assure either potability or freedom from radioactive contamination.

Over the first two to four weeks after the attack, thousands of short-term survivors will die of radiation sickness, particularly of infection secondary to radiation-induced lowering of resistance. The problem of mass infection is particularly ugly. Even assuming that a firestorm conveniently incinerates 500,000 of the dead in a one-megaton attack, there will remain some 300,000 or more decomposing human corpses in the Bay Area.

There will be no safe water supply or effective sanitation. The vectors of disease—flies, mosquitoes and other insects—will enjoy preferential survival and growth in the post-attack period because their radiation resistance is many times that of mammals. Most surviving humans will have reduced resistance to infection. It is hard to construct a scenario more likely to produce epidemic disease.

Finally, any likely population-targeted attack will assign many multi-megaton weapons to each major city, and therefore calculations based on a single one-megaton or 20-megaton strike are unrealistically conservative.

Preventive Medicine

Other scenarios—the so-called "counterforce" exchanges aimed primarily at missile sites or various city-trading hypotheses—presumably would result in less *immediate* death and injury. But they pose medical and social problems of equal magnitude in the longer run, even if they do not almost automatically escalate into full-scale exchanges.

Mass evacuation of cities in a nuclear crisis, the current favorite of civil defense enthusiasts, would in itself be seen as provocative by an adversary and therefore would increase risks. According to testimony before a Senate subcommittee by representatives of the Federal Emergency Management Agency, effective evacuation would require "only eight days" from warning time to completion.

It is, once again, a technique aimed at short-term biological survival, not social survival: to what would the dispersed urban residents return?

The danger of nuclear war is a public health problem of unprecedented magnitude. It is not, however, unprecedented in *type*. There are many other medical problems to which a coherent response is not possible and for which there are no cures. One medical (and social) strategy is still available in such cases: Prevention.

Footnotes

1.) Joint Committee on Atomic Energy, U.S. Congress, *Biological and Environmental Effects of Nuclear War: Summary Analysis of Hearings, June 22-26, 1969,* U.S. Government Printing Office, 1959; *New England Journal of Medicine,* 266 (1962), pp.1137-1144; S. Aranow, F.R. Ervin, V.W. Sidel, eds., *The Fallen Sky: Medical Consequences of Thermonuclear War,* Hill and Wang, 1963; H.N. Lewis, "The Prompt and Delayed Effects of Nuclear War,"*Scientific American,*241:1 (1979), pp. 35-47; U.S. Congress, Office of Technology Assessment, *The Effects of Nuclear War,* OTA-NS089, U.S. Government Printing Office, 1979. _____

2.) U.S. Arms Control and Disarmament Agency, "Urban Population Vulnerability in the United States," 1979.

3.) Lewis, "Prompt and Delayed Effects."

4.) Aranow, Ervin and Sidel, *The Fallen Sky.*

Chapter 16

The Economic Impact of Military Spending

J.J. Joseph

The single major expenditure in the United States economy is military spending. It accounts for more than 10 percent of the entire GNP and more than 50 percent of all Federal spending (other than trust funds). Small wonder then that all weapons—both nuclear and conventional—have serious effects long before their detonators are activated. Military spending has an explosive bearing on the Federal deficit and a shattering impact on social programs. It aggravates the unemployment problem while it enhances the profits of defense contractors. It deprives the economy of needed capital investment and places the nation at a disadvantage with its capitalist competitors. The negative effects of military spending extend to the international arena, particularly to developing countries. In an economic context, military spending both at present and projected levels, diminishes the nation's real security.

Military Budget Trends

The categories "national defense" or the "Department of Defense" do not include all the items which belong to "military spending." In the United States Government Budget, military spending is distributed among a number of government func-

FIGURE 16-1

TOTAL MILITARY SPENDING, 1982-1988

(in billions of dollars)

	1982	1983	1984	1985	1986	1987	1988
National defense	218.7	245.5	280.5	330.0	364.8	397.0	432.7
Interest attributable to national defense*	50.8	53.3	61.9	68.5	73.6	78.2	80.6
Veterans benefits	25.0	25.0	26.1	26.9	27.8	26.8	29.5
International affairs	15.3	17.1	16.8	16.3	15.8	15.6	16.1
Science, space, and technology	7.1	7.9	8.5	8.4	7.7	7.7	6.8
Energy	3.3	3.7	2.9	3.1	3.1	3.2	3.7
Total	320.2	352.5	396.7	453.2	492.8	530.3	569.4

*Interest attributable to military spending is estimated at 60% of total net interest.
approximately the proportion calculated by DeGrasse. *Military Expansion. Economic Decline.* pp. 234-235.

Source: *Budget of the U.S. Government*, FY 1984. p. 9-7

tions and agencies. A proper accounting of the real amount spent on the military should include the Department of Defense (about 70 percent of the total), the nuclear weapons activities in the Department of Energy (including research, development, testing, production, and weapons materials production), Veterans' benefits and services, the military space program in NASA, foreign military assistance and the portion of the federal debt service attributable to military spending.[1]

Both national defense and military spending are on the increase whether measured in current dollars or constant dollars. National defense expenditures for the six-year period 1977-1982 totalled $804 billion.[2] For the next six-year period 1983-1988, they will equal $2,051 billion—an increase of two and one-half times.[3] Even allowing for inflation, this represents a real increase of more than two times.

Table 1 shows the annual increase in both "national defense" budgets and total military spending. The statistics in Table 1, as in all the data in the Federal Budget for fiscal year 1984, assume an annual inflation increase between 4.4% and 4.7% for the years 1984 through 1988.[4]

In 1983 President Reagan and the Pentagon asked for a 10% increase in real spending. The Congress was disposed towards a 5% increase. The budget itself showed an annual increase over the previous year in national defense spending of 12.3% in 1983, 14.3% in 1984 and 17.6% in 1985. For procurement alone, (i.e. authorizations for weapons, ships, etc.) those annual increases are 24.5% for 1983, 17.2% for 1984 and 27.1% for 1985.

The defense budget for 1984 and later years will exceed those of any year since World War II. Table 2 compares the Reagan peace-time defense budget, in constant 1983 dollars, with the outlays of the Korean War and the Vietnam War.

It is clear from the chart that by 1984 the Department of Defense outlays (not to mention total military spending) will reach a new peak even in constant dollars.[5]

Military Spending and Budget Deficits

At current levels, the Federal deficit amounts to about 5% of the GNP and about 25% of the Federal budget. The huge deficits are a matter of concern to all segments of our society including public officials as well as a major section of the business community.

The National Governors Association adopted a resolution in March 1983 urging President Reagan and the Congress to reduce the deficit to 2% of the GNP by 1988.[6] *U.S. News and World Report* expressed the worry "that a continuous string of

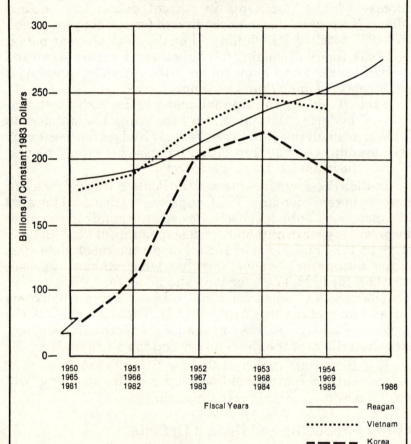

FIGURE 16-2
DEPARTMENT OF DEFENSE OUTLAYS
Constant 1983 Dollars

Source: Robert W. DeGrasse Jr.; *Military Expansion Economic Decline*. Council of Economic
Priorities, 1983.
Primary Sources: U.S. Department of Defense (Comptroller), unpublished data. Estimates for
1982 to 1986 from U.S. Department of Defense, Office of Assistant Secretary of Defense (Public
Affairs), *FY 1984 Department of Defense Budget*, January 31, 1983.

FIGURE 16-3
FEDERAL BUDGET SUMMARY, 1982-1984
(In Billions of Dollars)

	1982 Actual	1983 Estimate	1984 Proposed
Expenditures (Outlays)	728	805	848
Receipts	618	597	660
Deficits	(110)	(208)	(188)

Source: *Budget of the U.S. Government, FY 1984*, p. 9-7

large deficits will absorb private capital and thus push interest rates up once again to abort an economic recovery.[7] Federal Reserve Board Chairman Paul Volcker stated that the fear of deficits "clouds the future and contributes to market uncertainties."[8] Stanley Weiss, President of American Minerals, Inc. and founder of Business Executives for National Security, has said "You've heard of 'better dead than red'? This administration has a new slogan, 'better in the red than dead'. [We are spending] ourselves into insolvency."[9]

Most important, a Bi-Partisan Appeal of 500 leading corporate executives, investment bankers and others, founded by five former Secretaries of the Treasury and one former Secretary of Commerce campaigned throughout 1983 for reduced deficits. "Military strength in the years to come must go hand in hand with economic strength," they said. "Neither can be achieved unless huge projected...deficits are reduced drastically and permanently...the projected growth in defense outlays...is a significant contributor to the projected deficit..."[10]

Federal budget deficits are an old story—under both Republican and Democratic administrations. In the past fifty years there have been 42 deficits and only 8 surpluses. The last surplus—$3.2 billion—was in 1969. Between 1933 and 1983, the Federal debt has climbed from about $20 billion to $1,400 billion.

President Reagan decries a government policy of "tax and tax—spend and spend." However, before the middle of

President Reagan's term, the impossibility of increasing military spending and cutting taxes while at the same time balancing the budget, had become clear to all. The promise to reduce deficits was deferred to later years. The promise to eliminate deficits was converted to a proposed constitutional amendment.

War and military spending account for much of the Federal deficit. This was true of the Korean and Vietnam wars and recent history confirms the relationship. During each of the years 1978-1981 (three of Carter's and one of Reagan's) military expenditures were more than double the entire Federal deficit.[12] The deficits for 1982-1984, which are at an all-time high, are shown in Table 3).

The combined deficits of the 1950 and 1960 decades equalled only $75 billion. The 1983 deficit of $208 billion alone exceeds the total 5-year World War II (1941-1945) deficit of $175 billion.

To be sure, deficits have multiple causes. The massive tax reductions enacted in 1981, primarily for wealthy individuals and corporations, reduced government revenues and multiplied the current deficits. But the principal culprit is military spending.

From the point of view of Federal funding, military spending is almost exclusively responsible for the deficit. The Federal budget comprises two major funds—Trust and Federal. Trust funds refer to those outlays that are self-financing, such as Social Security, Medicare and Unemployment Insurance. Federal funds, which include military spendings, represent discretionary outlays subject to year-to-year decision by the Congress and the White House. Trust fund spending is generally lower than trust fund revenues. In 1982, 1983 and 1984, trust funds show a surplus.[13] The entire Federal deficit is in Federal funds, where military spending accounts for about half of all outlays. As the Council on Economic Priorities noted, "Trust funds...do not add to the federal deficit because they do not draw from general funds."[14] And further, "After subtracting self-funding programs from the federal budget and adding all military-related costs to the national defense function, we find that 48.6 per-cent of the federal government's general funds were spent on the military in fiscal year 1981. In fiscal year 1986, the Pentagon is expected to use 59.2 percent of the government's general funds."[15]

The deficit has also created problems with the U.S. allies in Western Europe. It was a major issue at the Economic Summit meetings of 1983. France asserted that Europe and others are paying for the American budget deficit. Their reasoning was that "the high interest rates resulting from the deficit attract dollars out of Europe for investment in the United States. This [tendency] is held to swell the value of the dollar on the exchange markets and increase the costs of those countries that must pay international bills, notably for oil, in American currency."[16]

Military Spending and Inflation

"Defense spending is the worst kind of government outlay precisely because it is so inflationary," the *Wall Street Journal* editorialized.[17]

Military spending is inflationary because it increases the overall volume of consumer demand, but does not produce extra commodity goods to meet this demand. If money and materials are spent producing something that people can buy, then inflationary pressures are balanced by the increased supply and prices are kept down. But no one can go to the supermarket and purchase a guided missile or an F-15 fighter. Thus military spending drives up domestic prices by putting money into the economy without increasing the supply of goods which can be purchased. The widening gap between supply and demand raises the prices of goods and is thus inflationary.

The imbalance between supply and demand is not the only way that Pentagon budgets fuel inflation. We have already seen how military spending contributes to Federal deficits. The Federal deficit is paid for by the issuance of Treasury notes, bills and bonds. The larger the deficit the more the government is forced to borrow. This "paper" money increases inflation.

A third contributing factor to inflation stems from the heavy use of raw materials in military production, particularly metals and alloys. This factor raises prices. From 1979-1980 cost increases for jet engines and electronic memories ranged from 14% to 35%. For critical raw materials, such as titanium and copper, inflation ranged from 38% to 650%. In fact, because military contractors work on a cost-plus basis, they tend to drive up the prices of raw materials affecting most civilian business.

A 1983 study by the Congressional Budget Office reported that "at no time in its history has the United States increased defense spending so rapidly without encountering, at about the same time, a substantial increase in inflationary pressures."[18] After the military buildup in World War I, World War II, the Korean War and the Vietnam War, the inflation rate jumped sharply. (See Table 4).

Because the recession of the early 1980s idled many industries and created high unemployment, administration eco-

FIGURE 16-4
INFLATION RATES
BEFORE AND AFTER PREVIOUS MILITARY BUILD-UPS

Start of Build-Up	Inflation Rate for 3 Prior Years	Inflation Rate for 3 Subsequent Years
1917 (W.W. I)	8.7	16.0
1941 (W.W. II)	1.5	6.2
1950 (Korea)	2.6	3.6
1965 (Vietnam)	1.4	3.3

Source: Congressional Budget Office, *Defense Spending and the Economy*, February 1983, p.5.

nomists contend that unlike Korea or Vietnam, this time the economy can absorb new military spending without stimulating new inflation.

However, the Council of Economic Priorities predicted that "as we climb out of the recession, backlogs in key military-related industries will bid up the prices in the high-technology sector. Soaring federal deficits, required to finance the build-up, will help push interest rates back to record levels, squeezing out new investment. These problems could short-circuit economic revitalization and lead to renewed inflationary pressures."[19]

A staff study for the Joint Economic Committee of the U.S. Congress reported "The defense buildup adds to inflationary pressures and widening deficits unless there are offsetting budget cuts or tax increase."[20] William Winpisinger, President of the International Association of Machinists, aptly called the Pentagon a "perpetual inflation machine."

Military Spending and Jobs

In 1982 and again in 1983, there were more than 11 million full-time unemployed. If discouraged workers and involuntary part-time workers are included, the unemployed would number at least 15 million. Our economic system does not begin to show the capacity to create the more than two million jobs needed each year just for new entrants to the labor force.

More available workers than available jobs is a permanent feature of the United States economy. Unemployment, rising and falling with the business cycle, is part of every capitalist system. The effect of technological displacement on unemployment is an ongoing phenomenon. To these classic forms of unemployment in the United States, there must now be added structural unemployment stemming from the permanent decline of certain smokestack industries. Part of this decline is due to the flight of capital which has redeployed many jobs beyond our borders. In 1977, U.S. transnational corporations employed more than seven million workers abroad.[21] Today this number is probably close to ten million. It is against this background that the relationship of military spending to jobs must be viewed.

The Pentagon has an economic unit called the Defense Impact Modeling System (DEIMS). Employing macroeconomic input-output models DEIMS is responsible for supplying estimates of jobs created per billion dollars of military spending Accordingly, Defense Secretary, Caspar W. Weinberger said, "You get 35,000 more jobs for every extra $1 billion you spend on national defense."[22] The statement implies that military spending *reduces* unemployment. But unemployment has increased sharply during the Reagan years. The Council on Economic Priorities compared military spending as a share of the gross domestic product versus unemployment for the U.S., U.K., France, West Germany, Sweden, Italy, Canada, and Japan for the period 1960-1979. They concluded that "higher levels of military spending generally correspond with greater unemployment among western industrial nations."[23]

What the Pentagon's computer fails to print out is that employment created by almost any other use of the same money would create *more* jobs than military spending does. Military procurement creates fewer jobs than cilivian. Modern arms production is more capital intensive than labor intensive. It requires a greater concentration of highly skilled engineers and technicians than does civilian industry. The percentage of production employees in defense industries is far *lower* than in other industries. For U.S. industry as a whole, the *average* ratio of production to total employees is 89.9% for the auto industry 73.5%; for ordnance and accessories, 47.3%; and for guided missiles only 27.8%.[24]

The Council on Economic Priorities found that employment impact of alternative uses of $1 bilion created the least jobs of all in missile production.[25] Employment Research Associates found that "contrary to long held and popular belief, military spending...does not create employment—it generates—unemployment."[26]

The Coalition for a New Foreign and Military Policy

demonstrated the superior job creating capacity of civilian spending. (See Table 5).

FIGURE 16-5

JOBS CREATED PER BILLION DOLLARS

Day care..	120,476
Mass transit......................................	79,300
Energy and conservation...........................	65,079
Military..	45,000

Source: Coalition for a New Foreign and Military Policy

Aside from capital versus labor intensive characteristics,[27] the Congressional Budget Office found two additional economic factors at play. "The employment effects of defense purchases are smaller than for non-defense, partly because wage and salary levels in defense industries average about 7 percent higher than in non-defense...In addition...defense purchases from industry tend to have smaller employment effects since some of the additional spending goes into higher profits."[28]

The theoretical effects of military spending on jobs may be clarified by reference to actual industries, companies and unions. In 1975, 90,300 members of the International Association of Machinists (IAM) were employed on military contracts— either industrial or governmental. By October 1978, as the military budget rose and procurement contracts went up, the number of IAM military-related jobs *declined* to 88,000.[29] In Virginia, Tenneco's Newport News Shipbuilding division, the Navy's largest contractor, employment was down from 1981.[30] At Lockheed, where defense contracts have increased steadily over the past decade, the labor force *declined* from 30,000 to 16,000.[31] As late as March 1983, the *Wall St. Journal* headlined "So Far, Arms Build-up Creates Few New Jobs, Major Contractors Say. The Reagan administration's defense build-up is producing more political controversy than job-creating contracts."[32]

A final negative economic impact of military spending on employment stems from the reduction in trade between the United States and socialist countries. Hundreds of thousands of jobs have been lost as part of a policy in which the U.S. attempts to weaken the USSR economically by boycotts and trade sanctions. There is a definite domestic price for such a policy—more unemployment in the United States. A good example is the Caterpillar Tractor Company of Peoria, Illinois. In 1982 it was forbidden from fulfilling its contract to supply pipe-laying equipment for the Soviet gas pipeline to Western Europe. KOMATSU, a competitive Japanese firm promptly undertook the business. Caterpillar sales would have generated jobs for 12,000 workers for one year. (Incidentally, Caterpillar lost almost $200 million in 1982 and its stock dropped sharply.)

Our Western allies do not share the U.S. economic policy towards the USSR. It is estimated that between two and four million West European and Japanese workers have jobs producing for socialist countries.

Defense Industry

From the standpoint of the economy, most of the impact of military spending has been negative, and from the standpoint of the poor, downright disastrous. Yet military spending is clearly advantageous for one sector of the economy, namely, the defense industry.

To a large degree the *raison d'etre* for military spending is the pressure from the alliance of the Pentagon and defense contractors—the military-industrial complex. Their influence on military spending, on R&D in universities, and on Congressional politics is well documented.[34] Numerous studies describe the methods of contracting and procurement, the waste and excess profits of major DOD contractors.[35]

The defense industry is one of the few in the economy which is practically recession proof. It has grown from 4.7% to 10% of the total goods-producing sector of the economy. The big ten DOD contractors are McDonnell Douglas, United Technologies, General Dynamics, General Electric, Boeing, Lockheed, Hughes Aircraft, Raytheon, Grumman and Chrysler.[36]

Military appropriations are the single most important source of investment and profit for corporate U.S. research and development costs of DOD contractors are paid by the government so that contracting firms stake relatively little capital of their own. Practically all defense contracts are let on a non-competitive cost-plus basis insuring high profits. The General Accounting Offices reported that profits before taxes for defense contractors were 56%— higher than any in the civilian sector.[37]

Military Spending and International Competition

Military production and spending diverts capital investment from the civilian sector. Such investment is essential for improving the efficiency of American factories and hence of keeping them competitive in the world economy. In the U.S., for every $100 available for domestic capital formation, $46 is spent for the military compared to $14 in West Germany and $3.70 in Japan.[38] "While the Japanese are busy working their fifth generation computer," said economist Lester Thurow of MIT, "we're busy building the MX."[39]

The share of the U.S. industry in the world auto market declined from 22.6% in 1962 to 13.9% in 1979. Other industries showing such declines included aircraft, telecommunications, agricultural machinery, railway vehicles and machine tools. Meanwhile, the share of foreign industry in the U.S. market increased sharply, notably in auto, steel, consumer electronics, machine tools, and textile machinery.

During these two decades of decline in world trade, the low level of capital investment was matched by a high level of military spending. As a share of the gross domestic product, U.S. military spending was higher in relation to capital formation than in 16 other Western nations studied by the Council of Economic Priorities.

The United States and the United Kingdom, where military spending was highest, lost ground to their competitors, particularly Japan and Germany where investment as a share of GDP was much higher. This correlation is described in Table 6. Insofar as the future "reindustrialization" of the United States is concerned, there are enormous implications in these data.

Alternative Uses of Military Spending

"The next time someone tells you defense spending is good or bad for the economy, ask: Compared to what?"[40]

The answer, no matter what, is always political. It always expresses a value judgment. For by now, it is quite clear that the nation's economy cannot afford both guns and butter.

In view of the fact that the impact of military spending on the Federal deficit, inflation, unemployment, and on an economy hungry for capital investment, the substitutes for reduced military spending practically spell themselves out. Basically, there are three possible choices (or a combination of two or all of them):

1. Restore social programs eliminated or reduced in recent years.

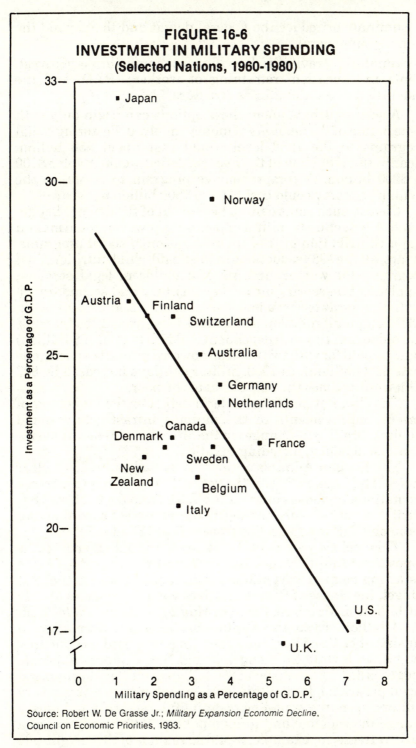

**FIGURE 16-6
INVESTMENT IN MILITARY SPENDING
(Selected Nations, 1960-1980)**

Source: Robert W. De Grasse Jr.; *Military Expansion Economic Decline*,
Council on Economic Priorities, 1983.

2. Eliminate or reduce the Federal deficit and thereby aid the economy in general.

3. Stimulate a revitalized civilian economy through investments in education, retraining of workers, R&D, and the restoration of an ailing infra-structure.

A serious debate about these options can begin only with some notion of the *amounts* of money involved. Restoring social programs to the 1982 level would cost about $50 billion. Meaningful reduction of the Federal deficit would involve $100 to $200 billion. A comprehensive program to revitalize the civilian economy could cost $300 to $500 billion per year.[41]

Clearly such sums cannot be met out of the defense budget alone. A reduction in military spending, however, could make a major contribution toward the restoration of social programs. In fact, all the 1983 reductions in Medicaid, child nutrition, food programs for women, infants and children, legal services, supplemental security income, elementary and secondary education, guaranteed student loans, energy and conservation, R&D, community development grants, mass transit, food stamps, and aid to families with dependent children (a total of $6 billion) could be paid for with two nuclear-powered aircraft carriers (one costs $3.44 billion). In 1983, military outlays increased by $33 billion—five times the cuts in aid to the poor.

The elimination of the Federal deficit or the launching of serious improvements in the nation's infrastructure would require more drastic changes in the direction of Federal government fiscal policy, including taxation.

The Reagan Administration's 1984 budget makes a clear choice. The fiscal policy for the years 1981 to 1988 is to increase the national defense claim on the GNP from 5% to almost 8%. During the same years non-defense government spending as a claim on GNP would decline from 18% to 11% of GNP.[42]

This policy judgment is at least candid. Some of the opposition to military spending is no more than a gesture. From a starting point of $284 billion for national defense in the 1984 budget, the House of Representatives voted a reduction of only $10 billion on March 23, 1983. On May 20, the Senate voted a cut of $4 billion. Even the Center for Defense Information, a consistent critic of Pentagon spending, proposed a cut of only $33 billion.[43] Only the Congressional Black Caucus alternate budget called for a transfer of $50 billion in military spending to social programs. It is at this level or higher that reductions in military spending would be meaningful and begin to imply a change in economic and foreign policies.[44] The adoption of a nuclear freeze, for example, would save sums of this magnitude for alternate civilian use.

International Impacts of Military Spending

On a world-wide scale, many of the economic effects of military spending (on rates of economic growth, impact on social services, inflation and employment) parallel those on the domestic level. However, because of the relative affluence of the U.S., the economic and social consequences of military expenditures are much more devastating in the international arena, particularly on developing countries, than in the domestic economy.

World-wide military spending is now over $600 billion annually.[45] On the average, countries are devoting 5% to 6% of their output to military ends. Military spending in 1982 was more than the entire income of 1,500 million people—one third of the world's population—living in the 50 poorest countries.

The volume and direction of world trade ebbs and flows with military spending as well as with recession. The arms business ranks in total sales just below the annual incomes of the world's fourteen largest national economies. Thirty-five billion dollars of these sales are in international arms trade. In the last ten years, the import and export of weapons have become an essential feature of world trade. The Olaf Palme Commission reported that "the arms export boom was one of the ways in which certain...developed economies adjusted to the financial changes of the 1970s. Through arms exports, they shifted part of their increased oil costs to developing countries, including oil-exporting countries."[47]

Waste and Diversion

The arms race and arms trade represent an enormous waste of resources and a diversion of the world economy.

To begin with, consider *nutrition*. Half a billion people throughout the world are severely undernourished. It has been estimated that funds equivalent to one percent of the military budgets of industrialized countries would be sufficient to close the gap of needed development assistance to agriculture.

As to *health*, the eradication of some of the most important communicable diseases would cost trifling amounts compared to the arms race. The World Health Organization (WHO) spent about $83 million over 10 years to eradicate smallpox in the world. That amount would not suffice to buy a single modern strategic bomber. The program to eradicate malaria which affects many more people in the world is dragging owing to lack of funds.[48]

Education also suffers. There are almost as many soldiers as teachers in the world. World military expenditures average $19,300 per soldier; public education expenditures average $380 per school child. In 32 countries, governments spend more for military purposes than for education and health care combined.[49]

As to the waste of people-power, about one half million scientists and engineers are employed in military research and development. About 25 million are in the armed forces alone. Around the world an estimated 100 million people are engaged in military-related occupations.

Natural resources of many types—some of them non-renewable—are squandered by military expenditures. The protection of the *environment* is also affected in many ways—from the diversion of financial and scientific resources to the deliberate and sometimes inadvertent dissemination of harmful radioactivity and toxic wastes.

Public services, health, education, housing, protecting the environment and social and economic progress generally need the resources which military spending consumes. Military spending is a global waste of financial resources, manpower, raw materials, technical skills and research and development capability.

Developing Countries

It is generally acknowledged among economists that one of the most serious problems of this century is the disparity of income between rich (industrialized) and poor (developing) countries.

At the United Nations, the 1970s were designated as the *Decade of Disarmament*; they were also called the *Second Development Decade*. Because disarmament failed, so did the called-for development. It is ironic and tragic that the poorer nations have adopted (or been coerced into) huge military expenditures themselves. The share of developing countries in the world military expenditures has doubled in the past two decades—from 10% to 20%. They account for three-quarters of the world's arms trade. Military spending increases the gap between rich and poor nations.

A United Nations report found that "military spending reduces economic growth in developing countries. The most recent econometric findings (for 69 countries in the 1950s and 1960s) show that increases in military spending had significant negative effects on rates of growth. On average, across countries a one percent increase in the military share of GDP was associated with a 23% reduction in the investment share of

GDP, and an 18% reduction in the share of agriculture."[50] On a political level, the U.S. government widely uses military spending to support military dictatorships.

Military spending and the arms race have also distorted the flow of bilateral assistance from developed to developing countries. They have diminished the priority accorded to economic aid. Military spending accentuates the emphasis on military solutions to international problems which are more often economic, cultural and/or religious in essence. Thus military spending often delays solutions to international problems and becomes a destabilizing factor in the overall picture of foreign policy.

The United Nations study observed: "By diverting vast resources away from production and growth, and by contributing to inflation and the economic crisis which have affected many countries, the arms race directly and indirectly impedes the full development of international exchanges...The arms race...contributes to maintaining and widening the gap between and within developed and developing countries and impedes cooperation between States, socio-economic progress generally and the promotion of a new international economic order."[51]

Military spending is both the supplier and consumer of dozens of local wars in the Middle East, Asia, Africa, and South and Central America. Worst of all, the so-called local wars often have far-reaching implications and could readily involve the major powers in a nuclear war.

Summary

From 1983 to the end of the decade, annual military spending is scheduled to rise from about $200 to $500 billion. It represents a rapidly growing percentage of the Federal budget. Military spending is responsible for the mounting annual Federal deficits (now in the order of $200 billion). Military spending fuels inflation by (a) increasing the Federal deficit, (b) pumping money into the economy without producing buyable goods, and (c) driving up the prices of critical materials.

Military spending contributes to unemployment. Jobs per billion dollars of investment are *lower* for military procurement than virtually any form of spending in the civilian sector of the economy. Military spending deprives the civilian sector of capital investment, thus contributing to the stagnation of the economy. Military spending commands more than half of all research and development costs and skilled personnel. Along with the shortage of investment capital, this concentration depresses innovation and productivity in civilian industries. Military spending adversely affects the competitive position of the U.S. in the world capitalist markets vis-a-vis Western Europe and Japan. U.S. foreign economic policy also puts our country at a disadvantage in competition for the world socialist market.

The expansion of military spending comes at the direct expense of social programs which are being sharply curtailed and in some cases eliminated. Restoration of social programs is one alternate use of military expenditures. Another is reduction in the Federal deficit. Still another is investment in the revitalization of the U.S. economy and its infrastructure.

The principal beneficiaries of military spending are the corporations (and their owners) who make up the military-industrial complex. "Defense" industry is the main recession-proof sector of the U.S. economy.

The negative effects of military spending—on economic growth, inflation, social services, and unemployment—are even worse in the international arena—particularly in developing nations than in the United States. Military spending accelerates the export of arms to the rest of the world contributing to many regional and local wars now raging with conventional weapons at great loss of life and risk of escalation to nuclear war.

Footnotes

1. Robert W. DeGrasse Jr. *Military Expansion Economic Decline,* Council on Economic Priorities, (CEP), 1983. p. 212 ff. The CEP definition of military spending also includes (properly) some smaller items such as a fraction of the Coast Guard, the Maritime Administration and the Impact Aid for Education program.

2. *Economic Report of the President* 1983, pp. 246-7.

3. *Budget of the United States Government,* Fiscal Year 1984, (hereafter cited as "1984 Budget").

4. Ibid., pp. 2-9.

5. As part of the political process, budget figures continue to change through most of the year - from the original submission of the President to the Congress in January, followed by Congressional Committee revisions, then House and Senate votes, then Conference Committee decisions, then First and Second Budget Resolutions, then specific appropriation bills, etc.

6. *The New York Times,* August 1, 1983.

7. *U.S. News and World Report,* February 7, 1982, p. 24.

8. Ibid.

9. Common Cause, Jan.-Feb. 1983, p. 30.

10. See Bi-Partisan Appeal two-page ad in *The New York Times,* April 6, 1983.

11. President Reagan campaigned for office on a fiscal platform of ending deficit spending for which Democrats were said to be mainly guilty. Business journals take pleasure in pointing out that President Franklin Roosevelt was the worst sinner. (In fact, of the total $197 bilion deficit in FDR's 12 years, eight years of New Deal spendig account for 14% while four World War II years were responsible for 86% of the 12-year total.) See *U.S. News and World Report* "Budget Deficits: The Endless River of Red Ink," Feb. 7, 1983.

12. *Economic Report of the President,* 1983, pp. 246-248.

13. *Special Analysis, Budget of the U.S. Government* 1984, p. C-1.

14. DeGrasse, op. cit., p. 140.

15. Ibid., pp. 14-15.

16. *The New York Times,* May 18, 1983.

17. *Wall Street Journal,* Jan. 22, 1980.

18. Congressional Budget Office, *Defense Spending and the Economy,* Feb. 1983, p. 4.

19. Robert DeGrasse, Jr., Paul Murphy, William Roger. *The Costs and Consequences of Reagan's Military Build-up,* Council on Economic Priorities, 1982.

20. Joint Economic Committee, *The Defense Build-up and the Economy,* Feb. 1982.

21. Obie G. Whichard, "Employment and Employee Compensation of U.S. Multinational Companies in 1977", *Survey of Current Business,* vol. 62,

no. 2, Feb. 1982, pp. 37-49.

22. *The New York Times*, Sept. 17, 1982.

23. CEP, *Cost and Consequences...*, op. cit., p. 24. This study also includes a useful bibliography of research on military spending and jobs. See pp. 24-26 and footnotes 34 through 40.

24. Jacques S. Gansler, *The Defense Industry*, MIT Press, 1982, p. 53.

25. CEP, *Cost and Consequences...*, op. cit., p. 27.

26. Employment Research Associates, *The Empty Pork Barrel*, 1982.

27. "The defense budget is always sold as a jobs program, but the defense industry labor force began to realize that, over time, defense dollars are not creating new jobs in those same factories. Every time defense procurement sags and recovers, the defense labor force shrinks, thanks in large part to the rising capital intensity of defense manufacturing. Here, as in other sectors of the economy, increasing machinery prices, more sophisticated raw materials and technology are consuming a larger share of the total dollar costs of a weapons system. The share going into wages is declining in relative terms." *Controlling Weapons Costs,* by Gordon Adams with Paul Murphy and Gray Rosenau, Council on Economic Priorities, 1983.)

28. Congressional Budget Office, *Defense Spending and the Economy,* Feb. 1983, p. 44.

29. Marion Anderson, *The Impact of Military Spending on the Machinists Union,* January 1978.

30. "Military Build-up Slow to Create Jobs," *The New York Times,* June 1, 1982.

31. *Mother Jones,* Sept.-Oct. 1982, p. 12.

32. *Wall Street Journal,* March 23, 1983.

33. Congressional Budget Office, op. cit., Feb. 1983, p. 13.

34. Certain geographical areas of the country also benefit by military spending especially where military bases, shipyards, and major military contractors are located. Contrariwise, the Pentagon budget is a major source of inequality and imbalance betwen Federal expenditures and Federal taxes. It contributes to the economic stagnation of certain regions of the country which do not have substantial military installations or contracts. (James R. Anderson, *Bankrupting America: The Tax Burden and Expenditures of the Pentagon by Congressional District,* 1982 Edition.

35. An excellent bibliography is in Gordon Adams, *The Iron Triangle: The Politics of Defense Contracting,* Council on Economic Priorities, 1981, 465 pp.

36. Council on Economic Priorities, *Newsletter*, August 1982.

37. Michael Parenti, "More Bucks from the Bang", *The Progressive,* July 28, 1980.

38. *The Freeze Economy*, op. cit., p.9. See also DeGrasse, op. cit. pp. 55-97.

39. *The New York Times,* Nov. 14, 1982.

40. Barry M. Blechman, Vice President, Roosevelt Center for American Policy Studies, in the *The New York Times,* Jan. 18, 1983.

41. Conservative estimates of the national cost burden for repairing the infrastructure are close to $3,000 billion over the next ten years (or $300 billion per year). The Department of Transportation estimates that just

maintaining non-urban highways in their current conditions (not improving them) would require more than $500 billion over the next ten years. Water systems in 756 urban centers will require $75 billion to $110 billion over the next 20 years. One in five bridges requires either major reconstruction or rehabilitation cost: about $33 billion. The Association of American Railroads estimates tracks, railbed and railyard improvements at about $90 billion for the next 10 years. The National Waterways Study recommends $32 billion for waterway projects, including locks and deepening 10 major ports. The billion dollars of construction work is needed. (*Industry Week,* March 7, 1983.)

42. *Budget of the United States Government* Fiscal Year 1984, pp. 3-14 and 3-15.

43. *Defense Monitor,* XII, 2, 1983.

44. The Labor Research Association proposed a reduction of $100 billion in military spending. *Economic Notes,* March 1983.

45. Ruth Leger Sivard, "World Military and Social Expenditures," 1982.

46. United Nations, "Economic and Social Consequences of the Arms Race and of Military Expenditures," 1978 edition, p. 39.

47. Independent Commission on Disarmament and Security Issues (Olaf Palme, Chair): "Military Spending: the Economic and Social Consequences," 1982.

48. United Nations, *op. cit.,* p. 27.

49. Sivard, *op. cit.,* p. 22 and p. 5.

50. Independent Commission, Olaf Palme, *op. cit.*

51. U.N. Report, *op. cit.,* p. 59.

Chapter 17

The Social-Psychological Dimension of the Arms Race*

Morris Schwartz

I would like to speak with you about the socio-psychological dimensions of the nuclear arms race, focusing especially on the mechanisms used by the Reagan Administration—and by past administrations—to perpetuate and justify the arms race. I will also discuss the psychological effects the arms race has had, and continues to have, on the thinking, feeling and behavior of the American public. And finally I will suggest some ways of approaching a solution to the problem of stopping the arms race, reversing course, and beginning to reduce and eliminate nuclear arms.

Let me begin by saying that we do not have an adequate frame of reference to fully understand the delicate, peculiar, fragile and unprecedented relationship between life and death, that exists today. Thus we have difficulty in assimilating the nuclear reality—difficulty in absorbing it, believing it, confronting it, coming to terms with it, and then acting to banish nuclear weapons so that they no longer threaten our existence.

When I talk about the psychology of the arms race I am referring to the psychology of President Reagan and his entourage, that is, all those who want to perpetuate and speed up the arms race so that we will spend 1.5 trillion dollars on it in

* Transcript of a speech delivered at Brandeis University

the next five years. This entourage consists of his civilian advisors and consultants, some cabinet officers and other officials, the Pentagon planners, defense strategists and experts, the scientists and technologists who service the Administration, and the armament industrialists who will profit from the billions we spend on arms. It is these people whose collective and social psychology as revealed in their plans and policies that I will interpret for you, not their individual psychology—for I have no inside information about their private thoughts, feelings, motivations and psychodynamics. However, I do not wish to leave the impression that the Reagan Administration is different from other administrations in regard to increasing our nuclear arsenal. It is not. It is only more aggressive, blatant, and demanding of economic resources in pursuing nuclear armament increases. Basically its policies are a continuation and acceleration of the policies of previous administrations.

In referring to the Reagan Administration and its proposals to speed up the arms race I am tempted to call them "the arms racers," but that would fall into the very psychological trap that I first want to warn you against: that is the *sanitizing of the language*. This psychological mechanism has been operating for along time and is not a Reagan invention. It is a deliberate attempt to clean up, tone down and neutralize the language; to disguise or conceal the meaning; to detach oneself from and objectify the real situation so that we do not experience the full horror of what is being discussed. It is an attempt to lull us into a false sense of security and to make the arms race and the nuclear weapons it produces ordinary occurrences and thus acceptable and unremarkable. It is hoped that the terms will, if they haven't already, infiltrate our vocabulary, become part of our every-day talk and thus reduce or deaden their emotional impact. Thus we have the term "nuclear device" which suggests a machine or gadget, while in reality it is an atom bomb that can kill and maim hundreds of thousands of people in an instant. As for the term "nuclear event," it sounds like an ordinary happening or occurrence that one might read about in the morning newspaper. What it means, in fact, is that a nuclear bomb has been dropped with all the horrific consequences for those in its orbit. Similarly with the term "nuclear exchange". It sounds like a friendly trade between acquaintances or business associates. In reality, it means a nuclear war has started. The term "pre-emptive strike" conveys the idea of a defensive and protective gesture, or "first strike" which sounds like a baseball game or union walk-out. In reality it means the initiation of an atomic war. I could go on and on with such terms as "counterforce," "strategic options," "acceptable losses,""surgical strike," "nuclear-tipped missiles," "collateral damage" and "peacekeeper" (for the de-stabilizing MX missile).

Let me end with one more term, that which refers to nuclear arms as "weapons of war". Here the attempt is to leave the impression that nuclear arms are like other weapons that are used in fighting a war. In truth they are not weapons, but rather instruments for extinguishing the human race, and if used would not be fighting a war but threatening the survival of the human race and the planet on which we live.

It is difficult to estimate how much and in what ways this sanitizing of the language has succeeded in deadening our responses so that we do not experience flesh and blood human beings in peril, so that we deny or are numbed to the potential possibility that all of human life might be obliterated. But it is quite clear that it is the intention of those who sanitize our language to induce such numbing, denial and normalization in us, and ordinariness for themselves, and to lull us into a false sense of security.

In the Administration's and "Defense" Department's attempts to sanitize the language, and in the attempts of others to expose this "nuke-speak" lies a struggle for providing the vocabulary to be used, and establishing the terms of discourse, in the nuclear arms race. It is also a struggle for the ways in which reality will be framed, defined and experienced, how our minds and feelings will encompass the current nuclear condition and the fate that is being prepared for us. In this struggle the Administration hides or distorts reality by subjecting us to a massive propaganda barrage that tries to explain, persuade, justify, and rationalize the necessity for increasing our nuclear arms. They do this by claiming our national security is at risk because of a window of vulnerability, and that we have to overcome Soviet nuclear superiority if we are to maintain a credible deterrent. All of these propaganda assaults and the attempts at sanitizing the language have the intended and unintended consequences of: normalizing the abnormal; making the concrete danger, abstract; splitting our thoughts from our feelings; technologizing the moral; making the insane, sane; mystifying the obvious; making the absurd, rational; transforming the horrendous into the everyday and making the unacceptable, acceptable.

The sanitized vocabulary is very much related to the next socio-psychological mechanism I shall discuss, namely the *de-*

humanizing attitudes and orientations utilized toward self and others. In devising nuclear war strategies the language is cold and calculating, it is abstract and logical, and it is technical. Charts, graphs, computer printouts are objective representations of cities and people. Means-ends sequences are analyzed, statistic probabilities are projected, logical deductions are made, alternative scenarios are portrayed, gain and loss is calculated, and possibility and opportunity are evaluated. What emerges are abstract conclusions that are formulated in such a way that, for example, the killing of 20-40 million Americans is considered an "acceptable loss." And by taking this "calculated risk" we might expect to inflict a loss of 100 million on the Russians, thus a victory for our side. In this social madness called nuclear war game playing, the role-players act like de-humanized automatons or robots, and thereby de-humanize themselves, us, the Russians, and all of humanity. We are asked to support such calculated madness, in order to achieve victory over the Russians. What is conspicuously absent in these technical calculations is the moral-human dimension. What is missing is the experience of specific human beings in danger, a reverence for human life, and a recognition of our interdependence with other nations and peoples. What is ignored is compassion for ourselves and our fellow human beings, and a poignant awareness of the monstrous evil that is being calculated and contemplated. Such objective considerations cry out for a focus on, and discussion of: ultimate concerns, the meaning of the human enterprise, recognition of our common humanity, and what it means to tempt the possibility of foreclosing the future. Einstein, anticipating the nuclear crisis, had this to say in his last signed statement, "we appeal as human beings, to human beings: Remember your humanity and forget the rest."

The third socio-psychological mechanism I would like to briefly discuss is the *polarization of the enemy.* In this regard the advent of the atom bomb has changed everything except the Administration's ways of thinking about the Russians. They are obsessed with the "Russian danger," stuck in the old channels and exaggerated stereotypes, of seeing "Them" in a world-wide contest with "Us." They paint the Russians as Evil Incarnate who want to take over the world, and us as the "Good" protector of the Free World. They see the Russians as preparing for war and conquest while we are only preparing to protect ourselves against their evil designs. They say the Russians are untrustworthy, treacherous and aggressive, whereas we are the opposite. George Kennan, the former Ambassador to the USSR and the author of the containment policy, has had much to say recently about how the Administration distorts, misrepresents and misinterprets Soviet society, intentions, strengths and weaknesses and motivations.[1] But the Administration continues to alarm us about Soviet military strength and nuclear might and emphasizes our weakness. There are many factors at work here: fear, suspicion, distrust, misunderstanding, ideological distortion, vested interest, and the need to confirm the convictions one held in the first place about the Soviets. What is clear is that such polarization serves at least two purposes for the Administration. It enables them to justify the heating up of the arms race and their demand for vast sums of money for arms, thus enabling arms manufacturers to make huge profits. And it provides the American public with a convenient, acceptable, U.S.-made object and scapegoat upon which to project its frustrations, fears, angers and hatreds. In addition, it makes it more and more difficult to come to terms with this polarized enemy. By engendering irreconcilable enmity toward the Russians it becomes virtually impossible to find bases for accommodation; and as we prepare for conflict with them we deny its suicidal potentialities. Such polarization diverts our attention from the central fact of our times: that in the nuclear age, at this time, we and the Russians share an inescapable common fate: we shall either live together on this planet or die together. Each possesses the power to unilaterally bring about our mutual death, but only both together, through negotiation and compromise, can assure continuing collective life.

A quote from George Kennan is appropriate here: "There is no issue at stake in our political relations with the Soviet Union—no hope, no fear, nothing to which we aspire, nothing we would like to avoid—which could conceivably be worth a nuclear war."[2]

Another socio-psychological mechanism put to work by the current Administration, is the production of delusions and deceptions, in order to keep fueling the fires of the nuclear arms race. A concise statement of these *delusions and deceptions* goes something like this. 1) *Nuclear war can be limited.* There is no way of ensuring such a limitation or controlling the course of a nuclear war, the probability is great that it will spread into a total nuclear war; 2) *We can prevail*, i.e., win in a nuclear war. There are no winners or losers. Everyone loses with millions of deaths on each side, and a contaminated, uninhabitable planet; 3) *We can provide a civil defense against a nuclear attack.* Millions of real, live, flesh and blood human beings will be incinerated, burst asunder, radiated and annihilated; 4) *We can recover from a nuclear attack*. It is most likely that chaos and panic will prevail and that those who survive will be so disoriented, psychotic, shell-shocked, depressed or catatonic that organized life as we know it will be impossible.

I believe that the persons generating these delusions and deceptions acutely feel the loss of security and stability, and that they feel afraid and powerless. They try to overcome and defend themselves against this feeling of powerlessness by seeking increased strength through a massive increase in nuclear arms, and they try to conquer their fear and reassure themselves by asserting that we can prevail if we do indeed multiply our nuclear arsenal. Thus as we escalate the arms race we increase the very devices that are responsible in the first place for our loss of security, and are left with a greater sense of vulnerability and insecurity.

A striking illustration of this delusion-deception mechanism is a statement by Deputy Undersecretary of Defense T.K. Jones: "Everybody's going to make it [in a nuclear war] if there are enough shovels to go around...Dig a hole, cover it with a couple of doors, and then throw three feet of dirt on top. It's the dirt that does it."[3] I ask myself in amazement and trembling, "Could he be serious? Does he really believe this?" If he does, it's a form of madness. If he doesn't then it is a mode of highly irresponsible deception. Or consider two statements by the Federal Emergency Management Agency: "A close look at the facts shows with fair certainty that with reasonable protective measures (including plans for evacuation that will require six days notice) the U.S. could survive nuclear attack and go on to recovery within a relatively few years," and "the other thing that the Administration has categorically rejected is the short-war, mutually assured destruction, it'll-be-over-in-20-minutes-so-why-the-hell-mess-around-spending-dollars-on-it—We're trying to inject a long-war mentality."[4] It is difficult to say whether these are self-deceptions based on delusions, or whether they are deliberate deceptions to delude the public. It is probably some of both: they believe some claims and not others, some partially and others fully.

If Administration officials are totally self-deluded and out of touch with reality about the consequences of a nuclear war then I begin to wonder if a form of social madness has already taken over. If, on the other hand, they are deliberately deceiving us, in order to hide the horrible truth that there is no protection from atomic war, and that the only way to protect ourselves is to prevent it, then we had better stop listening to them, discredit them, and discover our own truths.

I want now to discuss some socio-psychological mechanisms involved in the *quest for national security*. It is a fundamental need of the individual to feel safe and secure as a person. And it is a basic concern of a nation to provide for the security of its citizens and territory. An example of our quest for security is President Reagan's recent speech in which he promises to seek an impregnable defense in outer space. This, and the attempt to reassure ourselves that we can indeed be made secure through more and better nuclear arms, reflects a fundamental unwillingness on the part of our leaders to accept the fact that the basis for, and the nature of, our national security has changed radically: that it cannot be total for we will always be vulnerable to some degree, that it cannot be established and maintained unilaterally, and that it will not be found in increasing nuclear armaments. On the contrary, when this quest for national security is sought through more and better nuclear arms, it is pursued in a self-defeating way. Let me tell you why I believe this to be true. The more and better nuclear arms we build, the more frantic and frightened the Russians become and try to match us. The more they try to match us, the more frantic and threatened we feel and try more desperately to get ahead. The more we try to get ahead, the more insecure they become, and the harder they try to get ahead. If either side feels that the situation is de-stabilized, and one is beginning to fall too far behind then one might be tempted into dropping the bomb first. Or the power that thinks they are so far ahead might persuade itself that this time is propitious to initiate the dropping of the bomb. Thus the arms race becomes more and more insecurity producing for each and both, especially at times when either country feels it is more vulnerable or more powerful than the other. Under conditions of vulnerability and fear, the probability increases that one or the other of the antagonists might act rashly, irrationally or precipitously. Meanwhile, as these weapons of destruction pile up in such huge numbers that it is difficult to find targets for them, the possibility of a bomb being exploded by accident or miscalculation increases. As do the proliferation of nuclear weapons to other countries, and the possibility that a nuclear weapon might be manufactured or used by an "unstable" or "irresponsible" head of government, or by a terrorist. Thus we have a cyclical feedback mechanism in which more nuclear arms means less security. Therefore we have to conclude that our security is dependent upon helping the Russians feel more secure; and their security is dependent upon their helping us feel more secure. We can only insure our individual security by insuring our mutual security. We will thus be secure together or vulnerable and insecure together. It seems clear then that the nuclear arms race accomplishes the opposite of what it intends and hopes for, and that only a nuclear arms freeze, arms reduction and eventual disarmament might achieve the goal of national security that both countries are desperately striving for.

The last socio-psychological mechanism I shall describe is the defense establishment experts' and the Administration's cold warriors' *trained incapacity to accept our new reality*. It is a mechanism that undergirds the other socio-psychological processes I've described. It consists of a deficit in imagination, which makes them incapable of having the present and future consequences of the nuclear arms race realistically sink in at the emotional and cognitive level. This incapacity is constituted by restricted vision and constricted feeling, by an emotional addiction to, and reliance on, the bomb, by a passionate commitment to their pre-conceptions, by their inability to detach their stereotyped frames of reference, and by the need to maintain ideological purity. It means that our leaders cannot experience directly or hold emotionally the reality of the nuclear danger, i.e., that it might eventuate in a final act of destruction.

Our leaders are also incapable of accepting the fundamental existential fact of our nuclear age—vulnerability. Everyone is susceptible to instant destruction. In order to cope with the terror of the nuclear danger they are holding on to familiar ways of thinking about defense and making war—thinking about winning and losing, about inferiority and superiority, about being ahead and behind in nuclear arms. This striving to get ahead or keep ahead in order to prevail in a nuclear war gives them a sense of power and effectiveness. It enables them to project the possibility of success and thereby reduces the felt vulnerability. But it does not change the real vulnerability. It is especially difficult to repair this incapacity to confront our new reality when it serves such powerful defensive purposes and the actors constitute a closed group which perpetuates and reinforces its faulty thinking and feeling—a group whose members only pay attention to those who agree with them. Thus it appears difficult if not impossible to enter this closed circle of cold warriors with contrary recognitions and new ways of thinking and feeling about our nuclear situation.

Some of the socio-psychological mechanisms I have described—the sanitizing of the language, the de-humanizing orientations and attitudes of the nuclear warriors, the polarization of the Russians and Us, deceptions and delusions the self-defeating quest for unilateral national security and the incapacity in accepting our new reality—are all used consciously or unconsciously by our defense planners in the service of pushing the nuclear arms race.

Consciously, they see the increase of nuclear arms and the pursuit of an impregnable defense as a vehicle for preventing nuclear attack, and as ways of restoring our pre-eminence as the leading super-power. Unconsciously, they are reacting against feelings of impotence by trying to "take control" and stay in control of the nuclear situation. In addition they are protecting themselves against experiencing and facing the uncertainty and insecurity of the unknown that accompanies preparations for nuclear war and its unpredictable course and outcome. As for the rest of us, the Administration intends with these mechanisms to persuade us to accept and support their plans and policies, to keep us ignorant and passive, to numb us into quiescence and complacency, to minimize and blur our recognition of the dangers, and to keep us unaware of the vastness of the holocaust.

Meanwhile, the belligerent talk, declamations that we are not afraid to fight a nuclear war, threats that we are preparing to do so, and indeed will do so under certain circumstances, has had profoundly disturbing effects on segments of our society. John E. Mack, Professor of Psychiatry at the Harvard Medical School, has sent out 1000 questionnaires to students in grammar schools and high schools. He found that "the questionnaires showed that these adolescents are deeply disturbed by the threat of nuclear war, have doubts about the future, and about their own survival. There was an experience of fear and menace. There was also cynicism, sadness, bitterness and a sense of helplessness. They feel unprotected. Some have doubts about planning families and are unable to think ahead in any long-term sense."[5] In another report, Mack and a co-worker reported that to their respondents, planning seems pointless and ordinary values and ideals seem naive. In such a context, impulsivity, a values system of 'get it now', the hyperstimulation of drugs and the proliferation of apocalyptic cults that try to revive the idea of an afterlife while extinguishing individuality or discriminating perception, seem to be natural developments."[6]

As for those of us who are partially or fully sensitized to our socially mad nuclear situation, we inhabit a world in which we either practice denial, numb ourselves, sink into despair or anguish, are overhelmed by fear and anxiety, feel powerless and disoriented, or discover other ways of escaping from the impinging reality of the nuclear threat. Assigning this threat the seriousness it deserves means we are forced to lead schizoid lives: living in ordinary day-to-day reality and with the "other reality"—the threat that human life might be extinguished at any moment. We may have that "other reality" in the background or foreground of our consciousness, and we may work out different balances between the two realities, but the ominous dread haunts us as a continuing feature of our life, threatening us with absurdity and meaninglessness. We face a lingering uncertainty about how best to organize our lives when the existence of the future is in question. Some of us try to defend ourselves against the recognition of and confrontation with the threatening peril by single-minded pre-occupation with self, career, family, sex, money-making, status, power, or living for the moment. Yet when this doesn't work and the defenses break down or are set aside momentarily we find ourselves in internal conflict: attending and inattending to the nuclear threat; acting in relation to, or withdrawing from, it; asking ourselves whether and how to become activists and then turning away from the question. It is a conflict all of us face which may be temporarily resolved then struggled with again and again at various levels of difficulty. Finally, we may find a ground upon which to stand so that we can balance and integrate the two "realities" that envelop us. We have to learn to live with the ever-present threat of extermination of all we treasure and value knowing that it will be difficult to reduce and eliminate the nuclear arsenal, yet also knowing we must do all we can to minimize the social madness which increasingly threatens to overwhelm us.

What are the other social costs and consequences of the nuclear arms race? What are the effects on, and in, a society whose center of gravity is salvation? What happens to a society when it prepares for and threatens nuclear war?

It is of course difficult to answer these questions in a direct and unequivocal way as have economists in relation to the economy. They have shown how, when our society skews its expenditures toward defense, it does so at the expense of our human, public and social services. We do not have the evidence nor the research to demonstrate the general social damage that I believe is being done to individuals in our society, our institutions and our society as a whole. Thus I can only offer you my impressions of some of the ways in which nuclearism may be contributing to the unravelling of the social fabric.

As fear, dread, anxiety and powerlessness about the nuclear threat spread among individuals in society, it may be that they are precipitated into engaging in various irrational, defensive or destructive acts they previously had not contemplated or had restrained themselves from performing. These affective currents, combined with the felt insecurity and vulnerability occasioned by our nuclear situation, may induce desperation or despair and thus facilitate forms of behavior previously deemed unacceptable. Thus our norms and values erode and our daily life becomes more endangered. It is difficult to gauge how far feelings of increased insecurity, uncertainty and fragility have imbedded themselves in our individual and collective consciousness, and our unconscious. But I believe it has happened to a sufficient degree to endanger our democratic values; for under conditions of extreme threat and insecurity these are quickly dispensed with. This erosion of our democratic values is aided and abetted by the societal secrecy, surveillance and heightened security measures that accompany our nuclearism.

In addition, as the awareness that collective life can be terminated at any moment heightens, one possible response is that life's absurdity and meaninglessness is felt more acutely. As a consequence the restraints on "immoral", "unethical" or "indecent" behavior might diminish, as might the motivation for role-performance. What happens here is that civility, decency, concern for others, mutual responsibility, and other manifestations of "civilized" behavior are discarded in order to desperately pursue what is presumed to be in one's self-interest, or to indulge in forms of hedonism, narcissism and egocentricity which reduce the social bonds of solidarity. Furthermore, when collective life is experienced as absurd and one feels powerless to change the pathological normalcy, some might feel themselves adrift, without stable social anchors, compelled by fleeting social currents to participate in ways they have not self-consciously chosen and to which they have no moral commitment.

When we are treated by our leaders as "acceptable losses" in an atomic war, and are encouraged to accept the possibility of slaughtering millions of others if they deem it to be in our "national interest", powerful modes of de-humanization are already in play. We need to ask ourselves how far we have already been de-humanized and have de-humanized ourselves. Even if we were to avoid a nuclear war, by continuing on this path we would lose these more precious human characteristics, a compassion for the other, and a reverence for life.

One of the ways of preparing us for accepting the use of our stored violence is by normalizing it. That this normalization has already taken place is reflected in a new game called "Ultimatum: A Game of Nuclear Confrontation" distributed by

Yaquinto Publications of Dallas, Texas. The instruction manual states: "The object is to destroy relatively more of the enemy's population while minimizing one's own population loss. . . .The winner is generally the one who has destroyed more of his enemy's population than he himself lost."

When the stored violence in our nuclear arsenals is rationalized, normalized and accepted, as are the threats of readiness to use them, these instruments of extermination might begin to serve as invitations and models for the use of violence and force in everyday life. They could possibly facilitate the violence of those who are already so disposed, unconsciously legitimate it for some, and encourage the violence of those who are only tenuously restrained from it.

Finally, with the nuclear threat, and the nightmare it adumbrates becoming too horrible to contemplate, people defend themselves against full awareness of the nuclear situation. Thus by inattending, denying, escaping from, and numbing themselves to the nuclear threat they engage in various forms of reality distortion. By hatred and suspicion of, and projection on to, the "life-destroying" enemy, they parallel the social madness perpetuated on us by our leaders. When these irrationalities, defensive maneuvers and forms of social madness push aside, or overwhelm, a more objective reality orientation, organized social life in which respect and dignity for the individual is a central value becomes more and more difficult to maintain. And the sense of a common humanity, shared with all peoples of the world—a sense that is so necessary for our survival in this divided world—becomes virtually impossible to generate.

What is to be done then? How to get out of this horrendous nuclear situation we are already in, and into which we are sinking deeper and deeper?

I have no easy or exceptional solutions to offer, but to say that the struggle against the nuclear arms race and the nuclear arms menace must be engaged at various levels. First we must recognize fully that because of the existence of nuclear arms and our competition-conflict with Russia around them, we are an endangered species. At risk is our humanity, our flawed democratic-humane civilization, our individual and collective survival, and our habitable planet. We must absorb fully the awareness that the time is late and the danger is great.

Second, what is asked of us is a radical re-conceptualization of our framework for thinking about and experiencing the nuclear threat; and we need a radical emotional re-orientation toward each other and all of humanity.

Third, we must become acutely aware of the different psychological ways we are being persuaded and coerced into accepting the Administration's view of the nuclear situation. We must raise our own and other people's consciousness to resist their psychological manipulations. Fourth, we must convince ourselves and then try to convince the Administration that if we contribute to Russian security we will enhance our own, that it can no longer be us against them, that we either win together and preserve human life, or we lose together and annihilate it. Fifth, we must be clear about the ever-present danger of nuclear war and we must therefore join in the social movements that are expressing opposition to the continuation of the nuclear arms race and urging that the production of these weapons cease and their reduction begin. Sixth, we must insist that the nuclear arms race is a human and moral issue, and not a problem to be solved by experts—the technicians, the politicians and the military—alone. This means that we must express our moral revulsion toward nuclear arms and believe in and feel our power to make a difference, to make our voices heard, our votes count, and our impact felt. Seventh, we must retain our social sanity while recognizing and resisting the social madness being perpetrated on us. And finally, we must unite in what I would call the *Great Refusal.* Each of us separately and all of us together must undertake the varying forms of refusal to cooperate with the nuclear arms race that are appropriate to our situation and state of being. The danger is great, the threat is imminent, the crisis is severe, and the actions we take must be appropriate to the extreme situation in which we exist.

Footnotes

1. Kennan, George, *The Nuclear Delusion* (New York, Pantheon Books, 1982).

2. *Ibid*, p. 194-195.

3. Quoted in the *Defense Monitor*, 1982, Vol. XI, No. 5, p. 5.

4. *Ibid*, p. 5.

5. Mack, John E., "Psychosocial Effects of the Nuclear Arms Race," in *Bulletin of Atomic Scientists*, April 1981, pp. 19-20.

6. Beardslee, W. and Mack, John E., "The Impact on Children and Adolescents of Nuclear Developments," in APA Task Force No. 20, *Psychosocial Aspects of Nuclear Developments*, 1982, pp. 89-91.

PART IV

INTERNATIONAL ASPECTS OF THE ARMS RACE

Introduction

> I find the view of the Soviet Union that prevails today
> in large portions of our government and journalistic
> establishments so extreme, so subjective, so far re-
> moved from what any sober scrutiny of external reality
> would reveal that it is not only ineffective but danger-
> ous as a guide to political action.
>
> —George Kennan, former U.S.
> Ambassador to the Soviet Union

In his March 23, 1983 speech to the nation on defense spending
and policy, President Reagan repeated his earlier claim that the
Soviet Union enjoys a "margin of nuclear superiority" over the
United States. However, Simon Rosenblum's comparison of
American and Soviet nuclear capabilities and policies reveals
that it isn't so. The United States maintains a clear advantage
in the numbers game and, more importantly, the Soviets lag in
most areas of nuclear technology. Given that the latter is the
cutting edge of the arms race, there is no reason to fear
imminent Soviet superiority. Even Reagan's own Scowcroft
Commission has had to admit the absence of any "window of
vulnerability." Soviet military power cannot, of course, be
ignored. The Soviet Union could explode about 8,000 nuclear

weapons on North American territory, and has at least another 10,000 tactical nuclear weapons available for use in Europe. But as David Holloway's carefully analyzed companion piece demonstrates, parity and not superiority is the essence of Soviet nuclear policy. The Soviets have indeed increased their nuclear arsenal, but in this connection the following statement by Bernard Brodie, the first nuclear strategist, may be sobering: "Where the Committee on the Present Danger...speaks of 'the brutal momentum of the massive Soviet strategic arms buildup—a buildup without precedent in history,' it is speaking of something which no student of the American strategic arms buildup in the sixties could possibly consider unprecedented." Likewise, what the U.S.S.R. has done through its increase in conventional forces is to break a previous western monopoly on military activity in the Third World. And, on balance, Rosenblum argues, the Soviet Union is not making headway throughout the world.

The assumptions of U.S. defense policy represent a fundamental miscalculation of Soviet military development and policy. And this is by no means accidental. Alan Wolfe argues that there is a recurring tendency of American politicians to exploit the "Soviet threat" issue for political gain. The implication is that domestic politics within the U.S. rather than objective Soviet actions are responsible for the hardening of American defense policy. Indeed the escalation of Cold War rhetoric over the last number of years may be more a companion to the American weapons buildup than a cause; it is impossible to generate public support for multibillion dollar weapons systems, without "scaring hell out of the country," as Senator Arthur Vandenburg advised President Truman when the first large military appropriations of the Cold War were being planned.

If it is true, as argued in Part I, that it is indeed the United States which is striving for clear nuclear superiority and a "nuclear war-winning capability," much of the confusion over the "Russian threat" can be understood as essentially another weapon in the arsenal of our American hawks.

On the European front, the major issue is obviously the Cruise and Pershing II deployments. Dan Smith refutes the conventional wisdom that says NATO development of these two weapon systems is necessary to counter the Soviet SS-20s. He suggests that NATO's strategy is better explained as a product of tensions in the relationship between the United States and Western Europe than as a consequence of any radical change in the European nuclear theater. Indeed, a convincing case can be made that the existing balance is not unfavorable to NATO. Smith expresses the resentment, increasingly felt in Europe, that America's "limited nuclear war" strategies include destroying Europe in order to save it. The American proposals on intermediate-range nuclear weapons are so self-serving and counterproductive that even the former West German leader Helmut Schmidt has expressed his lack of faith in American negotiations.

The Cruise and Pershing deployment has obviously been a major catalyst in the emergence of a mass European peace movement. Diana Johnstone points out that on this issue the peace movement has the support of the majorities in most West European countries. Yet European governments are proceeding with deployment and the peace movement has yet to find a way to convert its popular support into political muscle. The Western European peace movement's horizons go well beyond particular weapons systems in their challenge to the historical domination of Europe by two hostile military blocs. E.P. Thompson's article indicates the increasing frustration felt by European peace activists about being held hostage by the two superpowers. The goal of a denuclearized Europe "from Poland to Portugal" is accurately understood as a fundamental challenge to both blocs and reflects a desire to remove all of Europe from the Cold War. The growth of an independent peace movement in Eastern Europe is obviously a necessary counterpart to this campaign. Suzanne Gordon gives us a picture of this movement sheltered by the church, maintaining an uneasy relationship with the "official" government peace committees and constantly in jeopardy of being crushed.

Western European peace movements, by demonstrating in the streets and mobilizing opinion against their own governments, have begun to achieve within a few years what almost four decades of Cold War policy has not—the encouragement of groups within the Eastern bloc that challenge the race toward nuclear war by both superpowers. And in turn, the existence of these Eastern European independents has helped Western peace movements refute the notion that Western militarism is necessary because there is no hope for internal antiwar pressure in Warsaw Pact countries. Yet, at the same time, disarmament agreements cannot wait upon the growth of democracy in the East. Indeed, the reality is that efforts for democracy in the East will be successful only when the arms race has been halted and the Cold War thawed.

Chapter 18

The Russians Aren't Coming

Simon Rosenblum

The more constructive East-West relationship which the
Allies seek requires tangible signs that the Soviet Union is
prepared to abandon the disturbing build-up of its military
strength, to desist from resorting to force and intimidation
and to cease creating or exploiting situations of crisis and
instability in the Third World.

-Soviet Military Power
published by the U.S. Department of Defense, 1981

Let us not confuse the question by blaming it all on our
Soviet adversaries...They too have made their mistakes;
and I would be the last to deny it. But we must remember
that it has been we Americans who, at almost every step of
the road have taken the lead in the development of this
sort of weaponry. It was we who first produced and tested
such a device; we who were the first to raise its destructiveness to a new level with the hydrogen bomb; we
who introduced the multiple warhead; we who declined
every proposal for the renunciation of the principle of
"first use"; and we alone, so help us God, who have first
used the weapon in anger against others, and against tens
of thousands of helpless noncombatants at that.

-George F. Kennan, Former U.S.
Ambassador to the U.S.S.R.

Ronald Reagan describes U.S. military vulnerabilities in the most sweeping terms: "In virtually every measure of military power the Soviet Union enjoys a decided advantage." His Administration vigorously declares that the Soviets are hell-bent on taking over the world. Indeed, the last decade has undoubtedly witnessed an upsurge in Soviet military strength which is still continuing. This has led many in the West to claim first, that the nuclear balance of power between East and West is beginning to tilt in favor of the East; and second, that Soviet determination to strengthen its forces suggests that it harbors expansionist designs.

It is first of all necessary to assess the Soviet military threat. An increasingly widespread contention is that the Soviet Union's strategic nuclear forces are "superior" to those of the United States and that the Soviets are aiming to fight and win a nuclear war. This prognosis has so pervasively and almost routinely been reported in the mass media that it is rapidly becoming commonplace, the hard-headed new realism for a hard-boiled age.

Are the Soviets stronger than the West? Differences in the composition of Soviet and American military forces make it all too easy to take a few figures out of context to alarm people about the military balance. The Soviets probably spend a larger proportion of their GNP for military purposes than does the U.S., and they have more missile launchers, more tanks and artillery pieces in Europe, more ships in their navy and a greater total megatonnage in nuclear weapons. Does this mean that they are ahead in the arms race?

The Numbers Game, or 'Who's on First?'

Where the Committee on the Present Danger in one of its brochures speaks of "the brutal momentum of the massive Soviet strategic arms buildup — a buildup without precedent in history," it is speaking of something which no student of the American strategic arms buildup in the sixties could possibly consider unprecedented.
—Michael Howard, Oxford University Professor

The United States has approximately 1,000 land-based intercontinental ballistic missiles (ICBMs) and the Soviets have about 1,500. The Russian missiles are bigger than the American ones. The U.S. and the Soviets have approximately equal numbers of strategic weapons, but Soviet warheads, too, are bigger. The United States has more B-52 bombers, but the Russian bombers are newer. Such facts are bandied about as if they were deciding factors in the who's ahead debate, but they

FIGURE 18-1
THE U.S.—SOVIET STRATEGIC ARMS RACE

	ICBMs		SLBMs		Long Range Bombers		Delivery Vehicles		Total Warheads		Total Megatons*	
	U.S.	USSR	U.S.	USSR	U.S.	USSR	U.S.	USSR	U.S.	USSR	U.S.	USSR
1990**	1,350	1,700	720	1,300	450	200	2,550	3,200	18,000	20,000	7,100	13,000
1985**	1,052	1,500	664	1,100	348	140	2,064	2,740	13,300	10,000	4,200	9,200
1982	1,052	1,400	632	950	348	140	2,032	2,490	11,000	8,000	4,100	7,100
1980	1,054	1,400	640	950	348	140	2,042	2,490	10,000	6,000	4,000	5,700
1978	1,054	1,400	656	810	348	140	2,058	2,350	9,800	5,200	3,800	5,400
1976	1,054	1,500	656	750	390	140	2,100	2,390	9,400	3,200	3,700	4,500
1974	1,054	1,600	656	640	470	140	2,180	2,380	8,400	2,400	3,800	4,200
1972	1,054	1,500	656	450	520	140	2,230	2,090	5,800	2,100	4,100	4,000
1970	1,054	1,300	656	240	520	140	2,230	1,680	3,900	1,800	4,300	3,100
1968	1,054	850	656	40	650	155	2,360	1,045	4,500	850	5,100	2,300
1966	1,054	250	592	30	750	155	2,396	435	5,000	550	5,600	1,200
1964	800	200	336	20	1,280	155	2,146	375	6,800	500	7,500	1,000
1962	80	40	144	20	1,650	155	1,874	290	7,400	400	8,000	800
1960	20	a few	32	15	1,650	130	1,702	150	6,500	300	7,200	600

* The figures shown are for "equivalent megatons," the most commonly used measure of aggregate explosive power. It is obtained by taking the square root of weapon yields above one megaton and the cube root of weapon yields below one megaton.

** Assumes no SALT Treaty limiting strategic offensive weapons. The numbers shown are extrapolations of official U.S. estimates provided in congressional testimony on the SALT II Treaty.

Source: *Ground Zero, Nuclear War: What's In It For You?* (New York: Pocket Books, 1982), p. 266.

are virtually meaningless. Actually, a straight-forward look at American military capabilities leads to the opposite conclusion.

A familiar charge hurled by those who warn of impending or present danger is that the Soviet Union has more strategic delivery vehicles than the United States. But those pointing to Soviet numerical superiority in missiles and bombers point only at the irrelevant. The number of missiles meant something in the days before multiple independently targetable warheads. Now that figure, at least as an indicator of offensive strength, has very limited utility. More relevant is the number of warheads and bombs (the things that actually kill people and demolish targets). The United States has 25 percent more of these.[1] Furthermore, measuring nuclear forces in numbers of missiles and warheads ("bean counts") doesn't really mean all that much. Weapon systems must be related to specific missions, i.e., their accuracy, speed and vulnerability, as well as the strategic doctrines of the superpowers. The Soviet advantage in the number of ICBM launchers, upon which Washington now bases its claims of Soviet superiority, has always been a sign of Soviet weakness rather than strength. That is why the Nixon administration explicitly conceded to the Soviet Union's higher number of ICBMs in the SALT I agreement. Henry Kissinger considered the treaty a major coup for America. The United States, he told Congress, was interested in warheads, not launchers. "This was the theory behind SALT I, which froze numbers of at-that-time single warhead systems in the Soviet Union against multiple warhead systems in the U.S.," he explained. The U.S. was able to develop solid fuel and precision multiple warhead missiles before the Soviet Union, which made it less dependent on land-based ICBMs and on a comparable number of heavy weapons. To make up for its lack of accurate multi-warheaded lighter missiles, the Soviet Union relied on heavier land-based ICBMs.

Another charge is that the Soviet Union's weapons possess greater "throw-weight" than those of the United States. This is a dishonest comparison because in the mid-1960s the U.S. Defense Department made a conscious and deliberate choice to trade in throw-weight for accuracy. As Henry Kissinger explained in his March 22, 1976 Dallas speech: "The Soviet Union chose a different course because of its more limited technological capabilities, it emphasized missiles with greater throw-weight compensated for their substantially poor accuracy." Soviet missiles are bigger because they are built in a style American missile designers regard as extremely old-fashioned. Ninety-five percent of Soviet missiles are powered by liquid fuel, which the U.S. stopped using for new military missiles some 20 years ago. Liquid fuel is volatile and corrodes delicate electrical circuity. The "throw-weight gap" exists because the Americans decided back in the 1960s that there was no point in building big missiles, a fact that has not stifled hawkish fury since over the Soviet lead in "heavy" missiles. The question is totally irrelevant, because the weight of a missile's warhead does not necessarily bear any relation to the size of the blast. For example: the latest American ICBM warhead, the Mark 12-A, is just two percent heavier than its predecessor, the Mark 12; yet its explosive blast is twice as large. So, the U.S. doesn't need heavy throw-weight to perform its strategic missions. Moscow on the other hand has long had to compensate for inferior accuracy technologies by increasing missile yields. Since a near ten-fold increase in yield only equates to a two-fold improvement in accuracy, this was less than ideal. By 1980, Moscow was finally able to test accuracies equal to those of the U.S. Minuteman 3 force (deployed since the early 1970s). Of all the people who complain about the Soviet SS-18, the only "heavy" missile in either superpower's arsenal, none proposes that the U.S. should, or needs to, build anything so huge. "In megatonnage, the Soviets are way ahead; it doesn't make a damn bit of difference," former U.S. SALT negotiator Paul Warnke says. "The fact that they might have a two-megaton warhead compared to our modest ones of something like 400,000 tons of TNT only makes one difference: How big is the hole going to be where the high school used to be?" In comparison with the SS-18, the MX has a higher chance of destroying missile silos because of its superior accuracy. In short, throw-weight tells little about a warhead's capacity to destroy area or hard targets. According to retired U.S. Admiral Eugene La Rocque:

> Comparing the sizes of American and Soviet missiles is like comparing the sizes of our calculators. Bigger doesn't mean better. We build our missiles smaller because our technology is more advanced. Our ICBMs have miniaturized, computerized guidance packages, more efficient rocket engines, thinner but more effective heat shields, greater accuracy and more compact, efficient hydrogen weapons.

The crucial advantages held by the U.S. over the U.S.S.R. are rarely mentioned in Washington today: the U.S. is 10 to 20 years ahead of Russia in microelectronics and increasing its lead, three or four generations ahead in precision guided-weapons systems, and 10 to 20 years ahead in surveillance techniques. America is at least five years ahead in computerization in general and increasing its lead in war gaming, antisubmarine warfare, signal processing and early-warning systems. The U.S. is also about a generation ahead on anti-tank and anti-aircraft missiles and is at work in several areas that the Soviets have hardly touched. Dr. William Perry, President Carter's Undersecretary of Defense for Research and Engineering summed up this American supremacy in military technology: "In precision-guided weapons..., the most significant application of technology to modern warfare since the development of radar, the United States has a substantial lead." In fact, the superiority of American military technology has made it far less expensive for the U.S. to modernize its strategic weapons systems. To improve the accuracy of the delivery systems of their strategic nuclear warheads, the Soviets have had to introduce a whole new generation of ICBMs, while the U.S., by merely improving its guidance system and, by introducing the MARK 12A warhead, has achieved the same result at one-sixth the cost.

The following dialogue from the Senate Foreign Relations Committee (April 29, 1982) reveals that the Reagan administration is fully aware of America's supremacy in nuclear weapons technology:

> Senator Charles Percy: "Would you rather have at your disposal the U.S. nuclear arsenal or the Soviet nuclear arsenal?"

> Defense Secretary Weinberger: "...I would not for a moment exchange anything because we have an immense edge in technology."

The Window of Vulnerability

The new scenario in Washington imagines a "limited" Soviet attack on all U.S. land-based missile forces and missile submarine bases. With a portion of their own ICBM forces, the Soviets could (this "window of vulnerability" scenario assumes) destroy most of the U.S. forces. The U.S. could not strike Soviet nuclear forces because American sea-based missiles are supposedly not sufficiently accurate and its bombers too slow. Nor would the U.S. attack Soviet cities for fear of retaliation against American cities, which had hitherto been spared. The U.S. deterrent would thus itself be deterred, and the U.S. would be compelled to back down in a confrontation with the Soviets. Indeed, with this scenario clearly understood, the Soviets would not actually have to undertake the attack in the first place to achieve their aims. The vulnerability of the U.S. land-based missiles would provide the Soviets with important political advantages.

But this scenario actually is a far-fetched concoction. Critics retort that this script is, in the words of Paul Warnke, former U.S. Chief Arms Control Negotiator, "inherently implausible." First, Soviet planners could not be confident that all U.S. ICBMs would be destroyed in a first strike. As physicists Bernard Feld and Kosta Tsipis from the Massachusetts Institute of Technology state: "...the assertion that the U.S. Minuteman force can now or in the future be destroyed with any degree of assurance by an all-out Russian counterforce attack (on Minuteman silos) seems to us to be a careless oversimplification, if not a deliberate exaggeration." Indeed, according to American intelligence sources, recent U.S. monitoring of Soviet missile tests shows that Moscow's nuclear arsenal isn't accurate enough to destroy existing American missile silos in a first strike. A source who has evaluated the top-secret test data told *The New York Times*: "Their accuracy isn't even within the ballpark of being able to launch a first strike against our Minuteman missile silos." Secondly, the U.S. would not have to respond to a "limited" Soviet attack on its land-based missiles by an all-out assault on Soviet cities. On the contrary, a whole range of Soviet military targets (such as naval and air bases, concentrations of conventional forces, and command, control and communications facilities) could be struck—there are over 20,000 such targets in the U.S. strategic operation plan—causing damage to the Soviet Union commensurate with that suffered by the U.S. Desmond Ball, an authority on strategic policy, points out that: "In any case, on that second strike, after they have knocked out your ICBMs, which is going to use up most of their ICBMs, what are you going to need accuracy for? The targets you are going to go after at that point are other military targets: airfields, army camps, tank concentrations, or urban industrial areas. Neither of those require high accuracy. In any case, the accuracy of sub-launched missiles these days is approaching that of the ICBMs. It is certainly good enough to do a lot of hard-target operations that in the past could not have been done by submarines."

But perhaps most important, after such a "limited" attack with thousands of nuclear warheads causing between 8 and 20 million casualties (according to the American Office of Technology Assessment), it is absurd to suppose that Soviet strategists could count on a cool decision by the United States to do nothing in retaliation. Common sense suggests that Soviet leaders could not possibly contemplate a first strike against

FIGURE 18-2
RELATIVE U.S./USSR STANDING IN THE MOST IMPORTANT BASIC TECHNOLOGY AREAS
(U.S. DOD Assessment)

Basic Technologies	1980			1982		
	U.S. Superior	U.S.-USSR Equal	USSR Superior	U.S. Superior	U.S.-USSR Equal	USSR Superior
Aerodynamics/fluid dynamics		●			●	
Automated control	●			●		
Conventional warhead (including chemical explosives)						●
Computer	▼ ●			●		
Directed energy		●		●		
Electro-optical sensor (including IR)	●			▲ ●		
Guidance and navigation	▲ ●			▲ ●		

Hydro-acoustic

Intelligence sensor

Manufacturing/production

Materials (light weight, high strength)

Microelectronic materials and integrated circuit manufacture

Non-acoustic submarine detection

Nuclear warhead

Optics

Propulsion (aerospace)

Power sources (mobile)

Radar sensor

Signal processing

Software

FIGURE 18-2 CONTINUED

Basic Technologies	1980			1982		
	U.S. Superior	U.S.-USSR Equal	USSR Superior	U.S. Superior	U.S.-USSR Equal	USSR Superior
Stealth (signature reduction technology)				•		
Submarine detection (including silencing)				◄•		
Telecommunications	•			•		

Notes:

1. This table is intended to provide a valid base for comparing **overall** U.S. and USSR **basic** technology, not the technology level in deployed military systems.
2. The technologies selected have the potential for significantly changing the military balance in the next 10 or 20 years. The technologies are not static; they are improving or have the potential for significant improvement.
3. The arrows denote that the relative technology level is changing significantly in the direction indicated.
4. The judgements represent averages within each basic technology area.

The table for 1980 is taken from *The FY 1981 Department of Defense Program for Research, Development and Acquisition. Statement by the Honorable William J. Perry, Under Secretary of Defense Research and Engineering to the 96th Congress, Second Session, 1980,* in U.S. House of Representatives, *Research and Development, Title II,* Hearings before the Committee on Armed Forces, Washington, D.C.: USGPO, 1980, Representatives, *Research and Development, Title II,* Hearings before the Committee on Armed Forces, Washington, D.C.: USGPO, 1980, p. 82. The 1982 table is taken from *The FY 1983 Department of Defense Program for Research, Development and Acquisition, Statement by the Honorable Richard D. DeLauer, Under Secretary of Defense, Research and Engineering, to the 97th Congress, Second Session, 1982,* p. 11-21.

U.S. land-based missiles unless they had gone collectively insane. Former U.S. Defense Secretary Robert McNamara clearly rejects hypothetical notions of Soviet first strike blackmail:

> The argument is without foundation. It's absurd. To try to destroy the 1,054 Minutemen, the Soviets would have to plan to ground-burst two nuclear warheads of one megaton each on each site. That is 2,000 megatons, roughly 160,000 times the megatonnage of the Hiroshima bomb. What condition do you think our country would be in when 2,000 one-megaton bombs ground-burst? The idea that, in such a situation, we would sit here and say, "Well, we don't want to launch against them because they might come back and hurt us," is inconceivable! And the idea that the Soviets are today sitting in Moscow and thinking, "We've got the U.S. over a barrel because we're capable of putting 2,000 megatons of ground-burst on them and in such a situation we know they will be scared to death and fearful of retaliation; therefore we are free to conduct political blackmail," is too incredible to warrant serious debate.

U.S. Qualitative Advantages

For all the talk recently about Russia's potential ability to destroy America's land-based missile force, the fact is that U.S. missiles are more reliable and accurate than Soviet missiles. The United States starts off with another key advantage in the new missile duel: approximately three-quarters of all Soviet strategic warheads are carried on silo-based ICBMs which are becoming more vulnerable to U.S. missiles. Only one-quarter of U.S. warheads are so based. Moreover, at least 50 percent of all American warheads are in submarines which cannot be destroyed by any of the ICBMs or SLBMs the Soviets are developing or have deployed. While the U.S.S.R. places most of its strategic eggs in one basket—increasing vulnerable land-based ICBMs—the U.S. is relying increasingly on invulnerable submarine-launched ballistic missiles. The United States has forty-one nuclear submarines, ten of the older Polaris class and thirty-one Poseidons, plus new Tridents coming onstream. The Polaris carries sixteen missiles with one to three warheads apiece. The Poseidon carries sixteen missiles each with nine to fourteen warheads, each one three times as powerful as the Hiroshima bomb. One or two Poseidon subs, which are invulnerable to attack at this time, could destroy most or all of the 218 Soviet cities with a population of 100,000 or more.

American naval chiefs seem certain that the Russians cannot seriously threaten their missile submarines in the foreseeable future. According to American navy intelligence analysts, the Soviets have never successfully tracked a single U.S. nuclear-missile submarine. But are the Soviet missile-submarines (SSBNs) safe from a preemptive strike by the U.S. Navy? The Soviet submarine missile force is somewhat more vulnerable than that of the United States, since U.S. anti-submarine warfare (ASW) in the Atlantic is far superior to that of the Soviet Union. Not only is American surveillance and information-processing technology more advanced, but a large number of Soviet submarines, the Yankee class, are equipped with missiles with ranges of the order of 1,300 nautical miles, forcing them to operate in the Atlantic Ocean to be able to hit even the Eastern United States. Here they are especially vulnerable to U.S. anti-submarine warfare. The United States has large sonar towers off the coast of Norway, off the Azores, and off the Japanese Islands. These are attached by cable to a giant computer processing center, which can dampen out all of the other noises in the ocean and leave in only the noises of Soviet submarines. All authorities on the subject agree that U.S. attack submarines, though out-numbered by their Soviet counterparts, are far more effective in locating and following Soviet ballistic missile submarines than vice versa.

The Soviet weakness will decrease as more and more of their submarines are equipped with missiles having ranges greater than 4,000 miles, thus being able to launch in the Arctic and Far Pacific. Nevertheless, even in such waters, the Soviets must be concerned about their submarine survivability since their ships are noisier and easier to detect and track than American submarines. New American satellite tracking systems (based on detection of distinctive head and/or wave patterns) would, if perfected, make Russian submarines "visible" even while on patrol in waters adjacent to the Soviet Union. When it becomes feasible for the U.S. Navy to locate Soviet submarines patrolling in the Barents Sea or the Sea of Okhotsk and to destroy them, then the deterrent available to the Soviets would at best be dubious. To better understand the entire picture, let us review the number of Soviet submarines that would have to be instantaneously destroyed. In mid-1979, the U.S.S.R. had about sixty-four missile submarines. Let us say that by the mid-1980s, the Soviets have approximately eighty SSBNs capable of running submerged for extended periods. That number may pose no problem for the techniques the U.S. is developing. And the job of destroying them is made easier by the fact that only fifteen percent are away from port at any time. Most could be hit in their pens.

There is "no doubt" the United States could stage a massive nuclear counterattack even if the Soviet Union struck first according to a recent highly-respected independent study by the Carnegie Endowment for International Peace. Rebutting Ronald Reagan's assertion that the Soviets hold a "margin of superiority," the study concluded that the U.S. arsenal "is not now vulnerable" and that the Soviets would be "very" vulnerable if their land-based missiles were knocked out first. Based on up-to-date information on the accuracy of Soviet missiles, on their lack of a comprehensive navigation-satellite system, on their lack of deep-water anti-submarine warfare system and other factors, a Soviet first-strike capability is not close at hand and may never be. On the other hand, based on new American guidance systems and the Navy's extensive and growing deep-water anti-submarine warfare capability, it has become increasingly clear that the United States is approaching the possibility of first-strike capability. The prestigious Boston Study Group similarly concluded that the Soviet nuclear build-up does not jeopardize the U.S. ability to carry out "assured destruction" in case of nuclear attack:

> A careful analysis of each of the [Soviet military] trends under consideration has led us to the conclusion that the degree of change...is often exaggerated and that the overall impact of current and likely future developments in Soviet forces does not warrant any new or special concern for the security of this country or its allies.

Even President Reagan's Scowcroft Report concluded, "to deter such surprise attack, we can reasonably rely both on our other strategic forces and on the range of operational uncertainties that the Soviets would have to consider in planning such aggression." George Kistiakowsky, the American scientist and Presidential Science Advisor, who was responsible for devising the implosion system of the first atom bombs, has published a record of his days in which he tells how President Eisenhower's policies were always frustrated by those who consistently exaggerated the Soviet military threat. He did not hesitate to declare that any analysis of the predictions that have been made of the Soviet military threat over the past 20 years will show that they have always been far-fetched. In the present context, Admiral Eugene Carroll (Ret.) has drily commented: "The window of vulnerability is the son of the missile gap." Leslie H. Gelb, head of the American State Department's

Bureau of Political and Military Affairs under President Carter, points out that just as Defense Secretary Weinberger would pick U.S. military technology over Russian:

> I have yet to meet a senior American officer involved in this subject who would trade the American arsenal for the Soviet one. Only those experts who focus exclusively on the Soviet superiority in land-based missiles think otherwise. And here the debate among the experts ascends to the level of theology.

While the U.S.S.R. is modernizing its military capabilties—and doing some things earlier and more quickly than the West had anticipated a few years ago—this build-up does not and will not, for the foreseeable future, jeopardize the United States' ability to respond flexibly and selectively, or all-out, to Soviet strikes. It may be true that, of late, Russia is spending more money than the U.S. on military weapons. Comparisons of U.S. and Soviet spending produced by the Central Intelligence Agency (CIA) are commonly used to demonstrate the alleged inferiority of American defense. Essentially, the CIA's methodology involves estimating what it would cost the U.S. to run the Soviet military system in U.S. dollars. But measurement in dollars is misleading and, in the CIA's own words, causes "an overstatement of Soviet defense activities relative to those of the United States." The most obvious example of this involves the cost of military personnel. Soviet conscripts receive 3.8 rubles per month, which is about $6 at official exchange rates. American volunteers are paid a minimum of $550 per month. Yet the CIA estimates assume equal pay for military personnel, which quickly translates into whopping Soviet military personnel costs because of the very large size of the Soviet army. It is also important to consider that the CIA restricts its comparisons to the U.S. and the Soviet Union, ignoring their allies. As Defense Secretary Brown put it in his 1979 Annual Report, "We are fortunate in having prosperous and willing allies who can help counterbalance the Soviet effort. The Soviets are not so fortunate. Moreover, they have felt obliged to allocate up to 20 percent of their total defense effort to the Far East and the PRC (China)."

Furthermore, there is no strict relationship between money and effectiveness in strategic weapons—or, for that matter, in anything. The Soviets are doing more, and they have become a formidable military power; but their methods are far more inefficient than America's; they get far less "bang for the buck" (or "rubble for the ruble"). Therefore, comparing military spending—in dollars or in rubles—does not bring us anywhere close to the essence of the military balance.

FIGURE 18-3
ESCALATION OF THE ARMS RACE

	U.S. (Action)	USSR (Reaction)
First nuclear chain reaction	Dec. 2/42	Dec. 24/46
First atom bomb exploded	July 16/45	Oct. 23/49
First H-bomb exploded	Nov. 1/52	Oct. 12/53
European alliances in effect	Oct. 24/49 (NATO)	May 14/55 (Warsaw Pact)
Tactical nuclear weapons in Europe	1954	1957
Accelerated buildup of strategic missiles	1961	1966
First supersonic bomber	1960	1975
First ballistic-missile-launching submarine	1960 (Polaris)	1968 (Yankee)
First solid rocket fuel used in missiles	1960	1968
Multiple warheads on missiles	1964	1973
Penetration aids on missiles	1964	None to date
High-speed re-entry bodies (warheads)	1970	1975
Multiple independently-targeted re-entry vehicles (MIRVs) on missiles	1970	1975
Computerized guidance on missiles	1970	1975

Source: Jim Wallis, ed., *Waging Peace* (New York: Harper and Row, 1982), p. 34.

Hardliners in the West, however, insist that the Soviets are now making a clear bid for superiority. Whilst there can be no doubt that the U.S.S.R. is striving very hard to achieve overall parity with the United States, the assumption that it is the pacesetter in the arms race is incorrect. The United States still enjoys a significant lead in the qualitative measures of strategic power (e.g., in the accuracy, reliability and survivability of its nuclear delivery system). What has occurred is that the growth in the size of the U.S.S.R.'s nuclear arsenal has diminished America's perceived advantage in strategic weaponry. That is not to say that America's nuclear war-making potential has in any way been reduced: both superpowers have long possessed sufficient firepower to destroy the world many times over, and both continue to expand their arsenals at rapid rates. What has changed is that the gap between U.S. and Soviet capabilities has narrowed over the last fifteen years. As Michael W. Johnson, formerly a senior analyst for the U.S. Army, noted: "Although much is made of the projected Soviet deployment of SS-18's and SS-19s and their capability of destroying all American land-based ICBMs, these Soviet ICBMs will merely be capable of doing in the 1980s what American ICBMs could do in the 1960s."

The Red Menance

If I had been the Soviet Secretary of defense, I'd have been worried as hell about the imbalance of force. And I would have been concerned that the United States was trying to build a first-strike capability. I would have been concerned simply because I would have had knowledge of what the nuclear strength was of the United States and I would have heard the rumors that the Air Force was recommending achievement of such a capability. You put those two things together: a known force disadvantage that is large enough in itself to at least appear to support the view that the United States was planning a first-strike capability, and, secondly, it would have just scared the hell out of me!

—Robert S. McNamara
former U.S. Secretary of Defense

Although the scenarios pertaining to supposed Soviet military capabilities are relatively easy to demystify, the newest twist is to focus on the more subjective plane of intentions. Richard Pipes, an important Reagan advisor and a pace-setter among this new school, has asserted that the U.S.S.R. "thinks it could fight and win a nuclear war." Pipes assures us that the Soviets would take the risk because having lost tens of millions in World War II, the Soviet leadership would not value life as we do in the West:

> The Soviet ruling elite regards conflict and violence as natural regulators of all human affairs; wars between nations, in its view, represent only a variant of wars between classes...Soviet doctrine emphatically asserts that while an all-out nuclear war would indeed prove extremely destructive to both parties, its outcome would not be mutual suicide; the country better prepared for it and in possession of a superior strategy could win and emerge a viable society...There is something innately destabilizing in the very fact that we consider nuclear war unfeasible and suicidal for both, and our chief adversary views it as feasible and winnable for himself.

Such bold conclusions, however, must be taken with a grain of salt. After he had been in his White House job only two months, Pipes told the Reuters News Agency that "there is no alternative to war with the Soviet Union if the Russians do not abandon communism." The burden of Pipes' (and others') case is that believing it could fight and survive a nuclear war, the U.S.S.R. would be prepared to launch one under certain circumstances. Of course, the Soviet Union is no innocent party in all of this. Its repressive political system fosters an unsentimental attitude toward the use of power. But one need not have any illusions on that score in order to maintain that the Soviet Union does not desire nuclear war. Raymond L. Garthoff, a former American diplomat, recently studied Soviet perspectives on the nuclear arms race and concluded: "The Soviet leaders believe that peaceful coexistence—with continued political and ideological competition—is the preferable alternative to an unrestrained arms race and to recurring high-risk politico-military confrontation; that detente and a relaxation of tensions is in the interest of the Soviet Union; and that nuclear war would not be."

There is nothing in Soviet behavior, history or ideology to suggest that the model of the Soviet leader waiting by the button until the computer predicts an "acceptable" casualty level is anything but a convenient Pentagon fantasy to support an unending arms race. Soviet leaders have committed some monumental crimes in the name of national security—mostly against their own people. And they have invaded countries on their borders. But the historic preoccupation with the defense of their homeland, and above all the uncertainties any leader faces about limiting the danger in a nuclear war, makes a holocaust by design totally implausible.

What about Reagan's claim that the effective use of civil defense (elaborate evacuation and shelter programs combined with the relocation of industry to underground sites hardened to the point of being able to withstand a nuclear blast) by the Russians wipes out the deterrent effect of the massive American nuclear arsenal? A 1978 CIA study assessed the Soviet civil defense program as having a negligible impact on Soviet leadership perceptions of the risks of launching a nuclear attack. Nor did the CIA feel that this situation would change in "the foreseeable future." As *The New York Times* editorialized: "Most students of Soviet society hold this [Reagan's arguments] to be a vast exaggeration. They think the known Soviet instruction manuals, shelter signs and civil defense drills are modest exertions; there is no evidence that the Russians have ever practiced evacuating a city. That would require a miraculous transformation of the Soviet transport and supply networks. And it would be futile. With the twist of a few dials, as former Defense Secretary Brown once observed, America's nuclear weapons could be retargeted to blanket the evacuation sites."

George Kennan, the historian and former American diplomat, feels that the view of the Soviet Union in "our governmental and journalistic establishments" is so distorted and exaggerated that it imperils the chances for a "more hopeful world." He now maintains that the view of the Soviet Union prevailing in the United States is "so extreme, so subjective, so far removed from what any sober scrutiny of external reality would reveal, that it is not only ineffective but dangerous as a guide to political action." It might be said that all this is a harmless (but expensive) fantasy, a kind of insurance policy against Armageddon. But unlike an insurance policy, the arms race directly affects the risk. By preparing for an implausible war the United States now makes other scenarios for nuclear wars—wars by accident and miscalculation—far more probable. "So far as nuclear war is concerned, we and the Soviet Union are in the same boat," Professor Roger Fisher of the Harvard Law School observed. "You can think of that physically. There is no way that we can make our end of the boat safer by making the other end more likely to tip over."

The Great Russian Bear Not Hibernating

> Soviet advantages notwithstanding, the United States
> is generally superior to the Soviet Union in those types
> of combat forces that are most appropriate for rapidly
> projecting power to areas remote from either homeland.
> —U.S. Joint Chiefs of Staff

Western rearmament advocates, in order to provide ammunition for their demands, frequently rely upon charges of
massive Soviet expansionism in the Third World. They claim
that since 1975, when the U.S. retreated from Vietnam, the
U.S.S.R. has expanded its military power. It has used its allies'
conventional forces, mainly Cubans and East Germans, to aid
revolutionary forces in Angola, Ethiopia, South Yemen and
Afghanistan, and to control strategic areas or chokepoints
(narrow waterways between land masses). This proves without
doubt, the Soviets are increasingly prepared to use troops, aid,
advisors and allies to protect "socialist" regimes from external
(Ethiopia) or internal (Afghanistan) challenges.

Cold war interpretations of Soviet foreign policy have been
given a new lease on life by recent developments in Africa. In
Angola, the Horn of Africa and Mozambique, Moscow and its
Cuban proxies, it is claimed, have spurned the spirit of detente
in a determined effort to subvert and infiltrate the African
continent. Communist military intervention in Africa on this
scale is indeed unprecedented. Moscow, at one and the same
time, proved it had now developed the capacity to deploy
military forces thousands of miles from their home base and the
willingness to play an active part in areas distant from its
traditional sphere of influence. However, Soviet goals in Africa
can be presented in a much less disquieting manner. Africa is,
now, increasingly an arena in which the U.S.S.R. and the West
(and also China) are competing for power and influence. This
marks less a new phase in Soviet expansionism than an
appraisal, in Moscow, that political developments on the
continent had weakened Western control and created opportunities for the extension of Soviet influence. Moscow is staking out
a claim for itself and trying to ensure that its weight can be
brought to bear and its objectives taken into account, when
decisions pertaining to Soviet interests are arrived at.

Whatever their motives, the entry of the Soviet Union into
African affairs has, by balancing Western hegemony, enabled
African governments to play off one against the other, hence
widening their room for maneuver. The assessment of the

Angolan conflict—the Soviets launching a massive airlift of armaments to Angola, along with 10,000 Cuban troops, to give the MPLA a decisive edge in the civil war there—reflects the pronounced tendency of hard-liners to squeeze the most disparate situations into the familiar and simple mold of Cold War thinking. It overlooks the fact that the Portuguese were only able to maintain their grip on their African empire for so long because of aid from NATO powers. Indeed, Russia had, throughout this period, been the only major power to afford material help to the liberation movements, in particular the MPLA which had been in the forefront of the battle against Portuguese colonialism. The U.S. and the U.K. only discovered their new roles as disinterested friends of Angolan freedom and independence after the overthrow of the Caetano dictatorship in Lisbon. President Nyerere of Tanzania recently made some pertinent observations on Western responses to Communist activities in the continent. He defended the role of the Cubans and Soviets and accused the U.S. of using Africa in the Middle East conflict and concluded that "current developments show that the greatest immediate danger to Africa's freedom comes from nations in the Western bloc." The past invasion and current subversion of Angola by U.S.-aided South Africa is a case in point.

But isn't the Soviet invasion of Afghanistan a first step toward their eventual goal of gaining control of Middle East oil? A quick look at the map reveals that the Soviets wouldn't need to go through Afghanistan to get to the Persian Gulf. The Soviet Republic of Azerbaijan and Turkmen and the Soviet-controlled Caspian Sea provide much closer and more direct access to Middle East oil fields than the treacherous passes of Afghanistan. The Soviet invasion of Afghanistan can best be explained by purely parochial concerns—political instability in a border country—rather than on some grand design for control of the Gulf. Any presumption of a Soviet "blueprint" for control of Mideast oilfields, moreover, is flatly contradicted by Moscow's alliance with Ethiopia. Ethiopia provoked a split with Somalia and, according to Keith Dunn of the U.S. Army War College, the consequence was that the Soviet Union "damaged its geopolitical situation in the Horn of Africa and caused it to lose access to the best port facilities in the area." And although they did what they could to promote the destabilization of America's model client state in Iran, the Soviets soon discovered that, despite their geographic advantage, the religiously charged upheaval in Iran was as much beyond their control as Washington's

Most Pentagon officials would probably concede there is a very low probability of a Soviet drive on the Persian Gulf. What worries them much more, in fact, is an internal conflict or regional dispute that jeopardizes the flow of oil. Afghanistan provided a convenient cover for Washington's plan to reassert U.S. military force in the Third World. President Carter pledged to use "any means necessary, including military force," to protect American oil supplies in the Persian Gulf—the use of "tactical" nuclear weapons was by no means ruled out. In a most ominous development, the Pentagon has deployed seven cargo ships—filled with equipment, supplies, fuel and water to support a marine amphibious brigade of 12,000 men—to the Indian Ocean, where they will serve as a floating arms depot for combat forces sent to Iran or elsewhere in the area. Washington has also created the Rapid Deployment Force (R.D.F.) which may be used to "deter" conflict by physically occupying the battlefield before the battle gets fully underway as well as to counter aggression by others. This non-nuclear equivalent of what might be called a "first-strike" deployment doctrine was unveiled in a little-noticed address by Zbigniew Brzezinski to the Economic Club of Chicago: the R.D.F., he said, "will give us the capacity to respond quickly, effectively, and even pre-emptively in those parts of the world where our vital interests might be engaged and where there are no permanently station-ed American forces." And given the growing tendency of conservative American leaders to exploit the "Soviet threat" issue for political gain, it is increasingly likely that Washington will engage in military "show of force" operations to demon-strate that it has the "will" to "stand up to the Russians" in contested areas abroad. Many top American policymakers have been contemplating intervention in places like El Salva-dor, Guatemala, South Yemen, Oman and the Western Sahara.

All in all, the U.S.S.R. has not exactly built a large empire in the years since 1945. Loss of Yugoslavia and Albania; loss and subsequent enmity of China; defeat in Indonesia; defeat of insurgencies in Malaysia and a half-dozen other countries; loss of influence in Algeria, Sudan, Somalia; major military and politicial investments written off in Iraq, Uganda, Guinea; transformation of Egypt into a U.S. ally hardly add up to what one would call a decisive march toward a Soviet-dominated world! The extent of Soviet expansion is much less impressive or daunting compared with the prodigious growth of America's imperial reach during these same thirty-five years. Besides, in the struggle to maintain and enlarge its world position and ensure a hospitable environment for American corporations, the United States has resorted to many of the same violent and reprehensible methods of foreign intervention as the Soviet Union. It has also installed or propped up authoritarian governments that are at best different in degree rather than in kind from Russia's totalitarian satellite and client states.

Since 1945, according to Brookings Institute, the U.S. has used military force 215 times to gain political or economic ends. Many believe that the U.S. has engaged in such military and economic commitments for the main purpose of preserving freedom and democracy. But the reality is that the top ten recipients of U.S. military and economic aid, according to Amnesty International, are also the world's top ten dictatorships or violators of human rights: South Korea, the Philippines Indonesia, Thailand, Chile, Argentina, Uruguay, Haiti, Brazil and formerly, Iran. Is there any way to justify U.S. support to these governments as "defending freedom"? According to testimony by Senator Alan Cranston, 51 countries or 69% of the nations receiving military grants from the U.S. are classified as "repressive regimes". These governments allow U.S. air and naval bases on their soil and offer a "favorable investment climate" for the U.S. multinational corporations: low wages, no unions, no strikes, cheap raw materials and no government regulations. All these countries have conditions "favorable" to U.S. business.

Because the United States has historically been allied with economic "imperialism" and the U.S.S.R. has not, the tendency has been for liberation struggles in the Third World to turn to the East for military and material aid. These alliances are as much due to a mixture of pragmatism and ideology in the Third World movements themselves as they are the work of Soviet expansionism. The tendency in the West to blame Russian meddling for developments in the Third World countries safeguards their own sovereignty. It is very dubious, for example, whether the many African liberation movements that have accepted Soviet arms have by this fact become Soviet satellites. It would be easy to argue from historical precedent that these movements seek nothing so much as national independence and ultimately find themselves hostile to both superpowers. Zimbabwe is an excellent example. After years of bloody civil war, the black majority regime, led by Robert Mugabe, makes it very clear that even though it got its arms from the Soviets, it wishes the closest possible economic relations with and aid from the West. The Angolan regime, likewise, has been recognized by all NATO powers except the United States, and is striving to reduce its links to the Eastern European and Soviet bloc. It is the incapacity of present U.S. policy to relate to these liberation movements that is the problem, rather than Soviet expansion in that area. As British writer David Holloway concludes: "The Soviet Union is indeed an important actor on the international stage, but it does not devise the plot, write the script, set the scene and direct the play as well."

The bottom line is not very favorable to the Soviet Union. On a good day, according to the Center for Defense Information headed by Admiral Gene LaRocque, Russia can command the allegiance of only 19 countries (out of 155). The Center's careful 1980 study, "Soviet Geopolitical Momentum," found that Soviet influence, in fact, has actually decreased since the late 1950s and their setbacks dwarf marginal Soviet advances in lesser countries. Robert McNamara, U.S. Secretary of Defense from 1961 to 1968 serving under Presidents Kennedy and Johnson, concurs:

> I, myself, believe that they've gotten weaker. That may sound naive when one says it in the face of what has clearly been an increase in the number of their conventional forces—not nearly as great, by the way, as many say, but still an increase. But I think they've gotten weaker because, economically and politically, there have been some very serious failures. In my opinion, they are in a weaker position today than they were fourteen to fifteen years ago.

The Soviet Navy

Yet, at the same time as it was closing the gap in strategic weaponry, the Soviet Union was also expanding its conventional (i.e. non-nuclear) arsenals. More and more voices can be heard alerting the West to a massive and frightening growth in Soviet naval forces. Again the extent of this expansion has been exaggerated. Soviet naval growth has been proportionately greater than the West's but starting from a much lower base line. Although the Soviet bloc does deploy more submarines, it has fewer nuclear-powered ones than the West, its fleet is technologically inferior and it lags behind in anti-submarine warfare. Moscow is building more ships but these are mainly small ones, frigates and destroyers. The United States has five amphibious assault ships which are gigantic: like small carriers, they weigh 40,000 tons and carry 25 helicopters and 15 VTOL planes. The U.S. has another 40 amphibious landing ships which weigh over 10,000 tons. The size of the ship determines its range, that is, how far away and how long it has the fuel and supplies to operate. With one exception, the largest amphibious landing ships in the Soviet Union weigh 4,000 tons. These small ships are designed to carry landing craft in the enclosed seas near the Soviet Union: the Baltic, the Mediterranean, the Sea of China, and the Sea of Okhotsk. Much of the growth of the Soviet Navy has been devoted to protecting their vulnerable nuclear submarines according to Michael McGuire, an expert on the Soviet Navy at the Brookings Institute. Nevertheless, the Soviets have, for the first time ever, created a navy of impressive dimensions. The navy has been transformed from a coastal defense force into a true ocean-going fleet. The Soviets have built a massive naval force which, according to the authoritative *Janes Fighting Ships* Report for 1980, "goes far beyond the needs of defense of the Soviet sea frontiers."

There is no question that there has been a Soviet naval buildup. The controversial issues have to do with its extent and significance. The Soviets do not have naval military bases abroad to give them the logistical flexibility they need to develop their navy further. They have port facilities in Angola and Vietnam where they can dock and refuel. However, unlike the base in Somalia which the Soviets lost, these are not real bases where they can store weapons, or set up an air bridge to bring in weapons to re-arm the Soviet navy.

Although the Soviets have in recent years been building the Kiev-class aircraft carrier, guided-missile aviation cruisers, and other surface ships designed to project power at a distance or to attack U.S. ocean supply lines to Europe and Japan, they have virtually no capacity to land an expeditionary force by sea. Because of the tremendous expense, the United States is the only country in the world that operates a fleet of aircraft carriers with modern supersonic aircraft. The Soviet navy still lacks true aircraft carriers which can accommodate high-performance combat planes with a deep-penetration attack capability like the U.S. carrier-borne A-6s and A-7s. The approximately 800 combat planes in the Soviet naval air force are no match for the combined U.S. Navy and Marine Corps airforces which have twice that number of planes, most of which can be launched from aircraft carriers. Russia's air-cargo planes have shorter range and cannot be refuelled in the air. As the U.S. Joint Chiefs of Staff noted in their 1982 *"Military Posture Statement,"* the lack of sea-based tactical air support greatly limits Soviet ability to carry out amphibious landing against heavy opposition." Thus, while there is no doubt that the Russians have a greater capability for intervention abroad than they had a decade ago, it falls far short of what the United States can bring to bear and, given Moscow's lack of true aircraft carriers, could not be used against any well-armed opponent. For these reasons, the Rand Corporation concluded that "gross Soviet capabilities to project power abroad do not remotely equal the U.S.'s" and could not sustain an occupation/invasion beyond its own immediate border state areas.

The chief object of Soviet naval policy is to counter Western naval forces. According to a Brookings Institute study:

> The primary mission of the Soviet navy continues to be defensive to protect the Soviet Union from Western sea-based strike forces and to deter the latter from intervening in regions, like the Middle East, close to Soviet shores.

The West may have lost unchallenged supremacy at sea; it still firmly outclasses its rival; and one may ask why the West should assume it has a natural right to rule the sea unhindered. The high seas cannot be thought of as an exclusive Western possession. Soviet naval forces are being used to "show the flag" and demonstrate Moscow's resolve to protect its new-found allies in Africa and Asia. By restricting America's capacity to use the threat of force to intimidate Third World governments, the Russian navy has deprived Washington of a favored instrument of coercion and thus further diminished America's perceived global power. For instance, the U.S. would probably be more hesitant to embark on a 1958 Lebanon-style marine landing now that Western control of the Mediterranean is no longer undisputed. The current U.S. naval buildup is, in fact, an effort to reestablish what Secretary of the Navy John Lehman calls "clear maritime superiority."

When expressed intelligibly, concern among NATO policy-makers has been directed at the loss of "overwhelming authority" on the world's seas and the freedom of action which went with it. As American military critic Michael Klare has argued:

> It is not Western shipping that is threatened by Soviet naval deployments, but Washington's strategy for continued Western hegemony in remote Third World areas. All one can say authoritatively at this point is that Russia's military build-up (especially after the Soviet-built airbase in South Yemen is completed) has equipped her with the means to play a global role and enhanced its ability to further its interests outside Europe. The upshot is that Moscow can now contemplate the type of action which Washington has taken for granted for a generation.

Conclusion: Towards Disarmament

> Despite all that has happened, I feel that the questions
> of war and peace and disarmament are so crucial that
> they must be given absolute priority even in the most
> difficult circumstances. It is imperative that all pos-
> sible means be used to solve these questions and to lay
> the groundwork for further progress. Most urgent of all
> are steps to avert a nuclear war, which is the greatest
> peril confronting the modern world.
>
> —Andrei Sakharov
> Soviet dissident

> The fact of a Soviet threat...cannot be denied...Ameri-
> cans need have no illusions about the Soviet system of
> repression.
>
> —The Pastoral Letter of the
> Bishops on War and Peace

Most of the current alarm about the "decline" of American
military power rests upon an alleged loss of strategic superiority to the Soviet Union. However, the constant government
assertion that the United States is inferior to the U.S.S.R. in
overall strategic power is simply not borne out by the facts.
Under close scrutiny, much of that assessment has been shown
to be based on questionable assumptions, and sometimes on
questionable facts, taking individual facts and events out of
their larger contexts; ignoring the limits on Soviet power and
the setbacks encountered by Moscow. The purpose here is not to
paint the Soviets as the innocent victims of the Cold War. It is
true that the Soviets have been building up their military and
that the strategic arsenals of the U.S. and the U.S.S.R. are now
more nearly equal than ever before. There are many uncertainties about Soviet intentions, just as in Soviet eyes there are
many uncertainties about current American developments.
David Holloway, in his recent book on Soviet military developments, is on solid ground with his polite but firm advice to
Western peace movements: "It is intellectually unsatisfying
and politically dangerous to ignore Soviet military power and
the threat it can pose to Western countries." Yet there is little, if
anything, about Soviet military trends that should provide
grounds for huge military increases in the West. "Never since
World War II," foreign policy analyst and advisor George
Kennan wrote in 1980, "has there been so far-reaching a

militarization of thought and discourse in the capital...An unsuspecting stranger could only conclude that the last hope of peaceful, non-military solutions had been exhausted—that from now on only weapons, however used, could count." Not only critics of the Pentagon are aware of America's military might. General David C. Jones, past chairman of the Joint Chiefs of Staff, expressed the opinion in his 1980 annual report to Congress that "I would not swap our present military capability with that of the Soviet Union nor would I want to trade the border problems each country faces." When asked if he would consider making such a trade, Jones' successor General John W. Vessey, Jr. simply replied: "Not on your life."

In short, while there are few grounds for complacency about the Soviets; they are improving their forces more, and more quickly, than intelligence analysts had predicted. However, neither are there grounds for panic. The American deterrent force remains secure and strong, and notions of impending Soviet "strategic superiority" have no operational meaning. The U.S. is still able to carry out its strategic missions, can still deter the Soviets from attacking, and can respond in limited fashion to limited strikes. As long as this is so, there is a "strategic balance." After all, President Carter said in his January, 1979 State of the Union address: "Just one of our relatively invulnerable Poseidon submarines, comprising less than 2% of our total nuclear force, carries enough warheads to destroy every large and medium-sized city in the Soviet Union."

Author Macy Cox, who worked on Soviet and East European Affairs for the CIA for many years, makes the point that the current U.S. concern about perceived changes in the international balance of military power has little to do with real military changes and nothing at all to do with Soviet understanding of the political implications of military power. A number of U.S. commentators now argue that the renewal of the image of the "Soviet threat" in the U.S. has much more to do with American internal political trends than with objective Soviet actions. Several sectors of American political life have traditionally used the Soviet spectre to strengthen their own hold on policy. By exaggerating Soviet abilities and intentions these groups prejudice public debate on East-West relations at precisely those moments when "detente" is most urgently needed. The present is a replay of history, albeit a more dangerous one. The past has been replete with "gaps." There was a bomber gap in the early 1950s that was later proven false—but only after U.S. production of B-52 bombers was well underway. In the late 1950s and early 1960s, the West was warned of a missile gap, and it was later shown to be fictional—

but only after the Pentagon had accelerated production of ICBMs and SLBMs. Herbert York, who had been associated with both President Eisenhower and President Kennedy at the center of the nuclear arms debate, refers to a steady flow of "phoney intelligence" from a variety of sources and tells us that "those who had all the facts of the matter knew there was no real basis to any of these claims about Russian intentions and capacities."

President Reagan's March 31, 1982 news conference was the occasion for unveiling the official response to the worldwide protest against the nuclear arms race. Reagan set the tone at the outset: "We all want peace," he said, and we all want to "lower the level of armaments"—but first the United States has to catch up with the Russians. Senator Mark Hatfield immediately labelled that approach for what it is—"voodoo arms control"—meaning that you must have more in order to have less. The new Big Lie is that the United States has somehow fallen into a catastrophically inferior position.

That blatant untruth has just been challenged on its own terms. An equally important consideration is the utter irrelevance of talk about superiority or inferiority when each superpower possesses such enormous overkill capacity. If the only aim of American nuclear strategy were to deter a Soviet first strike, the present U.S. arsenal could be diminished by at least 75 percent-instantly. If, on the other hand, Washington wants to achieve a first-strike potential of its own—without risking Soviet retaliation—it clearly has a way to go. That, it seems, is exactly what the U.S. administration's alarms are really all about. When Reagan speaks of a "window of vulnerability," he is not referring to American vulnerability to a Soviet first strike, but to U.S. vulnerability to Soviet retaliation. The rest of us are under no obligation to share that lunatic concern.

In May 1981, addressing West Point cadets on his commitment to higher military spending, President Reagan told them, "I am happy to tell you that the people of America have recovered from what can only be called a temporary aberration." Referring to the demise of SALT 2 he said, "any controversy now would be over which weapons the United States should produce and not whether it should forsake weaponry for treaties and agreements." After intensive interviewing of President Reagan and his chief nuclear weapons advisors, journalist Robert Scheer suggests that the American public is being deceived:

Instead of going to the people and saying, "Hey, listen,

we want to get back to the good old days of superiority," they pretend that we have actually fallen behind and are simply trying to catch up. Instead of talking openly about nuclear-war-fighting as they did in the first year of their Administration—before their poll-takers advised them to soften their rhetoric—they now stress the need for credible deterrence against the Soviet nuclear-war-fighters. But the neo-hawks have already said too much and written too much to conceal their true intentions.

If this attempt to deceive were simply a matter of special interest lobbying in some relatively unimportant area of our national life, then one might shrug and say, "So what's new about political chicanery?" But the danger is that these people are dealing with more than commonplace matters, even though most of the violence has so far been verbal. Because of their role in an Administration in which the President sympathizes strongly with their point of view, they have already profoundly affected the commitment to new weapons systems, systems that will make the world far more dangerous, while at the same time they have abandoned the possibility of arms control no matter how many hours we are willing to spend in negotiations with the Soviets.

But can the West trust the Russians to live up to a freeze or weapons reduction agreement? In the past 20 years, the U.S. and the U.S.S.R. have signed 14 lasting agreements which have not been violated by the Soviets. The Defense Department, the Joint Chiefs of Staff, the State Department, and the Arms Control and Disarmament Agency, in response to allegations that the Soviets have broken agreements, stated in the summer of 1980 in their joint position paper that "Soviet compliance performance under 14 arms control agreements has been good."

For the most part we do not have to rely on the honesty of the Soviets. For, as former CIA director William Colby, among others, has maintained, American intelligence could adequately monitor the Russians under such a comprehensive agreement. Soviet compliance can be checked using highly sophisticated satellites. The production and testing of intercontinental and medium-range missiles and aircraft, production of weapons grade fissionable material at specialized and highly visible plutonium production reactors and uranium enrichment plants, and testing of nuclear warheads can be verified easily by satellites, listening posts equipped with sensors and unmanned seismic stations. Indeed, the Russians now seem willing to accept on-site inspection·in regard to nuclear testing. To be truly effective, a freeze should involve a complete cutoff of warheads production—which the current freeze proposal does imply. Replacement of worn-out parts and maintenance of existing nuclear forces would, of course, be allowed until reductions can be mutually agreed upon.

To the extent that such means of detection are weaker or less certain—for example, for clandestine production of additional warheads out of existing surplus stocks of weapons-grade material, production of smaller missiles, or testing and installation of improved missile components—any cheating would have only small-scale effects, relative to the size, technology and potential uses of the existing arsenals (50,000 nuclear weapons). Herbert Scoville, former Director of the CIA for Science and Technology, emphasizes: "It is hard to see how any clandestine production that would significantly add to these numbers could escape detection by our intelligence." Cheating would be highly unlikely because the risk of detection would be considered relative to the benefits of the small scale activities that might be undertaken. Clearly the risks of undetected cheating would be far outweighed by the gains of (1) a halt to major missile production; (2) a considerable lessening of the chances of the spread of nuclear weapons to other countries; and (3) the reduced likelihood of nuclear war in comparison with the situation if the arms race continues unabated.

The world is now faced with a U.S.-paced arms race that is getting dangerously out of control. As Admiral Rickover, the father of the American nuclear Navy, told a Congressional committee: "We're spending too much on defense...I think we will probably destroy ourselves...We are in danger of arming ourselves into oblivion." When asked in May 1981 about arms negotiations with the Soviets, Paul Nitze said, "There could be serious arms control negotiations but only after we have built up our forces." How long would it take, he was asked? His reply, "In ten years." The immediate cause of World War III may well be the preparation for it!

Footnotes

1. It has been argued that the number of usable Soviet warheads is undercounted since the Soviets have a reloading and refiring capability with many of their missiles. The idea of loading huge, volatile, liquid-fueled missiles into silos heavily contaminated by nuclear fallout is, however, quite absurd. The only factual basis for such concern is that some Soviet missiles could be ejected from their silos before their engines were ignited ("cold launch") and the silos could therefore be reused. But as former Air Force Deputy Chief of Staff for Research and Development, General Kelly Burke, has testified, such reloading would take "on the order of two or three days as about a minimum time...If that area has been struck by our nuclear weapons, then it might not be possible for them to get in at all."

Key References

Aldridge, Robert C. *The Counterforce Syndrome*. Washington: Institute for Policy Studies, 1978.

Barnet, Richard. *Real Security*. New York: Simon and Schuster, 1981.

Blechman, Barry M. and Kaplan, Stephen S. *Force Without War, U.S. Armed Forces As A Political Instrument*. Washington: The Brookings Institute, 1978.

Calder, Nigel. *Nuclear Nightmares*. Harmondsworth, Middlesex: Penguin Books, 1981.

Carnegie Endowment for International Peace, *Challenges for U.S. National Security: A Preliminary Report*. Washington: 1981.

Cox, Arthur Macy. *Russian Roulette*. New York: Times Books, 1982.

Dunn, Keith A. "Power Projection or Influence: Soviet Capabilities for the 1980s," *Naval War College Review* (Sept., Oct. 1980).

Ford, Daniel, Kendall, Henry and Nadis, Steven. *Beyond the Freeze*. Boston: Beacon Press, 1982.

Garthoff, Raymond L. "Mutual Deterrence and Strategic Arms Limitation in Soviet Policy," *International Security* (Summer 1978).

Gervasi, Tom. *The Arsenal of Democracy II*. New York: Grove Press, 1981.

Holloway, David. *The Soviet Union and the Arms Race*. New Haven, Connecticut: Yale University Press, 1983.

Kaplan, Fred. M. *Dubious Spectre: A Skeptical Look at the Soviet Nuclear Threat*. Washington: Institute for Policy Studies, 1980.

Kennan, George. *The Nuclear Delusion*. New York: Pantheon, 1982.

Klare, Michael T. *Beyond the "Vietnam Syndrome"*. Washington: Institute for Policy Studies, 1981.

McGuire, Michael. "The Rationale for the Development of Soviet Seapower," *U.S. Naval Institute Proceedings* (May, 1980).

Scheer, Robert. *With Enough Shovels: Reagan, Bush and Nuclear War*. New York: Random House, 1982.

Thompson, E.P. *Beyond the Cold War*. New York: Pantheon, 1981

Chapter 19

War, Militarism, and the Soviet State

David Holloway

In the military structure of the world, the Soviet Union and the United States stand in a class by themselves. They mount the two largest military efforts and between them account for one half of the massive resources which the world devotes to arms and armed forces. There are, it is true, considerable differences between the military forces of the Soviet Union and the United States, but these are insignificant when compared with the differences between them and the forces of other states.

From the armed forces it maintains and the weapons it produces, it is clear that the Soviet military effort is large. It is difficult, however, to say precisely what resources it consumes. The Soviet Government publishes a figure for the defense budget each year, but this is of little help in estimating the military burden because it is not clear what the budget covers. In any event, observers outside the Soviet Union agree that the Soviet armed forces could not be paid for by the official defense budget without the help of very large hidden subsidies. Western attempts to assess Soviet defense spending must be treated with caution too because of the intrinsic difficulties of making such estimates.[1] It is evident, nevertheless, that only a major commitment of resources has enabled the Soviet Union in the last twenty years to attain strategic parity with the United States, maintain large well-equipped forces in Europe and along the frontier with China, extend the deployment of the Soviet Navy throughout the world, and engage in continuous modernization of arms and equipment.

A military effort of this scale necessarily has a far-reaching impact on the Soviet economy. An extensive network of military research and development establishments is required to develop armaments, while a major sector of industry is needed to produce them in quantity. The Soviet Union has amassed military power roughly comparable to that of the United States, even though its Gross National Product is only about half as large. Consequently, a higher rate of extraction of resources has been necessary, with consequences which will be examined below.

The maintenance of standing forces of some 4 millon people (mainly men) has not only economic, but also social and political consequences.[2] Institutional arrangements exist to draft a substantial proportion of each generation of young men into the armed forces. A considerable effort is made to ensure that reserves are available for mobilization if necessary. Voluntary military societies provide moral support for the armed forces and military training for the population at large. Secondary school children are given pre-induction military training from the age of fifteen. In recent years there has been a growing campaign of military-patriotic education which tries to instill in the population the values of patriotism and respect for military virtues. Party leaders seemingly believe that obligatory military service can help to foster social discipline and to bring the different nationalities closer together. They also appear to believe that association of the Party with the armed forces will strengthen Soviet patriotism and the commitment of the people to the existing political order.[3] At the highest political level the close relationship between Party and army has been underlined by the awarding to General Secretary Brezhnev of various military honors, including the rank of Marshal of the Soviet Union.

All this is a far cry from the vision of a socialist society which the founders of Marxism and the makers of the Bolshevik revolution held. Marxist thought has traditionally been marked by a strong antipathy to militarism, seeing war and armies as the product of the world capitalist system. Before 1917 socialists agreed that standing armies were instruments of aggression abroad and repression at home; the proper form of military organization for a socialist state would be the citizen army which would not degenernate into a military caste or create a military realm separate from other areas of social life. Although he had to lead the young Soviet republic against the White armies and foreign intervention, Lenin never succumbed to the worship of things military or tried to enhance his own authority by the paraphernalia of military command.

Why is it then that the country in which the first socialist revolution took place is so highly militarized? Why is Soviet military organization so different from original socialist concepts, with rank and hierarchy distinguished in a very marked way? Why is the defense sector accorded a special place in the economy? Why are the values of military patriotism given so much emphasis? The object of this essay is to examine the obstacles to disarmament and demilitarization in the Soviet Union and to see whether there exists in Soviet society the possibility of initiatives in that direction.

Methodological Issues

Soviet writers claim that there is nothing intrinsic to Soviet society that would generate arms production or armed forces, and that the military effort has been forced on the Soviet Union by the enmity of the capitalist world. This claim is not usually argued at length, and is based on a general statement about the nature of socialism rather than on a specific analysis of the Soviet system. A contrast is drawn with the fundamentally aggressive nature of imperialism and the incentives which the capitalist system offers for arms production. In this view Soviet military policy is purely a response to external stimuli. (Interestingly, the same writers often claim that Soviet society is, for various reasons, peculiarly suited to building up military power; among the reasons given are the disciplined, hierarchical, military-like organizations of the Party, and the planned economy which enables the Party to mobilize resources for military purposes.)[4]

A rather different view is given by those peace researchers who argue that the East-West arms race is now firmly rooted in the domestic structures of the two military superpowers. The military competition between East and West, it is claimed, did have its origins in international conflict, but has now become institutionalized in powerful military-industrial-scientific complexes. This is why the settlement of major political disputes in Europe in the early 1970s was not accompanied by any significant moves toward demilitarization. This argument points not to specific features of socialism or Russian history, but to characteristics which the Soviet Union shares with the United States.[5]

The Soviet Union has been subjected to this kind of critical analysis primarily since its emergence as a full-fledged military superpower. The attainment of strategic parity with the United States has made the Soviet Union seem to share full responsibility for the continuing arms race. Soviet arms policies in the 1970s have proved profoundly disappointing to those who hoped that the SALT I agreements would lead to a slackening of the arms race. They, and others, have come more insistently to ask: what drives Soviet arms policies? What are the domestic roots of those policies?

The problem of militarization is, however, wider than that of disarmament. Andreski has pointed out that the term militarism is used in a number of different senses: first, an aggressive foreign policy, based on a readiness to resort to war; second, the preponderance of military in the state, the extreme case being that of military rule; third, subservience of the whole society to the needs of the army, which may involve a recasting of social life in accordance with the pattern of military organization; fourth, an ideology which propagates military ideals.[6] In this essay I shall use the term militarization to refer to the third of these phenomena, specifying the others when necessary.

There are some helpful pointers to the relationships that have to be analyzed. The first of these is the interaction of internal and external factors. The particular form which socialist construction has taken in the Soviet Union cannot be understood without reference to the international context in which the Bolsheviks undertook the transformation of Russian society. Consequently, the militarization of Soviet society has to be examined in the light of international, as well as of domestic, relationships. Moreover, some attempt must be made to discuss what is specific to militarism in the Soviet Union, and what it shares with militarism elsewhere.

Secondly, it has been seen that different historical perspectives—some rooted in the Russian Empire, some in the Cold War—have been adopted, and this raises interesting questions about the way in which patterns of political relationships are reproduced in a given society. Although it is important to provide a historical perspective, there is the danger that the Russian tradition will be presented as monolithic, and that militarism will be seen as a genetic inheritance, transmitted from one generation (or even one social formation) to the next. This would be disheartening in its suggestion that no change is possible, and also wrong. The Russian political tradition is diverse, embracing not only militarism, but also the antimilitarism of Tolstoy and Kropotkin. The Soviet tradition too contains various strands, and the diversity is very wide if the views of contemporary dissidents are taken into account. Consequently it would be a mistake to begin this analysis by portraying this militarization as either inevitable or all-embracing.

War and the Soviet State

With the failure of revolution in Europe, the Soviet Union was left largely isolated in a hostile world. This helped to stimulate a great debate about the direction of socialist construction, and in the mid-1920s the idea of building "socialism in one country" began to gain ground in the Bolshevik Party. This idea, as E.H. Carr has noted, marked the marriage of Marxist revolutionary goals and Russian national destiny.[7] The policy of industrialization which was embarked on toward the end of the decade was the practical offspring of this marriage. In 1931 Stalin, now the dominant leader, who had set his own brutal stamp on the industrialization drive, justified the intensity of the policy by referring to the need to overcome Russia's backwardness and thus prevent other powers from beating her.

> Do you want our Socialist fatherland to be beaten and to lose its independence? If you do not want this you must put an end to its backwardness in the shortest possible time and develop genuine Bolshevik tempo in building up its Socialist system of economy. There is no other way. That is why Lenin said during the October Revolution: "Either perish, or overtake and outstrip the advanced capitalist countries."
>
> We are fifty or a hundred years behind the advanced countries. We must make good this distance in ten years. Either we do it, or they crush us.[8]

Although this justification was not explicitly military, it did prove a clear rationale for the development of the defense industry.

The German invasion of June 22, 1941 took Stalin by surprise, and found the Red Army in a state of unreadiness. The opening months of the war proved disastrous, with the German forces advancing to the outskirts of Moscow. Only by an enormous effort over the next four years was the Soviet Union able to halt the German advance, turn the tide of war, and push the German armies back to Berlin. The degree of industrial mobilization was much greater in the Soviet Union than in the other belligerent states, and Soviet losses of people and material were immense. The Soviet name for the war with Germany—the Great Patriotic War—symbolizes the appeal which Stalin made to the Soviet people's patriotism. In contrast to the bitter social and political tensions of the 1920s and 1930s, state and people were largely united in the common effort to defeat the Nazi enemy.[9]

Victory brought the Soviet Union gains in territory and influence which had seemed inconceivable in the early months of the war. But victory also brought political conflicts with the war-time allies, and these soon found their expression in intense military rivalry, which centered on the development of nuclear weapons and their means of delivery. By 1947 the Soviet Union had four major military research and development programs under way: nuclear weapons, rockets, radar and jet-engine technology. After Stalin's death the implications of this "military-technical revolution" became more pressing. The existence of nuclear weapons in growing stockpiles raised fundamental questions about the relationship of war to policy, and about the appropriate structure for armed forces in the nuclear age—questions which have dominated Soviet military policy ever since.

Khrushchev now put greater stress on peaceful coexistence between East and West, and set in motion major changes in military doctrine and military institutions. In the late 1950s and early 1960s he tried to devise a new military policy, based on nuclear-armed missiles, that would be militarily and diplomatically effective, while freeing resources for civilian purposes. He even floated the idea of restoring the territorial-militia element in the armed forces. But internal opposition, which was strengthened by a succession of international crises (the U-2 incident in 1960, the 1961 Berlin crisis, and the Cuban missile crisis of 1962) and by the Kennedy administration's buildup of strategic forces, finally defeated Khrushchev's efforts.[10]

If we can speak of a "Soviet military build-up," then its origins lie in the defeat of Khrushchev's policy. His successors have devoted considerable attention to the all-round strengthening of Soviet military power. A major increase in strategic forces has brought parity with the United States. The Ground Forces have been expanded, in particular along the frontier with China, and have received more modern equipment. The Air Forces too have been modernized. Soviet naval presence has been extended throughout the world. Arms transfers to third world countries have grown substantially in this period. Certainly Soviet policy has been subject to many rash and alarmist interpretations in the West, but the evidence does point to a steady and significant increase in Soviet military power since the early 1960s.[11]

In the first ten years after the end of the Second World War a clear bipolar structure emerged in world politics, with the United States and the Soviet Union as the dominant powers. Since that time new forces have emerged to transform the international system. The creation of the Third World as a political force was helped by the existence of the Soviet bloc, which could provide a counterweight to Western power.

The Soviet Union now possesses large armed forces, an advanced defense industry, and an extensive military R and D network. In no other area has the Soviet Union come so close to achieving the goal of "catching up and overtaking the advanced capitalist powers." As a consequence, the law of comparative advantage seems to operate in Soviet external policies, giving a major role to the military instrument. The Soviet Union conducts its central relationship with the NATO powers from a position of military strength and economic weakness. In Eastern Europe the Soviet Union has suffered political setbacks but has used military force, and the threat of military force, to underpin its dominant position. Soviet relations with China have now acquired an important military dimension with the build-up of forces along the Chinese frontier. In the Third World the Soviet Union has used arms transfers and military advisers as a major instrument of diplomacy. Thus in spite of the fact that the Soviet concept of the "correlation of forces," in terms of which international politics is analyzed, does not place primary emphasis on military force, military power has become a basic instrument of Soviet external policy.

It is not surprising that the present generation of Soviet leaders should see military power as the main guarantee of Soviet security and of the Soviet position in the world. The men now at the top levels of leadership came to positions of some power in the late 1930s, and Brezhnev and Ustinov are only the most prominent members of this generation to have had a direct part in managing the development and production of arms. Victory in the war with Germany, the attainment of strategic parity with the United States, and the long period at peace since 1945—these are regarded by this generation as among its greatest achievements. When one considers the course of Soviet history from 1917 to 1945, it is no surprise that this should be so.

It should be clear from this brief outline how important war and the preparation for war have been in the formation of the Soviet state. This is not to say that the course of Soviet development has been determined by forces outside the Soviet Union or that every event in Soviet history is to be explained in terms of external conditions. The rise of Stalin and his system of rule cannot be explained without reference to social, economic, and political conditions in the Soviet Union. Moreover, not everything in the Stalinist period can be seen as a response to external threats. The great purge of 1936-38 was justified in this way, but the justification was patently false and the purge greatly weakened the Red Army. But the Stalinist industrialization drive had as its major goal the development of heavy industry as the basis for economic growth and military power, and it was in these terms that it was justified.

This policy involved the extensive mobilization of the resources and energies of Soviet society and the extraction from society of these resources by the state, which then channelled them toward the ends laid down by the party leadership. The process was dominated by the Party-state apparatus which forced changes in social and economic relationships, extracted the resources from an often unwilling population, and managed the new economic system. In order to secure the loyalty of the Party-state apparatus special social and economic privileges and distinctions were introduced. (It was at this time that pre-revolutionary ranks began to be reintroduced into the Red Army.) The rate of extraction was very high, leaving the mass of the population with minimal living standards and sometimes (as when famine occurred) not even those. Coercion was an intrinsic part of this policy.

Victory in the war seemed to show that, whatever the "mistakes" of Stalin's policies in the immediate prewar years, the general emphasis on industrialization had been correct. After the war the high rate of extraction continued as industry was reconstructed and military rivalry with the West pursued. But since Stalin's death important changes have taken place which have a bearing on the questions of disarmament and demilitarization. The first is that the rate of economic growth has slowed considerably, provoking intensive debate about economic reform. It has been widely argued inside and outside the Soviet Union that the system of economic planning and administration was suited to the industrialization drive, but has now become a brake on industrial development and in particular on technological innovation. Second, terror has been abandoned as a system of rule and the Party leadership has been searching for new sources of legitimacy for the state. Repression of opposition and dissent still takes place, but greater effort has been made to secure popular support. Among the ways in which this has been done is through the provision of more and better goods and services to the mass of the population, and through appeals to nationalist sentiments. Third, as a result of the greater attention that has been paid to the living standards and welfare of the population, the priorities of resource allocation have become more complex than they were under Stalin.

The Defense Sector and the Soviet Economy

The organization of the defense sector is similar to that of the rest of Soviet industry.[12] The enterprises that produce arms and equipment are controlled by a series of ministries which have responsibility for the different branches of the sector. The work of these ministries is in turn planned by the central planning agencies (in line with the general policy laid down by the Politburo), since the activities of the defense sector must be coordinated with those of the rest of the economy. There are, however, special institutional arrangements in the defense sector which are designed to ensure that military production has priority claim on scarce resources. In this sense the defense sector is distinct from the rest of the economy.

Soviet military-economic policy is supposed to be guided by three main principles: (1) to maintain a high level of armaments production; (2) to ensure the flexibility of the economy (for example, in shifting from civilian to military production, in raising the rate of arms production or in introducing new weapons); and (3) to secure the viability of the economy in wartime.[13] These principles were elaborated in the 1930s and are still taken as the most important indicators of the state's economic potential—that is, of its ability to provide for the material needs of the society while producing everything necessary for war.

In spite of the flexibility recommended by these principles, the available evidence suggests that there is considerable stability in the defense sector and that this has a major influence on its mode of operation. The research institutes and design bureaus, where new weapons are created, are funded from the budget and their finances do not seem to depend directly on orders for specific systems. Coupled with the institutional continuity of the military R and D network, this provides the basis for a steady effort in the design and development of weapons. Consequently a strong tendency to create "follow-on" systems can be discerned. Stable production appears also to be a feature of the defense sector, with no major variation in output from year to year.

The managers of the defense industry form a coherent group with interlocking careers. There is, however, little evidence that they have acted together as a lobby. The one occasion on which they seem to have done so was in the period 1957 to 1965 when they took part, with some success, in resistance to Khrushchev's decentralization of the system of economic planning and management. In 1963, after some recentralization had taken place, Khrushchev indicated his dissatisfaction with Ustinov and the "metal-eaters" and complained that secrecy made it difficult to criticize the shortcomings of the defense industry.[14]

In the 1970s certain organizational features and management techniques—especially in the area of technological innovation—have been borrowed from the defense sector and applied in civilian industry.[15] This marks an attempt to use the defense sector as a model or dynamo of technological progress in the economy as a whole.

The priority of military production is a matter not only of central decisions, but also of the structure of industry and the attitudes of workers and managers. This was clearly illustrated by an article in *Literaturnaya Gazeta* in 1972 and the correspondence it provoked. The author of the article pointed out that in numerous ways—in prestige, in the priority given by other ministries (for example, in construction projects), in wages in cultural and housing facilities, in labor turnover—light industry fared worse than heavy industry.[16] One of the correspondents wrote that:

> the best conditions are given to the so-called "leading" branches. Then we have the remaining enterprises in Group A/heavy industry. Last in line are the Group B enterprises. Naturally the most highly skilled cadres —workers, engineers or technicians—find jobs or try to find them where the pay is highest, so they are concentrated in the "leading" branches of industry. What is more, these branches receive the best materials, the most advanced technology, the latest equipment etc. etc....Even at the same machine-building enterprise, in the production of "prestige" output and Group B output, there is no comparison in quality and in the attitude to the categories of output (in terms of technology, design work, management, pay, etc.).[17]

There is little doubt that within heavy industry the defense sector occupies the position of highest prestige, and therefore shows these features to the highest degree.

The Soviet system of economic planning and administration has not been altered fundamentally since it was first established. It remains a relatively effective mechanism for extracting resources from the economy and directing them to the goals set by the political leaders, and one of the most important of these goals has been the creation of military power. The defense sector occupies a key—and in some respects, a privileged—position in this system, not only in terms of central priorities, but also in terms of the organization of industry and the attitudes of workers and managers. The debates about economic reform have resulted in partial and piecemeal changes rather than in a fundamental transformation of the system. There has been a tendency over the last ten years to use the defense sector as a model for the rest of industry. In terms of the militarization of the Soviet economy, this is an ambiguous development. On the one hand, it testifies to a political concern about the performance of civilian industry; on the other, it highlights the special position and performance of the defense sector.

The Armed Forces and the Rationales for Military Power

There is little evidence of opposition inside the Soviet Union to Soviet military policy. Since 1965 there have been few if any indications of disagreement in the Party leadership about the level of military expenditure. This contrasts with the Khrushchev period, when military outlays did provide a focus of political argument. And in the dissident *samizdat* literature, although sharp criticism has been made of many features of Soviet life, few voices have been raised against the military policy of the Soviet state. Almost the only exception is the warnings which Andrei Sakharov has given the West of the growing military power of the Soviet Union; and Sakharov's background in nuclear weapons development makes him in this instance a very special case. Thus the situation is rather different from that in the United States, where militarism and racism formed the chief targets of protest in the 1960s and 1970s. There are many reasons for this difference, but the chief one appears to be that inside the Soviet Union the Soviet military effort is widely seen as legitimate and as pursuing legitimate goals. This is in spite of the fact that the burden of military expenditure is greater than in the NATO countries and that there are many competing claims for the resources which are devoted to defense.

One of the main reasons for the acceptance of Soviet military policy is no doubt that for the last thirty to thirty-five years the Soviet Union has enjoyed a period of peace and internal stability which stands in sharp contrast to the wars and upheavals of the first half of the century. The Soviet armed forces have seen very little combat since 1945—certainly nothing to compare with the military role of the American, British, and French forces. The Soviet claim that Soviet military strength is conducive to peace does not, therefore, fly directly in the face of reality. This is one reason why there has been, in the Soviet view, no contradiction between the processes of political detente and the growth of Soviet military power. Soviet military power is regarded as a crucial element in detente because it makes it impossible for the West to deal with the Soviet Union from a position of strength or to use its armed forces in an unfettered way throughout the world.[18]

Although Soviet forces have been engaged in relatively little combat since 1945, military power is certainly regarded by the Soviet leaders as contributing to their political purposes. The main object of that policy has been to prevent the West from conducting offensive actions—whether military or political—against the Soviet Union and its allies. Soviet military aid to Third World countries is to be seen in the same context. Since the 1960s the Soviet Union has come to use its military power—in the form of advisers and arms transfers—more frequently as a way of gaining influence and undermining Western power. (There may now be an economic element in Sovet arms tranfers: excess production can be exchanged—in some instances—for hard currency. But the primary rationale is still political.[19])

But military power has also been a major factor in Soviet relations with socialist states. The Soviet Union used military force in Hungary in 1956 and in Czechoslovakia in 1968 in order to maintain its dominant position in Eastern Europe. That position is underpinned by the ever-present threat of military force, even though that threat is not voiced openly. In the 1960s the confrontaton with China assumed a military form with the build-up of forces along the Chinese frontier. Thus apart from deterring offensive policies directed against the Soviet Union and helping to destroy Western domination in different parts of the world, Soviet military power has been used as an instrument to create and sustain Soviet domination over other states. Moreover, as Soviet military strength has grown, new roles have been found for it, particularly in the projection of power outside the Soviet frontiers. The intervention in Afghanistan illustrates the Soviet Union's growing ability to use its military power in this way, and—more important—its willingness to do so.

In the late 1960s the Soviet Union attained strategic parity with the United States and on that basis entered into negotiations to limit strategic arms.

Of course, it remains extremely difficult to say what constitutes parity or equality (does it mean equality with one particular state or with all potential enemies combined?), and acceptance of the principle still leaves great scope for disagreement both within and between the negotiating states. Moreover, the principle of parity provides a basis for negotiation between the Soviet Union and the United States only because they have so many more nuclear weapons than other states that the other nuclear powers can be left largely out of account. But does every state have the right to parity? Obviously not, since the Non-Proliferation Treaty represents a commitment of a kind to stop the spread of nuclear weapons. Negotiations between the superpowers on the basis of parity go along with the attempt to prevent other states from attaining that status. Precisely because the Soviet Union and the United States are using arms control negotiations in this double-edged way, they are likely to stimulate other states to acquire nuclear weapons of their own. Consequently arms control negotiations on the basis of parity are by no means the foundation for a process of radical demilitarization.

In spite of the acceptance of parity as the basis for negotiations to limit strategic arms, it remains true that there are major differences between Soviet and American strategic thought. American thinking has laid particular emphasis on the ability, under all circumstances, to inflict widespread destruction on the enemy's society. Soviet thinking, on the other hand, has been concerned to limit the damage to Soviet society in the event of nuclear war. Even in a relationship of parity Soviet policy has been directed toward limiting the vulnerability of the Soviet Union to nuclear attack and ensuring the viability of Soviet society in war-time. Whether this can be achieved seems very doubtful (even though viability is a relative term), but it does appear to be the rationale behind important elements of Soviet military, military-economic, and civil defense policies, and it does have important implications for the militarization of Soviet society.

A Military-Industrial State?

As a major instrument of Soviet external policy the armed forces naturally enjoy an important position in the Party-state apparatus. The Ministry of Defense and the General Staff are overwhelmingly staffed by professional officers who have spent all their careers in the armed forces. Since 1945 the post of Minister has, more often than not, been held by a professional soldier, although the present Minister, Ustinov, has spent most of his life in the defense industry. The chief functions of the Ministry and the General Staff are those of similar institutions in other countries: to draw up plans, develop strategy and tactics, gather and evaluate intelligence about potential enemies, educate and train the troops, and administer the whole network of military institutions. The Soviet Union, unlike the United States, does not have an extensive network of civilian institutions conducting research into military operations: operational analysis is done very largely within the armed forces.

The existence of a large military establishment within the state might be thought to pose difficult problems of civilian-military relations and to threaten the Party's dominant position in Soviet society. It is true that there have been elements of conflict and tension in Party-military relations, but the principle of Party supremacy has never seriously been threatened.

The Soviet Union embodies the apparent paradox of a militarized social system in which the military, while an important political force, is not the dominant one. This is not to say, however, that the armed forces—or, more particularly, members of the High Command—have played no role in the political crises of the post-Stalin period. In each case of leadership change—Beria's arrest and execution in 1953, Malenkov's defeat by Khrushchev in 1955, the defeat of the "anti-Party group" in 1957, and Khrushchev's fall in 1964—members of the High Command played some role. But military support was one factor among others, and probably not the decisive one. Moreover, Marshal Zhukov's disgrace in 1957, only months after he had helped Khrushchev to defeat the "anti-Party group" in the the Central Committee, shows that engaging in leadership politics can be a risky business for soldiers. The spectre of Bonapartism was conjured up by Khrushchev as a major justification for Zhukov's removal from office. Even though it appears to have been a contrived justification, it underlined the determination of the Party leadership to retain its supremacy over the armed forces. Military involvement has been made possible only by splits in the Party leadership, and on no occasion has it resulted in a conflict in which Party leaders were ranged on one side and the military on the other; the High Command has had its own internal politics and divisions.

The political quiescence of the armed forces is to be explained by reference not so much to the formal mechanisms of Party and secret police control as to the way in which military interests have been given priority in Party policy. To say this is not to minimize Stalin's brutal treatment of the armed forces or to deny that Khrushchev often pursued policies that were to the distaste of the High Command. But by stressing the importance of international conflict and national solidarity, the Party has provided an ideological framework which gives a clear meaning to the armed forces' existence. Party policy has also given the officer corps a privileged material position and a high status in Soviet society. Finally, the professional interests of the officer corps have been generally well served, especially in the allocation of resources to defense and in the opportunities for career advancement.

Since Stalin's death in 1953, and more particularly since Khrushchev's fall from power in 1964, officers have been given considerable freedom to discuss questions of military policy and a greater voice in the policy-making process. This has resulted from the general diffusion of power at the center of the Soviet state and has parallels in other areas of Soviet life where vigorous debates have been conducted about matters of policy. The Brezhnev Politburo has placed great emphasis on "scientific" policy-making and on expert and technically competent advice.

The diffusion of power has created what some writers refer to as "institutional pluralism."[20] Like all pluralism, however, it is imperfect in the sense that some groups and institutions have more power than others. In this respect the armed forces and the defense industry occupy a special position. The armed forces enjoy wide prestige as the embodiment of national power and integrity— a prestige which is enhanced by the extensive program of military-patriotic education. The Ministry of Defense and General Staff are institutions of undoubted competence, with a monopoly of expertise in military affairs: there are no civilian institutions able to challenge this expertise. The high priority given to the defense sector remains embedded in the system of economic planning and administration. The defense industry has been in the forefront of Soviet technological progress and is seen by the Party leaders as something to be emulated rather than restricted in the age of the "scientific-technical revolution." Finally, key aspects of military policy are shrouded in secrecy, and this limits criticism of the priority given to defense in resource allocation and of the way in which those resources are used.

This is not to suggest that the military policy of the Soviet state has been pursued against the wishes of the Party leadership. The final decisions on military policy rest with the Politburo and with the Defense Council, which comprises several leading Politburo members under Brezhnev's chairmanship. All the evidence points to a set of shared assumptions among the leaders about military power and military expenditure. There are differences of view, no doubt, but these appear to be marginal, and the overall policy seems to rest on a broad consensus.[21] It is, however, possible that this state of affairs will change in the post-Brezhnev leadership and that the level of military effort will become a contentious issue as it was under Khrushchev. Then the institutional power of the armed forces and the defense industry might be important in determining the outcome of the argument.

Can we speak then of a Soviet "military-industrial complex"? It is true that there is a large military establishment and a large defense industry. But the term itself often carries theoretical connotations that make it inapplicable to the Soviet Union. Sometimes it suggests a degenerate pluralism in which the balanced interplay in interests has been undermined by links between the armed forces and industry; in this sense it seems not to be appropriate because it implies too great a degree of pluralism—and it implies pluralism as a norm—for the Soviet Union. Sometimes it is implied that the driving force of arms policies is the pursuit of profit by capitalist enterprises; this too would be inappropriate, and for this reason Garaudy has argued that the Soviet Union has a "bureaucratic-military complex"—that is, a military-industrial complex without the economic driving-force.[22] An objection of a different kind is summarized in the statement that the Soviet Union does not *have* a military-industrial complex, but *is* such a complex. This is too sweeping a statement, but it does make the point that the history of the Soviet Union is so bound up with military power that it seems wrong to speak of a separate military-industrial complex acting within the state.

Whether or not we say the armed forces and the defense industry constitute a military-industrial complex in the Soviet Union matters less than the fact that they exhibit many features that are identified as a characteristic of such a complex. Because of the way in which the Soviet economic system is organized it does not exhibit these features in the same way, or to the same degree, as the American defense sector; but it does share them nevertheless. For example, competition is to be found in the weapons development process between offensive and defensive systems, with new technology in one area stimulating innovation in another. This may happen without any direct stimulus from outside. Second, the military R and D system shows considerable inertia in its operations, thus generating strong pressure for follow-on systems. Third, the R and D system does not appear to have a strong innovative dynamic of its own. Intervention by the political leadership is required for major innovations; but because the Party leaders have devoted so much attention to this area, such intervention is often forthcoming. Further, the military R and D system is not especially conducive to the cross-fertilization of technologies to produce new weapons, but this may happen as designers search for ways of meeting new requirements. Finally, the steadiness of Soviet arms policies may be accounted for, in part, by the planning to which weapons development and production are subject.

The Soviet military effort, which was created in the course of international rivalry, is now rooted in the structure of the Soviet state. This is not to say, of course, that the external stimuli have vanished. It is clear that foreign actions do impinge on Soviet arms policies and this can be seen both in the histories of specific weapons systems and in the direction of overall policy.[23] The advanced capitalist powers have set the pace in making major weapons innovations, and this has served to stimulate Soviet military technology. Of course it must be borne in mind that military power rests not only on the quality of military technology, but also on its quantity and on the way in which the troops are trained to use it. The arms competition between East and West consists of both qualitative and quantitative elements; although the balance of the two may change, the arms race has never been a question of one of these elements to the exclusion of the other. Western military technology has spurred Soviet weapons development, but has often been justified in terms of superior Soviet numbers.

It would be wrong therefore to deny the effects of foreign actions of Soviet arms policies. But it would be equally mistaken to see Soviet policy as merely a reaction to Western actions. Foreign influences are refracted through the Soviet policy-making process, in which Soviet perceptions, military doctrine, foreign policy objectives, and domestic influences and constraints come into play. The effect of foreign actions on Soviet policy is complex and not at all automatic. In many cases the foreign influences combine with domestic factors to speed up the internal dynamic of Soviet arms policies.[24] The very existence of large armed forces, a powerful defense industry, and an extensive network of military R and D establishments generates internal pressures for weapons development and production. The interplay of demands and invention gives rise to proposals for new and improved weapons. As a system progresses from conception to development, military and design bureau interests become attached to it, building up pressure for production. If it passes into production—and here a decision by the Party leadership is required for major systems—enterprise managers are likely to favor long production runs.

Although much of Soviet military policy-making is shrouded in secrecy, enough is known about the structures of the military-industrial-scientific complex to suggest that internal pressures are generated and considerable inertia built up in the military effort. It seems clear too that the removal of external stimuli, while it might alter Soviet arms policies in some important respects (for example, make it less technologically innovative), would not eliminate its driving-force entirely, because much of that force is derived from domestic sources. (Nor could one say that military power would wither away because it had no role: it has been noted already that as Soviet military power has expanded it has acquired new roles). The question then is: How are these domestic sources to be weakened?

Conclusion

This essay has tried to outline in general terms the domestic sources of the Soviet military effort. It has suggested that these sources are deeply embedded in Russian and Soviet history. Disarmament and demilitarization would involve therefore more than the surgical removal of some element of the Soviet state; it would have far-reaching effects throughout the whole society. Indeed, complete disarmament and demilitarization could come about only with the destruction of the international state system (and would not necessarily happen then). And although the "withering away of the state" is one of the anticipated consequences of communist construction, the Soviet Union has one of the most powerful and extensive state apparatuses in the world. Yet, although the sources of Soviet militarism are strong, this essay has tried not to present them as absolute, or to suggest that there is no scope for initiatives for demilitarization. There are some developments in the Soviet Union today which suggest that a change of direction is possible. It would be a serious error to overestimate their importance or the degree to which they can be influenced from outside the Soviet Union. Yet it would be an even greater mistake to suppose that no change is possible or that its direction could not be influenced from afar.

Soviet military policy contains several contradictions which may, with time, become more apparent and exert an influence on Soviet politics. Having attained equality of superpower status with the United States, the Soviet Union is now faced with a new set of questions about military power and the direction of its policy. The Soviet leaders have said that they are not striving for superiority, but they have made it clear that they will not fall behind the United States in military power. The Soviet Union has thus locked itself into a relationship of parity with the United States. At one level the maintenance of parity—along with the arms control negotiations which it underpins—provides the justification for Soviet military policy. At another level, however, the attainment of parity has meant that the Soviet Union has come to share full responsibility for the continuing arms competition. This has had a subtle, yet profound effect on the attitude of many people in the West to Soviet military policy. Many of those sympathetic to Soviet policy deemed it legitimate for the leading socialist state to catch up with the leading capitalist power; but sharing responsibility for the arms race is not regarded so favorably, especially in view of the danger of nuclear war. In a similar way, the continuation of a high level of military effort, even after parity has been attained, may help breed opposition inside the Soviet Union to the amassing of more military power. It is possible, for example, that Soviet militarism may emerge as a more important focus for dissident criticism, though the strength of nationalist sentiment (including dissident Russian nationalism) and the deep roots of legitimation should not be forgotten.

The Soviet Union shares with the United States the contradiction that growing military power does not bring stability even for superpowers. The accumulation of military power may only spur other governments to increase their own forces, thus nullifying the original gain. It is true that military power can further foreign policy, but it cannot ensure complete security in the nuclear age. The "Soviet military build-up" of the 1960s and 1970s has brought the Soviet Union political gains, but it has also helped stimulate countervailing actions, and it is highly doubtful whether, in the last analysis, Soviet security is more assured now than it was fifteen years ago. Moreover, the extension of Soviet military power throughout the world increases the risk that the Soviet Union will become embroiled in a military adventure which will arouse opposition at home, just as the American war in Vietnam did, or as did the Russo-Japanese war of 1904-05. The failure of military power to ensure security should, in principle, provide the opportunity of pressing the importance of pursuing non-military cooperative arrangements for security rather than seeking to provide one's own security at the expense of another's.

These contradictions would be of little importance if there were no possibility of giving them political significance. The

last fifteen years have been a period of consolidation and
conservative reform in the Soviet Union. But beneath the stable
surface, changes have been taking place which could result in
major shifts of direction in Soviet policy. The rate of economic
growth has been declining, thus increasing the prospect that
pressure for far-reaching reform will reemerge. Agricultural
performance has improved greatly, but at a very high cost,
again raising the prospect of reform. Other pressures exist for
changing the priorities of resource allocation—for example, in
order to speed up development of Siberia or to raise living
standards. The cumulative effect of such pressures might be to
weaken the position of the defense sector or to involve it more
deeply in nonmilitary functions. But it is not only the economic
system that has been the focus of debate; discussion has also
been taking place about the Soviet Union's proper relationship
to the rest of the world. Some have pressed for as great a degree
of autarky and isolation as possible; others have argued for a
more outward-looking approach which would recognize that
the world faces many problems which can be solved only by
common and concerted action.[25] With the impending change of
leadership these various factors may combine to create a
turning-point in Soviet politics. The present leadership, as has
been seen, has given immense importance to military power. It
is as yet unclear how the next generation, which will not have
been marked so deeply by the war, will view military power.

In pointing to these developments one should not forget the
militarizing pressures that were analyzed earlier in this paper.
Nor should one suppose that a change of course undertaken by a
Soviet leadership would amount to radical disarmament or
demilitarization. But the possibility for some change does exist
and it should be the aim of the peace movement to try to influence that change in the desired direction. There are considerable difficulties in seeking to influence Soviet policy from the
outside, for the political system is very impermeable, both in
physical and cultural terms: it is hard to gain access to the
policy-making process, and foreign attempts to influence policy
will automatically be viewed with suspicion.

There are, nevertheless, two courses to be pursued. The first
of these is directed at Western governments and should aim at
ensuring that they do not foreclose, through their own policies,
the possibility of Soviet moves toward disarmament and demilitarization. This course is a natural concomitant of efforts to
press Western governments in that direction too. But some
attempt is needed to take the Soviet dimension consciously into
account, and this means that the causes of Soviet militarism,

and the ways in which pressure on Western governments can also serve to influence the Soviet Union, need to be analyzed. Such influence need not necessarily be directed solely at disarmament, but could try to draw the Soviet Union into cooperative efforts to solve such problems as the world food supply. This might make it easier subsequently to work out cooperative, non-military security arrangements.

The second course is directed at the Soviet Union and should try to engage people there in a dialogue about the problems of disarmament and demilitarization. Such a dialogue should be as extensive as possible, and should not be confined to officials and representatives of officially approved bodies on the one hand, or to dissidents (whether in the Soviet Union or abroad) on the other. The variety of political views and currents in the Soviet Union is very wide, and dissident and official views overlap and shade into each other; there are, for example, strong nationalist tendencies in both official and dissident thinking, and dissident reformist views find an echo in official circles as well.[26]

The importance of this course is that vigorous debates about Russia's destiny and the proper path of Soviet development are taking place inside the Soviet Union and among Soviet emigres; in Eastern Europe too there is such argument about the future of state socialism. But the issues of disarmament and demilitarization—which are important for everyone's future—scarcely figure at all in these discussions, even though militarism and the lack of democracy are linked in the Soviet case. If these issues could be injected into the discussion, they would then be subject to a great deal of creative political thinking—and thinking, moreover, that is more attuned to the specific problems and conditions of the Soviet Union. Besides, it has been seen that the military burden in the Soviet Union is very heavy, but that its legitimation is also strong. Debate and discussion about the problems of Soviet militarism might help to weaken that legitimation.

It should not be supposed that everyone will welcome such discussion, and the attempt to generate it may well be regarded as unwarranted interference in the internal affairs of the Soviet Union. But in the nuclear age we are all affected by the military policies of the superpowers, and hence we surely have the right to try to influence them.

Footnotes

1.) The figures available on arms production and force levels give only the roughest indication of Soviet military production. They show no very sharp fluctuations since 1950, but they are too crude to register any but the most massive changes. The late 1950s and early 1960s appear to be the period of lowest effort. Western estimates of Soviet defense spending as a proportion of GNP seem to fit this pattern, with the Khrushchev years as the period when the proportion was lowest. Most estimates, derived by whatever means, fall into the range of 8 to 14 percent, with the lower estimates for the late 1950s and early 1960s. See, for example, the following: A.S. Becker, *Soviet National Income 1958-64* (1969), chapter 7; F.D. Holzman, *Financial Checks on Soviet Defense Expenditures* (1975); H. Block, in Joint Economic Committee, U.S. Congress, *Soviet Economic Prospects for the Seventies* (1973), pp.175-204; W.T. Lee, *The Estimation of Soviet Defense Expenditures 1955-75* (1977).

2.) *The Military Balance* (IISS, London) each year gives a figure for the manpower in the Soviet Armed Forces. In 1979 the figure is 3-6 million (*The Military Balance 1979-1980,* p.9). This does not include approximately 400,000 KGB and MVD troops. On top of these figures there are the 400,000 troops who engage in construction, railroad, farm, and medical work. See M. Feshback and S. Rapawy, in Joint Economic Committee, U.S. Congress, *Soviet Economy in a New Perspective* (1976), pp.144-52.

3.) Defense Minister Ustinov has declared that "service in the Soviet armed forces is a wonderful school of labour and martial training, of moral purity and courage, of patriotism and comradeship." *(Pravda,* November 8, 1979, p. 2). See T. Rakowska-Harmstone, "The Soviet Army as the Instrument of National Integration," in John Erickson and E.J. Feuchtwanger, eds., *Soviet Military Power and Performance* (1979), pp. 129-54.

4.) See, for example, *Markizm-Leninism o voine i armii* (1968), chapter 5.

5.) See in particular Dieter Senghaas, *Rustung und Militarismus* (1972).

6.) J. Gould and W.L. Kolb, eds., *A Dictionary of the Social Sciences* (1964), pp. 429-30.

7.) E.H. Carr, *Socialism in One Country, 1924-1926,*Vol.2 (1970), p.59.

8.) J.V. Stalin, *Problems of Leninism* (1947), p. 356.

9.) This is not to deny that there was opposition to the Soviet state during the war; but the memory of the war is very potent. See, for example, Chapter 12 of Hedrick Smith, *The Russians* (1976).

10.) On this period of Khrushchev's rule see especially Michel Tatu, *Power in the Kremlin* (1969).

11.) It is also possible to trace the "Soviet military build-up" to the Central Committee resolution "On the Defense of the Country" in

1929. But the present phase has its roots in the "revolution in military affairs" which was the subject of much discussion in the early 1960s.

12.) For a discussion of the organization and functioning of the defense sector, see my "Soviet Military R & D: Managing the Research-Production Cycle," in J. Thomas and U. Kruse-Vancienne, eds., *Soviet Science and Techology* (George Washington University for the National Science Foundation, 1977), pp. 179-229; for a more detailed discussion, see my two chapters in R. Amann and J. Cooper, eds., *Innovation in Soviet Industry* (forthcoming).

13.) *Markizm-Leninizm o voine i armii* (1968), pp.258-59.

14.) *Pravda*, April 26, 1963; Tatu, *Power in the Kremlin*, pp. 343-44.

15.) See especially Julian Cooper, *Innovation for Innovation in Soviet Industry*, Center for Russian and East European Studies, University of Birmingham, Discussion Paper, Series RCB/11, 1979, pp.87-92.

16.) A. Levikov, " 'A'; 'B,' " in *Literaturnaya Gazeta*, November 15, 1972, p. 11.

17.) *Literaturnaya Gazeta*, February 7, 1973, p. 10.

18.) See, for example, S. Tynshkevich, "Sootnoshenie sil v mire i faktory predotyrashcheniya voiny," *Kommunist vooruzhennykh sil*, no. 10 (1974), p. 16; N.A. Kosolapov, "Sotsialno-psikhologicheskie aspekty razryadki," *Voennaya sila i mezhdunarodnye tonosheniya* (1972), chapter 1.

19.) See *World Armaments and Disarmament. SIPRI Yearbook 1979*, pp.172-72; G. Ofer, "Soviet Military Aid to the Middle East," Joint Economic Committee, U.S. Congress, *Soviet Economy in a New Perspective* (1976), pp. 216-39.

20.) "The Soviet System: Petrification or Pluralism," in J. Hough, *The Soviet Union and Social Science Theory* (1977), pp. 19-48.

21.) For a discussion of marginal shifts of resources, see J. Hardt, "Military-Economic Implications of Soviet Regional Policy," prepared for Colloquium at NATO Economic Directorate, Brussels, April 1979.

22.) R. Garaudy, *The Turning-Point of Socialism* (1979), p. 138.

23.) A very clear example is Soviet atomic bomb development. See my *Entering the Nuclear Arms Race: The Soviet Decision to Build the Atomic Bomb*, Working Paper No. 9, International Security Studies Program, Wilson Center, Washington, D.C., 1979.

24.) See my "Research Note: Soviet Thermonuclear Research," *International Security*, winter 1979/80.

25.) For a discussion of the different trends, see W. Clemens, Jr., *The USSR and Global Interdependence* (1978).

26.) See, for example, the discussion in R. Medvedev, *On Socialist Democracy* (1975), chapters 3 and 4.

Chapter 20

Domestic Sources of the "Soviet Threat"

Alan Wolfe

"The principal threat to our nation, to world peace, and to the cause of human freedom is the Soviet drive for dominance... The Soviet Union has not altered its long-held goal of a world dominated by a single center—Moscow."[1] So spoke an organization called the Committee on the Present Danger, founded in 1976 on the premise that the United States, if it did not build up its defenses, would soon be impotent in the face of Soviet strength. The dual perception that the United States is becoming weaker while the Soviets are gaining strength, articulated so forcefully by the Committee, became a political issue in the election of 1980 and contributed in no small measure to the election of Ronald Reagan, a politician long identified with conservative views on defense policy. The debate that subsequently broke out about Russian intentions in the early years of the Reagan administration was not a new phenomenon. The frequency with which intellectuals and policy-makers concern themselves with the Soviet threat raises questions that go to the very heart of America's ability to survive as a democratic society. But if a Soviet military threat to the American system is not genuine—if it is exaggerated, distorted, and based upon self-serving needs—then the danger to Amer-

343

ica's democracy comes as much from within as from without, for in such a case there would be pressure to expand the military budget, curtail basic freedoms, and restrict open access to government on the basis of a premise that was false.

In this essay I will argue that much of the recent hysteria about the Soviet military build-up has a great deal to do with the dynamics of domestic politics. I will argue that in the past *U.S. perceptions of hostile Soviet intentions have increased not when the Russians have become more aggressive or militaristic, but when certain constellations of political forces have come together within the United States to force the question of the Soviet threat onto the American political agenda.*

Three Peaks of Hostility

There have been certain periods of time in which, although much attention was paid to the evils of communism, the U.S. did not actively pursue a directly provocative course with respect to Russia. And there have been other times when a concern with Soviet perceptions of American weakness have led to a veritable obsession with "standing up to the Russians."

For the purposes of this study, a high peak in the perception of the Soviet threat can be defined as having the following characteristics. First, some important group of policymakers issues a report making a claim that the Russians are getting stronger and the Americans weaker. This report is read and debated in the highest circles of policymaking, fashioning a new consensus about the Soviet danger. As a result of the new perception, certain steps are taken to demonstrate America's concern. The two most important indications of the new mood are a decision to increase the defense budget and a decision to demonstrate U.S. strength in some way, either through a direct intervention or through a symbolic display like moving the American fleet. Both kinds of action are meant by policymakers to prove American resolve. Therefore, a peak in the perception of the Soviet threat requires a conjuncture of an ideological offensive (as manifested in some new official statement about the rivalry between the two superpowers) combined with a manifest shift toward policies that tangibly demonstrate a firmer course.

Contrariwise, a dip in the perception of the Soviet threat would occur when either the ideology or the action was missing, or both. For our purposes, a trough in the hostile perception of the Soviet Union will be considered a period in which anti-Russian ideology did not correspond with a palpable rise in foreign policy belligerence to produce a new U.S. offensive in the world.

Based upon these criteria, postwar American policy has gone through three peaks and two valleys:

1. *The first peak:* the period of cold war initiation. Right after World War II ended until the early 1950s, a very negative interpretation of Soviet conduct began to win out in the United States. As a result, the basic decisions that began the cold war—such as developing the H-bomb—were made.

2. *The first valley:* the Eisenhower retrenchment. In spite of all the anti-communist rhetoric of John Foster Dulles, ideology did not correspond with action under Eisenhower. The defense budget did not increase and U.S. foreign policy actions designed to prove America's resolve to the Russians were relatively few.

3. *The second peak:* the cold war consolidation. Beginning in the late 1950s with the Gaither report, a number of defense specialists began to question the Eisenhower approach. The anti-Soviet ideology was carried forward but to it was added, especially between 1961 and 1962, a new American belligerence in foreign affairs, culminating in the Cuban Missile Crisis.

4. *The second valley:* detente. Starting fitfully in 1963 with Kennedy's American University speech and continuing into the Nixon administration, big-power cooperation began to increase. By the mid-1970s, the defense budget (as a percent of GNP) had decreased, foreign interventions, while more blatant, were less numerous, and SALT I was signed and ratified.

5. *The third peak:* Carter to Reagan. Two years into the Carter administration, just as a new strategic arms treaty with the Russians was concluded, a new wave of anti-Soviet hostility swept Washington. Ratification of SALT-II became impossible. Pressures to increase military spending, especially after the Iranian hostage crisis and the Soviet invasion of Afghanistan, became irresistable. In such an atmosphere, the strong rhetoric of Ronald Reagan seemed a tonic, leading to the election of a conservative president and the attempt to put into practice some of the more extreme anti-Soviet perceptions available in the United States.

The transformations from peak to valley and back to peak periods correspond with changes in several aspects of domestic politics. These aspects include: the pattern of party politics; cycles of presidential strength and weakness, inter-service rivalries, debates over the locus of foreign policy; and patterns of economic growth.

The Center Cannot Hold

The most striking feature that all three peaks of anti-Soviet hostility have in common is that the Democrats held the presidency. Does this mean that the Democrats are a war party? It does, but only because the Republicans force them to be. In order to understand the role that domestic politics play in raising the level of intensity of the Soviet threat, it is important to examine the way the two political parties treat foreign policy.

Hostile perceptions of the Soviet Union tend to occur under similar political conditions. First, a new president, generally a Democrat, assumes office. During this time, the right wing organizes itself around the notion of a Soviet threat, a politically safe issue for them since they are out of power and need not concern themselves with putting new policies into effect. Pressure from the right makes the newly installed president vulnerable. If there was equally strong pressure from the left, in favor of programs oriented toward greater equality and a foreign policy permitting smaller defense budgets, the new president would not be forced to lean rightwards. But without a strong left, Democratic presidents invariable adopt a more aggressive foreign policy as a way of protecting their political base. This also gives them the appearance of being bold and decisive, which cuts down some of the need to adopt aggressive domestic programs—ones that would antagonize big business and conservative interest groups. Eventually, the cold war fever that afflicts the Democrats spreads to the Republicans as well, until new fiscal or international realities bring anti-Soviet obsessions into more reasonable focus.

If the peaks of anti-Soviet hostility have certain political features in common, so should the valleys. And indeed, just as the former are dominated by Democrats pursuing cold war liberal policies, the later are dominated by Republicans with a different domestic political agenda. The Republican party, at the presidential level, did not have to face the same kind of domestic dilemmas that bedevil liberal Democrats. Eisenhower, for example, simply was not as vulnerable to the right. It is true that the right, in the form of Senator Joseph McCarthy and his allies, did try to attack the General, but the notion that such a conservative man as Eisenhower could be "soft" on communism was so ludicrous that this tactical mistake began McCarthy's downfall.

Nixon and Kissinger were in a similarly favorable position. Nixon hoped to fashion an "emerging Republican majority" by uniting the white working class of the North with conservatives in the South and West over a strategy of trying to roll back the social gains experienced by minorities during the 1960s. To accomplish this task, Nixon did need foreign policy bellicosity, but he could rely on largely symbolic anti-communism for domestic consumption while searching for big-power accommodations with the Soviet Union. Highly symbolic foreign policy militancy works better for Republicans than for Democrats, for the latter's vulnerability to the right means that they often have to combine action with words. The former, because they are the right, find that words suffice to shore up their domestic image of "toughness."

The shape of domestic political coalitions clearly has an impact in determining whether an administration will choose a highly negative image of Soviet conduct, leading to confrontation, or a big-power view, leading to some form of accommodation. This pattern continued under the presidency of Jimmy Carter, but with consequences that would add a new, and more dangerous, twist to the role that partisan politics played in exacerbating the Soviet threat.

When Carter assumed office, the length and intensity of the cold war had transformed many key features of American politics. By the late 1970s many Democrats had come to accept the Soviet threat as an indispensable part of their outlook on the world. Defense plants, hawkish labor unions, support for Israel, and macroeconomic stimulation had all combined with the power of military men, contractors and spies to produce a firm coalition in favor of increased defense spending and a renewed foreign policy militancy.

Jimmy Carter made the assumption that cold war sentiment could be effectively bought off through compromise and symbolic gestures—an assumption which failed to take account of the intense, indeed fanatical, quality of the resurgent cold warriors. Instead of coopting anti-Soviet hysteria, Carter's decision to appear tougher with the Russians simply intensified it, so that the more that Carter moved to the right, the further right the discourse shifted.

The net effect of the Carter presidency was to undermine thoroughly the appeal of dentente and to lead to the election of a Republican far more sincere in his articulation of the Soviet threat than Carter. When Ronald Reagan became president, a new stage in the relationship between domestic politics and foreign policy perceptions was reached, for under previous Republicans like Eisenhower and Nixon, cold war hysteria eventually subsided, whereas under Reagan it reached unprecendented new heights. Does this mean that the historic relationship between cold war perceptions and Democratic presidents has become obsolete? It would be an error to jump to that conclusion too quickly. Instead we should try to understand the significance of the Reagan electoral victory in the context of postwar party politics.

In both domestic and foreign policy, Reagan ran against the historical legacy of his own party. His domestic notions, emphasizing supply-side tax cuts, bore a much closer resemblance to deficit spending proposals than they did to the orthodox Republican belief in balanced budgets. And in foreign policy Mr. Reagan avoided the isolationist and cautious approach to world affairs in favor of an active and aggressive foreign policy that had been more associated with the Democrats than the Republicans. Indeed, in its basic essentials—rapid economic growth at home and an equally rapid expansion of military capacity abroad—the Reagan agenda was closer to the platform of John F. Kennedy than to any other postwar incumbent. In 1980, in short, the same dynamics described in this chapter were working, but they had come to affect the internal dynamics of the Republican Party more than they colored the composition of the Democratic Party.

If the Reagan administration continues to pursue foreign policy based upon the most negative possible interpretation of Soviet conduct, one would expect the Democrats, as the party of the opposition, to urge caution and restraint. If this were to take place, the entire pattern of postwar domestic input into foreign policy would reverse itself. However, there is reason to believe that the Reagan administration may not be able to continue its hawkish foreign policy, in which case the future patterns of party politics will remain confused and uncertain.

The effect of trying to put into practice some of the most extreme theories about Soviet behavior has had the impact of undermining the solidity of the fear of the Soviet threat. In 1980 the American people were clearly scared and anxious to do whatever they could to meet the challenge from the Soviet Union. Two years later there was talk of a nuclear freeze, major disputes between the allies, New Right distrust of Ronald Reagan, pressure to stretch out or even postpone defense expenditures just recently approved, and a sense that the whole wave of insecurity about Soviet military spending and aggression may have been exaggerated. The Reagan administration desperately wants to keep the third peak of anti-Soviet hostility at its height, but in spite of its best efforts, a relaxation of tensions may occur nonetheless.

There are some Democrats, associated with the neo-conservative wing of the Party, who already feel that Reagan has softened and needs to be criticized from a more pure anti-Soviet position. If they take the leadership in future elections, we will return to the pattern by which the Democrats adopt the more cold war positions. But a more likely scenario is that each party will divide between its more and less hawkish elements. The most extreme negative perceptions of the Soviet Union will unify both parties as they serve in opposition and campaign for office, but in the real world of limited funds, internal disputes within the Atlantic Alliance, the greying of the Soviet leadership, political transitions in the Kremlin, the local character of Third World disputes, and the changes taking place in Eastern Europe, no administration, of either political party, will be able to govern for long based on extreme cold war stereotypes. That will be the ironic legacy of the Reagan presidency.

The Presidency and Its Enemies

After Vietnam and Watergate, many observers think of a strong presidency as being responsible for some of the abuses of the American political system. Yet there is a peculiar way in which the peaks of anti-Soviet hostility correspond, not so much to the strength of the presidency, but to its weakness.

Much of American ideology is sympathetic to weak government, but the American economic system since the later part of the nineteenth century has demanded a strong one. Traditionally, therefore, there have been cycles in which activist presidents have expanded the power of the presidency, only to see its power watered down in later years. In the period since World War II, there have been a number of occasions when power seemed to be passing away from the presidency, commencing a cycle of weak executive power. It has been precisely during those periods when negative perceptions of an external enemy heightened, and one consequence was to preserve presidential power.

When Franklin Roosevelt died and was replaced by Truman, a reaction against presidential power set in. From the states, from Congress, and from the heartlands of America came demands to simplify life, to return power to the people, and to reestablish normality. For example, Truman's globally oriented advisors were telling him how important it was to retain some U.S. troops in Europe in order to maximize American leverage there after the war ended. But so strong was the demand for a more normal existence that Truman was effectively prevented from so doing; the troops came home. This experience with demobilization made it clear to presidential activists (like Clark Clifford) that unless steps were taken to curb such sentiment, all the gains that had been made by the executive since 1932 might be lost. Without a strong executive, men like Clifford reasoned, the U.S. would be unable to exercise world leadership; its role in the world's markets would be undermined by foreign competition; its welfare state would be in danger; and the entire political coalition that had brought the U.S. out of the depression and had fought the war would fall apart.

The rise of a negative perception of Soviet conduct must be seen in the light of these debates over presidential power. This is not to argue that the policymakers deliberately exaggerated the Soviet threat in order to keep the executive strong, but it is to suggest that the entire atmosphere associated with the fears of an external enemy is conducive to making the argument for strong presidential power seem more valid.[2]

One case of a fairly deliberate decision by the Truman administration to adopt a negative perception on Soviet conduct in order to protect the presidency came over the Truman Doctrine. Truman's advisors had convinced the president that securing public support for aid to Greece and Turkey demanded an "all out" speech portraying Soviet activities as a major threat to the security of the United States. To do so would be to ignore evidence that events in both countries were local in scope, the result of long historical forces, and not the result of Soviet "aggression." Two of the most prominent Soviet specialists in the U.S., George Kennan and Charles Bohlen, both strongly anti-communist, blanched when they saw a draft of Truman's speech because of its provocative overtones. Their objections were overruled on the grounds that in order to win Senate approval of a new foreign policy (the Senate was attracted to isolationism and was wary of giving up its role in foreign policy, as an aggressive doctrine like containment would force them to do), a militant anti-Soviet speech was essential.[3] Thus cold war perceptions were cultivated, not because of international affairs, but because of domestic political conditions.

In the 1960s, President Kennedy also rejected a "restricted concept of the presidency," and said that the nation's leader should become "the vital center of action in our whole scheme of government." Kennedy practiced what he preached. During his administration, tendencies toward concentrated power increased. Distrustful of the State Department, Kennedy placed responsibility for foreign affairs in the hands of a few men on his personal staff. Distrust of all agencies of power outside the presidency was characteristic of both the Kennedy and Johnson administrations. For them, highly dramatic foreign policy crises, requiring decisive presidential action, added to the glamor of their administrations, and also worked to still any thoughts that Congress, local elites, conservative defenders of the Constitution, or ordinary people might have about a simpler political system in which the president did not have such enormous power.

No president undermined the power of the executive more than did Richard Nixon through his clumsy attempts to expand it. Although a strong executive had in the past been favored by Democrats and opposed by Republicans, Nixon confounded the pattern by expanding presidential power in order to pursue conservative goals.

The Watergate scandal was thus both a boom and a bust to the believers in the active presidency that congregated around the Democratic Party. It disgraced Nixon and opened the way for the Democrats to re-occupy the White House. But at the same time, Nixon had given a bad name to presidential power, and a strong executive was still central to the practice of the Democratic Party. The biggest challenge facing the Carter administration was how to restore the legitimate authority of a strong presidency after both Vietnam and Watergate had reawakened the traditional American desire to fracture power and keep it weak.

Carter was not very successful at this task. Despite his best efforts to transform the energy crisis into the "moral equivalent of war," skepticism of emergencies had been too firmly ingrained in the American people to produce much of a response. When Carter discovered the cold war, making hair-raising speeches about Soviet intentions such as the one at Forrest College in 1978, he seemed mechanical and unconvincing, as if reading lines written for others.

As a result of Carter's inability to rally the country around stirring presidential leadership, the third peak in anti-Soviet hysteria did not follow the same script of the previous two. If anything, America's latest flirtation with the idea of a Soviet menace was inspired by Congress against an increasingly wishy-washy and hyper-moralistic president.

If the Carter presidency is an exception to the generalization that a relationship exists between presidential power and negative perceptions of the Soviet threat, the Reagan administration confirms the trend many times over. Ronald Reagan and his advisors came to power with a prepared agenda carefully worked out in advance. They were going to repeal the Great Society and as much of the New Deal as they could. They were going to try and obtain strategic superiority over the Soviet Union. They were going to redistribute income from the poor and middle class to the rich. Ironically, although the goals of the Reagan administration were conservative, the means were liberal, for it required an unusual presidential power to make changes as drastic as these. Ronald Reagan needed all the power he could get if he were to have a chance to roll back the welfare state and governmental power. One of the most important of Reagan's electoral victories in his first year was to win a procedural point by which Congress voted on his budget as a whole, not piece by piece. This enabled the administration to provide executive leadership missing since the days before Watergate.

The Reagan administration, like previous Democratic administrations, used the language of presidential prerogatives to argue for its point of view. When a resolution in the house calling for a nuclear freeze came within two votes of passage, the Reagan administration opposed it, not on grounds of content, but with the argument that it would tie the president's hands in negotiating with the Russians, a page lifted from Kennedy's book. So long as the Reagan administration successfully manages to raise the spectre of the Soviet threat at opportune momments, the Congress may continue to sacrifice its already waning powers.

But there are increasing signs of the unwillingness of Congress to play a passive role in these matters. In time of fiscal austerity, claims about the Russian menace often give way to budgetary prudence. Before the election of 1982, Congress was searching desperately for a method of holding down rapid increases in defense spending, and even some Republican members were secretly furious at the Reagan administration for its inflexibility in invoking the Soviet threat. After the administration lost 26 House seats in 1982, the way was prepared for a reassertion of Congressional power, culminating in a vote during the lame-duck session in December 1982 rejecting the "dense-pack" basing mode for the MX missile. This was a vote of historic significance, not only because Congress had not previously in the postwar period rejected a major weapon, but also because it indicated that when fiscal reality and anti-Soviet ideology clash, at least some policymakers can recognize reality and act accordingly. Under Ronald Reagan, the cycle of power may, despite the best efforts of the President, shift back to the Congress.

The Politics of Inter-Service Rivalry

The modern Executive is not only one branch of government among many, but a system of government unto itself containing numerous branches within it. As the presidency has become more vital to the governing of modern economy with a global foreign policy, the most important political conflicts begin to take place, not over it, but within it. Even within single branches of the executive, disputes over "turf" are likely to be serious. The most important of these disputes—arguments between the military services for a greater share of the defense dollar—are directly related to the peaks of anti-Soviet perception.

The sharpest example of the relationship between military infighting and the exaggeration of anti-Soviet perceptions before the Reagan administration took place as the cold war began. Both Franklin Roosevelt and Harry Truman had followed policies that tended to benefit the Army and the Navy at the expense of the Air Corps. But the Air Corps was convinced that the future belonged to airpower, for in the postwar period nuclear weapons were the number one reality, and it seemed as if the logical way to deliver such weapons was on airplanes.

In their campaign for hegemony, prominent Air Force officials found themselves distorting the Soviet threat, for they needed a credible external enemy as a rationale for their campaign. Air Force General Carl Spaatz, who led the fight for his service, blithely stated the case as follows: "The low grade terror of Russia which paralyzes Italy, France, England, and Scandinavia can be kept from our own country by an ability on our part to deliver atomic destruction by air. If Russia does strike the U.S., *as she will if her present frame of mind continues*, only a powerful air force in being can strike back fast enough, and hard enough to prevent the utter destruction of our nation."[4] (Emphasis added) When the war scare broke out over Czechoslovakia in the spring of 1948, the Air Force saw its chance. Air Force Secretary Stuart Symington created something called the 70-Group to lobby for greater funds for his service. He was successful. The military budget was entirely rewritten for FY 1949, and the share going to the Air Force had doubled. It had become clear to all how fanning the flames of the overseas crisis could be used to protect (and even expand) bureaucratic turf at home.

The Air Force had shown how one service branch, trying to solidify its hegemony over the others, could use an **exaggeration** of the Soviet threat to achieve its purposes. By the late 1950s, as the second peak of anti-Soviet belligerency was building up, the Army began to show how a branch that was losing power could also use the Soviet threat in order to regain its prestige. Strengthened by vastly increased budgets, the Air Force had become more complacent during the 1950s, convinced that the discovery of nuclear weapons had made the other services obsolete. Although Eisenhower had been an Army man, he went along with this point of view, for his fiscal conservatism pushed him to support the Air Force's claim of a "bigger bang for the buck." So sure was the Air Force of its superiority that it failed to notice a rising challenge from a new generation of Army officers.

A cosmopolitan Army Chief of Staff named Maxwell Taylor launched a campaign during the closing years of the Eisenhower era to return the army to its former position of prominence. Taylor was convinced of two things. First, though nuclear weapons were impressive, they were not as likely to be used in the "brushfire" wars the U.S. was likely to be fighting. Second, relying on them meant that the U.S. was becoming weaker, not stronger, for it was putting its military eggs in the wrong basket. Based on these points, Taylor, in various Department of Defense internal memoranda and in his popular book *The Uncertain Trumpet*, urged the U.S. to build more conventional arms. In addition, since any conflicts in Europe were likely to involve nuclear weapons (the stakes were that high), he urged that the U.S. think about areas of the world outside Europe, and especially about the Third World. To make it appear as if these countries were of vital and direct concern, Taylor and like-minded people claimed that the *real* enemy in such circumstances was the Russians. From this point of view, any revolution in the Third World was automatically a victory for the U.S.S.R. since it diminished the power and prestige of the United States.

Kennedy, as a Democrat, leaned toward the Army view of events. He made Taylor a major figure in his administration. He increased the budget of the Army. He sponsored the notion of counter-insurgency warfare around which the Army was staging its comeback. In short, domestic political considerations—especially the link between the Army and the Democratic Party—had much to do with the attractiveness of a new strategic theory in the early 1960s. Since no new theory could be implemented without a revised (and revived) version of the Soviet threat, the Soviet threat was duly revised (and revived). From now on, the Russians were seen as wanting to expand into the Third World in exactly the way an earlier generation viewed them as anxious to get their hands on France and Germany.

The costs of bringing peace to Washington's inter-service

rivalry were enormously high, as all participants realized. Furnishing each service with its own pet projects brought about the reality feared by conservatives since 1946: deficit spending, high taxes, and uncontrollable inflation. Indeed, by the time Nixon was elected, the economy seemed almost completely out of control, and at least one prominent reason for its erratic behavior was the drain that defense spending, especially but not exclusively Vietnam, had upon domestic economic performance.

Nixon began to realize that some attempt to make choices in national defense would have to be made. Although military men think of themselves as apolitical creatures, the pattern since 1950 shows that the Army tends to fare better under the Democrats and the Air Force under the Republicans. The Air Force budget increased (and the Army budget decreased) after 1953 when Eisenhower became president; this pattern was reversed again under Kennedy and Johnson; and it reversed again under Nixon and Ford.

Carter's inclination was to favor the Army, but fiscal realities prevented him from doing so. Unlike Nixon and Ford, Carter cancelled deployment of the B-1 bomber, although Congress kept alive the possibility of its revival. Moreover, both in PRM-10 and in his budget messages, Carter gave a more prominent role to conventional weapons, which remained the preserve of the Army and the Navy. By identifying the Middle East as a crucial problem area, Carter relied on lightening-quick deployment of tanks and helicopters, not massive nuclear weapons delivered from planes that fly in the stratosphere. Not surprisingly, the Army and the Navy were encouraged by these developments, while Air Force officials murmured dark hints about deteriorating national resolve.

During the Carter years allegations of the Soviet threat began once more to build-up, and, expectedly, the Air Force took the lead in the new crusade. Loss of the B-1 was a bitter blow to the Air Force, which in any case had seen the increased obsolesence of manned strategic bombers, upon which it once rested its future. By concentrating on the systems it lost, the Air Force complained that America's entire defense was in shambles, leading it to play a major role in the militaristic atmosphere of the late 1970s.

Once the Reagan administration took office, predictable statements about the Soviet lead in air force technology became routine on Capitol Hill. What was less routine was the attempt by the Reagan administration to expand the Air Force budget beyond all expectations. For fiscal 1983, for example, Reagan asked Congress to approve the following: $4.8 billion for a new version of the B-1 bomber; $4.46 billion for the MX; $860 million for two models of the C-5 cargo plane; $882 million for air launched cruise missiles; and a build-up of Air Force personnel from 580,000 to 640,000 over five years. The totals represented a 12.2 % "real" increase in the share of the military budget claimed by the Air Force.[5] Never before had one service branch obtained so much from one budget.

Not content with these increases in the Air Force budget, the Reagan administration has also been sympathetic to complaints from the Navy that it has been shortchanged in recent years. Reagan's Secretary of the Navy, John Lehman, is planning a Navy that would contain 600 ships and 1900 aircraft, and he states quite frankly that his goal is "maritime superiority." Convinced that in the future, resource wars between the U.S. and other societies will be on the agenda, the Reagan administration is attempting to create a global presence that would be effective, mobile, and capable of sustained action.

During the Reagan years, the pattern of inter-service rivalry, disturbing as it has become, has been complemented by a tendency for each of the services to divide into factions which use the Soviet threat against each other. The result is that the size and scope of the military budget seems to have as much to do with bureaucratic politics as with national security.

Foreign Policy Coalitions and the Soviet Threat

In a democratic society, foreign policy cannot be made directly by a small elite unconcerned about interest groups or public opinion. It is necessary to build a coalition of interests around a specific foreign policy, and to win public support for that policy through mass appeals. In this section I will argue that negative perceptions of Soviet conduct are an important device by which certain kinds of foreign policy coalitions try to win support for a change in the locus of U.S. foreign policy.

One of the most important disagreements within the foreign policy establishment until the late 1940s was between Europhiles, who thought of Europe as the quintessence of Western civilization, and Asia-firsters, who were concerned about bringing "civilization" to the East. Asia-firsters tended to be tied to businessmen interested in expanding into new markets and territories.[6] Generally associated with new and more competitive industries located in the West, they were conservative in their politics, and were suspicious of the use of big government for any purpose other than protecting U.S.

businessmen through tariffs. Since European markets had been tied up for centuries, they generally viewed the Third World avariciously, and typically had a special interest in Asia, where more potential consumers exist than anywhere else.

European-oriented policymakers viewed the Asia-firsters roughly the way box holders at the opera think of wrestling fans. Generally men of considerable hereditary wealth, long since removed from the nitty-gritty of making money, the Europhiles were concerned with long-term global stability, not immediate profit. With ties to both the financial world and the monopoly sector—and with a domestic ideology that stressed long term reform in the interests of preserving the system as a whole—these men were far more sympathetic to using the power of government to organize the world than their Asian inclined colleagues. They thought of the world in terms of nation-states, not specific business firms, and they wanted to see the American state be the unsurpassed power in the world. This meant a tolerance for high defense budgets, a standing army, support for foreign aid and covert intelligence, and a penchant for becoming involved in the affairs of other countries.

Underlying the debate between the Asia-firsters and the Euro-capitalists were differences in economics that made the issues so bitter. The Europhiles tended to be free-traders. In their view, capital should be free to move around wherever it can be most efficient, regardless of national boundaries.

Oppositon to the free trade principles of the European-oriented elite came, not unexpectedly, from nationalistic businessmen that needed protection to compete on the world's markets, from labor unions that wanted to protect their members' jobs, and from all those people who, for whatever reason, did not want their tax dollars propping up other governments around the world.

In the late 1940s, negative images of Soviet expansionism became the device by which free-trade liberals were able to overcome the inherently elitist aspects of their program and to sell it as having general appeal. By combining the free trade vision with the Soviet threat, the Europhiles were able to characterize protectionist and Asia-firsters as short-sighted, selfish, and uncharitable in the face of the world's problems. They were also being accused of being stingy on matters of national defense and of encouraging war and aggression. So long as the debate was posed in this fashion, the European-oriented free traders could dominate it, something they could never have been able to do without the Soviet threat. Thus the Russians were used to make a free trade program acceptable in a democratic society.

The first test of the political clout of the two foreign policy factions came in 1946 as the U.S. Congress considered a massive loan to the British. Conservative opposition, led by Ohio Senator Robert Taft, was fierce. Congressional leaders told Truman that the only way to pass the bill was to make a strongly anti-Soviet speech claiming that Britain's future was in danger from the Russians. Truman said no. Congressional leaders made the claim in any case, and the loan passed. Within two years, Truman would no longer be so reticent.[7]

The British loan, as conservatives correctly charged, was a foot-in-the-door for more elaborate aid proposals. European-oriented policymakers had in mind an audacious plan to reconstruct the entire economy of Western Europe with an aid program so vast that capital flows around the world would be permanently altered. When the idea was unveiled at Harvard University by Secretary of State George Marshall, the opposition mobilized. Passage of the Marshall Plan, most policymakers realized, would so commit the U.S. to the future of a capitalist Europe that there would be no turning back.

The Marshall Plan was, in the end, approved by Congress but only after Truman's war scare speech in March 1948. No longer could he refuse to arouse the spectre of the Soviet threat.

During the 1950s, the Asia-firsters made an attempted comeback under Senator Joseph McCarthy, who tried to purge the State Department of its European orientation and led an attack on the China experts who, to him, were not sufficiently enraptured by the anti-communists in that part of the world. As a result, the pro-European policies adopted in the late 1940s were in danger.

The sense of urgency about Europe that captivated Kennedy's advisors was thus reinforced by their perception that under Eisenhower the alliance had begun to atrophy. In the view of the Kennedy men, Eisenhower had made needless concessions to the Soviets in 1959 over Berlin and was going to make more at the 1960 summit.

But equally as important to the Kennedy administration as the firming up of the European alliance was its concern with the Third World. In Asia and Africa, newly independent countries were coming into existence every year. The West's policy toward the Third World had until then been a colonial one, which did not make much sense for the last half of the twentieth century. The Kennedy administration took the lead in trying to fashion a policy that would be more appropriate to this new reality than the simple business-dominated neo-colonialism of the Eisenhower administration.

So, the second peak of anti-Soviet hostility, like the first, had a foreign policy dimension, but not one directly related to U.S.-Soviet relations. Fear of the Russians was exaggerated in order to win support for foreign aid and a Third World orientation, just as in the first phase it was helpful in winning support for the Marshall Plan and a European orientation. The two peaks are not similar in terms of the specific focus of foreign policy, but they are quite similar in terms of the ways that negative perceptions of Soviet conduct helped build domestic support for a shift in foreign policy orientation.

To understand the sharp rise in anti-Soviet rhetoric that characterizes the Reagan administration, we must go back to the early 1970s and Richard Nixon. Nixon's administration had been a nightmare for the Europeanists. In three significant ways, Nixon attempted to break U.S. policy away from the Eurocapitalist vision. First, he wondered aloud about the relevance of NATO. Secondly, Nixon's opening with China was proof of his determination to upgrade Asia in the strategic thinking of the United States. Finally, Nixon's foreign economic policies repudiated all the crucial notions of the Europeanists. In 1971 Nixon suspended the Bretton Woods agreement that had organized the postwar world, and took the U.S. off the gold standard. Moreover, Nixon's Secretary of the Treasury, John Connally, was an unabashed economic nationalist who favored protectionist policies and a go-it-alone mentality.

As if this was not enough, American foreign policy was in even greater disarray because of the fallout from the Vietnam War. The American withdrawal from Vietnam stimulated a major debate in policymaking circles about the future locus of foreign policy. Some argued that only "core" areas of direct vital concern to the U.S.—especially Europe and the Middle East—required military intervention, while other areas like Africa were not worth the cost. Others argued that Vietnam was a failure of nerve on the part of the U.S., demanding an even greater commitment to the principles of cold war liberalism. The debate became extremely heated, and it burst into the public arena when the Carter administration took office in 1977. Carter initially seemed to side with the position that emphasized a primary commitment to the core areas, and this aroused the ire of all those who believed that the problem in Vietnam was a failure of American will.

The Carter administration came into power with two apparent objectives: restoring Europe to its central place after the shift adopted by Nixon, and developing a new U.S. stance vis-a-vis the Third World. The former task was urged most prominently by the Trilateral Commission, the ultimate voice in articulating European sympathies and closely linked to the Carter administration in outlook and personnel.

The pro-Europeanists around Carter—such as Cyrus Vance —were convinced that the U.S. overextended itself in Vietnam. They were strong believers in the notion that the U.S. should concern itself most explicitly with core areas like Europe and the Middle East and rely on non-interventionary solutions in other parts of the world, especially Africa. Their problem, therefore, was as follows. If they aroused the spectre of the Soviet threat, they put themselves in the position of alienating their foreign policy toward the Third World as well as risking the antagonism of Europe, since the Europeans had come to depend on the Soviet Union for trade. Make the cold war rhetoric too strong, Carter discovered, and Trilateralism went by the board. But make Trilateralism too dominant, he also found, and without the Soviet threat his administration would increasingly lose political popularity. The dilemma was one that Carter never could overcome. He pursued both policies at once, an economically oriented Trilateralism and, toward the end of his term, a military oriented cold war, but he was unable to obtain either. The third peak of the Soviet threat began under Carter, but did not reach its full height until a new administration came to power.

There are two aspects to the Reagan administration's approach to East-West affairs, and they contradict each other. On the one hand the U.S. is waging a geo-strategic war against the Soviet Union which requires European cooperation. On the other hand, the U.S. is waging an economic war against Europe that, ironically, demands Soviet compliance. For the Europeans to agree to Washington's demands to increase military spending and to stop trading with the Russians would involve the loss of jobs and a slowing of economic growth in Western Europe, which no incumbent government, conservative or socialist would accept. The only way this strategy can be successful is if the Russians cooperate by being aggressive and threatening. The lack of Soviet cooperation makes it difficult for the Administration to impose its will on Western Europe, leading to a major conundrum: to the degree that Reagan intensifies the cold war, he risks alienating Western Europe; to the degree that he seeks European cooperation against the Soviets, he undermines America's economic domination of the continent. Like the Carter administration, Reagan faces problems whichever way he turns; unlike Carter he has in general decided to resolve these dilemmas by explicitly moving toward a cold war posture, although occasional concessions to Western Europe such as revoking sanctions against firms supplying the Siberian pipeline are thrown in.

A major reason why the Reagan administration has been willing to risk confrontation with the European leaders is the feeling on the part of these men that Europe may not be crucial to the future health of American corporations as Asia and other parts of the non-European world. As corporations become multinational, as the division of labor become global, and the scarce resources located in every continent become essential for continued production, the key to American strength, or at least the strength of American firms, lies on their ability to operate on a global scale, shifting jobs from one place to another, obtaining what they need at the best possible price. In an unstable world, the Reagan administration seems to believe, the best guarantee of one's ability to maneuver is the possession of military forces sufficient to protect the global economic strength of the U.S.

Ronald Reagan's foreign policy confirms that external events are crucial to perceptions of the Soviet threat, but that those events do not directly involve the Soviet Union. I have suggested here that since 1945, factions within foreign policy coalitions have used the Soviet threat to shift American foreign policy from one direction to another. In the first cold war, the Asia-firsters were vanquished and a pro-European policy was organized around the Soviet threat. The second peak of anti-Soviet hostility occurred at a time when the U.S. sought the capacity to intervene in revolutionary struggles taking place in the Third World. Now, after a decade of indecision, global turmoil, and power-sharing, the Reagan administration seems set on undermining Trilateralism and pursuing a foreign policy rooted in nationalistic and unilateral sympathies. The cycle has been completed. Thirty years ago a cultivation of the Soviet threat was a key element in moving the U.S. from unilateral isolationism to pan-European cooperation. In the present context, the same Soviet threat becomes a lynchpin of a strategy to take the U.S. away from multilateral cooperation in favor of go-it-alone nationalism. The world in thirty years changed drastically; the role played by the Soviet threat in shifting the perspective of American foreign policy changed hardly at all.

Economic Transformations and Anti-Soviet Hostility

It is worth noting that there is a relationship between

overall economic conditions and the rise of the Soviet threat, but it is not the relationship that one might immediately expect. Negative perceptions of Soviet intentions generally peak after periods of recession, not during them. This is because increased military spending is as much a *political* as economic means to solidify growth coalitions oriented to domestic and international expansion.

In 1946, economists of every conceivable political stripe expected a letdown after the tremendous productive outpouring of World War II. Truman's economic advisors saw defense spending as a good way to avoid the expected recession. Indeed, NSC-68 recommended defense spending as a way of enhancing the economic growth of the United States. The only problem was that by the time NSC-68 was written, 1950, the postwar recessionary expectations had already passed. With the economy beginning its long postwar boom, the rise in defense spending that took place in the early 1950s was no longer "needed" to bring the country out of a trough.

Likewise, in the late fifties, foreign policy activists, critical of the Eisenhower administration's lean "New Look" pointed out that the economy would benefit from increased defense spending. Yet by the time they had an impact, in the first two years of the Kennedy administration, the economy had recovered and was in the process of racking up its best growth record in the postwar period.

Recent experience also conforms to this pattern. Since 1968 there has been a substantial downturn in the American economy. For most of the time, while Republicans held the presidency, slowed economic growth was not necessarily seen as a bad thing. There were some economists, however, who felt that the fall off in defense spending under Nixon and Ford could not be allowed to continue. But even as the Carter administration came into office and began to increase defense spending, the worst aspects of the recession had passed. A new recession began in 1981-1982—coinciding with Reagan's plan to throw money at the military—but it remains true that Carter's decision to upgrade the defense budget occurred after the previous recession had peaked in 1974.

Because increases in defense spending usually come after recessions one cannot simply make a simple correlation between overall levels of economic performance and the rise and fall of anti-Soviet perceptions. One must enrich an economic understanding of the problem with a political analysis.

Support for the cold war on the part of major manufacturers and large-scale labor unions has been close to axiomatic in the postwar period. A very strong political coalition that lobbies in favor of increased defense spending has come into existence, and, in order to make the case for a higher military budget, relies on the cultivation of an external threat.

One pattern that emerges in each peak period of anti-Soviet hostility is that a governing coalition comes into power based upon promises to the working class, minorities, and other disadvantaged groups. Many politicians, especially Democrats, find that they must make such promises in order to be elected. Once in power, when faced with the choice of taking from the rich or trying to expand the whole pie, they invariably choose the latter, since it is politically more acceptable. And when they try to expand the size of the economy, they discover that the public budget is an important source of economic growth. Committing themselves to an expansion of the budget, they further discover that among the many ways to spend the public's money, defense spending is the least controversial. Unlike public housing or medical care, which arouse the ire of private companies that provide those services for profit, defense spending has no direct opposition in the private sector. The purpose of defense spending is not, however, the short-term goal of taking the economy out of a recession, but a future oriented goal of sustaining a growth coalition organized around spending in order to expand the economy so that those at the bottom will be able to obtain more without detracting from the privileges of those at the top.

Alternatively, it is also clear that the valleys in hostility toward external enemies come when growth coalitions are not in power. Republican presidents (at least before Reagan) generally do not make extensive promises to working class people and minorities about enhanced social benefits. They often try to campaign on the fear of inflation, which is of more direct concern to middle class people, or on the basis of highly symbolic, non-economic issues like crime or national prestige.

During the third peak in anti-Soviet hostility, the relationship between growth politicians in power and a rise in foreign policy aggressiveness has continued, but in a new form. No longer are the Democrats the party that calls for rapid and extensive economic growth; that rhetoric shifted to the Republican party, and as it did, the most negative perceptions of the Soviet Union shifted along with it.

Ronald Reagan could never have become President, it seems safe to say, if he had run in 1980 on a traditional Republican platform of a balanced budget achieved through economic restraint. Instead, Reagan, knowing full well that

without working class votes his campaign was doomed, adopted the growth strategy that had worked so well in the past for
the Democrats. Supply-side economics which, when the Democrats were in power, was called Keynesianism, gave the Republican candidate the chance to enter the working-class cities like
Buffalo claiming to promise jobs. Reagan was elected in large
measure because he made a credible case that his economic
progam would restore prosperity.

For Reagan, as for the Democrats, the problem was not to
make promises but to carry them out. Reagan's economic advisors convinced him that a tax cut need not necessarily produce
huge deficits, since it would unleash economic activity that
would in turn increase revenues to the Federal government. In
the worldview of the Reagan administration, tax cuts would
finance growth that would finance the military, while military
spending would finance growth that would permit tax cuts. In
short, Reaganism saw once more the interconnection of a
growth strategy and the Soviet threat, since the later was
viewed as necessary to support the former.

Conclusion

America—in fact, the whole world—faces a clear and
present danger from the Soviet threat. It is, however, not the
threat from Russia that runs the risk of destroying democracy
in the United States but the threat posed by those who would
acquire extremely destabilizing weapons systems for reasons
that have little to do with national security and much to do with
politics. Because there is such a substantial political core to the
waxing and waning of the Soviet threat, the danger that faces
America from within can only be met *politically*. The threat
from those who try to exaggerate the Soviet threat will be met
only when a political challenge has been issued to the dominant
way that public business is conducted in the United States.

As I have tried to point out, the Soviet threat has become a
regular feature of American life because it is essential to each of
the following processes:

1.) It enabled the Democratic party (and now the
Republican party as well) to govern without developing
a program for reorganizing social life along positive
lines, while protecting itself from the demagoguery of
the right.

2.) It is a useful device to prop up the necessity of a
strong executive in the face of popular feeling that
political power should be broken up.

3.) It has enabled bureacratic vested interests—particularly in the miliatry services—to retain their hold over the federal budget.

4.) It has been the method by which foreign policy coalitions with unpopular ideas have mobilized public and interest group support for shifts in U.S. foreign policy.

5.) It has permitted advocates of greater economic growth to develop a method of stimulating the economy through federal spending without supporting controversial programs that would arouse business and conservative opposition.

The way to meet the threat from the Soviet Union is to create a progressive presence in the United States, one that can rectify the rightward tilt that exists on all foreign policy and defense issues. Contained in this unremarkable assertion are two imperatives. First, those who are attempting to build a progressive coalition in the U.S. must take foreign policy issues more seriously than they have. Without some curtailment of cold war rhetoric there simply will not be any advances in affirmative action, community control over economic development, labor organizing, or any other such issues. And secondly it means that the peace groups and anti-militarist organizations which have been concerned with foreign policy need to combine a preoccupation with moral witness and individual conscience with a larger political understanding of the world that illustrates why militarism has become such crucial aspect of American politics. When both of these changes occur, a solid base for an anti-militarist coalition will be laid.

Footnotes

1.) Committee on the Present Danger, *Common Sense and the Present Danger*, Cited in Alan Wolfe and Jerry Sanders, "Resurgent Cold War Ideology: The Case of the Committee on the Present Danger," in Richard Fagen (ed.), *Capital and the State in U.S. Latin American Relations* (Stanford: Stanford University Press, 1979).

2.) Bert Cochran, *Harry Truman and the Crisis Presidency* (New York: Funk and Wagnalls, 1973).

3.) Daniel Yergin, *Shattered Peace* (Boston: Houghton Mifflin Co., 1978), pp.282-283.

4.) Cited in Yergin, p. 341.

5.) Quoted in the *New York Times,* April 8, 1982, p. B8

6.) On the Asia-first outlook see Thomas McCormick, *China Market: America's Quest for Informal Empire* (Chicago: Quadrangle, 1967).

7.) For details on this period, see Richard M Freeland, *The Truman Doctrine and the Orgins of McCarthyism* (New York: Shocken Books, 1974).

Chapter 21

Cruise and Pershing II: Political and Strategic Issues

Dan Smith

NATO is haunted by an irony. In December 1979 it decided to deploy 572 new nuclear missiles to western Europe by the mid-1980—108 extremely accurate Pershing II ballistic missiles, and 464 extremely accurate ground-launched cruise missiles.[1] The plan is to put all the Pershing II's and 112 cruise missiles in West Germany, 160 cruise in Britain, 96 in Italy and 48 each in Belgium and the Netherlands. Prominent among the motives for the decision were desires to strengthen NATO's unity, restore US leadership of the alliance and provide a basis for a renewed detente with the USSR. The irony is that on all three counts the decision has had precisely the opposite result. No issue in NATO is more divisive than nuclear weapons in general and the new missiles in particular; US leadership still ebbs despite its strategic predominance; and the only argument these days about detente is whether it is dead or only sleeping.

December 1979 and Detente

American readers may be surprised to find included among the prominent motives the desire to provide a basis for detente. British readers would probably be similarly surprised. Our experience of the politics surrounding cruise and Pershing II missiles since the decision places it firmly in the context of the new cold war, of the hawkishness of Carter in his final year as President, of Reagan and of Thatcher. But not all the motives behind the December 1979 decision were common among all the actors, and circumstances have changed since the process within NATO which led to the decision was initiated in 1977. Among some of the western European governments, and most notably in Helmut Schmidt's West German administration, the renewal of detente was a major aim in the late 1970s and was seen to be quite compatible with the NATO decision on cruise and Pershing II missiles.

The December 1979 decision is commonly referred to as the 'double-track' (sometimes 'dual track') decision. The first track was the deployment of the new missiles; the second was the simultaneous offer to the USSR to start negotiations on limiting US and Soviet long-range, land-based nuclear missiles in the European theatre. The two tracks were announced in the same communique and were described as 'parallel and complementary approaches in order to avert an arms race in Europe caused by the Soviet TNF buildup, yet preserve the viability of NATO's strategy of deterrence and defence.[2] Since one of the main criticisms of the deployment of cruise and Pershing II missiles is that it will bring on a new round of the arms race, it is perhaps ironic to remember the expectations expressed at the outset. But, like all the best ironies, this one has a touch of tragedy about it.

The expectations and the logic on which they were based were far from outlandish. Had matters developed differently, they might well have been fulfilled. To understand them it is necessary to appreciate a series of premises widely shared in Europe in the late 1970s. Detente was and still is generally understood positively. Reaganism and the 'new right' in the USA have succeeded in associating detente with US weakness and attaching negative connotations to the term and the policies associated with it. In Europe, similar political groupings have not made the same headway on that issue. Thus, it remains an important issue as to which side is responsible for terminating detente—the USSR with its arms buildup and invasion of Afghanistan, or the USA and allies with cruise and Pershing II, MX, the scuttling of SALT II and the new rhetoric of confrontation. This positive connotation for detente was accompanied by a positive connotation for arms control. In Europe, neither was understood to mean succumbing to the USSR; both were seen as essential to reduced confrontation and reduced risks of nuclear war. However, those forces which were making such headway in the USA in undermining the domestic political consensus for arms control and detente were paralleled by similar forces in western Europe, making some headway though not as much.

· For a politician such as Helmut Schmidt, aware of those forces in his own country as well as in the USA, progress in detente and arms control depended on conceding something to the hawks. Among the many targets of the hawks in the late 1970s were the Soviet military buildup and modernisation programs in Europe and the 'gap' in NATO's deterrence that was supposed to be revealed by the introduction of the SS-20 land-based, intermediate-range nuclear missile in 1977. NATO had nothing similar. It was in this area that the concession was made. The USSR's buildup was consistently exaggerated through out the 1970s as it is today, and the concept of the gap in deterrence was entirely fallacious. NATO lacked land-based nuclear missiles capable of striking the USSR as a result of a deliberate decision: the Thor and Jupiter missiles of the late 1950s had been withdrawn because they were unnecessary, created inviting targets and were provocative. Instead, NATO had more accurate bombers and submarine-launched missiles— some from the USA, some from the UK and, depending on how one read the politics of it, possibly some from France as well. It was nonetheless conceded to the hawks that here was a serious cause for concern. The most public announcement of the concession was a speech in London by Helmut Schmidt in October 1977.[3] This speech has occasionally been regarded as a request by Schmidt on behalf of western Europe for cruise and Pershing II. It was no such thing. While he pointed to a disparity in nuclear forces in Europe, he called for it to be removed by arms control rather than rearmament. But the speech, like his entire conception of detente, was also firmly based on the view that defence and deterrence must be maintained. Two years later, the duality was encapsulated in the 'double-track' decision.

The tragic irony of all this is multi-faceted. Several of the logical steps along the way are unfounded. The gap in deterrence was and remains fallacious. So much has been willingly conceded even by advocates of the December 1979 decision: cruise and Pershing II missiles will not be aimed against new targets; there was no shortfall in NATO's nuclear destructive potential.[4] The disparity Helmut Schmidt acknowledged was in 'nuclear tactical and conventional weapons'. In overall nuclear weapons in Europe NATO's numerical superiority was some 7,500 to an estimated 3,500 for the Warsaw Pact.[5] In conventional forces, some Warsaw Pact numerical superiorities such as in tanks are at least off-set by other NATO advantages, such as in anti-tank weapons.[6] The concession to the hawks was entirely unwarranted.

The Hawks and U.S. Power

Perhaps more important, the concession did not and could not propitiate the hawks. A group as diverse as 'the hawks' has, almost by definition, a variety of opinions within it. Their characteristic chivvying around of statistics so that, despite the USA's numerical superiority in both strategic and total nuclear warheads combined with its more widespread global military presence and political influence, the USA is always shown as being 'behind' the USSR reflects a number of different political agendas.[7] For some, it reveals only a sincere alarm at what they believe their statistical maneuverings show. For others, the main point is increased military spending, either as a whole or for their favourite services, industries or corporations. For yet others, the basic thrust is related to domestic politics—either to securing immediate electoral advantage or to a grander project of reviving faith in basic American values. But for perhaps the most important grouping, the agenda lying behind alarmism about the USSR is the concern to re-establish American leadership of NATO and of the advanced capitalist states as a whole. The clearest statement of this is to be found in an important *Business Week* article.[3] This described the USA's political and relative economic decline by the late 1970s from its unchallenged pre-eminence of three decades previously. It charted it through economic performance, the defeat in Southeast Asia, the loss of political credibility and the energy crisis. It diagnosed the problem as 'a crisis of the decay of power'. As a solution, it proposed the USA should utilize the one strong card it still held—its continuing strategic leadership of the 'the free world.' Since the defence policies of the vast majority of advanced capitalist states are explicitly predicated on US capabilities, there is an objective basis for this strategy for the restoration of power. What it demands is an emphasis on the strategic threat from the USSR and the need for general rearmament under US leadership. The USA must itself set the example; others must follow. That sentence is a fair summary of policy under President Reagan.

Any thoughts about NATO's 'double-track' decision appeasing the hawks while providing a basis for renewed detente were caught up in the momentum of the new US policy (actually begun under Carter) and thoroughly trampled on. The expectation that NATO's decision might avert an arms race in Europe has been revealed as a naive misreading of US politics in the late 1970s. This dashing of hopes is encapsulated in the history of the arms control half of the 'double-track'. It lay neglected through 1980 and most of 1981, though development of cruise and Pershing II missiles and preparation of their European bases continued. Under heavy western European pressure it was picked up with President Reagan's announcement in November 1981 that he was now ready to enter negotiations on exactly the basis laid out in the original decision nearly two years before. His negotiating proposal offered the USSR non-deployment of cruise and Pershing II if the USSR would scrap all its SS-20 intermediate missiles together with the obsolete SS-4s and SS-5s. It was so unlikely to be accepted that one can only assume it was the intention it should be turned down. When informal discussions between the leaders of the US and Soviet delegations produced what might have been a fruitful avenue to explore, what followed was effectively a reprimand to Paul Nitze, leader of the US team. Meanwhile, the US Arms Control and Disarmament Agency was being partially dismantled so as to paralyse it. By March 1983 when Reagan announced a new negotiating position, a senior State Department official could be quoted as saying the negotiations were really all about convincing public opinion in western Europe about the need for deployment of cruise and Pershing II—i.e., they were nothing to do with arms control anymore.[9] Small wonder that in May 1983, Helmut Schmidt, still loyal to his reading of the 'double-track' decision, declared his belated scepticism about the sincerity of the USA in the negotiations.

The European Response

From the viewpoint of those wishing to reconstruct US power through emphasizing strategic leadership, and thus, in part, through deploying new US nuclear missiles in western Europe, real arms control is a mere irritant. It gets in the way of an unrestrained buildup of military power, which is the primary tactical objective, even if it might restrain Soviet military power. Detente and arms control are pre-eminently disposable in that viewpoint. That this risks a new arms race, intensified confrontation and hostility culminating in a nuclear war is entirely beside the point.

Appreciation of this in western Europe is, of course, one of the things which has ensured that the aim of strengthening NATO's unity has badly backfired. And in the course of that happening, the aim of restoring US political leadership has also failed, at least for a very large part of the populations. Opposition to nuclear weapons in western Europe means opposition to the core of NATO strategy and to its reliance on US capabilities. This is the irreducible political fact of the European disarmament movements.

The movements' resurgence began in late 1979 and early 1980, in the run-up to and immediate aftermath of the decision on cruise and Pershing II missiles. The pace was uneven across the different countries. The earliest signs were in the Netherlands and Belgium. Things were stirring in Britain after the turn of the year and soon began to move in Denmark and Norway. They were rather later in Italy and West Germany, but not by much. It was on the cruise and Pershing II missiles that the movements immediately focused, with national variations which reflected varying circumstances. In Britain, for example, emphasis was also placed on opposing preparations for civil defence and the purchase of the Trident missile system from the USA. In Norway, opposing cruise and Pershing II was linked to proposing a Nordic nuclear-free zone. In West Germany as in other countries, the issues broadened to encompass the whole US nuclear and military presence. By the last quarter of 1981 the movements were strong enough to mobilize about 2,500,000 people in demonstrations in almost every western European country.

These people and those others who do not march but support the movements' main demands are motivated in a variety of different ways. Different facets of the decline of detente and renewal of the cold war alerted them into a new and more active consideration of the issues and forced the problem of nuclear weapons onto the western European political agenda. In retrospect, it would be wrong to say that the December 1979 decision by NATO caused the movements, though not quite as wrong as the common assertion in the USA that they were a response to some of President Reagan's wilder statements. But it might be true to say that that decision was the main spark which ignited a tinder box, that there was a latent readiness to be concerned and active which only needed something to get it going. As E.P. Thompson has put it:

> If, after 38 years of gathering nuclear threat, and the insatiable and growing appetites of the nuclear armorers, some people had not stood up and started waving banners to each other across the globe, then one could properly have assumed that the human spirit had rolled over on its back and given up the ghost.[10]

Importantly, however, it is not just the human spirit which

has refused to give up the ghost, despite all temptations, but also the human intellect. The decision to deploy land-based missiles to Europe was taken in part because it was thought that providing reassurance about deterrence required highly visible systems.[11] Instead of putting the systems at sea in submarines—out of sight and safely out of mind—the people of western Europe were to have nuclear deterrence forced upon their consciousness anew. Faced with this, the consciousness of a large part of the western European populations drew conclusions which had not been in the thinking of the experts who drew up the plans. Visibility encouraged an examination of NATO strategy and it was found wanting. The unity which it was hoped the missiles decision would engender turned out to be a unity of opposition because the object around which unity was supposed to coalesce—NATO's nuclear strategy —is so utterly unappealing.

NATO and Limited Nuclear War

The concept of limited nuclear war is at the heart of NATO's strategy of flexible response. The strategy expresses a determination to respond to aggression at an 'appropriate' level of force, but if conflict cannot be contained at that level there is also the willingness to escalate the war to tactical nuclear weapons combined with the hope of containing it there. If we imagine a situation in which deterrence initially breaks down and war occurs, followed by NATO using nuclear weapons, followed by nuclear strikes from the Warsaw Pact, but a holding back on both sides before the prospect of all-out nuclear war, the result is 'limited' nuclear war—'limited' in the sense that 'only' Europe has been destroyed. It did not need some unthinking remarks by Ronald Reagan to reveal this; it takes only a moment's thought. But that moment's thought occurred to large numbers of people only when it was forced upon them.

NATO's strategy sits firmly in a deeply uncomfortable paradox. If the nuclear element of NATO's deterrence were only all-out nuclear war, that might well be thought incredible. This is one of two fundamental assumptions underlying flexible response. But if limited nuclear war becomes an option, that frightens the supposed beneficiaries of its deterrent effect. The argument that the option provides a more credible deterrent than all-out nuclear war depends on the view that a US President would more willingly release nuclear weapons to NATO forces for a limited use than for a massive strike against the USSR. Making it easier to start a nuclear war is, quite unaccountably for the experts, rather unsettling to most people.

Moreover, Europeans tend to take offence at the idea that the nuclear destruction of Europe is somehow a 'limited' act. And in any case, detailed analysis of the functioning of military systems of command and of the likely course of a nuclear war which starts limited suggests it will not stay limited for long.[12] In which case, any increase in the President's propensity to start a nuclear war can only be based on self-delusion. As an element of nuclear deterrence, the threat of limited nuclear war is both terrifying and incredible. The main drift of US nuclear strategy since at least the early 1970s, in common with NATO strategy, is to try to make nuclear war less likely by making it more likely. Wishing for unity around such a dangerous paradox is futile.

In matters like this, however, much depends on what kind of unity is thought important. As a study by the US Congressional Research Service put it, the consensus represented by the December 1979 decision was achieved:

> through a process of intense preparation and consultation during the 2 years preceding the decision, and reflected favorably both on alliance solidarity and American leadership.[13]

> But this was a unity of the experts, the bureaucrats, the military and the political leaders to whom they finally reported and recommended. Ordinary people were necessarily left out of this unity and it is they who have challenged it.

One now encounters in official circles in Washington and NATO a great impatience with western European opposition to the deployment of cruise and Pershing II missiles. 'It was the Europeans who asked for them,' is the plaintive cry. A statement like that contains a mixture of truth, half-truth and plain silliness. The truth in it is that political leaders in western Europe had consistently shown they were particularly worried about limitations on the technology of cruise missiles during the US-Soviet SALT 2 negotiations,[14] and that those leaders also fully supported the December 1979 decision. The statement is also a half-truth because it suggests the USA was simply providing what it was asked for, much to its surprise. In fact, NATO's High Level Group which undertook the 'intense' preparation was established in October 1977.[15] A year previously, President Ford had announced he had approved the proposal to start enginnering development of ground-launched cruise missiles.[16] With a range of 2,500 kilometres, their targets if based in the USA would be Canada, Central America or fish; logic suggested they were intended for deployment in western

Europe and perhaps, though less likely, Northeast Asia. Indeed, this American initiative was added to by most of the staff work for the High Level Group being done in Washington, DC.[17] The missiles were not foisted upon unwilling western European political leaders. Nor was there a completely autonomous request for the missiles from those leaders. Their request was worked up by the USA. Finally, the silliness is that very few Europeans 'asked for' cruise and Pershing II. The majority, when the matter was brought to their attention, appear to have decided they do not want them.

The scale of resistance to the cruise and Pershing II missiles, however, does not seem enough to prevent their deployment. In Britain and West Germany, governments are in power which seem likely to implement their share of the NATO plan against majority public opinion. The reasons why successfully mobilizing majority opposition on a single issue does not necessarily prove decisive in the electoral arena are too complex to be addressed here. In Britain, they owe much not only to the state of the competing parties in the 1983 elections, but also to the vagaries of the electoral system which gives a 'landslide' victory to a party supported by just 31 per cent of adult citizens.

Europe's Future

The deployment of cruise and Pershing II will not solve the problems which their imminent arrival has helped bring to the surface. The missiles have come to symbolise a strategy which becomes more unpopular the more widely it is understood. They have come to symbolize an arms race in which rational purpose has long since been sacrificed to power games, obsession with the latest technology and the drive of the arms manufacturers. And they encapsulate the dilemmas of the European situation intensifying confrontation, hardening the division of the continent and emphasizing in the western half a strategic dependence on the USA which is counter to increasing political and economic independence, divergences and conflicts of interest.

It is probably in the contradiction between the dependence on the USA symbolized by deployment of cruise and Pershing II and the contrary pressures of a thirty year trajectory away from economic and political dependence that the main hope lies for western Europe. And this is probably also the main hope for Europe as a whole. What is required is maturing, growing out of a situation bequeathed to us from the last World War so that it does not lead to the next one. For eastern Europe to mature away from domination by the USSR is a much less likely prospect than for western Europe to continue getting out from under the USA. But if this is to happen, it could be with a terribly dangerous outcome. Unless, along with its dependent partnership with the USA, western Europe also jettisons its dependence on nuclear weapons, the result could be the formation of a new nuclear bloc in world affairs. I referred above to the view that the threat of all-out nuclear war as the only deterrent threat is incredible as one of two assumptions behind flexible response. The other assumption is that NATO forces in Europe are inferior to the Warsaw Pact in non-nuclear weapons. Were this so, it would still not provide a logically sound basis for relying on nuclear weapons. But the fact is that it is not so. Without increasing military spending, western Europe is perfectly capable of mounting a credible conventional defence against any non-nuclear threat from the USSR. This can be done, moreover, by developing forces which are clearly capable only of defensive operations—providing deterrence, but no threat.[18] By showing the capability to resist conquest and exact a punitively high price for any attempt at it, and by showing that nuclear annihilation would gain precisely nothing for the aggressor, all options of military aggression can be closed down. Adopting this policy would reduce confrontation and hostility. It would thus reduce the likelihood of war and encourage conditions in which the division of Europe could begin to be eroded.

But to do this, western European states must shrug off their two politico-psychological dependencies of the modern age—on the USA and on nuclear weapons. Writing this essay in the middle of 1983, it is hard to be optimistic about the short-term prospects of achieving. The longer-term prospects, perhaps simply because they are longer-term, seem healthier. At the moment, mass movements exist which have it in them to be the main bearers of a new political maturity for western Europe. If they fade, hope will fade too.

Footnotes

1. In fact, it now appears the US Army has changed the plan for Pershing IIs. There will be 108 *launchers* but the current intention is to build about 385 *missiles*. See W.M. Arkin and R.W. Fieldhouse, 'Pershing and Cruise: No Room for Compromise', *ADIU Report*, Vol. 5, No. 2, March/April 1983 (Armament & Disarmament Information Unit, University of Sussex).

2. Communique issued at a Special Meeting of the NATO Foreign and Defence Ministers in Brussels, December 12, 1979, para. 11.

3. H. Schmidt, 'The 1977 Alistair Buchan Memorial Lecture,' (28 October 1977) *Survival*, Vol. XX, No. 1, January/February 1978 (International Institute for Strategic Studies, London).

4. See Walter Slocombe, U.S. Assistant Secretary for Defense, in Congressional Hearings, 10 April 1979, quoted by S. Lunn, *The Modernization of NATO's Long-Range Theater Nuclear Forces*, Report prepared for the Subcommittee on Europe and the Middle East of the Committee on Foreign Affairs, U.S. House of Representatives, by the Foreign Affairs and National Defense Division, Congressional Research Service, Library of Congress, December 31, 1980 (U.S. Government Printing Office, Washington D.C., 1981), p. 33.

5. On these figures and the uncertainties in them, see M. Leitenberg, 'Background information on tactical nuclear weapons (primarily in the European context)', in Stockholm International Peace Research Institute, *Tactical Nuclear Weapons: European Perspectives* (Taylor & Francis, London, 1978).

6. D. Smith, The Defence of the Realm in the 1980s (Croom Helm, London, 1980) Ch. 4.

7. See M. Kidron & D. Smith, *The War Atlas* (Simon & Schuster, New York, 1983), Maps 16-20.

8. 'The Decline of U.S. Power', *Business Week*, 12 March 1979.

9. By L.H. Gelb, in *The New York Times*, March 31, 1983.

10. E.P. Thompson, *The Defence of Britain* (END & CND, London, 1983), p. 3.

11. Lunn, *The Modernization of NATO's Long-Range Theater Nuclear Forces*, p. 20.

12. The best study is D. Ball, *Can Nuclear War Be Controlled?*, Adelphi Paper 169 (International Institute for Strategic Studies, London, 1981).

13. Lunn, *The Modernization of NATO's Long-Range Theater Forces*, p. 4.

14. *Ibid*, p. 18.

15. *Ibid*, p. 19.

16. During his second TV debate with candidate Carter; *Flight International*, 16 October 1976.

17. Lunn, *The Modernization of NATO's Long-Range Theater Nuclear Forces*, pp. 19-20.

18. For discussions, see A. Boserup, 'Nuclear Disarmament: Non-nuclear Defence' and B. Dankbaar 'Alternative Defence Policies and Modern

Weapon Technology', in M. Kaldor & D. Smith, eds., *Disarming Europe* (Merlin Press, London, 1982); also The Alternative Defence Commission, *Defence Without The Bomb* (Taylor & Francis, London, 1983).

Chapter 22

Western European Peace Movements

Diana Johnstone

A massive peace movement emerged across Western Europe in the early 1980's in opposition to the revival of the nuclear arms race. It may be defined as the effort by various concerned minorities to give effective expression to the opposition, on the part of a large majority of European populations, to a gravely significant change of course decided over their heads and against their wishes. Alva Myrdal, for one, prefers the term "resistance movement".

The NATO "double track" decision in December 1979 to deploy 572 American nuclear missiles in five European countries was a *fait accompli* foisted on the people of Europe without their consent. The "double track" part, the promise to pursue Soviet-American arms control negotiations that could cancel out the deployment altogether, was intended to obtain political consent by suggesting that perhaps nothing was really happening. In reality, however, the deployment of 108 Pershing II missiles in West Germany and 464 cruise missiles in West Germany, Britain, Italy, Belgium and the Netherlands would have far-reaching consequences. Europe's strategic position, international political role and domestic politics would be profoundly affected. European peoples were not consulted about these changes, nor even informed of the implications of the shift in NATO strategy. The peace movement can also be defined as an effort to arouse and spread awareness of the real meaning of these dangerous changes.

Such efforts were undertaken by a wide range of groups, different in each country. Internationalism is a common aspiration, difficult to achieve. In reality there are a number of peace movements which vary from country to country according to political mood, traditions, the nature of the groups that took up the new Euromissile issue, and the ways in which they relate this issue to others.

Britain

In Britain, the revival of the nuclear arms race quite naturally revived the old Campaign for Nuclear Disarmament (CND), founded back in 1958 by Bertrand Russell. It also inspired the creation in the spring of 1980 of the new European Nuclear Disarmament (END) movement, which overlaps with CND while trying to bring its political thinking up to date and involve it in the problems of continental Europe. CND and END dominate the British peace movement. CND is a mass organization, with over 50,000 national members ranging from clergy to communists and many more in local groups. END is basically a collection of intellectuals, including E.P. Thompson, Mary Kaldor and Ken Coates of the Russell Foundation, more daring in exploring the political implications of the nuclear arms race, disarmament and especially the problem of Europe's dominance by two hostile military blocs.

CND was down to 3,000 members when the NATO double decision gave it a new lease on life. In early 1980, the British government produced a civilian defense booklet called Protect and Survive advising British citizens to hide under tables or in cupboards in case of nuclear war. E.P. Thompson published his mordant answer, Protest and Survive, in March 1980 and the following month, he and other British intellectuals issued the appeal for European Nuclear Disarmament that launched END.

By calling for a de-nuclearized Europe "from Poland to Portugal", END was trying to move beyond the British-centered "unilateralism" of CND. The Campaign for Nuclear Disarmament's goal has always been Britain's unilateral renunciation of its own nuclear arsenal. This unilateralism is peculiarly British. In Europe, only Britain is both a nuclear power and an island. It has its own nuclear weapons to give up, and surrounding water to provide a sense of security. Moreover, this unilateralism has its roots in a period when Soviet nuclear arsenals were still rudimentary. The CND approach seemed insular and outdated to the END founders.

This does not mean that END is against unilateralism. Indeed, a certain consensus has emerged among peace researchers (the intellectual backbone of the peace movement) throughout Europe in favor of *reciprocal unilateralism*, that is, a process of disarmament patterned after the arms race itself, only in reverse. CND itself expounds this interpretation of unilateralism. In an October 1982 speech in Moscow, printed in *ENDpapers FIVE*, CND general secretary Bruce Kent defended unilateral action as a critical part of the disarmament process. "Amazingly," he said, "the arms race which accelerates by an unending series of unilateral steps is, according to the militarists, never to be allowed to go into reverse by the same process."

The consensus around reciprocal unilateralism is based primarily on the realization that arms control talks and treaties have served to keep the arms race going by channeling it into technologically new fields while reassuring public opinion that everything was safely under control. Disarmament requires a different approach. Even without negotiations, states would be able to signal to each other their willingness to change direction. The real problem is to create a favorable political climate for such a process.

END has tried to address this problem, the creation of a political climate in which nuclear disarmament might be possible not only in Britain, but in all of Europe. This leads the END intellectuals to criticize both the United States and the Soviet Union and the bloc system of NATO and the Warsaw Pact as a whole. They readily acknowledge that the United States has historically led the nuclear arms race at every stage and bears the greater responsibility. However, Soviet leadership bears a political responsibility for repressive practices within its own sphere which create a fearful, threatening image in Western Europe enabling the United States to dominate its European allies in return for the hope of protection. The Soviet Union has repeatedly expressed willingness to negotiate nuclear disarmament, and has made unilateral gestures to signal its good faith (such as troop withdrawals and the pledge not to resort to first use of nuclear weapons). However genuine, these expressions and gestures do not overcome the deep fear in Western Europe inspired by Soviet Communist Party methods of governing: intense unanimity, and a degree of secrecy that encourages outsiders to suspect the worst. END has therefore insisted on trying to link the peace movement in the West with the problem of human rights in the East.

The British peace movement flourished in 1980 and 1981, then suffered a psychological blow in the summer of 1982 when Conservative Prime Minister Margaret Thatcher led Britain to victorious war over Argentina in the Falkland Islands. Depressed Britain rediscovered the imperial joys of war-making in faraway places, complete with flashy modern technology. CND itself split over whether to brace the popular mood of bellicose jubilation by criticizing the war or to stick to the safer single issue of nuclear weapons. The popular Falklands War helped re-elect Thatcher in a landslide that deprived the Labor Party's most ouspoken critic of the war and of the nuclear arms race, Tony Benn, of his seat in the House of Commons.   An initial strength of the British nuclear disarmament movement seemed to be that its demands were incorporated into the official platform of a major political party, Labor. But this turned to a liability as the British Labor Party proved unable to explain or justify its platform, much less get elected on it.

The re-election of Thatcher in June 1983 amounted to a green light for the installation of cruise missiles in Britain, even though polls continued to show about half the population opposed. Popular enthusiasm over the Falklands War and Maggie Thatcher has given many peace activists the sinking feeling of being, not the spokespersons for a growing majority, but rather a minority whose growth is limited by deep-rooted cultural attitudes and who risk being marginalized as eccentrics—a common fate of moral protest in Britain.

The women, whose non-violent direct action against cruise missile base construction at Greenham Common was the main movement activity in early 1983, illustrate this domestic dilemma of the British movement. To grow, the movement would seem to need to transform some basic cultural attitudes. This is what the Greenham Common women are trying to do. Yet this very attempt, attacked by the nation's institutions and distorted by the mass media, risks associating the movement with an eccentric cultural image that could hasten its marginalization and decline.

Common language makes the British movement by far the most visible to Americans, who may tend to mistake the British "European Nuclear Disarmament" (END) movement for the *European* nuclear disarmament movement. The West German movement is much larger, more deeply rooted, more politically challenging on many levels. END has played a major role in helping to organize the European Nuclear Disarmament Conventions in Brussels in May 1982 and in West Berlin in May 1983 (a third will be held in Italy in 1984). But British insularity and traditional detachment from European politics limit, more than Americans may realize, the extent to which the English can play a leadership role in a European movement.

The Small Countries

The small countries of northern and central Europe have shown their vocation to play a key role in peace-making efforts. Citizens of those countries often combine a developed sense of civic responsibility with an international awareness that is rare in big, powerful nations.

In the neutral countries, notably Sweden, Austria and Finland, peace movements are in harmony with national policy. Their main contribution is thus to exert influence beyond their borders. Because of their position, they often understand both the Russians and the Americans. They provide ideas for diplomatic approaches and reflection on problems of peace and disarmament, such as the works of Nobel Peace Prize winner Alva Myrdal. Finally, the mere existence of these countries, notably Finland and Austria, is proof that it is possible to live a free and independent national life right on the border of the allegedly insatiably "expansionist" Soviet Union without nuclear arms or NATO to protect them.

In the small NATO countries, the movements against the NATO missile escalation have been so strong that the Pentagon and its cohorts are looking for ways to bypass them altogether in decision making.

Probably the strongest single movement against the NATO "double decision" developed in the Netherlands, home country of NATO's super pro-American secretary general Joseph Lums and arguably the most deeply loyal member country of the Atlantic Alliance in all of Europe. It was precisely Holland's close insertion in NATO plus its small-country awareness of international developments that alerted Dutch people earlier than some others to dangerous shifts in Pentagon-NATO strategy away from deterrence toward nuclear war-fighting.

The main organizational base of the Dutch movement is the Inter Church Peace Council (IKV) set up in 1966 by the main churches, both Protestant and Catholic, to nudge them into doing more for peace than make speeches. IKV general secretary Mient Jan Faber calls it a form of "self-criticism" and self-challenge instituted by the churches.

In 1977, the IKV launched a long-term campaign against nuclear weapons with the slogan: "Help rid the world of nuclear weapons. Let it begin in the Netherlands." Initially aimed at getting rid of short-range nuclear missiles already on Dutch soil, it was almost immediately obliged to turn to the struggle to keep new longer-range missiles from being brought in. For 1977 was also the year of the neutron bomb controversy. IKV worked with the newly-formed "Stop the N-Bomb" movement, whose organizers included Holland's small Communist Party. The neutron bomb proposal was withdrawn by Carter, but turned out to be merely the first public sign of the NATO "modernization" program made official by the NATO decision in December 1979. Forty-eight cruise missiles were earmarked for Holland.

The Dutch movement has been closely intertwined with the country's churches. In 1980, Pax Christi Netherlands took up IKV's recommendation for unilateral initiatives in Holland as a catalyst for multilateral disarmament, and advised Dutch Catholic bishops to develop new moral criteria encouraging nuclear disarmament. Shortly thereafter, on November 21, 1980, the General Synod of the Netherlands Reformed Church took the position that all nuclear weapons should be unilaterally removed from the Netherlands as a first step in curbing the nuclear arms race.

Unable to say "no" to the United States or "yes" to their own people, Dutch governments have adopted a policy of stalling indefinitely on the missile deployment question. In June 1983, the U.S. House of Representatives helped them by cutting appropriations to build the cruise missile base in Holland. Deployment may be politically impossible in the Netherlands, but the Dutch movement stresses that it will continue to struggle against nuclear weapons everywhere, East and West, on land or at sea.

Germany

As the center of East-West bloc confrontation and the main site for the scheduled nuclear missile deployment, Germany is the heartland of the new European peace movement. It is the only country scheduled to receive Pershing II missiles, particularly dreaded by Soviet leaders because of their short flight time of less than ten minutes from Russian targets. The German movement is the largest and most complex. What becomes of it will be decisive for the future of Germany and perhaps of Europe.

The German movement is made up of extremely disparate components with often conflicting outlooks. The main forces are ecological Greens, Protestants, part of the Social Democratic Party (SPD), the variegated post-1960's left identified with the "alternative scene", feminists and the small but efficient German Communist Party, sometimes regarded as a pariah by the others. A great deal of decentralized grassroots activity allows the various currents to develop in their own way.

The German movement is particularly inventive in its forms of action and rich in intellectual analysis. For historical and geographical reasons, the NATO "modernization" confronts Germans with a series of particularly crucial problems of securtiy and national identity. The missile deployment crisis has stimualted a series of reflections on strategy, defense, relations with Russia, and aspects of what is called the "German question" that go beyond what is usually understood elsewhere by a peace movement to become factors in a new political culture.

Strategic implications of Pershing II and cruise missiles are discussed in great detail by a large minority of well-informed citizens. Nowhere in the world do so many people know so much about American and Soviet weapons and strategy. The debate is enriched by the work of several independent peace research institutes, in Frankfurt, Hamburg, Munich and other cities, whose staff frequently include retired senior officers of the Bundesweher with NATO experience. Far from being moved by thoughtless emotion or Soviet manipulation, as their detractors allege, German opponents of the NATO deployment have thought through its implications for themselves perhaps more thoroughly than anybody anywhere, including the Pentagon.

The German movement is not ashamed of its emotions, however, and Protestant theologians are there to laud "fear" when it is fear for the future of humanity. This is the "Protestant Angst" Pentagon policy-maker Richard Perle referred to condescendingly as a sort of cultural hangup getting in the way of the serious business of preparing for nuclear war.

The combination of expertise and creative emotion is personified by the partnership between Green Party Bundestag members Gert Bastian, a retired NATO General, and American-educated Petra Kelly, who exhorts men to develop their sensitivity and women to develop their rationality in the construction of a new non-violent culture.

For the Social Democratic Party, the Eurostrategic missiles issue has been a deadly boomerang. In the dominant legend, at any rate, it was SPD chancellor Helmut Schmidt himself who launched the issue with his 1977 London speech complaining to the International Institute for Strategic Studies of the lack of arms "parity" in Europe. It is not clear just what Schmidt had in mind, other than his low opinion of President Jimmy Carter's ability to look after Europe's interests. The Schmidt speech has enabled the Reagan Administration to maintain that it was Germany, and a Social Democratic chancellor at that, that asked for the new American nuclear missiles to start with. Schmidt seems to have been hoodwinked by the cruise missile lobby in NATO. It is certain, however, that a majority of his own party never wanted the missiles and reluctantly agreed to the "double decision" in December 1979 only on the grounds that this was the only way to get the Americans and the Russians to include Eurostrategic weapons in the next round of arms control talks, that is, the SALT 3 that was expected to follow ratification of SALT 2. Totally committed to the *Ostpolitik* pioneered by Willy Brandt, Social Democrats were persuaded that further improvement in relations with Eastern Europe required extending detente to the military field, and this could be advanced by the "double decision" and subsequent scaling down of nuclear weapons in Europe.

Instead, they have got quite the opposite: no SALT 2, no SALT 3, truncated intermediate range forces talks in Geneva that by concentrating on a single category of weapons where the Russians are ahead virtually assure American deployment, and a new nuclear arms race that is scarcely compatible with detente. The American "nuclear umbrella", after being discreetly folded up with the shift to "graduated response" in the sixties, was being turned into an aggressive arm to threaten the USSR from close up. Europe was being transformed from a protected sanctuary into a nuclear missile launching platform and a prime target for an eventual Soviet pre-emptive strike.

One of the first to see what was happening was Erhard Eppler, a main link between the SPD and the Lutheran Church. Another early leader of opposition to the missiles is Oskar Lafontaine, the dynamic young mayor of Saarbrucken, who has gone so far as to hint that the German Federal Republic's permanent membership in NATO might not be written in the stars. However, it should be stressed that "the breakup of NATO" has been, at least at the outset, a theme raised not by the peace movement but by the Americans in order to frighten Europeans into accepting whatever defense measures the U.S. chooses to impose on them. The implied U.S. threat, usually in terms of "Congress and the American people won't understand if you say no", is: either you take these missiles and like them, or we'll go home and leave you to the Russians.

Thus a main theme of discussion around the German peace movement is alternative defense. Experts like retired General Christian Krause challenge the assumption that the Warsaw Pact has a conventional arms superiority requiring NATO to depend on nuclear weapons.

SPD *Ostpolitik* specialist Egon Bahr, in an annex to the Palme Commission report on "Common Security", has suggested a simple principle fo the creation of a nuclear weapons-free zone in central Europe: "All nuclear weapons should be withdrawn from European states which do not themselves possess nuclear weapons." This proposal realistically assumes that the powers already possessing nuclear arms are not about to give them up. But the dangers of their use would be reduced if they could not be employed on somebody else's territory. Bahr's proposal also stresses the need for conventional balance of forces in Europe.

Bahr sees a necessary division of labor between a movement, which can and should make "absolute demands", and a party, which must come up with compromises. Although there is great resentment within the peace movement against the SPD for accepting the NATO "double decision", SPD leaders themselves (and probably some others as well) tacitly welcome the movement for putting pressure on the Americans they would not dare put themselves. In its public positions, the SPD would like to stay close to the American Democratic Party, and has welcomed the Freeze Movement and the "No First Use" proposal which Germans can take up with less risk of being labelled "anti-American."

However, the high-handed way in which the Reagan administration has rammed through the Euromissile deployment has awakened a young generation to the "German question." Germans under 39 were all born after World War II, but no peace treaty has ever been signed and their country is still under military occupation by the victorious allied powers. The only really dangerous East-West border in Europe is the German-German border. Fear of Germany, of German reunification or of German rearmament, is the most fundamental historical reason for the division of Europe into hostile military blocs. One of the aspirations to be found in the German peace movement, expressed notably by Rudolf Bahro, is to develop such a clearly new, non-violent political culture in Germany that fear of the Germans can finally be dissipated in the rest of Europe. Bahro suggests that this would be the best contribution Germans could make to freeing Eastern European peoples from tight Soviet control.

Compatible with this aspiration is the East German conscientious objectors' movement, whose Church-supported effort to spread the slogan "Swords Into Ploughshares" has met with official suppression.

Soviet peace committee chairman Yuri Zhukov complained publicly at the mere announcement that "a so-called German question" would be discussed at the 1983 END Convention. Most of the German peace movement itself seems to prefer to avoid a subject which can arouse misunderstanding and hostility among Germany's neighbors. The two Germanies are where symmetrical peace movements in East and West might be most likely to emerge—to the alarm of much of the rest of Europe.

As missile deployment neared, a main worry in the peace movement was that authorities would try to isolate the movement from the majority by associating it with violence — perhaps by use of provocateurs. But by now its arguments are too widely known, its social base too broad. The peace movement will remain an important factor in German political life.

France

In the summer of 1983, Willy Brandt called on newly-elected French president Francois Mitterrand to propose a Franco-German socialist partnership to promote detente and disarmament in Europe. Mitterrand sent him packing. Since then, France has stood alone as the main bastion of the anti-peace movement in Europe.

With remarkable unanimity, French media have censored and distorted the strategic debate and portrayed the peace movement in neighboring countries as "baa-ing pacifists", ignorant sheep trembling before the superior military might of Soviet tanks and SS-20 missiles. This view of things has allowed French opinion-makers floods of self-congratulations about their own national spunk in adding to the French nuclear arsenal and applauding vigorously as the U.S. stations nuclear missiles in neighboring countries.

To Germans, at least, it has become clear that France is happy with a nuclear Maginot line running through German territory. For its part, the French government seems to hope that the German sense of insecurity may induce the Federal Republic to help pay for a French nuclear force which just might, who knows, help deter any eventual Soviet aggression. By its own arms program, nuclear testing in the Pacific, aggressive export policies and indifference to the dangers of proliferation, France is a main actor in the nuclear arms race and in the movement toward a worldwide plutonium economy. And all this with a left coalition government of Socialists and Communists.

The French left's electoral victory in mid-1981 at first

aroused hopes in the European left and peace movements that they had found a powerful new ally. Quite the contrary turned out to be the case. Largely ignorant of such matters, the French Socialists in office have remained dependent on right-wing Gaullists and pro-American propagandists for most of their notions about strategic questions. Mitterrand's strong support for the American missile deployment has been regarded by most of the French left as a clever way to keep the Reagan administration from destabilizing "socialist" France while making life difficult for the French Communist Party. The idea is that by pursuing a conspicuously anti-Soviet foreign policy, Mitterrand protects his economic austerity policy from criticism by his Communist partners, since anything negative they say can be accused of being Moscow-inspired retaliation for Mitterrand's foreign policy. This sort of provincial and Byzantine political calculation has made France in the early 1980's seem like a world off by itself.

Socialists and other people on the left who in other circumstances would have organized a protest movement against the missiles, if only out of anti-Americanism, do not want to embarrass Mitterrand. There is also the peculiar phenomenon of the French reaction to the suppression of *Solidarnosc* in Poland. This event arrived just in time to enable much of the French intelligentsia — especially the part that controls the media -to justify their final abandonment (for reasons too complex to treat here) of socialist ideals by blaming the Soviet Union. This has contributed to an anti-Soviet and anti-communist mood in France not at all mitigated by the presence of four Communist cabinet ministers in a government that is losing popularity.

An attempt by some people in the non-communist left to create a French branch of the European movement under the label CODENE (Committee for European Nuclear Disarmament) has proved unable to rally more than a handful of convinced anti-militarists. As for the French Communist Party (PCF), it has proved by a big peace march in 1982 and a "Fete de la Paix" in 1983 that it is the organization that can bring out the masses in the hundreds of thousands, but under simple slogans like "I love peace" that do not begin to inform the French of the issues as they are seen in neighboring countries. So long as it stays in the government, the PCF must limit its amibitions to staking out its claim to the peace movement turf and trying to influence Mitterrand to promote the European disarmament negotiations promised in the Socialist Party program.

Italy

As in other countries of southern Europe, the existence of an important communist party has been a serious handicap in the development of a strong peace movement. Everywhere, Socialists have seen the missile issue as a way to embarrass their rivals, the Communists. This factor has weighed heavily in Italy, the only southern European country scheduled to receive missiles (112 cruise missiles at the Comiso base in Sicily) and the only one where the Communist Party (PCI) is much bigger than the Socialist Party. For conservative forces in Italy, and in particular for the ambitious Socialist leader Bettino Craxi, the American desire to deploy nuclear missiles in Italy came as a godsend, providing them with a fresh excuse to keep the Communist Party out of the government, just when the old excuses were wearing out. The PCI had already endorsed NATO, broken its ties with Moscow and criticized Soviet policy. These used to be the conditions for being considered a "normal" party eligible for national government. But now, as Fiat chairman Giovanni Agnelli pointed out, it was given still another test to pass: approval of cruise nuclear missile deployment.

This political factor helps explain why the Italian government was the first in Europe to accept the missiles, even though scarcely anyone outside the Sicilian Mafia really wants them. With a Socialist defense minister, Lelio Lagorio, pushing through the missile base project, Craxi would hope to win a Reagan administration stamp of approval for his bid to be prime minister. And all the government coalition parties saw their interest in pleasing the Americans.

Anxious to avoid political isolation, the PCI took up the peace movement cautiously as a cross it had to bear, stressing that it is only part of a "broad movement" and letting itself be led by its allies in the Italian Catholic Workers Association (ACLI) or the small leftist parties PDUP (Democratic Party of Proletarian Unity) and Democrazia Proletaria. The PCI has marginalized those in its own ranks whose single-minded opposition to the cruise missiles could appear pro-Soviet and steered a course into the mainstream of the northern European peace movement, as close as possible to Willy Brandt.

However, the Italian movement has from the start been much more focused on North-South relations rather than on the East-West conflict. It is obvious to Italians that the missiles to be stationed in Sicily have nothing to do with defending Western Europe from the Warsaw Pact and everything to do with establishing a *de facto* protectorate over the Middle East and North Africa. The Comiso base clearly fits into an overall

U.S. strategy for involving Italy in policing the Mediterranean area, the Horn of Africa and the Arab world.

Another specifically Italian concern is the Mafia, which has been used by the U.S. since World War II to strengthen American influence in Sicily and which is certain to profit from construction of a major American base and from the recreational business likely to flourish around it. The Mafia was already in a period of aggressive expansion thanks to the heroin trade. The militarization of Sicily will be a further boon. This is an alarming development to the PCI and to other Catholic and political forces engaged in combat against the Mafia.

Opposition to the missiles has surely been widespread from the start in Italy. To the surprise of organizers, half a million people turned out for a peace demonstration in Rome on October 24, 1981. In a couple of months in 1982, over a million Sicilians signed a petition to suspend Comiso base construction. The petition was circulated by the Unitary Committee for Disarmament and Peace (CUDIP) headed by Comiso's former Communist mayor, Giacomo Cagnes.

The Italian peace movement's intellectual center is the weekly Pace e Guerra, whose regular coverage of the European movement is perhaps the best in Europe. Running as independents with PCI support, Luciana Castellia and several other prominent Pace e Guerra editors won with large margins in the June 1983 legislative elections, whose results came as an unexpected encouragement to the peace movement just when it was most needed. Probably more than any other, the Italian movement is attentive to the whole world scene and will try to fit its own special concerns into an international perspective.

The peace movement arose at the end of a decade, the 1970's, marked by the decline of the working class movement and the fragmentation of the left into separate and even antagonistic movements. The peace movement is the first of the new movements with the potential to put them back together in a new combination. Peace is a universal aspiration and need that could unify a new movement based on meeting genuine human needs.

For example, the peace movement has begun to link up with labor through studies of peaceful conversion of the arms industry, raising essential questions of investment priorities, job creation and democratic choice of what should be produced and for what purposes. The peace movement also readily connects with feminism, third world solidarity and various "marginalized" sectors of the population whose needs are neglected in favor of military spending. It also brings together libertarian and Christian currents opposed to the militarization of society.

Ready or not, the peace movement finds itself raising all the fundamental social issues. One of these is the problem of democracy in both Eastern and Western Europe. In Western Europe, the majority can freely express its opposition to government policy, but its wishes are ignored. In Eastern Europe, outside official channels, people are not allowed to express agreement with government policy. This absurdity has been brought to light by the Western peace movement in its contacts with independent peace groups in Eastern Europe, who do not consider themselves "dissidents" but who are not allowed to say for themselves what their governments insist on saying for them.

The peace movement, in all its diversity, which has only been suggested here, is the main progressive ferment in a period of extreme moral confusion and intellectual bewilderment. The only other force clearly at work for the recomposition of European society is its opposite, militarization. This seems to be the fundamental political contest in Europe in the early 1980's.

Chapter 23

From the Other Shore: Peace Movements in Eastern Europe

Suzanne Gordon

The journey East is not an easy one. To leave the Western sector we take the S-Bahn train from the Berlin Zoo station. The train—a collection of old-fashioned trolley cars outfitted with worn leather seats and interior oak trim, varnished and shinning like the dashboard of an antique automobile—crosses over the Berlin Wall to deposit us at the Friedrichstrasse station in East Berlin. As we make the five-minute journey, I discuss contingency plans with my friend and translator.

He as well as the other peace activists who arranged for me to meet with Pastor Rainer Eppelmann are more cautious today than usual. Since Eppelmann joined the late eminent East German physicist Robert Havemann to protest East German militarism, his phone and house have been bugged and peace activists in the West prefer to make appointments with him by courier. Time pressure made that impossible for my visit; our telephone call to Eppelmann has certainly alerted the East German police to the fact that a Western journalist will be arriving. If I am to convince the border guards that I am only a tourist making the typical day trip to inspect the accomplishments of East German communism, I must leave my tape recorder, reporter's notebook, even a simple pad of paper behind. Should they discover any odd and unexplainable paraphernalia, they would be likely to keep me from crossing.

Or they might try to stop my friend—a member of the Berlin Working Group for an Atomic-Free Europe—from crossing. With the growth of the East German peace movement, such restrictions on travel and harassment of activists are becoming more and more common. The week before our visit, a retired professor at East Berlin's Humboldt University was interrogated by the police and advised to curtail his church-related peace activity.

The following week, Mient Jan Faber, secretary general of the Dutch Interchurch Peace Council (IKV), was on his way to meet Eppelmann when he was unexpectedly denied entry. Although it is probably the most influential peace group in Western Europe, IKV has had relatively uninterrupted contact with church groups in East Germany. Subsequent inquiries proved that Faber's detention was not an arbitrary act of an overzealous border guard. He had been officially declared *persona non grata* in East Germany and IKV was informed that it had to reduce its contact with over eighty East German peace groups to a quarter that number.

Neither my friend nor I will know if the same thing will happen to us until we get to the border. There we separate I pass through a special checkpoint for tourists and he through a checkpoint reserved for West Berliners. If the East Germans decide to add his name to a growing list of political undesirables, he won't appear on the other side and I will have to proceed alone.

Fortunately, we both make it across and catch another subway to the Alexanderplatz—the once elegant square that is today a concrete wasteland with a huge radio tower balancing a restaurant rotunda at its peak. From there, we take a bus along the city's wide avenues, passing bright red billboards with pictures of larger-than-life Brezhnev clasping the hand of East German First Secretary Erich Honecker, as the two proclaim their commitment to world peace. At the city's northeastern edge, we walk by blocks of low, barracks-like apartment complexes and knock at a small stucco house sitting back from the road across from a communal garden.

A small, lean, wiry man, balding, with a thick pointed beard, hugs my friend and shakes my hand. He is wearing cut-off jeans and a bright orange sleeveless tee shirt. A sword and ploughshares medallion hangs from a leather string around his neck. Pastor Rainer Eppelmann ushers us in.

Pastor Eppelmann has become the symbol of a new kind of peace movement—a movement whose very existence may come as a surprise to many Americans. Although the American press has reported widely on peace activity in Western Europe, coverage of the East has, for the most part, been limited to chilling accounts of the arrest of Soviet dissidents and the continued repression of Poland's Solidarity Union. In general the American press has not provided information about the growth of peace movements in the Soviet Union and Eastern Europe.

Yet the news coming from behind the "Iron Curtain" is not as uniformly bleak as we may imagine. Courageous citizens in the Soviet bloc are beginning to express growing anti-war and anti-military sentiment. Pastor Eppelmann is one of them.

A minister in the East German Evangelical Protestant Church, Eppelmann originally became known for his efforts to reinvigorate a church that had fallen into disfavor after the Communist takeover. Like American clerics of the 1960s, who tried to make religion more socially and politically relevant, Eppelmann instituted a series of "Blues Masses," which used modern music and contemporary themes to attract young people. Then, he turned his attention to disarmament issues.

In July of 1981, he sent a letter to East German First Secretary, Erich Honecker, suggesting seventeen measures that might help prevent "the imminent annihilation of Europe." When Honecker failed to respond, he joined Robert Havemann in circulating what has since become known as the "Berlin Appeal," a carefully worded plea for a nuclear-free Europe, withdrawal of foreign troops from the two Germanies, and steps to discourage the increasing militarization of East German society. This last included a ban on production and sale of war toys, peace education—rather than military education—in the schools, an end to civil defense exercises, and the creation of a peace service (the equivalent of conscientious objectors' alternative service). The appeal was distributed in schools, factories, and churches and was signed by 2,000 East Germans.

These efforts have spread peace activity in East Germany. In February, 5,000 people attended a peace forum in Dresden, and that summer 2,000 people participated in a similar forum in Eppelmann's Berlin church. For the day-long event, the church was converted into an open forum with a "Hyde Park Corner," where participants could freely voice their opinions on a vast range of political subjects, and an anti-military museum displaying photographs of the horrors of war.

To Westerners this appears a commonplace church event. However, the museum exhibited photographs that directly contradict East Germany's official line that all wars to defend socialism are necessarily just ones and that the "Hyde Park Corner" was a space for freedom of expression that is not normally granted in the highly regulated East German society. For years, West German television, which reaches homes all over East Germany, had brought East Germany's news of peace activity in the West. Soon these same news reports were carrying accounts of growing peace activity in the German Democratic Republic (GDR), and Pastor Eppelmann has figured prominently in such reports.

Eppelmann speaks tirelessly for the next three-and-a-half hours. Before arriving, I had asked my friend if I should refrain from asking questions too critical of the GDR. "Don't censor yourself," he advised. "If Eppelmann chooses not to answer, that's his decision." I followed his advice and it was hard to imagine how the conversation could have been more frank and open. Speaking thoughtfully and judiciously, he would even stop me as I prepared to race on to another of the questions on my long list, because he had not fully replied to the previous one.

He voiced only one reservation. At the start of our interview, he asked me not to record the conversation in the standard question-and-answer talk format. An East German law forbids the publication of interviews if the State has not given written permission. Although he said I was free to quote him, he asked that I intersperse paraphrased segments throughout my article. A small point, it illustrates the tricky place of criticism in East German society. While tolerated, it is carefully limited by idiosyncratic legalisms.

Rainer Eppelmann is no newcomer either to the narrow confines of protest or to the penalties meted out to those who venture beyond acceptable debate. Raised in East Berlin, Eppelmann went to school in the Western sector until he was in the eleventh grade. The construction of the Berlin Wall abruptly ended his education and he left school to serve as an apprentice mason. Drafted into the army, he became a "bausoldat." A category unique to East Germany, the "construction soldier" is a "militarized" alternative to military service. He must submit to two months of military training, but he is not, thereafter, required to carry weapons. Although he must wear a uniform, he performs nonmilitary duties, building bridges and working on construction sites.

Eppelmann's first encounter with the military was characteristic of all his future dealings with East German officialdom. Soon after he was inducted, he was asked to take an oath required by all soldiers in any army to obey orders unconditionally. He refused. "I don't think I have ever met a person I could unconditionally follow," he says simply. His refusal earned him an eight-month jail sentence. After his release he became a theology student and later a minister.

East German authorities blame increased military spending and the militarization of daily life on the 1979 NATO "two-track" decision, which mandated the modernization of NATO's nuclear armory simultaneously with negotiations for nuclear disarmament. Eppelmann's experiences in the army, however, convinced him that this argument ignores history. "When I was a *bausoldat,*" he explains, "a sign in the mess hall reminded us that our heart belongs to the party and our fist to the enemy." In other words, they were telling us that there is no such thing as neutrality as far as the socialist camp is concerned."

There is nothing in the GDR, Eppelmann elaborates, that is not solved by a battle. There is the battle of agriculture and harvesting, which is fought and won by captains of harvesting machinery. For the battle of production, troops are marshalled in East German factories. Recently, the authorities have found yet another battleground—the schools—and added yet another group of soldiers to the ranks—kindergarten children, who are armed with state-purchased war toys.

When press reports from the West in the late 1970s brought him news of the escalating arms race and the breakdown of SALT II, as well as the activity of Western peace movements, Eppelmann began to criticize openly East Germany's military establishment as well as the East German Church's willingness to acquiesce to governmental policies. Like millions of protesters in the West, he decided it was time to take the future away from the politicians, foreign policy experts, and military strategists. "I do not think detente and disarmament is only a matter for the politicians in the United States and the Soviet Union," he says. "It is a matter for all people. We must begin to put forth proposals that increase confidence and trust between the state and the people."

Just as the silent acceptance of the "unalterable realities" of the nuclear age has been shattered in the West, so too it is being shattered in the Eastern bloc. The sounds and signs of opposition are less voluble and visible in Communist countries. Reporters assigned to cover the Eastern bloc do not receive press releases announcing mass demonstrations and teach-ins. No full-page ads in local newspapers and expensive television commercials will capture their attention. Nor will they be invited to attend lively debates of freeze resolutions in town meetings or the houses of parliament. But should curious journalists trouble to decipher the intricate codes of political discussion, they will find much to describe. If they know something about communication in the Eastern bloc, they will be even more impressed. For in communist countries, not only are those who question the status quo harassed and repressed, like-minded people must also use great ingenuity simply to communicate with one another.

Pastor Eppelmann, moving to the edge of his seat, asked me if I had noticed a full-page ad signed by West German peace activists, and some East Germans, that recently ran in the *New York Times*. Hadn't it made an impression? he asked. Hadn't it led to a series of actions? When I admitted that I had glanced at the ad but thought little about it, he was crestfallen. In East Germany, such public signs of protest aren't permitted; their appearance would indeed herald the coming of a new society.

Eppelmann's expectations for the newspaper ad seem distorted by the lens of scarcity. In the same way, our Western eyes often look at Eastern Europe through the equally distorting lens of plenty. Unless protest there takes on the forms and proportions to which we have become accustomed, we either ignore or dismiss it. So we regard 2,000 signatures on a petition as minuscule, and consider the presence of 5,000 people at a peace seminar too insignificant to note. In the Eastern bloc, those who have the courage to act openly may represent a silent majority who share the same fears and hopes but who hesitate to act on them.

In most Eastern European countries peace is official policy and is aggressively advertised. Eastern European countries all have their official peace committees, which are normally affiliated with the World Peace Council. Like the Soviet Peace Committee, they sponsor seminars and conferences and publish a variety of pamphlets and books. Some observers say these committees do have the support of ordinary citizens and that they are financed, in part, by voluntary contributions. The observers add that Eastern European peace committees have also been helpful in raising consciousness about the perils of nuclear war by disseminating information that would otherwise be unavailable. Although these committees may be founded upon the genuine desire of the people for peace, cautions E. P. Thompson, the British historian and leader of England's European Nuclear Disarmament (END), they "should be seen as...engaging in informal diplomatic relations with Western opinion." These groups, Thompson says, "may appear to conduct informal and flexible discussion," but they nonetheless pursue the "diplomatic aims of one side only, without any pretense to autonomy or spontaneity."

Westerners are not the only ones who are wary of official peace organizations. Citizens in Eastern Europe also regard them with suspicion. Thompson writes that the strong association of peace policy with states that simultaneously repress dissent and spend enormous sums preparing for war, has led East European citizens to have only the most perfunctory and superficial involvement with such organizations. Western peace activists who are interested in creating a pan-European peace movement with a genuine emancipatory and democratic thrust are therefore quite hesitant to legitimize state-controlled organizations and concentrate their energies on establishing contacts with the independent peace movements that have grown in countries like Czechoslovakia, Hungary, and East Germany.

In Czechoslovakia, a group called Charter 77 has been responsible for most unofficial peace activity. Formed in 1977, by former supporters of the Prague Spring and young people from the cultural underground, Charter 77 surfaced with a petition—signed by 1,000 Czechs—politely requesting the government to observe its constitutional commitment to human rights. Czech authorities did just the opposite: they began a campaign of harassment directed at the signers and organizers of the petition. Over the years, arrests, dismissals from jobs, and emigration have reduced the ranks of the group and today only a small core of dedicated dissidents continues to publish underground journals and pamphlets, and has recently begun to raise consciousness about peace and disarmament.

Recently Charter 77 published a letter of solidarity with the East German peace movement that illustrates how the group links the issue of peace with human rights. Charter 77, it reads, "shares your movement's specific aims. It considers that everywhere, in literally every country, it should be ordinary citizens, like you, who either individually, or as an unofficial group, should uphold the human right to live in peace."

A more tolerant political environment in Hungary has allowed an unofficial peace movement to grow alongside the official Hungarian National Peace Council. E.P. Thompson recently visited Hungary and has described the peace movement's curious position in Hungarian society. "Hungary," he writes in an END pamphlet, "is a remarkably open society today, in terms of the ideas which circulate widely in discussion groups, in the university, and in the schools. There is a delicate line between activities which are 'semi-legal'—that is, ideas and causes which may be canvassed informally, in small groups, but which may not be fully expressed in public meetings or in print; and 'semi-illegal' activities which are regarded by the authorities as 'oppositional,' such as *samizdat* (unauthorized duplicated publications, circulating usually in a few copies only) or underground university lectures."

So far, the semi-legal Hungarian peace movement has stayed on the safe side of the law. Its adherents come from three main groups: high school students, university students, and church-goers and priests. Secondary school students have formed the Anti-Nuclear Campaign, which distributes leaflets and peace badges in the schools and has taken over space in a Budapest park. In the university, two leading peace workers, Ferene Koszegi, a history student, and his wife, a student working on the problems of emotionally disturbed children, have organized small peace cells that have embraced the goals outlined in the Berlin Appeal. On June 12, 1982, when hundreds of thousands of Americans marched for peace in New York City, Koszegi and his co-activists held their own peace event—a meeting in which they discussed the prospects of total disarmament, the creation of a nuclear-zone in Europe, and their opposition to both Soviet SS-20s and NATO's Euromissiles.

The priests and church-goers who make up the third wing of the Hungarian peace movement have less global objectives. Since the 1960s, they have built up a network of some 300 "base communities"—small community groups—that work actively against militarism in their country. A number of priests have recently been either arrested or suspended for their participation in the struggle to create an alternative peace service, that is, a real conscientious objector status.

As Koszegi explains in the END pamphlet, nascent peace groups will face two major obstacles as their influence expands. Either Hungary's official National Peace Council will simply co-opt peace activity, using the unofficial peace group to revitalize its own image, Koszegi predicts, or it will face a challenge from its "friends" on the left. In the latter case these militant dissidents' more radical protest could lead it across the thin line of semi-illegality and thus invite state repression. Koszegi counsels Hungarian peace activists to work not only to increase their numbers and impact, but to establish a *modus vivendi* with the Hungarian National Peace Council. To insure its continued health, it must also reach out to Western peace groups whose support and encouragement are essential.

The Hungarian effort has in part been inspired by Eastern Europe's largest and most successful independent peace movement, that in East Germany. Tolerated because it is sheltered by the East German Protestant Church, it enjoys a status different from any other institution inside East Germany. To understand the East German peace movement, one must understand the church's prewar and postwar role in German society.

Before the division of Germany, the Lutheran Church had the allegiance of most German Protestants. Because of its collaboration with the Hitler regime, however, it lost its spiritual authority. Apart from a few courageous Christians, like Pastor Niemoller, the church offered no resistance to National Socialism. After the war, and the Allies' division of the country, the church tried to reclaim its spiritual hegemony by keeping alive the hope of reunification.

The Berlin Wall put an abrupt end to any immediate prospect of reunification and by 1969, the Church had reconciled itself with reality. The East German Church formally split off from its West German counterpart to form a separate federation of Evangelical churches inside the GDR. It has become a haven of sorts because a series of accords, negotiated with the communist state, have granted it privileges enjoyed by only one other group of East German citizens— artists and writers. In a society where all social and political activity—from participation in a football club to political meetings—is controlled by the state, church activists and cultural workers may engage in fairly open debate and may publish their writing (provided it reaches no more than a narrow circle of readers); they are often allowed to travel to meet with Westerners and travel to the West.

Rather than forcing citizens to feign an "atheism" to which they do not, in fact, subscribe, the state has used the Church's apparent freedom to legitimate its control. This relationship is nonetheless an ambiguous one.

What the East Germans refer to as "the Church's free space" has facilitated at least a partial discussion of state policies and priorities. In the late 1970s, ecologists used this "free space" to initiate a debate about environmental pollution—a problem that plagues East Germany as well as the West. Members of the Church's Federal Administration took part in the state-church dialogue and published a report entitled "Church and Society," which questioned both the state's economic planning and its emphasis on consumerism. The following year, members of the clergy travelled to the United States to attend a World Council of Churches meeting on "Environment, the Future, and Faith." Upon their return, they began an exploration of the impact of nuclear power plants; in 1981, the Church Synod suggested that East German authorities educate the population about the hazards of nuclear power. The state rejected this suggestion, but did not act to restrict this sort of debate—the two sides just agreed to disagree.

The birth of the ecological movement coincided with renewed interest in the problem posed by the increasing militarization of East German society. Until recently, military education programs—which had become an accepted, if unfortunate, fact of German life—were only required for students during the last two years of high school. But in 1978, the state went too far. The program to purchase military toys for kindergarten children created alarm among parents, who then looked to the Church for leadership. The Church hierarchy was pressured into proposing the creation of an alternative peace service that went beyond the "*bausoldaten.*" The results of this church-state encounter were as disappointing as the nuclear power debate. Moreover, in March 1982, the Church issued a statement solemnly announcing, "We are convinced that Christians can dare to do military service in spite of the risks this presents."

The Church's acquiescence to the state did not quash the environmental debate, and it has not silenced opposition to the military. The Berlin Appeal, peace forums in Dresden and Berlin, a movement to distribute over 20,000 badges depicting swords beaten into ploughshares in schools, factories, and churches, and a recent celebration of the "Peace Decade" all over East Germany have attracted thousands of Germans—old and young, workers, students, and intellectuals, Christians and non-Christians—all of whom look to the church for leadership and support.

Following the war and the construction of the Wall, the number of East Germans attending Sunday services and receiving the sacraments had fallen to a record low. Today that trend has reversed. Ironically, the new members who have so enhanced the Church's status also threaten its delicate relationship with the state. The Church's privileges depend on its ability to control the activities it sponsors. And although more vocal critics like Pastor Eppelmann are careful to follow the byzantine rituals that regulate debate, their continued activity could easily trigger a more general protest.

As long as the peace debate occupies a few intellectuals and a restricted number of Protestant faithful, it is safe, even useful, indulgence. Once it generates popular support and begins to challenge superpower domination, however, it becomes a luxury the authorities of both church and state may no longer be able to afford.

For now, Pastor Eppelmann and the burgeoning East German peace movement have successfully maneuvered through the tangle of church skittishness and state harassment. He and the East German peace movement are, however, constantly tracked by both church and state authorities. The security police routinely invite him to visit their offices for interrogatory chats and he is loathe to leave East Berlin for the trip to the West—even the short hop to West Berlin. In East Germany a common tactic used to limit dissent is simply to exile the dissenter, and Eppelmann fears he would not be allowed to return to his work and family in the East.

Dealings with church authorities also take up a great deal of time. "In a discussion I had with an established church official, " he recounts, "he told me that, speaking metaphorically, the church is like a cupboard full of cups. These cups signify a variety of services the Church performs—youth work, work with old people, community work, and peace work. He said he would not like to see the cupboard damaged and all the cups broken because of our peace work. I answered," Eppelmann continues, "that his portrait was not accurate. The peace question, I said, cannot be compared to one among many of these so-called cups. It is, rather, the entire cupboard."

To protect their vision of the "cupboard," church officials, Eppelmann says, are far more cautious than is necessary. When Church officials first heard about his "Blues Masses," they immediately warned him that the State Central Committee was considering preventative action, and they advised restraint. In fact, the state did not interfere and now the Blues Masses are accepted in the G.D.R. Nonetheless, when Eppelmann told church officials he would soon conduct a peace forum in his Berlin church, they again grew nervous and raised the specter of state intervention. And again, the peace forum took place—Hyde Park Corner, anti-military museum and all—without repercussions.

For this reason, Eppelmann feels moderately enthusiastic about the future. He is also encouraged by the growth of peace movements in other Eastern European countries and by the possibility of exchanges of ideas and support. "In the past, there has been very little solidarity among Eastern European peoples. That was true of Berlin in 1953, of Hungary in 1956, of Czechoslovakia in 1968, and now with Poland. There's always been curosity, even sympathy, between peoples in Eastern European countries, but it's never been translated into action.

That seems to be changing," he predicts, citing Charter 77's recent letter of support. "This is the first time I've seen that kind of action. Finally an East European state does more than just look at its own problems. It looks at what's happening in another Eastern European state."

Such hopeful signs do not blind Eppelmann to the pessimistic realities of life in the G.D.R. He is well aware, for example, that the peace movement's increasing popularity may well jeopardize its health. What the state worries about, Eppelmann explains, is not the simple expression of disagreement, but the number of people who express it. That explains why the security police are suddenly interested in the pacifist academies, and why police have recently begun to harass young people who wear swords-into-plowshares badges. What the police demanded of one professor was not that he stop participating in smaller peace meetings, but that he abandon the broader debate taking place at Eppelmann's church. Similarly, when the distribution of swords-into-plowshares badges exceeded a certain limit, and attracted attention in the West, then the police cracked down.

"Their main concern," Eppelmann says, "is not to limit the church but to limit the number of people who have access to information. They furthermore categorically refuse to allow the Church and the Church-sheltered peace movement to enter any other discussion or organization because they fear this would lead to a mass movement of dissent."

To create the conditions for real political detente, both inside their societies and between the superpowers, is what Eppelmann and the others are fighting for. Certainly they want to help rid the world of nuclear weapons. But they want to do more. "My task is to try to widen space and confidence to take advantage of the freedoms granted the Church to allow people to speak and think freely, as they did that one Sunday in June at Hyde Park Corner. People can then build on these experiences so they can speak out in their families and at work."

"This is something," he says at the end of a tiring but exhilarating session, "we East Germans must do for ourselves. It is not something that can be accomplished from the outside. We must learn to demand these freedoms because we East Germans are truly biological mysteries. We can walk even though we do not have a spine. And what we must do, first of all, is grow it back."

East/West Networking

The European peace movement, says Erhard Eppler, a leading West German peace activist and Social Democratic member of the Bundestag, is the "weak link in the Cold War." It is also the strongest link in a new kind of European alliance—one that does not accept the postwar division of Europe. To fight the Cold War consensus that Reagan, Thatcher, Kohl, and others are trying to resurrect, and to build a pan-European movement, European peace activists have spent a great deal of energy establishing contact with both official and unofficial groups in the Eastern bloc.

This East-West networking has stirred up a great deal of controversy. Most peace groups agree that it is important to prove that the desire for peace is not the exclusive property of the West and they reject the notion that any peaceful noises the Soviets and their East European allies make are just part of a giant conspiracy to dupe American opinion. On the other hand, there is widespread disagreement about strategy. If one wants to establish links with Eastern Europe peace activists to whom should one talk—official or unofficial groups? What issues do you raise with these groups? How much publicity should you court and create for your Eastern European counterparts? And how should you portray and promote the importance of these alliances?

Several European peace groups believe that Western peace activists should focus on creating contacts only with official peace committees in the Soviet Union and Eastern Europe. Obviously, Soviet or Communist party-dominated peace groups are the main proponents of this line. But some others, like Germany's Action Reconciliation (ASF) believe that it's a waste of time to cultivate unofficial groups in Eastern Europe. When I visited ASF's Berlin headquarters, a spokesperson curtly dismissed the idea of dealing with people like Pastor Rainer Eppelmann. "He is just turning himself into a dissident," she said, "a marginal figure who will have less, not more, impact on events in his country."

Other groups feel that one should not do anything to legitimate Soviet-style peace groups and should deal only with independents or dissidents. Still others admit that it is important to talk with official groups, but disagree about the extent of the cooperation. An example of this sort of conflict surfaced recently when Scandinavian women organized a march to the Soviet Union this past summer. The women—organizers of a march from Stockholm to Paris the previous year—recognized the compromises necessary to deal with the Soviet Peace Committee and World Peace Council, but felt it was important to bring their message of peace to the ordinary people they would meet on marches and demonstrations, as well as to the officials of the Soviet Peace Committee, whose ideas, they say, are subject to change. The marchers, however, were criticized by other peace activists who say the event merely legitimated the Soviets without affecting official policy.

Members of E.N.D. and I.K.V. believe it is important to speak to both official and unofficial groups. E.N.D. finds it useful to invite official groups to peace gatherings because this often allows unofficial representatives to attend the same meeting. The official groups want to have their views expressed and it's sometimes worth it to them to permit independents to come if that's the price.

I.K.V. also believes it's important to talk with official groups as long as certain ground rules are obeyed. When Wim Bartels, I.K.V.'s international secretary, participated in a recent meeting on nuclear catastrophe called by the Patriarch of the Russian Orthodox Church, he agreed to attend only if the Russians allowed him to address the conference plenary. The Russians negotiated, and suggested Bartels speak instead to a conference working group—a forum, they promised, that would be open to the press.

When he arrived and found the Soviets had closed the working group to the press, he withdrew in protest. Some groups criticized I.K.V.'s action because it severed important links that should be maintained. But Bartels feels his departure did not compromise I.K.V.'s relationship with the Soviets and that it is important to convince the Soviets of I.K.V.'s seriousness.

Although Bartels often talks with representatives of countries like Yugoslavia, Hungary, and Romania—countries that have declared their support for the concept of nuclear-free zones in Europe—he explains that I.K.V.'s real peace partners are the unofficial groups who are not just opposed to the nuclear arms race but who oppose the power race as well. "If you include all elements for peace—human rights, self-determination, and social justice," Bartel says, "then our partners are those groups in society that are looking for broader political alternatives, like Solidarity and Charter 77."

Many European peace activists debate the extent to which activists should bring up the sensitive problem of human rights. If, for example, you go to the Soviet Union or East Germany and complain about Afghanistan or Poland, you forego the possibility of cooperation with official groups. If you do not bring up human rights issues, you lose credibility with independent peace goups and dissidents.

The issue of human rights is particularly important when peace activists consider their relationship to Poland's Solidarity movement. As Daniel Singer, author of *The Road to Gdansk* explains, there are some within the Solidarity movement who are actively hostile to the European and American peace movements. They feel, Singer says, that their survival depends on a strong nuclear deterrent in Europe and America. If the peace movement is to woo them, Singer says, it must raise the issue of human rights far more aggressively.

Just how openly and aggressively any of these issues are raised is another point of contention. While Eastern European peace activists argue that continued contacts with Western peace activists are essential—both for inspiration and for their survival and safety—some activists contend that press attention from Western journalists and too much contact with Western activists only aggravates an already impossible situation. A representative of the International Fellowship of Reconciliation in Holland refused to go into the matter of his group's relationship with Eastern Europeans. The group argues that any open discussion about the activities of Eastern European activists merely incites the state, which, like an angry bee, will inevitably sting.

Those activists who are involved in more open exchanges are no less advocates of caution. All contacts with such groups, E.P. Thompson writes of Hungary, must be developed carefully. These groups exist "within a delicate balance of both internal and external forces. It is well that the Western peace movement should appreciate this and not rush in with amateurish enthusiasm."

Some would suggest they may not want to rush at all. Robert Borosage, director of the Institute for Policy Studies, is worried about the extent to which groups like END promote their contacts with the Eastern Europeans. "Although peace movements in the West inevitably talk to almost everyone across state lines and Cold War divides, it's important that one thing should be clear: the movement to end the arms race in the West cannot wait upon the growth of democracy in the East. Since democracy in the East will grow only when the arms race has stopped and the Cold War thawed, this means that the task of citizens in the Western peace movement is very challenging. They must change the direction of the leadership not only in the West but in the East as well. They must have such moral and political force that the leaders of the Soviet Union will be compelled to respond."

"Given the limits on political freedoms in the East," Borosage continues, "it's very unlikely that an independent peace movement there will play much of a role in the peace effort. Therefore the prospects and the fate of the peace movement in the West should not be made dependent upon the growth and health of independent peace groups in the East. Because those movements are very fragile indeed."

Chapter 24

Beyond the Cold War

E.P. Thompson

What, we must ask as we enter the 1980s, is the Cold War *about?* The answer to this question can give us no comfort at all. If we look at the military scene, then nothing is receding. On the contrary, the military establishments of both superpowers continue to grow each year. The Cold War, in this sense, has broken free from the occasions at its origin, and has acquired an independent inertial thrust of its own. What is the Cold War now about? It is about itself.

We face here, in the grimmest sense, the "consequences of consequences." The Cold War may be seen as a show which was put, by two rival entrepreneurs, upon the road in 1946 or 1947. The show has grown bigger and bigger; the entrepreneurs have lost control of it, as it has thrown up its own managers, administrators, producers, and a huge supporting cast; these have a direct interest in its continuance, in its enlargement. Whatever happens, the show must go on.

The Cold War has become a habit, an addiction. But it is a habit supported by very powerful material interests in each bloc: the military-industrial and research establishments of both sides, the security services and intelligence operations, and the political servants of these interests. These interests command a large (and growing) allocation of the skills and resources of each society; they influence the direction of each society's economic and social development; and it is in the interest *of* these interests to increase that allocation and to influence this direction even more.

I don't mean to argue for an *identity* of process in the United States and the Soviet Union, nor for a perfect symmetry of forms. There are major divergences, not only in political forms and controls, but also as between the steady expansionism of bureaucracy and the avarice of private capital. I mean to stress, rather, the *reciprocal* and inter-active character of the process. It is in the very nature of this Cold War show that there must be two adversaries: and each move by one must be matched by the other. This is the inner dynamic of the Cold War which determines that its military and security establishments are *self-reproducing*. Their missiles summon forward our missiles which summon forward their missiles in turn. NATO's hawks feed the hawks of the Warsaw bloc.

For the ideology of the Cold War is self-reproducing also. That is, the military and the security services and their political servants *need* the Cold War. They have a direct interest in its continuance.

This is not only because their own establishments and their own careers depend upon this. It is not only because ruling groups can only justify their own privileges and their allocation of huge resources to "defense" in the name of Cold War emergencies. And it is not only because the superpowers both need repeated Cold War alarms to keep their client states, in NATO or the Warsaw Pact, in line. All these explanations have force. But, at an even deeper level, there is a further explanation—which I will describe by the ugly word "psycho-ideological"—which must occasion the grimmest pessimism.

The Threat of the Other

The fear of the Other is grounded upon a profound and universal human need. It is intrinsic to human bonding. We cannot define whom "we" are without also defining "them"—those who are not "us". "They" need not be perceived as threatening: they may be seen only as different from "us"—from our family, our community, our nation: "They" are others who do not "belong". But if "they" are seen as threatening to us, then our own internal bonding will be all the stronger.

Throughout history, as bonding has gone on and as identities have changed, the Other has been necessary to this process. Rome required barbarians. Christendom required pagans, Protestant and Catholic Europe required each other. The nation state bonded itself against other nations. Patriotism is love of one's own country; but it is also hatred or fear or suspicion of others.

Let us return to today's Cold War. The condition of the Cold War has broken free from the "causes" at its origin: and the ruling interests on both sides have become ideologically addicted—they need its continuance. The Western Hemisphere has been divided into two parts, each of which sees itself as threatened by the Other; yet at the same time this continuing threat has become necessary to provide internal bonding and social discipline within each part.

Moreover, this threat of the Other has been internalized within both Soviet and American culture, so that the very self-identity of many American and Soviet citizens is bound up with the ideological premises of the Cold War.

There are historical reasons for this, which have less to do with the actualities of communist or capitalist societies than we may suppose. Americans, for a century or so, have had a growing problem of national identity. America has a population, dispersed across half a continent, gathered in from the four corners of the globe. Layer upon layer of immigrants have come in, and the new layers are being laid down today: Vietnamese and Thailanders, Cubans and undocumented Hispanic workers. Internal bonding tends to fall, not upon horizontal nationwide lines—the bonding of social class remains weak—but in vertical, fissiparous ways: local, regional, or ethnic bonding—the blacks, the Hispanics, the Poles, the Irish, the Jewish lobby. The resounding, media-propagated myth of United States society is that of an open market society, an upwardly-mobile free-for-all: its objective is not any communal goal but equality of ego-fulfillment for everyone.

But where, in all these centrifugal and individualistic forces is any national bonding and sense of American self-identity to be found? American poets and novelists have suggested better answers—America (they have suggested) might be the most internationalist nation in the world—but the answer that has satisfied America's present rulers is, precisely, in the Cold War. The United States is the leader of the "free world," and the Commies are the Other. They need this Other to establish their own identity, not as blacks or Poles or Irish, but as free Americans. Only this pre-existent need, for bonding-by-exclusion, can explain the ease by which one populist rascal after another has been able to float to power—even to the White House—on nothing but a flood of sensational Cold War propaganda. And anti-communism can be turned to other internal uses as well. It can serve to knock trade unions on their head, or to keep dissident radical voices or peace movements ("soft on Communism") on the margins of political life.

But what about the Soviet Union? Is there a similar need to bond against the Other within Soviet culture? I can speak with less confidence here. But there are indications that this is so.

The Soviet Union is not "Russia" but a ramshackle empire inherited from Tsarist times. It also has its own fissiparous tendencies, from Mongolia to the Baltic states. It has no need to invent an Other, in some fit of paranoia. It has been struck within active memory, by another, to the gates of Moscow, with a loss of some 20 million dead. One would suppose that the Soviet rulers, while having good reason for a defensive mentality, would need the Cold War like a hole in the head. They would want it to go away. And, maybe, some of them do.

Yet the Cold War, as ideology, has a bonding function in the Soviet Union also. This huge collection of peoples feels itself to be surrounded—it is surrounded—from Mongolia to the Arctic ice-cap to its Western frontiers. The bonding, the self-identity, of Soviet citizens comes from the notion that they are the heartland of the world's first socialist revolution, threatened by the Other—Western imperialism, in alliance with 1,000 million Chinese. The positive part of this rhetoric—the Marxist-Leninist, revolutionary bit—may now have worn exceedingly thin; but the negative part remains compelling. The one function of the Soviet rulers which commands consensual assent throughout the population is their self-proclaimed role as defenders of the Fatherland and defenders of the peace.

There is nothing sinister about that. But the bonding function of Cold War ideology in the Soviet Union is directly disciplinary. The threat of the Other legitimates every measure of policing or intellectual control. In Stalin's time this took the form of indiscriminate terror against "counter-revolutionaries." The measures of terror or discipline have now been greatly modified. This is important and this is hopeful. But the function of this disciplinary ideology remains the same.

What it does is to transform every social or intellectual conflict within the Soviet Union into a problem affecting the security of the state. Every critic of Soviet reality, every "dissident," is defined as an ally of the Other: as alien, unpatriotic, and perhaps as an agent of the West. Every impulse towards democracy or autonomy in Eastern Europe—the Prague Spring of 1968, the Polish renewal—is defined as a security threat to the Soviet frontiers and to the defensive unity of the

Warsaw powers.

Like the populist American denunciation of "Commies," the Soviet denunciation of "Western" penetration can be turned to every purpose imaginable in the attempt to impose internal discipline—but with the important difference that in the Soviet Union the attacks of the media and of political leaders are supplemented by more powerful and more intrusive security forces. Even juvenile delinquency, or the new wave of consumerism in the Soviet white-collar and professional groups, can be denounced as Western attempts to "subvert" Soviet society. And General Semyon Tsvigun, first deputy chairman of the KGB, writing recently in *Kommunist*, has instanced the "negative influence" of Western styles and pop music upon Soviet young people as examples of the "subversive" activities of the external "class enemy."

This is the double-bind which the Soviet people cannot break through. It is weary, but it works. And it works because the Cold Warriors of the West are eager to be in the same card-game, and to lead into the strong suits of their partners, the Cold Warriors of the East. The Western Warriors, by championing the cause of "human rights," in the same moment define the dissidents of the East as allies of the West and as security risks. It is a hypocritical championship on several counts, but we will leave this aside. It is utterly counter-productive, and perhaps it is intended to be so. It does no-one, except the Cold Warriors of the other side, any good.

The boycott of the Moscow Olympics is a case in point. Initially this may have been welcomed by some dissident intellectuals in Eastern Europe and among some Soviet Jews. It was to do them no good. A Russian friend tells me that, as an operation promoting liberty, it was a disaster. The boycott bonded the Soviet people against the Other. In a state of siege and isolation for half-a-century, the Olympics offered to open international doors and to give them, for the first time, the role of host on the world stage. They were aggrieved by the boycott not as Communists, but in their latent patriotism. They had allocated resources to the Olympics, they had rehearsed their dancers and their choirs. They were curious to meet the world's athletes and visitors. Critics of the Olympics were felt to be disloyal, not only by the security services, but also by their workmates and neighbours. The boycott hence made possible the greatest crack-down upon all centers of critical opinion in the Soviet Union in a decade. It was a gift, from the CIA to the KGB. Lord Killanan and the British Olympic team did the right thing, not only in support of the Olympic tradition but also in support of the cause of peace. But "dissent" in the Soviet Union has not yet recovered from the Western Cold Warriors' kind attentions.

It can be seen now, also, why the most conservative elements in the Soviet leadership—the direct inheritors of Stalin—*need* the Cold War. This is not only because some part of this leadership has arisen from, or spent some years in service of the bureaucratic-military-security complex itself. And it isn't only because the very heavy allocations to defense, running to perhaps 15 percent of the gross national product, must be justified in the eyes of the deprived public. It is also because these leaders are beset on every side by difficulties, by pressures to modernize, to reform or to democratize. Yet these pressures threaten their own position and privileges—once commenced, they might pass beyond control. The Polish renewal will have been watched, in the Soviet Union and in other Eastern European states, as an awful example of such a process—a process bringing instability and, with this, a threat to the security of the Communist world.

Hence Cold War ideology—the threat of the Other—is the strongest card left in the hands of the Soviet rulers. It is necessary for bonding. And the card is not a fake. For the Other—that is, the Cold Warriors of the West—is continually playing the same card back, whether in missiles or in arms agreements with China or in the suit of human rights.

We could not have led up to a more pessimistic conclusion. I have argued that the Cold War is now about itself. It is an ongoing, self-reproducing condition, to which both adversaries are in a reciprocal relationship of mutual nurture: each fosters the growth of the other. Both adversaries need to maintain a hostile ideological posture, as a means of internal bonding or discipline. This would be dangerous at any time; but with today's nuclear weaponry it is an immensely dangerous condition. For it contains a built-in logic which must always tend to the worst: the military establishments will grow, the adversary postures become more implacable and more irrational.

That logic, if uncorrected, must prove terminal, and in the next two or three decades. I will not speculate on what accident or which contingency will bring us to that terminus. I am pointing out the logic and thrust of things, the current which is sweeping us towards Niagara Falls. As we go over those Falls we may comfort ourselves that it was really no-one's fault: that human culture has always contained within itself a malfunction, a principle of bonding-by-exclusion which must (with our present technologies of death) lead to auto-destruct. We might have guessed as much by looking at the nettles in history's hedges.

The Role of Europe

All this perhaps will happen. I think it at least probable that it will. We cannot expect to have the good fortune of having our planet invaded, in the 1990s, by some monsters from outer space, who would at last bond all humanity against an outer Other. And short of some science fiction rescue operation like that, all proposals look like wish fulfillment.

Yet there is a contradiction. Today's military confrontation is protracted long after the historical occasion for it has come to an end. I share the view of a recent editorial comment in the *London Times* (October 2, 1981):

> The huge accumulations of weaponry which the two brandish at each other are wholly out of proportion to any genuine conflict of interests. There is no serious competition for essential resources, or for territory that is truly vital to the security of either, and the ideological fires have dwindled on both sides. In strictly objective terms a reasonable degree of accommodation should be easily attainable.

But if the Cold War is at once obsolete and inexorable, an on-going, self-reproducing road-show that has become necessary to ruling groups on both sides, can we find, within this contradiction, any resolution short of war?

Perhaps we can. But the resolution will not be easy. A general revolt of reason and conscience against the instruments which immediately threaten us—a lived perception, informing multitudes, of the human ecological imperative: this is a necessary part of the answer. For if the Cold War has acquired a self-generating dynamic, then, as soon as public concern is quieted by a few measures of arms control, new dangers and new weapons will appear. We must do more than protest if we are to survive. We must go behind the missiles to the Cold War itself. We must begin to put Europe back into one piece.

And how could that be done? Very certainly it cannot be done by the victory of one side over the other. That would mean war. We must retrace our steps to that moment, in 1944, before glaciation set in, and look once again for a third way.

If I had said this two years ago I would have despaired of holding your attention. But something remarkable is stirring in this continent today; movements which commenced in fear and which are now taking the shape of hope; movements which cannot yet, with clarity, name their own demands. For the first time since the wartime Resistance, there is a spirit abroad in Europe which carries transcontinental aspiration. The Other which menaces us is being redefined—not as other nations, nor even as the other bloc, but as forces leading both blocs to auto-destruction—not "Russia" nor "America" but their military, ideological and security establishments and their ritual opposi-tions.

And at the same time, as this Other is excluded, so a new kind of internal bonding is taking place. This takes the form of a growing commitment, by many thousands, to the imperatives of survival and against the ideological or security imperatives of either bloc or their nation states. In the words of the Appeal for European Nuclear Disarmament of April 1980:

> We must commence to act as if a united, neutral and pacific Europe already exists. We must learn to be loyal, not to "East" or "West", but to each other.

This is a large and improbable expectation. It has often been proclaimed in the past, and it has been as often disap-pointed. Yet what is improbable has already, in the past year, begun to happen. The military structures are under challenge. But something is happening of greater significance. The ideo-logical structures are under challenge also, and from *both* sides.

The Cold War had placed the political culture of Europe in a permanent double-bind: the cause of "peace" and the cause of "freedom" fell apart. What is now happening is that these two causes are returning to one cause—peace *and* freedom—and as this happens, so, by a hundred different channels, the trans-continental discourse of political culture can be resumed.

The peace movements which have developed with such astonishing rapidity in Northern, Western and Southern Europe— and which are now finding an echo in the East—are one part of this cause. They have arisen in response not only to a military and strategic situation but to a political situation as well. What has aroused Europeans most is the spectacle of two super-powers, arguing above their heads about the deployment of weapons whose target would be the "theater" of Europe. These movements speak with new accents. They are, in most cases, neither pro-Soviet nor manipulated by the Communist-influ-enced World Peace Council. Their objective is to clear nuclear weapons and bases out of the whole continent, East and West, and then to roll back conventional forces. Nor is it correct to describe them as "neutralist" or "pacifist." They are looking for a third way. A third way is an active way: it is not "neutral" between the other ways, it goes somewhere else.

The Western peace movements, in majority opinion, bring together traditions—socialist, trade unionist, liberal, Christian, ecological—which have always been committed to civil rights. They extend their support to the Polish renewal and to Solidarity, and to movements of libertarian dissent in the Warsaw bloc. And from Eastern Europe also, voice after voice is now reaching us—hesitant, cautious, but with growing confidence—searching for the same alliance: peace *and* freedom.

These voices signal that the whole thirty-five-year-old era of the Cold War could be coming to an end: the Ice Age could give way to turbulent torrents running from East to West and from West to East. And within the demands of the peace movements and also in the movements of lower profile but e-qual potential in Eastern Europe there is maturing a further—and a convergent—demand: to shake off the hegemony of the superpowers and to reclaim autonomy.

Europe Between the Superpowers

The question before Europeans today is not how many NATO forward-based systems might equal how many Soviet SS-20s. Beneath these equations there is a larger question: in what circumstances might *both* superpowers loosen the military grip which settled upon Europe in 1945 and which has been protracted long beyond its historical occasion? And how might such a retreat of hegemonies and loosening of blocs take place without endangering peace? Such an outcome would be profoundly in the interest, not only of the people of Europe, but of the peoples of the Soviet Union and the United States also—in relaxing tension and in relieving them of some of the burdens and dangers of their opposed military establishments. But what—unless it were to be our old enemy "deterrence"—could monitor such a transition so that neither one nor the other party turned it to advantage?

We are not, it should be said, describing some novel stage in the process known as detente. For in the early 1970's detente signified the cautious tuning-down of hostilities between states or blocs, but within the Cold War *status quo*. Detente (or "peaceful co-existence") was licensed by the superpowers: it did not arise from the client states, still less from popular movements. The framework of East-West settlement was held rigid by "deterrence": in the high noon of Kissinger's diplomacy detente was a horse-trade between leaders of the blocs, in which any unseemly movement outside the framework was to be discouraged as "de-stabilizing." Czechs or Italians were required to remain quiet in their client places, lest any rash movement should disturb the touchy equilibrium of the superpowers.

But what we can glimpse now is something different: a detente of peoples rather than states—a movement of peoples which sometimes dislodges states from their blocs and brings them into a new diplomacy of conciliation, which sometimes runs beneath state structures, and which sometimes defies the ideological and security structures of particular states. This will be a more fluid, unregulated, unpredictable movement. It may entail risk.

The risk must be taken. For the Cold War can be brought to an end in only two ways: by the destruction of European civilization, or by the reunification of European political culture.The first will take place if the ruling groups in the rival superpowers, sensing that the ground is shifting beneath them and that their client states are becoming detached, succeed in compensating for their waning political and economic authority by more and more frenzied measures of militarization. This is, exactly, what is happening now. The outcome will be terminal.

But we can now see a small opening towards the other alternative. And if we thought this alternative to be possible, then we should—every one of us—re-order all our priorities. We would invest nothing more in missiles, everything in all the skills of communication and exchange. All I can do now is indicate, briefly, programs which are already in the making.

One such program is that of limited nuclear-free zones. I have the honor to speak now in the Guildhall of the nuclear-free city of Worcester. I need not say here, Mr. Mayor, that this is not just a measure of self-preservation. It is a signal also, of international conciliation, and a signal which we hope will be reciprocated. Such signals are now arising across our continent. A Nordic nuclear-free zone is now under active consideration. And in the Southeast of Europe, the Greek government is pledged to initiate discussions with Bulgaria and Rumania (in the Warsaw pact) and with non-aligned Yugoslavia, for a further nuclear-free zone.

Such zones have political significance. Both states and local authorities can enlarge the notion to take in exchanges between citizens, for direct uncensored discourse. In Central Europe a zone of this kind might go further to take in measures of conventional disarmament also, and the withdrawal of both Soviet and NATO forces from both Germanys. This proposal is now being actively canvassed in East Germany as well as West—the East German civil rights supporter, Dr. Robert

Havemann, has raised the question directly in an open letter to Mr. Brezhnev—and is now being discussed, in unofficial circles, in Poland and Czechoslovakia as well.

The objectives of such larger zones is clear: to make a space of lessened tension between the two blocs; to destroy the menacing symbolic affront of nuclear weapons; to bring nations both East and West within reciprocal agreements; and to loosen the bonds of the bloc system, allowing more autonomy, more initiative to the smaller states.

But at the same time there must be other initiatives, through a hundred different channels, by which citizens can enlarge this discourse. It is absurd to expect the weapons systems of both sides to de-weaponize themselves, the security systems of both sides to fall into each other's arms. It is, precisely, at the top of the Cold War systems that deadlock, or worse, takes place. If we are to destructure the Cold War, then we must destabilize these systems from below.

I am talking about a new kind of politics which cannot (with however much goodwill) be conducted by politicians. It must be a politics of peace, informed by a new internationalist code of honor, conducted by citizens. And it is now being so conducted by the international medical profession, by churches, by writers and by many others.

Music can be a "politics" of this kind. There is, today, some generational cultural mutation taking place among the young people of Europe. The demonstrations for peace—Bonn, London, Madrid, Rome, Amsterdam—have been thronged with the young. The young are *bored* with the Cold War. There is a shift at a level below politics—expressed in style, in sound, in symbol, in dress—which could be more significant than any negotiations taking place in Geneva. The PA systems of popular music bands are already capable of making transcontinental sounds. The bands may not be expert arms negotiators; but they might blast the youth of Europe into each others' arms.

It has been proposed that there might be a festival—it might be called "Theater of Peace." Young people (although their elders would not be excluded) would be called to assemble from every part of the continent, bringing with them their music, their living theater, their art, their posters, their symbols and gifts. There would be rallies, workshops, and informal discussions. Every effort would be made to invite youth from "the other side," not in pre-selected official parties but as individual visitors and strays.

Conclusion

In conclusion, how do we put the causes of freedom and of peace back together? This cannot be done by provocative interventions in the affairs of other nations. And it certainly cannot be done by the old strategy of Cold War "linkage." If we look forward to democratic renewal on the other side of our common world, then this strategy is plainly counter-productive. No-one will ever obtain civil or trade union rights in the East because the West is pressing missiles against their borders. On the contrary, this only enhances the security operations and the security-minded ideology of their rulers. The peoples of the East, as of the West, will obtain their own rights and liberties for themselves and in their own way—as the Portuguese, Spanish, Greek and Polish people have shown us. What is needed, from and for all of us, is a space free of Cold War crisis in which we can move.

There might, however, be a very different kind of citizen's linkage in which, as part of the people's detente, the movement for peace in the West and for freedom in the East recognized each other as natural allies. For this to be possible, we in the West must move first. As the military pressure upon the East begins to relax, so the old double bind would begin to lose its force. And the Western peace movement (which can scarcely be cast by Soviet ideologists as an "agent of Western imperialism") should press steadily upon the state structures of the East demands for greater openness of exchange, both of persons and of ideas.

A transcontinental discourse must begin to flow, in both directions, with the peace movement—a movement of unofficial persons with a code of conduct which disallows the pursuit of political advantage for either "side"—as the conduit. We cannot be content to criticize nuclear missiles. We have to be, in every moment, critics also of the adversary posture of the powers. For we are threatened, not only by weapons, but the ideological and security structures which divide our continent and which turn us into adversaries. So that the concession which the peace movement asks of the Soviet state is—not so much these SS-20s and those Backfire bombers—but its assistance in commencing to tear these structures down. And in good time one might look forward to a further change, in the Soviet Union itself, as the long outworn ideology and structures inherited from Stalin's time gave way before internal pressures for a Soviet renewal.

What I have proposed is improbable. But, if it commenced, it might gather pace with astonishing rapidity. There would not be a decade of detente, as the glaciers slowly melt. There would be very rapid and unpredictable changes; nations would become unglued from their alliances; there would be sharp conflicts within nations; there would be successive risks. We would roll up the map of the Cold War, and travel without maps for a while.

I do not mean that Russia might become a Western democracy, nor that the West would go Communist. Immense differences in social systems would remain. Nations, unglued from their alliances, might—as Poland and Greece are now showing us—fall back more strongly into their own inherited national traditions. I mean only that the flow of political and intellectual discourse, and of human exchange, would resume across the whole continent. The blocs would discover that they had forgotten what their adversary posture was about.

Our species has been favored on this planet, although we have not always been good caretakers of our globe's resources. Our stay here, in the space of geological time, has been brief. No one can tell us our business. But I think it is something more than to consume as much as we can and then blow the place up.

We have, if not a duty, then a need, deeply engraved within our culture, to pass the place on no worse than we found it. Those of us who do not expect an afterlife may see in this our only immortality: to pass on the succession of life, the succession of culture. It may even be that we are happier when we are engaged in matters larger than our own wants and ourselves.

We did not choose to live at this time. But there is no way of getting out of it. And it has given to us as significant a cause as has ever been known, a moment of opportunity which might never be renewed. If these weapons and then those weapons are added to the huge sum on our continent—if Poland drifts into civil war and this calls down Soviet military intervention—if the United States launches some military adventure in the Middle East—can we be certain that this moment will ever come back? I do not think so. If my analysis is right, then the inertial thrust of the Cold War, from its formidable military and ideological bases, will have passed the point of no return.

The opportunity is *now*, when there is already an enhanced consciousness of danger informing millions. We can match this crisis only by a summoning of resources to a height like that of the greatest religious or political movements of Europe's past. I think, once again, of 1944 and of the crest of the Resistance. There must be that kind of spirit abroad in Europe once more. But this time it must arise, not in the wake of war and repression, but before these take place. Five minutes afterward, and it will be too late.

Humankind must at last grow up. We must recognize that the Other is ourselves.

PART V

OPPOSING THE ARMS RACE

Introduction

Reagan's nuclear strategy and foreign policy intersect, according to Richard Barnet, in the drive for a *Pax Americana.* Barnet maintains that we face the most dangerous moment since World War II as we are heading toward an all-out arms race, the consequences of which the country does not comprehend. The United States is at a crossroads: the choice is between the continued hostility to nationalist movements in the Third World and an irrational cold war combined with the rearmament necessary to maintain American hegemony, or an accommodation with a changing world. David Gold and Gordon Adams demonstrate that, if U.S. foreign policy moved away from confrontation and toward real national security, $50 billion could be removed from the defense budget "with no reduction in America's ability to defend itself." Similarly, the Congressional Black Caucus recently mapped out an alternative budget that would provide for the defense of U.S. borders and those of our allies while slashing funds for the interventionist Rapid Deployment Force and additional nuclear weapons systems. Reagan, however, is pursuing the militarist option full steam ahead and among the consequences is an escalating nuclear arms race. Not surprisingly, therefore, is the absence of any meaningful U.S. arms limitation initiatives.

Christopher Paine argues that Reagan's Strategic Arms Reduction Talks (START) proposal was based on the faulty premise of an American "window of vulnerability." In fact, at current rates of development the Soviets are projected to remain behind the United States in the number of warheads that can be delivered after absorbing an initial attack. If there is a "window of vulnerability," it is in the Urals. Not only would the START proposal have had a most unequal impact on the respective structure of nuclear forces held by the U.S. and the U.S.S.R. but, even more importantly, no qualitative controls on weapons development were included. Since the writing of Paine's article, Reagan has shifted gears and under the guise of a bipartisan arms control initiative now proposes the build-down scheme in which old missiles would be traded in for new ones. Again, there is the complete absence of qualitative controls which gives a green light to the further development and deployment of destabilizing "first-strike" weapons. Ironically, the changing warhead/missile ratio could mean that the build-down proposal would leave the United States with considerably fewer surviving warheads after a Soviet first strike. START would reduce the security of both sides.

It goes without saying that the greatest challenge to Reagan's nuclear buildup has been mounted by the Freeze movement which began in 1980 to organize around Randall Forsberg's engaging proposal. The Freeze has been dismissed by some in the peace movement as just arms limitation rather than true disarmament. But as Michael Kazin observes, a freeze by both superpowers would offer a profound opportunity for nuclear stability by limiting the emerging threat of first-strike weaponry. While not a proposal for complete nuclear disarmament, the Freeze would mean a dramatic reversal of the strategic arms race, a rejection of nuclear war-fighting capabilities and doctrine, and reduced fear of a first-strike by either the U.S. or the U.S.S.R.

Michael Klare provides a necessary caution with his discussion of conventional weapons that now possess the "kill radius" of small nuclear weapons. The development and use of "smart" conventional weapons will narrow the firebreak between the use of conventional and nuclear weapons. Klare, while recognizing the understandable priority of focusing on nuclear weapons, warns that the peace movement must make the connection between conventional rearmament, interventionary impulses and the growing risk of triggering nuclear annihilation. The difficulty, of course, is the ability of the mass movement to successfully focus on all weapons and examples of militarism.

Beside the Freeze, the most widely discusse disarmament proposal is a no-first-use declaration. The Union of Concerned Scientists (UCS) have joined others including McGeorge Bundy, Robert McNamara *et al.* in suggesting that NATO's conventional forces be upgraded to match those of the Warsaw Pact so that the threat of nuclear response will not be needed to deter Soviet conventional aggression against Western Europe. Jon Saxton's article represents the views of many who are troubled by what they perceive as UCS's clean bill of health to increased NATO conventional armaments when a conventional war could easily lead to the total destruction of Europe.(The available conventional fire power in Europe is now twenty times greater than in World War II.)

In fact, numerous studies, including that of the UCS, indicate that a relatively small expenditure on conventional weapons, defensive in character, could adequately bolster Europe's conventional deterrent. In the meantime, another danger is being created by the provocative escalation of "near nuclear" conventional weapons by NATO. For example, the increasingly talked about Airland Battle strategy for deep strikes against Soviet controlled territory with high technology conventional warheads is likely to be highly destabilizing since it increase Soviet incentives to launch their own pre-emptive strikes, probably with nuclear weapons.

A negotiated freeze would obviously release enormous amounts of money. These billions of dollars could be used to restore social program cuts, reduce the federal deficit, and to fund health, agricultural and education programs in the less developed countries. Additionally, as Lloyd Dumas suggests, the government should combine initiatives aimed at retraining and reemploying workers affected by the Freeze with funding for economic infrastructure projects such as railroads, mass transit, and the promotion of alternative energy and conservation measures. Some groups, like the Machinists Union, are proposing programs for rebuilding basic American industry by redirecting capital from military industries to industries badly in need of modernized productive capacities. Conversion from military production to civilian investment is a prerequisite to revitalizing the U.S. economy. Yet, as he acknowledges, such "peace conversion" is not a simple process. The prospects for success are intimately related to the successful implementation of innovative programs at both the local and national level. This was indeed done following World War II and there is no reason that it cannot be done again.

Probably no document in recent memory has received more press than the Catholic Bishops' Pastoral Letter. The Bishops evaluated nuclear weapons in relationship to "just-war" criteria and found absolutely no justification for the use of such weapons. Surely the Roman Catholic Bishops are correct to challenge superpower morality. At no time in history have we more urgently needed to clarify the legitimate purposes for which power is acquired and used. But the Bishops also wanted to create obstacles to any overhasty (or unilateral) attempts to do away with nuclear weapons. They describe their perspective on U.S.-Soviet relationships as one of "cold realism" and they attempted to balance the nuclear danger against the need to protect "the independence and freedom of nations and entire peoples." That is why the Bishops declared that the doctrine of deterrence may be considered temporarily as morally tolerable, on the condition that it serves as a means of bringing about a process of nuclear disarmament. McGeorge Bundy caught the sense of the Bishops' moral analysis when he commented "In our current debate (the Bishops') strict conditions may be more significant than their approval."

Deterrence, as Theodore Draper remarked elsewhere, now rivals freedom in the number of crimes committed in its name. The editors, not surprisingly, reserve for themselves the last word in a critique of a Harvard University study. Our quarrel with the Ivy League professors is over their support for the doctrine of extended deterrence which calls upon the threat or use of nuclear weapons to resist or deter perceived acts of conventional aggression which undermine American hegemony anywhere in the world. We emphasize that it is completely unjustified to call upon nuclear weapons to police a *Pax Americana*.

Short of significant change in international relations and domestic politics, the goal of "zero nuclear weapons" will be difficult if not impossible to achieve. Without some form of world govenment, full nuclear disarmament is not only utopian but quite possibly dangerous—Jonathen Schell, in the *New Yorker*, has recently made an intriguing but in the final analysis unconvincing case for complete nuclear disarmament under today's political structure. Our acceptance of a position of minimum deterrence is, like the Bishops', "strictly conditioned." Nuclear weapons must be pushed far into the background of world politics and their "use" limited to a single narrow purpose—to prevent the actual use of such weapons by others. Nuclear disarmament must be an idea whose time has come.

Chapter 25

A False START

Christopher Paine

Even while promising to abide by the SALT II agreement as long as the Russians do, President Ronald Reagan continues to criticize it for "simply legitimizing the arms race," and for its failure to close the notorious "window of vulnerability," which allegedly encourages Soviet leaders to believe they could destroy the U.S. land-based missile force.

With these strategic concerns firmly engraved in the public record, one would expect the Administration's Strategic Arms Reduction Talks (START) proposal to address them. It doesn't. The proposal omits *qualitative* controls over the arms race altogether, and the particular combination of *quantitative* restraints envisioned will do nothing to lessen land-based missile vulnerability. In fact, the most likely ratios of forces under the proposal make the problem even worse.

The START Proposal

The START proposal is built around a one-third cut in the number of warheads carried by U.S. and Soviet land- and sea-based long-range ballistic missiles. These warheads would be reduced from their present total of approximately 7,500 on each side to 5,000 over a period of perhaps five to ten years. The reductions in warheads would be accompanied by a parallel reduction in missiles to 850 on each side, with no more than 2,500 warheads permitted on the remaining land-based missiles.

Upon close examination, this proposal appears largely designed to wrap the Administration's ambitious strategic modernization program in an insulating blanket of arms control. While representing a baby-step forward in its recognition that "more is not necessarily better," START is vulnerable to the same criticism President Reagan leveled at SALT—"it simply legitimizes the arms race." In support of this proposition, one may observe the following:

—The proposal concerns only the *number* of long-range ballistic missiles and warheads. It does not address, and thus will not constrain, new *types* of ballistic missiles, bombers and long-range cruise missiles, reentry vehicles and warheads. START would thus allow this and future Administrations to recoup reductions in ballistic missile warheads by following through on the planned deployment of some 5,000 cruise missiles on 240 B-52 G/H and 100 B-1 bombers, not to mention that additional warheads could be carried by the so-called "Stealth" bomber now under development. Since measures to control long-range nuclear-armed cruise missiles have been postponed to an as yet ill-defined "second phase" of the negotiations, it would appear that Reagan intends to use the threat of their unconstrained deployment as a lever to induce the Soviets to accept the deep reductions in land-based ICBM warheads which he contends are essential for "stability." In return, the United States will offer as yet undisclosed restraints on air-launched cruise missiles.

This is similar to the strategy pursued by President Carter in March 1977 when he tried to squeeze the Soviets with the Hobbesian choice of the Vladivostok ballistic missile ceilings without cruise limitations or heavy-missile "Deep Cuts" with cruise constraints. Predictably, the Soviets rejected both, and are likely to do the same this time around. At the very least, such pressure tactics will complicate and protract the negotiations. Although considerably behind the United States in cruise missile technology, the Soviets can be expected eventually to exploit this loophole in the START proposal if it is allowed to remain open.

—The proposal exempts nuclear armed submarine-launched cruise missiles, and does not even address the modernization or reduction of some 17,000 nuclear weapons which can be deployed on a wide variety of short-range torpedoes, air defense missiles, depth charges, anti-submarine rockets, battlefield missiles, artillery and aircraft. The proliferation of warheads for this "tactical" dimension of the arms race would be allowed to continue, and indeed, might be given increased impetus under the President's narrowly construed "reductions" program.

—The reduction in land-based ICBM warheads to no more than 2,500 involves no sacrifices for the United States, as the 25 percent of its nuclear deterrent forces carried by ICBMs is already 350 warheads *below* the proposed ceiling. The Soviet Union, on the other hand, is some 3,400 warheads *above* it, the consequence of deploying some 70 percent of its nuclear deterrent on ICBMs, and thus it would have to scrap some 350 to 1,000 missiles, depending on the particular combination of single warhead and MIRVed missiles chosen.

—The proposal will easily accommodate the planned modernization of the U.S. ICBM force by allowing the replacement of 2,150 existing .17-megaton and .34-megaton warheads with up to 2,500 high-yield, accurate "silo-killing" warheads such as the 600-kiloton advanced ballistic reentry vehicle.

—Likewise, reductions from the current level of 5,300 submarine-launched ballistic missile warheads to levels consistent with the combined limit of 5,000 warheads could be accomplished through the already planned retirement of some 3,000 40-kiloton Poseidon missile warheads, deployed on 19 Lafayette-class submarines which were not selected for modernization with the Trident I missile. These Poseidon warheads are now awaiting retirement pending the phase-in of the new Ohio-class submarine equipped with Trident I and II missiles. For example, there would be room under the proposed ceilings to deploy 250 eight-MIRV MX on land, retain the current 12 Lafayette-class submarines equipped with Trident I missiles, and deploy the ten already authorized Ohio-class submarines equipped with Trident II silo-killing missiles (six high-yield warheads per missile).

—By failing to constrain deployments of more accurate and higher yield weapons, the Reagan START proposal fails to close the "window of vulnerability." In fact it would appear to open it wider for both sides, but especially for the Soviet side, by dramatically reducing the number of Soviet ICBMs while allowing new deployments (MX and Trident II) aimed at increasing U.S. capabilities to destroy Soviet silos.

—U.S. nuclear and non-nuclear means for destroying Soviet ballistic missile submarines also would not be constrained by the proposal. Since the Soviet geostrategic and technological

432 Search for Sanity

position with respect to both the offensive and defensive aspects of submarine warfare is weaker than the American, the increased Soviet reliance on sea-based systems required by Reagan's proposal, coupled with its lack of restraints on U.S. anti-submarine and countersilo weapons programs, may cause the Soviets to reject the proposal on purely military grounds alone, quite apart from its political deficiencies in requiring unequal concessions on the Soviet side.

—As for the Administration's assertion that its proposal would lead to greater "stability" in a crisis, this is far from being the assured outcome. Currently, the ratio of Soviet ICBM warheads to U.S. silos is about five to one. Assuming deployment of an eight-MIRV MX in fixed silos or some other readily targetable land-based mode, this ratio would remain at best something close to five to one, even after reductions are implemented. Thus the pressure for some kind of multiple aimpoint scheme for the MX would persist under a START treaty regime, but the Soviets' potential for deploying large numbers of additional warheads to overwhelm the system *would* be limited under START. However, the ratio of U.S. ICBM warheads to Soviet ICBM targets would be *improved* from about 1.5 to one to about five to one. Simultaneously, significant additional counterforce capability could be deployed via the Trident II, boosting the U.S. warhead-to-silo ratio to about eight to one. When they favor the Soviet Union—as they have in recent years—ratios considerably less than this one are said to be terribly destablizing. However, when the tables are turned in favor of the United States, the situation is described by Reagan Administration officials as one of "restoring" strategic stability. This kind of strategic doublethink bodes ill for meaningful arms negotiations.

Despite the overwhelming evidence of the past decade that parity is the best that can be obtained from the nuclear arms competition, the Reagan Administration seems to be trying to resurrect a U.S. "assured" or "disarming" second-strike capability—an ability to counter hypothetical Soviet conventional or limited nuclear attack with a range of preemptive nuclear retaliatory strikes which could disarm Soviet forces. Apparently the Administration believes it can attain this goal through a judicious combination of limited arms reductions and significant arms modernization.

Reagan's Opposition to the Freeze

Other than the terms of the proposal itself, what additional evidence is there to support this view?

There is the Administration's steadfast opposition to the freeze, and the frequent statements of senior government officials supporting this position. The Administration opposes the nuclear freeze resolution offered by Senators Edward Kennedy and Mark Hatfield on the grounds that it would leave the Soviets with "a definite margin of superiority."

Aside from the technical irrelevance of the Administration's objection—the resolution does not require an immediate freeze but merely immediate negotiations on "when and how" to obtain one, leaving the way open for making desired reductions in the price of a freeze—the constant assertion that the United States is inferior to the Soviet Union in overall strategic power is simply not borne out by the facts. But even if it were, it would not constitute a *sufficient* argument against the freeze: if we are indeed behind now, why should we necessarily be any *less* behind in the future? Sadly, the President's assertion during his March 31, 1982 news conference that "the Soviet's great edge is in their ability to absorb our retaliatory attack and hit us again" is simply incoherent. Such a capacity cannot usefully be regarded as an "edge." First, taking advantage of it would involve the deliberate sacrifice of tens of millions of Soviet citizens. Second, were we to strike the Soviet Union in an initial attack, we too could absorb their retaliatory blow and hit *them* again. The President was not expressing a Soviet advantage, but an inevitable reality of mutual assured destruction. What is most disturbing about the statement is that the President obviously feels that the United States should take steps to assure that the Soviets could *not* "hit us again."

In fact, the whole debate over the desirability of a freeze essentially revolves around the ostensible size and characteristics of Soviet and U.S. "residual" forces—that is, those hypothetically remaining after a first "exchange" of nuclear weapons has occurred. The Reagan Administration believes the U.S. force should contain an "enduring" land-based component of high accuracy capable of destroying Soviet ICBM silos, hardened command posts, and other targets in a possibly "protracted" nuclear war. It also wants a B-1 bomber for "post-attack reconnaissance" and destruction of mobile and "deeply buried" targets. These and other nuclear weapons programs would be stopped by a freeze, and thus the United States could find itself at a disadvantage in prosecuting the prospective second and third rounds of a nuclear war. Those who advocate a freeze find this nuclear war-fighting posture conceptually and morally impossible to assimilate.

The Reagan Administration further believes that a "protracted" nuclear war capability is essential for deterring Soviet "nuclear coercion" and conventional attacks against NATO allies and Japan, because such large-scale conventional and limited nuclear threats could best be countered by the threat of a U.S. nuclear second strike which would disarm Soviet forces in a given theater of operations, or if necessary, completely destroy the Soviet nuclear deterrent.

Moreover, the Administration apparently believes that the Soviet Union has outstripped the United States in building preemptive nuclear war-fighting capabilities which it believes are essential for deterrence. Specifically, officials allege that the Soviet force of some 668 SS-18 and SS-19 missiles, carrying some 5,240 warheads under SALT II counting rules (the actual number is less) is capable of destroying virtually all of the 1,052 missiles in the U.S. ICBM force. Thus in opposing the freeze, the Reagan Administration frequently makes the following argument: either the United States must rectify the "war-fighting" imbalance in "residual" ICBMs by deploying a new, ostensibly more survivable, land-based ICBM (MX) which can threaten Soviet ICBMs, or a program to deploy such a missile must be used at the bargaining table to bring about "unequal reduction to (allegedly) more equal levels."

The American Advantage

Is the current Soviet preemptive threat really greater than the U.S. threat, and is this provocative quest for "leverage" at the table in Geneva really necessary in order to obtain an equitable agreement?

By the Reagan Administration's own estimate, Soviet ICBM accuracy improvements will not be fully deployed until the latter half of the decade. Under questioning, Defense Secretary Caspar Weinberger admitted that the Pentagon's public assessment concerning Soviet ICBM capabilities "are mixtures of projections and current abilities." In fact, there is still time for a freeze to have a considerable effect in arresting Minuteman's hypothetical demise.

More importantly, however, the United States actually poses a greater preemptive threat to the *total* Soviet deterrent force than the Soviet Union poses to the *total* U.S. force. Because some 5,200 warheads—some two-thirds of the Soviet nuclear deterrent—are concentrated in only 668 MIRVed SS-18 and SS-19 missiles, these missiles are theoretically vulnerable to preemptive attack from the 2,150 U.S. ICBM warheads, 900 of which have an accuracy-yield combination explicitly designed to attack hardened silos. A relatively small number of additional weapons would be needed to destroy Soviet non-alert strategic bombers (the entire force) and the 85 percent of the Soviet submarine-launched ballistic missile force usually in port on any given day. Thus Pentagon planners can nominally destroy some 80 percent of the Soviet strategic deterrent in a preemptive attack on paper while using up less than a third of the U.S. arsenal.

The Soviet planner, by contrast, would have to plan on using some 2,000 ICBM warheads (one-quarter of their total force) to destroy the bulk of the U.S. ICBM force (just one-quarter of the U.S. deterrent.) Only one-third of the U.S. submarines are in port at any given time, and roughly one-third of the U.S. bombers are kept on alert and would likely survive a surprise attack. Thus on paper the Soviet planner can destroy on the order of 55 percent of the U.S. deterrent in a surprise attack.

The point of reviewing these obviously arbitrary, and for the most part, foolish scenarios is to demonstrate that the "window of vulnerability," which the Reagan Administration contends is the major obstacle to a freeze, either does not exist—because of one's judgement of the technical and operational complexities involved—or exists for *both* sides, in which case the Soviets have a larger "window" than the United States.

Assuming that this analysis has also been performed by the Reagan Administration, one is tempted to conclude that the continuing official preoccupation with Soviet ICBM "superiority" is less a sincerely held conviction than a deliberate ruse to lead the START talks down a blind alley, thereby generating an impression of Soviet intransigence at the bargaining table which will justify completion of the planned nuclear buildup.

Certainly no one in the Administration manifests much anxiety over the prospect of *not* reaching an agreement. The President manages to betray his lack of enthusiasm for arms control even when he and his advisors are consciously *trying* to project a "peace-loving" image. For example, his Memorial Day announcement that START talks would begin June 29 included a less-than-stirring call for "treaties that can *someday* bring about a reduction in the terrible arms of destruction."

Escalating the Arms Race

Former Arms Control and Disarmament Agency (ACDA) Director Eugene Rostow was more than willing to acknowledge publicly the President's subliminal arms control timetable. Rostow told the annual meeting of the American Institute of Aeronautics and Astronautics, "Unless collective security is fully and visibly restored, we in ACDA are going to wear out the seats of a good many pairs of pants during the next couple of years." Arms control negotiations, he warned, are not "a substitute for programs designed to restore the military balance with the Soviet Union."

The Administration is having a tough time finding support within its own ranks even for ratification of two minor agreements negotiated during the Nixon-Ford years—the Threshold Test Ban and Peaceful Nuclear Explosion Treaties. Rostow told the Senate Foreign Relations Committee that he had "run into a profound stone wall" in trying to talk "whole phalanxes and battalions" of officials out of their belief that "given the uncertainties of the nuclear situation and the need for new weapons and modernization, we are going to need testing, and perhaps testing above the 150-kiloton limit."

Consistent with this view, the Administration recently submitted a revised budget request for nuclear weapons testing and production, raising the level of the requested increase from $800 million to $1.2 billion over this year's $4.5 billion nuclear weapons budget, yielding a total of $5.7 billion for the coming year. If passed this represents an astounding 70 percent increase in the nuclear weapons budget in just two years.

What will we do with all these new weapons? "Protracted" nuclear wars are thought to require many more warheads than strategically unfashionable "spasm" wars. "We don't believe a nuclear war can be won," Secretary of Defense Weinberger told ABC News in June. Nevertheless he vowed, "We are planning to prevail if we are attacked."

"Prevailing with pride," remarked White House advisor Thomas C. Reed at the Armed Forces Communications and Electronics Association meeting in June 1982, "is the principal new ingredient of American foreign policy."

Chapter 26

A Call To Halt The Arms Race

To improve national and international security, the United States and the Soviet Union should stop the nuclear arms race. Specifically, they should adopt a mutual freeze on the testing, production and deployment of nuclear weapons and of missiles and new aircraft designed primarily to deliver nuclear weapons. This is an essential, verifiable first step toward lessening the risk of nuclear war and reducing the nuclear arsenals.

The horror of a nuclear holocaust is universally acknowledged. Today, the United States and the Soviet Union possess 50,000 nuclear weapons. In half an hour, a fraction of these weapons could destroy all cities in the northern hemisphere. Yet, over the next decade, the U.S.A. and U.S.S.R. plan to build over 20,000 more nuclear warheads, along with a new generation of nuclear missiles and aircraft.

The weapon programs of the next decade, if not stopped, will pull the nuclear tripwire tighter. Counterforce and other "nuclear warfighting" systems will improve the ability of the U.S.A. and U.S.S.R. to attack the opponent's nuclear forces and other military targets. This will increase the pressure on both sides to use their nuclear weapons in a crisis, rather than risk losing them in a first strike.

437

Such developments will increase hairtrigger readiness for a massive nuclear exchange at a time when economic difficulties, political dissension, revolution and competition for energy supplies may be rising worldwide. At the same time, more countries may acquire nuclear weapons. Unless we change this combination of trends, the danger of nuclear war will be greater in the late 1980s and 1990s than ever before.

Rather than permit this dangerous future to evolve, the United States and the Soviet Union should stop the arms race.

A freeze on nuclear missiles and aircraft can be verified by existing national means. A total freeze can be verified more easily than the complex SALT I and II agreements. The freeze on warhead production could be verified by the Safeguards of the International Atomic Energy Agency. Stopping the production of nuclear weapons and weapon-grade material and applying the Safeguards to U.S. and Soviet nuclear programs would increase the incentive of other countries to adhere to the Nonproliferation Treaty, renouncing acquisition of their own nuclear weapons, and to accept the same Safeguards.

A freeze would hold constant the existing nuclear parity between the United States and the Soviet Union. By precluding production of counterforce weaponry on either side, it would eliminate excuses for further arming on both sides. Later, following the immediate adoption of the freeze, its terms should be negotiated into the more durable form of a treaty.

A nuclear-weapons freeze, accompanied by government-aided conversion of nuclear industries, would save at least $100 billion each in U.S. and Soviet military spending over the rest of the decade. This would reduce inflation. The savings could be applied to balance the budget, reduce taxes, improve services, subsidize renewable energy, or increase aid to poverty-stricken third world regions. By shifting personnel to more labor-intensive civilian jobs, a nuclear weapons freeze would also raise employment.

Stopping the U.S.-Soviet nuclear arms race is the single most useful step that can be taken now to reduce the likelihood of nuclear war and to prevent the spread of nuclear weapons to more countries. This step is a necessary prelude to creating international conditions in which: further steps can be taken toward a stable, peaceful international order; the threat of first use of nuclear weaponry can be ended; the freeze can be extended to other nations; and the nuclear arsenals on all sides can be drastically reduced or eliminated, making the world truly safe from nuclear destruction.

Scope of the Freeze

1.) Underground nuclear tests should be suspended, pending final agreement on a comprehensive test ban treaty.

2.) There should be a freeze on testing, production and deployment of all missiles and new aircraft which have nuclear weapons as their sole or main payload. This includes:

U.S. Delivery Vehicles	Soviet Delivery Vehicles
In Production:	*In Production:*
Improved Minuteman ICBM	SS-19 ICBM
Trident I SLBM	SS-N-18 SLBM
Air-launched cruise missile	SS-20 IRBM
(ALCM)	Backfire bomber
In Development:	*In Development:*
MX ICBM	SS-17, SS-18, SS-19
Trident II SLBM	ICBM improvements
Long-range ground- and sea-	New ICBM
launched cruise missiles	New SLBM (SS-N-20)
(GLCM, SLCM)	
Pershing II IRBM	
New bomber	

3.) The number of land- and submarine-based launch tubes for nuclear missiles should be frozen. Replacement subs could be built to keep the force constant, but with no net increase in SLBM tubes and no new missiles.

4.) No further MIRVing or other changes to existing missiles and bomber loads would be permitted.

All of the above measures can be verified by existing national means of verification with high confidence.

The following measures cannot be verified nationally with the same confidence, but an effort should be made to include them:

5.) Production of fissionable material (enriched uranium and plutonium) for weapon purposes should be halted.

6.) Production of nuclear weapons (bombs) should be halted.

There are two arguments for attempting to include these somewhat less verifiable steps. First, with a halt to additional and new delivery vehicles, there will be no need for additional bombs. Thus, production of weapon-grade fissionable material and bombs would probably stop in any event. Second, the establishment of a *universal* ban on production of weapon-grade fissionable material and nuclear bombs, verified by international inspection as established now for non-nuclear-weapon states under the Nonproliferation Treaty and the International Atomic Energy Agency, would greatly strengthen that treaty and improve the prospects for halting the spread of nuclear weapons.

The Agreement to Freeze

The U.S. and Soviet governments should announce a moratorium on all further testing, production and deployment of nuclear weapons and nuclear delivery vehicles, to be verified by national means. The freeze would be followed by negotiations to incorporate the moratorium in a treaty. The negotiations would cover supplementary verification measures, such as IAEA inspections; and possible desirable exceptions from the freeze, such as an occasional confidence test.

This procedure follows the precedent of the 1958-1961 nuclear-weapon test moratorium, in which testing was suspended while the U.S.A., U.S.S.R. and U.K. negotiated a partial test ban treaty.

Relation to SALT Negotiations

The bilateral freeze is aimed at being introduced in the early 1980s, as soon as sufficient popular and political support is developed to move the governments toward its adoption.

The freeze would prevent dangerous developments in the absence of a SALT treaty. It would preclude exploitation of loopholes in past treaties and, at the same time, satisfy critics who are concerned that the SALT process may not succeed in stopping the arms race.

The freeze should not replace the SALT negotiating process, but should supplement and strengthen it. The freeze could be adopted as a replacement for SALT II or as an immediate follow-on, with the task of putting the moratorium into treaty language the job of SALT III.

The Case for a Nuclear-Weapons Freeze

There are many reasons to support a halt to the nuclear arms race at this time:

Parity—There is widespread agreement that parity exists between the U.S. and Soviet nuclear forces at present.

Avoiding "Nuclear Warfighting" Developments—The next generation U.S. and Soviet nuclear weapons improve "nuclear warfighting" capabilities—that is, they improve the ability to knock out the enemy's forces in what is termed a "limited" nuclear exchange. Having such capabilities will undermine the sense of parity, spur further weapon developments and increase the likelihood of nuclear war in a crisis, especially if conflict with conventional weapons has started. It is of overriding importance to stop these developments.

Stopping the MX and New Soviet ICBMS—Specifically, a freeze would prevent the deployment of new and improved Soviet ICBMs, which are expected to render U.S. ICBMs vulnerable to preemptive attack. This would obviate the need for the costly and environmentally-destructive U.S. mobile MX ICBM, with its counterforce capability against Soviet ICBMs. That, in turn, would avoid pressure for the U.S.S.R. to deploy its own mobile ICBMs in the 1990s.

Stopping the Cruise Missile—The new U.S. cruise missile, just entering production in an air-launched version and still in development in ground- and sea-launched versions, threatens to make negotiated, nationally-verified nuclear arms control far more difficult. Modern low-flying, terrain-guided cruise missiles are relatively small and cheap and can be deployed in large numbers on virtually any launching platform: not only bombers, but also tactical aircraft, surface ships, tactical submarines, and various ground vehicles. They are easy to conceal and, unlike ICBMs, their numbers cannot be observed from satellites. If the United States continues the development and production of cruise missiles, the U.S.S.R. will be likely to follow suit in 5-10 years; and quantitative limits on the two sides will be impossible to verify. A freeze would preclude this development.

Preserving European Security—A freeze would also prevent a worsening of the nuclear balance in Europe. To date the U.S.S.R. has replaced less than half of its medium-range nuclear missiles and bombers with the new SS-20 missile and Backfire bomber. The United States is planning to add hundreds of Pershing II and ground-launched cruise missiles to the forward-based nuclear systems in Europe, capable of reaching the U.S.S.R. Negotiations conducted *after* additional Soviet medium-range weapons are deployed are likely to leave Europe with more nuclear arms on both sides and with less security than it has today. It is important to freeze before the Soviet weapons grow to large numbers, increasing pressure for a U.S. response and committing both sides to permanently higher nuclear force levels.

Stopping the Spread of Nuclear Arms—There is a slim chance of stopping the spread of nuclear weapons if the two superpowers stop their major nuclear arms race. The freeze would help the U.S.A. and U.S.S.R. meet their legal and political obligations under the Nonproliferation Treaty. It would make the renunciation of nuclear weapons by other countries somewhat more equitable and politically feasible. In addition, a U.S.-Soviet freeze would encourage a halt in the nuclear weapons programs of other countries which are known or believed to have nuclear weapons or nuclear technology. These are Britain, France and China, with publicly-acknowledged nuclear weapons programs, and India, Israel and South Africa, without acknowledged programs.

Timing—There is a unique opportunity to freeze U.S. and Soviet nuclear arms in the 1980s. The Soviets have offered to negotiate the further deployment of their medium-range nuclear forces and submarine-based forces. Given the pressure to respond to new weapons on both sides and the existing nuclear parity, an equally opportune time for a freeze may not recur for many years.

Popular Appeal—Campaigns to stop individual weapon systems are sometimes treated as unilateral disarmament or circumvented by the development of alternative systems. The pros and cons of the SALT II Treaty are too technical for the patience of the average person. In contrast, an effort to stop the development and production of all U.S. and Soviet nuclear weapons is simple, straight-forward, effective and mutual; and for all these reasons it is likely to have great popular appeal. This is essential for creating the scale of popular support that is needed to make nuclear arms control efforts successful.

Economic Benefits—Although nuclear forces take only a small part of U.S. and Soviet military spending, they do cost some tens of billions of dollars annually. About half of these funds go to existing nuclear forces, while half are budgeted for the testing, production and deployment of new warheads and delivery systems. A nuclear-weapon freeze, accompanied by government-aided conversion of nuclear industries to civilian production, would yield several important economic benefits:

—About $100 billion each (at 1981 prices) would be saved by the United States and the Soviet Union over the period from 1981 to 1990 in unnecessary military spending.

—The saving could be applied to balance the budget; reduce taxes; improve services now being cut back; subsidize home and commercial conversion to safe, renewable energy resources; or increase economic aid to poverty-stricken third world regions, thereby defusing some of the tinderboxes of international conflict.

—With the shift of personnel to more labor-intensive civilian jobs, employment would rise. At the same time, the highly inflationary pressure of military spending would be mitigated.

Verification

The comprehensive nature of a total freeze on nuclear weapons testing, production, deployment (and, by implication, development) would facilitate verification.

Long-range bomber and missile production would be proscribed. The letter of assurance attached to the draft SALT II Treaty that the U.S.S.R. will not increase its rate of production of Backfire bombers indicates not only *deployment* but also *production* of the relatively large aircraft and missiles in question can be observed with considerable confidence. While concealed production and stockpiling of aircraft and missiles is theoretically possible, it would be extraordinarily difficult to accomplish with no telltale construction or supply. Any attempt would require the building or modification of plants and the development of new transport lines that are not operational at present. It would also involve high risks of detection and high penalties in worsening relations without offering any significant strategic advantage.

Verification of a ban on *tests* of missiles designed to carry nuclear weapons can be provided with high confidence by existing satellite and other detection systems. Here, too, a comprehensive approach is easier to verify than a partial or limited one.

Verification of aircraft, missile and submarine *deployments*, by specific quantity, is already provided under the terms of the SALT II and SALT I Treaty language. Verifying *no* additional deployments or major modifications will be considerably easier, in fact, than checking compliance with specific numerical ceilings in a continually changing environment.

Verification of a comprehensive nuclear *weapon test* ban, the subject of study and negotiation for many years, has been determined to be possible within the terms of the existing draft comprehensive test ban treaty.

Chapter 27

The Freeze: From Strategy to Social Movement

Michael Kazin

The single issue has long been a staple of American politics. From the pre-Civil War abolitionists to woman suffragists in the late nineteenth and early twentieth centuries to anti-war organizers in the 1960s and 70s, activists who focus their energies on a solitary cause have been able to transform the views of millions and to sway the decisions of state. In the process, they catalyzed movements which—with a broader agenda and a vital internal life—penetrated deep into the nation's political culture.

The outcry against nuclear weapons, with the nuclear freeze campaign at its core, has not yet matured into that type of movement. As I write (in the summer of 1983), the movement has in fact suffered reverses which throw into question its ability to stop the production of a single missile, much less survive to have a more profound effect upon American society. In May, 1983, the House of Representatives passed a freeze resolution by over 120 votes, but only after Republicans and conservative Democrats delayed the decision by two months and deprived freeze campaigners of the clear victory they had expected. Moreover, only weeks after the vote on that symbolic resolution, the House appropriated funds for the MX and

Pershing-II missiles—extremely accurate, high-speed weapons which peace groups had lobbied vigorously to stop.

An additional roadblock lies in the high visibility enjoyed by elite critics of the freeze—even those critics who are not identified with the Reagan administration. Leslie Gelb, national security correspondent for the *New York Times* and the Harvard Nuclear Study Group—largely composed of professors who are, like Gelb, former policy makers—oppose the freeze in the name of "practical arms control" and privileged knowledge of the complexity of arms negotiations.[1] They seek to manage the arms race, rescuing it from the political pressure of "extremists" whether resolute hawks or advocates of a total freeze on new weapons. Above all, the arms controllers want to leave expert representatives of the super-powers alone to make cautious, gradual decisions, free from sustained public scrutiny or dissent. Although he came into office as a strong critic of past arms control treaties, Ronald Reagan has sounded more and more like a convert to this way of thinking. In 1983, he largely shelved bellicose threats against the USSR and began to speak of his desire for verifiable reductions and an end to the nuclear danger. Thus, in a predictable process, elite writers and politicians have learned to acknowledge the protests in order to dilute and circumvent their impact.

Despite these developments, I believe the freeze campaign remains the best hope for building a long-term movement against nuclear weaponry. The freeze was launched in the spring of 1980 with a statement written by Randall Forsberg (the same time as the more radical Appeal for European Nuclear Disarmament, drafted by E.P. Thompson). The freeze was conceived as a demand which millions of Americans could understand. In this way it would be a contrast to earlier, abortive efforts to stop individual weapons, or efforts to help pass the more complicated SALT-II Treaty. Quickly, the freeze became the major alternative to Reagan's nuclear policy and the shared chorus of an elaborate medley of groups opposed to the arms race. This coalition is still new, fragile, and of uneven strength—both socially and regionally. Against the well-entrenched plans of the two super-powers, its victory is obviously not assured. However, I think an honest evaluation of what the anti-nuclear groundswell has already accomplished must acknowledge the indispensability of a popular, forceful demand for a freeze. The troubles of the freeze campaign are a problem for us all.

What follows then is one activist's perspective on the politics of the movement against nuclear weapons. Throughout the essay, I assume that nuclear disarmament is a process which, once seriously undertaken, will take many years to complete. There will be multiple shifts of official rhetoric and policy, tactical alliances and international crises along the road to a saner world. Peace activists have to look beyond the next vote in Congress or the dangers posed by the latest weapons system. The twin needs for immediate victories and a long-term movement committed to disarmament will often clash. To grasp either pole exclusively, however, is a grave mistake. It took many decades and a variety of tactics to win the abolition of slavery and votes for women. The elimination of nuclear arsenals would mean the reversal of a pattern of human behavior—the search for security in better weapons—that is as old as recorded history. It will require the timing of a canny politico, the savvy of a good community organizer, and the vision of a messianic prophet. Without all three, the mass desire for peace will not become a movement that can sustain itself until the end is in sight.

All peace activists, whatever their opinion of the freeze concept, should learn to think *strategically*. While unilateral disarmament may be morally virtuous, it is a political impossibility. Furthermore, advocating the speedy elimination of American weapons does not protect the movement from being folded into the agenda of liberal politicians or the Democratic Party. On the contrary, to demand one's ultimate goal and nothing less leaves the shaping of policy ever more firmly in the hands of those who would continue the Cold War through more pragmatic means than Reagan employs. Only by posing significant but realistic goals, and mobilizing a coalition to win them can we put the anti-war movement on the offensive.

Accomplishments of the Freeze

The originators of the freeze campaign viewed it as a political strategy to hasten their goal of nuclear and conventional disarmament. What has the freeze achieved since the spring of 1980?

First, it provided an easily understood yet profound rallying cry for Americans who, since the bombing of Hiroshima, dreaded nuclear war but seldom found a way to convert their fear into activism. The movement against nuclear testing in the late 1950s and early 1960s mobilized a wide array of organizations and enjoyed, according to the Gallup Poll, almost 80 percent public support.[2] Yet, the 1963 US-USSR Treaty banning tests in the atmosphere caused the movement to dwindle into a small band of campaigners known mostly to each other. The freeze, because it demands a halt to the production, deployment, and testing of all nuclear weapons and delivery systems, cannot easily be co-opted by a super-power agreement which would allow the continued stockpiling of warheads and the refinement of any first-strike missiles.

The constituency the freeze campaign has engaged is truly massive. It represents several "mainstream" parts of the population as well as the liberal left which embraced the issue with a unanimity and enthusiasm not seen since the last American soldier left Indochina. The vast majority of religious institutions strongly support the freeze; Methodists, Presbyterians, and especially Roman Catholics lend funds and meeting space as well as spiritual legitimacy. From a wide range of professional groups—most prominently physicians but also lawyers, research scientists, architects, journalists, and academics in every field - come articulate and well-publicized critiques of administration policy.

A sizeable contingent of middle-level labor officials (though few members of the AFL-CIO Executive Board) endorse the freeze, condemn the bloated military budget, and recognize the necessity of industrial conversion. Officials from the Machinists (IAM), Clothing and Textile Workers (ACTWU), Food and Commerical Workers (UFCW), Service Employees (SEIU), and National Education Association (NEA) are the most visible, but anti-nuclear sentiment is also widespread among the rank and file. Polls consistently show a majority of blue-collar workers supporting the freeze.[3] In 1982, the annual convention of the California Labor Federation would have endorsed that state's freeze initiative if an alarmed Lane Kirkland hadn't threatened to put the 1.8 million-member body into receivership.

The freeze's original identity as a project for white liberals and its reluctance to address the ongoing urban economic crisis have hampered the campaign's spread to blacks and Latins. Yet, the pattern of the 1982 election (in which freeze initiatives swept every non-white urban community where they were on the ballot), the strong endorsement by the Congressional Black Caucus, and candidate Jesse Jackson's enthusiasm for the issue indicate the depth of support among Afro-Americans, passive as it may seem to whites. In Alabama, where traditional conservatism and high employment in military industries have limited the campaign to handfuls of veteran peace and civil rights organizers, the only city council to pass a freeze resolution as of spring 1983 was that of Tuskegee, a predominantly black university town.

The second major success of the freeze strategy has been to

translate the apolitical horror of a possible nuclear war into electoral clout. The tactic of mounting local and state initiatives was begun in November, 1980, by Randy Kehler and others at the Traprock Peace Center in western Massachusetts. The initiatives neatly combined a method for recruiting grassroots volunteers and staff members with a way to put pressure on elected officials. By the end of 1982, the freeze had won the votes of about 30 percent of the American electorate and lost only one of ten state referenda (in Arizona). In the cynical words of Alexander Cockburn and James Ridgeway, "Freeze resolutions have become almost cognate to voting for mom and apple pie."[4]

This respectability helped parry Reagan's wild attempts to connect freeze leaders with the KGB, and it enabled the campaign to win House endorsement, albeit in diluted form. It also sparked a successful lobbying campaign in December, 1982, against the dense-pack basing mode for the MX missile. In March, 1983, when Reagan clothed a new anti-ballistic missile program in exotic space-age garments, pro-freeze speakers gained almost equal time to expose it as a dangerous fantasy.

In addition, buoyed by the popularity of the freeze, a group of sixty to seventy anti-militarist Congresspeople have become more consistent and aggressive in opposing new weapons systems such as the B-1 and Trident-II and in challenging interventionist policies in every area of the world but the Mideast. The "Vietnam Syndrome" is once more alive and kicking at the Capitol. These House members - there is not one Senator willing to risk "statesmanlike" status - include Ron Dellums, Barbara Boxer, and Don Edwards from the San Francisco Bay Area, Pat Schroeder from Colorado, Byron Dorgan from North Dakota, John Conyers from Michigan, Barney Frank and Ed Markey from Massachusetts, and Ted Weiss and Thomas Downey from New York. They hold down the beachhead of hope for a new foreign policy until the peace movement and its allies acquire the clarity of purpose and electoral strength to elect a Congress willing to reject the Pentagon's expansionist mission as well as its affection for cost-plus contracts.

The fact that these anti-militarist representatives come mainly from districts of high unemployment hints at a third result of the freeze, one the press has largely neglected in its rush to chronicle purely anti-nuclear activities. Econmics has become integral to the politics of peace. Early in 1983, the annual freeze convention endorsed and many local organizers helped plan Jobs With Peace Week, which was held in mid-April. At public hearings from Boston to Albuquerque, legislators and neighborhood activists proposed urban "peace budgets"—what cities could afford if the military didn't drain away half their taxes. In Los Angeles County (the nation's most populous), 71 union locals which originally joined together to work in the California freeze initiative turned their energies to formulating and promoting the dream budgets.

The national freeze campaign itself has published the best available guide to initiating the conversion of military industry to civilian production. Entitled *The Freeze Economy*, the long pamphlet details which American communities would be affected by a halt to nuclear weapons production and tells peace activists how to both address the potential unemployed and to develop a strategy for "alternative use planning," including support for Rep. Ted Weiss's job-replacing Defense Economic Adjustment Act. *Freeze Economy* editors Dave McFadden and Jim Wake manifest a sensitivity to the dilemma of defense workers that more "radical" advocates of disarmament often lack. "When a worker or a labor representative expresses concern about job security in the wake of a freeze," they write, "it is helpful to demonstrate that there is not only concern, but some concrete steps that are being taken to address the problem at the national level. Economic conversion, it must be acknowledged, is not a simple process. The prospects for success are intimately related to the successful implementation of innovative programs on both the local and national level."[5]

Problems for the Freeze Movement

This is a formidable balance sheet to show for three years of work: a broad and politically astute movement has been launched. Still, the arms race has not been halted and the deployment of ever more deadly "modernized" weapons hurtles ahead, almost heedless of opposition both here and abroad. Moreover, as Michael Klare and other left students of the military have charged, the freeze does not address crucial changes in the Pentagon's conventional arsenal. Klare predicts that these "near-nuclear weapons" may soon take the place of tactical or battlefield nuclear warheads (see article in this anthology). Is the freeze irrelevant to ever-advancing developments in military technology?

Unfortunately, it is one thing to journalistically expose the Pentagon's latest designs and quite another to strongly challenge their funding and deployment. A strategy which requires opposing each new weapons system would quickly exhaust organizers and cause their grassroots support to shrink. The demand for a complete nuclear freeze does risk encouraging a "nuclear pacifism" while conventional weapons proliferate. But it is also the only feasible way to coherently attack the arms race at its most vulnerable point. The freeze is a simple concept. It does not require the public to know the grisly details behind all the acronyms the technologists of death concoct. Unity behind a concept that has shown its ability to move millions is far preferable to a welter of organizations, each claiming that a different weapon is most central to military power in the 1980s.

Of course, actually winning a freeze is a far more difficult task than was establishing the popularity of the idea. Outside the circle of anti-militarists I mentioned, there is no Congressional support for scrapping the deployment of Cruise and Pershing-II missiles in Western Europe. Other new weapons, with the exception of the MX, are even less controversial than the Euromissiles and, as always, are propelled along by the "iron triangle" of Pentagon, Armed Services committees, and aerospace corporations.[6] The tradition of allowing the President to make foreign policy—unless, as in Vietnam, he fails miserably—also works against a thoroughgoing opposition to the nuclear buildup. Many lawmakers have become well-versed in bewailing "the threat to the future of mankind" while voting to fund every billion-dollar missile and space war R&D program that comes to the floor. They are, in the phrase of one peace activist, "freeze phonies."

Part of the problem admittedly lies with the single-mindedness of freeze strategy itself. While necessary to the growth of the movement that now exists, the demand that unites also tends to limit political sophistication and tactical flexibility. In my experience, few of the people who devote themselves to the repetitive but utterly essential tasks of local organizing know much about the history of the Cold War, the mechanisms of weapons procurement, or the trade-off between conventional and nuclear weaponry. Randall Forsberg is always ready with a well-documented response to Reagan's latest offer to the Soviets, but educational seeding at the grassroots has been sorely neglected.

The gathering storm of the presidential campaign will also test the movement's ability to engage in electoral politics without being imprisoned inside "lesser evil" boundaries. Whomever the Democrats nominate will give vigorous lip service to the freeze. Predictably, he will attempt to yoke mainstream peace organizations and leaders to his campaign while avoiding any firm commitment to propose a freeze at Geneva or to scrap the current administration's gargantuan missile modernization program. He will magnify rhetorical differences with

Reagan's bellicose stand but keep his powder dry.

Faced with such a choice, freeze activists must carve out an independent strategy and pursue it vigorously. They have to make clear that the goal of a *complete* halt to all phases of the arms race cannot be shelved or satisfied with half-measures. It would be ludicrous, however, to ignore the presidential race or favor a marginal third party. The overwhelming majority of citizens who want to brake the nuclear buildup will vote for Reagan's only serious opponent, whomever he may be. But a pro forma endorsement of the Democratic candidate must be accompanied by a heightened effort, dubbed "Project '84" by national freeze staff members, to elect pro-freeze representatives and Senators. In 1982, several national "peace-PACs" tested the waters, contributing to a handful of Congressional races and achieving mixed results. A more concentrated, better funded campaign—one in which local freeze campaigns are directly involved—could be a critical element in close races. Spearheaded by millionaire businessman Harold Willens, the 1982 California freeze initiative raised over $3 million. That sum of money alone, intelligently distributed, would cover the entire budget of six anti-militarist candidates for the House and perhaps two for the Senate.

A Range of Tactics

Independence also means acting outside the circumscribed terrain of parliamentary democracy. Involvement in elections does not have to compromise the principles of a mass movement. As the history of the movement against the Vietnam War attests, politicians will manipulate the popular desire for peace even if radicals righteously condemn them and counsel abstention. However, the freeze campaign must pursue its own tactics as well: street demonstrations in conjunction with our European allies, teach-ins and other dramatic educational events, local campaigns against corporations and think-tanks which design and manufacture nuclear weapons, declarations by city councils that their localities are "nuclear free zones," etc. Their ecological purism aside, the Greens in West Germany provide a good example of a movement which combines electoral work with a rich assortment of "extra-parliamentary" activities. Even without a viable third party of the left, we are also strong enough to move with confidence both on the streets and in the legislatures. With the exception of violence, I see no justification for reading any tactical approach out of the movement. As Roger Spiller, Vice-Chair of Britain's Campaign for Nuclear Disarmament, advises, "Any well-thought-out activity, whose aim is to further public understanding of the issues, must be good and must be welcomed and supported, even if it is not one's own preferred course of action."[7]

In California, for example, opponents of the arms race have used a variety of tactics to "bring home" the dangers of nuclear weapons in varied but complementary ways. They have particularly targeted the civil defense plans of the Federal Emergency Management Agency (FEMA). Scores of private and public hospitals in the state refuse to provide beds for FEMA's post-attack Civilian Military Contingency System. Many county boards of supervisors will not cooperate with its $4.2 billion nuclear evacuation scheme. And several boards of education reject its "duck-and-cover" survivalist curriculum. Meanwhile, residents of northern Mendocino County pack hearings by the hundreds to shout their disapproval of the Navy's plan to dump aging nuclear submarines into the neighboring Pacific Ocean. Most dramatically, thousands of civilly disobedient adults and children have been arrested (many of them two or three times) for blockading the gates of the Livermore Laboratories, where new weapons are designed, and the Vandenberg Air Force Base, launching pad for the MX testing program.

Freeze activists are not responsible for most of this activity, and there are tensions between some adherents of "direct action" and those who favor the tactics of strict legality.[8] Accusations that only those who "put their bodies on the line" are effective foes of nuclear weaponry echo the worst attitudes of leftists in the late 1960s. Conversely, ridiculing the sit-ins for their counter-culture style ("it seemed like all of Berkeley went to jail," a friend quipped about a recent blockade of the Livermore Labs) often misses the positive effect a determined moral stand can have on previously apathetic witnesses. The point is to mix a variety of tactics in such a way that the movement enhances its overall strength—both within Congress and among the general population. To elevate a single means of protest above all others is a form of fetishism particularly harmful to a young movement.

The growing popularity of civil disobedience among peace activists owes much to the accomplishments of the freeze campaign. The blockades, sit-ins, and women's encampments would not have attracted many participants or extensive news coverage without a well-publicized, legitimated alternative to the official gospel on nuclear weaponry. For years, the Berrigan brothers and their associates took courageous steps to draw attention to nuclear obscenity. But their acts were solitary ones until Americans began to organize around the proposal drafted by Randall Forsberg in the spring of 1980. Thus, the media's habit of identifying the "freeze movement" with every action taken against the arms race, while fuzzy on specifics, implies a larger truth. The freeze has been a thin but effective glue binding together diverse groups and sub-issues into a force capable of challenging the guiding assumptions of the national security state.

The Freeze and the Soviet Union

But how will the freeze-as-strategy develop into the freeze-as-a-social-movement that can oppose militarism and the Cold War of which nuclear weapons are the linchpin? I purposely use the term "Cold War" rather than "imperialism." In the service of capitalism, the United States still terrorizes, exploits, and entices much of the world, but it is not alone in this role—as the people of Afghanistan and Poland can testify.

Perhaps the most important lesson the European peace movement has taught us is that the division of the globe between East and West cripples the advance toward peace and a democratic form of socialism in both spheres. In Europe especially, each major country is a military client of one of the super-powers; "neutralism" becomes a curse denoting those naive enough to believe extrication from suicidally armed camps is either possible or desirable. In the Third World, revolutionary regimes that were established to emancipate their people from poverty and organized violence exist under constant fear of attack and thus are increasngly militarized. National liberation may depend on guns, but a liberated society cannot be built in an atmosphere of fear and rigid discipline.

Many peace activists in the United States differ with this image of two super-powers engaged in a reciprocal process of threatening the future of civilization. They instead depict the Soviet Union as playing a rather innocent game of catch-up with the United States in the arms race and answer each reference to Soviet actions in Eastern Europe or Central Asia with a plea to consider American-sponsored atrocities in El Salvador, Guatemala, and the Philippines.[9] Americans who criticize Soviet policy only stir up irrational fears of the Russian bogey and play into Reagan's hands, the logic runs. Far better to direct peacful fire at our own government which, after all, has refused to disavow a first strike and has provoked fears of a "limited nuclear war" in Europe.

What this argument neglects is the basic dynamic of the Cold War. Each side views a gain by the other—be it a new ally, a favorable election result, or a new defector—as a lost piece on the geopolitical chessboard. This zero-sum game, played constantly in Moscow and Washington, constricts the space for even deeply reformist change, as in Chile a decade ago or Poland more recently, much less revolution. To open up that space, we have to attack the game at its source. Focusing on American intervention alone will not do that, because it doesn't unearth the root: two competing imperialisms, each, for different reasons, determined to stop the autonomous development of societies within its own sphere of influence.

Therefore, the bilateral emphasis of the freeze should be extended into a broader consciousness that infuses the entire disarmament movement. Richard Barnet's observation that, "neither communism nor capitalism remain credible philosophical systems for organizing society in the contemporary world," can be the starting point for an alternative perspective that refuses to be intimidated by the ideology or weaponry of either super-power.[10] The Soviets may endorse the freeze proposal and portray themselves as faithful allies of the peace movement, but their missiles are just as deadly and their reluctance to stop building any new weapons system is just as firm as that of their counterparts along the Potomac. As E.P. Thompson has written: "It is futile for the peace movement to place its trust in any heavily armed nuclear state and especially one where the information available to its citizens is strictly controlled and where public opinion can scarcely influence the rulers."[11]

This does *not* mean that peace workers should make their demand for a freeze and deep reductions in nuclear arsenals dependent upon progress in the human rights behavior of Soviet bloc governments. "Linkage" is a posture reserved for cynical administrations in Washington who care little about either disarmament or the universal application of the Bill of Rights. The peace movement has a far different task: to unequivocally denounce both Soviet and U.S. actions which threaten peace and strangle freedom - whether a behind-the-scenes clampdown on independent unions in Poland or an escalated offensive against social revolution in Central America. This requires loud protest when independent disarmament activists are hustled off the streets of Moscow and sent into prison, psychiatric hospitals, or exile. Such protests may be politically wise for Americans, but they are also acts of principle. No government should be left alone to preach peace while simultaneously repressing its people when they demand concrete steps to achieve it.[12] Citizens on both sides of the divide must join in tearing down the barriers of Cold War, or mutual suspicions will grow. One day the barriers may burst into unquenchable flames.

At the same time, the foreign and military policy of the United States is based upon an image of Soviet power which the peace movement must challenge. The nuclear arsenal of the USSR is inferior, both in quality and quantity, with one exception: land-based ICBMs which are the most vulnerable leg of the deadly "triad". Moreover, Soviet troops, despite the blood they have spilled in Afghanistan, are deployed only along Soviet borders. Andrew Cockburn and others have revealed how primitive is the technology of the Red Army and how unmotivated are its troops.[13] The Politburo may issue brave statements about "the rising tide of socialism," but they are primarily concerned with the difficulties of keeping order within an unstable empire.

Creating an Alternative

Airing the truth about Soviet power is only preliminary to the task of developing new guidelines for American policy. In the last few years, several supporters of the peace movement have proposed excellent alternative military budgets which have unfortunately failed to draw much attention - either in the mass media or among freeze activists themselves.[14] There are minor differences of emphasis among the various proposals, but all agree on the following: first, that "national security" would be enhanced by cutting all funds for first-strike nuclear weapons and new delivery systems like the B-1 bomber; second, the use of interventionary forces, especially the Rapid Deployment Force, would only initiate wider conflicts in the Third World; and, third, most conventional weapons in the planning stages are ridiculously over-priced and do not even function according to their own specifications. Together, the cuts proposed would delete about one-third of the current outlay for defense.

Whether or not limiting increases in the military budget remains a popular pastime on Capitol Hill, these carefully-drawn alternatives will be the basis of any long-range restructuring of American foreign and military policy. Their authors—a mixture of intellectuals, lawmakers, and organizers—recognize that the armed forces of the United States can only be significantly reduced and their mission altered through a joint process of mass education, protest, and electoral success. The alternative budgets implicitly acknowledge that the disarmament movement will progress only so far without expanding its indictment into a politics combining democratic and peaceful ideals with concrete measures that can win the support of the majority of Americans who favor a "strong defense". At the core of all these proposals is a simple truth with which I believe most citizens—after a healthy debate—would agree: more weapons to fight a "protracted" nuclear war or to intervene overseas only make the nation more insecure.

But how to generate mass support and activism around an alternative military budget? The key is to design a program which unites all the social groups—unionists, blacks, Latins, women, the unemployed, liberal professionals—who are excluded ed from Ronald Reagan's new America and will continue to suffer from an unplanned and undemocratic economy, whether the administration in power is of the right or center. Thus, organizers should inform workers that defense plants are more capital intensive than any other industry. Also, few people of color get hired to produce or service goods for the military (unless they are in unifrom) and, when they do, their chances for advancement are slim. Freeze activists should adopt the argument developed by Seymour Melman and popularized by Jobs With Peace—that funds spent on the military rob an already troubled economy of people and resources. Fear of a nuclear holocaust may subside, but the military will continue to gobble up dollars and technology needed to achieve long-term prosperity, much less the humane goal of a full-employment economy.

For the freeze to make the transition from a strategy to a sustained movement, it will also have to build an internal life which allows diverse segments of the population to participate. Peace organizations now draw most of their recruits from the white, well-educated stratum which also forms the core of the environmental and feminist movements. This group, while responsible for giving the freeze a strong jolt of globally-oriented idealism, also expresses a style that can alienate potential volunteers from other strata: loose organization, decision-making by consensus rather than majority vote, and a promotional style which swings between dire predictions of the end of the world and pathetic slogans like "Nuclear war means never having a nice day" and "You can't hug your kids with nuclear arms." There is passion aplenty, but not enough respect for the limited time and different priorities of those outside the young, middle-class core. As Dick Greenwood of the International Association of Machinists complains, "You go to these meetings, and everyone's got their own thing—all those autonomous organizations—you talk, talk, talk. It's almost a group grope."[15]

To move away from such self-limiting characteristics, peace activists should learn from the behavior of good labor and community organizers. Tolerance towards individuals with varying degrees of commitment, political opinions, and verbal expressions is one lesson. A flexible rhetorical style and accountability to the decisions of a coalition is another. Obviously, not all participants will develop into dedicated organizers against nuclear weaponry. But when the success of a movement depends on its public image as well as on the content of its message, those who run the offices, write the leaflets, and staff the tables at shopping centers must be able to address a range of concerns and not merely parrot the slogans of the moment.

I began by mentioning reform movements in American history which transcended the single issue on which they originally focused. Common to abolitionists, woman suffragists, and radical opponents of the Vietnam War was an understanding that their "issue" was the key to unraveling the threads which held a brutal and immoral society together. None of these movements worked a fundamental transformation of America, but each succeeded in politicizing large segments of the population in a leftward direction. Because they won their cardinal demand, both the anti-slavery and suffrage forces were responsible for thrusting a major social group (black men and white women) onto the political stage, although the roles they assumed were not what either movement's founding visionaries would have preferred.

The freeze specifically and the peace movement in general have pinpointed a central dilemma of our era: how to find security in a civilization that could be utterly destroyed in a matter of hours. Confronting that dilemma also means taking on some of the basic problems of humanity, whether governed by capitalist or socialist ideologies: the primacy of military considerations in foreign policy, the ever-widening gap between rich and poor nations, destructive alliances hardened through almost forty years of Cold War and, ultimately, a mass psychology in which competition rides in the saddle. "The public discussion of the problems presented by nuclear weaponry which is now taking place in this country," wrote George Kennan recently, "is going to go down in history, I suspect (assuming, of course, that history is to continue at all and does not itself fall victim to the sort of weaponry we are discussing), as the most significant that any democratic society has ever engaged in."[16]

For Kennan's prediction to come true, the freeze movement

will have to do more than stop the missiles from flying—which itself would be an awesome accomplishment. It will have to become skilled at threading a path between two political extremes: a radical purism which abstains from electoral involvement and expects Americans to eventually see its chosen light, and a cautionary "realism" that thinks only of the next task and assumes that ending the arms race will require no unsettling changes in the social and economic order. The freeze has been the core of an unprecedented upsurge against the danger of nuclear war. Now, with or without the spur of Ronald Reagan in the White House, it must evolve into a movement that can both act effectively to win its "single issue" and inspire people to dedicate their lives to achieving the age-old dream of a world without war.

Footnotes

1. Leslie Gelb, "A Practical Way to Arms Control," *New York Times Magazine*, June 5, 1983, pp. 33-42; The Harvard Nuclear Study Group, *Living With Nuclear Weapons* (New York, 1983), pp. 207-9.

2. Cited in Paul Boyer, "From Activism to Apathy: What Happened to the Anti-Nuclear-Weapons Movement After 1963?," unpublished paper, p. 4. Boyer, a professor of history at the University of Wisconsin-Madison, notes that opposition to testing was "highly volatile, fluctuating markedly depending on the state of Soviet-American relations." Support for the freeze on the other hand, has grown during a period of hostility between the two super-powers.

3. For example, in late 1982, manual workers supported it by 71 percent and labor union families by 74 percent. The overall total was 71 percent. *The Gallup Report*, January 1983, p. 13. Later polls affirm these statistics.

4. "The Freeze Movement Versus Reagan," *New Left Review* 137 (January-February, 1983), p. 15.

5. *The Freeze Economy*, edited by Dave McFadden and Jim Wake, p. 34. The pamphlet is available for $2.50 from the National Freeze Clearinghouse in St. Louis.

6. Gordon Adams, *The Iron Triangle: The Politics of Defense Contracting* (Washington, 1981).

7. "Together We Stand; Divided...," *Sanity: Voice of CND*, April 1983, p. 3.

8. For an entertaining expression of these disagreements, see Marcy Darnovsky, "Smile and Say 'Freeze'," *Radical America* (July-October, 1982), p. 7-9.

9. See Norman Solomon, "Letter to E.P. Thompson: Europe, Russia, and the U.S. Missiles" and Thompson's response, "Peace is a Third-Way Street," in *The Nation*, April 16, 1983, p. 469-481.

10. Richard Barnet, "Two Bumbling Giants: The Superpowers' Outdated Policies in a Nuclear World,' p. 68, in *Waging Peace: A Handbook for the Struggle to Abolish Nuclear Weapons*, ed. Jim Wallis (San Francisco, 1982).

11. E.P. Thompson, "END and the Soviet 'Peace Offensive," *The Nation*, February 26, 1983, p. 233.

12. I don't believe, however, that Soviet apologists, such as those in the U.S. Peace Council, should be excluded from the ranks of the peace movement. To bar "Communists" would evince a fear of political differences, embitter and divide activists over a side-issue of civil liberties, and set a harmful precedent which could be used against any controversial faction. It is better to educate ourselves about the aims of the Soviets and their supporters and then to defeat them in open debate. For the exclusionist argument, see Ronald Radosh, "The 'Peace Council' and Peace," *The New Republic*, January 31, 1983, p. 14-18.

13. Andrew Cockburn, *The Threat: Inside the Soviet Military Machine* (New York, 1983).

14. For examples, see The Boston Study Group (which included Randall Forsberg), *Winding Down: The Price of Defense* (San Francisco, 1982); Ed Glennon, "Military Budget Manual, Fiscal Year 1983 Edition," National SANE Education Fund, 1982; Cong. Ronald Dellums, "Defense Sense," *The Nation*, August 21-28, 1982, p. 133, a short description of H.R. 6696, an alternative budget which, in July, 1982, attracted 55 votes in the House.

15. Quoted in Bruce Shapiro, "Movement Looks for the Union Label," *Nuclear Times*, April 1983, p. 18.

16. *The Nuclear Delusion: Soviet-American Relations in the Atomic Age* (New York, 1982), p. 201.

Chapter 28

The Inescapable Links: Interventionism and Nuclear War

Michael Klare

While the U.N. General Assembly was meeting in New York to consider the paths to disarmament, the world was moving closer to a nuclear war. At the onset of the 1982 U.N. Special Session on Disarmament, not one but two nuclear powers—Israel and Great Britain—were engaged in military hostilities (in the Falklands and in Lebanon)—while other nations allied with the superpowers were at war elsewhere in the world. Although none of these conflicts appeared to threaten the outbreak of a nuclear war, it is not hard to imagine how some future incidence of such conflict could blow out of control and trigger a nuclear confrontation. Indeed, a careful analysis of current world trends leads inevitably to the terrifying conclusion that the world is likely to experience an increasing number of military conflicts, and that these conflicts will raise an ever-growing risk of nuclear escalation.

The growing risk of nuclear war is the result not of any single factor but rather of the convergence of a number of concurrent developments. These include recent developments in the *nuclear* field—particularly the introduction of so-called "Counterforce" weapons like the MX missile which offer the potential for a first-strike nuclear attack—but also include developments in the political and diplomatic field, as well as in the area of non-nuclear, *conventional* weapons. Indeed, the world of conventional armaments is experiencing a revolution every bit as profound as the revolution in nuclear arms, and this transformation in conventional arms *is making nuclear war more likely*.

The growing link between conventional arms and nuclear war reflects the fact that recent technological innovations in weapons design—the development of new explosives and of "smart" bombs and missiles (precision-guided munitions, or PGMs) with near-100% "kill probability"—have made conventional arms far more lethal and destructive than ever before. As a result, future wars fought with modern conventional weapons are likely to produce extremely high levels of violence and destructiveness (witness the devastation caused by the Israeli "incursion" into Lebanon), and thus could produce the conditions under which one side or another may feel tempted or compelled to use nuclear weapons. In fact, this is the most likely way in which a nuclear war would begin. And given the growing inclination of the major nuclear powers to intervene in local Third World conflicts, the risk of such conflagrations is increasing with every passing day.

There is, therefore, a direct link between conventional arms and interventionism on one hand, and nuclear escalation and global catastrophe on the other. Unfortunately, the American peace movement has tended to ignore this link, and to address the issues of interventionism and nuclear war separately. Thus, many elements of the anti-nuclear movement believe that our overriding task is to eliminate nuclear weapons, and that then, and only then, can we turn our attention to the control of conventional forces. In their (quite understandable) desire to curb nuclear weapons, some disarmament groups, such as the Union of Concerned Scientists, have even proposed *increases* in U.S. conventional forces as part of a nuclear-restraint policy. Other groups, on the other hand, have argued that interventionism is the overriding issue and that nuclear disarmament is a secondary priority. It should be obvious from the above, however, that the issues of interventionism and nuclear war *cannot be separated* and that therefore the peace movement must view them as a linked issue which must be addressed with a unified analysis and a unified strategy. Indeed, *only* a strategy that links interventionism and nuclear war can address the driving forces behind global violence today.

In order to fully appreciate the absolute necessity of this linkage, it is essential that we examine the current world trends that are making a nuclear war more likely:

1. *Conventional weapons are becoming more like nuclear weapons in their capacity to destroy large concentrations of people.* As a result of recent developments in explosives and weapons technology, arms designers are now able to develop conventional weapons that have the destructive effect of small nuclear weapons. Thus U.S. and West German designers have created "cluster bombs" which scatter anti-personnel "bomblets" capable of killing or maiming all unshielded human beings in a very large area—as much as 75 square city blocks. And because of all the opposition to nuclear weapons in Europe, NATO planners are accelerating the development of other conventional weapons with the effective "kill radius" of a small nuclear weapon.

2. *At the same time, nuclear weapons are becoming more like conventional weapons in their capacity to destroy relatively confined geographic areas.* Just as conventional weapons designers are being encouraged to "think big" in order to create weapons of near-nuclear destructiveness, nuclear weapons designers are being encouraged to "think small" in order to create "mini-nukes:" weapons with the same "kill radius" as large conventional weapons. The aim of this effort is to produce conventional arms and nuclear arms which are essentially interchangeable—thereby making it easier to switch from one to the other.

3. *The so-called "firebreak" between conventional war and nuclear war is vanishing.* At one time, there was a large "firebreak" between the most powerful conventional weapons and the smallest nuclear weapons—thus making it easier for political leaders to prevent escalation across that all important gap. As a result of #1 and #2, however, that gap is disappearing rapidly. Because there is virtually no distinction (in terms of killing power) between the largest conventional weapons and the smallest nuclear weapons, it will be that much easier for military commanders to justify the transition from conventional to nuclear combat—promising at first to use mini-nukes or neutron bombs only, but inevitably starting the chain reaction towards full-scale thermonuclear conflict.

4. *Meanwhile, conventional wars are becoming far more ferocious and destructive than ever before.* As we have seen in the Falklands crisis and in Lebanon, any war fought with modern conventional weapons is likely to produce very high levels of violence and destructiveness. With the introduction of PGMs, moreover, every shot fired is likely to score a direct hit, so that a PGM-intensive war will produce very high casualties on both sides no matter who eventually "wins" the war. And it is

exactly in this sort of ferocious, violent conflict that a military commander—fearing the loss of his forces to the conventional weapons of his enemy—might move up the ladder of escalation to his most powerful conventional weapons and then cross the very narrow gap to mini-nukes, and then to ever more powerful nuclear munitions.

5. *Furthermore, more and more countries are acquiring the capacity to fight high-intensity conventional wars.* At one time, large conventional armies and sophisticated conventional weapons were the exclusive prerogative of the superpowers and their closest allies. Today, however, many Third World countries have large armies, and—thanks to the military aid policies of the superpowers and the booming arms trade—very large stockpiles of modern weapons. Indeed, in their hunger for profits, the major arms suppliers have sold Third World countries even their most advanced and sophisticated weapons, such as the *Exocet* missiles used by Argentina to sink the British destroyer Sheffield. What this means, of course, is that future wars occuring almost *anywhere* in the world will be fought with the same magnitude of violence and destruction we would expect in a superpower conflict in Europe. This reality is particularly frightening because:

6. *There are more hotspots and war zones in the world than ever before.* After World War II, the superpowers exercised substantial control over the military activities of their clients and allies, thereby limiting wars largely to those they themselves initiated or participated in. Today, the East-West rivalry is as intense as ever, but the diminution of superpower domination has allowed other rivalries to flourish—North-South rivalries, intra-Third World disputes, religious conflicts like the Iran-Iraq war, territorial disputes such as the Falklands, and so forth. If present trends continue, many of these rivalries will erupt into major regional conflagrations. And because the flow of sophisticated arms into the Third World is only likely to accelerate in the years ahead, these wars will be fought at ever-increasing levels of violence and destructiveness. This is scary enough. But what is especially frightening about all this is that:

7. *The superpowers appear increasingly prone towards intervention in local Third World conflicts.* Despite assurances of restraint, the two superpowers are expanding their interventionary capabilities and assumed policies that make such action increasingly likely. After Vietnam, the U.S. Government—under pressure from a war-weary populace—assumed a stance of non-interventionism in internal Third World conflicts (the so-called "Vietnam Syndrome"). Under the guise of the

Nixon Doctrine, U.S. leaders turned to "surrogate gendarmes" like Iran and Indonesia to protect U.S. interests in the Third World. With the fall of the Shah, however, Washington lost its faith in surrogates and began planning for a renewed U.S. interventionary posture abroad. The Iranian hostage crisis and the Soviet invasion of Afghanistan gave popular legitimacy to this stance, of course, but the basic decisions—e.g., to establish the Rapid Deployment Force (RDF) and to deploy a naval fleet in the Indian Ocean—were made before those two events. Since coming to office, Mr. Reagan has accelerated the expansion of the RDF and other U.S. interventionary capabilities, and has explicitly threatened to use those capabilities against various foes, including the guerrillas in El Salvador, against Cuba, against Libya, and so forth. Indeed, the buildup in interventionary forces—especially the RDF and U.S. naval forces—is the principal motive behind Reagan's massive military build-up. The Soviet Union, meanwhile, has also demonstrated a greater propensity for intervention abroad. It has already provided logistical support for major military operations by its allies in Angola, Cambodia, and Ethiopia, and has intervened with its own forces in Afghanistan. And while Moscow has so far avoided direct involvement in the Polish crackdown, future Soviet involvement in Poland or other Eastern European countries is entirely possible. Given the superpowers growing propensity for intervention, therefore, and the aforementioned proliferation of likely war zones, it is obvious that we face a very real risk of U.S. or Soviet military involvement in some not-too-distant conflict—or even joint intervention by both super-powers. And that leads to the greatest nightmare of all: if we add points 1,2,3,4,5,6, and 7 together, item 8 appears inevitable.

8. *The world is now facing a greater risk of nuclear war than ever before.* No one can predict future events, but the logic of this conclusion appears inescapable.

Given the fact that the world is likely to experience an increasing incidence of localized wars of ever-increasing levels of violence and destruction, and given the fact that the super-powers appear more inclined than ever to intervene in such conflicts, and given the fact that such conflicts are likely to produce extremely high numbers of casualties in very short amounts of time, and assuming that one or the other super-power might face a potentially disastrous military defeat in such an environment—when you add all these up, and plug in the vanishing firebreak between conventional and nuclear weapons, it seems painfully obvious that we face a very real threat of nuclear catastrophe.

This is, indeed, a terrifying litany. But its purpose is not so much to alarm, as to demonstrate the absolute necessity of linking nuclear disarmament to anti-interventionism and controls on the international arms trade. Any approach that fails to make this linkage would not address the most dangerous factor in the arms race today: the *convergence* between interventionary impulses, the revolution in conventional arms, and the risk of nuclear annihilation.

The linkage between anti-interventionism and nuclear disarmament is not only a strategic *necessity*, it also provides an unprecedented *opportunity* for the peace movement. First of all, it provides the basis for coalitions between the anti-nuclear movement and the various anti-interventionary movements (e.g., the movement against U.S. intervention in El Salvador). Even more important, it provides the basis for coalitions with all those Americans—the poor, the elderly, the minorities, the handicapped—who are suffering as a result of Reagan's campaign to shift Federal resources from the social sector to the military budget. (Because the bulk of Reagan's defense buildup is committed to conventional and interventionary forces—as much as 85%—only a cutback in such programs will result in significant military budget reductions.) Finally, it provides the basis for linking the widespread persistence of the Vietnam Syndrome to the growing outpouring of anti-nuclear sentiment.

For all these reasons, but most of all because of the terrifying arithmetic I described before, it appears absolutely essential to me that the peace movement view anti-interventionism and nuclear disarmament as related tasks of a unified struggle. Indeed, it seems to me absolutely inescapable that the only way that we can prevent an interventionary war fought with conventional weapons from escalating into a nuclear war is by preventing the interventionary war in the first place.

Chapter 29

A No First Use Declaration

Union of Concerned Scientists*

Nuclear warfare is not merely an extension of conventional warfare to a higher level of violence. It is an entirely different phenomenon. Modern conventional warfare can produce vast death, destruction, and suffering, but at its worst, conventional warfare leaves populations and structures for recuperation. General, all-out nuclear war would destroy the peoples, institutions, and cultures of the targeted nations, as well as damage the rest of the planet to an unpredictable but dangerous degree. The survival of the engaged nuclear powers, their allies, and many other nations depends upon preventing, permanently, the outbreak of general nuclear war.

Prevention of general nuclear war is, therefore, an objective of absolute priority, an objective which must be pursued for the indefinite future, in times of calm and in times of international crisis, even during actual hostilities. Prevention must be at the heart of U.S. and alliance policy and strategy. Dependence on the threat or the use of nuclear weapons to achieve national or allied purposes should be reduced to a minimum, since any such dependence creates the risk of initiation and escalation of nuclear war. There is no present substitute for the threat of nuclear retaliation to deter the hostile use of nuclear weapons.

*Text was prepared for the Union of Concerned Scientists by Vice Admiral John Marshall Lee.

But it is not similarly inescapable to rely on nuclear forces to deter or defeat conventional attack or to accomplish other military operational objectives. To depend on the threat or use of nuclear weapons for these tasks will with high probability, sooner or later, in one crisis or another, bring on disaster.

Such nuclear dependence is, however, the basic U.S. and NATO strategy and has been so for a generation. This strategy assumes a Soviet superiority in conventional forces that can be met, ultimately, only by U.S. nuclear weapons. In the case of NATO, the U.S. has repeatedly declared its determination, if conventional defenses were to fail, to initiate the use of nuclear weapons. In a number of other actual or potential situations, from Dien Bien Phu to the Persian Gulf, where conventional forces appeared unable to deal with a situation, the U.S. has contemplated using nuclear weapons. The nuclear concept is built intimately into U.S. and NATO assumptions, plan, organization, posture, doctrines, and programs. The bulk of U.S. strategic study in the postwar era has been devoted to refining ideas for nuclear posture and nuclear employment designed not only to strengthen deterrence but also to seek concepts for using nuclear weapons in action without necessarily escalating to a general nuclear exchange. In the last analysis, our strategy is a nuclear strategy.

In the early days of the atomic era, when atomic weapons were few in number and largely in U.S. hands, such a nuclear-based strategy was at least plausible. During that period, the U.S. could have used nuclear weapons and survived the Soviet response, badly damaged but still functional. In the last twenty years, however, with enormous arsenals deliverable by both sides, the probability has become overwhelming that neither the U.S. nor the Soviet Union would survive. The logic of the nuclear-based strategy has evaporated.

Today, the nuclear weapon is not operationally usable. Its only rational function—and this function is essential—is nuclear deterrence: to prevent the use of nuclear weapons by others. To call on the nuclear weapon for any other role will be, in the long run, fatal. In the words of Field Marshal Lord Carver, present U.S. and NATO nuclear-dependent strategy is "either a bluff or a suicide pact."

This critical dilemma can be resolved and U.S. and alliance policy and strategy can be put on a rational footing by a declaration that the U.S. will not be the first to use nuclear weapons in any hostilities—the No-First-Use declaration. The No-First-Use declaration will signal a decisive shift in fundamental national and alliance policy of thirty years' standing. It will demand thorough rethinking of strategic doctrine and extensive military and political analysis and debate in the U.S. and allied nations, including public discussion and the development of public support. Further, it will require substantive change in military doctrines, plans, forces, and programs. This preparatory process will not be quick, easy, or lacking in strong opposition in the U.S. and among the allies. The discussions and debates will themselves be productive, however, in enhancing public understanding and, ultimately, national and alliance unity of purpose and concept.

The effect of a No-First-Use declaration will be profound. On the political side, alliances will ultimately be strengthened and relations with the Soviet Union, especially in times of tension, made less apocalyptic. On the military side, restricting the role of nuclear weapons to nuclear deterrence or retaliation will cause basic changes in the conventional as well as the nuclear forces, markedly lowering the risk of nuclear conflict.

Political effect of No-First-Use

For a generation, our allies have based their security on U.S. readiness to use nuclear weapons in defense against conventional attack. A No-First-Use declaration may initially be viewed as undermining that deterrence. However, the allies are conscious of the irrationality of defense by the threat of suicide. They are aware that they cannot be "defended" by nuclear warfare, but would be destroyed by it. And while the allies depend on the power of nuclear deterrence, they recognize the danger of its failing catastrophically, sooner or later, in one crisis or another. The allies need, as we do, a rational strategy offering reasonable hope for long-term survival.

In allied nations, as in the U.S., a spectrum of views has emerged on the relative merits of No-First-Use and the nuclear deterrence of conventional attack. Arriving at a meeting of the minds, here and abroad, will depend on reaching several shared appreciations:

◻ The distinction between conventional and nuclear war is of overpowering significance. Some elements in allied countries, scarred by the tragic experiences of the two great wars of this century fought on their soil, virtually equate conventional and nuclear war.

◻ Under No-First-Use, conventional war would not surely escalate to nuclear war, as many now assume.

◻ A sound conventional defense which provides a powerful conventional deterrent and, if called upon, a good promise of operational success, is within reach at manageable political and economic cost.

□ The present strategy of first-use will very probably lead to the catastrophe of nuclear war; it is intellectually and morally insupportable; it is internally divisive for the nations of the alliance.

Once such points are broadly agreed upon, a No-First-Use strategy will be seen as a major advance in security for all allies. Allies will readily appreciate the impact of No-First-Use on several existing problems. One perennial weakness of our alliances has been concern about American reliability in crises. Some Europeans, in particular, have long doubted that the U.S. would actually use its nuclear weapons against a Warsaw Pact conventional attack, when the consequence would be the near certainty of its own destruction. An even more corrosive variant of this fear is that the U.S. and the USSR will find some way to confine nuclear operations to the territory of their allies and cooperate to maintain their own countries as sanctuaries. There are also those who fear that the U.S., provoked by excessive hostility to the USSR, could trigger hostilities needlessly.

No-First-Use would alleviate these concerns. The allies could be confident that the U.S., substantially relieved of the prospect of its own immediate destruction, deeply conscious of the importance of its allies to U.S. security, and with its own large forces in the front line, would fully participate in a mutual conventional defense. Nor would U.S. nuclear support be eliminated. It would be in reserve as a powerful deterrent of hostile nuclear attack before and during hostilities; and if, tragically, the USSR were to break the nuclear barrier, it would be a ready retaliatory force.

Other cracks in the unity of purpose of the U.S. and allied nations would be ameliorated by No-First-Use. We would all be largely freed from the absurdity of defending ourselves by threat of suicide. We would be liberated, in great measure, from the inhuman prospect of inflicting millions of deaths, on our own initiative, on mostly innocent people. We would be functioning under a comprehensible policy and strategy that would justify the necessary military measures—a strategy that would give grounds for hope for the long future.

The transition of the alliances to a No-First-Use basis will be laborious, time consuming, and probably stormy. Advocates of No-First-Use, in the U.S. and in allied nations, face a major task. The U.S. clearly must be ready to share in strengthening the conventional defense. Once No-First-Use is in effect, however, the alliances will be on a rational and realistic military footing with a sensibly reduced risk of nuclear catastrophe. Our alliances will be stronger and more dependable.

Predicting Soviet actions and reactions cannot be done with accuracy and is not attempted here. There are, however, a number of considerations that would flow from a U.S. No-First-Use declaration that the USSR might weigh in its decision-making.

Given the profound Soviet mistrust of the U.S. and its allies, as well as the impossiblity of predicting any nation's action under ultimate stress, the USSR may never place complete confidence in U.S. No-First-Use. Nevertheless, the Soviets will analyze the national and inter-allied discussion and debate on the subject, and will observe the associated military measures. This should lead them to a cautious belief that No-First-Use is at least accepted policy and strategy in the West. Such a belief would support the apparent Soviet interest in maintaining the non-nuclear barrier. With its powerful, numerically superior conventional forces, enormous geographical expanse, and central strategic position, the USSR is nearly invulnerable to conventional attack; the U.S. and its allies cannot seriously contemplate invading the Soviet Union. Thus, as long as any hostilities remain conventional, the Soviet homeland should seem basically secure. If the nuclear barrier were breached, however, the USSR and its allies would almost certainly be destroyed as functioning societies. Even under the stress of conventional warfare, and—the extreme case—even with that warfare going badly for the USSR, avoiding escalation to nuclear weapons would be profoundly in the Soviet interest. Furthermore, cutting their losses, pulling back from unsuccessful external adventures, and awaiting a better opportunity would be in keeping with enduring Communist dogma and Russian historical experience. In sum, a U.S. No-First-Use declaration, with its related measure, could give Soviet decision-makers additional grounds to avoid a dangerous hair-trigger nuclear posture, to refrain from nuclear preemption, and to adhere to their own recent No-First-Use declaration.

One important consequence of these factors is to invalidate the common assumption that any major hostilities involving the U.S. and the USSR would surely be, or quickly become, nuclear.

Military Effect of No-First-Use

The effect of No-First-Use on the allied military structure would also be fundamental. A basic assumption now shared by the U.S. and its allies is that the nuclear weapon is available as the final arbiter in major hostility. If conventional operations go badly or major objectives cannot otherwise be achieved, nuclear forces can properly be called on. In brief, nuclear operations are legitimate operations of war, usable when needed. Under No-First-Use, that assumption would no longer hold. The ultimate reliance on nuclear weapons to shore up conventional operations would be eliminated; nuclear first-use would be outside the boundaries of legitimacy for U.S. forces. No American combat commander would expect or recommend nuclear support of his operations, just as today he would neither expect nor recommend the use of other prohibited weapons such as nerve gas or biological weapons.

The mission of the conventional forces would be to succeed conventionally. The mission of the nuclear forces would be definite and limited—to deter or, failing that, to retaliate against hostile use of nuclear weapons. Each side would, of course, find it essential to provide for the possibility of the other using nuclear weapons in violation of the No-First-Use declaration, or for nuclear operations being triggered by accident, mistake, insubordinate initiative, or third parties. A nuclear threat would still exist, and each side would need to be able to retaliate. But reliance on nuclear forces to shore up our own conventional operations would be eliminated.

The conventional forces would no longer be, in the final analysis, a trip-wire for nuclear war. They would have to fulfill their mission themselves, without a nuclear crutch. That would require conventional forces capable of deterring, or if necessary stopping, conventional attack against essential objectives. Nuclear weapons and nuclear concepts are now deeply intertwined with nearly every element of the forces; all aspects would need to be reexamined and modified. The composition, size, structure, and priority of various combat, support, and infrastructure elements would be altered to some degree. Adequate stocks of nonnuclear combat consumables would be given a higher priority. Organization, task assignments, reserve force concepts, training, doctrines, manuals, operational plans, and tactical concepts would all feel the impact. Weapon research, development, and procurement programs would need some redirection. Perhaps most important, the sense of mission of the conventional forces, at all levels, would be revolutionized; from top to bottom the conventional forces would know that the whole combat responsibility was theirs, that nuclear weapons were not available to cover inadequacy, incompetence, or failure. The basic dignity of the conventional combat forces would be restored. The effect on their outlook, tone, and determination—and consequently on their effectiveness—would be substantial.

The nuclear forces would also change. Nuclear weapons whose functions can be discharged conventionally, such as antiarmor (neutron bomb), antiair, and antisubmarine, would lose their *raison d'etre*. The present dangerous and vulnerable accumulation of tactical weapons located in or near potential combat zones would surely be rethought. Presumably, tactical weapons could be thinned out and moved to less provocative locations, greatly reducing pressures to use these weapons before losing them and also clearing out the prime targets for hostile preemptive attacks. The longer-range nuclear forces, theater and strategic, would also be altered. With an exclusively retaliatory mission, first-strike characteristics would be given less weight; the very short flight time and high accuracy of the proposed Pershing II, for example, would presumably be recognized as provocative and destabilizing rather than a deterrent. Invulnerability, reliability, and endurance would gain priority in strategic force programming. The bottomless requirements for nuclear forces generated by nuclear "war-fighting" scenarios would have even less validity; a straightforward deterrence and retaliatory mission for the nuclear forces should restrict requirements. It might be possible, at long last, to answer for nuclear weapons the question "How much is enough?"

Under No-First-Use, it will be essential to make clear that any hostile first-use of nuclear weapons will be met by nuclear retaliation. This will require maintaining the means, the preparations, and the plans—including graduated plans—for making retaliation certain. No-First-Use neither eliminates nuclear requirements nor nuclear danger. However, if the Soviet Union and its people are convinced they will be safe from our nuclear weapons unless, and only unless, their weapons are used against us or our allies—the No-First-Use concept—the nuclear dangers will be markedly reduced and genuine security greatly enhanced.

A No-First-Use declaration would demand and would generate major, substantive, military changes—changes both in concepts and in forces. Some have argued that No-First-Use would be merely declaratory diplomacy, that the decision whether to use nuclear weapons will be made on the basis of perceived national interest at the moment of crisis. This argument fails to recognize the weight a No-First-Use declaration would have after it had been built into our thinking, our preparations, and our military structure. While it will be operationally possible to violate the No-First-Use declaration and use nuclear forces, the weight of legitimacy, expectation, preparation, planning, and operations will all be against such action.

In essence, the U.S. and its allies will have calmly evaluated their true individual and collective interest and decided that nuclear war is inevitably destructive to that interest. No-First-Use, then, will not leave the nuclear decision to a moment of nearly intolerable stress in the heat of crisis; the U.S. and its allies will have made that decision and built it in advance into their entire military postures.

Arguments Against No-First-Use

Renunciation of the first-use of nuclear weapons would strike at the foundation on which the U.S. and its allies have built their military defense for a generation. Quite naturally, the proposal has produced a number of opposing arguments. Some of these arguments—in particular the impact on the cohesion of our alliances, considerations bearing on Soviet decision-making, and the argument that a No-First-Use declaration would be without operational significance—have been discussed above.

The following four opposing arguments are probably the most significant of the remaining issues:

(1) It is not possible to provide a conventional counter to Soviet conventional strength within the limits of economic and political practicability.

(2) It is essential to prevent major conventional war as well as nuclear war; let us take the steps needed to enhance conventional strength but not declare No-First-Use, because No-First-Use would erode nuclear deterrence of conventional attack and make conventional war more likely.

(3) Limited nuclear war can be controlled and may be needed in an ultimate crisis; let us not close out the option.

(4) Soviet communism is a malignant force dedicated to global domination; it must be stopped regardless of cost.

Discussion of these points follows.

1.Conventional Defense

It is not possible to provide a conventional counter to Soviet conventional strength within the limits of economic and political practicality.

Since the U.S. post-World War II demobilization, it has

been an article of faith, here and abroad, that the Soviet Union has overwhelming conventional superiority. It has been taken as a given that in Central Europe, the Warsaw Pact could rapidly overrun NATO conventional defenses and that in other potentially contested areas around the Soviet periphery the USSR could rapidly prevail. This presumption of unmatchable Soviet conventional dominance is challenged herein; the following sections of this report (Parts II and III) argue that:

In Central Europe:

□ NATO enjoys the intrinsic advantage of the defender: that defense can be sustained with forces numerically smaller than those needed by the attacker. The existing numerical balance in men and weapons is within the generally accepted range for successful defense.

□ The common assessment of Soviet conventional dominance, while it fully considers NATO limitations, gives inadequate weight to some of the problems facing the Warsaw Pact, notably the questionable reliability and effectiveness of Soviet satellites, and the limitations and vulnerabilities of Warsaw Pact communications.

□ NATO has in existence powerful conventional forces and ongoing programs for the enhancement of these forces. There are a number of material, organizational, and operational improvements, at manageable cost, that can substantially strengthen the defense. Taken together, these factors bring within reach a conventional defense able to powerfully deter conventional aggression and, if necessary, able to contain or repel conventional attack with high confidence.

□ NATO superiority in advanced micro-technology exists and promises to continue. It is in this technological area that decisive and economical advances in weapons and control systems are most probable. Critical fields in which NATO can exploit its technological superiority with powerful effect include search and surveillance, target acquisition and fire control, communications, navigation command and control, and electronic warfare.

Outside Europe:

□ There are no targets for U.S. or allied attack where nuclear weapons would have a critical advantage over conventional weapons. Nuclear exchanges, however limited, would be greatly to the disadvantage of the U.S. and its allies in operations around the Soviet periphery or at sea. The risk of escalation would be acute. First-use of nuclear weapons by the U.S. or its allies would therefore be irrational.

2.Deterring conventional war

It is essential to prevent major conventional war as well as nuclear war; let us take the steps needed to enhance conventional strength but not declare No-First-Use, because No-First-Use would erode nuclear deterrence of conventional attack and make conventional war more likely.

This argument against a No-First-Use declaration was made in an exaggerated form by General Haig while he was Secretary of State. No-First-Use, he said, is "tantamount to making Europe safe for conventional aggression." Without the threat of nuclear response to conventional attack (i.e., without "extended deterrence"), the risk of undertaking such an attack would be greatly reduced. Consequently, conventional war would be more likely to occur. Conventional war alone would be a major disaster and it would also be likely to trigger nuclear war. On the operational level, if the threat of tactical nuclear response to conventional attack is removed, the attacker could concentrate his forces and add power to the attack. In brief, advocates of this argument recommend improving the conventional forces to reduce dependence on nuclear weapons while retaining the threat of first-use to maintain extended deterrence.

There are serious problems with this attempt to maintain the deterrent value of nuclear first-use:

▫ The threat of nuclear response to conventional attack is indeed very powerful, but it is an unacceptable risk for NATO to rely on such extended deterrence to succeed invariably for the indefinite future. A single failure, whether in the first or the nth East-West crisis, would spell catastrophe. A solid conventional defense, on the other hand, is a strong deterrent to conventional attack, and if that deterrence were to fail, the outcome, though tragic, could be faced and survived.

▫ There is substantial doubt on both sides of the Atlantic and both sides of the Iron Curtain that NATO would, in fact, use nuclear weapons to stop a Warsaw Pact conventional advance in view of the probability of mutual destruction. (In particular, it is difficult to conceive of the Federal Republic of Germany concurring in tactical nuclear employment when most of the weapons of both sides would presumably be aimed initially at targets in West Germany.) NATO's confidence in its nuclear defense, under first-use, is therefore limited and uncertain—a source of weakness.

□ Under a first-use policy there is a high probability that any major hostility will become nuclear; this danger will be a source of political weakness in crisis.

□ Concentration of forces offers advantages not only to the attacker but also to the counter-attacking defender; in any case, modern conventional weapons increasingly threaten concentrated forces.

The overriding problem with nuclear deterrence of conventional attack, however, is that under that strategy the option to use nuclear weapons first will always exist, and will always be the dominating military consideration, in calm and in crisis. Without No-First-Use, the essential basic change in nuclear thinking will not occur among government leaders, the military, or the public. Basing security on a threat of suicide will increasingly disaffect the public. Military commanders, in plans and in actual operations, will be driven to calling for nuclear support whenever they face difficult tasks. National leaders, working under the appalling stress of crises, with partial, delayed, and dubious information, will be under enormous pressure to issue the nuclear command. On the Soviet side, the desired change in perception will not take place. The Soviets will have no reason to consider the nuclear threat reduced or to refrain from hair-trigger postures. The pressures on the Soviets to avoid crossing the nuclear barrier will not be powerfully reinforced.

Such extended nuclear deterrence, therefore, does not provide security. Instead, it weakens public morale, it undercuts the ultimate resolution of conventional forces, it overloads national leaders, and it makes catastrophic nuclear war more probable. Conventional attack can rationally be deterred or met only with conventional forces.

On the immediate, practical level, it is unrealistic to advocate a solid conventional defense and, simultaneously, a first-use option. The necessary steps on the conventional side will not be taken and sustained unless the conventional mission is seen as clear, possible to achieve, and critically necessary for national and allied security. There is simply not the incentive to do what needs to be done on the conventional side while the nuclear option exists. According to NATO Supreme Allied Commander of Europe, General Bernard Rogers, "We have mortgaged our defense (of Western Europe) to a nuclear response " (*New York Times*, 10-14-82).

Changing fundamental national and alliance policy, taking the extensive doctrinal and material steps to implement that change, and conveying the change convincingly to deeply mistrustful Soviet opponents cannot be done without broad public and official support throughout the alliance. These objectives cannot be attained and maintained without a clearcut public position that is widely accepted as rational and feasible and that offers a realistic hope for genuine security and a substantial, even if incomplete, release from the nuclear trap. A No-First-Use declaration is indispensable.

3. Limited Nuclear War

Limited nuclear war can be controlled and may be needed in an ultimate crisis; let us not close out the option.

The last twenty years have seen the development of concepts and plans, and the procurement of weapons and equipment for "controlled," "limited," and most recently "protracted" nuclear war-fighting strategies. These strategies aim to produce a broader deterrence and, if used, to limit the range of destruction. The military objective of these strategies is to gain some operational advantage without escalating to full-scale nuclear exchange. These operations would try to halt a conventional attack, for example, or give the firing side a recognizable lead in the remaining nuclear balance, or wreck the opponent's political and military control system. These strategies envision a nuclear war fought to a successful conclusion. Their supporters argue that nuclear "war-fighting" capabilities enhance deterrence of hostilities generally and deterrence of escalation during hostilities, that limited nuclear war may be a necessary last resort at a critical moment, and that it should therefore not be debarred by a No-First-Use declaration.

However, the various limited nuclear war concepts have several overriding defects. Planning for limited nuclear war produces virtually bottomless requirements for nuclear forces: weapons, delivery vehicles, and systems of command, control, communications, and intelligence. Such planning is the primary stimulus for very large increases in nuclear forces and contributes to a corresponding buildup by the other side which must, under war-fighting concepts, again be matched.

No one has been able to produce a scenario for limited nuclear operations, on whatever scale, that would clearly work to U.S. and allied advantage. Scenarios with "favorable" outcomes depend upon a whole series of dubious assumptions. None has a firm stopping point. In the real world, they would, on balance, work to our operational disadvantage, produce more or less localized chaos, and almost irresistibly escalate.

The concept of limited nuclear war lowers the nuclear threshold. If the first critical breach of the nuclear barrier is thought to offer some possibility of success without ultimate disaster, the fateful decision, at some moment of terrible stress, will be dangerously more probable.

The decisive argument against limited nuclear war, however, is the high probability of unlimited escalation. Limited nuclear operations are fundamentally not manageable. For limited nuclear war to remain limited—to be brought to a stop short of complete catastrophe—the two sides, during actual nuclear exchange, would have to first work out and observe mutually tolerable operational limits—mutually accepted restraints on the kinds and locations of the targets they fired at and the numbers, sizes, and kinds of weapons they used. In addition, and this is even less conceivable, both sides would have to arrive at an agreed outcome, a stopping point, while still in mid-exchange, and with each side still possessing more than ample nuclear forces to carry the exchange up further steps and finally to destroy the other. They would have to do this with different information, different weapons, different operational concepts and mechanisms, under apalling stresses of event and time, with the continued existence of both literally in the balance, while pursuing diametrically opposed objectives, in the midst of "limited" but substantial nuclear exchanges and the resulting death, destruction, and chaos. In such circumstances, the chances of successful limitations are remote indeed.

In short, limited nuclear war, or any firing of nuclear weapons in anger, however limited, has a prohibitively high probability of escalating to a full-scale exchange and catastrophe for both sides. We should not initiate such use nor, for reasons given in the previous section, should we use the threat of limited nuclear war for extended deterrence. Preserving limited nuclear war options should not be allowed to stand in the way of No-First-Use.

4. If Defense Fails

> Soviet communism is a malignant force dedicated to global domination; it must be stopped regardless of cost.

The remaining general argument against No-First-Use poses the ultimate nuclear dilemma. What should be done in case nonnuclear defense fails?

It is the argument of this paper that under a No-First-Use declaration, with the consequently improved conventional concepts and posture, the U.S. and its allies would maintain a powerful conventional deterrence, and were that deterrence to fail, they could defend conventionally with high probability of success.

High probability is, of course, not certainty. There has never been nor can there be a way to predict the outcome of such hostilities with complete assurance; there are too many unknowns, too many contingencies, too much blind chance. There is, and there always will be, some possibility of the defense failing to hold.

Some argue that the Soviet advance must then be stopped by nuclear weapons, at any cost, including the common destruction of the nuclear powers and their allies. This is a counsel of despair; national suicide is not a rational solution. The only sane approach in the nuclear age is to fight on, conventionally, as long as it may take and as costly as it may be. When the situation is finally restored, there will at least be peoples, cultures, and national structures to carry out the rebuilding and restoration.

Implementation of a No-First-Use Declaration

It is the basic recommendation of this report that a process leading to a No-First-Use declaration be set in motion forthwith.

The public debate and the alliance decisions required by a declaration of No-First-Use will need time to complete. The implementation of the military measure will stretch over a number of years. To await completion of this entire process before making a No-First-Use declaration, as some have argued, would be to postpone it indefinitely; it will always be possible to question the completeness of military preparations. On the other hand, an immediate No-First-Use declaration is neither politically nor diplomatically possible; there must first be broad agreement nationally and internationally, and steps needed to implement No-First-Use must be at least in progress.

To achieve No-First-Use in a reasonable time scale, therefore, discussions within and between U.S. and allied governments should be started at once, leading to general agreement on the desirability of a No-First-Use declaration and on the military measure that the declaration would require. As soon as broad agreement has been reached and the program of military measures adopted and adequately advanced, the U.S. should formally issue a No-First-Use declaration.

Improving NATO's Defense

There are a number of weaknesses and inadequacies in

NATO's posture which can and should be corrected if NATO is to face confidently the Warsaw Pact without the option of first-use of nuclear weapons. Under No-First-Use it will no longer be possible to excuse deficiencies with the facile statement that NATO will use nuclear weapons in the event of failure. General Maxwell Taylor, former Chairman of the Joint Chiefs of Staff, has written that No-First-Use will itself not be credible and stabilizing unless the alliance moves to implement necessary improvements in the conventional balance.

The steps that need to be taken to improve NATO's conventional defense fall into four categories. First, NATO must be able to make rapid political decisions and deploy promptly covering forces, as well as other forces in Europe and reinforcements from overseas. Second, a number of operational improvements should be made, including the construction of tank obstacles and field fortifications, and better use of reserve forces to cover the threat of a long war. Third, NATO should cultivate its advantage in the use of high technology. Finally, gaps in NATO's ability to sustain military operations should be closed.

Political and Military Readiness

The alliance must be capable of acting quickly and effectively in times of crisis. A sudden Warsaw Pact buildup followed immediately by an attack is not the only or even the most probable way that war would start, but it represents a critical test of NATO's defense. In this instance, the Warsaw Pact decides when to commence its mobilization, concealing the action as best it can. If NATO detects the Pact mobilization and promptly makes its decision, NATO would begin mobilizing within three or four days, and the balance of deployed and available forces should allow for a successful defense. If NATO's decision is delayed, however, and the difference between the initiation of the two mobilizations is extended to a week or more, the Pact's level of superiority in deployed forces grows beyond a danger point and remains high.

Traditionally, NATO's alliance of sovereign nations has reached decisions unanimously. Consequently, rapidity of an alliance-wide decision to move to a high state of readiness, to deploy in-theater forces, and to mobilize and reinforce cannot be assured. This problem exists with or without No-First-Use.

But with a policy of first-use, the problem can be glossed over by counting on escalation to nuclear weapons to compensate for slow decision-making. With No-First-Use, such indecision is not an option. On the Central European Front the matter is complicated by the presence of forces of six nations (seven, if France is counted). Since German, American, and British sectors cover the most probable invasion corridors, it is likely that these three nations will have to act ahead of their allies. Preparations to do so should not be left for improvisation during a crisis.

A more practical approach is to rely on the use of light infantry forces capable of extremely rapid mobilization and deployment along the Central Front. Armed with modern anti-armor weapons, these forces could be garrisoned close to or within their assigned sectors, and be bolstered very rapidly with reserves from the immediate area who are intimately familiar with the terrain. By exploiting the defensive value of the terrain in these areas, these forces would delay, wear down, and channel the attack while masking the counterattack by NATO's more heavily equipped divisions. Unequivocally defensive, the light forces would have the additional virtue that they could, in a crisis, be brought to full readiness without exacerbating an already tense political situation.

Readiness could also be significantly improved by completing the U.S. POMCUS program.[1] The POMCUS objective is currently set at six division-sets (plus support units) in Europe three in the Northern Army Group Sector (NORTHAG) and three in the Central Army Group Sector (CENTAG). In NORTHAG, a logistics base for immediate support of the arriving forces will also be required. At present, four division-sets have been placed in Central Europe, and two are yet to be authorized. The full program will provide for the early arrival and readiness of a powerful mobile reserve in each Army Group sector. It would substantially improve the force balance at the most critical point in the build-up process, two weeks after the Warsaw Pact commences mobilization.

Obstacles and Field Fortifications

Professor John Keegan of Britain's Royal Military College at Sandhurst writes, "It is an almost bizarre hiatus in the NATO defense system that no fortifications have been constructed on its fronts." This is contrary to all previous military practice, although nothing in the military revolution of our time is revolutionary enough to suggest that there is no longer any use for obstacles and field fortifications. Yet for political reasons, the construction of obstacles and field fortifications is blocked in West Germany. Farmers along the Central Front have resisted efforts to place such objects in their fields, and perhaps more important, the objective of German reunification has resulted in resistance to the construction of "permanent" barriers along the border.

A system of tank-and-mechanized-vehicle obstacles backed by field fortifications is essential. Obstacles, such as ditches, minefields, and concrete forms, are relatively cheap to build. They require little more than earth-moving machinery, explosives, and concrete for their construction. Fixed fortifications include prepared emplacements for use by tanks and artillery, as well as observation posts for calling and controlling the use of long-range artillery, antitank clusters, or remotely controlled precision-guided munitions. Such fortifications could also include numerous small concrete bunkers to provide shelter and support for light infantry forces.

The effectiveness of modern artillery fire, relying on modern means of reconnaissance, makes large permanent fortifications ineffective and a waste of resources. A more useful approach is to rely on numerous small, hardcover installations, which can be camouflaged, and distributed randomly. They can also be simulated by inexpensive decoys to improve survivability. Moreover, these structures, together with man-made obstacles, should be arranged in depth, taking maximum advantage of the terrain, to require successive penetrations by attacking forces. Since such fortifications would be priority targets for Soviet artillery, duplication and redundancy in the control system is also necessary.

NATO need not rely exclusively on fixed obstacles and barriers built in peacetime and therefore known to and planned for by the Warsaw Pact. New developments allow obstacles to be created when needed, for example, by employing projectable mine-fields or buried explosive hose. Buried explosive hose, a small-bore plastic hose no harder to lay than domestic gas piping, would be buried four to five feet below the surface. When pumped full of an explosive "slurry" and detonated, it creates a tank obstacle that is impassable without special equipment. During periods of low tension, the pipes would be inert. Under crisis conditions, they could be rapidly filled from tankers. Piping of this sort could be laid in a variety of patterns over wide areas of the Central Front.

NATO should place highest priority on those measures designed to improve its ability to respond to a Warsaw Pact attack after a short period of mobilization. The alliance must, however, also continue its efforts to meet the threat of a protracted conflict. Some analysts suggest that NATO should add as many as eight new divisions to its current force posture to prepare adequately for this contingency. Such an improvement need not necessitate costly increases in the number of military personnel or a return to conscription in the U.S., Great Britain, and other nations which do not currently use a draft. The same end may be achieved by increasing the number of U.S. and allied reserve divisions. Reserve forces can provide a powerful supplement to active-duty forces at approximately half the cost per unit.

Deep Interdiction

The Soviet method of attack is based on striking with successive echelons. As the lead echelon is worn down, a second, fresh element replaces it, and the lead echelon pulls back to recover. If the oncoming echelons were subjected to effective attack before commitment, their combat power would be reduced, their movement slowed, and plans disrupted. The ultimate objective of the defense is to hit reserve echelons so powerfully as to essentially stop them and thus isolate the lead echelon. This could be accomplished by deep air interdiction strikes against troops and their lines of communication and supply depots, as well as against airfields and support installations in Poland, Czechoslovakia, and East Germany.

The interdiction problem is being analyzed and molded into a unified concept in the U.S. Army General Staff (where it has been given the name "Airland Battle 2000") and at SACEUR's headquarters. Existing and forthcoming target-accusation systems, delivery systems, and munitions show promise of making such attacks effective. The required large volume of modern munitions and systems will be expensive, and countermeasures can be expected and will have to be overcome. However, the basic idea is sound. It takes advantage of NATO's superiority in advanced micro-technology and targets a potential vulnerability in the Warsaw Pact.

It should also be emphasized that these advanced weapons and control systems can be brought to bear in the zone of contact. Their range and flexibility are such that their fire can be called in whenever needed, anywhere along the front. In many cases, it may prove preferable to let the opponent do the work of transporting himself to the front, and then to hit him where we have all the advantages of real-time intelligence.

Advanced Technology

NATO has a lead over the Warsaw Pact in a number of critical areas of military technology which must be preserved and exploited. Such innovations have historically played an important role in warfare, and have often provided one side or the other with a decisive edge. Important examples include the 1973 Arab-Israeli war and the more recent clashes between Syrian and Israeli forces in Lebanon. Under today's conditions of rapid technological change, failure to exploit technology fully would be a critical error.

Precision-guided munitions (PGMs) are an outstanding example of the potential of technology. Until recently, most weapons were relatively inaccurate devices that damaged their targets more through saturation than precision. Artillery, for example, is an area weapon; aerial bombing, before the "smart" bomb, relied on volume. By contrast, a PGM is designed to hit directly and destroy its target with a probability of 50 percent or more in battle conditions. The effectiveness of PGMs was recently demonstrated in the Falkland Islands operations, where both sides inflicted very serious damage using air-launched PGMs. PGMs are under development that will carry multiple, target-seeking, and target-discriminating warheads. A single PGM round can give a promise of multiple kills of targets such as tanks, artillery pieces, and infantry-fighting vehicles.

When coupled with tank obstacles and fortifications, PGMs can provide a very powerful antidote to the tank. Although much has been made of the limitations of the antitank guided missiles (ATGMs), such limitations are to be expected with any new technology. Improved ATGMs, along with new and multiple sensors, guidance systems, discriminators, and firing systems are likely to overcome many of the current shortcomings. Furthermore, as experience grows and more ATGM systems are produced, their quality will improve, the costs of their production should decrease, and their field reliability will increase. And, as troops gain familiarity with ATGMs, tactical and operational improvements will be developed and proficiency will be increased.

PGMs will also be invaluable in attacking targets deep in enemy territory: advancing attack-echelons, lines of communication, airfields, and support installations. While aerial bombardment has been the tool for deep interdiction in the past, it is likely to be restricted in the future by the high concentration and effectiveness of air and ground defense systems. PGMs, however, can cause greater damage to deep targets with less exposure and lower losses than can piloted aircraft. Long-range ground-launched, air-launched, and sea-launched cruise missiles of high accuracy, and possibly carrying multiple, non-nuclear warheads, would be able to provide this capability.

The PGM is but one of the areas where technological

innovation is significantly changing conventional warfare. In fact, there is scarcely an area of military operations, equipment, and control that is untouched by new developments in electronics, materials, and computers. NATO enjoys a considerable advantage in all of these technologies. It would of course be a mistake to overemphasize technological solutions, or to rely exclusively on any one particular system. In the case of PGMs, for example, their overall effectiveness is sensitive to the development of electronic and other countermeasures. Nevertheless, it is important to recognize that technology has and will continue to play a very significant role in modern warfare.

Stockpiles of Combat Supplies

Major NATO-Warsaw Pact hostilities will consume combat supplies at an unprecedented rate because of the way forces are concentrated and firepower is massed. A "day of supply" today, in fuel, spares, replacements, and especially ammunition, is much larger and more expensive than in the past. Investments in stockpiles have had a low priority because of the assumption that major NATO-Warsaw Pact hostilities would rapidly escalate to nuclear warfare. As a result, the stockpiles of combat consumables for the Central European area are at a dangerously low level. In war simulations, a number of NATO elements exhaust some of their supplies in just two weeks of intensive combat. Under No-First-Use, it is essential to raise these stocks to an interim goal of thirty days of supply, and in the long term, to a level of not less than forty-five days. As a first step, NATO should increase stockpiles for its standing divisions to cover an additional two weeks of combat.

Defense in Rear Areas

NATO's air bases, command centers, and supply depots would be subject to heavy attack by Warsaw Pact air forces during wartime. A number of relatively inexpensive steps can be taken to enhance the survivability of these facilities and installations. The construction of combat aircraft shelters on allied air bases in Central Europe to protect against bombing attacks is one critical example. These have not been built for the large numbers of air reinforcements which would arrive in the first days of the buildup. Failure to construct this highly effective and relatively inexpensive defense for the vulnerable, very costly, and vital air reinforcement may be the most notable false economy in the NATO defense program.

Cost Estimates

In the preceding section, various steps that NATO might take to improve its conventional force posture were outlined. Some of these measure are already called for in the Long-Term Defense Program adopted by NATO in 1978. These initiatives will require a higher level of priority under No-First-Use. Other improvements that we are recommending extend beyond the scope of the 1978 NATO program. The most important of these measures are those that would improve NATO's defensive strength during the critical period shortly after an outbreak of hostilities. Their costs are outlined briefly below.

▢ The least expensive improvements to NATO's conventional capability are those which involve construction. This category includes the construction of tank obstacles, field fortifications, and air-base shelters, which can be made out of basic materials like steel, concrete, and dirt. Using such materials, construction of an obstacles-and-fortifications network along the Central Front could cost less than $1 million per kilometer. Total costs would be less than $1 billion for Central Europe, spread over a six-year period. Over the same period, it is estimated that the construction of shelters at allied air bases in Europe would cost an additional $300 million.

▢ NATO's deficiency in the area of war stocks and reserves is more costly to correct. While some of NATO's troops are prepared to conduct military operations for more than fifteen days, many are not. The cost of equipping one division for an additional fifteen days of combat is conservatively estimated to cost at most $1.4 billion, spread over six years. As a first step, NATO should increase the ability of its standing forces to maintain combat for an additional fifteen days, so that each unit is capable of conducting operations for no less than thirty days. The cost of such improvements for twenty-nine divisions would be roughly $40 billion.

▢ To insure the availability of equipment for American reinforcements travelling from the United States it is necessary to improve POMCUS and sealift capabilities. Pre-positioning equipment in Europe for two additional U.S. divisions would cost less than $3 billion over six years. These equipment-sets would supplement the four POMCUS sets already funded. Alternatively or in addition, the capability to ferry supplies by sea from the U.S. to Europe could be improved at a cost of about $4 billion in six years. The total cost of implementing both the POMCUS and sealift improvements would thus be approximately $7 bilion.

To strengthen their defensive capabilities for a protracted period of combat, the U.S. and its NATO allies could increase the availability of reserve divisions. Preparing five additional U.S. reserve divisions to supplement active-duty forces would cost $28 billion, including training and thirty days of war-reserve stocks. Three additional allied reserve divisions would cost approximately $5 billion each, assuming that training and thirty days of war reserve stocks were also included. The total cost of these improvements would be roughly $43 billion.

Taken together, the cost of the improvments outlined above would amount to less than $100 billion over a period of six years. Estimating the costs of additional measures, such as the creation of a light infantry reserve force along the Central Front, is beyond the scope of this study. However, it is unlikely that the costs of these additional measures would cause the overall costs of improvements required by a No-First-Use declaration to exceed spending levels that are within an acceptable range of political and economic feasibility.

Since 1978, alliance members have agreed to increase defense spending by 3 percent annually. From 1978 to 1980, this goal was almost met, and NATO's defense budget now totals $300 billion annually. The $100 billion in costs projected for high priority improvements—obstacles and fortifications, combat consumables, pre-positioning of supplies, and reserve forces—would entail roughly a 2 percent annual increase in real terms. This is within the current level of 3 percent increases and considerably below the 4 percent increases recently advocated for the 1983-1988 period by General Bernard Rogers, the Supreme Allied Commander of Europe. (A 4 percent annual increase over six years would result in a total increase in expenditures of more than $200 billion.)

In the U.S., a large deficit and major cuts in social programs have created opposition to large increases in defense spending, and similar conditions exist in Western Europe. This suggests that the optimal approach for funding the requisite components in conventional defenses would be to reallocate funds now intended for nuclear weapons procurement. Funding for implementing conventional improvements could come from a reallocation of military priorities among the NATO member nations. Money allocated to nuclear weapons procurement, such as the MX missile or B-1 bomber in the U.S. and the

Trident submarine in the U.K., could be shifted to meet the costs of many of these higher priority conventional programs.

Not all of the improvements suggested above can be implemented quickly. Some of these steps are likely to require a few years to gain acceptance, and when accepted, to be implemented. On the other hand, adoption of a No-First-Use policy would create pressures and inducements that would lower the political obstacles faced by an improvement program based on the continued reliance on nuclear weapons for defense.

Footnotes

1. POMCUS (Pre-Positioned Material Configured to Unit Sets) pre-positions the equipment for a number of U.S.-based divisions and support units in Central Europe. When mobilization is ordered, the personnel can be flown directly to their equipment and supplies in Europe and be deployed promptly.

Chapter 30

Nuclear Diplomacy: The Peace Movement and Declaring No First Use

Jon Saxton

On June 12, 1982 nearly one million people rallied in New York's Central Park calling for a nuclear freeze, nuclear disarmament, and for a reorientation of national priorities to fund human needs.

Since that day the American peace movement has been attempting to maintain and broaden the active participation of the American people in the cause of peace. The Campaign for a Nuclear Weapons Freeze has done well at the polls and in Congress. Some people have taken up the European initiative in campaigning for nuclear free zones in cities around the country. Unilateral and unconditional disarmament remains the goal of others. But the movement for nuclear disarmament faces serious difficulties in sustaining and expanding its base of active support.

The Reagan Administration is opposed to serious arms control efforts and is intent on deploying a new generation of nuclear weapons. As opposition to these weapons grows, so does the attempt to undermine popular support for the peace movement. The specter of the Soviet threat both at home and abroad has been recast in a style appropriate to the new fundamentalist fervor, while a critical "window of vulnerability" in the West's deterrent has been identified. These and a variety of other tactics threaten to intimidate and confuse popular support for the peace movement and help set the stage for the planned deployment of the new weapons.

It is in the face of these developments that the idea of a campaign for a no-first-use of nuclear weapons pledge has emerged. It deserves serious consideration. Under certain conditions a no-first-use campaign could be a logical "next step" in the process of building a popular disarmament movement and in bringing the arms race to a halt. This essay presents an evaluation of the no-first-use proposal in light of the history of American nuclear policy and practice, and the recent experience of the disarmament movement.

The Historical Record

For thirty-eight years the United States has followed a policy of using nuclear weapons, if need be, in military or political conflicts that threaten American global interests. The history of American nuclear diplomacy is just now being told, and it clearly demonstrates the extent to which both the capability and the expressed willingness to use nuclear weapons have served to "guarantee" American political and economic power around the world.

To understand the historical record we must first appreciate two fundamental aspects of nuclear weapons. The first of these is first strike capability. To have first strike capability the U.S. must be able to strike and destroy virtually all of the Soviet Union's intercontinental nuclear forces before they can be launched in retaliation. This is a capability that Robert Aldridge fears the U.S. is close to achieving.[1]

The second dimension is what I propose to call nuclear-use capability.[2] Nuclear-use capability encompasses all of the ways in which nuclear weapons can be employed in an aggressive or offensive manner to achieve certain policy objectives. The policies of "limited nuclear war" and of "escalation dominance", as articulated by the Reagan Administration are an expression of perceived advantage in nuclear use capability. In essence, the Reagan Administration conceives of having strategic or tactical advantages which could make a policy of threatening nuclear use credible. With these two dimensions of nuclear weapons in mind let us look at the record.

From 1945 until the mid 1960's, by virtue of an overwhelmingly superior nuclear capability as measured by numbers of deliverable warheads, forward based systems in Europe, and the vulnerability as well as the unreliability of Soviet nuclear weapons, the U.S. had first strike capability. The U.S. had the ability to pre-emptively destroy the Soviet nuclear arsenal. The U.S. also had nuclear-use capability; that is, Washington enjoyed both the capability and the policy of threatening the use of nuclear weapons in a limited attack. During the Truman Administration American military planners grappled incessantly with the problem of developing an integrated nuclear policy, finally settling on one which expressed the willingness and determination of the U.S. to use nuclear weapons first. During both the Berlin Crisis in 1948 and the Korean conflict in 1950 Truman signalled American nuclear-use capability. In the former he deployed "nuclear-capable" bombers; in the latter he made public statements of his resolve to use "every weapon we have" to settle the conflict.[3]

It was during the Eisenhower-Dulles years of the 1950's that American nuclear weapons policy became most explicitly a "first-use" policy. President Eisenhower told the United Nations in December 1953 that "Atomic weapons have virtually achieved conventional status within our armed forces."[4] In 1955, Secretary of State Dulles remarked, "Where these things can be used on strictly military targets for strictly military purposes, I see no reason why they shouldn't be used just exactly as you would use a bullet or anything else."[5] These sentiments reflected internal documents on strategic policy. Among them, NSC 162/2, a top-secret statement on American military policy approved by Eisenhower in 1953, which stated that "the United States will consider nuclear weapons to be as available for use as other munitions" should the Soviet Union or China threaten U.S. global interests.[6] Although there have always been disagreements among American nuclear strategists, the overall trend in the development of nuclear strategy was clearly in the direction of making nuclear weapons more useable, more flexible, and more credible both for limited ends, and, if necessary, for an all-out nuclear attack.[7] This policy development also had its practical applications.

American nuclear weapons doctrine has always had the public face of a purely defensive deterrent to Soviet nuclear or massive conventional attack. However, Daniel Ellsberg and others have documented 18 instances of U.S. nuclear threats against other countries.[8] The list includes Korea (1950), China (1953, 1958), Iraq (1958), Guatemala (1954) and Berlin (1948, 1961). A Brookings Institute study of 215 American military interventions between 1945 and 1975 shows that the highest success rate was achieved by American actions that combined nuclear with conventional forces.[9] The capability to use nuclear weapons in this manner required that successive U.S. administrations have confidence in the clear superiority of U.S. forces. This superiority, and the demonstrated willingness to use such weapons (as the U.S. had shown in Japan), lent credibility to nuclear threats in this era of American nuclear diplomacy.

Not surprisingly, the use of such nuclear threats largely subsided after the Soviet Union achieved, in the late sixties, a survivable retaliatory capability. By finally deploying a survivable intercontinental ballistic missile force, the Soviets developed a *deterrent* to American nuclear use capability. The fact that Moscow could now strike back undermined the ability of the U.S. to credibly threaten the use of nuclear weapons. Nuclear parity helped produce a period of detente. The United States retained a large numerical and technical superiority over the Soviet Union. But effective parity could be maintained because the Soviets could now inflict enormous damage even if the U.S. launched the first strike. American military planners did not accept the inevitability of rough parity with the Soviet Union. It was during detente that the MX, the Pershing, the different types of cruise missiles, and the Trident II missile were conceived, and research and development programs started. Every one of these nuclear missiles was designed to have the accuracy to destroy super-hardened Soviet missile silos and command centers. Such extraordinary accuracy has no utility as a deterrent. The capacity to destroy hard targets is useful only if the targetted missiles are in their silos. The development of this whole new generation of first strike weapons indicates the existence of a major effort to overcome the Soviet deterrent to American nuclear use capability by restoring a credible American military threat to Soviet strategic forces.

The U.S. has been developing extraordinary new technologies in anti-submarine warfare, as well as improved command, control, communications and intelligence (C^3I) capabilities. When these developments are combined with the new counterforce systems, American confidence in its nuclear superiority might be restored. Nuclear use capability may again become a credible element of American force projections. Particularly important to these developments is the placement of the Pershing II and cruise missiles in Europe. Having such weapons on the Soviet border will do much to put the Soviets back on the defensive. These missiles are a critical element in the aggressive renewal of the doctrine of containment under the Reagan Administration.

From this perspective it is easy to see why the Freeze Campaign is so strongly resisted by the current administration.

The freeze would block deployment of the new generation of first-strike weapons and would effectively undermine the American effort to overcome the Soviet deterrent to American nuclear use capability. Any doubts about the role that this new generation of weapons is meant to play have been eliminated by Secretary of Defense Caspar Weinberger's Defense Posture Statement which calls for the capability for the U.S. to "prevail" at any level of nuclear conflict.

Liberals and No First Use

The recent upsurge in public concern over the arms race can be traced to the emerging awareness of the role that nuclear weapons have played and are being designed to play in American foreign policy. The impetus for a campaign to elicit an American no-first-use pledge follows directly from this growing mass awareness, but it takes on different meanings depending upon how the history of American nuclear diplomacy is understood. The no-first-use idea was really brought to the attention of the American public by McGeorge Bundy, Robert McNamara, George Kennan and Gerard Smith, all former high officials in defense and national security affairs. In the Spring '82 issue of *Foreign Affairs*, they argued that the U.S. should study the possibility of renouncing the first use of nuclear weapons in Europe. Their arguments are both important and limited. They understand, on some level, that the concept of a "limited" nuclear war is dangerous. They are also worried about the political tensions that have emerged within NATO over the scheduled deployment of the Pershing and cruise missiles. Bundy, et.al. argue that a no-first-use pledge, coupled with a commitment to a compensatory conventional build-up, would alleviate the strains in the Alliance and lead to a more believable deterrent to a Soviet invasion of Western Europe: "The political coherence of the Alliance, especially in times of stress, is at least as important as the military strength required to maintain credible deterrence. Indeed the political requirement has, if anything, an even higher priority...if a consensus is re-established on a military policy that the peoples and governments of the Alliance can believe in, both political will and deterrent credibility will be reinforced."[10] The emphasis on the importance of the political coherence of the Alliance, a coherence based upon American predominance, runs throughout their argument.

Bundy, McNamara and other defense liberals view the Reagan Administration's belligerent and casual references to a nuclear war confined to Europe as having unnecessarily exacerbated conflicts within the Alliance. From their perspective, a no-first-use pledge is a perfect vehicle to eliminate much of the divisive nuclear issue and to begin the process of forging a more moderate alternative to the aggressive Reagan defense posture. In particular, there are four principle objectives that they believe could be achieved. A no-first-use pledge could:

1. defuse the European popular movements against nuclear weapons;

2. enable the United States to retain its nuclear forces in the NATO command, and even to build-up and modernize those forces, without publicly maintaining any aggressive intentions;

3. provide a justification for extracting higher conventional military force commitments from the Allies, thereby assuaging domestic American critics of the large share of the burden that falls on the U.S.;

4. enable the Pentagon to deploy the latest generation of high-powered conventional forces and to incorporate into NATO the latest American battle doctrines and force structures.

This last point is particularly important. The U.S. military is facing growing popular opposition to nuclear weapons and the still troublesome problem of nuclear parity with the Soviets, both of which limit the projection of American power overseas. The Pentagon tried for two decades to compensate for the loss of the nuclear "big stick" through the enlistment of regional proxies such as the Shah in Iran and Somoza in Nicaragua. This policy has clear limitations. Liberation movements have a way of developing when confronted by such brutal dictatorships. Vietnam also taught Washington some hard lessons about the effectiveness of even massive forces against an indigenous revolutionary movement. The Pentagon has learned its lessons well and has developed a new concept for projecting and protecting American interests around the world.

The Rapid Deployment Force (RDF) is the centerpiece of this new concept. It is meant to be a very large integrated assemblage of air, land and sea forces capable of rapid interdiction into crises anywhere in the world. This force will carry tactical nuclear weapons and a range of new conventional weapons that have been described as "near nuclear" by military analysts.[11] The force is structured around a new battlefield doctrine, Airland Battle 2000. In the Airland Battle doctrine emphasis is on pre-emptive, extremely concentrated and simultaneous attacks against enemy front-line positions, supply lines, and reserve forces, utilizing the broadest range of weapons of mass destruction. The field manual explains: "By extending the battlefield and integrating conventional, nuclear, chemical and electronic means, forces can exploit enemy vulnerabilities anywhere...Fighting this way, the U.S. Army can quickly begin offensive action by air and land forces to conclude the battle on its terms."[12] *U.S. News and World Report* has described this doctrine as "highly sensitive politically because it seems so aggressive as to hold out the possibility of a U.S. attack" in its overriding emphasis on large-scale offensive and pre-emptive warfare.[13] The RDF will essentially be an ever-ready "Gulf of Tonkin", a military force that, by introducing American troops quickly and decisively into foreign conflicts, is more likely to generate patriotic support than cynical indifference as American casualties are incurred. The RDF has been described as a trip wire force, likely to get America into wars and perhaps into a nuclear war. For the Pentagon however, this new force, along with the commitment to several new aircraft-carrier based Naval task forces, represents the future of U.S. interventionary capabilities. Given these ominous new developments in the Pentagon's battlefield and force structure planning, it becomes clear that the Bundy et.al. proposal for a no-first-use pledge coupled with a mandate to build-up American conventional forces abroad, is a formula for a new and perhaps even more dangerous era of American force projection.

It is unfortunate that in a recent report the Union of Concerned Scientists (UCS), heretofore one of the most consistent advocates of non-militaristic applications of scientific knowledge, has adopted almost verbatim the recommendations of Bundy et.al.[14] In this otherwise helpful and technically accurate report, the UCS advocates the adoption of the Airland Battle 2000 doctrine, the exploitation of the American advantage in Precision Guided Munitions (PGM's), and the new generation of near-nuclear explosives. It also recommends readiness improvement in Europe that envisions nearly a thousand miles of above ground fortifications, all at a cost of "only" 100 billion dollars over 5 or 6 years. The Union of Concerned Scientists recommends these measures to augment NATO's defense capabilities even though the report notes that "NATO enjoys the intrinsic advantage of the defender: that the defense can be sustained with forces numerically smaller than those needed by the attacker. *The existing numerical balance in men and weapons is within the generally accepted range for successful defense.*"[15] (emphasis added). The UCS has proposed these measures to reassure military and political critics and to lure the Pentagon into support of the no-first-use idea. However, what has really happened is that the liberal defense establishment has lured the UCS into its newest ideas of how to increase American military force projection capabilities overseas.

This turn-around of the UCS's best intentions illustrates the pitfalls of ignoring the historical role of American nuclear diplomacy and intervention around the world over the past three decades. It also demonstrates the dangers of focusing on the threat of nuclear weapons alone. The existence of nuclear weapons poses a grave danger to our survival. But the major part of that danger lies in the policies that define their use. Those policies have always included nuclear weapons, but only as part of an overall military posture that envisions conventional war and counter-insurgency as the most likely and most important types of combat. The process of separating the movement against nuclear weapons from their overall role in American military planning can lead to a self-defeating understanding of their dangers and how to eliminate them. It can lead otherwise sensible people to advocate exchanging mass destruction in the form of nuclear weapons for mass destruction in the form of near-nuclear weapons.

No First Use and the Road to Peace

A no-first-use campaign designed to build the growing grass-roots resistance to the militarization of Western society, rather than appeasing military elites on both sides of the Atlantic, might become an important vehicle to carry the world a little further along the road to peace. The Boston chapter of the Mobilization for Survival (a national coalition of 140 peace, disarmament, social justice and feminist organizations) has begun to develop such a project. This no-first-use project is designed to fit the existing and possible future needs and goals of the peace movement, as they develop on the foundation that the Freeze Campaign has helped create.

The Freeze Campaign has done wonders in focusing popular attention on the dangers of nuclear weapons. It has been able to capture much of the spontaneous upsurge of concern that arose in the early months of the Reagan Presidency over the talk of nuclear war in Europe, and direct it into a popular mandate for arms control. The freeze effort relies on the clear and simple idea that a mutual and verifiable freeze on the production, testing and deployment of nuclear weapons is the logical first step in controlling the nuclear arms race. Parity or rough equivalence should be maintained by freezing the Soviet and American nuclear forces in place, so that neither might upset the balance and thereby initiate another round in the deployment of massive overkill. A freeze at parity can then lead to negotiations on mutual and balanced reductions in nuclear stockpiles. This in turn should lead to a lessening of the dangers of nuclear annihilation. The ultimate goal is to totally eliminate the danger of nuclear war, probably through the internationally supervised dismantling of all of the nuclear weapons held by all countries. However, the immediate concern is to stop the arms race now, before the situation of parity is destabilized.

The tremendous popularity of the freeze has pushed it into direct confrontation with the Reagan Administration and into the halls of Congress. However its very simplicity has also become a source of some difficulties in maintaining its appeal with the general public. The Freeze Campaign is finding itself somewhat strapped by its reliance on the logic of parity. Freeze critics, including Reagan himself, have agreed with the idea of freezing the arms race at parity, while arguing that parity is still far away. The administration argues that all those who favor a freeze should support the deployment of the new generation of American nuclear weapons because they will bring the U.S. into a position of parity with the Soviets. To freeze now, they say, would be to lock the United States into a position of inferiority. The struggle for a freeze threatens to become bogged-down in the immensely technical questions of what constitutes parity, what is a balanced reduction, and other such problems. These arguments have frequently been used to weaken and delay arms control negotiations in the past. If the opponents of the Freeze Campaign are successful in this tactic, the American public may retreat back into passive toleration of the nuclear guarantee that was originally fostered by years of the "peaceful atom" campaign and of tediously slow arms control negotiations.

The Freeze Campaign is not unaware of this danger, and in many communities it is beginning to relate the nuclear issue to that of conventional military force. Once again, however, the argument relies on the need for parity, and the same questions about what constitutes parity, this time for conventional forces, are again being posed. Unwilling to abandon the central idea of equivalency upon which much of its popular support is based, the Freeze Campaign will have to struggle hard to maintain both its popular support and its focus on an immediate halt to the arms race. The loss of either would seriously weaken its potential as a truly significant grass-roots arms control initiative.

To prevent the freeze from being stymied and to further strengthen the disarmament movement, it is important to resist the attempt to confine the nuclear debate to technical questions. It is at this point that a no-first-use campaign may be able to complement the efforts of the freeze. It can raise political and military policy questions and educate the public on the particularly aggressive history of American interventionary and nuclear policy. These are questions that the Freeze Campaign either cannot or will not raise.

The popular upsurge of concern about nuclear weapons is based on the growing awareness that the possible use of such weapons has become routinized within military and political strategy. It is this growing awareness of the role of nuclear weapons that produced such passionate negative reactions in the West, and that many in the disarmament movement feel needs to be confirmed. A no-first-use campaign would highlight the fact that it is the strategic policy as much as the strategic weapons that threatens to lead us into nuclear war.

Few Americans know that some 14,000 tactical nuclear weapons are stationed around the world with American troops, fully integrated into modern battlefield planning. Few Americans know that these weapons can be fired from cannon and grenade launchers, or deployed as land mines, depth charges and ship-to-ship missiles. A no-first-use campaign would highlight the extent to which nuclear weapons have become a mainstay of the American military, and how the dangers posed are not confined to Europe, but extend to Africa, the Middle East, Central America and elsewhere.

At the Second Special Session on Disarmament at the United Nations in June 1982, the Soviet Union unilaterally pledged never to be the first to use nuclear weapons. The United States, as it has for decades, rebuffed the Soviet initiative and refused to reciprocate. The continual refusal by the U.S. to make such a pledge should be troubling to all people concerned with nuclear arms control. The most frequent excuse offered by American policy makers is that America's commitments to NATO require a first use policy to guarantee Western Europe's security. Alexander Haig has remarked that a no-first-use pledge would be "tantamount to making Europe safe for conventional aggression."

It has become clear however, that the main reason for American intransigence on the issue of first use is that important sectors of the American defense community feel that the U.S. should not relinquish the ability to credibly threaten nuclear sanctions. This is why the struggle for a no-first-use pledge within the United States is so important. To successfully challenge this dangerous aspect of American military doctrine would be a significant step towards reversing thirty-eight years of unceasing development of new nuclear weapons with greater nuclear-use capability. A campaign for a no-first-use pledge can succeed only if it is adopted as an expression of the popular will of the American people. A no-first-use pledge could only carry weight if it were a matter of public vigilance by the American people. At no time has the mobilization of such a popular democratic will for peace been a more pressing goal.

The peace movement is becoming more and more convinced of the importance of establishing and maintaining channels of democratic access to the formulation of military and political policy. The trend within the Regan Administration is clearly towards more secrecy and more controls on the free exchange of information.[16] Complementing these anti-democratic measures has been the revival of accusations and innuendos suggesting peace movement complicity with Soviet aims. President Reagan himself has repeatedly suggested that the expression of popular concern in the West over America's nuclear policies undermines U.S. strength and bargaining power.

We must view this revival of the "Soviet Threat" and "Official Secrets" for the purpose of intimidating popular dissent from official policies with great apprehension. However the peace movement is slowly coming to a common understanding of such tactics and is beginning to articulate consensus on the question of the Soviet threat: the Soviet Union has done nothing and could do nothing that would justify the initiation of nuclear war. No matter what one thinks of the Soviet Union, its intentions, motivations, behavior or goals, they cannot be used to justify nuclear warfare or policy based upon the threat of nuclear war.

The standing threat to use nuclear weapons first, or under any conditions is politically, morally, ethically and humanly irresponsible. It is not the Soviet Union that is responsible for this American stance, it is America. And it is American intentions, foreign policy goals and defense commitments that must be evaluated by Americans if an end to the arms race is to be achieved. The absence of a clear and honest policy that seeks to eliminate the existence of and reliance upon nuclear weapons is in itself an abrogation of the values and standards of responsible national conduct.

A no-first-use pledge achieved not by decree, but as an expression of the popular will of the American people, and based upon public vigilance in maintaining that pledge, would be a truly significant step towards arms control and disarmament. If both the Soviet Union and the United States were to pledge no-first-use, then the question could become, "What is the use of these weapons?"

However the attempt to achieve such a pledge at the cost of substituting "non-nuclear" weapons is ill-conceived. Peace will not come through the reshuffling and restructuring of American military forces. Peace and disarmament will come only through the process of redefining national priorities. This would mean re-evaluating the vast nexus of economic and political exploitation that the American military is designed to protect and sometimes expand. It would also mean the establishment of new international channels for the resolution of international conflicts.

Though such possibilities remain far off in the future, the successful achievement of a no-first-use pledge coupled with resistance to a conventional build-up, would have an important impact on the short-term likelihood of international conflict erupting into nuclear war. With the precedent of a popular veto of "big stick" diplomacy, the American and European peace movements might be able to gain some important footholds in the struggle to create the kind of democratic participation necessary to give peace a chance.

Footnotes

1. See Robert Aldridge, *The Counterforce Syndrome,* Institute for Policy Studies, Washington, D.C.,1978;*First Strike*, South End Press, Boston, 1983; and Chapter 7 in this volume.

2. See the interview with Daniel Ellsberg in this volume (Chapter 3).

3.) Quoted in George Herken, *The Winning Weapon—The Atomic Bomb in the Cold War 1945-1950*, Vintage Books, New York, 1982, p.332

4. Quoted in John Lewis Gaddis, *Strategies of Containment*, Oxford U. Press, 1982, p. 151.

5. *Ibid.* p. 151.

6. *Ibid.* p. 151.

7. See for example, Lawrence Freedman, *The Evolution of Nuclear Strategy*, St. Martins, 1982, sections 3,4,5; also Gaddis, *op.cit.;* and Thomas C. Schelling, *Arms and Influence,* Yale U. Press, 1966.

8. Daniel Ellsberg, "Call to Mutiny", in E.P Thompson and Dan Smith, eds, *Protest and Survive,* Monthly Review Press, N.Y., 1981; also Konrad Ege and Arjun Makhijani, "U.S. Nuclear Threats: A Documentary History", *Counterspy,* vol. 6, no. 4, July-August 1982; David Holloway, *The Soviet Union and The Arms Race,* Yale U. Press, 1983, p. 51.

9. Barry M. Blechman and Stephen S. Kaplan, et. al., *Force Without War,* The Brookings Institution, Washington, D.C., 1978, pp. 98-108.

10. McGeorge Bundy, George Kennan, Robert S. McNamara and Gerard Smith, "Nuclear Weapons and the Atlantic Alliance", *Foreign Affairs,* Spring 1982, p. 766.

11. See Michael T. Klare, "The Era of Super-Violence", *MERIP Reports,* January 1983.

12. Quoted in Martha Wenger, Airland Battle Doctrine", *MERIP Reports,* January 1983, p. 13.

13. *Ibid.,* p. 12.

14. See the UCS Report in this volume (Chapter 29).

15. Union of Concerned Scientists Report on No First Use, Feb. 1, 1983, p. 13. Also see footnote 5, p. 29 where it is explained that Soviet estimates of the force ratio necessary to "decisive superiority" range from 3 to 1 to 8 to 1 in all categories of forces. These are well above the existing force ratios that now exist between the Warsaw Pact and NATO. These latter now stand at between 1 to 1, and 1.7 to 1.

16. See Anthony Lewis, "Reagan vs. Madison," *New York Times,* op. ed., 3/17/83; The Campaign for Political Rights, "Organizing Notes", vols. 6&7, 1982 & 1983, Washington, D.C.

Chapter 31

The Pastoral Letter of the U.S. Bishops on War and Peace

"The whole human race faces a moment of supreme crisis in its advance toward maturity." Thus the Second Vatican Council opened its treatment of modern warfare.[1] Since the council, the dynamic of the nuclear arms race has intensified. Apprehension about nuclear war is almost tangible and visible today. As Pope John Paul II said in his message to the United Nations concerning disarmament: "Currently the fear and preoccupation of so many groups in various parts of the world reveal that people are more frightened about what would happen if irresponsible parties unleash some nuclear war."[2]

As bishops and pastors ministering in one of the major nuclear nations, we have encountered this terror in the minds and hearts of our people—indeed, we share it. We write this letter because we agree that the world is at a moment of crisis, the effects of which are evident in people's lives. It is not our intent to play on fears, however, but to speak words of hope and encouragement in time of fear. Faith does not insulate us from the challenges of life; rather, it intensifies our desire to help solve them precisely in light of the good news which has come to us in the person of Jesus, the Lord of history. From the resources of our faith we wish to provide hope and strength to all who seek a world free of the nuclear threat. Hope sustains one's capacity to live with danger without being overwhelmed by it; hope is the will to struggle against obstacles even when they appear insuperable. Ultimately our hope rests in the God who gave us life, sustains the world by his power and has called us to revere the lives of every person and all peoples.

The crisis of which we speak arises from this fact: nuclear war threatens the existence of our planet; this is more menacing threat than any the world has known. It is neither tolerable nor necessary that human beings live under this threat. But removing it will require a major effort of intelligence, courage and faith. As Pope John Paul II said at Hiroshima: "From now on it is only through a conscious choice and through a deliberate policy that humanity can survive."[3]

As Americans, citizens of the nation that was first to produce atomic weapons, which has been the only one to use them and which today is one of the handful of nations capable of decisively influencing the course of the nuclear age, we have grave human, moral and political responsibilities to see that a "conscious choice" is made to save humanity. This letter is therefore both an invitation and a challenge to Catholics in the United States to join with others in shaping the conscious choices and deliberate policies required in this "moment of supreme crisis."

The Catholic tradition has always understood the meaning of peace in positive terms. Peace is both a gift of God and a human work. It must be constructed on the basis of central human values: truth, justice, freedom and love. This pastoral constitution states the traditional conception of peace:

> Peace is not merely the absence of war. Nor can it be reduced solely to the maintenance of a balance of power between enemies. Nor is it brought about by dictatorship. Instead, it is rightfully and appropriately called 'an enterprise of justice' (Is. 32:7). Peace results from that harmony built into human society by its divine founder and actualized by men as they thirst after ever greater justice."[4]

The protection of human rights and the preservation of peace are tasks to be accomplished in a world marked by sin and conflicts of various kinds. The church's teaching on war and peace establishes a strong presumption against war which is binding on all; it then it examines when this presumption may be overriden, precisely in the name of preserving the kind of peace which protects human dignity and human rights.

The Just-War Criteria

The moral theory of the "just war" or "limited war" doctrine begins with the presumption which binds all Christians: we should do no harm to our neighbors; how we treat our enemy is the key test of whether we love our neighbor; and the possibility of taking even one human life is a prospect we should consider in fear and trembling. How is it possible to move from these presumptions to the idea of a justifiable use of lethal force?

Historically and theologically the clearest answer to the question is found in St. Augustine. Augustine was impressed by the fact and the consequences of sin in history—the "not yet" dimension of the kingdom. In his view, war was both the result of sin and a tragic remedy for sin in the life of political societies. War arose from disordered ambitions, but it could also be used in some cases at least to restrain evil and protect the innocent. The classic case which illustrated his view was the use of lethal force to prevent aggression against innocent victims. Faced with the fact of attack on the innocent, the presumption that we do no harm even to our enemy yielded to the command of love understood as the need to restrain an enemy who would injure the innocent.

The determination of *when* conditions exist which allow the resort to force in spite of the strong presumption against it is made in light of *jus ad bellum* criteria. The determination of *how* even a justified resort to force must be conducted is made in light of the *jus in bello* criteria. We shall briefly explore the meaning of both.[5]

Just Cause. War is permissible only to confront "a real and certain danger," i.e., to protect innocent life, to preserve conditions necessary for decent human existence and to secure basic human rights. As both Pope Pius XII and Pope John XXIII made clear, if war of retribution was ever justifiable, the risks of modern war negate such a claim today.

Competent Authority. In the Catholic tradition, the right to use force has always been joined to the common good; war must be declared by those with responsibility for public order, not by private groups or individuals.

The requirement that a decision to go to war must be made by competent authority is particularly important in a democratic society. It needs detailed treatment here since it involves a broad spectrum of related issues. Some of the bitterest divisions of society in our nation's history, for example, have been provoked over the question of whether or not a president of the

United States has acted constitutionally and legally in involving our country in a *de facto* war, even if—indeed, especially if—war was never formally declared. Equally perplexing problems of conscience can be raised for individuals expected or legally required to go to war even though our duly elected representatives in Congress have in fact voted for war.

Comparative Justice. Questions concerning the *means* of waging war today, particularly in view of the destructive potential of weapons, have tended to override questions concerning the comparative justice of the positions of respective adversaries or enemies. In essence: Which side is sufficiently "right" in a dispute, and are the values at stake critical enough to override the presumption against war? The question in its most basic form is this: Do the rights and values involved justify killing? For whatever the means used, war by definition involves violence, destruction, suffering and death.

Right Intention. Right intention is related to just cause—war can be legitimately intended only for the reasons set forth above as a just cause. During the conflict, right intention means pursuit of peace and reconciliation, including avoiding unnecessarily destructive acts or imposing unreasonable conditions (e.g. unconditional surrender).

Last Resort. For resort to war to be justified, all peaceful alternatives must have been exhausted. There are formidable problems in this requirement. No international organization currently in existence has exercised sufficient internationally recognized authority to be able to either mediate effectively in most cases or to prevent conflict by the intervention of U.N. or other peacekeeping forces. Futhermore, there is a tendency for nations or peoples which perceive conflict between or among other nations as advantageous to themselves to attempt to prevent a peaceful settlement rather than advance it.

We regret the apparent unwillingness of some to see in the United Nations organization the potential for world order which exists and to encourage its development. Pope Paul VI called the United Nations the last hope for peace. The loss of this hope cannot be allowed to happen. Pope John Paul II is again instructive on this point:

> I wish above all to repeat my confidence in you, the leaders and members of the international organizations, and in you, the international officials! In the course of the last 10 years your organizations have too often been the object of attempts at manipulation on the part of nations wishing to exploit such bodies. How-

ever, it remains true that the present multiplicity of violent clashes, divisions and blocks on which bilateral relations founder, offer the great international organizations the opportunity to engage upon the qualitative change in their activities, even to reform on certain points their own structures in order to take into account new realities and to enjoy effective power.[6]

Probability of Success. This is a difficult criterion to apply, but its purpose is to prevent irrational resort to force or hopeless resistance when the outcome of either will clearly be disproportionate or futile. The determination includes a recognition that at times defense of key values, even against great odds, may be a "proportionate" witness.

Proportionality. In terms of the *jus ad bellum* criteria, proportionality means that the damage to be inflicted and the cost incurred by war must be proportionate to the good expected by taking up arms. Nor should judgements concerning proportionality be limited to the temporal order without regard to a spiritual dimension in terms of "damage," "cost" and "the good expected." In today's interdependent world even a local conflict can affect people everywhere; this is particularly the case when the nuclear powers are involved. Hence a nation cannot justly go to war today without considering the effect of its actions on others and on the international community.

The principle of proportionality applies throughout the conduct of the war as well as to the decision to begin warfare. During the Vietnam War our bishops' conference ultimately concluded that the conflict had reached such a level of devastation to the adversary and damage to our own society that continuing it could not be justified.[7]

Jus in Bello

Even when the stringent conditions which justify resort to war are met, the conduct of war (i.e., strategy, tactics and individual actions) remains subject to continuous scrutiny in light of two principles which have special significance today precisely because of the destructive capability of modern technological warfare. These principles are proportionality and discrimination. In discussing them here we shall apply them to the question of *jus ad bellum* as well as *jus in bello;* for today it becomes increasingly difficult to make a decision to use any kind of armed force, however limited initially an intention and in the destructive power of the weapons employed, without facing at least the possibility of escalation to broader, or even total, war and to the use of weapons of horrendous destructive potential. This is especially the case when adversaries are "superpowers," as the council clearly envisioned:

> Indeed, if the kind of weapons now stocked in the arsenals of the great powers were to be employed to the fullest, the result would be the almost complete reciprocal slaughter of one side by the other, not to speak of the widespread devastation that would follow in the world and the deadly after effects resulting from the use of such weapons.[8]

When confronting choices among the specific military options, the question asked by proportionality is: once we take into account not only the military advantages that will be achieved by using this means, but also all the harms reasonably expected to follow from using it, can its use still be justified? We know, of course, that no end can justify means evil in themselves, such as the executing of hostages or the targeting of non-combatants. Nonetheless, even if the means adopted is not evil in itself, it is necessary to take into account the probable harms that will result from using it and the justice of accepting those harms. It is of utmost importance in assessing harms and the justice of accepting them to think about the poor and helpless, for they are usually the ones who have the least to gain and the most to lose when war's violence touches their lives.

In terms of the arms race, if the *real* end in view is legitimate defense against unjust aggression and the means to this end are not evil in themselves, we must still examine the question of proportionality concerning attendant evils. Do the exorbitant costs, the general climate of insecurity generated, the possibility of accidental detonation of highly-destructive weapons, the danger of error and miscalculation that could provoke retaliation and war—do such evils or others attendant upon and indirectly deriving from the arms race make the arms race itself a disproportionate response to aggression? Pope John Paul II is very clear in his insistence that the exercise of the right and duty of people to protect their existence and freedom is contingent on the use of proportionate means.[9]

Finally, another set of questions concerns the interpretation of the principle of discrimination. The principle prohibits directly intended attacks on non-combatants and non-military targets. It raises a series of questions about the term "intentional," the category of "non-combatant" and the meaning of "military."

These questions merit the debate occurring with increasing

frequency today. We encourage such debate, for concise and definitive answers still appear to be wanting. Mobilization of forces in modern war includes not only the military, but to a significant degree the political, economic and social sectors. It is not always easy to determine who is directly involved in a "war effort" or to what degree. Plainly, though, not even by the broadest defintion can one rationally consider combatants entire classes of human beings such as school children, hospital patients, the elderly, the ill, the average industrial worker producing goods not directly related to military purposes, farmers and many others. They may never be directly attacked.

Direct attacks on military targets involve similar complexities. Which targets are "military" ones and which are not? To what degree, for instance, does the use (by either revolutionaries or regular military forces) of a village or housing in a civilian populated area invite attack? What of a munitions factory in the heart of a city? Who is directly responsible for the deaths of non-combatants should the attack be carried out? To revert to the question raised earlier, how many deaths of non-combatants are "tolerable" as a result of indirect attacks—attacks directed against combat forces and military targets which nevertheless kill non-combatants at the same time?

These two principles in all their complexity must be applied to the range of weapons—conventional, nuclear, biological and chemical—with which nations are armed today.

Moved by the example of Jesus' life and his teaching, some Christians have from the earliest days of the church committed themselves to a non-violent lifestyle.[10] Some understood the Gospel of Jesus to prohibit all killing. Some affirmed the use of prayer and other spiritual methods as means of responding to enmity and hostility.

As Catholic bishops it is incumbent upon us to stress to our own community and to the wider society the significance of this support for a pacifist option for individuals in the teaching of Vatican II and the reaffirmation that the popes have given non-violent witness since the time of the council.

In the development of a theology of peace and the growth of Christian pacifist position among Catholics, these words of the pastoral constitution have special significance: "All these factors force us to undertake a completely fresh reappraisal of war."[11] The council fathers had reference to "the development of armaments by modern science (which) has immeasurably magnified the horrors and wickedness of war."[12] While the just war teaching has clearly been in possession for the past 1,500 years of Catholic thought, the "new moment" in which we find ourselves sees the just-war teaching and non-violence as distinct but interdependent methods of evaluating warfare. They diverge on some specific conclusions, but they share a common presumption against the use of force as a means of settling disputes.

Both find their roots in the Christian theological tradition; each contributed to the full moral vision we need in pursuit of a human peace. We believe the two perspectives support and complement one another, each preserving the other from distortion. Finally, in an age of technological warfare analysis from the viewpoint of non-violence and analysis from the viewpoint of the just-war teaching often converge and agree in their opposition to methods of warfare which are in fact indistinguishable from total warfare.

The New Moment

At the center of the new evaluation of the nuclear arms race is a recognition of two elements: the destructive potential of nuclear weapons and the stringent choices which the nuclear age poses for both politics and morals.

The fateful passage into the nuclear age as a military reality began with the bombing of Nagasaki and Hiroshima, events described by Pope Paul VI as a "butchery of untold magnitude."[13] Since then, in spite of efforts at control and plans for disarmament (e.g. the Baruch Plan of 1946), the nuclear arsenals have escalated, particularly in the two superpowers. The qualitative superiority of these two states, however, should not overshadow the fact that four other countries possess nuclear capabilities and a score of states are only steps away from becoming "nuclear nations."

This nuclear escalation has been opposed sporadically and selectively, but never effectively. The race has continued in spite of carefully expressed doubts by analysts and other citizens and in the face of forcefully expressed opposition by public rallies. Today the opposition to the arms race is no longer sporadic or selective, it is widespread and sustained. The danger and destructiveness of nuclear weapons are understood and resisted with new urgency and intensity. There is in the public debate today an endorsement of the position submitted by the Holy See at the United Nations in 1976: the arms race is to be condemned as a danger, an act of aggression against the poor, and a folly which does not provide the security it promises.[14]

Papal teaching has consistently addressed the folly and

danger of the arms race; but the new perception of it which is now held by the general public is due in large measure to the work of scientists and physicians who have described for citizens the concrete human consequences of a nuclear war.[15]

In a striking demonstration of his personal and pastoral concern for preventing nuclear war, Pope John Paul II commissioned a study by the Pontifical Academy of Sciences which reinforced the findings of other scientific bodies. The Holy Father had the study transmitted by personal representative to the leaders of the United States, the Soviet Union, the United Kingdom and France, and to the president of the General Assembly of the United Nations. One of its conclusions is especially pertinent to the public debate in the United States:

> Recent talk about winning or even surviving a nuclear war must reflect a failure to appreciate a medical reality: any nuclear war would inevitably cause death, disease and suffering of pandemonic proportions and without the possibility of effective medical intervention. That reality leads to the same conclusion physicians have reached for life-threatening epidemics throughout history: prevention is essential for control."[16]

This medical conclusion has a moral corollary. Traditionally the church's moral teaching sought first to prevent war and then to limit its consequences if it occurred. Today, the possibilities for placing political and moral limits on nuclear war are so minimal that the moral task, like the medical, is prevention. As a people, we must refuse to legitimate the idea of nuclear war. Such a refusal will require not only new ideas and new vision, but what the Gospel calls conversion of the heart.

We see with increasing clarity the political folly of a system which threatens mutual suicide, the psychological damage this does to ordinary people, especially the young, the economic distortion of priorities—billions readily spent for destructive instruments while pitched battles are waged daily in our legislatures over small amounts for the homeless, the hungry and the helpless here and abroad. But it is much less clear how we translate a no to nuclear war into a national policy and an international system which more adequately reflect the values and vision of the kingdom of God.

The Use of Nuclear Weapons

Establishing moral guidelines in the nuclear debate means addressing first the question of the use of nuclear weapons. That question has several dimensions.

It is clear that those in the church who interpret the gospel teaching as forbidding all use of violence would oppose any use of nuclear weapons under any conditions. In a sense the existence of these weapons simply confirms and reinforces one of the initial insights of the non-violent postion, namely, that Christians should not use lethal force since the hope of using it selectively and restrictively is so often an illusion. Nuclear weapons seem to prove this point in a way hitherto unknown.

For the tradition which acknowledges some legitimate use of force, some important elements of contemporary nuclear strategy move beyond the limits of moral justification. A justifiable use of force must be both discriminatory and proportionate. Certain aspects of both U.S. and Soviet strategies fail both tests as we shall discuss below. The technical literature and the personal testimony of public officials who have been closely associated with U.S. nuclear strategy have both convinced us of the overwhelming probability that major nuclear exchanges would have no limits.[17]

On the more complicated issue of "limited" nuclear war, we are aware of the extensive literature and discussion which this topic has generated. [18] As a general statement, it seems to us that public officials would be unable to refute the following conclusion of the Pontifical Academy of Sciences:

> Even a nuclear attack directed only at military facilities would be devastating to the country as a whole. This is because military facilities are widespread rather than concentrated at only a few points. Thus, many nuclear weapons would be exploded.
>
> Furthermore, the spread of radiation due to the natural winds and atmospheric mixing would kill vast numbers of people and contaminate large areas. The medical facilities of any nation would be inadequate to care for the survivors. An objective examination of the medical situation that would follow a nuclear war leads to but one conclusion: Prevention is our only recourse.[19]

Moral Principles and Policy Choices

In light of these perspectives we address three questions more explicitly: 1) counter-population warfare; 2)initiation of nuclear war; and 3) limited nuclear war.

1. Counter-population Warfare. Under no circumstances may mass slaughter be used for the purpose of destroying population centers or other predominantly civilian targets. Popes have repeatedly condemned "total war," which implies such use. For example, as early as 1945 Pope Pius XII condemned nuclear warfare "when it entirely escapes the control of man" and results in "the pure and simple annihilation of all human life within the radius of action."[20] The condemnation was repeated by the Second Vatican Council:

> Any act of war aimed indiscriminately at the destruction of entire cities or of extensive areas along with their population is a crime against God and man itself. It merits unequivocal and unhesitating condemnation."[21]

2. Therefore, a serious moral obligation exists to develop non-nuclear defensive strategies as rapidly as possible.

We recognize the responsibility the United States has had and continues to have in assisting allied nations in their defense against either a conventional or a nuclear attack. Especially in the European theater, the deterrence of a *nuclear* attack may require nuclear weapons for a time, even though their possession and deployment must be subject to rigid restrictions.

The need to defend against conventional attack in Europe imposes the political and moral burden of developing adequate, alternative modes of defense to present reliance on nuclear weapons. Even with the best coordinated effort—hardly likely in view of contemporary political division on the question—development of an alternative defense position will still take time.

In the interim, deterrence against a conventional attack relies upon two factors: the not inconsiderable conventional forces at the disposal of NATO and the recognition by a potential attacker that the outbreak of large-scale conventional war could escalate to the nuclear level through accident or miscalculation by either side. We are aware that NATO's refusal to adopt a "no-first-use" pledge is to some extent linked to the deterrent effect of this inherent ambiguity. Nonetheless, in light of the probable effects of initiating nuclear war, we urge NATO to move rapidly toward the adoption of a "no-first-use" policy, but doing so in tandem with development of an adequate alternative defense posture.

3. Limited Nuclear War. It would be possible to agree with our first two conclusions and still not be sure about retaliatory use of nuclear weapons in what is called a "limited exchange." The issue at stake is the *real* as opposed to the *theoretical* possibility of a "limited nuclear exchange."

We recognize that the policy debate on this question is

inconclusive and that all participants are left with hypothetical projections about probable reactions in a nuclear exchange. While not trying to adjudicate the technical debate, we are aware of it and wish to raise a series of questions which challenge the actual meaning of "limited" in this discussion.

—Would leaders have sufficient information to know what is happening in a nuclear exchange?

—Would they be able under the conditions of stress, time pressure and fragmentary information to make the extraordinarily precise decision needed to keep the exchange limited if this were technically possible?

—Would military commanders be able in the midst of the destruction and confusion of a nuclear exchange to maintain a policy of "discriminate targeting?" Can this be done in modern warfare waged across great distances by aircraft and missiles?

—Given the accidents we know about in peacetime conditions, what assurances are there that computer error could be avoided in the midst of a nuclear exchange?

—Would not the casualities, even in a war defined as limited by strategists still run in the millions?

—How "limited" would be the long-term effects of radiation, famine, social fragmentation and economic dislocation?

Unless these questions can be answered satisfactorily, we will continue to be highly skeptical about the real meaning of "limited." One of the criteria of the just-war tradition is a reasonable hope of success in bringing about justice and peace. We must ask whether such a reasonable hope can exist once nuclear weapons have been exchanged. The burden of proof remains on those who assert that meaningful limitation is possible.

Deterrence in Principle and Practice

The moral challenge posed by nuclear weapons is not exhausted by an analysis of their possible uses. Much of the political and moral debate of the nuclear age has concerned the strategy of deterrence. Deterrence is the heart of the U.S.-Soviet relationship, currently the most dangerous dimension of the nuclear arms race.

1. The Concept and Development of Deterrence Policy. The concept of deterrence existed in military strategy long before the nuclear age, but it has taken on a new meaning and significance since 1945. Essentially deterrence means "dissuasion of a potential adversary from initiating attack or conflict, often by the threat of unacceptable retaliatory damage."[23] In the nuclear age deterrence has become the centerpiece of both

U.S. and Soviet policy. Both superpowers for many years now have been able to promise a retaliatory response which can inflict "unacceptable damage." A situation of stable deterrence depends on the ability of each side to deploy its retaliatory forces in ways that are not vulnerable to attack (i.e., protected against a "first strike"); preserving stability requires a willingness by both sides to refrain from deploying weapons which appear to have a first-strike capability.

This general definition of deterrence does not explain either the elements of a deterrence strategy or the evolution of deterrence policy since 1945. A recognition of the different elements of deterrence strategy and the evolution of the policy requires a series of distinct judgements. They include: an analysis of the *factual character* of the deterrent (e.g. what is involved in targeting doctrine); analysis of the *historical development* of the policy (e.g. whether changes have occured which are significant for moral analysis of the policy); the relationship of deterrence policy and other aspects of *U.S.-Soviet affairs;* and determination of the key *moral questions* involved in deterrence policy.

2. *The Moral Assessment of Deterrence.* The distinctively new dimension of nuclear deterrence were recognized by policy-makers and strategists only after much reflection. Similarly, the moral challenge posed by the nuclear deterrence was grasped only after careful deliberation. The moral and political paradox posed by deterrence was concisely stated by Vatican II:

> Undoubtedly, armaments are not amassed merely for use in wartime. Since the defensive strength of any nation is thought to depend on its capacity for immediate retaliation, the stockpiling of arms which grows from year to year serves, in a way hitherto unthought of, as a deterrent to potential attackers. Many people look upon this as the most effective way known at the present time for maintaining some sort of peace among nations. Whatever one may think of this form of deterrent, people are convinced that the arms race, which quite a few countries have entered, is no infallible way of maintaining real peace and that the resulting so-called balance of power is no sure genuine path to achieving it. Rather than eliminate the causes of war, the arms race only serves to aggravate the position. As long as extravagant sums of money are poured into the development of new weapons, it is impossible to devote adequate aid in tackling the

misery which prevails at the present day in the world. New approaches, based on reformed attitudes, will have to be chosen in order to remove this stumbling block, to free the earth from its pressing anxieties, and give back to the world a genuine peace."[24]

The moral duty today is to prevent nuclear war from ever occurring *and* to protect and preserve those key values of justice, freedom and independence which are necessary for personal dignity and national integrity. In reference to these issues, Pope John Paul II judges that deterrence may still be judged morally acceptable, "certainly not as an end in itself but as a step on the way toward progressive disarmament."

Two questions have particularly concerned us: 1) the targeting doctrine and strategic plans for the use of the deterrent, particularly their impact on civilian casualties; and 2) the relationship of deterrence strategy and nuclear war-fighting capability to the likelihood that war will in fact be prevented.

Moral Principles and Policy Choices

Targeting doctrine raises significant moral questions because it is a significant determinant of what would occur if nuclear weapons were ever to be used. Although we acknowledged the need for a deterrent, not all forms of deterrence are morally acceptable. There are moral limits to deterrence policy as well as to policy regarding use. Specifically, it is not morally acceptable to intend to kill the innocent as part of a strategy of deterring nuclear war. The question of whether U.S. policy involves an intention to strike civilian centers (directly targeting civilian populations) has been one of our factual concerns.

This complex question has always produced a variety of responses, official and unofficial in character. The NCCB committee has received a series of statements of clarification of policy from U.S. government officials. Essentially these statements declare that it is not U.S. strategic policy to target the Soviet civilian population as such or to use nuclear weapons deliberately for the purpose of destroying population centers.

These statements respond, in principle at least, to one moral criterion for assessing deterrence policy: the immunity of non-combatants from direct attack either by conventional or nuclear weapons.

These statements do not address or resolve another very troublesome moral problem, namely, that an attack on military targets or militarily significant industrial targets could involve "indirect" (i.e., unintended) but massive civilian casualties. We are advised, for example, that the U.S. strategic nuclear targeting plan (SIOP—Single Integrated Operational Plan) has identified 60 "military" targets within the city of Moscow alone, and that 40,000 "military" targets for nuclear weapons have been identified in the whole of the Soviet Union.[25] It is important to recognize that Soviet policy is subject to the same moral judgement; attacks on several "industrial targets" or politically significant targets in the United States could produce massive civilian casualties. The number of civilians who would necessarily be killed by such strikes is horrendous.[26] This problem is unavoidable because of the way modern military facilities and production centers are so thoroughly interspersed with civilian living and working areas. It is aggravated if one side deliberately positions military targets in the midst of a civilian population.

A second issue to concern us is the relationship of deterrence doctrine to war-fighting strategies. We are aware of the argument that war-fighting capabilities enhance the credibility of the deterrent, particularly the strategy of extended deterrence. But the development of such capabilities raises other strategic and moral questions. The relationship of war-fighting capabilities and targeting doctrine exemplifies the difficult choices in this area of policy. Targeting civilian populations would violate the principle of discrimination—one of the central moral principles of a Christian ethic of war. But "counterforce targeting," while preferable from the perspective of protecting civilians, is often joined with a declaratory policy which conveys the notion that nuclear war is subject to precise rational and moral limits. We have already expressed our severe doubts about such a concept. Furthermore, a purely counterforce strategy may seem to threaten the viability of other nations' retaliatory forces, making deterrence unstable in a crisis and war more likely.

While we welcome any effort to protect civilian populations, we do not want to legitimize or encourage moves which extend deterrence beyond the specific objective of preventing the use of nuclear weapons or other actions which could lead directly to a nuclear exchange.

These considerations of concrete elements of nuclear deterrence policy, made in light of John Paul II's evaluation, but applying it through our own prudential judgements, lead us to a strictly-conditioned moral acceptance of nuclear deterrence. We cannot consider it adequate as a long-term basis for peace.

This strictly conditioned judgement yields *criteria* for morally assessing the elements of deterrence strategy. Clearly, these criteria demonstrate that we cannot approve of every weapons system, strategic doctrine or policy initiative advanced in the name of strengthening deterrence. On the contrary, these critieria require continual public scrutiny of what our government proposes to do with the deterrent.

On the basis of these criteria we wish now to make some specific evaluations:

1. If nuclear deterrence exists only to prevent the *use* of nuclear weapons by others, then proposals to go beyond this to planning for prolonged periods of repeated nuclear strikes and counterstrikes, or "prevailing" in nuclear war, are not acceptable. They encourage notions that nuclear war can be engaged in with tolerable human and moral consequences. Rather, we must continually say no to the idea of nuclear war.

2. If nuclear deterrence is our goal, "sufficiency" to deter is an adequate strategy; the quest for nuclear superiority must be rejected.

3. Nuclear deterrence should be used as a step on the way toward progressive disarmament. Each proposed addition to our strategic system or change in strategic doctrine must be assessed precisely in light of whether it will render steps toward "progressive disarmament" more or less likely.

Moreover, these criteria provide us with the means to make some judgements and recommendations about the present direction of U.S. strategic policy. Progress toward a world freed of dependence on nuclear deterrence must be carefully carried out. But it must not be delayed. There is an urgent moral and political responsibility to use the "peace of a sort" we have as a framework to move toward authentic peace through nuclear arms control, reductions and disarmament. Of primary importance in this process is the need to prevent the development and deployment of destabilizing weapons systems on either side; a second requirement is to ensure that the more sophisticated command and control systems do not become mere hair triggers for automatic launch on warning; a third is the need to prevent the proliferation of nuclear weapons in the international system.

In light of these general judgements *we oppose* some specific proposals in respect to our present deterrence posture:

1. The addition of weapons which are likely to be vulnerable to attack, yet also possess a "prompt hard-target kill" capability that threatens to make the other side's retaliatory forces vulnerable. Such weapons may seem to be useful primarily in a first strike;[27] we resist such weapons for this reason and we oppose Soviet deployment of such weapons which generate a

fear of a first strike against U.S. forces.

2. The willingness to foster strategic planning which seeks a nuclear war-fighting capability that goes beyond the limited function of deterrence outlined in this letter.

3. Proposals which have the effect of lowering the nuclear threshold and blurring the difference between nuclear and conventional weapons.

In support of the concept of "sufficiency" as an adequate deterrent and in light of the present size and composition of both the U.S. and Soviet strategic arsenals, *we recommend:*

1. Support for immediate, bilateral, verifiable agreements to halt the testing, production and deployment of new nuclear weapons systems.[28]

2. Support for negotiated bilateral deep cuts in the arsenals of both superpowers, particularly those weapons systems which have destabilizing characteristics; U.S. proposals like those for START (Strategic Arms Reduction Talks) and INF (Intermediate-Range Nuclear Forces) negotiations in Geneva are said to be designed to achieve deep cuts; [29] our hope is that they will be pursued in a manner which will realize these goals.

3. Support for early and successful conclusion of negotiations of a comprehensive test ban treaty.

4. Removal by all parties of short-range nuclear weapons which multiply dangers disproportionate to their deterrent value.

5. Removal by all parties of nuclear weapons from areas where they are likely to be overrun in the early stages of war, thus forcing rapid and uncontrollable decisions on their use.

6. Strengthening of command and control over nuclear weapons to prevent inadvertent and unauthorized use.

These judgements are meant to exemplify how a lack of unequivocal condemnation of deterrence is meant only to be an attempt to acknowledge the role attributed to deterrence, but not to support its extension beyond the limited purpose discussed above. Some have urged us to condemn all aspects of nuclear deterrence. This urging has been based on a variety of reasons, but has emphasized particularly the high and terrible risks that either deliberate use or accidental detonation of nuclear weapons could quickly escalate to something utterly disproportionate to any acceptable moral purpose. That determination requires highly technical judgements about hypothetical events. Although reasons exist which move some to condemn reliance on nuclear weapons for deterrence, we have not reached this conclusion for the reasons outlined in this letter.

Nevertheless, there must be no misunderstanding of our profound skepticism about the moral acceptability of any use of nuclear weapons. It is obvious that the use of any weapons which violate the principle of discrimination merits unequivocal condemnation. We are told that some weapons are designed for purely "counterforce" use against military forces and targets. The moral issue, however, is not resolved by the design of weapons or the planned intention for use; there are also consequences which must be assessed. It would be a perverted political policy or moral causistry which tried to justify using a weapon which "indirectly" or "unintentionally" killed a million innocent people because they happened to live near a "militarily significant target."

Even the "indirect effects" of initiating nuclear war are sufficient to make it an unjustifiable moral risk in any form. It is not sufficient, for example, to contend that "our" side has plans for "limited" or "discriminate" use. Modern warfare is not readily contained by good intentions or technological designs. The psychological climate of the world is such that mention of the term "nuclear" generates uneasiness. Many contend that the use of one tactical nuclear weapon could produce panic, with completely unpredictable consequences. It is precisely this mix of political, psychological and technological uncertainty which has moved us in this letter to reinforce with moral prohibitions and prescriptions the prevailing political barrier against resort to nuclear weapons. Our support for enhanced command and control facilities, for major reductions in strategic and tactical nuclear forces, and for a "no first use" policy (as set forth in this letter) is meant to be seen as a complement to our desire to draw a moral line against nuclear war.

Any claim by any government that it is pursuing a morally acceptable policy of deterrence must be scrutinized with the greatest care. We are prepared and eager to participate in our country in the ongoing public debate on moral grounds.

The need to rethink the deterrence policy of our nation, to make the revisions necessary to reduce the possibility of nuclear war and to move toward a more stable system of national and international security will demand a substantial intellectual, political and moral effort. It also will require, we believe, the willingness to open ourselves to the providential care, power and word of God, which call us to recognize our common humanity and the bonds of mutual responsibility which exist in the international community in spite of political differences and nuclear arsenals.

Footnotes

1.) *Catholic Social Teaching Since Pope John,* (Maryknoll, N.Y.: 1976). D.J. O'Brien and T.A. Shannon, eds., *Renewing the Earth: Catholic Documents on Peace, Justice and Liberation,* (N.Y.: 1977). A. Flannery, OP, ed., *Vatican Council II: The Conciliar and Post Conciliar Documents,* (Collegeville, Minn.: 1975); W. Abbot, ed., *The Documents of Vatican II,* (N.Y.: 1966). Both the Flannery and Abbot translations of the pastoral constitution are used in this letter.

2.) John Paul II, Message to the Second Special Session of the United Nations General Assembly Devoted to Disarmament, (June 1982), 7 (hereafter: Message U.N. Special Session 1982).

3.) John Paul II, Address to Scientists and Scholars, 4; Origins, 10 (1981) p. 621.

4.) Pastoral Constitution, 78.

5.) For the analysis of the content and relationship of these principles cf: R. Potter, "The Moral Logic of War," *McCormick Quarterly* 23 (1970) p. 203-233; J. Childress in Shannon, cited, p. 40-58.

6.) John Paul II, World Day of Peace Message 1983, p. 11.

7.) USCC, Resolution on Southeast Asia (Washington: 1971).

8.) Pastoral Constitution, p. 80.

9.) John Paul II, World Peace Message, 1982, p. 12

10.) Representative authors in the tradition of Christian pacificism and non-violence include: R. Bainton, *Christian Attitudes Toward War and Peace,* (Abington: 1960) Ch. 4, 5, 10; J. Yoder, *The Politics of Jesus,* (Grand Rapids: 1972), *Nevertheless: Varieties of Religious Pacifism,* (Scotsdale: 1971); T. Merton, *Faith and Violence: Christian Teaching and Christian Practice,* (Notre Dame: 1968); G. Zahn, *Conscience and Dissent,* (N.Y.: 1967); E. Egan, "The Beatitudes of Works of Mercy and Pacifism," in T. Shannon, ed., *War or Peace: The Search for New Answers,* (N.Y.: 1980) p. 169-187; J. Fahey, "The Catholic Church and the Arms Race," Worldview, 22 (1979) p. 38-41; J. Douglass, *The Nonviolent Cross: The Theology of Revolution and Peace,* (N.Y.: 1966).

11.) Pastoral Constitution, p. 80.

12.) Same, p. 80.

13.) Paul VI, World Day of Peace Message, 1967; in Documents, p. 198.

14.) Statement of the Holy See to the United Nations (1976) in *The Church and the Arms Race;* Pax Christi-USA (N.Y.: 1976) p. 23-24.

15.) R. Adams and S. Cullen, *The Final Epidemic: Physicians and Scientists on Nuclear War,* (Chicago: 1981).

16.) Pontifical Academy of Sciences, "Statement on the Consequences of the Use of Nuclear Weapons," in Documents, p.241.

17.) The following quotations are from public officials who have served at the highest policy levels in recent administrations of our government:

"It is time to recognize that no one has ever succeeded in advancing any persuasive reason to believe that any use of nuclear weapons, even on the smallest scale, could reliably be expected to remain limited." McG. Bundy, G.F. Kennan, R.S. McNamara and G. Smith, "Nuclear Weapons and the Atlantic Alliance," *Foreign Affairs* 60 (1982) p. 757.

"From my experience in combat there is no way that (nuclear escalation)...can be controlled because of lack of information, the pressure of time and the deadly results that are taking place on both sides of the battle line." Gen. A.S. Collins Jr. (former deputy commander in chief of U.S. Army in Europe), "Theater Nuclear Warfare: The Battlefield," in J.F. Reichart and S.R. Sturn, eds., *American Defense Policy*, 5th ed., (Baltimore: 1982) p. 359-360.

"None of this potential flexibility changes my view that a full-scale thermonuclear exchange would be an unprecedented disaster for the Soviet Union as well as the United States. Nor is it at all clear that an initial use of nuclear weapons—however selectively they might be targeted—could be kept from escalating to a full-scale thermonuclear exchange, especially if command-and-control centers were brought under attack. The odds are high, whether weapons are used against tactical or strategic targets, that control would be lost on both sides and the exchange would become unconstrained." Harold Brown, Department of Defense Annual Report FY 1979 (Washington: 1978). Cf. also: "The Effects of Nuclear War" (Washington: 1979; U.S. Government Printing Office).

18.) For example, cf.: H.A. Kissinger, *Nuclear Weapons and Foreign Policy* (N.Y.: 1957), *The Necessity for Choice* (N.Y.: 1960); R. Osgood and R. Tucker, *Force, Order and Justice* (Baltimore: 1967); R. Aron, *The Great Debate: Theories of Nuclear Strategy* (N.Y.: 1965); D. Ball, "Can Nuclear War Be Controlled?" Adelphi paper No. 161 (London: 1981); M. Howard, "On Fighting a Nuclear War," *International Security* 5 (1981) p. 3-17.

19.) Statement on the Consequences of the Use of Nuclear Weapons, in Documents, p. 243

20.) Pius XII, Address to the VIII Congress of the World Medical Association, in Documents, p.131.

21.) Pastoral Constitution, p. 80.

22.) M. Bundy, *et al.,* "Nuclear Weapons," cited; K. Kaiser, G. Leber, A. Mertes, F.J. Schulze, "Nuclear Weapons and the Preservation of Peace," *Foreign Affairs* 60 (1982), p. 1157-70: cf. other responses to the Bundy article in the same issue of *Foreign Affairs*.

23.) W.H. Kincade and J.D. Porro, *Negotiating Security: An Arms Control Reader* (Washington: 1979).

24.) Pastoral Constitution, p. 81.

25.) S. Zukerman, *Nuclear Illusion and Reality,* (N.Y.: 1982); D. Ball, cited, p. 36; T. Powers, "Choosing a Strategy for World War III," *The Atlantic Monthly* (November 1982) p. 82-110.

26.) Cf. The coments in Pontifical Academy of Sciences "Statement on the Consequences of the Use of Nuclear Weapons."

27.) Several aspects in strategic theory would place both the MX and Pershing II missiles in this category.

28.) In each of the successive drafts of this letter we have tried to state a central moral imperative: that the arms race should be stopped and disarmament begun. The implementation of this imperative is open to a wide variety of approaches. Hence we have chosen our own language in this paragraph, not wanting to either be identified with one specific political initiative or to have our words used against specific political measures.

29.) Cf. President Reagan's Speech to the National Press Club (Nov. 18, 1981) and Address at Eureka College (May 9, 1982). Department of State, "Current Policy" pp. 346 and 387.

Chapter 32

How To Cut The Defense Budget Now

David Gold and Gordon Adams

There is underway now in Washington—and to a great extent in the rest of the nation as well—the first serious debate over the national security policies since the end of World War II. Some members of Congress and growing numbers of citizens have begun to realize that the rapid increase in military spending under this Administration is creating a massive sense of national insecurity. Tension between the superpowers appears greater today than at any time since the Cuban missile crisis.

At the same time, a revived and politically potent defense lobby—combined with Washington's largest and most powerful bureaucracy, the Pentagon—has shown no signs of restraint, heady with the attitude that all weapons are necessary and all must be bought at once. The Defense Department's procurement process is spinning out of control, weapons costs are rising dramatically, and Pentagon leaders seem unwilling to impose any limits or priorities.

As the debate proceeds, it seems to us critical for the emphasis to move from the broad question of disarmament and a nuclear freeze—those issues that E.P. Thompson, Randall Forsberg and literally millions of supporters have so correctly forced upon the nation—to a detailed and realistic discussion of the national security posture that is needed to replace the distorted vision of the Reagan Administration. In our view, military outlays can be significantly reduced—*perhaps by as much as $50 billion*—with no reduction in America's ability to defend itself.

To aid the current discussion, and to help shape the immediate proposals, we'll suggest several ways to achieve cuts in military spending. These suggestions only touch on the much needed longer-term re-evaluation of U.S. foreign policy, which could stimulate even more dramatic reductions.

Strategic Weapons and Arms Control

Growth in strategic weapons can be halted, and the nuclear force reduced, without harming America's ability to deter a Soviet nuclear attack.

The Administration's active pursuit of a complete overhaul and major expansion of the U.S. nuclear arsenal is wasteful and unnecessary. The MX missile is designed to replace the Titan and supplement the Minuteman land-based missiles; the Trident submarine and missile system to replace the Poseidon system; the B-1 to replace the B-52 and to be supplemented by the "stealth" bomber; the cruise missile to supplement strategic and European theater forces; the Pershing 2 to succeed the Pershing 1 in Europe; and some 17,000 new nuclear warheads to supplement and replace current ones. Combined with improvement in early warning systems and communications, continued work on submarine and air defense systems, and accelerated research and testing of ballistic missile defense systems, the Administration's "strategic modernization" package will cost at least $260 billion—in the end, probably far more—over the next half-decade.

This package is redundant and destabilizing. The B-1 will be ineffective against more sophisticated Soviet air defense systems and it will be unnecessary—the modified B-52 can perform as both a conventional bomber and a cruise missile carrier. The MX would be a formidable threat to the Soviet Union and a lucrative, and vulnerable, target for Soviet missiles. The Congressional Budget Office has concluded that MX will add very little to the survivability of the U.S. deterrent. With single warhead missiles being planned for the 1990s, the costly MX can be dispensed with. Eliminating the B-1 and the MX could save $13.5 billion in the Pentagon's 1984 authorization request.

Moreover, the proliferation of sea-launched cruise missiles would make verification of future arms agreements more difficult. Nuclear-tipped cruise missiles could be transported on almost any type of ship, and once they were deployed, neither the United States nor the Soviet Union could determine how many the other side had or whether they carried nuclear or conventional warheads.

But worse, the Reagan program allocates money for improvements that are quite unnecessary and imply a shift in America's nuclear strategy. The most important feature of the strategic package is not its additional megatonnage or its new warheads. It is the substantial improvement in guidance systems, making missiles far more accurate than before and far more able to destroy hardened targets. Such accuracy is not necessary for a strategy based on mutual deterrence, which requires only that a portion of the arsenal be capable of surviving a first strike and inflicting unacceptable damage on the aggressor. In the 1960s, the Defense Department estimated that nuclear forces would need the equivalent of 400 megatons of explosive power to inflict an unacceptable level of damage on the Soviet Union. Since both sides have many times the equivalent of 400 survivable megatons in their arsenals, the conditions for deterrence have existed for a long time and could exist at even far lower levels of force.

While many advocates of nuclear disarmament—Thompson, Jonathan Schell and others—maintain that there is no real distinction between mutual deterrence and the "winnable nuclear war" policy of some in the Reagan Administration, there is at least one difference. Deterrence implies a limitation of arms, an "enoughness" at some point, whereas the winnability school argues that nuclear weapons are weapons like any others and can always be improved and added to. In the last decade this latter view has been embodied in such strategies as "counterforce targeting" and "limited" nuclear warfare, and the technology has advanced to the point where it is possible to envision them as guidelines for actual military operations.

"Nuclear superiority" is a phrase without meaning as long as each superpower retains a survivable deterrent. It is easy, and relatively inexpensive, to deny superiority to another; it is practically impossible and prohibitively expensive to achieve it oneself. Moreover, for those worried about the survivability of land-based missiles and bombers, it should be emphasized that the U.S. submarine force will be survivable for decades, given America's lead in both submarine and antisubmarine warfare technology.

It is important to recognize that there is both a quantitative and a qualitative arms race. A decision against a new generation of nuclear weapons—the MX, Trident, cruise missile and the B-1 bomber—would not affect the utility or survivability of current strategic weapons (the submarine force in particular) and could be a significant first step toward a freeze and mutual reductions. Arms control talks could then focus on a process of having each side give up advantages step by step. The U.S. lead in warhead technology and submarine warfare could be a bargaining chip against the Soviet advantage in "throw weight" and megatonnage. So long as the reductions do not threaten either side's deterrent, they can continue until the deterrent itself is negotiable.

European Theater

Roughly half of the military budget is keyed to Europe, and the Administration makes much of the need for both a nuclear and a conventional buildup there to counter the "superiority" of the Soviet Union. Here too, it is necessary to move cautiously and offer a clear alternative.

The argument for deploying Pershing 2 and cruise missiles in Europe is that without them a Soviet Union superior in conventional arms could carry out a lightning armored thrust across the central European plains, sweeping NATO forces aside in a rush to the sea. This scenario simply does not conform to reality. As Robert McNamara has noted, "The conventional balance is not as favorable to the Soviets as is often assumed...We overstate the Soviets' force and underestimate ours." According to the International Institute for Strategic Studies, NATO and Warsaw Pact nations are equal in military personnel. Moreover, about half of the Warsaw Pact divisions are made up of Eastern Europeans, hardly the most reliable force in wartime. The superior number of Warsaw Pact tanks (27,500 to 11,800) is countered by NATO's vastly superior supply of anti-tank weapons (193,000 to 68,000 according to former Undersecretary of Defense William Perry). While the Soviet Union has more fighter and attack aircraft than the United States, the United States has nearly a two-to-one superiority in more sophisticated aircraft. NATO forces appear more than adequate to deter and counter those of the Warsaw Pact.

At the nuclear level, assertions of Soviet superiority are misleading. The 470 Soviet SS-4, SS-5 and SS-20 missiles are deterred by America's two Polaris subs, with 32 multiple-warhead missiles, and 64 British and 98 French medium-range missiles. In addition, both sides have vast supplies of nuclear warheads that can be delivered by long- and medium-range fighter and attack aircraft. In warheads—the category that most reliably indicates total destructive capability—the United States and NATO have a superiority of roughly three to one, counting battlefield, fighter-carried and missile versions.

Both sides maintain enough conventional and nuclear forces in Europe to make it a wasteland in case of war. Both sides are deterred.

If the Pershing 2 and ground-launched cruise missile programs were halted, that would save $1.3 billion in the fiscal 1983 budget. The "enhanced radiation" warhead, popularly known as the neutron bomb, is also not essential, and elimination of that program would save billions.

Some Pentagon officials assert that a massive buildup of conventional forces is the necessary concomitant of a denuclearized Europe. While these forces should not be allowed to rust, NATO/Warsaw Pact parity suggests that in the short run only gradual modernization is required. In the long run, both sides would benefit greatly from progress in the troop reduction talks in Vienna, lessening even further the likelihood that Europe could again be a theater of military conflict.

Chemical weapons designed for potential use in Europe are also included in the Reagan budget, justified by the assertion that they were used by the Soviet Union in Afghanistan and by Vietnam in Cambodia. The Administration plans to commit almost $800 million to chemical warfare programs in 1984, up 50 percent in two years. Arkansas Senator David Pryor, who has been drawn into the debate because the Administration wants to open a binary nerve gas plant in Pine Bluff, Arkansas, has argued that a new chemical warfare race "would commit the United States to at least $6 billion over the next five years." He and other critics have also pointed out that the current U.S. chemical arsenal is an adequate deterrent to any attack by the Soviet Union.

Although both sides in Europe train with chemical weapons, battlefield use of them presents formidable problems. The cumbersome equipment required would make fighting extremely difficult. Because of winds, neither side would know for sure which troops were vulnerable when or where. Moreover, the political complications of trying to deploy chemical weapons in Europe would further threaten NATO unity; as Senator Pryor notes, "The Europeans are not going to let nerve gas on their soil." Here, too, the United States and the Soviet Union have much to gain from arms control.

Overseas Intervention

The Reagan military budget also includes vast sums for upgrading U.S. power to intervene overseas. There are two major components of this effort—a massive increase in the size of the Navy and a buildup of the Rapid Deployment Force. Both are dubious in military terms and neither is consistent with a U.S. foreign policy aimed at non-intervention.

Over the next decade, the Administration proposes increasing the size of the Navy from 400 ships to 600, thus expanding the number of carrier-led battle groups from 13 to 15 (with the possibility of additional groups built around refurbished World War II battleships). The cost of this buildup is staggering: each battle group would take almost $20 billion to construct and another $20 billion to maintain over its life, excluding inflation. And carrier-led battle groups are militarily inefficient. They are large and slow and easy targets for an opponent with sophisticated equipment, especially naval bombers, cruise missiles and long-range "smart" missiles, as the Falklands war indicated. Indeed, much of the weaponry in a battle group is designed for self-defense, not for intervention.

One reason advanced for the new battle groups is to counter what is described as a large buildup of Soviet naval forces, thus permitting the United States to maintain its dominance over the sea lanes and its "show-the-flag" exercises around the world. But this justification is thin: most Soviet vessels are small and must keep close to Soviet coasts. The real reason for the groups is to reassert U.S. control over the course of political and economic events in the less developed world, substituting military force for diplomatic acumen and economic reform. However, current U.S. naval forces, already immense, are more than adequate even for these purposes. If these purposes are redefined, as is desirable, the naval force could be smaller, more mobile and less expensive.

The Rapid Deployment Force shows the same weaknesses. At a cost of at least $6 billion in fiscal 1984, the Administration plans to purchase container ships, start production of new cargo aircraft, and train and equip 229,000 Army, Navy and Marine troops for rapid deployment to crisis areas. This force is ostensibly designed for the Middle East, planners citing a Soviet invasion of Iran as the most likely emergency they expect to face.

The risks of this strategy are enormous. To deploy a significant force against such an invasion would require the creation of bases in Middle Eastern countries that either have unstable governments or are hostile to the United States because of Israel. And since the Rapid Deployment Force could not realistically respond to a Soviet thrust into Iran, it is more likely to be used in other parts of the globe against inferior local armies where there is no Soviet involvement. The link with an interventionist foreign policy is clear. If the United States intends to permit events to follow their own course, as was done in Nicaragua and Zimbabwe during the Carter Administration, rather than try to hold back the flood tides of change, its current deployment capabilities—the Marine Corps and the airborne forces in the Army—are more than adequate. Futher buildup is redundant.

Personnel

Defense Department personnel costs are immense. Salaries and benefits for the 1 million civilians and 2.1 million soldiers who make up the Pentagon's labor force are almost half of the current defense budget. While this percentage would drop under the proposed Reagan program, the dollar amount would rise. Some have suggested reinstituting the draft as a means of reducing costs and increasing numbers, but the problem discussed most often by military leaders is retaining people with skills and training, not attracting new recruits. The need to retain skilled people has increased over the last decade as the military has moved to more sophisticated equipment. A new draft would only make the problem worse, since draftees are less likely to have career ambitions than volunteers.

Some personnel reforms could help. Pay scales could be changed so that top officers receive less and noncoms and junior officers more. The "up-or-out" policy of retiring officers who are not promoted after a certain number of years could be revised; many would be content to remain majors and colonels, just as many corporate employees continue their careers even if they don't become vice-presidents. Preventing retired personnel from drawing both a full pension and a full salary in another government position could save additional money. And substantial savings could result from a shift in the orientation of military policy toward smaller strategic forces, a smaller Navy and smaller overseas troop deployments.

Waste

Pentagon waste, particularly in weapons-procurement procedures, amounts to somewhere between $10 billion and $30 billion a year, according to budget director David Stockman. Part of the problem is simple mismanagement, much of which can be remedied, and part of it is the lack of accountability within the closed system linking the Defense Department, military contractors, and key members of Congress. As Stockman has said, the main source of waste is "strong clients with weak claims." Or, in the words of Arizona Representative John Rhodes, "Eisenhower was obviously right when he said that the military-industrial complex needed to be watched—it does, and it isn't being watched to the point that it must be in the future."

In April 1981, seeking to defuse Pentagon critics, Undersecretary of Defense Frank Carlucci announced 32 basic reforms, including decentralization of procurement decisions, elimination of some regulations, an end to "buying-in" (giving Congress an unrealistically low estimate and then increasing costs once production is underway) and modification of the present bidding procedures, by which two-thirds of all negotiated contracts are bid on by a single supplier.

The Pentagon's opinion of these reforms was reflected in the fact that the cost of 47 principal weapons systems *rose* 114 percent from December 1981 to March 1982. And the truth is that, like past efforts, they just won't work. They do not focus on the real managerial and political sources of excessive costs: the lack of discipline among contractors and the close relationship between industry and the Pentagon. In many cases, contractors dream up their new weapons systems and prepare proposals based on their own inflated estimates of costs. The Pentagon relies on those figures, examines the expenditures only casually, and is motivated to obtain whatever weapon is promised at whatever costs. Once the procurement process is underway, no matter how wasteful the system, an army of titans is needed to reverse the political steamroller.

We believe the cost estimates should be more closely controlled, contractors who perform poorly should not receive new contracts, and greater competition should be required in contract bidding. Congress also needs to revive the few agencies that, however inadequately, monitored costs and contractor performance—including the Renegotiation Board (killed in 1978) and the Cost Accounting Standards Board (killed in 1980)—and to increase the authority of the General Accounting Office and the Defense Contract Audit Agency. In addition, Congress must curb the tendency of the Defense Department to buy weapons of excessively high technology, made ever more sophisticated as they go through the research and production process. High technology is not of itself undesirable, but stopping short of the last margin of sophistication and producing simpler weapons over a longer period would help reduce costs. Moreover, less complex weapons would ease the problems of maintenance and parts replacement, improving overall readiness.

The kind of reforms we are talking about here must be distinguished from those recently advocated by James Fallows, Gary Hart, and other Pentagon critics, who have attacked the Pentagon's elaborate gold-plated weaponry. Reform in the way weapons are purchased is important, but it is not the same thing as substituting simple technologies for complex ones so as to wage war more easily. If the objective is to reduce the risk of conflict while preserving national security, enormous stockpiles of weapons that are even simpler to use are not the solution—and in fact may only make unacceptable objectives easier to achieve.

As this discussion suggests, the Defense Department and especially Congress are missing the point on the military budget. More spending is not buying more security. It is throwing money at a series of non-problems, or at the wrong problems. The nuclear balance is even and requires a freeze and then reductions. European theater forces must be deployed in ways that reduce the likelihood of conflict. Current conventional forces are, in general, adequate for defense. Personnel costs can be restrained. Finally, the procurement mechanism requires deep-rooted reforms, not cosmetic changes. At heart, the problem is one of widening the range of alternatives and making the defense policy process more accountable to Congress and to the American public.

Chapter 33

Converting the Military Economy

Lloyd Dumas

The persistence of high levels of military spending over the last three and a half decades of what has officially been called "peacetime" has been a primary source of the ongoing stagflation from which the U.S. has suffered since 1969. It is therefore inconceivable that more than fleeting,cosmetic improvements in the economic situation in the U.S. can be achieved while the military budget is being expanded. In fact, substantial reductions in military spending, along with the transference of resources now in the military sector of the economy to productive, civilian-oriented activity, are a prerequisite to returning the U.S. economy to health and vigor. Such transference has been called "economic conversion," and the problem of carrying it out smoothly and efficiently so as to replace the previous military activity not merely with some civilian alternative activity but with economically viable alternative activity is the main focus of this chapter. This must, of course, begin with a thorough understanding of the parameters of the process.

Technological resource conversion. A major part of the problem of converting technologists from military to civilian oriented work is rooted in the differential requirements for successful military and civilian technological development. Present day high-technology military products are extremely com-

539

plex, and are designed with an effort to squeeze every possible ounce of performance out of the product. Whether or not this extra performance capability actually has military significance, the presumption that it does clearly underlies the practice of weapons research and development. This has led to the assignment of large teams of technologists to the design of weapons systems, each, in effect, developing and designing a part of a part. Accordingly, the need to become an expert in a very narrow range of knowledge has led to extreme specialization of engineers and scientists engaged in military-related work. In addition, the extreme priority attached to military funding, combined with the common practice of procuring weapons on an effectively cost-plus basis and the pressure for even small increments in weapons capability, has led to strong emphasis on the cost implication of design. In fact more expensive designs will certainly result in increases in sales revenue and typically in profit as well to the firms which generate them.

Successful design for the civilian market place, on the other hand, requires very heavy emphasis on the implication of the specific design for the cost of producing the ultimate product. This implies that designers, rather than being extremely specialized, should have a fairly clear concept of the overall design of the product and the interactions of its subcomponents. This, together with a basic understanding of the effects on cost of modifying the design in one way or another, will enable them to trade off changes in one part of the design against changes in the other to achieve desired product performance at the lowest possible cost. Keeping production cost down enables the price to be kept at a level which will make the product attractive to potential customers and hence bring expanded sales and profit to the firm.

Because of these differences, engineers and scientists performing defense work must be retrained and re-oriented before they can be successful in civilian research and development. Complete retraining is clearly not required, since much of the mathematical, scientific, and engineering knowledge they already have is also required for civilian work. But despecialization and increased cost sensitivity are required to establish firm connection with civilian design realities.

The length of the retraining process depends on the specific individual involved, the nature of his/her previous education and experience and the particular pair of activities between which the transfer is taking place. Clearly, a civil engineer moving between design work on jet fighters and design work on corporate jets will require less extensive retraining than one transferring from jet fighter design to bridge building. Yet it is possible to give a reasonably generalized range estimate for retraining time. It is unlikely to require less than six months or more than two years. In all likelihood, retraining and reorientation will ordinarily take a year to a year and a half.

The conversion process must also be extended to the educational institutions responsible for the training of engineers and scientists. These institutions have altered their curricula to emphasize specialization, especially in areas and sub-areas of interest to the military, and strongly de-emphasize training in cost-related matters. Instruction in mundane civilian-oriented areas like, for example, power engineering, was curtailed or eliminated, particularly at the "best" schools. All this may have been an appropriate institutional response to the changing shape of the high prestige opportunities available to their graduates. And yet, these changes meant that even those engineers and scientists who did go directly into civilian areas were to some extent less than optimally trained for the development of civilian-oriented technological progress. Existing engineering and scientific institutions, once reoriented, should be fully competent to carry out transitional retraining of the sort needed to produce a smooth and efficient conversion process.

The inability of military-oriented engineers and scientists to move into civilian-oriented research and development without conversion retraining is indicated by the commonly observed tendency of technologists, laid off because of the termination of a defense contract, to move to another geographic area to follow the contracts, accept non-engineering or nonscientific work, or simply remain unemployed until the contracts return. This tendency has been read by some as an indication that civilian technology is not starved by the diversion of technological personnel to military areas as I have argued, since they are not grabbed up by civilian research programs when they do become unemployed. But the failure of these technologists to be readily absorbed into civilian industry is due to the inappropriateness of their training and experience, not an overall lack of demand and certainly not a lack of national or commercial need. This point is periodically illustrated by such events as the development of a critical shortage of engineers qualified to design new non-nuclear power plants in the early 1970's side by side with the existence of a substantial pool of unemployed military-oriented engineers.[1]

Management conversion. The management of military industrial firms operates in a very different atmosphere from that which prevails in civilian-oriented enterprise. Defense firms have, in practice, only one customer—the United States

Government. They cannot sell their products to civilian customers in any case, and can sell to foreign governments only with the direct and specific approval of the U.S. Department of Defense. Even so, weapons sold to foreign governments were originally designed, developed, and produced for sale to the U.S. Government.

The one-customer orientation produces a very different sales and marketing situation from that faced by civilian firms. Rather than knowing how to run an effective electronic and print media advertising campaign, how to survey markets for public acceptance of a new product line, how to price a product for penetration into new markets or expansion of existing ones, etc., it becomes critical to know the minute detail of the Armed Services Procurement Regulations, to develop good working relationships with key government procurement personnel, and to be able to lobby effectively with members of the Congress.

Furthermore, the military industrial firm sells its product before it is produced, a very different situation from that faced by typical civilian manufacturers. This, combined with the availability of "progress payments," i.e. installment payments made by the government as different stages of the production process are completed, greatly alters the nature of the financing function, substantially lowering the need for equity funds. (This, of course, also tends to make the rate of return on equity, the conventional measure of profit rate, extremely high in military firms.)

Another critical difference is that the single customer does not itself have to sell its product in a market place. It does not therefore have to worry either about the effects on the ultimate price of its "product," of paying too much for the goods it buys, or the danger of its being forced into loss or bankruptcy by a drop in its sales if the equipment it purchases does not perform well.[2]

This strongly interacts with a third critical factor, the extremely high priority accorded to defense procurement, which is currently supported by national consensus. This not only assures that the Defense Department will continue to be a very rich customer, but also that its purchase decisions will be readily validated by both the Congress and the President. Thus, the wealthy customer that the military industry services faces no economic market test, and only the very loosest political contraints.

The net effect of these last two factors has been to guarantee at least higher *revenues* and typically higher *profits* to those military firms which are most effective in running up the cost of the products which they are contracted to produce, often regardless of whether or not these products perform as expected. A management operating in such a *milieu* will become very effective at finding ways of producing at high cost. But this sort of management training and experience is completely inappropriate to successful operation in civilian markets, where *holding costs down* is the crucial skill.

One of the most striking examples of the contrast between the way in which products are produced for military as opposed to civilian markets lies in the comparison of the Boeing 747 and the Lockheed C5A cargo plane. Both of these planes are jumbo jets of roughly comparable size, but the former was designed and produced for sale to commercial civilian airlines and the latter for sale to the U.S. Air Force. The 747 is a smooth flying, highly reliable aircraft flown daily by most of the world's major airlines, and is as energy efficient when fully loaded as a Volkswagen "beetle" carrying only its driver. The C5A has been plagued by severe operating difficulties, including cracking of the wing pylons, crash-producing failures of the rear cargo door, and considerable landing gear problems. The Air Force has acknowledged that a cargo version of the 747 could carry a larger payload than the C5A.[3] In 1971, the 747 was selling at about $23 million per plane as against the $60 million per plane cost of the C5A.[4] Furthermore, the wing defects of the C5A, which reduced its estimated service life by more than 70 percent, were projected to cost some $1.3 billion to repair, nearly doubling the original cost estimates for the program.[5]

That managements of military firms are in a sense rewarded for high cost production, even in the face of low product quality and performance, is illustrated by the following listing of article headlines, excerpted from *The New York Times:*

1.) "Nine Spy Planes Lost in Crashes, Pentagon Says" (March 23, 1979)...these planes were developed by Lockheed.

2.) "X Factor Continues to Raise Luftwaffe's Starfighter Toll" (July 4, 1972)...report of the 154th crash of this plane designed by Lockheed.

3.) "Lockheed's Step Is Costliest Ever: $800 Million Write-off on Tristar..." (November 23, 1974)...report of financial loss by Lockheed in its development of the L1011 commercial jet.

4.) "C5A Jet Repairs to cost $1.5 Billion" (December 5, 1975).

5.) "Lockheed Rises to Top as Defense Contractor" (December 11, 1975).

And, of course, this is the same firm whose management was granted a $250 million loan guarantee by the Federal Government.

Clearly, one cannot expect managers accustomed to operating in a situation in which there is no risk, high costs are not merely tolerated but become the path to success, and only one rich customer need be serviced, to operate successfully in risky, cost sensitive, multi-customer civilian markets without substantial retraining and re-orientation. When unconverted military industrial managements have turned their attention to production of civilian products for state and local governments, the results have borne a striking resemblance to their military operations in both cost and performance. Consider, for example, the Bay Area Rapid Transit (BART) system in San Francisco whose prime contractor was the Rohr Company, a firm which made its reputation in aerospace and related operations. Although the system was supposed to be in operation by 1968, prototypes were still crashing in 1971.[6]. A few weeks after it opened in 1972, the computer-controlled network experienced a number of breakdowns, including one instance in which a train "failed to slow down at the end of the line, barreled through a sand barrier, and did a nosedive into a parking lot."[7] As of late 1975, up to half the cars were out of service at any given time, "causing delays and standing room only for San Francisco commuters, who have dubbed it Bay Area Reckless Transit."[8] By 1971, estimates for the cost of the system had grown from $792 million to $1.4 billion.[9]

There is little question, that whether military oriented managements are turned to the supervision of the production of goods and services sold in the civilian marketplace or for civilian use by government, they must be retrained and re-oriented as a prerequisite for successful conversion.

For managers, as for engineers and scientists, the length of the retraining process for any given individual depends upon that particular person's education and experience, though it is likely to be somewhat less sensitive in the managerial than in the technological case. Similarly, the nature of the activities between which transference is being made influences both the length and nature of the retraining. In general it is likely that the retraining and re-orientation period will take on the order of six to eighteen months. Existing business and related schools at universities around the country should be capable of carrying out this transitional educational process, most likely with less internal readjustment than would be required at institutions engaged in retraining engineers and scientists. Management training centers of various large civilian-oriented cor-

FIGURE 33-1
BUDGET SAVINGS FROM A NUCLEAR FREEZE
(FY 1983-1987 ... and Beyond)

— Systems Which Would Be Directly Halted By A Freeze —

System or Program	Savings FY 1983-1987 (In Billions)	...And Beyond (In Billions)
MX Missile	$23.9	$60-$70 through year 2000*
B-1B Bomber	$27.2	Depends on how quickly Stealth bomber is developed
Trident I Submarine-launched Ballistic Missile (SLBM)	$ 2.5	$10 (for outfitting 12 Poseidon subs and 8 subs)
Air-launched Cruise Missile (ALCM)	$ 5.2	$5 to $6 under current plans
Sea-launched Cruise Missile (SLCM)	$ 0.8	At least $10.2 (depends on decision on how many to deploy)
Pershing II Missile Ground-launched Cruise Missile (GLCM)	$ 1.1	$5 to $6 for ground-launched cruise missile and Pershing through 1986
Nuclear Warhead Production Nuclear Warhead Development & Testing Nuclear Materials Production	$11.5 $ 3.6 $ 6.0	At least $21 through 1987. No estimate beyond
TOTAL**	$81.8	$190-$205 (Includes Trident II and Stealth)

FIGURE 33-1
BUDGET SAVINGS FROM A NUCLEAR FREEZE
CONTINUED

— Systems Which Would Be Halted After 1987 By A Freeze —

Trident II Missile (now in R&D)	$21.5 total program cost**
Stealth Bomber (now in R&D)	$30 through 1991***

— Systems Which Might Be Reduced Or Eliminated Once A Freeze Takes Effect —

Ballistic Missile Defense	$10-$25 total program cost****
Strategic Air Defense	$2.5 through 1987
Command, Control & Communications	$7 added through 1987***
Trident Submarine	$30 total program costs (20 subs), $11.75 through 1987

* Based on 20 year cycle in dense pack basing mode without ABM or other modifications which may be necessary
** In constant 1982 dollars — total costs, with inflation, will be higher
*** Figures on Stealth, C3, and Strategic Air Defense, from *Aviation Week and Space Technology,* October 12, 1982, pp. 18-20
**** Program costs are uncertain because final decisions have not been made on BMD.

Source: Unpublished data obtained from the U.S. Congressional Budget Office. April. 1982, adjusted to reflect a reduced MX missile authorization, for FY 1983. The $84.2 billion five-year total reflects budget authority — most of this will be spent in outlays during the five-year period.
Background Sources: Center for Defense Information. *Preparing for Nuclear War: President Reagan's Program;* Department of Defense. *Selected Acquisition Reports* as of March 31. 1982; Department of Defense: R. D. T. and E Programs. *Department of Defense Budget for Fiscal Year 1983. Office of Management and Budget. Major Themes and Additional Budget Details. FY 1983.* Thanks to SANE and the Coalition for a New Foreign Policy for much of the work on which this is based — *Economic Benefits of the Freeze.*

porations should also be available to aid in the process.

Conversion of production and low-level administrative workers. With the possible exception of a few highly skilled workers, the primary problem in channeling production and administrative workers into civilian oriented work lies not in the need for re-education but rather in the *numbers* of people involved. Roughly six million people in the United States are directly employed in military-related work by the Pentagon and by military-oriented industry. Clearly, the bulk of these employees are production workers and low-level administrative employees, including clerical workers.

Re-orientation to the standards of work of civilian enterprises will undoubtedly be required, since the lack of pressure toward efficiency generated by cost plus pricing permeates the system, and it is possible that additional vocational training will be required for some of these employees. This latter training is not so much to undo the effects of having been employed in military-related work as such (as in the case of engineers, scientists and managers), but rather to bring their skill into more perfect congruence with the best civilian opportunities available. The transition problem is simpler here because of the lesser nature of the re-education required, but more difficult because many more people are potentially involved.

The civilian re-employment of the workers displaced by cutbacks in military expenditures creates a potential problem for the unions involved, since workers may be transferred into industries or lines of work in the ordinary jurisdiction of unions other than those to which they currently belong. The seriousness of this problem depends on the particular form of organization of the unions involved, craft unions being clearly less likely to be affected than industrial unions. With the teamsters organizing teachers and the steelworkers organizing workers at nuclear weapons facilities these days, the problem has been somewhat mitigated. Nevertheless, this issue must be taken seriously, if, among other reasons, one is to avoid opposition to economic conversion by leaders of unions with an inordinately short-term and parochial view. As we have seen, continued high military expenditure is economically destructive, and in the long term, its inflation and unemployment-generating effects hurt defense workers as well as the large numbers of non-defense workers who constitute the vast majority of the U.S. labor force.

Capital equipment and facilities. Some of the industrial equipment and facilities currently employed in the service of the military are sufficiently general purpose in nature to be directly usable in civilian-oriented work. But some, such as certain types of extremely high capability machine tools, specialized shipbuilding facilities and highly specialized equipment for working with extraordinarily toxic materials (such as plutonium) are not so directly transferable. As to machinery whose civilian applicability suffers mainly from the excessive cost derived from its excessively high performance capability, the equipment should be usable for civilian operations if some sort of special one-time write-offs or tax breaks are allowed to overcome the cost penalty.

Those industrial facilities which do not so much possess excess capabilities as the *wrong* capabilities will have to be reconstructed, which cannot be effectively done until specific plans have been developed for the particular alternative purpose to which those facilities are to be turned. Similarly, military bases are unlikely to be appropriate, without some degree of alteration, for efficient performance of a civilian oriented activity.

Nuclear weapons facilities represent an interesting special case. In planning for conversion of nuclear weapons facilities there tend to be two common problems specifically related to the physical facility. The first is the existence of plant and equipment highly specialized to the storage, handling and processing of nuclear materials. At the manufacturing end (places like the Rocky Flats plant near Denver), there may be glove boxes, dust and fume control devices, remote manipulators, etc. At the storage and shipping end (places like the Seal Beach Naval Weapons Station near Los Angeles), there are earth-covered storage bunkers, special handling containers, etc. And at the waste storage facilities (like those in Hanford, Washington), large—and now thoroughly contaminated—tanks and associated facilities are found. This leads directly to the second problem, the problem of radioactive contamination.

It would be extremely surprising if there were a single nuclear weapons facility that was untouched by continuing radiation problems. It is certain that manufacturing facilities and waste facilities dealing with nuclear materials house at least some equipment that is heavily contaminated. In addition, leakages of radioactive materials into the soil at all such locations are a virtual certainty, rendering portions of the site and perhaps associated water supplies hazardous. The extent to which it is possible to effectively de-contaminate this equipment and these areas can only be determined by a thorough analysis of each facility. If there are storage areas from which nuclear materials cannot be removed for health, safety or whatever reasons, extreme care must be taken to avoid establishing new activity on the site that could threaten their integrity. If such materials have already been lost into the immediate environment, care must be taken to avoid further dispersal in the process of modifying the facility or in the nature of the new activity to be established.

The meaning of both these problems is that some parts of nuclear weapons facilities may have to be reckoned as a dead loss in planning conversion. But this is not equivalent to saying that activities carried on at such facilities are non-convertible. Even if the whole physical facility were unusable for productive civilian alternatives (a rare event), the labor force is an extremely valuable resource.

Preparing capital equipment and facilities for conversion is primarily a matter of assessing in detail what changes in layout, direct equipment and facilities, and supporting equipment and facilities are implied by the chosen civilian alternative. Given such an assessment, it should not be difficult to estimate both financing requirements and the time needed from start to finish for the actual physical conversion. This will in turn enable development of a financial plan, as well as effective coordination of this phase of the resource conversion process with the others.

Intra-regional concentration and the conversion problem. Property taxes, which were the subject of the famed taxpayer revolt of 1978 that began with the passage of Proposition 13 in California, constitute only about one-fifth of the average individual's tax burden. These taxes flow to state and local governments, primarily to finance local services such as education, road repair, health care, police, fire and sanitation services, as well as public welfare. Federal income taxes, on the other hand, are responsible for nearly half the individual's direct tax burden. Almost two-thirds of what the U.S. Office of Management and Budget defines as "relatively controllable" federal outlays (those essentially decided upon year-by-year) went for military purposes. In 1977, the average U.S. citizen paid $2.50 in federal income tax for every dollar paid in state and local property tax. Thus, the part of the individual's tax burden taken as "military tax" can be roughly estimated as somewhere between $1.10 and $1.60 per dollar of property tax.

While the incidence of military tax corresponds essentially to the pattern of per capita income, the military expenditures which the tax supports are distributed in a very different pattern. Military spending tends to be concentrated in relatively distinct geographic pockets, which are to be found in all major geographic sectors of the U.S. Examples include the San Francisco Bay area, Seattle, the Dallas-Fort Worth metroplex, and the Boston-Cambridge area. This combination of high concentration and geographic dispersion has important political and economic implications.

Politically, one would be hard-pressed to devise a geographic pattern which would provide better leverage. The Congressional representatives elected by constituencies which include one or more of these pockets, feel themselves compelled to support military programs that they perceive are in the interest of the people by whom they were elected, providing them with continued employment. They come to believe that their continued election depends upon the effectiveness with which they can aid in at least maintaining, if not expanding, the flow of military funds to their district. Accordingly, they may become salespeople for the military industry in their area.

Geographic concentration guarantees that the impact of alterations in the pattern, and particularly the magnitude, of military expenditure will not go unnoticed. The geographic dispersion of these pockets maximizes the likelihood that, through the normal process of congressional *quid pro quo* vote trading, support for maintenance or expansion of military expenditures will continue. This is particularly true to the extent that military spending pockets are focused in the districts of key Congresspeople.

In a recent study, James Anderson of Michigan State University analyzed the distribution of direct military tax dollar burden counterposed against the distribution of military spending by state, major metropolitan area and by congressional district.[10]

When both the military expenditure inflows and the military tax outflows are taken into consideration, the usual picture of military spending as a broad-gauge boon to the nation's economy takes on a different cast, for the pattern is one of vastly unequal distribution of burdens and benefits. A total of 305 of the nation's 435 congressional districts are, according to Anderson's calculations, net losers. (Of all the east coast states, only Maryland and Connecticut have more congressional districts with more net inflow than outflow.) Not a single state in the entire mid-country has more net inflow than outflow districts; the same is true of the South, where even Texas, second in the nation in total prime military contracts, has 14 out of 24 districts which are net losers. The two regions of the U.S. experiencing the greatest economic stagnation difficulties, the Northeast and the Midwest, are severely drained: 79 of the 104 congressional districts in the Northwest are net losers, as are 95 of the 100 districts in the upper Midwest.[11]

Within states, the disparities can be extreme. In Mississippi, for example, the state as a whole has a net excess of military spending over military tax of $1.3 billion. Yet, in Anderson's words, "Four out of its five congressional districts, comprising the northern four-fifths of the state's population and land area suffer a net drain...About $1.6 billion of Pentagon spending is concentrated entirely within the southeastern corner of the state..."[12] Texas, too, is a case in point. The Dallas-Fort Worth and San Antonio metropolitan areas experienced net inflows in fiscal 1977 of $862 million and $932 million, respectively, at the same time that the military tax burden was producing a net drain of $964 million in Houston.

It is not the intention here to analyze in any great detail the status and power in the Congress of the representatives of the net inflow areas, particularly in the House of Representatives where sheer numbers and complexity greatly magnify the task. However, a quick look at the 96th Congress, i.e., that which held office just *prior* to the sharp conservative pro-military shift that accompanied the Reagan election of 1980, indicates some interesting, though highly tentative results.[13] The largest net gain congressional district in the nation (nearly $1.6 billion) was, and is that of Congressman Wright of Texas, the House Majority Leader. Nearly a dozen representatives from the top 50 net inflow districts sat on the House Armed Services Committee; 9 sat on the Budget, Appropriations, or Ways and Means Committees, a dozen more on the Rules or Government Operations Committees. But, on the whole, the picture in the House was sufficiently ambiguous to require a much closer look before drawing firm conclusions.

In the Senate, the picture was a bit simpler and more clear. The ten states which had the largest net inflow according to the Anderson study were (in descending order): California, Virginia, Texas, Missouri, Connecticut, Mississippi, Washington, Hawaii, New Mexico and Maryland. Among the senators from these states were: the Senate Majority Whip; the Chair, Ranking Minority Member and three other members of the Armed Services Committee; the Chair of the Appropriations Committee and the Chair of its Defense Appropriations Subcommittee; and the Chair and five other members of the Governmental Affairs Committee. It is also interesting to note that 12 of the 17 members of the Armed Services Committee represented net inflow states, and only two represented a state without a single net inflow district (Iowa)—there are 12 such states.

What emerges here is a reasonably clear indication that in terms of direct dollar tax outflows and offsetting direct dollar return flows of military expenditures, the vast majority of the nation suffers a net loss even when viewed in simplistic, money flow terms. The military tax, offset against expenditures, produces a net dollar drain in more than 70 percent of the nation's congressional districts. Furthermore, a cursory glance at the Congress, even prior to its new conservative tilt, gives some indication (particularly in the Senate) that the pattern of expenditure relative to taxation has either resulted in or has been caused by a substantial congressional power base of representatives of areas with direct and substantial political economic stakes in military expenditure decisions, and a clear upward bias for reasons not necessarily related to either national security realities or the general economic well-being of the nation.

The primary economic implication of the geographic pattern of military-related facilities is that macroeconomic policies such as income tax reductions and money supply increases cannot cope with the problem of stimulating the economy so as to effectively produce a smooth absorption of the resources freed from military use into civilian activities. Such policies average their effects broadly over the nation. But what is required here are policies which will reach specifically into these pockets of military concentration and redevelop them. Only in this way can the temporary economic dislocation which accompanies any major structural change be held to a minimum, and the economic reconstruction of the United States thus be accomplished without real hardship.

Policies for Successful Conversion

An economically and socially successful conversion process requires considerable planning and preparation. First, a careful analysis must be performed to identify appropriate civilian alternatives into which the resources released from military-related activities may be effectively channeled. Second, a program for efficiently preparing the resources for their new civilian-oriented functions must be carefully developed. Finally, in the case of the human resources involved, various social services must be provided during the period of transition including income maintenance, employment services, and relocation and educational assistance where required. Consider each of these problems in turn.

Civilian alternatives for military-related resources. In a broad policy sense, it is not at all difficult to identify economically and socially productive alternatives for the employment of resources now devoted to unproductive military use.

One need only consider those vital social services and important areas of the economic infrastructure that are either presently in an advanced state of decline or clearly undergoing serious progressive retrenchment. Urban mass transit, housing, intercity rail transportation, police and fire services, mental and physical health care, standard education and vocational training, special education, care for the elderly, day care, etc., all would benefit enormously from a transfusion of resources from military programs, and that would clearly produce a major increase in the nation's economic and social welfare.

Besides such directly socially conscious alternatives, general redirection of resources into the production of "standard of living" goods and services, from machine tools to bubble gum, would revitalize the civilian economy. This revitalization would play a major role in creating the conditions under which the goal of full employment without significant inflation becomes economically achievable. And major gains in social welfare would clearly follow this kind of economic redevelopment.

But while broad prescriptions are important from the viewpoint of policy and perspective, an effective conversion process requires the detailed specification of particular alternatives for each facility, and each area undergoing this transformation.

The first step is to analyze the nature and quantity of all the productive resources involved in the transformation: the types and numbers of machines and their capabilities, the sorts of buildings (including their layout), the skill and experience mix of the labor force, and the characteristics of the site, including its size, terrain and location. The second step is to lay out a list of alternatives whose requirements for productive resources most closely correspond with what is currently available, as indicated by the resource analysis of the first step. Seeking alternatives which best match the capabilities of the present mix of resources minimizes dislocation and disruption by reducing the need for labor force hiring, firing, and retraining, and new equipment purchases. This tends to minimize the social cost of transition, as well as its direct financial cost. Furthermore, playing to the strengths of existing capabilites also increases the probability of success in the new activities. To some extent, the initial resource analysis will in itself suggest at least broad classes of feasible alternatives. For example, a manufacturing firm which owns considerable metalworking equipment and employs a fair amount of machinists would be more likely to convert successfully to the manufacture of metal office furniture or railroad cars than to the production of detergents or cosmetics.

This list of alternatives should not be conceived in purely industrial terms. Public and private non-manufacturing projects, in areas such as pollution control, education, transportation, etc. are also major alternative productive uses of resources. For example, it may well be that the prime civilian-oriented use for a particular naval facility may be as a major sewage treatment complex, medical center, or new university campus, rather than as an industrial park. It would be a serious mistake to think too narrowly at this critical stage of developing alternatives.

Finally, the "success potential" of each of the alternatives should be evaluated. In the case of conversion of industrial facilities to civilian production this primarily involves a study of what is called the "marketability" of the product, which involves an analysis of the demand for the product at the ranges of price that would permit a sufficient margin of profit (after covering costs) to make this product line attractive to the producer. In the case of public or non-profit projects, the evaluation should involve an analysis of the social need for such a project in that region, as well as its estimated cost. In either case, the accuracy and realism of estimates of both one-time conversion costs and subsequent continuing post-conversion production costs play a critical role in determining the feasibility and attractiveness of any proposed alternative.

To the extent that there is less than a perfect match between the labor requirements of even the best civilian alternatives for a given military enterprise and its preconversion labor force, there will be a need to channel some of the labor force into productive civilian activities wholly outside of that particular enterprise. For example, it is extremely unlikely that all or even most of the engineers and scientists currently employed by military industries would be required for any reasonable civilian alternative activities to which these industries would turn. This is no particular problem, in the sense that there are many civilian activities outside these particular converted industries in which the services of such personnel would be of great value. We need to think in terms of sufficient (particularly labor) resources released from military activity, and not simply sufficient alternatives to convert present military bases and firms into civilian facilites.

A combine of unions representing workers at Lucas Aerospace, one of the largest aerospace firms in Europe (headquartered in the United Kingdom) has through the joint efforts of its organized engineers and shop floor production workers, produced a collection of alternative products tailored to the

Lucas facilities and workforce. Known as the "Corporate Plan," this proposed set of alternatives consists not only of civilian products in general, but of what the Combine has called "socially useful" products in particular.

Transition support services. Workers undergoing occupational transition, whether or not it is part of a process of conversion from military to civilian economy, must find ways of connecting with new job opportunities, getting whatever retraining is necessary, financing a move when relocation is required, and keeping body and soul together during the period between jobs. The burden of meeting all their needs can be greatly eased by the availability of appropriate social services.

Not all of the workers involved in the conversion process will be changing employers, and those who will not do not have to worry about locating new job opportunities or maintaining their income. They may or may not require retraining, and probably will not require relocation, but even when retraining or re-location is necessary it should be possible to finance them at least partially through employers, though perhaps with some public supplementation.

Those individuals who must change employers will generally have much greater need for social services. Besides direct income maintenance assistance, they will likely require temporary public replacement of some employment fringe benefits—in particular group medical and dental insurance plans. An effective public program of employment services will be critical in making them aware of the nature and location of the new employment opportunities which best match their skills. Along with counseling services, this will be of vital importance in enabling them to plan whatever specific retraining they may need. In addition, the employment service will facilitate the process of direct placement of dislocated employees into new jobs. To make the transition even smoother, the government could provide special tax or other incentives for employers to sign conditional employment contracts with potential employees during this period that in effect guaranteed the prospective employees a job with that organization upon successful completion of a mutually agreed upon program of retraining. In this way, individuals requiring retraining that could be expected to stretch over a perod of time from six months to a year would have some assurance that undertaking training into a particular area of civilian expertise would provide them with attractive re-employment. Aside from any direct government benefits, private enterprises (whether businesses or private nonprofit institutions) would gain from the increased certainty in planning such agreements would imply.

Operating the entire conversion process along the lines suggested will tend to minimize the amount of geographic relocation required. This is important because moves over extended distances tend to be very disruptive of family and friendship ties. While people develop social roots after living in an area for a prolonged period, their ability to re-establish roots in a new area should not be underestimated. This is particularly true of young people, who often actively seek a new area in which to live and grow. In fact, the general population lived in a different house than that in which they lived in 1965, and nearly 25% of this group had moved to a different state.[11]

At any rate, the high degree of geographic concentration of military-related facilities virtually guarantees that some relocation will be required for some individuals. This is particularly true for engineers and scientists since they are concentrated within pockets of the defense industry much more highly than they would be likely to be in any civilian-oriented industry. But, the engineers and scientists who work in military industry have already developed a pattern of extraordinarily high geographic mobility as a result of their occupational need to follow the shifting defense contracts. So the prospect of one more move, coupled with the enhanced likelihood of future geographic stability, should not be an overly difficult thing with which to cope.

Expenses incurred in relocation for the purpose of re-employment in a new area are already tax deductible. Supplemental government relocation allowances for one time, conversion-connected single moves, along with aid in locating new housing, should go far in further easing the difficulties of relocating for those who must do so.

It is extremely important to the successful revitalization of the U.S. economy and society that the conversion process have a defined end. In order to avoid establishing new kinds of unhealthy dependencies, any effective conversion process must be designed to put itself out of business. The permanent existence of a very small version of the machinery for easing economic transitions may be of real value in a dynamic economy, but great care must be taken to avoid giving birth to large, new self-perpetuating conversion bureaucracies.

During each of the past several years, a bill containing one model for institutionalizing effective conversion planning has been introduced into both houses of Congress. The bill, called the Defense Economic Adjustment Act, embodies a local authority, low bureaucracy, people-oriented conversion planning concept. The Act is looked upon as one model for achieving effective ongoing conversion planning on a contingency basis. It is put forth in that spirit here, with full acknowledgment that in this area too there are undoubtedly a number of other workable alternative formulations.

The bill would require the establishment of a tripartite Alternative Use Committee at every military base and military industrial facility in the U.S., consisting of one-third representatives of the workforce at that facility, one-third representatives of the facility's management and one-third representatives of the local community without direct connection to that facility. These local committees would be funded independently and would have complete control over the process of drawing up conversion plans for their facility. The diverse interests of each of the three groups would combine to insure a serious planning effort.

The local Alternative Use Committees would be provided with access to all information at the facility which they would need to develop the plan. They would also be supplied with a conversion Guidelines Handbook produced by a central, national Defense Economic Adjustment Council.

This national council (consisting of one third each: Cabinet members, representatives of nondefense business, and labor unions), with a maximum staff of 15 persons, would serve mainly to encourage the preparation of civilian public projects at the Federal, State and local levels—projects which could create markets for converted defense contractors. It would also serve as an information coordinator. Though the council may serve an advisory function, it would have no authority to enforce its advice.

When a facility actually underwent a major cut in defense work, the ready conversion plan would be put into effect. Workers would be retrained for civilian operation. During the period of changeover, they would be eligible for income support equal to 90 percent of the first $20,000 and 50 percent of the next $5,000 of their previous income and continuation of medical coverage, pension and other benefits for up to two years. Those who could not be employed at the converted facility would also be given re-employment assistance and relocation allowances. The money to finance worker benefits would come from a pooled fund into which every defense contractor would be required to pay 1.25 percent of its total military contract value. (The tax is on revenue rather than profit to avoid accounting manipulation of profit figures.) As a rough estimate, the entire economic conversion process can be expected to take from two to four years. It will involve a great deal of detailed planning (mostly on a local basis) and careful implementation, at the cost of a considerable investment of time and effort. However the economic and social benefits which will accrue as a result of this investment are truly enormous.

The evidence of the failure of present economic policies is ubiquitous. The progressive weakening of the domestic and international strength of the U.S. and its influence as a world power cannot be reversed until the nation discards the illusory pursuit of strength and influence through military expansionism for the hard realities of economic redevelopment. And this can only come via the conversion process.

Footnotes

1.) *New York Times* (July 27, 1972).

2.) In fact, if the equipment and/or personnel operating it perform poorly, this can often be blatantly turned into an argument for further increases in the military budget, as for example was the case in the aftermath of the failed attempt to rescue the U.S. hostages held in Iran in 1980. If the military had had even more money, the argument went, it could afford to buy equipment that would perform better!

3.) Finney, John W. "C5A Jet Repairs to Cost $1,5 Billion." *New York Times* (December 5, 1975).

4.) Melman Seymour, *The Permanent War Economy* (New York: Simon and Shuster, 1974), p. 85.

5.) *Op. Cit.*, John Finney.

6.) "Bart in Transit," *Newsweek* (January 12, 1976).

7.) *Ibid.*

8.) *The New York Post* (December 15, 1971).

9.) Anderson, J.R. *The Impact of the Pentagon Tax on U.S. Congressional Districts,* (Lansing, Michigan: Employment Research Associates, 1979).

10.) Minnesota, Wisconsin, Iowa, Illinois, Michigan, Indiana, and Ohio.

Chapter 34

Real Security: An Alternative Foreign Policy

Richard Barnet

No one has a good word to say about Ronald Reagan's foreign policy. Liberals criticize the Administration for doing what it said it would do—promoting a mindless arms race in the name of national security, supporting murderous regimes in places such as El Salvador in the name of anti-communism, and striving clumsily to organize the world into an anti-Soviet crusade. Right-wing ideologues attack the President with rising fury because he does not do any of these things swiftly enough to suit them and has shown himself to be more "pragmatic" in some respects than they would like. The policy-making professionals, recalling Reagan's campaign promises to make "coherence" the guiding principle of his foreign policy, look on in amazement as the competing barons of the new foreign policy establishment carry on open warfare in the press.

It is easy to point to a succession of foreign policy failures, difficult to find the successes. The most immediate and conspicuous failure is in El Salvador. The Administration came into office determined to demonstrate that military force could once again be used to stem the "decline of American power." If *Pax Americana* could no longer be maintained throughout the non-socialist world, it could at the very least be enforced in our traditional backyard. The choice, the Reaganites believed, was between the sentimentality of Jimmy Carter's human rights policy and the historic dictates of the Monroe Doctrine. El Salvador seemed to provide a perfect test. It was a small country on which the Soviet Union had no claims—one that had been unmistakably in the American orbit for as long as anyone could remember. As a result of a coup in 1979, followed by a government in which some progressive Christian Democrats briefly took part, the ruling junta could be presented as a moderating voice seeking to mediate between the extreme Right and extreme Left.

No sooner was Reagan installed in the White House than El Salvador became the war cry. Secretary of State Alexander Haig spent his early days creating headlines on the subject, sending high officials to Europe to enlist them in the new crusade against peasant guerrillas in that tiny country. The Reaganites were confident that the American people were spoiling for a war to win—a war that would blot out the ignominy of Vietnam. Modest shipments of Soviet arms by way of Nicaragua and Cuba provided a perfect pretext for U.S. intervention. Here was a place at last where our military could demonstrate its muscle and change history.

According to the Reagan game plan, the United States could be mobilized around the El Salvador issue, and so could the allies who, conventional conservative opinion had it, would be greatly reassured by the decisions of the new Administration. In their rush to respond to the new anti-communist crusade, more nettlesome issues that divided the alliance would conveniently be forgotten. The war fever would free the public enthusiasm for the $1.5 trillion the Administration planned to spend on the military. The headlines would focus on the brave little war in El Salvador and would crowd out the pictures of unemployed on the street, soup kitchens, and other politically burdensome aspects of the Reagan recovery plan.

But nothing worked according to plan. The situation in El Salvador proved far less tractable than the Reagan Cold Warriors had anticipated. From the outset, the Administration deceived itself—much as the Johnson administration had in Vietnam—by underestimating the degree of popular revulsion in El Salvador against the government and by exaggerating the relatively small factor of outside aid. Just as in Indochina more than 15 years earlier, an American government sought to legitimate its intervention into a civil conflict by arguing that it was really an international war. But instead of signaling the final victory over the "Vietnam Syndrome," the Reagan administration's call to arms in Central America proved that many Americans had, indeed, learned the lessons of Vietnam.

The El Salvador intervention has elicited the most effective public protest in the United States since the Vietnam war. The opposition, which has included powerful elements of the Catholic hierarchy, became so strong that the State Department abruptly reversed itself and told the press it was making too much of the little war in Central America. From a moral standpoint, it turned out to be the worst battlefield imaginable—a tiny country run by a government that, according to the Catholic Church, has murdered 30,000 people and turned 13 per cent of the population into refugees. In Europe, El Salvador quickly captured the public imagination as Vietnam had. European leaders perceived that the Reaganites were poor practitioners of *Realpolitik*. Just as it was easy for De Gaulle to use Vietnam to dramatize France's independence from the United States, it became morally and politically satisfying for today's leaders of Holland, Germany, and France to oppose the United States on an issue in which they had so little at stake themselves.

The Administration is now caught in El Salvador. Even as the civil war intensifies, and headlines report massacres on an ever larger scale, Washington certifies that human rights are now respected to the point that military aid can be substantially increased. Other forms of military intervention have also been announced as the United States sinks deeper into involvement in what is now a regional conflict in Central America—a conflict for which decades of U.S. policy bear heavy responsibility.

Reagan's Ideology

A second conspicuous failure of Ronald Reagan's first year in office was U.S. policy toward Europe. Moving quickly to convert its ideology into policy, the Administration sought to drum up support for its huge military program by invoking that old standby, the Soviet menace. But Reagan succeeded only in terrifying many Europeans about the nature of American intentions. Defense Secretary Caspar Weinberger's posturing over the neutron bomb—he convened a press conference to inform the world we were making the weapons whether the Europeans liked it or not—and the redoubled effort to force the early deployment of European theater nuclear weapons brought more than two million people into the streets in protest. When Reagan himself speculated about the possibility of nuclear war in Europe, he was, indeed, expressing nothing more than nuclear orthodoxy, and his intent was to reassure the Europeans that the nuclear umbrella was still there. But so isolated are the nuclear theologians from popular attitudes, so little understanding do they have of the way things have changed since the days of John Foster Dulles and Konrad Adenauer, that the President was amazed when his words produced panic.

The Reagan ideology calls for delaying negotiations with the Soviet Union until the needed increments in U.S. military buildup are in place. But by the end of his first year in office, the President was forced to give a ringing endorsement to arms limitation in Europe—in the so-called Zero Options speech—to stem the rising tide of Continental protest. Negotiations have begun on an inherently non-negotiable U.S. position—a demand for the removal of all Soviet missiles in Europe in exchange for a U.S. promise not to put some in.

The Administration, like much of the press in the United States, underestimated and misunderstood the European peace movement. The movement is divided, and it has had as much difficulty in developing a coherent response to the tragic events in Poland as the governments have had, but it is very much alive. At its heart is a growing fear that the traditional security policies the United States is urging on the governments of Europe will lead straight to nuclear war.

The peace movement is growing in the United States, too. Increasingly, the churches here and abroad are raising fundamental moral and political questions about nuclear "defense." A recent Gallup poll in the United States found that 47 per cent of the respondents believe a nuclear war within five years is "likely," and many believe they would have no better than a fifty-fifty chance of surviving. A national security policy in a democracy can be successful only if it meets two tests: it must provide as much realistic protection as possible in a dangerous world, and it must make people believe that they are reasonably safe. By both criteria, the Reagan foreign policy is a fiasco.

Even Poland illustrates how difficult it is to turn Reagan rhetoric and ideology into policy. For the President, Poland was a cheap Cold War victory. It provided a pretext for trying to squeeze the Soviets with a series of sanctions that offer no hope whatever of reforming the Kremlin leaders. But from the start, economic realities such as the grain trade with the Soviet Union could not be jeopardized. Reagan could lament the fate of the Polish workers on the international airwaves while rolling back the rights and privileges of American workers, but he could not work his will in Eastern Europe any more than he could in Western Europe or Central America.

As Michael Klare has pointed out, this Administration's approach bears a certain resemblance to the Kennedy administration's. Under the cover of a massive nuclear rearmament campaign, the Reaganites are committed to resuming counterinsurgency warfare against national liberation movements. But guerrilla movements around the globe are better armed than they were in the 1960s, thanks to the generosity of both superpowers in spreading sophisticated hardware around the Third World.

Political movements are certainly no easier to destroy with weapons in the 1980s than they were in the 1960s and 1970s; indeed, three factors have made the task harder. First, the proliferation of advanced weaponry has given advantages to small nations and insurrectionary movements. (Unaccountably, the United States has given advanced rockets that can sink an aircraft carrier to some of the very countries we wish to impress by parading our Navy in their waters.) Second, the "Vietnam syndrome" is still with us. When democratic governments resort to strategies of annihilation, they can't avoid alarming and outraging their own populations. The role of the Catholic Church, especially with respect to El Salvador, imposes an important political limitation on the White House. Third, the ideological foundations of counterinsurgency have been destroyed. The brutality and sacrifice involved in conducting highly visible and brutal wars against bands of peasants can be legitimated only if the guerrillas are seen as part of a worldwide communist conspiracy. But ever since the Sino-Soviet dispute, the U.S. rapprochement with China, and the Soviet Union's emergence as the only nation in the world surrounded by hostile communist powers, that particular fiction has been hard to maintain.

This is a dangerous Administration that wishes to adopt the paranoid credo of the Committee on the Present Danger as official U.S. policy, but dares not act on every irresponsible impulse. It is an Administration that can be easily ridiculed for its incompetence, but a serious critique must dig below eccentricities to understand that the most alarming aspect of the policy is its continuity.

I do not mean to ignore some important differences between Jimmy Carter and Ronald Reagan. Carter entered the White House with some intimations, at least, of the dangers we face, while Reagan seems to have none. Carter set some admirable goals, but failed to attain them because he was unable to explain or defend his more realistic concerns and his more sophisticated approach toward the world force of revolutionary nationalism. In the Reagan administration, belligerent talk, the willingness to conduct a full-scale counterinsurgency war in El Salvador, dogfights with Libyan aircraft, and the preference for hectoring the Soviet Union instead of negotiating with it have all contributed to the deterioration of the international situation and to the insecurity of the American people. But it is a serious error to ascribe all these developments to the plans, prejudices, and politics of the Reagan administration.

By the time Reagan took office, a number of his basic assumptions had already been accepted at least as working hypotheses by the Carter administration. An arbitrary percentage increase in the military budget had been ordered, not on the basis of a new analysis of American military needs or a clearer understanding of the function of the new weapons but as a symbolic measure to stem "the decline of American power." The assumption that there was a connection between Pentagon funding and American power to influence allies, to manage crises like that in Iran, and to prevent the Soviet Union from building up its arms preceded Reagan.

The military spending under Reagan is greater and cuts in domestic programs more severe than contemplated by Carter, but his Administration, too, had planned major additions to the nuclear arsenal. The Carter administration had proceeded with production of the neutron bomb and deployment of theater nuclear weapons. (Indeed, the Reagan administration has shown greater willingness to moderate its rhetoric out of deference to the European allies than Carter demonstrated at the time of the Soviet attack in Afghanistan, when he plunged ahead unilaterally with a range of sanctions the Europeans could not support.) Moderation, which Carter had shown in Nicaragua, was being abandoned in El Salvador before he left office. By Inauguration Day, the United States was once again hostage to a hopeless client.

American Foreign Policy at a Low Ebb

The foreign policy of the United States is now in crisis. We face the most dangerous moment in our national history since World War II. We are heading toward an all-out arms race, the consequences of which we do not comprehend. Our government is engaged in a massive military buildup without any sign that it has a political or military strategy that would carry out its stated objectives. A careful reading of the Pentagon budget does not show that additional billions for "defense" will provide significant additional military capabilities. It is even less clear what new political objectives such new capabilities would offer.

At a time when the Soviet Union is more isolated than it has been since 1945, the U.S. government is devoting its diplomatic energies to isolating itself. The web of relationships we have developed with the other leading industrial countries of the world in the last three decades is seriously frayed. Those relationships have long been in need of repair, but they cannot be ignored or scrapped, as some of the Reagan people seem to believe, without courting great dangers. The industrial powers of Europe and Japan are no longer clients, and cannot be treated as such.

The political problems facing the industrial world and the East-West confrontation itself are further complicated by the now chronic economic crisis of the West. There is little hope of significant recovery of the economic momentum that characterized the brief period of *Pax Americana* (1945-1971) without fundamental reform of the world monetary system and a new set of ground rules for conducting world trade that would make it possible for billions of people in the Third World to participate for the first time in international society. There will be no prosperity for the West if the world population continues to grow but billions remain outside the economy, unable to act either as producers or consumers.

Some time ago, West German Chancellor Helmut Schmidt pointed to some of the similarities between our time and the period before World War I. Then, too, the flow of world politics was out of control. The great war that took the flower of a generation and doomed great empires broke out because no one could think of a way to stop it. The arms race reflex, commitments hastily made, a preoccupation with national prestige instead of national welfare—these all contributed to the first catastrophe of the century. Most historians ascribe the second and greater catastrophe which began in 1939 to world economic breakdown. The economic rivalry and confusion produced the soil of desperation in which Hitlerian madness could flourish.

Fortunately, disturbing historical analogies do not have the force of physical laws, but they do provide us with essential opportunities to learn and change. Recently, there have been some encouraging examples of social learning and change: serious environmental damage has been reversed, in some instances, by human intervention, and the industrial nations have figured out how to use less energy. To be sure, progress in these matters is modest compared to the need, but there has been no learning at all, and no change, with regard to the most basic problems of national security. In recent years the situation has become far more dangerous. Americans—and Russians—are less secure today than they were in the mid-1970s.

Why have we been so slow to learn the basic lessons of national security in the nuclear age? In part, because our evolutionary history is against us. For 10,000 years or so, the grisly arithmetic of the arms race did make a difference: it was undoubtedly better to have more bows and arrows than the other side, and it was better still to have more tanks and ships and aircraft. But in the nuclear age, when the weapons become suicidal, the connection between violence and politics snapped, even though it still shaped our thinking.

Americans find it especially difficult to think realistically about nuclear weapons because for about twenty years after they were first devised, this country alone derived power and influence from them. President Eisenhower was able to threaten the Chinese with the use of the atomic bomb to end the Korean war. The shadow of nuclear weapons hung over the Berlin crisis of 1961 and the Cuban Missile Crisis of 1962. But by the time the last explicit nuclear threat was made—President Carter's "Doctrine" that called for using nuclear arms to keep the Russians in check in the Persian Gulf—it was no longer credible; the U.S. near monopoly that made earlier threats look serious had been lost. It is the growing recognition of this reality in Europe and now, increasingly, in the United States that is fostering a new peace movement and a revived search for an alternative security system.

A real security policy would begin with some fundamental questions—not about the Russians, the Chinese, much less the Libyans, but about ourselves. What are we trying to protect? How much protection is possible in the nuclear age? How much can we do by ourselves? What should we ask of other nations?

The purpose of our national security policy is to protect people, property, and the values we cherish. The power we need is not the power to destroy other societies, or even to remake them, but to renew our own society. That is the legitimate purpose of a national security policy. It has been clear for a long time that we cannot honor that purpose acting alone; we must have close relations with other countries, and we must work with them to create the conditions in which prosperity and democracy can be maintained here. Such relationships are not built by multi-million-dollar arms deals or obsolete alliances, but by new rules of international society that can create economic and political stability.

The United States, despite its revolutionary origins, is by nature a conservative country. Despite the diffusion of power in the world, it still possesses the most powerful economy and the longest geopolitical reach. The national interest of the United

States is stability. A national security policy must, therefore, aim at producing as stable an international environment as possible for the orderly evolution of American society.

However, the concept of stability shared by both major parties and embodied in bipartisan foreign policy for a generation and a half is hopelessly obsolete. The American view remains today what it was in the time of John F. Kennedy: we will seek to support governments that are non-repressive and forward-looking: but since such governments do not exist in most places in the world, we will not hesitate to support dictatorships of the Right in order to suppress national liberation movements. The United States is prepared to abandon its stated ideals and expose itself to the world as a force favoring reaction and repression because it fears popular movements. Independence movements and social forces, which by nature are unpredictable, have been viewed consistently as threats for two reasons: first, it is assumed they will inevitably come to be dominated by the Soviet Union. This concern is not supported by a careful reading of recent history. There is overwhelming evidence that virtually every national liberation movement has sought to avoid dependence on any great power. The Vietnamese, the Angolans, and other national liberation movements have consistently sought diplomatic relations with the United States. Vietnam has become heavily dependent on the Soviet Union, but only after hopes of entering into normal relations with the United States were dashed. It is clear that the Cubans did not and still do not desire the degree of economic dependence on the Soviet Union that the U.S. embargo has made necessary. Why should they?

A second and increasingly significant argument for our counterrevolutionary preoccupation has to do with resources. What used to be advanced by the Left as a scandalous critique of American imperialism is now routinely invoked by generals and admirals testifying before Congressional appropriations committees: that the mission of our military is to protect corporate access to raw materials around the world.

Most of the expense of the military goes not to nuclear weapons but to the "general purpose" forces whose primary function is to keep nationalist left-wing governments from coming to power in "strategic" areas. There is a strong suggestion that where such governments come to power, U.S. investments will no longer be welcome and our country will be denied access to vital resources.

Indeed, much evidence suggests that revolutionary regimes may try to change the terms on which multinational corporations are permitted to participate, and may strike a harder bargain in selling resources—but sell them they will. A new government struggling to remake a poor country desperately needs capital, and will not reject opportunities to earn it. That Cuban soldiers were offered as guards for the Gulf Oil refinery in Angola, and that Gulf accepted them, are better indications than Reagan's rhetoric of world realities.

Reformulating American Foreign Policy

A serious national security policy would confront the historic moment we now face. We are at the end of a 500-year period of colonialism and imperialism. National liberation struggles have occurred and continue around the world. The United States can only temporarily prevent such movements from coming to power. Our greatest success in counterinsurgency warfare was achieved almost 30 years ago in Guatemala, and today Guatemala is engulfed in a civil war rooted in the unresolved conflicts of that time. A quarter of the country is in the hands of a guerrilla movement that regards the United States as the enemy, the sponsor of a generation of official terrorism. We should have learned something from the 1954 CIA-arranged coup: Short-term military success does not buy long-term stability.

The Reagan administration seems unwilling to face the decisions its own policy is forcing on the nation. Quite simply, the United States lacks the military power to carry out a worldwide policy of counterrevolution. If we are to take seriously the counterinsurgency goal, even the projected military budget is not nearly enough. To carry out such a policy without conscription would be unthinkable, for the costs of maintaining a volunteer military force adequate to the security task this Administration has defined would be prohibitive. But the Administration wisely shies away from conscription because it recognizes that the draft would be a referendum on foreign policy, and that while fighting the "Russians" in El Salvador or Libya may be a stirring idea for Reagan's right-wing backers, it looks quite different to those who would have to go do the fighting.

A national security policy that promotes stability for the United States must rest on a fundamentally different conception of the U.S.-Soviet relationship from that put forward by the present Administration or by its predecessors. President Reagan's notion that the Soviet Union could be pressed to drop out of the arms race by a major U.S. armaments buildup is a fatuous hope. More than 65 years of experience suggest that the Soviet leaders are quite capable of extracting whatever sacrifices may be necessary from the Soviet people to continue the arms race, and that they have been determined since the Cuban Missile Crisis not to fall behind.

The Soviet Union faces some severe problems. As its top officials look out from the Kremlin, they see a net tightening around them: a U.S.-Chinese military alliance, Europe and Japan being pressed by the United States to rearm, and increasing restlessness among the nations of Eastern Europe. At the same time, the Soviet Union is a formidable military power bent on achieving a capacity to match U.S. might in virtually every sphere. It is clear that the Soviet Union cannot be threatened into reform or into withdrawal from regions it controls. It cannot be made less dangerous by playing on the paranoia of its leaders. Aiming more missiles at the Soviet Union will inevitably result in more missiles aimed at the United States.

The starting point of an American security policy must be coexistence with the Soviet Union. The alternative is war, and war would mean the end of the American experiment, if not the end of civilization or even of the species. But there cannot be coexistence with the Soviet Union on any basis other than the principle of sovereign equality. The Reagan Administration's stated objective of military superiority must once more be abandoned; it is absolutely crucial that both sides recognize that military superiority is unattainable. This point can be telegraphed in many ways. Both sides would have to state explicitly that they will refrain from using or threatening the use of nuclear weapons except in response to nuclear attack. (The U.S. refusal to accept a "no-first-use" policy heightens anxiety not only in the Soviet Union but in Europe, particularly when the President speaks openly of plans for a limited nuclear war.) A proposal to freeze further production of nuclear weapons and to ban the deployment and testing of such weapons under international agreement, subject to easy verification by satellite, would be an important contribution to stability.

The world would still be a dangerous place. The weapons stockpiles would remain, but the superpowers would have made clear to one another that they have abandoned the hope of a technological breakthrough in the arms race. The freeze would symbolize surrender of the fantasy of nuclear victory. However, the U.S.-Soviet relationship cannot be stabilized by a mere freeze; it would have to be followed by serious negotiations for radical reductions in nuclear stockpiles. There can be no stability without an end to the U.S.-Soviet arms race, which cannot be ended unless we change the structures internal to each society that keep the arms race going.

Clear political commitment in the direction of demilitarization offers the most reliable evidence of peaceful national intentions. A substantially less crowded parking lot at the Pentagon and at the Ministry of Defense in Moscow, or the conversion of military plants to civilian production, would provide more reassurance than satellite photos of missile silos, as important as they are. If Soviet consumers began to get the priority attention showered on the Soviet military-industrial complex, if Soviet tanks began to look as dowdy as Soviet hotel elevators, one could reasonably conclude that something important had happened. A serious program of conversion would require the leaders on both sides to confront powerful interests that have a bureaucratic and ideological commitment to the arms race. That in itself would be impressive evidence of a turn toward peace.

The United States and the Soviet Union must also seek equality in the order of battle. We need simple, clear rules prohibiting the further deployment of Soviet as well as American military forces outside their own borders. We need mutually agreed-upon restrictions on how each superpower can deploy its military power—rules that would outlaw future interventions of the kind we have seen in Vietnam, the Dominican Republic, Chile, Angola, Czechoslovakia, Hungary, and Afghanistan. We should offer the Soviets a broad agreement that embodies the principle of parity on which they have long insisted—a concession that sacrifices no legitimate interest of the United States. Both superpowers should accept clear ground rules that bar the use of military force by themselves or their proxies in the Third World. Unless efforts are made to isolate revolutionary struggles from U.S.-Soviet military competition, superpower confrontations in the Third World are likely to spark general war.

Finally, a new national security strategy must recognize the true sources of this nation's strength. The greatest threat to the United States is posed not by Russian missiles, much less Soviet ideas, but by our failure to manage our own society. The brutal economic medicine of the Reagan administration inspires little confidence even among those who benefit spectacularly from the tax write-offs, subsidies, and other transfer payments from the poor to the rich. While welcoming the loopholes, subsidies, and bailouts provided by Uncle Sam, large investors do not seem to have much confidence in the long-term prospects of the economy. The official unemployment rate (which understates the problem) is approximately nine percent as a national average, and is far higher in distressed areas. Most significant, neither political party seems ready to offer a plan for harnessing this nation's enormous strengths to produce a stable, prosperous society.

The lack of effective domestic policy poses a critical threat to our national security in several ways. First, it undermines the morale of the people. When some of our cities look as if a war has already occurred, when millions of young women and men face only the most dismal future, the level of alienation and distress in the society threatens its very cohesion. An observer from space looking down at Washington D.C., where decisions are made to spend trillions to counter the Russian threat, would see the capital city in an advanced state of social dissolution: many thousands ill-housed and ill-fed; crime so widespread that fear stalks the city; a drug trade so pervasive that its underground economy—millions of dollars over which neither government nor legitimate business can have any control—is about the only growth industry; an education system in such a shambles that a whole generation is irretrievably handicapped.

The traditional guns versus butter argument misses the point. Excessive military spending produces the same consequences as military defeat: it gives foreign governments greater control over the life of the country. Because we have failed to develop a national security policy that provides real protection for American citizens against real dangers, Japanese car makers and Arab oil producers have been able to inflict needless damage on millions of Americans. It is a sign of the intellectual and moral bankruptcy of our politicians that they confront these problems by threatening the industrious Japanese and Europeans instead of taking the innovative steps that would make us better competitors.

The Reagan administration has cut at the very investments that would most improve our security—investments in the future of the United States. To think that an uneducated, unemployable population of young people does not pose a threat to the security and stability of the country is to live in a dream world. To cut back on investment in safe, renewable sources of energy in the name of economy is to leave the country dangerously vulnerable. Whether the oil glut continues or not, there is nothing that would improve the security of the nation and the stability of the economy as much as an orderly transition to a safer, less vulnerable energy system.

A Nuclear-Free World

The threats at which we throw most of our money are rather implausible compared to the more urgent threats that face the American people. Yes, the Russians could invade Western Europe, but for 30 years or more no Western intelligence service has put much credence in that threat. Still, billions of dollars go year after year into an incredible defense against that threat, based on plans to blow up Germany with nuclear weapons. Yes, the leaders of Western Europe might bow to Soviet blackmail and abandon the Western alliance, although at this point the Reagan administration is doing a much better job than the Russians pushing them out. Yes, the Soviet leaders might decide one day to launch their missiles against the United States. Once the button is pushed there is nothing we can do to defend the country, nor is there much more we can do than we have already done to discourage such a lunatic decision. If the Soviets are not sobered now by the near certainty that some large portion of the 30,000 nuclear weapons in our arsenal would strike their territory in a retaliatory attack, it is difficult to see why they would be deterred if we doubled the number.

Americans are becoming less and less secure because we are pouring our money and our energy into pointless efforts to head off those remote threats or into trying to thwart nationalist revolutions in poor countries that need not be threats at all. While squandering funds and talent on the remote threats, we are diverting energy and resources in a way that threatens our very survival as a free society. As we hover on the threshold of a new century, the most urgent national security requirement is the establishment of a world security system from which the shadow of war can be lifted. A nuclear-free world is the only stable environment for a secure human race. The task of our age is to create the political machinery, the economic structure, and above all the new modes of human relationship that could convert this idea from a pious phrase in Jimmy Carter's Inaugural Address into a practical political vision.

We cannot approach such a goal without the hard work of developing a new international monetary system, of dealing with the problem of world debt, especially in the Third World, of establishing new ground rules for integrating the former colonial nations into a world economic order. The Reagan administration shows almost no interest in these problems and, indeed, suggests that somehow they are annoying byproducts of U.S.-Soviet confrontation.

Over its 200-year history, the United States has exerted more influence in the world through its ideas than through its weapons. A democratic system, however imperfect, struggling to achieve human values and offering unprecedented levels of comfort for the ordinary citizen, has excited hope throughout the world. But increasingly, the leaders of other countries are coming to the conclusion that neither the United States nor the Soviet Union has useful ideas for the times we live in, that we are both frozen in the past.

In a dangerous age, economic and political stability is a more important national goal than ever for the United States. But to isolate ourselves from great historical currents, either by ignoring them or by trying vainly to turn them back, is to condemn ourselves to impotence. The economic system on which our power rests is in deep trouble. So also are the alternative economic systems, including social democracy and socialism. But in the chaos of this moment, the United States has greater means than any other nation to develop a new democratic economy that meets basic needs, encourages creativity, and civilizes power. Unless we do so, there will be no security for Americans. But it is a hopeless goal unless it becomes the central task that commands our energy, imagination, and resources. Power is, indeed, indispensible to national security in a dangerous world. But we must not continue to blind ourselves to the true sources of our power.

Chapter 35

A Modest Proposal: Deep-Cuts in Nuclear Weapons

George Kennan

Adequate words are lacking to express the full seriousness of our present situation. It is not just that we are for the moment on a collision course politically with the Soviet Union, and that the process of rational communication between the two governments seems to have broken down completely: it is also—and even more importantly—the fact that the ultimate sanction behind the conflicting policies of these two governments is a type and volume of weaponry which could not possibly be used without utter disaster for us all.

For over 30 years wise and far-seeing people have been warning us about the futility of any war fought with nuclear weapons and about the dangers involved in their cultivation. Some of the first of these voices to be raised were those of great scientists, including outstandingly that of Albert Einstein himself. But there has been no lack of others. Every president of this country, from Dwight Eisenhower to Jimmy Carter, has tried to remind us that there could be no such thing as victory in a war fought with such weapons. So have a great many other eminent persons.

When one looks back today over the history of these warnings, one has the impression that something has now been

577

lost of the sense of urgency, the hopes and the excitement that initially inspired them, so many years ago. One senses, even on the part of those who today most acutely perceive the problem and are inwardly most exercised about it, a certain discouragement, resignation, perhaps even despair, when it comes to the question of raising the subject again. The danger is so obvious. So much has already been said. What is to be gained by reiteration? What good would it now do?

Look at the record. Over all these years the competition in the development of nuclear weaponry has proceeded steadily, relentlessly, without the faintest regard for all these warning voices. We have gone on piling weapon upon weapon, missile upon missile, new levels of destructiveness upon old ones. We have done this helplessly, almost involuntarily: like the victims of some sort of hypnotism, like men in a dream, like lemmings heading for the sea, like the children of Hamlin marching blindly behind their Pied Piper. And the result is that today we have achieved, we and the Russians together, in the creation of these devices and their means of delivery, levels of redundancy of such grotesque dimensions as to defy rational understanding.

I say redundancy. I know of no better way to describe it. But actually the word is too mild. It implies that there could be levels of these weapons that would not be redundant. Personally, I doubt that there could. I question whether these devices are really weapons at all. A true weapon is at best something with which you endeavor to affect the behavior of another society by influencing the minds, the calculations, the intentions, of the men that control it; it is not something with which you destroy indiscriminately the lives, the substance, the hopes, the culture, the civilization of another people.

What a confession of intellectual poverty it would be—what bankruptcy of intelligent statesmanship—if we had to admit that such blind, senseless acts of destruction were the best use we could make of what we have come to view as the leading elements of our military strength.

To my mind, the nuclear bomb is the most useless weapon ever invented. It can be employed to no rational purpose. It is not even an effective defense against itself. It is only something with which, in a moment of petulance or panic, you commit such fearful acts of destruction as no sane person would ever wish to have upon their conscience.

There are those who will agree, with a sigh, to much of what I have just said, but will point to the need for something called deterrence. This is, of course, a concept which attributes to others—to others who, like ourselves, were born of women, walk

on two legs, and love their children, to human beings, in short—
the most fiendish and inhuman tendencies.

But all right: accepting for the sake of argument the
profound iniquity of these adversaries, no one could deny, I
think, that the present Soviet and American arsenals, present-
ing over a million times the destructive power of the Hiroshima
bomb, are simply fantastically redundant to the purpose in
question. If the same relative proportions were to be preserved,
something well less than 20% of those stockpiled would surely
suffice for the most sanguine concepts of deterrence, whether as
between the two nuclear superpowers or with relation to any of
those other governments that have been so ill-advised as to
enter upon the nuclear path. Whatever their suspicions of each
other, there can be no excuse on the part of these two governments for holding, poised against each other and poised in a
sense against the whole northern hemisphere, quantities of
these weapons so vastly in excess of any rational and demonstrable requirements.

How have we got ourselves into this dangerous mess?

Let us not confuse the question by blaming it all on our
Soviet adversaries. They have, of course, their share of the
blame, and not least in their cavalier dismissal of the Baruch
Plan so many years ago. They too have made their mistakes;
and I should be the last to deny it.

But we must remember that it has been we Americans who,
at least every step of the road, have taken the lead in the
development of this sort of weaponry. It was we who first
produced and tested such a device; we who were the first to raise
its destructiveness to a new level with the hydrogen bomb; we
who introduced the multiple warhead; we who have declined
every proposal for the renunciation of the principle of "first
use"; and we alone, so help us God, who have used the weapon in
anger against others, and against tens of thousands of helpless
non-combatants at that.

I know that reasons were offered for some of these things. I
know that others might have taken this sort of a lead, had we
not done so. But let us not, in the face of this record, so lose
ourselves in self-righteousness and hypocrisy as to forget our
own measure of complicity in creating the situation we face
today.

What is it then, if not our own will, and if not the supposed
wickedness of our opponents, that has brought us to this pass?

The answer, I think, is clear. It is primarily the inner
momentum, the independent momentum, of the weapons race
itself—the compulsions that arise and take charge of great

powers when they enter upon a competition with each other in the building up of major armaments of any sort.

This is nothing new. I am a diplomatic historian. I see the same phenomenon playing its fateful part in the relations among the great European powers as much as a century ago. I see this competitive buildup of armaments conceived initially as a means to an end but soon becoming the end itself. I see it taking possession of people's imagination and behavior, becoming a force in its own right, detaching itself from the political differences that initially inspired it, and then leading both parties, invariably and inexorably, to the war they no longer knew how to avoid.

This is a species of fixation, brewed out of many components. There are fears, resentments, national pride, personal pride. There are misreadings of the adversary's intentions—sometimes even a refusal to consider them at all. There is the tendency of national communities to idealize themselves and to dehumanize the opponent. There is the blinkered, narrow vision of the professional military planner, and his tendency to make war inevitable by assuming its inevitability.

Tossed together, these components form a powerful brew. They guide the fears and the ambitions of men. They seize the policies of governments and whip them around like trees before the tempest.

Is it possible to break out of this charmed and vicious circle? It is sobering to recognize that no one, at least to my knowledge, has yet done so. But no one, for that matter, has ever been faced with such great catastrophe, such inalterable catastrophe, at the end of the line. Others, in earlier decades, could befuddle themselves with dreams of something called "victory." We, perhaps fortunately, are denied this seductive prospect. We have to break out of the circle. We have no other choice.

How are we to do it?

I must confess that I see no possibility of doing this by means of discussions along the lines of the negotiations that have been in progress, off and on, over this past decade, under the acronym of SALT. I regret, to be sure, that the most recent SALT agreement has not been ratified. I regret it, because if the benefits to be expected from that agreement were slight, its disadvantages were even slighter; and it had symbolic value which should not have been so lightly sacrificed.

But I have, I repeat, no illusion that negotiations on the SALT pattern—negotiations, that is, in which each side is obsessed with the chimera of relative advantage and strives to retain a maximum of the weaponry for itself while putting its

A Modest Proposal 581

opponent to the maximum disadvantage—I have no illusion that such negotiations could ever be adequate to get us out of this hole. They are not a way of escape from the weapons race; they are an integral part of it.

Whoever does not understand that when it comes to nuclear weapons the whole concept of relative advantage is illusory— whoever does not understand that when you are talking about absurd and preposterous quantities of overkill the relative size of the arsenals has no serious meaning—whoever does not understand that the danger lies not in the possibility that someone else might have more missiles and warheads than we do but in the very existence of these unconscionable quantities of highly poisonous explosives and their existence, above all, in hands as weak and shaky and undependable as those of ourselves or our adversaries or any other mere human beings: whoever does not understand these things is never going to guide us out of this increasingly dark and menacing forest of bewilderments into which we have all wandered.

I can see no way out of this dilemma other than by a bold and sweeping departure—a departure that would cut surgically through the exaggerated anxieties, the self-engendered night-mares, and the sophisticated mathematics of destruction, in which we have all been entangled over these recent years, and would permit us to move, with courage and decision, to the heart of the problem.

President Reagan recently said, and I think very wisely, that he would "negotiate as long as necessary to reduce the numbers of nuclear weapons to a point where neither side threatens the survival of the other."

Now that is, of course, precisely the thought to which the present observations of mine are addressed. But I wonder whether the negotiations would really have to be at such great length. What I would like to see the President do, after due consultation with the Congress, would be to propose to the Soviet government an immediate across-the-boards reduction by 50 percent of the nuclear arsenals now being maintained by the two superpowers—a reduction affecting in equal measure all forms of the weapon, strategic, medium-range, and tactical, as well as all means of their delivery—all this to be implemented at once and without further wrangling among the experts, and to be subject to such national means of verification as now lie at the disposal of the two powers.

Whether the balance of reduction would be precisely even— whether it could be construed to favor statistically one side or the other—would not be the question. Once we start thinking that way, we would be back on the same old fateful track that has brought us where we are today. Whatever the precise results of such a reduction, there would still be plenty of overkill left— so much so that if this first operation were successful, I would then like to see a second one put in hand to rid us of at least two-thirds of what would be left.

Now I have, of course, no idea of the scentific aspects of such an operation; but I can imagine that serious problems might be presented by the task of removing, and disposing safely of, the radioactive contents of the many thousands of warheads that would have to be dismantled. Should this be the case, I would like to see the President couple his appeal for a 50 percent reduction with the proposal that there be established a joint Soviet-American scientific committee, under the chairmanship of a distinguished neutral figure, to study jointly and in all humility the problem not only of the safe disposal of these wastes but also the question of how they could be utilized in such a way as to make a positive contribution to human life, either in the two countries themselves or—perhaps preferably— elsewhere. In such a joint scientific venture we might both atone for some of our past follies and lay the foundation for a more constructive relationship.

It will be said: this proposal, whatever its merits, deals with only a part of the problem. This is perfectly true. Behind it there would still lurk the serious political differences that now divide us from the Soviet government. Behind it would still lie the problems recently treated, and still to be treated, in the SALT forum. Behind it would still lie the great question of the acceptability of war itself, any war, even a conventional one, as a means of solving problems among great industrial powers in the age of high technology.

What has been suggested here would not prejudice the continued treatment of these questions just as they might be treated today, in whatever forums and under whatever safeguards the two powers find necessary. The conflicts and arguments over these questions could still proceed to the heart's content of all those who view them with such passionate commitment. The stakes would simply be smaller; and it would be a great relief to all of us.

What I have suggested is, of course, only a beginning. But a beginning has to be made somewhere; and if it has to be made, is it not best that it should be made where the dangers are the greatest, and their necessity the least? If a step of this nature could be successfully taken, people might find the heart to tackle with greater confidence and determination the many problems that would still remain.

It will also be argued that there would be risks involved. Possibly so. I do not see them. I do not deny the possibility. But if there are, so what? Is it possible to conceive of any dangers greater than those that lie at the end of the collision course on which we are now embarked? And if not, why choose the greater—why choose, in fact, the greatest—of all risks, in the hopes of avoiding the lesser ones?

We are confronted here, my friends, with two courses. At the end of one lies hope—faint hope, if you will—uncertain hope, hope surrounded with dangers, if you insist. At the end of the other lies, so far as I am able to see, no hope at all.

Can there be—in light of our duty not just to ourselves (for we are all going to die sooner or later) but of our duty to our own kind, our duty to the continuity of the generations, our duty to the great experiment of civilized life on this rare and rich and marvelous planet—can there be, in the light of these claims on our loyalty, any question as to which course we should adopt?

In the final week of his life, Albert Einstein signed the last of the collective appeals against the development of nuclear weapons that he was ever to sign. He was dead before it appeared. It was an appeal drafted, I gather, by Bertrand Russell. I had my differences with Russell at the time as I do now in retrospect; but I would like to quote one sentence from the final paragraph of that statement, not only because it was the last one Einstein ever signed, but because it sums up, I think, all that I have to say on the subject. It reads as follows:

We appeal to you as human beings to human beings:
Remember your humanity, and forget the rest.

Chapter 36

Living Without Nuclear Weapons

Paul Joseph and Simon Rosenblum

We are entering the most dangerous decade in human history. A third world war is not merely possible, but increasingly likely. Economic and social difficulties in advanced industrial countries, crisis, militarism and war in the third world compound the political tensions that fuel a demented arms race...As each side tries to prove its readiness to use nuclear weapons, in order to prevent their use by the other side, new more "usable" nuclear weapons are designed and the idea of "limited" nuclear war is made to sound more plausible. So much so that this paradoxical process can logically only lead to the actual use of nuclear weapons.
—Appeal for European Nuclear Disarmament
April 28, 1980

Robert Jay Lifton has maintained that universities have failed to address the nuclear predicament seriously, either in their classrooms or in the scholarship they sponsor. In his 1982 commencement address, president Derek Bok announced that Harvard University, as an institution, was joining the nuclear debate by commissioning a book on the subject—a new twist on the "publish or perish" scenario! Bok wanted the book to be "an

objective account of the basic facts about nuclear arms control."
Although he said no single book could express all the views on
the subject represented in the university, the study would
express Harvard's "institutional responsibility to educate the
public as a whole." Accordingly, five of the institution's most
responsible figures—all members of one or both of Harvard's
foreign policy institutes—were given responsibility to produce
the study.*

What is the nuclear debate all about? How did we get here?
What should our strategy be? What policy options do the United
States and its allies have? What can be done about the nuclear
predicament? These are the questions (p. 9) that *Living With
Nuclear Weapons* attempted to answer. What emerged is a
document that searches a middle ground between the peace
movement and the most extreme hawks inside the defense establishment and Reagan administration. As we shall learn, in its effort
to avoid "atomic escapism," the Harvard study ends up by
making its peace with the fundamentals of America's nuclear
weapons strategies.

Before evaluating the Harvard study, it is useful to map out
current developments in the nuclear arms race and their impact
on world peace and security. From there we will judge how
Harvard measures up.

The Current Situation

The fragile East/West nuclear balance is rapidly being
undermined, as has been noted by the International Commission on Disarmament and Security Issues chaired by Swedish
Prime Minister Olaf Palme, which opened its report with the
assertion that "the world seems to be marching inexorably
toward the brink of a new abyss." This is due even more to
dramatic technical improvements in nuclear weapons than to
the steady buildup of nuclear arsenals (both sides already have
preposterous accumulations of overkill.) These innovations
have led to strategic and intermediate-range nuclear weapons
that are highly accurate and reach their targets more quickly
These more effective counterforce weapons are destabilizing
because weapons that are designed to be used against the other
side's weapons must be used first. This is a change from the
doctrine of deterrence, under which nuclear weapons were
designed to be used only in retaliation to a nuclear attack. In

---

*The authors are Albert Carnesale, Paul Doty, Stanley Hoffman,
Samuel Huntington, and Joseph Nye, Jr. Scott Sagan as staff
assistant drafted the text and was later added as a sixth author.

addition, the instability of the international situation and the uncertain position of the United States within it has both exacerbated current tensions and increased the number of potential crisis points in which nuclear weapons might be used. The Stockholm International Peace Research Institute points out the danger:

> The Soviet-American arms race is about to take yet another great leap forward. This new spiral in the arms race will be by far the most dangerous. Large numbers of nuclear weapons will be deployed which will be seen as useful for fighting a nuclear war but useless for nuclear deterrence. And military technology is developing a number of weapons systems which will strengthen the perception that nuclear war is fightable and winnable.

"Usable" nuclear weapons are now coming into style. These new weapons are designed to attack the opponent's nuclear forces. In the ultimate scenario they would disarm the enemy and hold its population hostage. The deployment of such weapons is just now beginning and will put pressure on the superpowers to launch their weapons first in times of crisis and to place their nuclear forces on an automatic "launch-on-warning" status in peacetime. The result will be the stimulation of the fears, the temptations, and the compulsions of a "first-strike" mentality among the political and military leadership of the superpowers. The arms race is being turned into a giant game of bluff with a hair-trigger which, once pulled, could touch off a cataclysm of unimaginable proportions.

For years, the arms race has been justified by many as a deterrent to nuclear war. In theory at least, nuclear war remains "unthinkable" so long as neither side can launch an attack without facing massive retaliation in return. But the changing technology of nuclear weapons means that they are far less effective deterrents than they once were. Previously, no surprise attack could be expected to destroy the other side's offensive forces. Most of these forces would be left undamaged—far more than enough to inflict lethal destruction on the aggressor nation's populace and civilization. In such a war, there could be no winner. That strategic nuclear balance was referred to as "mutual assured destruction" ("MAD") and it provided a significant (although by no means absolute) degree of security. It is that tentative stability which is being eroded today as MAD has come to be replaced by a more sinister strategy which sees nuclear weapons not as the means of deterring war but of winning it.

What we are faced with, in other words, is an arms race that is getting dangerously out of control. The danger is represented both by changing nuclear weapons technology and by the growing influence of nuclear use theorists. As these nuclear use theorists ("NUTS") increase their influence at the expense of those who believe in mutual assured destruction ("MAD"), one can truly say that the world is going from MAD to NUTS!

These dangers raise an important question: what should be the goals of U.S. nuclear policy? Let's look first at the answers offered by the Harvard study.

Harvard Rates a C-

The authors of *Living With Nuclear Weapons* employ the concept of deterrence as the benchmark for its evaluation of American nuclear policy. The problem is that deterrence has several different applications. (The number of variants and refinements has led Theodore Draper to observe dourly that deterrence "may yet equal liberty for the number of crimes committed in its name".) The first concept presented by the Harvard study is called "basic deterrence" and is defined as developing the capabilities that will deter a nuclear attack by the Soviet Union on the United States. So far, so good. As long as there is a world with nuclear weapons, this goal of American policy is not only unobjectionable, but necessary. No U.S. leader or peace movement can accept a situation where the Soviet Union has a nuclear arsenal and the U.S. does not. Nor can there be agreement to a situation where the U.S.S.R. has a decisive edge over the U.S. So far we agree with Harvard.

The first problem emerges when we consider exactly what capabilities are necessary to achieve basic deterrence. Most analysts would argue that fewer than 400 atomic bombs would be enough to produce destruction that the other side finds unacceptable. Most citizens would probably find one bomb, particularly if it landed near their house, "unacceptable." At any rate, with 10,000 strategic weapons, the U.S. currently possesses far more than would be necessary to achieve any conceivable definition of unacceptable damage. The weapons to secure basic deterrence are already in place. Yet Harvard, as we shall see, endorses new nuclear weapons that not only go beyond basic deterrence but tend to undermine it.

A second problem arises when Harvard discusses another goal of U.S. nuclear policy, that of "extended deterrence." Extended deterrence is defined as "helping to deter a nuclear or conventional attack on U.S. allies." The authors note that the U.S. has extended a commitment to defend other countries including NATO Europe, Japan and South Korea, from possible Soviet nuclear attacks. Harvard also points out that the credibility of the U.S. nuclear guarantee has been questioned as it became apparent that the Soviet Union can respond to an American attack on the Soviet Union. If the U.S.S.R. can effectively retaliate against the U.S., how secure can American allies feel about U.S. promises to attack the Soviet Union on their behalf? In this instance, American policy makers fear that both the military and political effectiveness of nuclear weapons in areas other than direct confrontation between Moscow and Washington has disappeared.

What the Harvard study skirts around but never makes absolutely clear is that extended deterrence is the application of the threatened use of nuclear weapons to protect the full range of U.S. economic, political and military interests. Eugene Rostow, former director of the U.S. Arms Control and Disarmament Agency, is more honest when he argues that a goal for nuclear weapons is to "permit us to use military force in defense of our interests with comparative freedom." In fact, Rostow has argued that "the nuclear weapon is a pervasive influence in all aspects of diplomacy and of conventional war." He would like to restore our past capability, where in a crisis, "we could go forward in planning the use of our conventional forces with greater freedom precisely because we knew the Soviet Union could not escalate beyond the local level." The problem, as Paul Warnke, former U.S. chief negotiator, warns, is that those weapons designed to secure extended deterrence, lead instead to war-fighting doctrines. As Warnke points out:

> Today, however, there are disturbing signs of a growing reliance on nuclear weapons as an instrument of foreign policy—to gain political ends, not just to prevent nuclear attacks. Some advisors to the current Administration have stated categorically that we should "devise ways to employ nuclear war rationally." Other Administration officials have maintained that the goal of our nuclear arsenal should be to prevent others from using conventional military force against our own conventional force as we see fit. And the argument that nuclear arms are useful only for deterrence seems now to be losing ground to the argument that we can and should shape our forces to fight, survive and win a nuclear war.

Most strategists who accept the policy goal of extended deterrence feel that U.S. nuclear forces must be modernized. What starts out under the term "deterrence" moves, through an important redefinition of that term, to an endorsement of attempts to achieve nuclear warfighting capabilities. Harvard is no exception to this tendency. Despite arguing that "an effort to re-establish American nuclear superiority would not appear to be worth the assured costs and risks" (p. 158), Harvard ends up endorsing the Pershing II and cruise missile in Europe, the Trident submarine and its counterforce D-5 missile, and is at least ambivalent on the MX. In addition, Harvard does not oppose American first-use policy which is seen as vital to preserving U.S. credibility with its allies. Each of these weapons systems presents a danger to peace. Harvard supports NATO's "two-track" policy of introducing the Pershing II and cruise missile while simultaneously trying to reach an intermediate-range nuclear weapons agreement with the Soviet Union. The justification for this stance is both to respond to the Soviets' SS-20, and to demonstrate America's political commitment to its European allies. Harvard argues that "if these objectives can be met without the missile deployments, we should be satisfied" (p. 168). In the meantime, it appears that both weapons are being deployed.

The deployment of the Pershing II and cruise missile in Western Europe introduces a qualitatively different danger of nuclear war in the European theater. The Pershing II is of special significance because it is highly accurate and could reach missile silos, and command and control installations in the western part of the Soviet Union. If the Soviet Union is pushed to adopt a launch-on-warning response, the deployment of Pershing II missiles may guarantee a much greater risk of accidental Soviet launch. So a decision taken ostensibly to enhance the security of NATO will instead undermine it.

It must be remembered that the SS-20, by virtue of its medium range and geographical deployment, cannot be targeted against American strategic weapons—unless, of course, the U.S. places land-based weapons in Europe! Consequently, the former director of the International Institute of Strategic Studies in London, Christophe Bertam, has described as "analytically dubious" the comparison between Soviet SS-20 missiles and the projected American missiles. Many others, including McGeorge Bundy, special assistant for national security affairs to Presidents Kennedy and Johnson, have noted that the SS-20 does not give the Soviet Union any significant nuclear capability against Western Europe that it did not have before a single SS-20 was deployed.

If the U.S. and NATO need a "bargaining chip" to reduce the Soviets' SS-20s, the addition of more submarine warheads would serve that purpose without lowering the nuclear threshhold. The logic of a primarily sea-based deterrent has even been embraced by Helmut Schmidt, who recently (February 1983) told *The Washington Post,* "sea-based systems would suit our geographic and strategic conditions better" than the Pershing and cruise missiles. The United States is resistant to putting its European "deterrent" out to sea because it would lack—at least at this point in technological development—the precision accuracy to be a credible "first-strike" weapon.

What about the MX? To support the new land-based missile Pentagon officials orginally postulated an implausible scenario: suppose the Russians should launch an attack on U.S. missile silos but hold back a sizeable portion of their silo-based missile force to deter the United States from retaliating against Soviet cities. In such a case, military experts claim the U.S. must have weapons accurate enough to wipe out those silos. The alternative, retaliation against Soviet urban-industrial targets, would only bring retribution against American cities. It is not very difficult to find objections to this scenario. Even President Reagan's Scowcroft Report acknowledged that there is no "window of vulnerability" as concerns the security of America's land-based nuclear weapons (though the members of the commission supported the MX).

Harvard remains schizophrenic on the window of vulnerability and the resultant need for the MX missile to close it. While considering a number of scenarios in which a nuclear war might start, the Harvard study explicitly rejects the plausibility of a limited attack against U.S. land-based missiles (the Minuteman): "The Minuteman-only scenario...is far less likely than many other possible paths to nuclear war. These surprise attack scenarios preoccupy all too many defense analysts whose talents would be far better applied to preventing more likely dangers" (p. 53). Yet, later, the authors of *Living With Nuclear Weapons* repeatedly refer to the problem of the vulnerability of land-based missiles and the consequent need to modernize the U.S. ICBM inventory as a result.

Harvard adopts a similar stance with regard to the Trident II (or D-5) missile. Now in development and scheduled for deployment on the new generation of submarines, this new missile would carry 8-10 warheads capable of destroying hardened targets, including Soviet ICBM silos. As with the MX, the Trident carries significantly new counterforce capabilities. Harvard vacillates, but ends up supporting the Trident II missile. Taken together these new weapons are a significant addition to U.S. nuclear warfighting capabilities.

A third goal of nuclear policy is crisis stability or minimizing the incentives for either side to strike first in an international crisis. Here a nuclear war might start, not from the belief that a victory is possible, but from desperation, from the feeling that in a deep crisis war is inevitable. As each side continues to develop counterforce capabilities that threaten the other side's retaliatory forces, the temptation to use vulnerable missiles may become overwhelming. If war does start and these missile are not used, the other side may destroy them. Counterforce and international crisis lead to a "use them or lose them" mentality.

The authors of *Living With Nuclear Weapons* recognize the possibility that these new weapons may undermine crisis stability. In fact they point out that if crisis stability was the only goal of U.S. nuclear policy, our arsenal should consist of inaccurate, invulnerable missiles with very long flight times so that Soviet leaders need never fear that their forces could be destroyed in a surprise attack. The weapons would be for retaliation only. The problem, at least for Harvard, is that deterrence based on such an arsenal would no longer be *credible*, that is, the prospect of actually using nuclear weapons would drop to zero because mutual suicide would be the only possible outcome. Most people would welcome such a development. But the Harvard professors are smarter than the average citizen. They point out that nuclear weapons could no longer be used on behalf of U.S. allies and interests. And since this is considered a valid goal, the authors end up with basic approval of the weapon systems that form Reagan's modernization package. Unfortunately, the counterforce capabilities of the MX, Pershing II, Trident II, and cruise missiles (to a lesser extent) also undermine crisis stability. And counterforce nuclear weapons, by virtue of their destabilizing effect, not only threaten our opponents but reduce our own security. George Kennan has stated the essence of the matter as follows:

> I believe that until we consent to recognize that the nuclear weapons we hold in our own hands are as much a danger to us as those that repose in the hands of our supposed adversaries there will be no escape from the confusions and dilemmas to which such weapons have now brought us, and must bring us increasingly as time goes on.

Such thinking is simple. Probably too simple for the level of sophistication that we have come to expect from Harvard.

Harvard and the Freeze

More and more people are questioning the stability of the nuclear balance of terror. From inside the political and military systems, there are voices of warning: the late Lord Mountbatten and George Kennan, scientists such as Jerome Wiesner and Solly Zuckerman. Even some governments are producing plans for nuclear reductions. There has been a tremendous outpouring of new and revised ideas for ending the arms race: Nuclear-Weapon-Free Zones, freezing the production of nuclear weapons, closing military research establishments, renouncing the first use of nuclear weapons, negotiated and reciprocated monitoring, cutting by half existing nuclear stockpiles, etc. Many consider that priority should be given to the limitation and reduction of systems that are particularly destabilizing.

The proposal for a freeze on the testing, production and deployment of nuclear weapons is the best known and widely supported of these proposals. A freeze by both superpowers would offer a profound opportunity for nuclear stability by limiting the emerging threat of first-strike weaponry and by breaking the impasse that prevents major reductions in current stockpiles of nuclear arms. While not a proposal for complete nuclear disarmament, it would mean a dramatic reversal of the strategic arms race, a rejection of nuclear warfighting capabilities and doctrine, and a great reduction in the fear of first-strike, by either the U.S. or the U.S.S.R. Randall Forsberg, the originator of the freeze proposal, sums up its significance:

> The freeze would not eliminate the existing capability of the U.S. and the U.S.S.R. to bring about global nuclear holocaust. As few as 100 nuclear weapons on each side, half of one percent of the current arsenals, could devastate the U.S. and U.S.S.R. beyond any previous historical experience and perhaps beyond recovery as industrial societies. To end the danger of nuclear war the nations must not merely freeze nuclear weapons but abolish them. The freeze represents a modest but significant step toward abolition. It would terminate the technological arms race and shut down entirely this wasteful and dangerous form of human competition.

In light of their support for the extended deterrence doctrine it should not be surprising that the nuclear freeze proposal gets little support from Harvard. They claim, in particular, that a comprehensive freeze would be difficult to verify. The authors do not address the arguments of arms control experts who have testified that the more inclusive a freeze the *easier* verification will be. As an alternative, Harvard proposes that the number of nuclear warheads possessed by the U.S. and U.S.S.R. be capped and that additions be compensated for by an equal number being withdrawn. Unfortunately, such a proposal could bring a first-strike capability closer. Old, rather imprecise systems would be replaced by nuclear weapons possessing greater speed and accuracy. The replacement proposal would only reduce the number of targets that had to be hit and increase the chances of hitting them. Greater instability would be the only possible result.

Future historians are bound to wonder why the Harvard contribution to this, the most important of all national debates, decided to stifle, rather than nurture, the largest attempt ever made by ordinary American citizens to derail the U.S.-Soviet rivalry from the track of self-defeating military competition. Our analysis of strategic nuclear policy suggests that the Harvard study moves in precisely the wrong policy direction. Robert Jay Lifton unfortunately seems to be correct in his condemnation of the universities' failure in the nuclear debate as representing "a moral and intellectual scandal." By getting caught up in the internal "logic" of the arms race and the dictates of extended deterrence, the Harvard professors have revealed themselves to be too clever by half. In fact they almost flunk the course.

Towards a Non-Nuclear World

Living with nuclear weapons, no matter how few, will remain dangerous for humanity. The eminent British historian A.J.P. Taylor puts it this way: "In the old days the deterrent (conventional arms) worked nine times out of ten. Now presumably it (nuclear arms) will work 99 out of a 100. But if the past experience is any good...the hundreth occasion will come." The history of international politics provides no reassurance that nuclear weapons will not be used again. Jonathan Schell is surely right to suggest that our present societies are based on a "lie that we all have come to live—the pretense that life lived on top of a nuclear stockpile can last." In assuming that because there has been a nuclear peace for about four decades this situation will continue indefintely, many are behaving like the person falling from the top of a fifty-story building who announces when passing the tenth floor, "so far, so good." Perhaps no catastrophic nuclear war at all will take place between now and the year 2000. But reaching the year 2000 without disaster only qualifies the world to try to continue to coexist with the bomb thereafter. It is one thing to be sanguine about the chance that nuclear peace will endure to the year 2000, quite another to be confident about the year 3000. The United Nations in paragraph 47 of the Final Document of the 1978 Special Session on Disarmament appropriately concludes: "Nuclear weapons pose the greatest danger to mankind and to the survival of civilization. It is essential to halt and reverse the nuclear arms race in all its aspects in order to avert the danger of war involving nuclear weapons. The ultimate goal in this context is the complete elimination of nuclear weapons."

"So, why not abolish nuclear weapons?" "Why not cleanse this small planet of these deadly poisons?" The authors of *Living With Nuclear Weapons* ask these questions and answer that we cannot. "Mankind's nuclear innocence, once lost, cannot be regained. The discovery of nuclear weapons, like the discovery of fire itself, lies behind us on the trajectory of history; it cannot be undone. Even if all nuclear arsenals were destroyed, the knowledge of how to reinvent them would remain and could be put to use in any of a dozen or more nations. The atomic fire cannot be extinguished. The fear of its use will remain a part of the human psyche for the rest of human history" (p. 5). Harvard condemns us to a future history in which the threat of nuclear war will remain forever. But are we doomed to such an existence?

We do not think so, although we want to avoid, in our answer to Harvard, easy and utopian solutions. One part of the problem is that only a very radical stage of reducing existing arms stockpiles could in a purely physical sense make the world safer. It has been estimated that either superpower could start dismantling its nuclear weapons at a rate of ten percent a year, and still have the capacity to completely destroy the other superpower several times over after 20 years of such a program. While the ultimate goal of complete and general nuclear disarmament is very far away, it is imperative that some cap be placed on the arms race right away.

Another part of the problem is that it would be naive, given the present state of world affairs, to expect that immediate nuclear disarmament is a realistic possibility. The current anarchy of international politics creates insecurity that makes self-protection prudent and weapons necessary. Obviously, if one nation has no nuclear weapons, and its adversary acquires a few, then that side would have decisive leverage. The problem is how to reduce the number of nuclear weapons and sever the connection between those weapons and world politics, all the while retaining stability and security. Several initial steps have been suggested in this book. They include the adoption of a mutual freeze on the testing, production, and deployment of nuclear weapons and a declaration of no first use. George Kennan, former U.S. ambassador to the Soviet Union, has suggested an across-the-board 50 percent reduction in the U.S. and Soviet stockpiles "without further wrangling among the experts." This is something both sides can safely afford to do. But even after dismantling and destroying thousands of nuclear warheads, each side would be left with destructive power equal to several hundred thousand Hiroshimas. The threat of war would not be ended.

Within the current constraints of international politics, a minimum nuclear deterrent will best secure stability. Under pure deterrence a relatively small number of nuclear weapons can give a country the capacity for assured destruction provided that they are invulnerable to preemptive attack. It is generally thought that 200 single-warhead missiles, based largely at sea, would be adequate for this purpose. In this sense we agree with the Catholic bishops in their pastoral letter on war and peace where they reach "a strictly conditioned moral acceptance of deterrence" as a way station on the road towards nuclear disarmament.

Such a minimal deterrent assigns a minimal policy task to nuclear weapons. Quite simply, pure deterrence allows no excess baggage (i.e. extended deterrence). All forms of linkage between nuclear weapons and political influence would be severed. Otherwise, as Allen Krass and Dan Smith argue in their contribution to this book, minimum deterrence would present an unstable situation in which one or both superpowers endeavored to get an edge on the other. It would be necessary to pay careful attention to the nature of technological developments in nuclear weapons systems in order to guarantee that the balance would not become unglued. Minimum deterrence is obviously not as good as a world without nuclear weapons and the Catholic bishops correctly, we believe, emphasize that they "cannot consider it adequate as a long-term basis for peace." But as Robert C. Johansen notes, "Compared to a nuclear warfighting capacity a minimum deterrent posture increases stability and the likelihood of peace, not because the deterring threat is immediate, but precisely because the threat is pushed far into the background and its use limited to a single narrow purpose—to prevent the first explosion of nuclear weapons."

Ultimately, significant reductions in nuclear arsenals and a much reduced threat of nuclear war depend on a dramatic alteration in the international political climate. It is not enough to entertain different ways of reducing the number of weapons.

We must also think about changes in the political and economic conditions of the U.S., the U.S.S.R., and the other nuclear capable countries. Particular attention must be paid to those conditions that generate tensions that lead to war. Nuclear arsenals cannot be considered out of context. They developed due to particular interests, especially the foreign policy and military interests of the United States. Unless the structure of those interests is changed dramatically, only marginal progress towards disarmament can be expected. We are not talking about pie in the sky plans for world government, but more of developing an imperative for peace that flows from changes occurring *within* each country.

The movement developing these changes would have to develop a resounding critique of extended deterrence and of the foreign policy interests that lie behind the development of the extended deterrence doctrine. Richard Barnet has argued that future American prosperity requires a fundamental shift of position of the U.S. within the world system. In particular, the U.S. must create different relations—relations that are not exploitative—with Third World countries. In similar fashion, creating a stable structure of peace will also require a new global position for the United States. Imaginative arms control measures are simply not enough. For in the final analysis the creation of a non-nuclear world will necessitate deep-seated changes in the interests that created nuclear weapons in the first place.

These considerations are entirely absent from Harvard's discussion of the conditions of peace. The authors of *Living With Nuclear Weapons* argue that peace would be best preserved through a balance of power. With great enthusiasm they recall the historical periods, especially the 19th century, where countries were able to avoid major conflicts through a structure of regulated competition. Harvard does note some of the differences between the 1800s and the present. Where there used to be five or six countries with relatively equal influence, there are now only two superpowers. The comparatively minor conflicts that broke out in the 19th century did not threaten the existence of the world. Now both superpowers are armed with nuclear weapons. In this sense Harvard recognizes that we cannot create a structure of peace by recreating the Congress of Vienna where, in 1815, Europe agreed to the methods by which they would disagree.

But in another sense Harvard remains mired in the distant past. The authors of *Living With Nuclear Weapons* make several suggestions for improving the chances of peace. But these suggestions remain focused on the rules of conducting international affairs. The possibility that responsibility for the arms race lies within the economic, political, and military interests that comprise the power structure of the U.S. is passed over in silence. So is any discussion that the possibility of securing genuine peace will come only with significant changes in those interests.

Harvard calls for better communication between Moscow and Washington. Fine. Harvard calls for working to reduce the tension that exists in certain regions such as the Middle East. Fine. Harvard even recognizes that the ability of any government to change the Soviet system is limited. Fine. But Harvard continues to hold that a balance of power will best preserve the peace. The authors of the study ignore the necessity of changing the concept of national interest that prevails in the U.S. Ultimately this is a failure of political imagination.

We can have a world without nuclear weapons. But to have it we must broaden our attack. Issues such as American foreign policy, the size and composition of our defense budget, even international economic arrangements, are vitally connected to the goal of nuclear disarmament. Developing meaningful change is dependent on a peace movement that moves beyond nuclear weapons to address these broader concerns. This will take time.

While recognizing the need for broad change, the peace movement must also pay attention to immediate considerations that preserve as much stability as possible in a world that all recognize to be filled with fear and terror. Minimum deterrence is one way to preserve that stability. The adoption of minimum deterrence will certainly lower the chances that a nuclear war will start. The task is very difficult—but also very possible. It consists in preserving nuclear stability in the short run while working to eliminate the conditions that produced nuclear weapons in the first place. In that project lies the best chance of protecting the planet, not the phony realism of learning to live beside the forces that can destroy us in a half hour.

Key References

Aldridge, Robert, *First Strike*, (Boston: South End Press, 1983).

Barnet, Richard, *Real Security*, (New York: Simon and Schuster, 1981).

Calder, Nigel, *Nuclear Nightmares*, (Middlesex, England: Penguin 1981).

Draper, Theodore, "Dear Mr. Weinberger—An Open Reply to an Open Letter" *New York Review of Books*, November 4, 1982.

Ege, Konrad and Makhijani, Arjun, "U.S. Nuclear Threats: A Documentary History," *Counterspy*, July-August 1982.

Harvard Nuclear Study Group, *Living With Nuclear Weapons*, (New York: Bantam Books, 1983).

Johansen, Robert C., "Toward an Alternative Security System," *Alternatives*, Winter 1983.

Kennan, George, "A Modest Proposal" *New York Review of Books*, July 16, 1981.

Lifton, Robert Jay and Falk, Richard, *Indefensible Weapons*, (New York: Basic Books, 1982.)

Mandelbaum, Michael, *The Nuclear Question*, (New York: Cambridge University Press, 1979).

Nitze, Paul, "Atoms, Strategy, and Policy," *Foreign Affairs*, January 1956.

Schell, Jonathan, *The Fate of the Earth*, (New York: Alfred A. Knopf, 1982).

Taylor, A.J.P., *How Wars Begin*, (New York: Atheneum, 1979).

The Independent Commission on Disarmament and Security Issues, *Common Security*, (New York: Simon and Schuster, 1982).

Warnke, Paul, "Nuclear War as a Foreign Policy Option," Talk delivered at St. John the Divine, New York, March 7, 1982.

About the Contributors

GORDON ADAMS is director of the Defense Budget Project at the Center on Budget and Policy Priorities, and the author of *The Iron Triangle: The Politics of Defense Spending* (Council of Economic Priorities).

ROBERT ALDRIDGE was formerly an aerospace engineer at the Lockheed Corporation. He is author of *First Strike! The Pentagon's Strategy for Nuclear War* (South End Press).

EDWARD ANDERSON is professor of mechanical engineering and director of the industrial engineering division at the University of Minnesota. From the late 1940s to the mid 1960s, he worked on inertial guidance systems for ICBMs.

DESMOND BALL is a fellow at the Strategic Studies Center, Australian National University, Canberra, Australia. He is the author of *Politics and Force Levels in the Kennedy Administration* (University of California Press) and numerous articles on nuclear strategy.

RICHARD BARNET is a senior fellow of the Institute for Policy Studies in Washington D.C. His books include *Real Security: Restoring American Power in a Dangerous Decade* (Simon and Schuster) and *Roots of War* (Penguin).

LOUIS RENE BERES is a member of the political science department at Purdue University. He is the author of *Apocalypse: Nuclear Catastrophe in World Politics* (University of Chicago Press) and *Mimicking Sisyphus: America's Countervailing Nuclear Strategy* (Ballinger).

LLOYD DUMAS is associate professor of political economy at the University of Texas, Dallas. He has written on the impact of military expenditures on the domestic economy and is the editor of *The Political Economy of Arms Reduction* (Westview Press).

DANIEL ELLSBERG began his career as a specialist for the Pentagon on nuclear command and control systems. His public release of the "Pentagon Papers" in 1971 marked a break with a career that spanned the administrations of four presidents. He recently wrote the introduction "Call to Mutiny" in *Protest and Survive* (Monthly Review Press).

RANDALL FORSBERG is director of the Institute for Defense and Disarmament in Brookline, Massachusetts. Known widely as the "author of the freeze," since 1968 she has done theoretical and practical work opposing the nuclear arms race.

JACK GEIGER is a member of Physicians for Social Responsibility and the author of numerous articles on the medical consequences of nuclear war.

HAYES GLADSTONE is a candidate for a master's degree in international affairs at the Fletcher School for Law and Diplomacy.

DAVID GOLD is director of the Institute on the Military and the Economy. He is the co-author of *Misguided Expenditure: An Analysis of the Proposed MX System* (Council on Economic Priorities) and of articles on nuclear weapons and the impact of military spending.

SUZANNE GORDON is assistant editor of *Modern Times* magazine and author of *Off Balance: The Real World of Ballet* (Pantheon) and *Lonely in America* (Simon and Schuster).

DAVID HOLLOWAY lectures in politics at the University of Edinburgh and is author of *The Soviet Union and the Arms Race* (Yale University Press).

DIANA JOHNSTONE is the European correspondent for *In These Times.*

J.J. JOSEPH is an economist with the Labor Research Association. He has extensive business experience in both government and business.

PAUL JOSEPH is associate professor of sociology at Tufts University. He is the author of *Cracks in the Empire: State Politics in the Vietnam War* (South End Press) and "From MAD to NUTs: The Increasing Danger of Nuclear War."

MICHIO KAKU is professor of nuclear physics at the Graduate Center of the City University of New York and director of the Institute for Peace and Safe Technology. He is co-editor with Jennifer Trainer of *Nuclear Power: Both Sides.*

MARY KALDOR is a research fellow at the Social Policy Research Unit, University of Sussex, England. Her most recent book is *The Baroque Arsenal* (Hill and Wang).

FRED KAPLAN reports regularly on military affairs for *The*

Boston Globe and is a Washington correspondent for *Nuclear Times.* He is the author of *The Wizards of Armageddon* (Simon and Schuster).

MIKE KAZIN teaches U.S. history at Stanford University. He has worked on the freeze campaign since the spring of 1981 and has written on the politics of nuclear weapons for *The Nation, Nuclear Times, Socialist Review,* and *The Oakland Tribune.*

GEORGE KENNAN is at the Institute for Advanced Study at Princeton University. He is the author of numerous books on the Soviet Union. The most recent is *Nuclear Delusion* (Pantheon). He is the recipient of the Albert Einstein Peace Prize.

MICHAEL KLARE is a fellow at the Institute of Policy Studies in Washington D.C. and author of several books including *Beyond the Vietnam Syndrome: U.S. Intervention in the 1980s* (IPS Books).

ALLAN KRASS is professor of physics and science at Hampshire College. He is the author of "The Evolution of Military Technology and Deterrence Strategy" (*SIPRI* Yearbook, 1981).

ADMIRAL GENE LAROCQUE is director of the Center for Defense Information in Washington D.C.

CHRISTOPHER PAINE is the staff assistant for arms control with the Federation for American Scientists in Washington D.C.

KARL PIERAGOSTINI is currently a member of the political science department at the University of Vermont. Work for his contribution on verification was conducted while an analyst for the Institute for Defense and Disarmament Studies.

SIMON ROSENBLUM is a member of the National Executive of Project Plowshares, a Canadian peace organization. He is co-editor of *Canada and the Nuclear Arms Race* (James Lorimer) and a member of the Federal Council of the New Democratic Party.

JON SAXTON is a member of Mobilization for Survival and an organizer of its No First Use Campaign. He is also a graduate student in sociology at Brandeis University.

MORRIS SCHWARTZ is professor of sociology at Brandeis University. He is currently investigating the cultural and social-psychological consequences of the arms race and preparing a rebuttal to the Harvard Study Group's *Living With Nuclear Weapons*.

DAN SMITH is a member of the council for the Campaign for Nuclear Disarmament. He is the author of *The Defense of the Realm in the 1980s* and co-editor of *Protest and Survive* and *Disarming Europe*.

JOHN STEINBRUNER is director of foreign policy studies at the Brookings Institute.

E.P. THOMPSON, historian and writer, is on the coordinating Committee of European Nuclear Disarmament. He is the author of *The Poverty of Theory*, *The Making of the English Working Class*, and *Beyond the Cold War*.

ALAN WOLFE is a professor of sociology at the City University of New York in Queens and is a member of *The Nation's* editorial board. His most recent book is *America's Impasse: The Rise and Fall of the Politics of Growth* (South End Press).

DANIEL YERGIN is a professor of government at Harvard. He is the author of *Shattered Peace* and *Global Insecurity: Energy, Society, and Upheaval in the Rest of this Century*.